HANDBOOK *of*

Imagination and
Mental Simulation

Edited by

Keith D. Markman ◆ William M. P. Klein ◆ Julie A. Suhr

Psychology Press
Taylor & Francis Group
New York   Hove

Psychology Press
Taylor & Francis Group
270 Madison Avenue
New York, NY 10016

Psychology Press
Taylor & Francis Group
27 Church Road
Hove, East Sussex BN3 2FA

International Standard Book Number-13: 978-1-84169-887-8 (Hardcover)

Library of Congress Cataloging-in-Publication Data

Handbook of imagination and mental simulation / edited by Keith D. Markman, William M.P. Klein,
  Julie A. Suhr.
    p. ; cm.
  Includes bibliographical references and indexes.
  ISBN-13: 978-1-84169-887-8 (alk. paper)
  ISBN-10: 1-84169-887-3 (alk. paper)
  1. Imagination. I. Markman, Keith D. (Keith Douglas), 1967- II. Klein, William Martin, 1966- III.
Suhr, Julie A.
  [DNLM: 1. Imagination. BF 408 H236 2009]

BF408.H286 2009
153.3--dc22   2008016089

Visit the Taylor & Francis Web site at
http://www.taylorandfrancis.com

and the Psychology Press Web site at
http://www.psypress.com

Contents

SECTION I   The Mental Simulation of Action and Behavior

SECTION II   Mental Simulation and Memory

SECTION III   Counterfactual Thinking: Simulating the Past

SECTION IV   Alternatives and Alternate Selves

SECTION V   Perspective Taking: Simulating Other Minds

SECTION VI   *Simulating and Preparing for the Future*

Overview

Keith D. Markman, William M.P. Klein, and Julie A. Suhr

You hold in your hands a collection of essays on the topic of mental simulation. Since the early 1980s, researchers have been examining fascinating questions regarding the nature of mental simulation: the act of imagination and the generation of alternative realities. Some researchers have focused on what happens in the brain when an individual is mentally simulating an action or forming a mental image, whereas others have focused on the consequences of mental simulation processes for affect, motivation, and behavior.

The purpose of gathering these essays is to achieve a novel and stimulating integration of work on imagination and mental simulation from a variety of perspectives. It is our hope that such a multidisciplinary volume will encourage an exchange of ideas that will benefit psychology. Although a number of excellent volumes have recently been published that examine the role of time perspective in decision making and social psychology more generally (e.g. Loewenstein, Read, & Baumeister, 2003; Sanna & Chang, 2006), we have elected to cut an even wider swath. Thus, the present volume includes chapters on mental representation; simulated movement and its relationship with actual motor movement; visual imagery; and how individuals use mental simulation to infer the thoughts, feelings, and intentions of others. Our goal is to forward the notion that a wide range of mental simulation phenomena share a commonality of underlying processes. To so, we have invited neuroscientists, developmental psychologists, cognitive psychologists, social psychologists, and clinical psychologists to unite under the same umbrella. By the end of this book, it should be clear that mental simulation is associated with a multifaceted but well-integrated array of biological, neurological, psychological, and social processes.

Before moving on to a description of the contents of this volume, we would note that this book was inspired by several seminal papers on mental simulation, including Kahneman and Tversky's (1982) initial propositions regarding the simulation heuristic; Taylor, Pham, Rivkin, and Armor's (1998) article on mental simulation and coping; and Johnson and Sherman's (1990) chapter entitled "Constructing and Reconstructing the Past and Future in the Present" that appeared in Higgins and Sorrentino's *Handbook of Motivation and Cognition* (Volume 2). We thank these individuals for their imagination, creativity, and foresight.

The book is organized into six sections that, we believe, offer a cogent characterization of the current state of mental simulation research.

I. THE MENTAL SIMULATION OF ACTION AND BEHAVIOR

Section I begins by describing some neurophysiological and cognitive underpinnings of motor behavior, empathic understanding, planning, and intention formation. In the opening chapter, Decety and Stevens (Chapter 1) review neurophysiological evidence indicating that actions are centrally represented in the brain, and that these action representations lie at the interface between individuals and their physical and social environments. According to Decety and Stevens, simulation of movement precedes and plans for upcoming physical action and activates the same cortical and subcortical structures that are responsible for motor execution. Moreover, they argue, motor simulation provides a "gateway to human social understanding" by allowing the motor system to resonate when it perceives the actions, emotions, and sensations of others. This capability of the motor system provides individuals with the primary means by which individuals can understand each other and can therefore be considered a basic form of intersubjectivity.

Beilock and Lyons (Chapter 2) also focus on the important role of motor simulation in accounting for performance differences between experts and novices. According to the work reviewed, skill expertise is not merely reflected during actual (i.e., on-line) unfolding of performance but is also observable off-line in terms of experts' superior ability to mentally simulate skill-relevant actions. In turn, recent work demonstrates that individuals need not be explicitly attempting to act for them to call on the motor systems used during the actual execution of a task. Apparently, skill-level differences also exist with regard to this type of covert action simulation during speech and text comprehension, and such differences can have an impact on preference judgments for encountered objects. In all, this work suggests that the manner in which experts mentally simulate mastered actions may be just as important for the study of skill learning and performance as understanding the on-line production of such actions.

Kosslyn and Moulton (Chapter 3) continue to stress the utility of motor simulation in their chapter about mental imagery and implicit memory (i.e., memory that cannot be voluntarily called to mind). Kosslyn and Moulton review evidence suggesting that imagery can be used to access implicit memories and describe how imagery can actually be used to alter such stored information (via mental practice), which in turn can affect behavior. In particular, these authors devote significant attention to the notion that imitation via observation of another's actions (either real or imagined) is a crucial mechanism underlying mental practice because it bridges observation and action, and they review the neural bases of such imitative learning.

Chapters 4 and 5 shift the focus from the representation and simulation of motor actions to the implications of associative representations stored in memory for mental simulation and subsequent behavior. In Chapter 4, Amit, Algom, Trope, and Liberman note that pictures and words have always been used as different means of representation, and they apply construal-level theory (CLT) to elucidate the idea of a distance-related difference between pictures and words. According to CLT, proximal and distal events are processed in a different manner, and extending this idea to words and pictures, Amit et al. propose that words typically serve to represent objects that are distal in time, space, society, or culture, whereas pictures serve to represent objects that are proximal along dimensions of distance. An important consequence of this distant-dependent means of representing words and pictures is that people tend to think of recent events in pictures but of more distant events in words. Moreover, because a word is at a higher level of construal than is a picture, the former is better able to function as a conveyor of information. Thus, perhaps pictures are not necessarily "worth a thousand words."

Faude-Koivisto, Wuerz, and Gollwitzer (Chapter 5) conclude this section by contrasting implementation intentions and mental simulations with regard to how they function during the planning stage of goal pursuit (see also Oettingen & Kappes, Chapter 26). According to the evidence reviewed, mental simulation (a planning process by which possible means or paths to a goal are explored) is associated with an explorative, open-minded processing style, whereas implementation intention formation (a process that leads to the selection of a critical situation, which is then linked to a goal-directed response) is associated with a closed-minded processing style. Moreover, the differential activation levels of the mental representations of implementation intentions and mental simulations underlie the distinct information-processing modes that these two self-regulation tools trigger. In addition, Faude et al. provide novel insights into the process by which implementation processes promote goal attainment by demonstrating that the formation of an implementation intention enhances the coactivation of the two components that comprise such intentions, namely, the mental representation of the anticipated situation and the goal-directed behavior.

II. MENTAL SIMULATION AND MEMORY

The chapters in Section II examine the role of mental simulation in producing false memories (Chapters 6 and 7) and explore commonalities and differences in the processes that underlie individuals' ability to engage in "mental time travel"—to remember the past and to imagine the future (Chapters 8 and 9). Bernstein, Godfrey, and Loftus (Chapter 6) review recent findings on false memories (i.e., memories for experiences that never occurred) and propose several potential mechanisms to account for the creation of false memories. According to Bernstein et al., the probability that an individual will come to believe that an event is generally plausible and that it likely occurred in the past depends, in part, on the ease with which the event is processed. Moreover, for processing fluency to increase plausibility and autobiographical belief, they hypothesize that individuals must be unaware of the actual source of the fluency. Thus, the creation of false memories depends on misattributions of processing fluency. Bernstein et al. then describe the results of studies employing a "revelation" paradigm in which individuals unscramble key words in the context of remembering life events. Their data suggest that successfully unscrambling life event-related anagrams produces an experiential "rush" of fluency that is misattributed to confidence that the related event did, in fact, occur.

Next, Lynn, Barnes, and Matthews (Chapter 7) review the extant evidence regarding the usefulness of hypnosis as a recall-enhancement procedure and conclude that hypnosis often produces false, yet believed-in memories. Lynn et al. then focus on mechanisms that might account for the creation of false memories via hypnosis. In particular, they examine the role of expectancies, arguing that prehypnotic beliefs that hypnosis facilitates recall, as well as suggestions implying that hypnosis involves an altered state, generate expectancies that hypnotic and posthypnotic recall will be improved. Moreover, because individuals expect that hypnosis will enhance the accuracy of their memories, hypnosis increases individuals' motivation to search for memories and to report imagined events or guesses as real memories.

In Chapter 8, Szpunar and McDermott examine the premise that recollection of the past is, in fact, a fundamental component of envisioning the future. Invoking the notion of autonoetic consciousness initially forwarded by Tulving, Szpunar and McDermott explain how in simulating the future individuals sample elements of remembered events to help generate potential future scenarios. Thus, episodic memory appears to be an inherently constructive system that enables people to simulate both their personal past and future. Empirical evidence to support this notion comes from two sources. First, it has been shown that personal past and future thoughts are selectively impaired in populations known to show deficits in episodic memory (e.g., amnesiacs, depressives, young children), and second, recent neurophysiological data indicate that several regions in the brain's posterior cortex are similarly engaged during personal past and future thought. Interestingly, however, Szpunar and McDermott also note that various additional brain regions consistently show activity differences in favor of simulating the future relative to remembering the past, and that these regions are the same as those that have been identified in studies that require participants to mentally simulate motor movements, harkening back to work described by Decety and Stevens (Chapter 1), Beilock and Lyons (Chapter 2), and Kosslyn and Moulton (Chapter 3).

Whereas Szpunar and McDermott (Chapter 8) focus on commonalities between retrospection and prospection, Van Boven, Kane, and McGraw (Chapter 9) focus on their differences. Van Boven et al.'s basic premise is that past tense mental simulation (e.g., imagining a vacation that occurred 2 years ago) is more constrained—more subject to "reality checks"—than is future tense mental simulation (e.g., imagining a vacation occurring 2 years in the future), and that the greater constraints on retrospection than prospection reflect a general temporal asymmetry in retrospection and prospection. The judgmental implications of such a temporal asymmetry are numerous. For instance, Van Boven et al. present evidence indicating that mental simulation in the past tense feels less imaginative and more difficult than mental simulation in the future tense. Moreover, individuals' mental representations of past events tend to be more concrete than their mental representations of the future (see Amit et al., Chapter 4), people think about emotional events in the past in a less-extreme fashion compared with their thoughts about emotional events in the future, and they tend to have more optimistic views about their futures compared with more realistic and mixed views about their pasts. In all, Van Boven et al. argue that temporally asymmetric constraints in imagining hypothetical and real events are important to consider if one is interested in achieving a more accurate understanding of mental simulation in everyday life.

III. COUNTERFACTUAL THINKING: SIMULATING THE PAST

The chapters in this section explore antecedents to and consequences of counterfactual thinking—the consideration of alternative past possibilities. Although several other chapters in this volume make contact with the counterfactual thinking literature (Chapters 9, 13, 26, 27, and 28), the three that appear in this section are completely devoted to expanding our understanding of counterfactuals. Byrne and Girotto (Chapter 10) describe the effects of context on (a) the inferences that individuals tend to draw from counterfactual conditionals and (b) the sorts of features that individuals focus on when they simulate counterfactual alternatives. With regard to the first, Byrne and Girotto demonstrate how knowledge of the facts (i.e., known facts vs. presupposed facts) affects the inferences that individuals are willing to make when they reason about counterfactual possibilities, and with regard to the second, they describe recent empirical evidence indicating that an individuals' role—reader of a hypothetical series of events versus actor actually experiencing those events—can differentially affect the construction of counterfactual alternatives. Specifically, readers tend to focus on a protagonist's controllable actions, such as choices, whereas actors, who have more information available to them regarding the features of a problem-solving phase, are consequently more likely to generate counterfactuals that focus on problem features.

Chapters 11 and 12 both examine the influence of counterfactual thinking on creativity, problem solving, emotion, and motivation, but they do so in different ways. Wong, Galinsky, and Kray (Chapter 11) focus on how counterfactual thinking has an impact on subsequent task performance by instantiating a "mindset," or process of thought that tunes information processing, attention, and thought production. The initial work described by Wong et al. uses a counterfactual priming procedure to instantiate a mindset that elicits a relational processing style—"a structured form of thought involving a consideration of relationships and the associations between a set of stimuli" (Wong et al., p. 168). Priming this mindset has the effect of enhancing decision-making accuracy and performance on creative association tasks. Next, Wong et al. describe how the relational processing style is more likely activated by generating subtractive counterfactuals (i.e., those that remove antecedent elements when reconstructing reality), whereas generating additive counterfactuals (i.e., those that add antecedent elements to reconstruct reality) tend to activate an expansive processing style that broadens conceptual attention. In support, the authors present empirical evidence indicating that additive counterfactual thinking mindsets enhance performance on idea-generation tasks, whereas subtractive counterfactual mindsets enhance performance on association tasks.

In contrast to Wong et al.'s (Chapter 11) focus on process activation via counterfactual thought, Markman, Karadogan, Lindberg, and Zell (Chapter 12) examine how counterfactual thought content has emotional, motivational, and behavioral consequences for the individual. The first part of Markman et al.'s chapter focuses on the functional benefits of counterfactual thinking as specified by the reflection and evaluation model (REM). According to the REM, the emotional and motivational effects of counterfactual thinking occur via an interaction between counterfactual direction (upward vs. downward) and counterfactual processing mode (reflective vs. evaluative). Counterfactuals that elicit negative affect are more likely to have preparative and motivational value, whereas counterfactuals that elicit positive affect are more likely to reap emotional benefits. In turn, the motivational effects of counterfactuals are moderated by the regulatory fit between the counterfactual and contextually salient goal means. Markman et al. then shift their focus to considering some dysfunctional implications of counterfactuals, including the role of upward counterfactuals in eliciting self-blame, the possibility that downward counterfactuals can lower personal standards of moral and ethical conduct, and the self-defeating and ruminative consequences of upward counterfactual thinking in nonrepeatable situations and for individuals who are depressed and state oriented.

IV. ALTERNATIVES AND ALTERNATE SELVES

The chapters in Section IV examine the judgmental implications of considering alternative outcomes and explore the phenomenology and motivational consequences of simulating alternate selves. Sanna, Schwarz, and Kennedy (Chapter 13) lead off the section by proposing and describing evidence for a general model of judgmental biasing and debiasing. According to Sanna et al., the production and reduction of judgmental biases are a function of the joint influence of accessible thought content and accompanying metacognitive experiences. As a default, individuals consider their metacognitive experiences relevant to what they are thinking about and thus draw on such experiences as a source of information that qualifies the implications of accessible thought content. Thus, focal thoughts give rise to bias when they are easy to bring to mind (see also Bernstein et al., Chapter 6) but attenuate bias when they are difficult to bring to mind. Conversely, thoughts about alternatives attenuate bias when they come to mind easily but increase bias when they are difficult to bring to mind. More generally, what individuals conclude from their metacognitive experiences depends on the nature of the experience and the particular naive theory of mental processes that is applied. However, if the informational value of the metacognitive experience to the judgment at hand is discredited, judgments will instead be solely based on accessible declarative information. Sanna et al. apply their model to a range of judgmental phenomena, including the hindsight bias, temporal confidence shifts, the planning fallacy, and the impact bias.

Chapters 14–16 focus on the phenomenology and motivational effects of imagining alternate selves. Taylor, Shawber, and Mannering (Chapter 14) examine the phenomenon of imaginary companion creation by young children, describing the typical features of an imaginary friend and exploring whether invisible friends are experienced as extensions of the self or as autonomous agents. In addition, Taylor et al. cite empirical evidence suggesting that children develop personal relationships with their imaginary companions and posit that invisible friends provide a vehicle for communicating narratives. Despite children's detailed descriptions and emotional attachments to their invisible friends, however, the vast majority of them appear to understand that invisible friends are pretend.

Klinger's chapter (Chapter 15) examines daydreaming, which he defines as nonworking thought that is either spontaneous or fanciful. After establishing some basic properties of daydreams (e.g., dimensions of thought flow, duration of thought segments, proportion of thoughts that are daydreams), Klinger describes the critical role played by goals and current concerns in determining daydream content. According to Klinger, a current concern (i.e. having a goal) sensitizes an individual to respond to cues associated with goal pursuit, and for this reason goal-related cues are processed automatically, receive priority in processing, and are reflected in daydream content. Klinger also advances the proposition that daydreaming is a mental default, a notion that is supported by recent neurophysiological evidence indicating that mindwandering entails activity in neural pathways that are known to be associated with the resting mind. Speculating on the evolutionary advantage of a default state of mental rest that spontaneously processes goal pursuits, Klinger suggests that (a) while a person is occupied with one task, such a system reminds the individual of their larger agenda; (b) the system provides opportunities for spontaneous problem solving; (c) daydreams serve as a form of mental rehearsal; and (d) daydreams act as a form of review of past behavior that can help individuals gain insights that might improve their future performance.

To conclude the section, Green and Donahue (Chapter 16) describe a psychological theory of transportation into narrative worlds that suggests that becoming immersed in a story can have powerful emotional and persuasive consequences. According to Green and Donahue, during transportation, readers' imaginative resources have them feeling removed from their surroundings and completely engaged in the world created by the author. After outlining how transportation is related to and distinct from other forms of mental simulation, the authors focus on some of the psychological processes underlying the transportation experience. For instance, transportation appears to link vivid images with beliefs implied by the story and thereby increase the story's persuasive power.

Moreover, transportation appears to facilitate belief change by reducing counterarguing about the issues raised in the story, making narrative events seem more like personal experiences, and inducing character identification that subsequently leads the reader to place greater weight on statements made by those characters. Green and Donahue conclude their chapter by considering some evolutionary advantages to transportation, including enhancing the complexity of individuals' theory of mind (see also Saxe, Chapter 17), adapting to the social world, creating a sense of immortality, and enhancing natural selection benefits.

V. PERSPECTIVE TAKING: SIMULATING OTHER MINDS

Section V examines the psychological processes (e.g., theory of mind, empathy, perspective taking) that individuals use to infer the mental states of others (see also Decety & Stevens, Chapter 1). Saxe (Chapter 17) leads off the section by reviewing developmental, social psychological, and neurophysiological evidence suggesting that the same theories of mind that are used to explain and predict our past, present, and future actions are also used to explain and predict the actions of others. Citing results from brain-imaging studies, Saxe notes that (a) certain brain regions (the right temporoparietal junction, in particular) are implicated specifically in explaining actions in terms of mental state causes; (b) these brain regions are distinct from those implicated in action execution and action perceptions; and (c) these same brain regions are used for attributing mental states to one's self. Moreover, Saxe posits that the brain regions that are implicated in theory of mind for others would not be recruited while individuals actually acted or reasoned based on a false belief but would be recruited when individuals subsequently explained those actions in terms of false beliefs.

The main thrust of Batson's chapter (Chapter 18) on empathic concern is to draw a distinction between two different ways of perceiving another's situation: the *imagine-other* perspective, by which one imagines how another person sees their situation, and the *imagine-self* perspective, by which one imagines how one would see the situation if one were in the other's position. According to self-report data, when confronted with a person in clear distress, an imagine-other and imagine-self perspective each produce an emotional response, with the former producing other-related thoughts and relatively pure empathic concern, and the latter producing self-related thoughts and direct personal distress. In addition, Batson reports neuroimaging data supporting the notion that an imagine-other perspective evokes empathic concern: activation of motivational-affective areas of distress or pain coupled with a lack of activation of sensory areas of pain. According to the empathy-altruism hypothesis, an imagine-other perspective should lead to relatively pure altruistic motivation, whereas an imagine-self perspective should elicit a mixture of altruistic and egoistic motivations.

Chapters 19 and 20 then tackle the issue of empathic accuracy: How good are we at correctly inferring the specific content of another person's covert thoughts and feelings? Myers and Hodges (Chapter 19) suggest that over time people increasingly rely on schemas and mental simulations (i.e., internally generated constructs as opposed to externally cued ones) to infer what another person is thinking or feeling. Interestingly, these authors take the position that although reliance on such heuristic strategies can occasionally lead to inaccuracies, for the most part the use of mental simulations and schemas/stereotypes improves empathic accuracy. Among the beneficial consequences of employing simulations and stereotypes cited by Myers and Hodges are that (a) they allow one to fill in gaps of information about another that are inaccessible or unavailable to the perceiver; (b) they reduce the amount of effort required in an interaction because the perceiver does not have to expend as much energy detecting subtle cues provided by the target person; and (c) even when the use of simulations and stereotypes leads to inaccuracies, the consequences of such inaccuracies are often not nearly as negative as one might fear.

Although Epley and Caruso (Chapter 20) generally agree with Myers and Hodges (Chapter 19) that "the ability to accurately adopt someone's perspective is better than chance but less than perfect" (p. 296), these authors elect in their chapter to focus on barriers to accurate perspective taking. First, they argue, individuals need to actively think about another's mental state when it is appropriate to do so, but in fact empirical evidence suggests that individuals often fail to activate the mental process of perspective taking. Second, to experience, simulate, or infer the perceptions of others, people must get over their own perspectives. In fact, empirical evidence indicates that initial egocentric assessment is likely to serve as a starting point in judgment, and subsequent attempts to adjust or correct such starting points tend to be insufficient. Finally, overcoming one's egocentric perspective often requires using some other information in its place to infer another's perspective (see also Myers & Hodges, Chapter 19). On this point, Epley and Caruso argue that, "If people are inclined to overcome egocentrism and rely on stored knowledge when they are adopting the perspective of someone who appears different from them, and if self-interest is a basic piece of stored knowledge that people use when thinking about others, then adopting the perspective of another person in the midst of conflict can actually make matters worse rather than better" (p. 304).

VI. SIMULATING AND PREPARING FOR THE FUTURE

The final section of the book explores how individuals render predictions about the future (chapters 21 and 22), define themselves with regard to their temporally extended future selves (Chapters 23 and 24), employ future selves as a means of self-regulation (Chapters 25 and 26), and alter their outlooks regarding the future for preparative benefit (Chapters 27 and 28). Klein and Zajac (Chapter 21) begin their chapter by identifying various dimensions of optimism, including the important distinction between absolute judgment (i.e., estimated chance of experiencing a future life event) and comparative judgment (i.e., estimated chance relative to the chances of another person or persons). It is the comparative measure of personal risk that is most commonly used to measure "unrealistic optimism." Klein and Zajac then examine how different conceptualizations of optimism might be related and report empirical evidence indicating that conditional risk perceptions—risk perceptions conditioned on changes in future behavior—are the only type of risk perception associated with intentions to change behavior, and that there appears to be little or no correlation between dispositional optimism and situational optimism. Finally, Klein and Zajac explore the causes and consequences of optimism, noting that single-event optimism can be caused by egocentrism, self-enhancement and self-protection motives, and preparation for negative feedback (see also Zeelenberg & Pieters, Chapter 27, and Carroll & Shepperd, Chapter 28). Overall, empirical evidence appears to indicate that whereas unrealistically optimistic beliefs lead to negative consequences (e.g., lower reported intentions to stop engaging in risky behaviors), dispositional optimism has mostly beneficial consequences.

Next, Dunn, Forrin, and Ashton-James (Chapter 22) take a close look at affective forecasting errors—the tendency for individuals to be miscalibrated with regard to their predictions for how they are going to feel in the future after certain events occur and their actual emotional responses to these events once they do occur. To account for such errors, Dunn et al. use Epstein's cognitive-experiential self theory (CEST), which posits that humans make sense of themselves and the world around them via two distinct information-processing systems: the rational system and the experiential system. According to Dunn et al., forecasters tend to adopt an analytical approach toward imagining their emotional responses to future events, but this approach is problematic because emotional experiences often stem from more holistic responses to events. Moreover, the cold, logical approach of the rational system neglects to account for either the psychological defenses initiated by the experiential system or the hot, visceral factors that will shape future feelings and behaviors and overly relies on abstract, quantitative information in generating affective forecasts, when in fact such information has little influence on actual emotions. Finally, Dunn et al. present evidence that discrepancies between forecasts and responses to the emotional experiences that those forecasts are meant to predict can be reduced, by both usurping the rational system's resources—leaving the experiential system free to take the lead in information processing—and enhancing forecasters' ability to tune in the experiential system.

According to early instantiations of temporal self-appraisal (TSA) theory, past selves are temporally extended selves that can vary in proximity to the current self. In Chapter 23, Perunovic and Wilson illustrate how the TSA approach may also be extended to the investigation of future self-appraisal (see also Libby & Eibach, Chapter 24). To begin, these authors note how subjective proximity has an impact on subjective valence, as individuals appear to be more motivated to evaluate close temporal selves favorably because those selves reflect directly on current identity. In addition, individuals appear to reap the benefits of anticipated future glory by drawing it subjectively closer to the present while viewing threatening future failures as more remote. Finally, Perunovic and Wilson present recent evidence suggesting that anticipated future goals have a greater motivational impact when they feel psychologically imminent rather than remote. Thus, subjective temporal distance may play a pivotal role in self-regulation for effective goal pursuit.

In a related vein, Libby and Eibach (Chapter 24) examine how imagery perspective functions in defining the temporally extended self (see also Kosslyn & Moulton, Chapter 3). Illustrating this connection, recent work is described indicating that those who were told to reflect on the broader meaning of a specific life event for their life as a whole were subsequently more likely to visualize it from the third-person perspective than those told to focus on the details of the event in isolation. Furthermore, in a study on high school memories, participants reported experiencing more third-person imagery when their past selves were inconsistent with their present selves than when they were consistent, regardless of whether those past selves were perceived to be negative or positive. According to Libby and Eibach, thinking about events in terms of their relations to broader themes in one's life rather than focusing on the concrete experience appears to be responsible for the effect of self-change on imagery perspective (i.e., from first- to third-person perspective). Finally, Libby and Eibach report that picturing voting from the third-person as opposed to the first-person perspective the night before election day led voters to be more likely to turn out to the polls the following day. Overall, then, imagery perspective appears to function in defining the temporally extended self-concept, influencing judgments about the self and guiding behavior.

Chapters 25 and 26 explore how future selves can be employed as a means of self-regulation. Oyserman and James (Chapter 25) devote significant attention to the motivational consequences of possible selves—future-oriented aspects of self-concept that represent what one expects to become or hopes to avoid becoming. According to Oyserman and James, possible selves serve a self-improvement function insofar as they link vivid images of oneself in a future state to current action that can be taken to move toward positive and away from negative future selves. In addition to linking possible selves theory with other self-regulation models, Oyserman and James outline a process model by which possible selves are likely to influence self-regulation and outcomes. Elements of this model include (a) whether the discrepancy between the present and possible self is clear; (b) whether the possible self seems attainable or preventable; (c) whether the possible self is linked to another possible self in the same domain but of opposite valence; (d) whether the possible self is linked to strategies; and (e) whether the subjective experience of effort at working toward a goal is interpreted as meaning that the goal is important. According to Oyserman and James, if these and other requirements are not met, individuals are likely to be oriented toward the present rather than the future and so will not engage in persistent self-regulation.

In Chapter 26, Oettingen and Kappes describe self-regulatory mechanisms that allow individuals to successfully respond to negative feedback. The first part of the chapter describes Oettingen's model of fantasy realization (see also Klinger, Chapter 15), which posits that conjointly envisioning the future and reality (i.e., mental contrasting; see also Markman et al., Chapter 12) links them together in a manner suggesting that reality obstructs the realization of a desired future. This linkage elicits a necessity to act that activates expectations of success. When such expectations are high, individuals will actively commit to striving for the desired future, whereas when such expectations are low, individuals will refrain from doing so. In turn, Oettingen and Kappes describe recent evidence indicating that mental contrasting with high expectations allows individuals to process negative feedback effectively, protect their self-views from the threat posed by negative feedback, and explain negative feedback in an optimistic way. Moreover, mental contrasting effects appear to transfer from one task to another and across domains, suggesting that acquiring mental contrasting as a self-regulatory strategy can help foster achievement on a more general level. In all, the fantasy realization model contributes to research on goal pursuit by specifying the processes by which individuals form goal commitments.

The final two chapters in the book (Chapters 27 and 28) examine mental strategies that individuals use to prepare for the future. Zeelenberg and Pieters (Chapter 27) point out that when decisions are important, individuals tend to think about how they would evaluate their outcomes in light of the outcomes forgone (see also Chapters 10–12). Such prefactual thoughts often arouse feelings of anticipatory regret, and according to Zeelenberg and Pieters, decision makers tend to regulate their regrets by behaving in a manner that minimizes the likelihood that they will actually experience this emotion in the future. The authors then describe a regret regulation perspective that specifies the various types of strategies that decision makers might use to prepare for their anticipated experience of regret. These include goal-focused strategies, such as decreasing one's standards; decision-focused strategies, such as improving decision quality, delaying or avoiding decisions, increasing decision justifiability, or transferring decision responsibility; alternative-focused strategies, such as ensuring decision reversibility and avoiding feedback about forgone alternatives; and feeling-focused strategies, such as bracing for the worst (see also Carroll & Shepperd, Chapter 28).

Finally, and fittingly, Carroll and Shepperd (Chapter 28) close out the volume by examining preparedness—a need state that represents a readiness to respond to future uncertainty. According to Carroll and Shepperd, "preparedness provides the proximal motivation that drives people to utilize the functions of mental simulations and expectations to prepare for possible future outcomes before they arise" (p. 437), and it "provides a framework for understanding the translation of memories into mental simulations that generate the future expectations, which in turn guide plans and intentions to respond to future uncertainty" (p. 437). Thus, Carroll and Shepperd use the preparedness construct to link together many of the processes described in other chapters that ultimately subserve this need state, including the link between retrospection and prospection (Chapters 8 and 9), the preparatory and affective functions of mental simulations (Chapters 11 and 12), emotional inoculation via downward revision of future outlooks (Chapter 22), and the manner in which mental simulations elicit expectancies regarding future behavior (Chapters 5, 6, 7, 25, 26, and 27), as well as a general readiness to act (Chapters 1, 2, and 3).

It has been said that your imagination will set you free. We hope that the work described in this volume stimulates psychologists and nonpsychologists alike to reflect on our ability to simulate the past, the present, and the future and to consider the implications of this ability for feeling, judging, thinking, knowing, and behaving. As the reader shall see, mental simulations have the ability to both enhance our lives and lead us astray. In all, however, it should become clear that how we imagine, what we imagine, and why we imagine are essential components of what it means to be human.

REFERENCES

Johnson, M. K., & Sherman, S. J. (1990). Constructing and reconstructing the past and future in the present. In E. T. Higgins & R. M. Sorrentino (Eds.), *Handbook of motivation and cognition: Foundations of social behavior* (Vol. 2, pp. 482–526). New York: Guilford.

Kahneman, D., & Tversky, A. (1982). The simulation heuristic. In D. Kahneman, P. Slovic, & A. Tversky (Eds.), *Judgment under uncertainty: Heuristics and biases* (pp. 201–208). New York: Cambridge University Press.

Loewenstein, G., Read, D., & Baumeister, R. (2003). *Time and decision: Economic and psychological perspectives on intertemporal choice.* New York: Sage.

Sanna, L. J., & Chang, E. C. (2006). *Judgments over time: The interplay of thoughts, feelings, and behaviors.* New York: Oxford University Press.

Taylor, S. E., Pham, L. B., Rivkin, I., & Armor, D. A. (1998). Harnessing the imagination: Mental simulation, self-regulation, and coping. *American Psychologist, 53*, 429–439.

List of Contributors

Daniel Algom
Tel-Aviv University
Tel-Aviv, Israel

Eleanor Amit
Tel-Aviv University
Tel-Aviv, Israel

Claire E. Ashton-James
University of British Columbia
Vancouver, British Columbia, Canada

Sean Barnes
State University of New York at Binghamton
Binghamton, New York, USA

C. Daniel Batson
University of Kansas
Lawrence, Kansas, USA

Sian L. Beilock
University of Chicago
Chicago, Illinois, USA

Daniel M. Bernstein
Kwantlen University College
Surrey, British Columbia, Canada

Ruth M.J. Byrne
Trinity College Dublin, University of Dublin
Dublin, Ireland

Patrick Carroll
The Ohio State University—Lima
Lima, Ohio, USA

Eugene M. Caruso
University of Chicago
Chicago, Illinois, USA

Jean Decety
University of Chicago
Chicago, Illinois, USA

John K. Donahue
University of North Carolina at Chapel Hill
Chapel Hill, North Carolina, USA

Elizabeth W. Dunn
University of British Columbia
Vancouver, British Columbia, Canada

Richard P. Eibach
Williams College
Williamstown, Massachusetts, USA

Nicholas Epley
University of Chicago
Chicago, Illinois, USA

Tanya S. Faude-Koivisto
University of Konstanz
Konstanz, Germany
New York University
New York, New York, USA

Noah D. Forrin
University of British Columbia
Vancouver, British Columbia, Canada

Adam D. Galinsky
Northwestern University
Evanston, Illinois, USA

Vittorio Girotto
University IUAV of Venice
Venice, Italy

Ryan D. Godfrey
University of California, Riverside
Riverside, California, USA

Peter M. Gollwitzer
New York University
New York, New York, USA
University of Konstanz
Konstanz, Germany

Melanie C. Green
University of North Carolina at Chapel Hill
Chapel Hill, North Carolina, USA

Sara D. Hodges
University of Oregon
Eugene, Oregon, USA

Leah James
University of Michigan
Ann Arbor, Michigan, USA

Joanne Kane
University of Colorado, Boulder
Boulder, Colorado, USA

Andreas Kappes
Universität Hamburg
Hamburg, Germany

Figen Karadogan
Ohio University
Athens, Ohio, USA

Lindsay A. Kennedy
University of North Carolina at Chapel Hill
Chapel Hill, North Carolina, USA

William M. P. Klein
University of Pittsburgh
Pittsburgh, Pennsylvania, USA

Eric Klinger
University of Minnesota, Morris
Morris, Minnesota, USA

Stephen M. Kosslyn
Harvard University
Cambridge, Massachusetts, USA

Laura J. Kray
University of California, Berkeley
Berkeley, California, USA

Lisa K. Libby
Ohio State University
Columbus, Ohio, USA

Nira Liberman
Tel-Aviv University
Tel-Aviv, Israel

Matthew J. Lindberg
Ohio University
Athens, Ohio, USA

Elizabeth F. Loftus
University of California, Irvine
Irvine, California, USA

Steven Jay Lynn
State University of New York at Binghamton
Binghamton, New York, USA

Ian M. Lyons
University of Chicago
Chicago, Illinois, USA

Anne M. Mannering
University of Oregon
Eugene, Oregon, USA

Keith D. Markman
Ohio University
Athens, Ohio, USA

Abigail Matthews
State University of New York at Binghamton
Binghamton, New York, USA

Kathleen B. McDermott
Washington University, St. Louis
St. Louis, Missouri, USA

A. Peter McGraw
University of Colorado, Boulder
Boulder, Colorado, USA

Samuel T. Moulton
Harvard University
Cambridge, Massachusetts, USA

Michael W. Myers
University of Oregon
Eugene, Oregon, USA

Gabriele Oettingen
New York University
New York, New York, USA
Universität Hamburg
Hamburg, Germany

Daphna Oyserman
University of Michigan
Ann Arbor, Michigan, USA

Wei Qi Elaine Perunovic
University of New Brunswick
Fredericton, Canada

Rik Pieters
Tilburg University
Tilburg, The Netherlands

Lawrence J. Sanna
University of North Carolina at Chapel Hill
Chapel Hill, North Carolina, USA

Rebecca Saxe
Massachusetts Institute of Technology
Cambridge, Massachusetts, USA

Norbert Schwarz
University of Michigan
Ann Arbor, Michigan, USA

Alison B. Shawber
University of Oregon
Eugene, Oregon, USA

James A. Shepperd
University of Florida
Gainesville, Florida, USA

Jennifer A. Stevens
College of William and Mary
Williamsburg, Virginia, USA

Julie A. Suhr
Ohio University
Athens, Ohio, USA

Karl K. Szpunar
Washington University, St. Louis
St. Louis, Missouri, USA

Marjorie Taylor
University of Oregon
Eugene, Oregon, USA

Yaacov Trope
Tel-Aviv University
Tel-Aviv, Israel

Leaf Van Boven
University of Colorado, Boulder
Boulder, Colorado, USA

Anne E. Wilson
Wilfred Laurier University
West Waterloo, Ontario, Canada

Elaine M. Wong
Northwestern University
Evanston, Illinois, USA

Daniela Wuerz
Ludwig-Maximilians-University Munich
Munich, Germany
New York University
New York, New York, USA

Laura E. Zajac
University of Pittsburgh
Pittsburgh, Pennsylvania, USA

Marcel Zeelenberg
Tilburg University
Tilburg, The Netherlands

Ethan Zell
Ohio University
Athens, Ohio, USA

Section I

The Mental Simulation of
Action and Behavior

1 Action Representation and Its Role in Social Interaction

Jean Decety and Jennifer A. Stevens

There is a large body of evidence to support the idea that actions are represented in the brain via specific computational mechanisms underpinned by neural structures similar to those recruited during action execution. Examination of the processes that mediate motor representation singularly offers a window into the automatic and covert planning-to-execution motor translations that occur during voluntary movement sequences. Indeed, motor representation and its role in the evaluation and planning of action has come to be known as a categorically distinct modality of representation. One by-product of this organization is the functional connection motor representation appears to serve between the mind and the body, a relation encapsulated within the thesis of embodied cognition. Because motor representation inherently involves aspects of both body and mind, it presents as the most obvious candidate for wedding this dichotomy. But the functional connection has also surfaced through the number of studies demonstrating that action or the simulation of it relates to a variety of mental operations, including action understanding, object naming, self-identity, and memory. Theories of embodied cognition impart the notion that the current motor state pervades all of our cognitive states and emotions.

Recent progress in cognitive neuroscience suggests a critical role for motor representations in social interaction (e.g., Beilock & Lyons, Chapter 2, this volume; Sommerville & Decety, 2006). In the case of understanding purposeful movement, information about the movement properties of an action and the typical end state that it embodies (i.e., its consequence or effect on another person) is processed, with the latter typically given higher priority than the former (Prinz, 2003). Accordingly, action representations are shared in that they invoke similar states of mind, including emotions across individuals. Specifically, motor representation underlies the development and maintenance of empathetic responses to another's situation (Decety & Jackson, 2004; see also Batson, Chapter 18, this volume). In this chapter, we present action representation as a meaningful construct that presupposes interaction with the environment, whether or not voluntary movement by the self or another subsequently occurs. Action representation, by means of the neural activity and attention the simulation requires, can serve as a facilitative strategy for physical performance of motor actions in typical and atypical populations. Moreover, it provides the basis for social interaction, including action understanding, social facilitation, imitation, and empathy by offering a means for individuals to take on another's perspectives (Sommerville & Decety, 2006).

MOTOR SIMULATION AT THE ORIGIN OF VOLUNTARY MOVEMENT

Voluntary movement is the unfolding of a planned outcome. The current motor state is compared against the desired endpoint and a movement plan is generated and then realized. Theorists in biomechanics suggest that this translation occurs within the internal models (IMs) (Kawato & Wolpert, 1998). IMs take into account the proprioceptive cues about the current motor state and an understanding of how that state can be transformed into the joint torques and muscle forces required for the upcoming action. Essentially, they mimic the behavior of the sensorimotor system, thereby enabling determinations about the motor commands required to perform specific tasks and predictions about the consequences of those commands. The external or environmental features that are generally coded include target location, direction, and distance (Bhat & Sanes, 1998; Moody & Zipser, 1998; Paulignan, Frak, Toni, & Jeannerod, 1997), and following the visual registration of a target, an action pattern toward it is generated; the IMs provide a covert place where afferent information can be translated into efferent commands or vice versa. This idea is historically related to the notion of "schema" (Neisser, 1976) and "motor program" (Keele, 1968) from cognitive psychology. A number of studies have used behavioral aftereffects to demonstrate the instantiation of motor adaptation or IMs (e.g., Conditt, Gandolfo, & Mussa-Ivaldi, 1997; Shadmehr & Mussa-Ivaldi, 1994), while functional neuroimaging methods have documented shifts in cortical activity that occur as a function of newly acquired motor sequences (Clower et al., 1996; Shadmehr & Holcomb, 1997).

Motor images, similar to IMs, are covert simulations of planned behavioral performances. However, they are unique in that they can be explicitly generated and evaluated, providing a window into the planning-to-execution translation that precipitates voluntary movement (Jeannerod, 2003). For example, the mental rehearsal of a motor act, and the time needed to do so, provides insight into the representational features of the movement (Crammond, 1997). Essentially, motor images may be considered mental representations that mimic those processes that occur on-line and covertly during everyday movement situations.

The buildup to the link among motor representation, simulation of movement in the planning-to-execution translation, and the relative importance of motor simulation in cognitive and social constructs began with studies demonstrating a tight link between internal action processing (representation) and external action performance (execution). Specifically, they share behavioral and neural structure.

NATURE AND NEUROPHYSIOLOGICAL SUBSTRATE OF MOTOR REPRESENTATIONS

Psychophysical studies on motor imagery demonstrate similar temporal patterns between physically and mentally performed actions. The base of these studies is the finding that mental movement time reflects biomechanic movement properties, namely, movement time as a function of movement accuracy, a relation mathematically identified as Fitts law (Fitts, 1954). For both single-trajectory and repetitive movements, movement time is a logarithmic function of movement distance and target size. Movement time increases with distance but decreases with size because large targets require less correction to maintain accuracy. For example, it takes similar amounts of time to complete actual or imagined handwriting in small and large amplitudes: Large-size handwriting covers more distance, while small-size handwriting has a decreased margin for error (Decety & Michel, 1989). The effect of path width on real and imagined walking speed (Choudhury, Charman, Bird, & Blakemore, 2007; Decety & Jeannerod, 1996; Stevens, 2005) and of target size on real and imagined pointing (Sirigu et al., 1996) is mediated by a similar function: Movements of the same distance take more time as movement space decreases. While similar temporal patterns arise in real and imagined motor movement times, there is not always temporal equivalency. When traversing distances of greater than 5 m, movement times are significantly faster in the imagined condition, perhaps the result of the same foreshortening effect that has been found to influence judgments of distance in the frontal plane (Calmels, Holmes, Lopez, & Naman, 2006; Stevens, 2005).

Less-direct behavioral paradigms also illustrate that biomechanical-specific considerations underlie motor representation. A study by Georgopolous and Massey (1987) revealed movement initiation to be a function of the upcoming reach amplitude, suggesting that a mental simulation of the action precedes and is temporally dependent on the size of the upcoming action. That is, the larger the movement to be made, the longer the delay between trial onset and initiation of physical movement trajectory. Of special importance, studies conducted by Shiffrar and Freyd (1990, 1993) on apparent motion demonstrated that perception of biomechanically impossible, direct movement paths are avoided when enough time to perceive the completion of biomechanically possible, indirect movement paths is given. Observers perceive an arm moving through a barrier at short stimulus onset asynchronies (SOAs) (<300 ms) but perceive the arm moving around a barrier during longer SOAs (>400 ms). This result reveals that a preference for perception of natural action paths occurs once a cognitive identification of the relevant features of the biomechanic entity and movement context can be made.

Other experiments demonstrated a link between physical and mental state through shifts in cognitive processing time based on congruency between the individual's physical position and the cognitive task performed. In general, when the cognitive task and the individual's motor state are incompatible, the task is completed less quickly. Arm swings take longer to imagine when individuals stand with an arm extended horizontally, while the same pose does not affect time needed to imagine running in place. Standing on one leg has the opposite effect: Imagined running in place is slowed, while arm swings are not (Stevens, 2005). Response times for left-/right-hand identifications are quicker when the orientation of the stimulus hand is compatible with the orientation of the observer's hand (Parsons, 1994; Shenton, Schwoebel, & Coslett, 2004). Consistent with the theory that observers imagine their own hand moving into the position of the stimulus hand as a solution strategy, brain activity during a left-right hand identification task has been found to occur in the sensory and motor cortices and in the cerebellum (Parsons et al., 1995). Motor-evoked potentials observed in the hand resulting from transcranial magnetic stimulation to contralateral motor cortex are higher and stretch reflex response is quicker when there is congruency between the current hand position and an imagined hand movement (Fourkas, Ionta, & Aglioti, 2006; Li, Stevens, Kamper, & Rymer, 2005).

Overall body posture has been found to affect some specific cognitive processes. For example, standing in an awkward posture degrades performance on spatial but not object working memory (VanderVelde, Woollacott, & Shumway-Cook, 2005). Error rates for mental imagery tasks involving inspection are lowest when individuals are in a horizontal position (lying on one's side, right ear down), whereas in tasks of composition, errors are lowest when the individual is in a supine position (lying on one's back) (Mast, Ganis, Christie, & Kosslyn, 2003). In the memory domain, positive thoughts are more readily recalled while seated in an upright versus a slumped position (Wilson & Peper, 2004), and retrieval of events is quicker when the current body posture is congruent with that of the event recalled (Dijkstra, Kaschak, & Zwaan, 2007). For example, a memory of waving to a person is recalled more quickly while actually standing up and waving.

These postural effects are in line with the recent formulations of embodied cognition, which regard the motor state as a characteristic of being that permeates all human processing (see Garbarini & Adenzato, 2004). The concept of embodiment may be rightly traced back to Gibson's theory of affordances, a notion that characterized the human in a continual state of perception for action in the environment (Gibson, 1979). It is critical to know what we can physically accomplish in any given situation, be it flee, fight, eat, or hug. But, the engagement of our motor system can also influence and be influenced by judgments, memory, or attention-cognitive processes traditionally considered aspects of mind, not body. For example, individuals are faster to respond with a pull toward themselves when a likeable trait is presented (but are faster to respond with a push away if the person imagines him- or herself in the opposing location) (Markman & Brendl, 2005). Thus, although Gibson restricted his theory of affordances to a discussion of perception and action, physical state and the perception of its capabilities may have more global effect.

Neuroimaging studies have reliably outlined striking overlap in neural patterns of activation associated with physical and imagined movement. Most consistently, both activate the supplementary motor area (SMA), the premotor cortex (PMC), and the cerebellum (e.g., Decety et al., 1994; Michelon, Vettel, & Zacks, 2006; Naito et al., 2002; Stephan et al., 1995) (see Figure 1.1 for anatomical definitions).

The role of primary motor cortex in motor representation remains ambiguous because its activation is less consistent across subjects and studies (e.g., Roth et al., 1996). Moreover, damage to

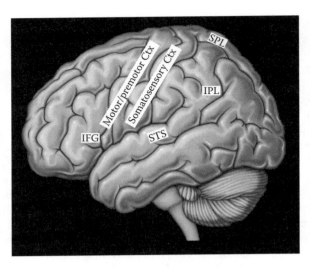

FIGURE 1.1   A lateral view of a human left hemisphere. IFG, inferior frontal gyrus; STS, superior temporal sulcus; IPL, inferior parietal lobule (Brodmann areas 39 and 40); SPL, superior parietal lobule (Brodmann areas 5 and 7); and cerebellum. Note that the IFG corresponds to the ventral premotor cortex in monkeys in which area F5 is located. The premotor cortex has a central role in the selection of movements. Neurons in the posterior portion of the STS are triggered by the sight of actions performed by others, but not during the execution of action. The SPL is involved in coding space and in directing spatial attention in relation to the control of body movements. The left IPL mediates motor representations, and the right IPL/temporoparietal junction is critical for the sense of agency. Ctx, cortex.

this area does not affect an individual's ability to imagine movements at time intervals similar to those needed to complete physical performance (Sirigu et al., 1995). Significant activation in primary motor cortex has been found during on-line simulation of physical movement, but only when the movements are compatible with the biomechanical capacities of the observer (Stevens, Fonlupt, Shiffrar, & Decety, 2000). In that neuroimaging study, participants were presented with static images of a human model in different positions as well as objects in different spatial configurations. Members of the pairs were presented in sequence, so that one position seemed to move into the other. The participants were asked to rate the trajectories of the perceived motion path. For the human model, the perceived motion was either a possible or an impossible biomechanical path. The results indicated that the left primary motor cortex at the level of the upper limb area, the parietal cortex in both hemispheres, and the cerebellum were selectively activated when participants perceived possible paths of human movement. In contrast, no selective activation of these areas was found during conditions of biomechanically impossible movement paths.

The parietal cortex plays a significant role in motor imagery tasks, particularly when the movements are tied to visual coordinates in space. Patients with damage to the parietal cortex display selective impairment in imagined finger movements and imagined pointing as compared to control subjects or patients with damage to primary motor cortex (Sirigu et al., 1996). A case study examining the effects of right hemisphere parietal damage (resulting in left neglect) on imagery processing revealed a dissociation between the speed-accuracy trade-off recognized by real movements and the movement time function associated with imagined movements regardless of hand used, or imagined to be used, to complete the action (Danckert et al., 2002). Parietal cortex damage has also been found to affect the ability to verbally identify when one becomes aware of an intention to move. While control participants and individuals with cerebellar damage were found to retain the ability to indicate the start of a realization of an intention to move, individuals with damage to either left or right parietal cortex could not (Sirigu et al., 2004). This finding suggests that the parietal cortex may offer a unique location for conscious processing during motor representations.

FACILITATIVE EFFECTS OF ACTION REPRESENTATION ON MOTOR PERFORMANCE

There is a natural and practical application of the overlap between mentally simulated and physically executed action: Mental practice may be used to facilitate subsequent physical performance. The value in using mental imagery to enhance performance in sport is not new and has been well documented for decades (see Feltz & Landers, 1983; Kosslyn & Moulton, Chapter 3, this volume). Mental practice is believed to benefit the individual by improving motor and motivational skills during performance in a stressful situation. Several studies have been able to characterize demonstrable physical changes as a result of mental practice. An important study conducted by Wehner, Vogt, and Stadler (1984) showed early on that motor imagery results in increased muscular activity, but the increases are limited to those muscles relevant to the imagined motor movement. Mental practice has been linked to significant increases in muscle strength (Yue & Cole, 1992); however, this effect may depend on the kind of action that is mentally practiced. For example, Yue and Cole examined effects of a 4-week mental practice on hypothenar (fifth-digit) muscles and found increases in muscle strength. In contrast, Herbert and colleagues (Herbert, Dean, & Gandevia, 1998) examined effects of an 8-week mental practice on elbow flexor muscles and found no significant increase in muscle strength.

What *is* new is the literature from cognitive neuroscience that has exposed the cortical and subcortical mechanisms that serve both imagined and executed action. Shifts in brain activation can occur as a function of mental practice. Jackson and colleagues demonstrated two regions of increased activation that occur during motor performance following several days of motor imagery practice: increase in the orbitofrontal cortex activation and a decrease in activation in the cerebellum (Jackson, Lafleur, Malouin, Richards, & Doyon, 2003; Lafleur et al., 2002). However, in a study with a relatively large sample size ($N = 54$), cortical and subcortical activity during motor execution and motor imagery conditions for a hand sequence task did not differ greatly across novel and skilled conditions, a result that indicates that imagery engages relevant features of the motor execution network and may be used in its stead as a modality of practice (Lacourse, Orr, Cramer, & Cohen, 2005). The effectiveness of mental practice in influencing subsequent physical performance likely depends on the formation of meaningful representations. For example, activation of motor planning and behavior regions appears to be specific to a first-person relationship between an imagined movement and the self (Decety et al., 1994; Parsons et al., 1995). Decety and colleagues (1994) found motor cortical activity when participants imagined their own hand completing grasps (first-person perspective of action), but when the participants observed an alien hand completing grasps (third-person perspective of action) high activation was found in visual cortical areas. These results suggest that only images formed from the first-person perspective or with the biomechanics of the self in mind will have a positive effect on subsequent physical performance. Indeed, participants that imagine a novel action as they place themselves in another's position, as if they are completing the task observed, learn the task better (Lozano, Hard, & Tversky, 2006).

Because of the tight link between the neural encoding of represented and executed action and the downstream responses activated by mental rehearsal, the effect of mental practice may be likened to the facilitatory effects of priming. During mental rehearsal, the motor pathways that will be recruited during subsequent motor performance are activated at a quicker rate, resulting in a more rapid response time or more accurate performance. The effects of priming on improved performance have been demonstrated in a number of studies across a number of behavioral domains, most notably memory retrieval (Baddeley & Hitch, 1993).

Investigations on the value of mental practice in sport continue, but the use of simulated movement as a motor enhancement strategy has also become more common within the context of rehabilitation. Specifically, stroke survivors with hemiparesis (weakness on one side of the body) have demonstrated functional improvements in hand or leg performance following a course of simulated motor practice (Dickstein & Deutsch, 2007; Jackson, Doyon, Richards, & Malouin, 2004; Stevens &

Stoykov, 2003). Using transcranial magnetic stimulation, Cicinelli and colleagues (2006) found that motor imagery significantly enhanced the cortical excitability of motor cortex in the hemisphere affected by stroke in a postacute stage. The changes in excitability corresponded to the muscle area used in the imagined movements, and no differences were observed with respect to the stroke lesion locations. This result suggests that as long as the motor cortex is active, motor imagery may be used to facilitate its response, which may then translate downstream to result in better motor execution. Thus, while earlier brain imaging and patient studies may have found variable motor cortex activity mediating motor imagery, this study demonstrated that motor imagery invariably mediates motor cortex activity in the stroke survivor.

COMMON CODING AND THE MIRROR NEURON SYSTEM

One influential theory, known as the *common coding hypothesis*, suggests that somewhere in the chain of operation that leads from perception to action, the system generates derivatives of stimulation and antecedents of action that are commensurate in the sense that they share the same system of representational dimensions (e.g., Prinz, 2003). The core assumption of the common coding hypothesis is that actions are coded in terms of the perceivable effects (i.e., the distal perceptual events) they will generate. Performing a movement leaves behind a bidirectional association between the motor pattern it was generated by and the sensory effects that it produces. Such an association can then be used backward to retrieve a movement by anticipating its effects (Hommel, 2004). These perception-action codes are also accessible during action observation, and perception activates action representations to the degree that the perceived and the represented actions are similar (Wilson & Knoblich, 2005).

EVIDENCE FROM NEUROPHYSIOLOGY

Neurophysiological evidence for the common coding hypothesis comes from a variety of electrophysiological studies, which have demonstrated that (a) motor representations are involved in both action production and perception of others actions, and (b) these representations are organized as goal-directed motor schema. The existence of a mechanism directly matching action and perception was demonstrated by single-cell recordings in the monkey that have discovered neurons in the posterior region of the inferior frontal gyrus (IFG; ventral PMC in monkeys) that selectively discharge both during the execution of actions and during the observation of the same actions executed by conspecifics. These sensorimotor neurons are called *mirror neurons* (Rizzolatti, Fadiga, Gallese, & Fogassi, 1996).

Subsequent work has revealed that mirror neurons in the PMC respond on the basis of the goal of an action, not merely its motor components. In nonhuman primates, a subset of mirror neurons responds when the final part of an action, crucial in triggering the response when the action is seen entirely, is hidden and can only be inferred (Ulmità et al., 2001). By automatically matching the agent's observed action onto its own motor repertoire without executing it, the firing of mirror neurons in the observer brain simulates the agent's observed action and thereby contributes to the understanding of the perceived action. Subsequent studies have shown that some neurons display mirror properties between motor and other modalities such as audition (Kohler et al., 2002), indicating that single neurons are concerned with some actions regardless of the modality through which a given action is inferred (i.e., it is the consequence of the action that seems to represented).

Such neurons are not restricted to the PMC but have also been recorded in other areas of the brain, notably in the posterior parietal cortex (area PF) in relation to actions performed with objects. A single-cell electrophysiological study with monkeys reported that inferior parietal mirror neurons, in addition to recognizing the goal of the observed motor acts, discriminate identical motor acts according to the context in which these acts are embedded, for instance, grasping a piece of food to eat versus grasping the same item to place (Fogassi et al., 2005). The authors further argued that because the discriminated motor act is part of a chain leading to the final goal of the action, this neuronal property allows the monkey to predict the goal of the observed action and thus to "read" the intention of the acting individual.

Another cortical region, the superior temporal sulcus (STS), responds to the observation of actions done by others. In the macaque monkey, Perrett and coworkers (1989) have found that there are neurons in the superior part of the STS that are sensitive to the sight of static and dynamic information about the body. The majorities of these cells are selective for one perspective view and are thought to provide viewer-centered descriptions that can be used in guiding behavior. For some cells in the lower bank of STS, the responses to body movements were related to the object or to the goal of the movements. Movements effective in eliciting neuron responses in this region include walking, turning the head, bending the torso, and moving the arms. A small set of STS neurons discharges also during the observation of goal-directed hand movements. Moreover, a population of cells, located in the anterior part of the STS, responds selectively to the sight of reaching but only when the agent performing the action is seen attending to the target position of the reaching (Jellema, Baker, Wicker, & Perrett, 2000). In addition, the responses of a subset of these cells are modulated by the direction of attention (indicated by head and body posture of the agent performing the action). This combined analysis of direction of attention and body movements suggests a role for neural activation in the STS during the detection of intentional actions. These two regions (i.e., posterior STS and PMC) are reciprocally connected via the posterior parietal cortex. Thus, in the monkey, there seems to be a circuitry composed of the STS, area PF, and F5 that codes the actions of others and maps these actions onto the motor repertoire of the observer.

In humans, a number of cognitive (e.g., Loula, Prasad, Harber, & Shiffrar, 2005) and functional imaging studies demonstrated the involvement of motor representation during the perception of action performed by others (e.g., Hamzei et al., 2003). Notably, one functional magnetic resonance imaging (fMRI) study showed that the activation pattern in the PMC elicited by the observation of actions performed by another individual follows somatotopic organization (i.e., different parts of the body are represented in an orderly sequence in a number of cortical regions, such as the primary motor cortex and the somatosensory cortex) related to the observed action. Watching mouth, foot, and hand actions elicits different sites in the premotor and superior parietal cortices, which are normally involved in the actual execution of the observed actions (Buccino et al., 2001). Interestingly, when participants watched movements without objects, only the PMC was activated, while when the actions observed involved objects, the parietal cortex became activated. Thus, it seems that the PMC activation is not dependent on the movement having an objectified goal.

Studies related to the phenomenon of apparent motion offer compelling evidence for the involvement of motor representation in the perception of bodily movements in humans (Shiffrar & Pinto, 2002). For instance, Stevens and colleagues (2000) adapted the apparent biological motion paradigm to present participants in the scanner with a human model in different postures. Depending on the activation conditions, the subjects were shown either possible or impossible biomechanical paths of apparent motion. The left primary motor cortex and parietal lobule in both hemispheres were selectively activated when the participants perceived possible paths of right limb human movement. No activation in these areas was detected during conditions of impossible biomechanical movement paths. Thus, only the perception of actions that conform to the motor capabilities of the observer evokes motor representations in the observer.

Further evidence suggests that activation of the mirror neuron system is mediated not only by whether the actions are motorically plausible for the observer, but also by the observer's level of expertise performing the action. For instance, one fMRI study demonstrated that expert ballet dancers show stronger activation of premotor and parietal cortices when watching other ballet dancers than do novices. The extent of premotor and parietal activation in these areas is greatest when dancers observe their own style of dance versus another kinematically similar dance style (Calvo-Merino, Glaser, Grèzes, Passingham, & Haggard, 2005). Interestingly, this finding—less activation in novices than in experts—cannot be interpreted in terms of neural efficiency because this latter interpretation would predict exactly the opposite pattern of results. Indeed, neural efficiency assumes that higher ability in a cognitive task is associated with more efficient neuronal processing of this task. Such efficiency is reflected in decreases in neural work (e.g., glucose metabolic rate). For instance, Lamm, Bauer, Vitouch, and Gstättner (1999) documented significant event-related potential differences between good and poor performers in a visuospatial task. The poor performers showed higher activity in the posterior parietal region, and their topography was more extended into the frontocentral regions. Thus, the greater activation of the frontoparietal circuit during the perception of dancing movements by experts fits neatly with the involvement of motor representations during observation of action when there is congruence between subjects' own motor repertoire and perceived actions performed by others (see also Beilock & Lyons, Chapter 2, this volume).

The effect of similarity between the observer's motor repertoire and the perceived action was also demonstrated in one fMRI study during which participants were shown video clips of themselves and of others lifting a box and had to judge the beliefs of the actors about the weight of the box. Results demonstrated activity in a number of cortical regions involved in motor control, namely the dorsal PMC, left parietal cortex, and right cerebellum, when participants made judgments about their own actions as well as those of others (Grèzes, Frith, & Passingham, 2004).

Interestingly, there is some evidence that the motor resonance system is present not only in adult brains but also in young children. An electroencephalographic study with intracranial recordings on a 36-month-old child showed that corresponding areas of the sensorimotor cortex were activated when the child watched another person drawing with his right hand and when the child drew with her own right hand (Fecteau et al., 2004). Recent work suggests that the functional relation between action production and action perception has its roots in infancy. Previous research has revealed that, after successfully searching at one hiding location (A), infants typically revert to that location after watching a hiding event in which the object is hidden in a new location (B; called the "A not B error"). Longo and Bertenthal (2006) established that perseverative errors to the initial hiding location also occurred after 9-month-old infants only watched the experimenter hide the object at the A location. These new data suggest that infants motorically simulate the actions of others during action observation.

The fact that action representations encode both the means of an action (e.g., the motor properties) and the typical end associated with it, with the latter having precedence over the former, suggests that the mirror system might underlie our ability to identify the goals of particular motor acts. Indeed, many researchers have suggested that the covert simulation or emulation of one's own action representations during action observation enables us to anticipate the likely outcome of other's actions (e.g., Sommerville & Decety, 2006; Wilson & Knoblich, 2005).

Recent neuroimaging work provides evidence for specific cortical regions within the mirror system that appear to be responsible for encoding goals. Notably, one fMRI study investigated goal detection in participants who watched short movies in which an actor reached toward one of two adjacent objects and picked up the object. On subsequent trials, the goal alone, trajectory alone, neither dimension or both or only one dimension varied in a random fashion (Hamilton & Grafton, 2006). The authors predicted that neural regions responsive to a change in another person's goal should show a greater response to novel goals than repeated goals but should not distinguish trajectories. They focused on three potential regions of interest for goal representation: the IFG, the intraparietal sulcus (IPS), and the right STS. They found that two cortical regions in the left IPS were specifically sensitive to goals. These two regions showed a greater response to a novel goal than a repeated goal, and the hemodynamic response function was reduced when the second video clip depicting the same goal was presented, irrespective of the trajectory taken by the hand.

To what extent does the mirror system underwrite or contribute to more sophisticated aspects of action understanding? Some authors have suggested that the mirror system may support mental state attribution via simulation (e.g., Blakemore & Decety, 2001), a proposal that is in keeping with theories in philosophy of mind that postulate that psychological state understanding is based on off-line reproduction of behavior and introspection (e.g., Goldman, 2002; Gordon, 1986; Harris, 1989).

In contrast, other authors have suggested that the mirror system's primary function concerns more basic aspects of action analysis (Wilson & Knoblich, 2005).

Numerous functional neuroimaging studies investigating mental state attribution across a variety of tasks (false belief understanding, attribution of intentions, mentalistic descriptions of object motion, evaluation of other's knowledge states, etc.) have documented several cortical areas outside the mirror system that are reliably activated during mental state reasoning tasks: the right posterior STS, temporal poles, the amygdala, and the medial prefrontal cortex (Frith & Frith, 2003; Siegal & Varley, 2002, for reviews). Moreover, studies with patients showed that damage to several regions in the prefrontal cortex impairs theory of mind abilities (e.g., Happé, Brownell, & Winner, 1999). Such findings suggest that the mirror system alone cannot support mental state attribution (Saxe, 2005, Chapter 17). However, questions remain regarding the potential developmental relation between the mirror system and the mentalizing system (Sommerville & Decety, 2006), as well the extent that the neural circuits specialized in theory of mind are specific to that function (Decety & Lamm, 2007; Stone & Gerrans, 2006).

Overall, the mirror neuron mechanism may subserve different functions, including action understanding (Rizzolatti & Craighero, 2004), empathy (Decety & Jackson, 2004; Meltzoff & Decety, 2003; Preston & de Waal, 2002), imitation (Brass & Heyes, 2005), and social facilitation. This last function is supported by direct neurophysiological evidence from a study conducted by Ferrari and coworkers (Ferrari, Maiolini, Addessi, Fogassi, & Visalberghi, 2005). The authors reported a series of single-neuron recordings in monkeys; the studies addressed observation of eating behavior. Their results indicate that such an observation significantly enhanced eating behavior in the observer, even when only the sound of eating actions was played. They suggested that eating facilitation triggered by observation or listening of eating actions can rely on the mirror neuron system of ventral PMC that provides a matching between the observed/listened action and the executed action. An fMRI study by Cheng, Meltzoff, and Decety (2007) demonstrated that motivation to eat modulates the mirror-neuron system. Greater signal change was detected in the IFG, the superior temporal gyrus, and the superior parietal cortex when hungry participants were observing the grasping of food as compared to when they were satiated. Further, the hemodynamic response in the right IFG correlated with subjective assessments of the motivation to eat as measured by subjective ratings. No such correlation was detected when participants were observing grasping objects.

FROM SOCIAL MIRRORING TO EMPATHIC UNDERSTANDING

In everyday life, imitation is remarkably prevalent. For instance, people unconsciously mimic others' postures, vocalization, mood, and mannerisms. This tendency to automatically mimic and synchronize one's own behavior with others facilitates the smoothness of social interaction and may even foster empathy (Hassin, Uleman, & Bargh, 2005; in this volume, see also Batson, Chapter 18, and Myers & Hodges, Chapter 19). For instance, one study demonstrated that participants who had been mimicked by the experimenter were more helpful and generous toward other people than non-mimicked participants (Van Baaren, Decety, Dijksterhuis, van der Leij, & van Leeuwen, in press; Van Baaren, Holland, Kawakami, & van Knippenberg, 2004). These researchers also found that these beneficial consequences of mimicry were not restricted to behavior that was directed toward the mimicker, but included behavior directed toward people not directly involved in the mimicry situation. Interestingly, autistic individuals who are profoundly impaired in social and emotional abilities do not show spontaneous mimicry of facial expressions but can do voluntary mimicry just fine (McIntosh, Reichmann-Decker, Winkielman, & Wilbarger, 2006). Such a core deficit in involuntary motor resonance may be the seed for their profound impairment in basic emotional connectedness.

Social mirroring does not require anything new to be learned or an understanding of the meaning of the imitated action. It is based on matching the current behavior of another with similar-looking actions of one's own. Such a matching may rely on the mirror-neuron system. However, an important difference between monkey and humans needs to be considered. The mirror neurons in monkey respond only to goal-directed actions and not to movements. In contrast, interference between observation and action has been documented in participants watching movements with no obvious goal (Brass, Bekkering, & Prinz, 2001; Kilner, Paulignan, & Blakemore, 2003). Furthermore, PMC activation has been reported in humans during the observation of meaningless movements (Grèzes, Costes, & Decety, 1998). It should be noted, however, that there is no direct neuroimaging evidence in support of the neural mechanism that underpins automatic mimicry. Of the neuroimaging studies that examined action observation and imitation, each required participants to consciously attend to the stimuli and the task. Conscious attention, however, is not a component of the mimicry phenomenon, which is unconscious and vanishes as soon as the individual becomes aware of his or her mimicry. It is highly plausible that part of the mirror neuron circuitry contributes to the lower-level processing involved in mimicry. However, the functional impact of top-down, controlled processes on the mirror neuron system remains to be demonstrated. The various forms of imitation—ranging from automatic mimicry to reproducing an action intentionally off-line—may well constitute a continuum from simple acts to complex ones for which executive functions, including attention and response selection, are at play.

Over the last decade, an impressive number of findings from both behavioral and cognitive neuroscience approaches strongly support a direct connection between the neural and cognitive systems involved in producing one's own action and the systems involved in perceiving the actions of others. This direct link between perception and action has several consequences (and adaptive values), including social mimicry, social facilitation, and stereotype activation, that may influence the subsequent behavior of the perceiver (e.g., Chartrand & Bargh, 1999).

The perception-action mechanism accounts for emotion sharing and empathy (Decety, 2002; Decety & Jackson, 2004, 2006; Preston & de Waal, 2002). This model posits that perception of emotion activates in the observer the neural mechanisms that are responsible for the generation of similar emotion. This mechanism was previously proposed to account for emotion contagion. Indeed, Hatfield, Cacioppo, and Rapson (1993) argued that people catch the emotions of others as a result of afferent feedback generated by elementary motor mimicry of others' expressive behavior, which produces a simultaneous matching emotional experience. For example, while watching someone smile, the observer activates the same facial muscles involved in producing a smile at a subthreshold level, and this would create the corresponding feeling of happiness in the observer. Indeed, viewing facial expressions triggers expressions on one's own face, even in the absence of conscious recognition of the stimulus (e.g., Dimberg, Thunberg, & Elmehed, 2000). Interestingly de Gelder and colleagues (de Gelder, Snyder, Greve, Gerard, & Hadijkhani, 2004) demonstrated that observing fearful body expressions produces increased activity not only in brain areas associated with emotional processes but also in areas linked with representation of action and movement. These results indicate that the mechanism of fear contagion automatically prepares the brain for action.

Making a facial expression generates changes in the autonomic nervous system and is associated with feeling the corresponding emotion. In a series of experiments, Levenson, Ekman, and Friesen (1990) instructed participants to produce facial configurations for anger, disgust, fear, happiness, sadness, and surprise while heart rate, skin conductance, finger temperature, and somatic activity were monitored. They found that such voluntary facial activity produced significant levels of subjective experience of associated emotions as well as specific and reliable autonomic measures. An fMRI experiment confirmed and extended these findings by showing that when participants are required to observe or to imitate facial expressions of various emotions, increased neurodynamic activity is detected in the STS, the anterior insula, and the amygdala, as well as areas of the PMC corresponding to the facial representation (Carr, Iacoboni, Dubeau, Mazziotta, & Lenzi, 2003).

Further evidence for the involvement of the perception-action coupling mechanism has been documented in imitation of facial expressions. In one study, participants watched movies of facial expressions and hand movements while sitting passively and under imitative and motor control conditions (Leslie, Johnson-Frey, & Grafton, 2004). The authors documented activation of the left pars opercularis, bilateral premotor areas, right STS, bilateral SMA posterior temporooccipital, and cerebellar areas during both hand and face imitation. Passive viewing of facial expressions selectively involved the right ventral premotor area, whereas imitation of facial expressions yielded bilateral activation.

PAIRED DEFICITS IN EMOTION EXPRESSION AND EMOTION RECOGNITION

The finding of paired deficits between emotion production and emotion recognition also provides strong arguments in favor of the perception-action matching model. Notably, a lesion study carried out with a large number of neurological patients reported that damage within the right somatosensory-related cortices (including primary and secondary somatosensory cortices, insula, and anterior supra-marginal gyrus) impaired the judgment of other people's emotional states from viewing their face (Adolphs, Damasio, Tranel, Cooper, & Damasio, 2000). Another study with brain-damaged patients indicated that recognizing emotions from prosody draws on the right frontoparietal cortex (Adolphs, Damasio, & Tranel, 2002). These findings strongly support the hypothesis that the recognition of emotion in others requires the perceiver to reconstruct images of somatic and motoric components that would normally be associated with producing and experiencing the emotion signaled in the stimulus.

Moreover, there are several dramatic case studies that support the idea that similar neural systems are involved both in the recognition and in the expression of specific emotion. For instance, Adolphs and collaborators (Adolphs, Tranel, Damasio, & Damasio, 1995) investigated S. M., a 30-year-old patient, whose amygdala was bilaterally destructed by a metabolic disorder. Consistent with the prominent role of the amygdala in mediating certain negatively valenced emotions such as fear, S. M. was found to be impaired at both the recognition of fear from facial expressions as well as in the phenomenological experience of fear. In another case, N. M, who suffered from bilateral amygdala damage and left thalamic lesion, was found to be impaired at recognizing fear from facial expressions and exhibited an equivalent impairment of fear recognition from body postures and emotional sounds (Sprengelmeyer et al., 1999). The patient also reported reduced anger and fear in his everyday experience of emotion. There is also evidence for paired deficits for the emotion of disgust. Calder and colleagues (Calder, Keane, Manes, Antoun, & Young, 2000) described patient N. K., with left insula and putamen damage, who was selectively impaired at recognizing social signals of disgust from multiple modalities (facial expressions, nonverbal sounds, and emotional prosody) and who was less disgusted than controls by disgust-provoking scenarios. Further and direct support for a specific role of the left insula in both the recognition and the experience of disgust was recently provided by an fMRI study in which participants inhaled odorants producing a strong feeling of disgust and, in another condition, watched video clips showing the facial expression of disgust. It was found that observing such facial expressions and feelings of disgust activated the same sites in the anterior insula and anterior cingulate cortex (ACC; Wicker et al., 2003).

SHARING PAIN WITH OTHERS

The expression of pain provides a crucial signal that can motivate caring behaviors in others. It is thus an ecologically valid way to investigate the neural systems involved in empathy and evaluate to what extent there is an overlap between the neural response to self-experienced pain and pain perceived in others. It is already well known that a restricted number of neural regions are involved in the processing of painful stimuli, including the ACC, the insula, the somatosensory cortex, the periacqueductal gray (PAG), the thalamus, and the ventral prefrontal cortex (Price, 2000). Further, these regions are differentially involved in the sensory, affective, and motivational aspects of pain processing. One of the first fMRI studies of empathy for pain demonstrated that the ACC, anterior insula, cerebellum, PAG, and brain stem were activated when healthy participants experienced a painful stimulus as well as when they observed another person receiving a similar stimulus, but only the actual experience of pain resulted in activation in the somatosensory cortices and in dorsal ACC (Singer et al., 2004). Similar results were also reported by Morrison and colleagues (Morrison,

Lloyd, di Pellegrino, & Roberts, 2004) from a study in which participants were scanned during a condition of feeling a moderately painful pinprick stimulus to the fingertips and another condition in which they witnessed another person's hand undergo similar stimulation. Both conditions resulted in common hemodynamic activity in a pain-related area in the right dorsal ACC. Common activity in response to noxious tactile and to visual stimulation were restricted to the right inferior Brodmann's area 24b. In contrast, the primary somatosensory cortex showed significant activations in response to noxious tactile but not visual stimuli. The different response patterns in the two areas are consistent with the ACC's role in coding the motivational-affective dimension of pain, which is associated with the preparation of behavioral responses to aversive events. These findings are supported by an fMRI study in which participants were shown still photographs depicting right hands and feet in painful or neutral everyday-life situations and asked to imagine the level of pain that these situations would produce (Jackson, Meltzoff, & Decety, 2005). Significant activation in regions involved in the affective aspect of pain processing, notably the dorsal ACC, the thalamus, and the anterior insula was detected, but no signal change was seen in the somatosensory cortex. Moreover, the level of activity within the ACC was strongly correlated with subjects' mean ratings of pain attributed to the different stimuli.

In a follow-up fMRI study, Jackson, Brunet, Meltzoff, and Decety (2006), again using pictures of hands and feet in painful scenarios, instructed the participants to imagine and rate the level of pain perceived from two different perspectives (self versus other). Results indicated that both the self and the other perspectives are associated with activation in the neural network involved in the processing of the affective aspect of pain, including the dorsal ACC and the anterior insula. However, the self-perspective yielded higher pain ratings and recruited the pain matrix more extensively, including the secondary somatosensory cortex, the midinsula, and the posterior part of the ventral ACC. Adopting the perspective of the other was associated with increases in the right temporoparietal junction. In addition, distinct subregions were activated within the insular cortex for the two perspectives (anterior aspect for others and more posterior for self). These neuroimaging data highlight similarities in the neural circuits associated with self and others' perspectives. However, these data also demonstrate some distinctiveness as a critical aspect of human empathy. The experience of one's own pain is associated with more caudal activations (within area 24), consistent with the spinothalamic nociceptive projections, while the perception of pain in others is represented in more rostral (and dorsal) regions (within area 32). A similar rostrocaudal organization is observed in the insula, which is coherent with its anatomical connectivity and electrophysiological properties. For instance, painful sensations are evoked in the posterior part of the insula (and not in the anterior part) by direct electrical stimulation of the insular cortex in neurological patients (Ostrowsky et al., 2002).

Altogether, shared neural circuits between self and other at the cortical level have been documented for emotion recognition and pain processing. Such a system prompts the observer to resonate with the emotional state of another individual, with the observer activating the motor representations and associated autonomic and somatic responses that stem from the observed target. This basic mechanism gives rise to shared feelings and affects between self and other on which mature empathy and moral reasoning develop.

CONCLUSION

In this chapter, we reviewed behavioral and neurophysiological evidence that support the notion that actions are centrally represented in the brain. These action representations are at the interface between the individual and the individual's physical and social environment. They subserve various nonconscious aspects of cognition and social interaction. Simulation of movement has come to be recognized as a distinct modality of representation. It may be most aptly characterized as the fundamental and mental counterpart to motor behavior. Simulation of movement precedes and plans for upcoming physical action and activates the same cortical and subcortical structures that mediate motor execution. But, the pragmatic value in motor simulation is that, at its core, it is the gateway to human social understanding. An embodied perspective moves us away both from a mentalistic view of cognition and from a dualistic view of a mind/body. It considers cognitive processes as rooted in bodily experience and interwoven with action in the world and interaction with other people. The fundamental ability of the motor system to resonate when perceiving actions, emotions, and sensation provides the primary means by which we understand others and can therefore be considered as a basic form of intersubjectivity.

Of course, human social cognition cannot be reduced to this primitive, yet essential, level of processing, which constitutes the primary means of self-other connectedness. Self-awareness and agency are crucial for navigating the shared nature of our joint representations and are essential properties of any autonomous agent (Decety & Sommerville, 2003). Indeed, social cognition relies both on similarities and differences between individuals. To be an agent is to influence intentionally—through cognitive self-regulation—one's functioning and life circumstances. This sense of agency constitutes a major dimension of moral experience: Without agency we would not feel responsible for our actions. Social cognition is a product of a complex reciprocal interplay of intrapersonal, behavioral, and environmental determinants. It relies on both domain-general mechanisms and embodied domain-specific representations, tailored by millions of years of evolution. Evolution has constructed layers of increasing complexity, from nonrepresentational to representational (cf. Amit, Algom, Trope, & Liberman, Chapter 4, this volume) and meta-representational mechanisms, which need to be taken into account for a full understanding of human social cognition.

REFERENCES

Adolphs, R., Damasio, H., & Tranel, D. (2002). Neural systems for recognition of emotional prosody: A 3-D lesion study. *Emotion, 2*, 23–51.

Adolphs, R., Damasio, H., Tranel, D., Cooper, G., & Damasio, A. (2000). A role for the somatosensory cortices in the visual recognition of emotion as revealed by three dimensional lesion mapping. *Journal of Neuroscience, 20*, 2683–2690.

Adolphs, R., Tranel, D., Damasio, H., & Damasio, A. (1995). Fear and the human amygdala. *Journal of Neuroscience, 15*, 5879–5891.

Baddeley, A. A., & Hitch, G. (1993). The recency effect: Implicit learning with explicit retrieval? *Memory & Cognition, 21*, 146–155.

Bhat, R. B., & Sanes, J. N. (1998). Cognitive channels computing action distance and direction. *Journal of Neuroscience, 18*, 7566–7580.

Blakemore, S.-J., & Decety, J. (2001). From the perception of action to the understanding of intention. *Nature Reviews Neuroscience, 2*, 561–567.

Brass, M., Bekkering, H., & Prinz, W. (2001). Movement observation affects movement execution in a simple response task. *Acta Psychologica, 106*, 3–22.

Brass, M., & Heyes, C. (2005). Imitation: Is cognitive neuroscience solving the correspondence problem? *Trends in Cognitive Sciences, 9*, 489–495.

Buccino, G., Binkofski, F., Fink, G. R., Fadiga, L., Fogassi, L., Gallese, V., et al. (2001). Action observation activates premotor and parietal areas in a somatotopic manner: An fMRI study. *European Journal of Neuroscience, 13*, 400–404.

Calder, A. J., Keane, J., Manes, F., Antoun, N., & Young, A. W. (2000). Impaired recognition an experience of disgust following brain injury. *Nature Neuroscience, 3*, 1077–1078.

Calmels, C., Holmes, P., Lopez, E., & Naman, V. (2006). Chronometric comparison of actual and imagined complex movement patterns. *Journal of Motor Behavior, 38*, 339–348.

Calvo-Merino, B., Glaser, D. E., Grèzes, J., Passingham, R. E., & Haggard, P. (2005). Action observation and acquired motor skills: An fMRI study with expert dancers. *Cerebral Cortex, 8*, 1243–1249.

Carr, L., Iacoboni, M., Dubeau, M. C., Mazziotta, J. C., & Lenzi, G. L. (2003). Neural mechanisms of empathy in humans: A relay from neural systems for imitation to limbic areas. *Proceedings of National Academy of Science USA, 100*, 5497–5502.

Chartrand, T. L., & Bargh, J. A. (1999). The chameleon effect: The perception-behavior link and social interaction. *Journal of Personality and Social Psychology, 76*, 893–910.

Cheng, Y., Meltzoff, A. N., & Decety, J. (2007). Motivation modulates the activity of the human mirror system: An fMRI study. *Cerebral Cortex*, 17, 1979–1986.

Choudhury, S., Charman, T., Bird, V., & Blakemore, S.-J. (2007). Development of action representation during adolescence. *Neuropsychologia, 45*(2), 255–262.

Cicinelli, P., Marconi, B., Zaccagnini, M., Pasqualetti, P., Filippi, M. M., & Rossini, P. M. (2006). Imagery-induced cortical excitability changes in stroke: A transcranial magnetic stimulation study. *Cerebral Cortex, 16*, 247–53.

Clower, D. M., Hoffman, J. M., Votaw, J. R., Faber, T. L., Woods, R. P., & Alexander, G. E. (1996). Role of posterior parietal cortex in the recalibration of visually guided reaching. *Nature, 383*, 618–621.

Conditt, M. A., Gandolfo, F., & Mussa-Ivaldi, F. A. (1997). The motor system does not learn the dynamics of the arm by rote memorization of past experience. *Journal of Neurophysiology, 78*, 554–60.

Crammond, (1997). Motor imagery: Never in your wildest dreams. *Trends in Neurosciences, 20*, 54–57.

Danckert, J., Ferber, S., Doherty, T., Steinmetz, H., Nicolle, D., & Goodale, M. A. (2002). Selective, non-lateralized impairment of motor imagery following right parietal damage. *Neurocase, 8*, 194–204.

Decety, J. (2002). Naturaliser l'empathie [Empathy naturalized]. *L'Encephale, 28*, 9–20.

Decety, J., & Jackson, P. L. (2004). The functional architecture of human empathy. *Behavioral and Cognitive Neuroscience Reviews, 3*, 71–100.

Decety, J., & Jackson, P. L. (2006). A social-neuroscience perspective on empathy. *Current Directions in Psychological Science, 15*, 54–58.

Decety, J., & Jeannerod, M. (1996). Mentally simulated movements in virtual reality: Does Fitts' law hold in motor imagery? *Behavioural Brain Research, 72*, 127–134.

Decety, J., & Lamm, C. (2007). The role of the right temporoparietal junction in social interaction: How low-level computational processes contribute to meta-cognition. *The Neuroscientist, 13*, 580–593.

Decety, J., & Michel, F. (1989). Comparative analysis of actual and mental movement times in two graphic tasks. *Brain & Cognition, 11*, 87–97.

Decety, J., Perani, D., Jeannerod, M., Bettinardi, V., Tadary, B., Woods, R., et al. (1994). Mapping motor representation with positron emission tomography. *Nature, 371*, 600–602.

Decety, J., & Sommerville, J. A. (2003). Shared representations between self and others: A social cognitive neuroscience view. *Trends in Cognitive Sciences*, 7, 527–533.

De Gelder, B., Snyder, J., Greve, D, Gerard, G., & Hadijkhani, N. (2004). Fear fosters flight: A mechanism for fear contagion when perceiving emotion expressed by a whole body. *Proceedings of the National Academy of Science, 47*, 16701–16706.

Dickstein, R., & Deutsch, J. E. (2007). Motor imagery in physical therapy practice. *Physical Therapy, 87*, 942–53.

Dijkstra, K., Kaschak, M. P., & Zwaan, R. A (2007). Body posture facilitates retrieval of autobiographical memories. *Cognition, 102*, 139–149.

Dimberg, U., Thunberg, M., & Elmehed, K. (2000). Unconscious facial reactions to emotional facial expressions. *Psychological Science, 11*, 86–89.

Fecteau, S., Carmant, L., Tremblay, C., Robert, M., Bouthillier, A., & Théoret, H. (2004). A motor resonance mechanism in children? Evidence from subdural electrodes in a 36-month-old child. *NeuroReport, 15*, 2625–2627.

Feltz, D., & Landers, D. (1983). Effects of mental practice on motor skill learning and performance: A meta-analysis. *Journal of Sport Psychology, 5*, 25–57.

Ferrari, P. F., Maiolini, C., Addessi, E., Fogassi, L., & Visalberghi, E. (2005). The observation and hearing of eating actions activates motor programs related to eating in macaque monkeys. *Behavioural Brain Research, 161*, 95–101.

Fitts, P. M. (1954). The information capacity of the human motor system in controlling the amplitude of movement. *Journal of Experimental Psychology, 47*, 381–391.

Fogassi, L., Ferrari, P. F., Gesierich, B., Rozzi, S., Chersi, F., & Rizzolatti, G. (2005). Parietal lobe: From action organization to intention understanding. *Science, 308*, 662–667.

Fourkas, A. D., Ionta, S., & Aglioti, S. M. (2006). Influence of imagined posture and imagery modality on corticospinal excitability. *Behavioural Brain Research, 168*, 190–196.

Frith, U., & Frith, C. D. (2003). Development and neurophysiology of mentalizing. In: C. D. Frith and D. Wolpert (Eds.), *The neuroscience of social interaction* (pp. 45–75). New York: Oxford University Press.

Garbarini, F., & Adenzato, M. (2004). At the root of embodied cognition: Cognitive science meets neurophysiology. *Brain & Cognition, 56*, 100–106.

Georgopolous, A., & Massey, J. T. (1987). Cognitive spatial-motor processes. *Experimental Brain Research, 65*, 361–370.

Gibson, J. J. (1979). *The ecological approach to visual perception.* Boston: Houghton Mifflin.

Goldman, A. I. (2002). Simulation theory and mental concepts. In J. Dokic and J. Proust (Eds.), *Simulation and knowledge of action* (pp. 2–19). Philadelphia: Benjamins.

Gordon, R. M. (1986). Folk psychology as simulation. *Mind and Language, 1*, 158–171.

Grèzes, J., Costes, N., & Decety, J. (1998). Top-down effect of strategy on the perception of human biological motion: A PET investigation. *Cognitive Neuropsychology, 15*, 553–582.

Grèzes, J., Frith, C. D., & Passingham, R. E. (2004). Infering false beliefs from the actions of oneself and others: An fMRI study. *NeuroImage, 21*, 744–750.

Hamilton, A. F., & Grafton, S. T. (2006). Goal representation in human anterior intraparietal sulcus. *The Journal of Neuroscience, 26*, 1133–1137.

Hamzei, F., Rijntjes, M., Dettmers, C., Glauche, V., Weiller, C., & Büchel, C. (2003). The human action recognition system and its relationship to Broca's area: An fMRI study. *NeuroImage, 19*, 637–644.

Happé, F., Brownell, H., & Winner, E. (1999). Acquired "theory of mind" impairments following stroke. *Cognition, 70*, 211–240.

Harris, P. L. (1989). *Children and emotion.* Oxford, England: Blackwell.

Hassin, R., Uleman, J., & Bargh, J. (Eds.). (2005). *The new unconscious.* New York: Oxford University Press.

Hatfield, E., Cacioppo, J. T., & Rapson, R.L. (1993). Emotional contagion. *Current Directions in Psychological Science, 2*, 96–99.

Herbert, R. D., Dean, C., & Gandevia, S. C (1998). Effects of real and imagined training on voluntary muscle activation during maximal isometric contractions. *Acta Physiol Scand, 163*, 361–368.

Hommel, B. (2004). Event files: Feature binding in and across perception and action. *Trends in Cognitive Sciences, 8*, 494–500.

Jackson, P. L., Brunet, E., Meltzoff, A. N., & Decety, J. (2006). Empathy and the neural mechanisms involved in imagining how I feel versus how you would feel pain: An event-related fMRI study. *Neuropsychologia, 44*, 752–761.

Jackson, P. L., Doyon, J., Richards, C. L., & Malouin, F. (2004). The efficacy of combined physical and mental practice in the learning of a foot-sequence task after stroke: A case report. *Neurorehabilitation and Neural Repair, 18*, 106–111.

Jackson, P. L., Lafleur, M. F., Malouin, F., Richards, C. L., & Doyon, J. (2003). Functional cerebral organization following motor sequence learning through mental practice with motor imagery. *Neuroimage, 20*, 1171–1180.

Jackson, P. L., Meltzoff, A. N., & Decety, J. (2005). How do we perceive the pain of others: A window into the neural processes involved in empathy. *NeuroImage, 24*, 771–779.

Jeannerod, M. (2003). The mechanism of self-recognition in humans. *Behavioural Brain Research, 142*, 1–15.

Jellema, T., Baker, C. I., Wicker, B., & Perrett D. I. (2000). Neural representation for the perception of the intentionality of actions. *Brain and Cognition, 44*, 280–302.

Kawato, M., & Wolpert, D. (1998). Internal models for motor control. In G. R. Bock & J. A. Goode (Eds.), *Novartis foundation symposium 218: Sensory guidance of movement* (pp. 291–307). West Sussex, England: Wiley.

Keele, S. W. (1968). Movement control in skilled motor performance. *Psychological Bulletin, 70*, 387–404.

Kilner, J. M., Paulignan, Y., & Blakemore, S. J. (2003). An interference effect of observed biological movement on action. *Current Biology, 13*, 522–525.

Kohler, E., Keysers, C., Umiltà, M. A., Fogassi, L., Gallese, V., & Rizzolatti, G. (2002). Hearing sounds, understanding actions: Action representation in mirror neurons. *Science, 297*, 846–848.

Lacourse, M. G., Orr, E. L., Cramer, S. C., & Cohen, M. J. (2005). Brain activation during execution and motor imagery of novel and skilled sequential hand movements. *Neuroimage, 27*, 505–519.

Lafleur, M. F., Jackson, P. L., Malouin, F., Richards, C. L., Evans, A. C., & Doyon, J. (2002). Motor learning produces parallel dynamic functional changes during the execution and imagination of sequential foot movements. *Neuroimage, 16*, 142–157.

Lamm, C., Bauer, H., Vitouch, O., & Gstättner, R. (1999). Differences in the ability to process a visuo-spatial task are reflected in event-related slow cortical potentials of human subjects. *Neuroscience Letters, 269*, 137–140.

Leslie K. R., Johnson-Frey, S. H., & Grafton, S. T. (2004). Functional imaging of face and hand imitation: Towards a motor theory of empathy. *NeuroImage, 21,* 601–607.

Levenson, R. W., Ekman, P., & Friesen, W. V. (1990). Voluntary facial action generates emotion-specific autonomic nervous system activity. *Psychophysiology, 27,* 363–384.

Li, S., Stevens, J. A., Kamper, D. G., & Rymer, W. Z. (2005). The movement-specific effect of motor imagery on the premotor time. *Motor Control, 9,* 119–128.

Longo, M. R., & Bertenthal, B. I. (2006). Common coding of observation and execution of action in 9-month-old infants. *Infancy,* 10, 43–59.

Loula, F., Prasad, S., Harber, K., & Shiffrar, M. (2005). Recognizing people from their movement. *Journal of Experimental Psychology: Human Perception and Performance, 31,* 210–220.

Lozano, S. C., Hard, B. M., & Tversky, B. (2006). Perspective taking promotes action understanding and learning. *Journal of Experimental Psychology: Human Perception & Performance, 32,* 1405–1421.

Markman, A. B., & Brendl, C. M. (2005). Constraining theories of embodied cognition. *Psychological Science, 16,* 6–10.

Mast, F. W., Ganis, G., Christie, S., & Kosslyn, S. M. (2003). Four types of visual mental imagery processing in upright and tilted observers. *Brain Research: Cognitive Brain Research, 17,* 238–247.

McIntosh, D. N., Reichmann-Decker, A., Winkielman, P., & Wilbarger, J. L. (2006). When the social mirror breaks: Deficits in automatic, but not voluntary mimicry of emotional facial expressions in autism. *Developmental Science,* 9, 295–302.

Meltzoff, A. N., & Decety, J. (2003). What imitation tells us about social cognition: A rapprochement between developmental psychology and cognitive neuroscience. *Philosophical Transactions of the Royal Society, London Series B, 358,* s491–s500.

Michelon, P., Vettel, J. M., & Zacks, J. M. (2006). Lateral somatotopic organization during imagined and prepared movements. *Journal of Neurophysiology,* 95, 811–822.

Moody, S. L., & Zipser, D. (1998). A model of reaching dynamics in primary motor cortex. *Journal of Cognitive Neuroscience, 10,* 35–45.

Morrison, I., Lloyd, D., di Pellegrino, G., & Roberts, N. (2004). Vicarious responses to pain in anterior cingulate cortex: Is empathy a multisensory issue. *Cognitive, Affective, and Behavioral Neuroscience, 4,* 270–278.

Naito, E., Kochiyama, T., Kitada, R., Nakamura, S., Matsumura, M., Yonekura, Y., et al. (2002). Internally simulated movement sensations during motor imagery activate cortical motor areas and the cerebellum. *Journal of Neuroscience, 22,* 3683–3691.

Neisser, U. (1976). *Cognition and reality: Principles and implications of cognitive psychology.* San Francisco: Freeman Press.

Ostrowsky, K., Magnin, M., Ryvlin, P., Isnard, J., Gueno, M., & Mauguière, F. (2002). Representation of pain and somatic sensation in the human insula: A study of responses to direct electrical cortical stimulation. *Cerebral Cortex, 12,* 376–385.

Parsons, L. M. (1994). Temporal and kinematic properties of motor behavior reflected in mentally simulated action. *Journal of Experimental Psychology: Human Perception and Performance, 20,* 709–730.

Parsons, L. M., Fox, P. T., Downs, J. H., Glass, T., Hirsch T. B., Martin, C. C., et al. (1995). Use of implicit motor imagery for visual shape discrimination as revealed by PET. *Nature, 375,* 54–58.

Paulignan, Y., Frak, V. G., Toni, I., & Jeannerod, M. (1997). Influence of object position and size on human prehension movements. *Experimental Brain Research, 14,* 226–234.

Perrett, D. I., Harries, M. H., Bevan, R., Thomas, S., Benson, P. J., Mistlin, A. J., et al. (1989). Frameworks of analysis for the neural representation of animate objects and actions. *Journal of Experimental Biology, 146,* 87–113.

Preston, S. D., & de Waal, F. B. M. (2002). Empathy: Its ultimate and proximate bases. *Behavioral and Brain Sciences, 25,* 1–72.

Price, D. D. (2000). Psychological and neural mechanisms of the affective dimension of pain. *Science,* 288, 1769–1772.

Prinz, W. (2003). Experimental approaches to action. In J. Roessler & N. Eilan (Eds.), *Agency and self-awareness* (pp. 175–187). Oxford, England: Oxford University Press.

Rizzolatti, G., & Craighero, L. (2004). The mirror-neuron system. *Annual Review of Neuroscience, 27,* 169–192.

Rizzolatti, G., Fadiga, L., Gallese, V., & Fogassi, L. (1996). Premotor cortex and the recognition of motor actions. *Cognitive Brain Research, 3,* 131–141.

Roth, M., Decety, J., Raybaudi, M., Massarelli, R., Delon-Martin, C., Segebarth, C., et al. (1996). Possible involvement of primary motor cortex in mentally simulated movement: A functional resonance imaging study. *NeuroReport, 7*, 1280–1284.

Saxe, R. (2005). Against simulation: The argument from error. *Trends in Cognitive Sciences, 9*, 174–179.

Shadmehr, R., & Holcomb H. H. (1997). Neural correlates of motor memory consolidation. *Science, 277*, 821–825.

Shadmehr, R., & Mussa-Ivaldi, F. A. (1994). Adaptive representation of dynamics during learning of a motor task. *Journal of Neuroscience, 14*, 3208–3224.

Shenton, J. T., Schwoebel, J., & Coslett, H. B. (2004). Mental motor imagery and the body schema: Evidence for proprioceptive dominance. *Neuroscience Letters, 370*, 19–24.

Shiffrar, M., & Freyd, J. J. (1990). Apparent motion of the human body. *Psychological Science, 1*, 257–264.

Shiffrar, M., & Freyd, J. J. (1993). Timing and apparent motion path choice with human body photographs. *Psychological Science, 4*, 379–384.

Shiffrar, M., & Pinto, J. (2002). The visual analysis of bodily motion. In W. Prinz and B. Hommel (Eds.), *Common mechanisms in perception and action: Attention and performance* (Vol. 19, pp. 381–399). Oxford, England: Oxford University Press.

Siegal, M., & Varley, R. (2002). Neural systems involved in "theory of mind." *Nature Reviews Neuroscience, 3*, 463–471.

Singer, T., Seymour, B., O'Doherty, J., Kaube, H., Dolan, R. J., & Frith, C.D. (2004). Empathy for pain involves the affective but not sensory components of pain. *Science, 303*, 1157–1161.

Sirigu, A., Cohen, Duhamel, J. R., Pillon, B., Dubois, B., Agid, Y., et al. (1995). Congruent unilateral impairments for real and imagined hand movements. *NeuroReport, 6*, 997–1001.

Sirigu, A., Daprati, E., Ciancia, S., Giraux, P., Nighoghossian, N., Posada, A., et al. (2004). Altered awareness of voluntary action after damage to the parietal cortex. *Nature Neuroscience, 7*, 80–84.

Sirigu, A., Duhamel, J.-R., Cohen, L., Pillon, B., Dubois, B., & Agid, Y. (1996). The mental representation of hand movements after parietal cortex damage. *Science, 273*, 1564–1568.

Sommerville, J. A., & Decety, J. (2006). Weaving the fabric of social interaction: Articulating developmental psychology and cognitive neuroscience in the domain of motor cognition. *Psychonomic Bulletin & Review, 13(2)*, 179–200.

Sprengelmeyer, R., Young, A. W., Schroeder, U., Grossenbacher, P. G., Federlein, J., Buttner, T., et al. (1999). Knowing no fear. *Proceedings of the Royal Society (Series B: Biology), 266*, 2451–2456.

Stephan, K. M., Fink, G. R., Passingham, R. E., Silbersweig, D., Ceballos-Baumann, A. O., Frith, C. D., et al. (1995). Functional anatomy of the mental representation of upper extremity movements in healthy subjects. *Journal of Neurophysiology, 73*, 373–386.

Stevens, J. A. (2005). Interference effects demonstrate distinct roles for visual and motor imagery during the mental representation of human action. *Cognition, 95*, 329–350.

Stevens, J. A., Fonlupt, P., Shiffrar, M. A., & Decety, J. (2000). New aspects of motion perception: Selective neural encoding of apparent human movements. *NeuroReport, 11*, 109–115.

Stevens, J. A., & Stoykov, M. E. (2003). Using motor imagery in the rehabilitation of hemiparesis. *Archives of Physical Medicine and Rehabilitation, 84*, 1090–1092.

Stone, V. E., & Gerrans, P. (2006). What's domain-specific about theory of mind? *Social Neuroscience, 1(3–4)*, 309–319.

Ulmità, M. A., Kohler, E., Gallese, V., Fogassi L., Fadiga, L., Keysers, C., et al. (2001). I know what you are doing: A neurophysiological study. *Neuron, 31*, 155–165.

Van Baaren, R. B., Decety, J., Dijksterhuis, A., van der Leij, A., & van Leeuwen, M. L. (in press). Being imitated: Consequences of non-consciously showing empathy. In J. Decety & W. Ickes (Eds.), *The social neuroscience of empathy*. Cambridge, England: MIT Press.

Van Baaren, R. B., Holland, R. W., Kawakami, K., & Van Knippenberg, A. (2004). Mimicry and prosocial behavior. *Psychological Science, 15*, 71–74.

VanderVelde, T. J., Woollacott, M. H., & Shumway-Cook, A. (2005). Selective utilization of spatial working memory resources during stance posture. *NeuroReport, 16*, 773–777.

Wehner, T., Vogt, S., & Stadler, M. (1984). Task-specific EMG characteristics during mental training. *Psychological Research, 46*, 389–401.

Wicker, B., Keysers, C., Plailly, J., Royet, J. P., Gallese, V., & Rizzolatti, G. (2003). Both of us disgusted in my insula: The common neural basis of seeing and feeling disgust. *Neuron, 40*, 655–664.

Wilson, M., & Knoblich, G. (2005). The case of motor involvement in perceiving conspecifics. *Psychological Bulletin, 131*, 460–473.

Wilson, V. E., & Peper, E. (2004). The effects of upright and slumped postures on the recall of positive and negative thoughts. *Applied Psychophysiogical Biofeedback, 29*, 189–195.

Yue, G., & Cole, K. J. (1992). Strength increases from the motor program. Comparison of training with maximal voluntary and imagined muscle contractions. *Journal of Neurophysiology, 67*, 1114–1123.

2 Expertise and the Mental Simulation of Action

Sian L. Beilock and Ian M. Lyons

INTRODUCTION

What makes expert performance different from novice skill execution? At first glance, one might suggest that the answer is simple. It is the quality of overt behavior that separates exceptional performers from those less skilled. We can all point to many real-world examples of such performance differences—just try comparing any professional athlete to his or her recreational counterpart. Although actual performance is one component that differentiates experts from novices, overt performance outcomes are only part of the key to understanding skill learning, performance, and expertise. That is, skill-level differences not only are reflected in one's *on-line* task performance (i.e., the real-time unfolding of skill execution and its corresponding performance outcomes), but also are reflected *off-line*, in situations in which individuals are not overtly acting. In the current chapter, we focus our attention off-line on the mental simulation of action in an attempt to shed light on expertise differences in action perception, representation, and production. Such knowledge not only informs the question of what makes an expert different from his or her novice counterpart but also makes salient the robust and widespread influence that mental simulation has on our understanding and representation of information we encounter—even in situations in which individuals have no intention to act.

CHAPTER OVERVIEW

We begin by drawing on the literature in sport psychology, motor learning and control, and cognitive neuroscience to explore how the *explicit* ability to mentally simulate one's own action might differ as a function of one's motor skill level. This type of mental simulation is often termed *motor imagery* and has been defined as reenacting movements without overt execution (Decety, 1996a, 1996b; Decety & Stevens, Chapter 1, this volume). We first outline the cognitive and neural substrates of motor imagery and then consider (a) how motor imagery differs as a function of one's skill level and (b) the implications motor imagery carries for on-line performance and its outcome.

We next turn to recent work in cognitive psychology and cognitive neuroscience investigating how the perception of stimuli in one's environment can prompt *automatic* and *covert* mental simulation of action in the perceiver—even though the perceiver has no intention to act. This type of simulation, often termed *motor resonance*, is the process by which action observation activates the same neural substrates as those recruited when a perceiver performs an action by themselves (Prinz, 1997; Schütz-Bosbach & Prinz, 2007; Zwaan & Taylor, 2006). The conception of motor resonance is supported by monkey and human work demonstrating that overlapping neural regions (e.g., premotor and motor cortex) are involved in the observation and production of action (Decety & Grezès, 1999; Gallese, Fadiga, Fogassi, & Rizzolatti, 1996). Such findings have been taken to suggest that our motor system not only plays a central role in planning actions to be executed, but also participates in the representation and understanding of actions as well (Garbarini & Adenzato, 2004).

The idea that both observing and planning actions share a common neural substrate suggests that merely thinking about action may call on motor-based neural processes. That is, higher-level cognitive processes not directly involved in motor production such as language comprehension

(Zwaan & Taylor, 2006) may be rooted in the mental simulation of action. We ask how this may differ as a function of one's expertise performing the action in question. Together, the work presented in this chapter suggests that a complete understanding of high-level performance not only requires consideration of on-line performance differences across the learning continuum, but also consideration of skill-level differences in the off-line mental simulation of action.

EXPERTISE AND THE EXPLICIT MENTAL SIMULATION OF ACTION

As mentioned, the *explicit* ability to mentally simulate an action without overt execution is often termed motor imagery (Decety, 1996a, 1996b). What is the relationship between motor imagery and execution itself? According to psychophysiology and neuroscience work of the past several decades, there is a *functional equivalence* between action execution and the mental simulation of action (e.g., see Decety & Grezès, 1999; Jeannerod, 1994). That is, motor imagery and execution share common neural substrates (Decety, 1996a; Jeannerod & Frak, 1999). For example, when individuals are asked to imagine themselves writing, increases in regional cerebral blood flow (rCBF) are seen in prefrontal brain regions, the SMA (supplementary motor area), and the cerebellum—similar to the activation patterns found during actual writing movements (Decety, Philippon, & Ingvar, 1988).

Added support for the notion of imagery/action equivalence comes from work demonstrating that the duration of mentally performed movements often does not significantly differ from physically executed movements. For example, mentally performing graphic tasks, such as drawing a cube or writing a sentence, is underlain by similar temporal organization as when actually performing such actions (Decety & Michel, 1989). The time used to mentally simulate moving one's hand or arm to match the orientation depicted in a presented hand stimulus has also been shown to mimic actual execution time (Parsons, 1994). Temporal congruence between imagined and executed actions is not merely limited to specific effectors but has been demonstrated at the whole-body level as well. In a recent chronometric comparison of actual and imagined movements in elite gymnasts, Calmels, Holmes, Lopez, and Naman (2006) found that the overall time to perform versus image a complex gymnastic vault did not significantly differ. This was true whether the vault was imaged from an internal (first-person) or external (third-person) perspective (in this volume, see also Kosslyn & Moulton, Chapter 3, and Libby & Eibach, Chapter 24).

Despite these similarities between motor imagery and action production, there are differences between mentally simulated and overt movement as well. For example, in the above-mentioned Decety and Michel handwriting study (1989), primary motor area (M1) activation was found in actual but not imagined writing. In fact, several studies have found that motor imagery and actual performance show overlapping activity in premotor and SMAs but not in primary motor cortices (see Guillot & Collet, 2005). This suggests that actual and imaged movements overlap most specifically in terms of the planning and programming of behavior rather than behavior execution (Decety, 1996a, 1996b). This is consistent with the notion that motor imagery and physical performance share common processes at higher, cognitive levels of the motor control hierarchy but differ at the level at which performance outcomes actually occur (MacKay, 1989).

EXPERTISE AND MOTOR IMAGERY

To the extent that motor imagery recruits at least some of the same cognitive and neural processes involved in actual execution, it follows that those with particularly specialized bodily experiences ought to mentally simulate actions differently than those without such experiences. That is, experience performing particular actions should be reflected in the mental simulation of action sequences in one's domain of specialization. Support for this notion can be found at both a behavioral and neurophysiological level.

In the chronometric comparison of imaged versus executed springboard dives, Reed (2002) found differences between motor imagery and physical performance that were dependent on skill expertise. Specifically, unlike novices and experts, intermediate divers tended to image their dive sequences significantly slower than they performed them. Reed suggested that such temporal differences in imaged and actual dives may reflect schematic differences in skill representation. Whereas novices have sparse dive knowledge and experts' knowledge may be automatized such that it is relatively closed to explicit introspection and report (Beilock & Carr, 2001; Beilock, Wierenga, & Carr, 2002), intermediate divers may be slowed during imagery by large amounts of dive-relevant knowledge that is represented in a nonautomated form.

Recent neuroimaging work shows that patterns of neural activation also differentiate motor imagery in expert and novice athletes. Using functional magnetic resonance imaging (fMRI), Milton, Solodkin, Hlustik, and Small (2007) compared neural activity while six professional golfers and seven novice golfers (who had less than 2 years of golfing experience) mentally simulated their preshot routines. Results showed that novices primarily activated posterior limbic and basal ganglion (BG) regions of the brain when mentally simulating their preshot routine. BG activation may be indicative of the effortful simulation of shot-related processes and procedures that are not yet fully automatized in novices (see Packard & Knowlton, 2002, for a review of the role of the BG in motor learning). The authors interpreted the posterior limbic activation in the posterior cingulate (PC) to reflect the filtering out of nonrelevant task information (for a review of the role of the PC in sensory monitoring, see Vogt, Finch, & Olson, 1992). Greater PC activation for novices relative to experts, then, may indicate that novices' preshot simulations may fail to successfully block out details less central to the motor-planning components of the action about to be performed. Experts, on the other hand, showed greater activity than novices in regions more closely related to precise visuomotor simulation, namely in the superior parietal lobe (SPL), left dorsal premotor (left PMd) and occipital (OCC) cortices. These regions are part of a broader action-simulation network (Rizzolatti, Fogassi, & Gallese, 2001), and their greater recruitment during experts' preshot routines suggests that part of what experts do in shot preparation is mentally simulate the specific motor sequence about to be performed. Taken together, these data indicate that expert and novice golfers recruit qualitatively different neural networks during preshot routines, and that this may reflect differences in the content of the mental simulation of the actions about to be produced.

MOTOR IMAGERY AND PERFORMANCE

Regardless of the above-mentioned skill-level differences in motor imagery, if the mental simulation of action relies on at least some of the same neural substrates as on-line execution—and this is true whether one is a novice or experienced performer—then manipulating the way in which individuals image execution should have an impact on performance outcomes, just as if performance execution itself were similarly manipulated.

Novice sensorimotor skill execution is thought to be attended in a step-by-step fashion. In contrast, well-learned skills are believed to be based on more automated control structures that run largely outside of explicit attentional control (Beilock & Carr, 2001; Jackson, Ashford, & Norsworthy, 2006; Maxwell, Masters, & Eves, 2000). As a result, when attention is distracted away from primary skill execution, novel skill execution that depends on explicit attentional control suffers. In contrast, attention prompted to a component process of execution disrupts the proceduralized processes of skilled performers. Work in golf putting (Beilock, Bertenthal, McCoy, & Carr, 2004), baseball batting (Gray, 2004), and soccer dribbling (Beilock, Carr, MacMahon, & Starkes, 2002) showed that when individuals are asked to perform a secondary task (e.g., monitor a series of tones for a specified target tone) that distracts attention away from primary skill execution (e.g., dribbling a soccer ball through a series of cones as fast as possible), novice performance is harmed while skilled performance is not. However, when individuals are asked to pay attention to component processes of execution (e.g., in soccer dribbling, the side of the foot that most recently contacted the ball), skilled performance is harmed and novice skill execution is spared.

These skill-level differences carry implications for how limitations in the time available for the setup and execution of one's skill will have an impact on performance. For example, because attention takes time to deploy (Posner & Snyder, 1975; Shiffrin & Schneider, 1977), conditions that limit the ability to explicitly monitor and adjust skill execution parameters (e.g., limited performance time) should benefit the proceduralized performance of experts. Conditions that encourage explicit attentional control (allowing as much performance time as desired) should aid novice performance based on declarative knowledge that must be explicitly controlled in real time. And, indeed, we have found support for this assertion. Beilock et al. (2004) had novice and skilled golfers execute a series of golf putts under speeded conditions in which individuals were told to putt as fast as possible (while still being accurate) or under conditions in which time constraints were not an issue. Although novices performed better under unlimited execution time in comparison to speed conditions, skilled golfers showed the opposite pattern.

We tested whether the above-mentioned expertise differences might occur not only by manipulating on-line performance but also by manipulating the motor imagery that precedes execution as well. Beilock and Gonso (2008) had novice and skilled golfers first *image* and then *execute* a series of golf putts on an indoor putting green under both speeded and nonspeeded imagery and putting instructions. For the speeded condition, participants were told to perform the putt/image as quickly as possible without sacrificing accuracy. In the nonspeeded condition, participants were explicitly told they had as much time as needed to complete the putt/image. When imaging their putts, participants stood over the ball with the club in their hand and pressed a button on the club (connected wirelessly to a computer) to indicate when they began and ended their image. When actually putting, an experimenter recorded (with a stopwatch) the time participants took to complete each putt. Timing results demonstrated that individuals followed instructions in both the putting and imagery conditions, putting and imaging faster under speeded relative to nonspeeded instructions.

Subsequent putting accuracy was then assessed as a function of imagery condition (i.e., speeded vs. nonspeeded imaging) and as a function of actual on-line performance condition (i.e., speeded vs. nonspeeded putts). This 2 (imagery instruction: speeded, nonspeeded) × 2 (putting instruction: speeded, nonspeeded) experimental design allowed for an assessment of the effect of different imagery conditions on actual putting execution independent of the conditions under which the putting task was performed. Likewise, this design also allowed for an assessment of the impact of different putting instructions on actual performance outcomes independent of the particular imagery condition that preceded putting.

Regardless of imagery instructions, novices should perform at a higher level (i.e., putt more accurately) under the nonspeeded putting instructions relative to the speeded putting instructions. This is because the former condition should provide more of an opportunity to explicitly monitor and control execution processes. In contrast, experts should putt more accurately under the speeded relative to the nonspeeded putting instruction condition as the speeded condition should prevent experts' attention from being devoted to skill processes and procedures best left outside conscious control. As mentioned, previous work in our lab has confirmed these predictions regarding the manipulation of actual performance time (see Beilock et al., 2004). In terms of imagery instructions, if imagined and executed actions do share overlapping neural substrates (Decety, 1996a), and imaging an action serves to recruit and fine-tune the motor processes used during actual action execution (similar to the processes involved in motor resonance), then manipulating imagery speed should have the same impact on subsequent putting accuracy as manipulating putting execution itself. As can be seen in Figure 2.1, this is exactly what occurred.

Novices putted less accurately (i.e., a higher putting error score) following either putting *or* imagery instructions in which speed was stressed. Skilled golfers showed the opposite pattern for *both* putting and imagery instructions. Critically, there was no Expertise × Putting instruction × Imagery instruction interaction. In other words, the impact of the imagery instructions on subsequent putting performance did not depend on the type of instructions given for the execution of the putt itself and vice-versa. Thus, manipulating either imagery or putting time appears to

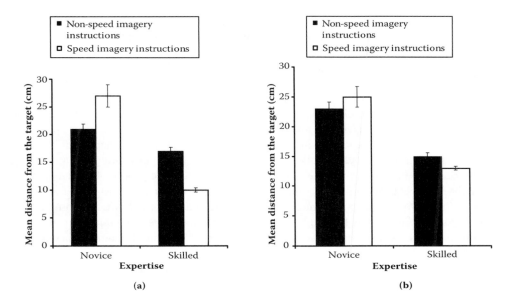

FIGURE 2.1 (a) Mean distance (cm) from the center of the target that the ball stopped after each putt following the nonspeed and speed putting instructions for the novice and skilled golfers. (b) Mean distance (cm) from the center of the target that the ball stopped after each putt following the nonspeed and speed imagery instructions for the novice and skilled golfers. Error bars represent standard errors. (Reprinted from S. L. Beilock and S. Gonso, *The Quarterly Journal of Experimental Psychology*, 2008.)

have similar yet independent effects on overt performance outcomes in a manner dependent on an individual's level of golf expertise.

One might wonder whether the impact of motor imagery on golf putting performance could be accounted for by imagery-induced alterations in putting time. That is, did individuals merely putt faster following speeded imagery instructions, which in turn impacted their performance outcomes? Putting time (defined as the time from when individuals put the ball on the starting position to ball contact) did not differ as a function of whether putts occurred after speeded imagery or nonspeeded imagery, ruling out the possibility that the impact of imagery on putting performance outcomes was merely due to imagery-induced alterations in putting time.

EXPERTISE AND COVERT MENTAL SIMULATION

In the preceding section, we explored the cognitive and neural substrates governing the *explicit* mental simulation of action (often termed motor imagery) and asked how this may differ as a function of skill level. We also considered the implications of functional equivalence between imagery and action in terms of skill-level differences in the impact of motor imagery on performance. In this next section we move beyond explicit or overt motor imagery and instead examine expertise differences in the automatic and covert mental simulation of action—even when there is no intention to act. Such work demonstrates that motor skill expertise carries implications beyond the playing field, having an impact on phenomena as diverse as language comprehension and one's preferences for particular objects they encounter in their environment.

LANGUAGE COMPREHENSION

Rather than our representations of objects and events, we read about being limited to amodal or propositional code that is arbitrarily related to the concepts it represents, language comprehension appears to be interconnected with the sensorimotor experiences implied by the text one reads or the words one hears spoken. Support for this assertion comes from a number of different findings. For example, when individuals make sensibility judgments about sentences by pushing a button that is either close to or far away from their bodies, the sentence's implied action direction interacts with the direction of the response (Glenberg & Kaschak, 2002). For instance, reading the sentence "Close the drawer" increases the time needed to respond with a movement directed toward the body (the opposite direction of the implied action) relative to a response involving movement directed away from the body (the same direction as the implied action). Similarly, sensibility judgments of sentences such as "Can you squeeze a tomato?" are facilitated when participants are primed with an associated hand shape (a clenched hand) relative to an inconsistent hand shape (a pointed finger; Klatzky, Pellegrino, McCloskey, & Doherty, 1989). Reading about performing a motion-directed act (e.g., "Eric turned down the volume") has also been shown to activate motor plans associated with actually producing this action (a counterclockwise hand movement; Zwaan & Taylor, 2006). This interaction between the actions implied by language and motor behavior performed concurrently with comprehension has been taken to suggest that language comprehension is interconnected with the systems involved in the understanding and planning of actions (Barsalou, 1999; Glenberg & Kaschak, 2003).

Converging evidence from cognitive neuroscience supports this idea. For example, reading action words associated with the leg and arm (e.g., "kick," "pick") activates brain areas implicated in the movements of these body parts (Hauk, Johnsrude, & Pulvermüller, 2004), and reading action-related sentences such as "I bit the apple" or "I kick the ball" activates the same areas of premotor cortex as those activated during the actual movement of mouth and leg effectors, respectively (Tettamanti et al., 2005). A recent study using transcranial magnetic stimulation (TMS) suggests that activation of the motor substrates governing the actions one reads about (i.e., motor resonance) is actually an important component of comprehension rather than a superficial by-product. Pulvermüller and colleagues (Pulvermüller, Hauk, Nikolin, & Ilmoniemi, 2005) found that when stimulation was applied to arm or leg cortical areas in the left hemisphere, lexical decisions to words denoting arm or leg actions were, respectively, facilitated. This finding suggests that these motor-related cortical areas play an important role in understanding linguistic descriptions of body-relevant actions.

To the extent that our comprehension of action-related language is grounded in the systems that support action execution, then those who have experience interacting with the objects and performing the actions they read about may represent this information very differently than those who do not have such experience. Despite demonstrations of motor resonance in language comprehension, little work has explored whether differences in motor skill expertise augment or attenuate these motor resonance effects. In a series of studies, we have been exploring this issue by examining differences in how novice and expert athletes represent both everyday and sport-specific objects and actions they read about.

In a first experiment, Holt and Beilock (2006) had ice hockey experts and novices read sentences describing hockey and nonhockey situations. The nonhockey situations depicted everyday objects and individuals (e.g., "The child saw the balloon in the air"). The hockey situations were hockey specific (e.g., "The referee saw the hockey helmet on the bench"). A picture of a target object was presented after each sentence. Participants judged as quickly as possible whether the target was mentioned in the preceding sentence. The target either matched the action implied in the sentence (match) or did not (mismatch) (see Figure 2.2). The correct response to all target items, whether matches or mismatches, was always "yes." Filler items that were not mentioned in the preceding sentence required a "no" response and were used to equate the number of yes and no responses across the experiment. Although the correct response to all target items was always yes, the action orientation of some items (i.e., matches) corresponded more closely to the action implied in the sentence that preceded these items than the action orientation of other items (i.e., mismatches). Building on the initial logic and work of Zwaan and colleagues (see Stanfield & Zwaan, 2001; Zwaan, Stanfield, & Yaxley, 2002), we hypothesized that if individuals mentally represent per-

Non-hockey sentence	Picture
Scenario 1:	
(A) The child saw the balloon in the air.	(A)
(B) The child saw the balloon in the bag.	(B)
Scenario 2:	
(A) The woman put the umbrella in the air.	(A)
(B) The woman put the umbrella in the closet.	(B)

Hockey sentence	Picture
*Scenario 1:	
(A) The referee saw the hockey helmet on the player.	(A)
(B) The referee saw the hockey helmet on the bench.	(B)
**Scenario 2:	
(A) The fan saw the hockey net after the player slid into it.	(A)
(B) The fan saw the hockey net after the puck slid into it.	(B)

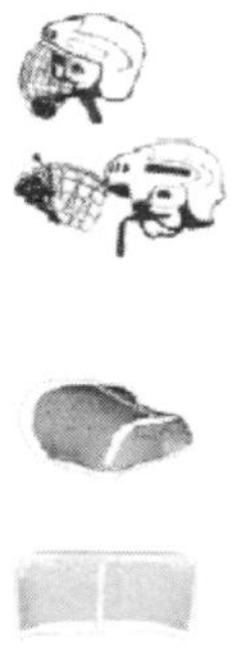

*Helmet has different configuration depending on whether or not it is on a player.
**Net is either knocked over or upright depending on who or what collides with it.

FIGURE 2.2 Examples of experimental stimuli. Picture A serves as a "match" for Sentence A and a "mismatch" for Sentence B. Picture B serves as a "match" for Sentence B and a "mismatch" for Sentence A. (Reprinted from "Expertise and Its Embodiment: Examining the Impact of Sensorimotor Skill Expertise on the Representation of Action-Related Text," L. E. Holt and S. L. Beilock, 2006, *Psychonomic Bulletin & Review, 13,* 694–701.)

ceptual qualities and action possibilities of the information they comprehend linguistically, then responses should be facilitated for matches relative to mismatches.

We predicted that both novice and expert hockey players would show the match-mismatch effect (i.e., responding faster to items that matched the action implied in the preceding sentence versus items that did not) for *nonhockey* objects and individuals because both novices and experts presumably have the same amount of knowledge and experience interacting with such everyday items. This result would replicate Zwaan et al.'s (2002) work in which only common objects were examined. However, if experience has an impact on the mental simulation of actions one reads about, then individuals with hockey expertise should show the match-mismatch effect for the hockey-specific items, while hockey novices should not.

Both novice and expert hockey players were able to understand the sentences they read (as indicated by high accuracy levels). In addition, participants responded faster to everyday items that matched the action implied in the preceding sentence versus those that did not, suggesting that participants' representations contained information about the sensorimotor qualities of the objects and individuals they read about. However, only those with hockey knowledge and experience showed this effect for the hockey scenarios. This finding is consistent with the hypothesis that a highly specific set of motoric experiences (e.g., athletic expertise) plays an important role in mediating the effect of the mental simulation of action on language comprehension.

In a second experiment, Holt and Beilock (2006) presented novice and expert football players with pictures of football players performing actions that either matched or did not match actions implied in preceding sentences. Critically, we manipulated the extent to which the action implied in the sentence was football specific (an action one would only perform were one a football player, e.g., a quarterback handing off to a receiver) versus not football specific (an action performed by a football player but that everyone should have performed in the past, e.g., a football player sitting down on a bench). Embedding both football-specific actions and non-football-specific (everyday) actions within the domain of football provides a stronger test of the prediction that knowledge and experience performing an action lead to covert action simulation when reading about that action. This is because even novices in a given domain should show evidence of this type of representation, provided they have experience performing the action in question. Under this view, both novices and experts should respond faster to a picture of a football player performing an everyday action that matches the action implied in a preceding sentence relative to a picture of an action that does not. In contrast, for football-specific actions, only those who have knowledge and experience performing the action should show the effect. This is exactly what was found. Thus, the ability to differentiate action orientations (suggesting one is representing sensorimotor information associated with the objects and individuals they are reading about) is not just a function of general domain knowledge but is dependent on specific experience one has performing the actions and interacting with the objects in question.

These findings are consistent with the idea that action possibilities are activated and simulated when individuals perceive specific objects or events, with this link dependent on the extent to which one has experience performing such actions. However, it should be noted that these results could be explained by a purely perceptual simulation of the sentences that involves no contribution from the motor system at all. We have turned to fMRI as a means to address this issue.

When listening to hockey-related action sentences, if hockey experts are mentally simulating the actions in question, they might show greater activation in motor-related regions of cortex relative to nonaction sentences. Novices would not be expected to show this pattern of activity. The specific pattern of neural activation obtained will help to elucidate precisely which components of the motor system underlie an experience-dependent influence of the mental simulation of action on language comprehension (or if the motor system is involved at all). Moreover, another interesting question that fMRI techniques may help to elucidate concerns whether those who have extensive visual experience watching actions (e.g., sports fans) but no actual playing experience show patterns of neural activation when comprehending hockey-action sentences more similar to novices, experts, or neither. Thus, the influence of visual and motoric expertise on language processing can be directly compared at the neural level—an important step in understanding how various forms of skill acquisition contribute to the read-about off-line representation of actions.

In a study aimed at addressing the issues outlined, we recruited hockey novices (who had neither hockey-playing nor hockey-watching experience), hockey experts (Division I intercollegiate hockey athletes), and hockey fans (who were carefully screened to have no hockey-playing experience but extensive hockey-watching experience). During fMRI scan acquisition, all subjects listened to sentences describing hockey actions (e.g., "The hockey player received the pass") and nonhockey actions (e.g., "The individual pushed the doorbell"). No overt behavioral task was performed in the scanner to prevent contaminating activation patterns related to comprehending the sentences with activation corresponding to stimulus-driven responses or overt preparation to perform the action described.

After exiting the scanner, individuals performed a version of the behavioral task used by Holt and Beilock (2006) described in this section. Specifically, participants were presented with the same hockey and nonhockey action sentences they had listened to during scanning followed by presentation of pictures of individuals performing actions that either did or did not match those implied in the sentence. We were interested in whether the match-mismatch effect found in Holt and Beilock (2006) for hockey stimuli varied as a function of hockey experience (i.e., fans, experts, novices) and how it related to neural activation when merely listening to hockey-action sentences.

All participants responded faster to pictures that matched the everyday actions implied in the sentences versus pictures that did not (i.e., the match-mismatch effect), replicating the work of Holt and Beilock (2006). This was not the case for the hockey actions. Only hockey players and hockey fans showed a match-mismatch effect for hockey-related sentences. Novices showed no difference in their response times for hockey action pictures that matched the action implied in the sentence versus those that did not.

To further elucidate the role of expertise in motor simulation and language comprehension, it is necessary to relate the neural activation observed while participants listened to hockey-action sentences with the aforementioned behavioral results. Interestingly, both ice-hockey experts and fans showed greater activation for hockey-action relative to nonhockey action sentences in a premotor region devoted to the planning and selection of actions (left lateral PMd). Novices did not show this pattern of activation, and activation for novices in this region while listening to hockey-action sentences was significantly less than both hockey players and hockey fans. Moreover, left PMd activity during hockey-action sentences positively correlated with the postscan behavioral task (i.e., the difference in response time to pictures that matched the hockey action implied in the sentence versus those that mismatched). Specifically, those individuals showing the greatest match-mismatch effect for hockey-related sentences showed the greatest amount of activation in the PMd region specifically for hockey-action sentences. Such results suggest that when individuals with either motor or visual expertise listen to domain-relevant action sentences, they recruit premotor regions involved in the planning and coordination of action execution. Although one might be surprised that hockey fans (with no playing experience) activated motor-planning areas when listening to hockey action sentences, such effects are consistent with work suggesting convergence in the systems used to perceive and perform actions (such as work on the human "mirror system"; for a review, see Garbarini & Adenzato, 2004). That is, the visual experience the hockey fans have may result in the recruitment of premotor areas involved in higher-level action planning when fans hear hockey actions described—at least more so than novices who have had no hockey-playing or -watching experience.

Together, these behavioral and neurophysiological findings suggest that we represent our surroundings, at least in part, via covert mental simulation of how we might execute an observed behavior or act on the objects we encounter, and importantly, that these simulations can differ as a function of one's action experience in a particular domain. Nonetheless, can we broaden this conception of bodily influence to include more than just the representation of action? That is, does the mental simulation of action serve functions beyond comprehension? The answer appears to be "yes." For example, by calling on and simulating one's own action-related experiences, one may better understand the actions, intentions, and goals of others—a potentially crucial component of social interaction (Decety & Grezès, 2006; Wilson & Knoblich, 2005). Moreover, simulation of such experiences can affect both the on-line interaction with and off-line representation (i.e., in the object's absence) of social objects (for a review, see Niedenthal, Barsalou, Winkielman, Krauth-Gruber, & Ric, 2005). Next, we consider work showing that automatic simulation of specific motor experiences can even influence one's preferences for stimuli in their environment.

PREFERENCE JUDGMENTS

If (a) individuals mentally simulate acting on the objects they perceive in their environment, (b) this mental simulation of action differs as a function of skill level, and (c) people prefer to act in ways that create less motor interference, then (d) individuals should report *liking* objects that are easier to act on—even though they have no intention to act. That is, the mental simulation of action may go beyond having an impact on representation and comprehension, influencing individuals' preferences for the stimuli they encounter. In an attempt to test these ideas, Beilock and Holt (2007) presented skilled and novice typists with two separate letter dyads on a screen and asked participants to indicate the dyad they preferred (Beilock & Holt, 2007). The dyads fell into one of two categories: dyads that would be typed with the same finger using standard typing methods (e.g., FV) or dyads that would be typed with different fingers (e.g., FJ). Each dyad pair always involved one dyad from each category, a paradigm first used by van den Bergh, Vrana, and Eelen (1990). Because typing is thought to involve the overlap of successive key strokes (Rumelhart & Norman, 1982), typing two letters with the same finger should result in more motor interference than typing two letters with different fingers, as the former case requires that the same digit essentially be in two places at once (or in very close succession).

As can be seen in Figure 2.3, skilled typists preferred dyads typed with different fingers (i.e., dyads *not* functionally incompatible) significantly more than chance. Novices did not show this preference. Importantly, participants were unaware of the link between our study and typing, and when asked, could not explicate how the letter dyads typed with the same versus different fingers differed. Why might skilled typists show the letter dyad preference that novices do not? If typing experience results in an association between specific letters and the motor programs used to type them and perceiving letters results in the activation of these motor plans (Prinz, 1997; Rieger, 2004), then such covert simulation of typing should provide information about the relative interference involved in acting on the letters presented. Moreover, if individuals prefer to act in ways that reduce interference, then they should prefer letter dyads that, when enacted, produce the least amount of motor interference.

To explicitly test these claims, while making their preference judgments on some trials in a first experiment, participants held a typing pattern in memory that involved the same fingers that would be used to type the presented dyads. If holding this pattern consumes the motor system in such a way that it can no longer inform typists' preference judgments, such preferences should disappear. As can be seen in Figure 2.3, this is exactly what was observed. A second experiment showed that this motor interference was specific to the digits actually involved in typing the dyads. When expert typists held a motor pattern in memory involving fingers *not* used to type the dyads, the preference remained (see Figure 2.3). Thus, covert mental simulation of acting on the information one is

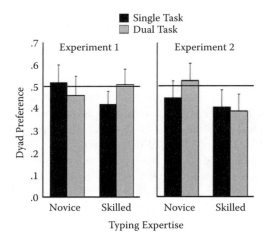

FIGURE 2.3   Letter dyad preferences in the single-task and dual-task blocks for novice and skilled typists in Experiments 1 and 2. The dark line at .5 represents chance. Error bars represent 95% confidence intervals. (Reprinted from "Embodied Preference Judgments: Can Likeability Be Driven by the Motor System?" by S. L. Beilock and L. E. Holt, 2007, *Psychological Science, 18,* 51–57.)

presented with not only has an impact on preference judgments but also is limited to information motorically resonant with the specific effectors involved in the simulated action.

IMPLICATIONS FOR THE ACQUISITION OF EXPERTISE

The behavioral and neurophysiological findings presented thus far suggest that we represent our surroundings, at least in part, via covert mental simulation of how we might execute an observed behavior or act on the objects we encounter. Moreover, by considering the influence of motor skill expertise on such simulations, we see the robust nature—and wide-ranging influence—mental simulation can have on cognitive tasks with no overt action component. These findings carry implications for understanding what makes an expert performer different from his or her novice counterpart, and they also shed light on how best to teach complex skills (with and without overt motor components) to others.

For example, motor imagery has been widely used as a rehabilitation technique for stroke and other patients who wish to regain finer motor control in certain tasks (for a review, see Dickstein & Deutsch, 2007). Motor imagery has also been used to train surgeons in complex surgical procedures (Hall, 2002; Rogers, 2006), to promote the learning and retention of complex athletic tasks (Driskell, Copper, & Moran, 1994; Feltz & Landers, 1983; Martin, Moritz, & Hall, 1999), and for the transfer of motor skills. For example, Gentili, Papaxanthis, and Pozzo (2006) demonstrated that imagery training using one arm can transfer to improved performance using the opposite arm. Mentally simulating an action, as reviewed in this chapter, is thought to activate the neural substrates involved in action production. It is perhaps not surprising, then, that simulation of certain actions benefits subsequent performance. Nonetheless, the full potential of this finding has yet to be exploited, not only as a rehabilitation or motor-learning technique but also as a potential means of acquiring more complex cognitive skills that do not involve overt action components, such as reading comprehension or spatial reasoning (see also Kosslyn & Moulton, Chapter 3, this volume).

Moreover, it is not just the explicit mental simulation of action that can improve performance. Action observation can result in improved performance as well. Vogt (1995) found that either observing or performing sequential arm movements resulted in similar improvement in the temporal consistency of executing such movements, suggesting that, in some cases, action observation facilitates subsequent motor performance as much as action production itself. In terms of higher-level cognitive skill learning, Glenberg and Robertson (1999) demonstrated that individuals more readily learned to operate a compass when they read about its operation *and* watched an actor physically enact the operation in comparison to individuals who only read about the actions. Although both groups gained similar levels of knowledge concerning compass operation, the group who watched the individual act on the object ultimately performed at the highest level on a subsequent novel compass navigation task. If watching an individual operate a compass results in the mental simulation of action in the perceiver that captures the action possibilities the compass affords, then subsequent performance should be facilitated in comparison to conditions in which such action possibilities are not made salient—exactly what was found.

Finally, the above-mentioned observation and imagery learning effects not only apply to skills with explicit action components (e.g., athletic tasks) but also can carry implications for the learning of skills that involve no overt action. Glenberg, Guttierez, Levin, Japuntich, and Kaschak (2004) found that when first- and second-graders either manipulated or mentally simulated acting on objects described in the text they read, they showed markedly better comprehension and later memory for the text in comparison to children who simply reread the text without actively simulating its content. Thus, learning that involves the mental simulation or observation of action improves comprehension and retention of action-related text. And, as reviewed in this chapter, such learning is likely the result of activation of the neural substrates that are involved in performing the actions one reads about, activation that provides an elaborate and robust situational representation that aids in comprehension and retention.

CONCLUSIONS

At the beginning of this chapter, we posed the question of what makes an expert different from his or her novice counterpart. Although there is a large body of research that examines on-line performance as a means to understand skill-level differences, we have begun to look at the off-line mental simulation of action as a means to understand expertise. Our current work, as well as related work from other laboratories, reveals that skill expertise is not merely reflected during the actual unfolding of performance, but can also be seen off-line in terms of the ability to mentally simulate skill-relevant actions. We began by reviewing work suggesting a strong degree of functional equivalence between motor imagery and overt execution and then asked whether imagery content might differ as a function of one's skill level or whether motor imagery might have an impact on performance differently for expert and novice individuals. We then moved on to work demonstrating that one need not be explicitly attempting to act in order to call on the motor systems used during the actual execution of a given task. We demonstrated skill-level differences in covert action simulation during text and speech comprehension and showed how such simulation differences can have an impact on one's explicit preference judgments for the particular objects one encounters. Together, this work suggests that understanding how experts imagine executing and cognitively represent the actions they have mastered may prove just as important for the study of skill learning and performance as understanding how skilled actions themselves are produced.

ACKNOWLEDGMENT

This work was supported by Institution of Education Sciences grant R305H050004 and National Science Foundation grant BCS-0601148 to S. L. Beilock.

REFERENCES

Barsalou, L. W. (1999). Perceptual symbol systems. *Behavioral & Brain Sciences, 22,* 577–660.
Beilock, S. L., Bertenthal, B. I., McCoy, A. M., & Carr, T. H. (2004). Haste does not always make waste: Expertise, direction of attention, and speed versus accuracy in performing sensorimotor skills. *Psychonomic Bulletin & Review, 11,* 373–379.
Beilock, S. L., & Carr, T. H. (2001). On the fragility of skilled performance: What governs choking under pressure? *Journal of Experimental Psychology: General, 130,* 701–725.
Beilock, S. L., Carr, T. H., MacMahon, C., & Starkes, J. L. (2002). When paying attention becomes counterproductive: Impact of divided versus skill-focused attention on novice and experienced performance of sensorimotor skills. *Journal of Experimental Psychology: Applied, 8,* 6–16.
Beilock, S. L., & Gonso, S. (2008). Putting in the mind versus putting on the green: Expertise, performance time, and the linking of imagery and action. *The Quarterly Journal of Experimental Psychology: Human Experimental Psychology, 61,* 920–932.
Beilock, S. L., & Holt, L. E. (2007). Embodied preference judgments: Can likeability be driven by the motor system? *Psychological Science, 18,* 51–57.
Beilock, S. L., Wierenga, S. A., & Carr, T. H. (2002). Expertise, attention, and memory in sensorimotor skill execution: Impact of novel task constraints on dual-task performance and episodic memory. *The Quarterly Journal of Experimental Psychology: Human Experimental Psychology, 55,* 1211–1240.
Calmels, C., Holmes, P., Lopez, E., & Naman, V. (2006). Chronometric comparison of actual and imaged complex movement patterns. *Journal of Motor Behavior, 38,* 339–348.
Decety, J. (1996a). Do imagined and executed actions share the same neural substrate? *Cognitive Brain Research, 3,* 87–93.
Decety, J. (1996b). The neurophysiological basis of motor imagery. *Behavioral Brain Research, 77,* 45–52.
Decety, J., & Grezès, J. (1999). Neural mechanisms subserving the perception of human actions. *Trends in Cognitive Sciences, 3,* 172–178.
Decety, J., & Grezès, J. (2006). The power of simulation: Imagining one's own and other's behavior. *Brain Research, 1079,* 4–14
Decety, J., & Michel, F. (1989). Comparative analysis of actual and mental movement times in two graphic tasks. *Brain and Cognition, 11,* 87–97.

Decety, J., Philippon, B., & Ingvar, D. (1988). rCBF landscapes during motor performance and motor ideation of a graphic gesture. *European Psychiatric Neurological Science, 238,* 33–38.

Dickstein R., & Deutsch, J. E. (2007). Motor imagery in physical therapist practice. *Physical Therapy,* 87, 942–953.

Driskell, J. E., Copper, C., & Moran, A. (1994). Does mental practice enhance performance? *Journal of Applied Psychology, 79,* 481–492.

Feltz, D. L., & Landers, D. M. (1983). The effects of mental practice on motor skill learning and performance: A meta-analysis. *Journal of Sport Psychology, 5,* 25–57.

Gallese, V., Fadiga, L., Fogassi, L., & Rizzolatti, G. (1996). Action recognition in the premotor cortex. *Brain, 119,* 593–609.

Garbarini, F., & Adenzato, M. (2004). At the root of embodied cognition: Cognitive science meets neurophysiology. *Brain and Cognition, 56,* 100–106.

Gentili, R., Papaxanthis, C., & Pozzo, T. (2006). Improvement and generalization of arm motor performance through motor imagery practice. *Neuroscience, 137,* 761–772.

Glenberg, A. M., Gutierrez, T., Levin, J., Japuntich, S., & Kaschak, M. P. (2004). Activity and imagined activity can enhance young children's reading comprehension. *Journal of Educational Psychology, 96,* 424–436.

Glenberg, A. M., & Kaschak, M. P. (2002). Grounding language in action. *Psychonomic Bulletin & Review, 9,* 558–565.

Glenberg, A. M., & Kaschak, M. P. (2003). The body's contribution to language. In B. Ross (Ed.), *The psychology of learning and motivation* (Vol. 43, pp. 93–126). New York: Elsevier Science.

Glenberg, A. M., & Robertson, D. A. (1999). Indexical understanding of instructions. *Discourse Processes, 28,* 1–26.

Garbarini, F., & Adenzato, M. (2004). At the root of embodied cognition: Cognitive science meets neurophysiology. *Brain and Cognition, 56,* 100–106.

Gray, R. (2004). Attending to the execution of a complex sensorimotor skill: Expertise differences, choking and slumps. *Journal of Experimental Psychology: Applied, 10,* 42–54.

Guillot, A., & Collet, C. (2005). Contribution from neurophysiological and psychological methods to the study of motor imagery. *Brain Research Reviews, 50,* 387–397.

Hall, J. C. (2002). Imagery practice and the development of surgical skills. *American Journal of Surgery, 184,* 465–470.

Hauk, O., Johnsrude, I., & Pulvermüller, F. (2004). Somatotopic representation of action words in the human motor and premotor cortex. *Neuron, 41,* 301–307.

Holt, L. E., & Beilock, S. L. (2006). Expertise and its embodiment: Examining the impact of sensorimotor skill expertise on the representation of action-related text. *Psychonomic Bulletin & Review, 13,* 694–701.

Jackson R., Ashford K., & Norsworthy G. (2006). Attentional focus, dispositional reinvestment, and skilled motor performance under pressure. *Journal of Sport & Exercise Psychology, 49–68.*

Jeannerod, M. (1994). The representing brain: Neural correlates of motor intention and imagery. *Behavioral and Brain Sciences, 17,* 187–245.

Jeannerod, M., & Frak, V. (1999). Mental imaging of motor activity in humans. *Current Opinion in Neurobiology, 9,* 735–739.

Klatzky, R. L., Pellegrino, J. W., McCloskey, B. P., & Doherty, S. (1989). Can you squeeze a tomato? The role of motor representations in semantic sensibility judgments. *Journal of Memory & Language, 28,* 56–77.

MacKay, D. G. (1989). *The organization of perception and action.* New York: Springer-Verlag.

Martin, K. A., Moritz, S. E., & Hall, C. R. (1999). Imagery use in sport: A literature review and applied model. *The Sport Psychologist, 13,* 245–268.

Maxwell, J. P., Masters, R. S. W., & Eves, F. F. (2000). From novice to no know-how: A longitudinal study of implicit motor learning. *Journal of Sport Sciences, 18,* 111–120.

Milton, J., Solodkin, A., Hlustik, P., & Small, S. L. (2007). The mind of expert motor performance is cool and focused. *NeuroImage, 35,* 804–813.

Niedenthal P. M., Barsalou, L. W., Winkielman, P., Krauth-Gruber, S., & Ric, F. (2005). Embodiment in attitudes, social perception, and emotion. *Personality and Social Psychology Review, 9(3),* 184–211.

Packard M. G., & Knowlton, B. J. (2002). Learning and memory functions of the basal ganglia. *Annual Review of Neuroscience, 25,* 563–593.

Parsons, L. M. (1994). Temporal and kinematic properties of motor behavior reflected in mentally simulated action. *Journal of Experimental Psychology: Human Perception and Performance, 20,* 709–730.

Posner, M. I., & Snyder, C. R. R. (1975). Attention and cognitive control. In R. L. Solso (Ed.), *Information processing and cognition: Loyola Symposium*. Hillsdale, NJ: Erlbaum.

Prinz, W. (1997). Perception and action planning. *European Journal of Cognitive Psychology, 9,* 129–154.

Pulvermüller, F., Hauk, O., Nikolin, V. V., & Ilmoniemi, R. J. (2005). Functional links between motor and language systems. *European Journal of Neuroscience, 21,* 793–797.

Reed, C. L. (2002). Chronometric comparisons of imagery to action: Visualizing versus physically performing springboard dives. *Memory and Cognition, 30,* 1169–1178.

Rieger, M. (2004). Automatic keypress activation in skilled typing. *Journal of Experimental Psychology: Human Perception and Performance, 30,* 555–565.

Rizzolatti, G., Fogassi, L., & Gallese V., (2001). Neurophysiological mechanisms underlying understanding and imitation of action. *Nature Reviews Neuroscience, 2,* 661–670.

Rogers, R. G. (2006). Mental practice and acquisition of motor skills: Examples from sports training and surgical education. *Obstetrics & Gynecology Clinics of North America, 33,* 297–304.

Rumelhart, D. E., & Norman, D. A. (1982). Simulating a skilled typist: A study of skilled cognitive-motor performance. *Cognitive Science, 6,* 1–36.

Schütz-Bosbach, S., & Prinz, W. (2007). Perspective coding in event representation. *Cognitive Processing, 8,* 93–102.

Shiffrin, R. M., & Schneider, W. (1977). Controlled and automatic human information processing: II. Perceptual learning, automatic attending, and a general theory. *Psychological Review, 84,* 127–190.

Stanfield, R. A., & Zwaan, R. A. (2001). The effect of implied orientation derived from verbal context on picture recognition. *Psychological Science, 12,* 153–156.

Tettamanti, M., Buccino, G., Saccuman, M. C., Gallese, V., Danna, M., & Scifo, P. (2005). Listening to action-related sentences activations fronto-parietal motor circuits. *Journal of Cognitive Neurosciences, 17,* 273–281.

Van den Bergh, O., Vrana, S., & Eelen, P. (1990). Letters from the heart: Affective categorization of letter combinations in typists and nontypists. *Journal of Experimental Psychology: Learning, Memory, Cognition, 16,* 1153–1161.

Vogt, B. A., Finch, D. M., & Olson, C. R. (1992). Functional heterogeneity in cingulate cortex: The anterior executive and posterior evaluative regions. *Cerebral Cortex, 2,* 435–443.

Vogt, S. (1995). On relations between perceiving, imagining and performing in the learning of cyclical movement sequences. *British Journal of Psychology, 86,* 191–216.

Wilson, M., & Knoblich, G. (2005). The case for motor involvement in perceiving conspecifics. *Psychological Bulletin, 131,* 460–473.

Zwaan, R. A., Stanfield, R. A., & Yaxley, R. H. (2002). Language comprehenders mentally represent the shape of objects. *Psychological Science, 13,* 168–171.

Zwaan, R. A., & Taylor, L. J. (2006). Seeing, acting, understanding: Motor resonance in language comprehension. *Journal of Experimental Psychology: General, 135,* 1–11.

3 Mental Imagery and Implicit Memory

Stephen M. Kosslyn and Samuel T. Moulton

INTRODUCTION

Alan Paivio's research had an enormous influence on the development of cognitive psychology. Using rigorous experimental methods, he showed that mental imagery plays a key role in human memory. The mountain of work he produced documented in detail his thesis that there are at least two ways to encode information, verbally and visually—and memory is enhanced when both of these types of codes are used (e.g., Paivio, 1971, 1986; see also Amit, Algom, Trope, & Liberman, Chapter 4, this volume).

Paivio focused on what has since been characterized as *explicit* memory: memory for facts and events that can be called to mind at will (see Schacter, 1987, 1996; Squire, 1992). However, much of what we know consists not of facts or events that we can consciously recollect (e.g., for many of us, the name of the lead singer of U2) but rather of ways to behave or tendencies to process information in certain ways in certain situations. We know how to drive, eat with a knife and fork, and maybe even how to bow correctly in Japan. Much of such knowledge is *implicit*: It cannot be voluntarily called to mind but rather is evoked by specific cues to guide our behavior (cf. Schacter, 1987, 1996).

We consider two closely related topics. First, we briefly review evidence that imagery can be used to access implicit information stored in memory. Next, we focus on the idea that imagery can be used to alter such stored information, which in turn can affect our later behavior.

USING IMAGERY TO ACCESS IMPLICIT MEMORIES

One of the remarkable aspects of mental imagery is that we can use it to access at least some aspects of implicit information stored in memory. By definition, such information cannot be retrieved directly, but we sometimes can access it indirectly—by noting how it affects our mental images. For example, when people are asked to imagine grasping an object, the time they take depends on exactly how they are asked to take hold of it. For instance, imagine seeing a hammer sitting on a table and reaching down, picking it up by the handle; compare this to when you imagine placing the back of your hand on the table and sliding your hand under the handle, grasping the hammer with your palm facing up; then compare this to when you reach down and pick it up only with your thumb and forefinger. You would take different amounts of time to simulate these behaviors, and the relative amounts of time would mirror the time you would take to perform the corresponding actual actions (e.g., Beilock & Lyons, Chapter 2, this volume; Decety & Stevens, Chapter 1, this volume; Frak, Paulignan, & Jeannerod, 2001; Jeannerod, 2001; Johnson, 2000; Parsons, 1994; Parsons & Fox, 1998; Sekiyama, 1982, 1983). The participants in these studies were not consciously aware of the biomechanical information they take into account when mentally simulating the actions any more than a seal solves differential equations when catching a ball on its nose.[1]

Many sorts of studies have used mental imagery to tap into implicit information stored in memory. For example, in one study researchers asked participants to take part in two experiments (Decety, Jeannerod, & Prablanc, 1989). In the first experiment, participants were blindfolded and asked to imagine walking a specific distance to a goal and to press a button when they arrived. In the second experiment, the participants actually walked that distance, and the time they took to reach the goal was recorded. In both imagined and actual walking, the greater the distance, the longer the participants took. Moreover, the participants took remarkably similar amounts of time to imagine walking as they required when actually walking. This finding nicely lines up with what we would expect based on the idea that imagery taps into implicit memories that control movements.

But, now we need to consider a wrinkle: In another experiment, these researchers asked the participants to imagine wearing a heavy backpack (25 kg) and to repeat the same two tasks. When mentally simulating this situation, they imagined that they would require more time to walk longer distances than they did when not wearing the backpack, but in fact when actually tested they walked as quickly as before (sans backpack). Apparently, the participants did not realize that they would simply expend more energy to keep up their previous pace with the heavy load (Decety et al., 1989; see also Decety, 1996). Thus, imagery is not a "royal road" to implicit memory. Rather, imagery also reflects our explicit expectations (e.g., that people walk slower with backpacks), which operate jointly with implicit knowledge to govern imaged scenarios.

Moreover, our images are only as good as the implicit information we have stored, even when that information may be relatively abstract. For situations in which we lack real-life experience (and thus lack the corresponding specific implicit information associated with those experiences), our imagery can be prone to flaws. Here is a particularly vivid example of how gaps in our implicit knowledge can lead imagery to go astray: Participants were asked to look at a picture of a tube wound into a spiral on the ground (looking a little like a coiled snake). They were asked to imagine a ball put in one end of the tube and then "shot out the other end at high speed." The participants were then asked to indicate the path they thought the ball would take when it flies out. McCloskey, Caramazza, and Green (1980; see also McCloskey & Kohl, 1983) found that many people believed that the ball would continue to fly along a curved path. In point of fact, in this situation a ball would continue along the tangent of the circle, in a straight line. Because we lack real-life experience with certain scenarios (e.g., projectiles exiting curved tubes), we use scenarios in which we do have real-life experience (e.g., projectiles exiting straight tubes) or knowledge of relatively abstract principles (presumably gleaned from such experiences) to simulate such events. The limits and biases of our everyday physical experiences and the generalizations we make from them often lead us to adopt incorrect views of physics (which may be one reason it took so many centuries for the correct principles to be discovered; Caramazza, McCloskey, & Green, 1981). These limits and biases of experience are reflected in limits and biases of our stored, implicit information, which form the basis for our occasionally faulty images.

In short, there is good evidence that imagery is sensitive to implicit information stored in memory. But, it is one thing to reflect the influence of such information and another to alter it. In the following section, we consider the role of imagery in actually entering new implicit information into memory. By "new," we include modifications of information that is already present in memory; we note that rarely is anything *entirely* new for an adult, but rearrangements of preexisting material nevertheless can produce representations that previously did not exist.

USING IMAGERY TO STORE IMPLICIT INFORMATION

An impressive body of evidence demonstrates that mental imagery can produce new implicit memories that help people to learn new activities. This evidence lies in the domain of mental practice. The key assumption underlying mental practice is that the representations stored in memory during such practice later can guide one to perform the corresponding actual activity.

IMAGERY AND MENTAL PRACTICE?

Mental practice hinges on visualizing oneself moving and imagining what it would feel like to move that way in space. Several types of imagery are involved in mental practice: Not only does one "see oneself" perform an action (a visual image), but also one is aware of the spatial relations of objects and their parts (spatial images), the sounds associated with an action (auditory images), and the bodily sensations that accompany movements (kinesthetic images). Not only are the objects and their parts being visualized stored in memory but also the movements are governed by information stored in implicit memory (cf. Vieilledent, Kosslyn, Berthoz, & Giraudo, 2003).

Numerous experiments have shown that the content of imagery during mental practice affects later behavior. Consider a now-classic study of mental practice in golfing (Woolfolk, Parrish, & Murphy, 1985; see also Powell, 1973), which dramatically illustrated the role of imagery in mental practice. In this study, the researchers first asked college students to putt a ball into a hole, and an initial "putting score" was recorded. The researchers then sorted the participants into three groups (ensuring that the participants in each group had comparable levels of skill at the outset, but otherwise randomly assigning participants to groups) and gave different instructions for mental rehearsal to each group. The participants in one group were asked to visualize putting a golf ball right into the hole (this was the "positive imagery" group); those in a second group were asked to putt a golf ball so that it just missed the hole (the "negative imagery" group); and those in the final group (the control group) were simply asked to visualize putting with no specific instructions about how to visualize. Following mental practice, the participants putted again, and another score was recorded. The results were dramatic: After mental practice, the participants in the positive imagery group performed 30.4% better than they had initially. The participants unlucky enough to have been assigned to the negative imagery group actually got worse, now scoring 21.2% more poorly than they had initially. (This decreased performance could reflect poor motor programming, "imagined frustration," or a number of other possible factors.) Those in the control group got only a bit better (9.9%).

One can use mental practice right before actually performing or well in advance of performing the movement. David Hemery (1988) interviewed 63 of the world's top athletes and reported that some 80% relied on imagery to enhance performance (see also Suinn, 1985; Ungerleider & Golding, 1991). Such mental practice is not confined to sports but rather applies to all activities. For example, when tenor sax player Gerry Bergonzi toured with Dave Brubeck, he used mental practice while he was on airplanes. He was on the road so often that he did not have many other opportunities to practice—mental or otherwise (H. G. Cox, Jr., personal communication, September 2001). Mental practice is especially useful for one-shot or dangerous events, when one does not have the luxury of actually performing them numerous times or when actual practice is too dangerous (for reviews of the literature and classical theories of mental practice and relevant findings, see Feltz & Landers, 1983; Grouios, 1992a; Jones & Stuth, 1997; Romero & Silvestri, 1990; Rushall & Lippman, 1998; Suinn, 1997; and Taktek, 2004).

For example, consider how surgeons "practiced" prior to performing a grueling 33-hr operation to separate twins who were born joined at the tops of their heads (so that even parts of their brains had melded together). This was an extraordinarily difficult and complex operation. Not only did 60 people participate on the medical team, but the surgery involved many complex steps; at its conclusion, the twins had no skulls above their foreheads (their heads were described in one report as being like "eggcups"), and the surgeons had to remove tissue from the boys' thighs to create a membrane to cover their exposed brains. (The surgeons' plan was to build the rest of the skulls out of pieces of bone salvaged during the operation supplemented by bones from cadavers.) A key part of the preparation for this operation was mental practice:

> "When I do a real operation, I play the videotape ahead of time in my mind," Dr. Shapiro said.
> Dr. Sklar said, "We were discussing this imaginary videotape for a long time."
> "I do the case in my head," said Dr. Maria Ortega, an anesthesiologist. "I must have done it 100 times. Every time, a problem would come up and I would find a solution and do it again. Every time I ran it in my head, it went faster. I'm sure everybody did the case 100 times."
> By the day of the surgery, Dr. Ortega said: "I was excited. I was elated. I was so confident. We had planned and talked and beaten each other over the head and challenged each other. We were ready. It was like the big game. 'Yes! Yes! Send me out there, coach!'" (Grady, 2003, p. 33)

Another compelling example of real-life mental practice comes from the field of power line maintenance. Because the penalty for error in this profession is so high (e.g., electrocution), individuals who inspect and maintain power lines do not have the luxury of learning through trial and error. In many cases, their job requires an extraordinarily complex set of movements. For instance, some high-voltage cable inspectors are flown to high-power lines via a helicopter, navigate from the helicopter to the 100-foot-high cable (while wearing a mesh full-body "hot suit" that acts as a Faraday cage), then traverse the cable on their hands and knees looking for areas that need repair.[2] David Harding, a power lineman for National Grid, reports how he uses mental practice to prepare for his work:

> I find I mentally practice a task in my head many times before I go up the pole and actually perform it. If I know what I'll be doing the next day I catch myself going over it in my head over and over again at home till I realize what I'm doing and I say to myself, "What the hell am I doing?" … I do this even with tasks I've performed hundreds of times before. Even when I roll up on a motor vehicle broken pole accident with police and fire on scene and lights flashing everywhere, I still take a couple seconds to go over the pole in my head and think about how my rigging will change as I'm moving conductors. (D. Harding, personal communication, May 2007)

As fascinating—and even compelling—as such testimonials are, they count for little in science. Is there evidence that mentally practicing an activity leads people to learn new skills or to perform a familiar activity better? Researchers have studied the efficacy of mental practice in almost every conceivable sport, including table tennis (Lejeune, Decker, & Sanchez, 1994); martial arts (Park, 1993); diving (Grouios, 1992b); golf (McBride & Rothstein, 1979); horseback riding (Fischer, 1995); racquetball (Gray, 1990); foul shooting in basketball (Clark, 1960); soccer (Salmon, Hall, & Haslam, 1994); football (Fenker & Lambiotte, 1987); rugby (Evans, Jones, & Mullen, 2004); volleyball (Johnston, 1971); rowing (Barr & Hall, 1992); figure skating (Rodgers, Hall, & Buckolz, 1991); track and field (Ungerleider & Golding, 1991); marksmanship (Whetstone, 1993); softball (Calmels, Berthoumieux, & d'Arripe-Longueville, 2004); shot put (Gassner, 1997); gymnastics (Palmer, 1971); sit-ups (Kelsey, 1961); field hockey (Wiegardt, 1998); wrestling (Mills, Munroe, & Hall, 2000–2001); swimming (Yamamoto & Inomata, 1982); goaltending in ice hockey (McFadden, 1983); tennis (Rahahleh & Al-Khayyat, 2001); kayaking (Millard, Mahoney, & Wardrop, 2001); cricket (Gordon, Weinberg, & Jackson, 1994); tenpin bowling (Wollman, Hill, & Lipsitz, 1985); dart throwing (Mendoza & Wichman, 1978); and even weight lifting (Hale, 1982). Researchers have also considered the effects of mental practice in activities as diverse as playing a musical instrument (Theiler & Lippman, 1995), conducting an orchestra (Bird & Wilson, 1988), and landing an airplane (Prather, 1973). Finally, although scientists have yet to study the effect of mental rehearsal on the surgical separation of conjoined twins, they have demonstrated its benefit for training basic surgical skills (Sanders, Sadoski, Bramson, Wiprud, & van Walsum, 2004).

WHEN DOES MENTAL PRACTICE WORK?

With such a great variety of studies of so many different activities, it is not surprising that not all studies have reported effects of mental practice (Corbin, 1972; Richardson, 1967). However, the majority of studies clearly showed that mental practice does improve performance; in fact, mental practice is one of the few "performance-enhancing" activities that a committee of the National Academy of Science found to be effective (Druckman & Swets, 1988). Let us take a closer look at exactly when mental practice is effective.

Driskell, Copper, and Moran (1994) performed a meta-analysis of the results from every well-conducted study of mental practice (i.e., that relied only on mental practice, and not other manipulations such as relaxation, and that included a no-practice condition or group) they could find in the literature. Although their most fundamental conclusion was that mental practice is generally effective, they also identified five factors that explain why it does not always work or does not work as effectively as it does in other circumstances.

1. One cannot entirely substitute mental practice for actual practice. Even though mental practice is better than nothing, usually physical practice is still better. However, although this general conclusion is correct, it does not apply to each and every individual case. Several studies have reported that mental practice can be just as good as actual practice (see Richardson, 1967; Weinberg, 1982). Clearly, mental practice will increasingly approximate actual practice to the extent that one has accurate images (cf. Suinn, 1984, 1994). Thus, feedback from actual performance, which allows one to tune images appropriately, should be critical. And in fact, some studies have reported that mixing actual practice with mental practice is not only better than mental practice alone, but can actually be better than purely physical practice (e.g., Riley & Start, 1960; Stebbins, 1968; Trussell, 1952; Weinberg, 1982). This last finding has not always stood up well (Hird, Landers, Thomas, & Horan, 1991), but nevertheless mixing physical practice with mental practice should enhance the effects of mental practice.

2. The amount of benefit from mental practice depends on the activity. As expected if the result of mental practice is to store implicit information, one is more likely to benefit if the task has a large "cognitive" component. That is, mental practice is more effective when tasks (such as playing basketball) require one to search for, organize, compare, and contrast information, as well as to make evaluations and decisions. If the task simply requires exerting force, maintaining balance, or other sorts of muscular control, mental practice is not as effective. Nevertheless, mental practice is better than nothing even for such tasks.

This finding is not surprising, given that mental simulations help one to organize, compare, and contrast information and make evaluations and decisions. What may be surprising, however, is that mental practice is not a purely intellectual activity: It also affects strength and other more physical aspects of behavior. For example, researchers found that simply imagining moving the fingers improved muscle strength almost as much as isometric exercises (22% improvement from imagery vs. 30% from isometric exercises; Yue & Cole, 1992; see also Yue, Wilson, Cole, & Darling, 1996). This makes sense because we know that imagining that one is performing an action actually engages the parts of the brain that control the muscles themselves (Kosslyn, Thompson, Wraga, & Alpert, 2001; Wraga, Thompson, Alpert, & Kosslyn, 2003). By repeatedly engaging the motor control processes responsible for a specific finger movement, participants in this experiment were able to hone those processes and, as a result, increase actual muscle strength.[3]

Imagining that one is activating the muscles repeatedly could have at least three effects: (a) It could actually strengthen the appropriate muscles. In fact, researchers have shown that when people imagine performing an action, very much the same pattern of muscles twitch—in the same order—as are used during the real thing (for reviews, see Grèzes & Decety, 2001; Jeannerod, 2001; Jeannerod & Decety, 1995). This correspondence in muscle activity has been shown in a variety of sports, including skiing (Suinn, 1980), basketball, rowing, horseback riding, swimming, and water skiing (Bird, 1984). However, one probably will not strengthen the muscles much by doing this; after all, one activates them just below the level needed to produce an actual movement. (b) Feedback from the stimulated muscles might strengthen the motor program that triggers the muscles. This is the classic *psychoneuromuscular theory* (which has been credited variously to Carpenter, 1894; Jacobson, 1932; Washburn, 1916). However, mental practice works even when the relevant muscles are temporarily immobilized, which prevents them from sending pertinent signals back to the brain (Yue et al., 1996). In addition, paralyzed and nonparalyzed individuals show the same changes in brain activity during mental practice, suggesting that neuromuscular feedback is not vital for mental practice effects (Cramer, Orr, Cohen, & Lacourse, 2007). (c) The central programs that activate muscles may become more efficient simply through being used more often. Aside from explaining the aforementioned data from immobilized and paralyzed participants, this account best explains the shifts in brain function associated with mental practice (e.g., Jackson, Lafleur, Malouin, Richards, & Doyon, 2003). Other possible mechanisms exist as well. For example, perhaps mental practice enhances strength by "giving yourself permission to go all the way."[4] We often hold in reserve some strength, not allowing ourselves to exhaust all of our physical resources. An image of yourself "going all the way" and "seeing" that this happy abandon leads only to positive consequences may short-circuit our safeguards, allowing us to exert more force than normal. This is, however, at present only a speculation.

3. The longer one waits between mental practice and performance, the smaller the effect of mental practice. In fact, the benefit of mental practice drops to half its initial level after 2 weeks. After 3 weeks, the effects are so small that we could debate whether they are present at all. Is mental practice mimicking what happens in actual practice? Yes, it is. The benefits of actual practice also drop off with elapsed time, probably for the same reason: Memories typically degrade with time. However, once implicit memories become firmly entrenched, they do not decay much over time (Schacter, 1996); one supposedly never forgets how to ride a bicycle. Is the same true for mental-practice-induced implicit memories? One recent study suggests that the answer is "yes." In this study, participants either imagined typing or actually typed a set of key sequences and were tested 1 month later on these same key sequences and new key sequences. The mental practice group performed as well as the physical practice group for the practiced sequences, and both groups performed better on the practiced sequences than the new sequences (Wohldmann, Healy, & Bourne, 2007). These findings indicate that implicit memories generated through mental practice persist over time as much as implicit memories generated through physical practice.

4. In general, both novices and experts benefit from mental practice, but novices benefit more if the task involves heavily cognitive components (such as arranging moves into a sequence) than if it is more physical (e.g., focused on strength per se), whereas experts benefit to the same degree for both types of tasks. For novices, basic actions must be assembled into longer sequences, but experts have long since stored such sequences in memory (and probably have even made them automatic). For experts, mental practice may serve to remind them of which aspects of the situation need to be attended to and may alert them to junctures where they sometimes make mistakes (see Beilock & Lyons, Chapter 2, this volume).

5. The total optimal amount of time to devote to mental practice is about 20 minutes. More or less time reduces the benefit. Too little mental practice may not lead to the salubrious effects noted, and too much can lead one to incorporate errors into motor programs. That is, if one goes too long without actual feedback, one may come to be practicing the wrong moves and thus later will have to dig out of a hole, first unlearning these flawed behaviors. In addition, it is possible that too much mental practice is boring, and people thereby lose concentration (cf. Driskell et al., 1994).

THE IMITATING BRAIN

How can forming images result in implicit information being stored in memory (even if such information consists of modifying representations that were previously stored)? One key idea is that mental practice relies on creating *images you can imitate* (this notion extends the early "social learning" ideas of Carroll & Bandura, 1982). Let us start by thinking about normal imitation: Someone makes a series of gestures, and someone else mimics these movements. We rely on imitation so much, from learning to drive to learning to dance, that we take it for granted. If one could not watch someone else dance and imitate what they did, one would be forced to rely purely on explicit instruction and trial-and-error learning, which might be good enough to master the twist but is no way to learn the tango. Our point is that imitation is a key mechanism that underlies mental practice (whether or not mental practice is best in combination with physical practice or explicit instruction). The benefits of imitative learning motivated the founder of modern Germany, Otto von Bismarck, to observe that fools learn from experience, but the wise person learns from the experience of others.

Imitation is in fact an amazing, almost miraculous, feat: Visual input (watching someone else) somehow gets converted to a "program" in the observer's brain, which then allows that person to make the same movements. How can observing someone else perform an act then allow you, with your different body and different point of view, to do the same?

THE NEURAL BASES OF IMITATION

Two recent discoveries can help us begin to understand how imitation works. First, researchers have found neurons in part of the frontal lobe that fire very selectively as an animal makes specific movements; some of these neurons fire as the animal grasps but not as it points or reaches, and others fire as it points but not as it grasps or reaches, and so on (Gentilucci et al., 1988; Perrett, Mistlin, Harries, & Chitty, 1990; Rizzolatti et al., 1988). These neurons represent a "vocabulary" of basic movements, and once triggered they lead the animal to produce a particular movement. Second, researchers have found that some of these basic-movement neurons respond even when the animal only observes another animal (or person) perform a specific behavior, even if the animal does not perform the action. These neurons have been dubbed *mirror neurons*. Again, each individual neuron responds only when a specific action is observed (e.g., Gallese, Fadiga, Fogassi, & Rizzolatti, 1996; for review, see Rizzolatti & Craighero, 2004). And, we have good reason to believe that such neurons exist in the human brain; although responses of individual neurons have not been monitored in humans as they watch others behave, the results of neuroimaging studies have revealed activation in the appropriate parts of the frontal lobe when people watch someone else gesture (Decety et al., 1997; Grafton, Arbib, Fadiga, & Rizzolatti, 1996; Grèzes, Armony, Rowe, & Passingham, 2003; Rizzolatti et al., 1996; for review, see Rizzolatti & Craighero, 2004). Given the similarities between the monkey and human brain, it is extremely likely that the human brain also is graced with mirror neurons.

We do not need a large leap of logic to suppose that mirror neurons play a key role in imitation. Mirror neurons do not simply register when one perceives specific actions; they also produce the corresponding behavior, and voila! we can do what we see. Why would the mirror neurons register perceived actions sometimes, but other times also produce those actions? The frontal lobes are known to contain many neurons with the job in life of inhibiting other neurons. Such inhibitory neurons can "turn off" performance when we do not want to imitate (probably most of the time). If the frontal lobes must actively intervene to stop us from imitating what we see, then it makes sense that young babies "automatically" imitate much of what they see (such as sticking out tongues); in fact, even 2-day-old infants can imitate facial expressions (Field, Woodson, Greenberg, & Cohen, 1982). The frontal lobes are the last lobes to become fully mature and do not inhibit behavior as effectively when we are very young, which we speculate might help to explain why "acting childish" is a synonym for acting impulsively, with little self-control.

IMITATING IMAGINED ACTIONS

Similarly, we do not need a large leap of logic to forge a connection between such neural machinery and the role of imagery in mental practice. Neuroimaging has shown that visual mental imagery activates about 90% of the same bits of the brain that are activated during the corresponding perceptual task (Ganis, Thompson, & Kosslyn, 2004). Moreover, there is much evidence that imagining something can later be mistaken for having seen it (for review, see Kosslyn, 1994). Thus, mental images can "stand in" for actual observation and—presumably—affect performance via the same neural mechanism that allows actual observation to affect performance: mirror neurons.[5] Furthermore, with imagery you can "see" things normally impossible in real observation, most notably yourself performing an act. Psychophysiology research by Fourkas, Avenanti, Urgesi, and Aglioti (2006) suggests that imagining oneself from an external (i.e., third-person) perspective activates the same mirror neuron regions involved in the observation and execution of motor acts. Therefore, mental practice might work not only by allowing you to imitate imagined others but also by allowing you to imitate an imagined version of yourself. Moreover, we can speculate further that one can imitate the spatial and motor images, as well as visual feedback, experienced when one actually performs an action. In such images, one would "see" (and feel) things from a first-person perspective.

But, why do we need visual imagery at all to practice mentally? Why not just imagine the kinesthetic "feel" of flexing our muscles? We need visual imagery in mental practice for the same reason we need visual percepts during actual practice: We are practicing not only moving our bodies or limbs but also moving in relation to objects in the world. We need to relate our images to what we would see in the corresponding situation, and thus we cannot rely simply on kinesthetic images, but rather must use visual and spatial images as well.

Mental practice occurs when one imitates actions in an image but does not trigger the behaviors themselves (Berthoz, 1996; Jeannerod, 2001). Neuroimaging studies have shown that virtually all of the brain areas that plan and control actual motor acts also plan and control imagined motor acts, although to a lesser degree and in a task-specific (and probably strategy-specific) manner (Porro et al., 1996; Roth et al., 1996; for review, see Crammond, 1997; Decety & Stevens, Chapter 1, this volume; Jeannerod & Frak, 1999).[6] Evidence suggests that the degree of overlap in functional neuroanatomy between imagined and performed acts increases with practice (i.e., as one learns a particular motor sequence), and that the changes in brain activation that occur as a result of actual practice correspond to those changes that occur as a result of mental practice (Lacourse, Orr, Cramer, & Cohen, 2005; Lafleur et al., 2002).

Although the vast majority of neuroimaging evidence is limited to the types of relatively simple motor tasks participants can perform in an functional magnetic resonance imaging (fMRI) or positron-emission tomographic (PET) scanner (e.g., foot tapping), a noteworthy exception comes from Ross, Tkach, Ruggieri, Lieber, and Lapresto (2003). In this study, golfers of different skill levels mentally rehearsed their golf swings while in a brain scanner. As expected, motor-related brain regions were activated when participants imagined teeing off. And, just like the studies of finger and toe tapping conducted earlier, the extent of this activation varied with skill: Golfers with higher handicaps actually used more of their brains during golf imagery than those with lower handicaps.

Researchers have also used transcranial magnetic stimulation (TMS) to show that the parts of the brain that control fine movements are activated by mental imagery. TMS is a relatively new technique by which a coil is placed on the skull at a location known to be over a specific part of the cerebral cortex. A large electrical current is run very briefly through the coil, which produces a strong, but very brief, magnetic pulse. This pulse in turn induces the neurons under the coil to fire (Pascual-Leone, Walsh, & Rothwell, 2000). Researchers have used this technique to stimulate the parts of cortex that control specific muscles; with the appropriate level of magnetic field strength, the TMS causes slight twitching of those muscles. Remarkably, if a person is imagining performing an activity that uses specific muscles, less TMS is required to get those particular muscles to twitch. The mental practice activates the appropriate brain area to a slight degree, which then requires less TMS to trigger the muscles (Fadiga, Craighero, & Olivier, 2005; see also Fadiga et al., 1999; Hashimoto & Rothwell, 1999).

Additional evidence that imagery engages brain systems used to control movements comes from studies of patients with Parkinson's disease. This disease depletes the amount of the neurotransmitter dopamine in parts of the brain that control movements and thereby disrupts the ability to move smoothly and well. Researchers asked patients with Parkinson's disease to reproduce a sequence of finger movements. As expected, these patients made the movements slowly. In addition, these researchers asked the patients not to move but instead to reproduce the movement sequence solely in their heads and report when they had finished. The patients imagined the sequence more slowly than normal, even though no actual movement was produced. This is as expected if the same neural mechanisms are used to produce real movements and to mentally simulate them (Dominey, Decety, Broussolle, Chazot, & Jeannerod, 1995).

MENTAL PRACTICE: STEP BY STEP

Mental practice has different aspects, which are handled separately by different systems in our brains. Take something as seemingly simple as practicing a golf swing. How complicated could that be? Let us take a look, step-by-step.

We can divide mental practice into four phases: storing images, initial mental rehearsal, image correction, and advanced mental rehearsal.

PHASE I. STORING IMAGES

At the outset of learning a new skill (which may rely on rearranging sets of relatively simple movements that have been previously represented), one needs to store in memory a clear representation of what one would like to achieve. Fortunately, our brains store what we pay attention to, so to store an appropriate image one needs to observe what a master of the trade does. (We note, however, that it is possible that one's previous experience limits what one can notice and store, and that one must incrementally develop increasingly more refined images as one becomes more adept in the skill. But our point is that the image one does encode, within whatever limitations one has, serves a key role at the outset of learning a new skill.) One needs to observe carefully, however, because the quality of later imagery depends on the quality of initial information encoding. To profit from a good golf coach, one needs to observe very carefully how he or she stands and positions his or her shoulders, feet, and head and exactly how he or she moves at different phases of the swing. A good coach will help a student by explicitly pointing out each key feature and perhaps even exaggerating some of them so that the student will be sure to notice the critical information. The goal here is to store the appropriate information as deep representations in long-term memory (Kosslyn, 1980) as well as associations between sequences of such representations; these associations will allow one later to generate a series of images.

Here is a crucial point: We can store not only static images but also images of moving objects (including a person's limbs). This is important because one usually does not want to learn a new pose, such as holding a salute; rather, we want to learn a new way to act, which involves motion. In fact, researchers have found that recalling images of moving objects activates those parts of the brain that register movement during perception (Goebel, Khorram-Sefat, Muckli, Hacker, & Singer, 1998; Grossman & Blake, 2001; see also Slotnick, Thompson, & Kosslyn, 2005). And, as predicted on the basis of the observation that imagery and perception share many of the same underlying brain mechanisms, imagining a moving object or pattern can alter perception. For example, have you ever stared at a waterfall for a few minutes and then turned your gaze to a stationary object? If so, you have probably noticed an illusion: The stationary object will seem to be moving upward, in the opposite direction as the waterfall. A very similar illusion can be induced simply by visualizing a moving pattern and then viewing a stationary one, which is good evidence that imagining movement engages brain mechanisms used in perceiving movement (for review, see Kosslyn, Thompson, & Ganis, 2006).

PHASE II. INITIAL MENTAL REHEARSAL

If one has stored the appropriate information in implicit memory and can generate the corresponding mental images and then inspect them, is this enough to learn that swing? After all, we have claimed that one can imitate images. There are two problems with this simple idea: The first is that one does not actually study oneself. The coach has a different body than the student's, and thus the student needs to transform the image ("fine-tuning" it) so that the movements fit his or hers. The second is that one may have moved one's eyes while studying the coach, fixing attention on one part of his or her movements at a time—and hence stored a series of separate images. So, one needs to integrate what has been stored piecemeal into a single, flowing action. To learn a single motion, such as arching the back, a single dose of mental practice may be enough. But to learn complex motions (such as a golf swing) and to assemble a set of motions into a single sequence, repeated episodes of mental practice are required. Each specific movement needs to be imitated correctly, in the right sequence, with just the right timing and amount of force. If one has a good image of the coach, it is possible to notice when one is not doing the mental practice properly and to correct the mental actions.

PHASE III. IMAGE CORRECTION (RE: THE BEST LAID PLANS OF MICE AND MEN)

Mental practice is only as good as the images used. Thus, perhaps paradoxically, an important part of mental practice is real practice. Particularly at the outset, feedback is necessary; one needs to see what actually happens when the mentally practiced motor programs (i.e., sequences of commands that control movements) are implemented in real life.[7] Thus, prior to actually performing the move, one should visualize oneself doing it—and then compare what actually happens when the act is performed to what was expected to happen on the basis of the mental simulation.

However, to take full advantage of feedback, some researchers have argued that in most activities one first must have shifted the image from an *external perspective* (seeing oneself as if from another person's point of view, from the "outside") to an *internal perspective* (seeing the situation as one would when actually performing the action, from the "inside"; Hale, 1994; see also Libby & Eibach, Chapter 24, this volume). In interviewing gymnasts who had qualified for the Olympics, researchers found that most of them reported using internal imagery to mentally practice; in sharp contrast, an otherwise similar group of gymnasts who had not qualified for the Olympics reported mostly using external imagery (Smith, 1987).

Why should the image perspective matter? After one generates images from an internal perspective, one can easily compare what happens when actually performing the action with what was expected to happen based on imagery. Indeed, when people were asked to take the two perspectives while their brains were scanned as they imagined making actions, researchers found that taking the internal perspective activated the part of the brain that most sensitively registers tactile sensations, the *somatosensory cortex*, more than did taking an external perspective. This cortex may allow us to "feel what would happen" when we move, which is crucial for comparing an imagined action to an actual action (Ruby & Decety, 2001; other brain areas were also activated differently when people adopted one or the other perspective, which clearly demonstrates that different processes underlie taking each of the two perspectives). And, based on such matching, one can tune imagery appropriately, changing it to improve both the image itself and the corresponding actions.

PHASE IV. ADVANCED MENTAL REHEARSAL

Advanced mental practice has the goal of making a complex performance automatic, of not only storing a set of new motor movements as implicit memories but also associating each movement with cues that will immediately trigger it in the proper setting. Part of this process involves making the sequence of small actions so cohesive that the entire sequence becomes a single unit. We do not want to be lost in thought before we hit each ball. The distinction between "conscious and effortful" versus "unconscious and automatic" is directly reflected by the existence of two separate brain systems for learning. One system relies on consciously using mental representations, and the other system relies on responding unconsciously to stimuli. The first sort of learning has been dubbed *cognitive learning*, whereas the second has been called *habit learning* (Mishkin & Appenzeller, 1987). As a first pass (which is undoubtedly an oversimplification), the cerebral cortex is crucial for the first sort of learning, whereas the basal ganglia (structures deep within the brain) and cerebellum ("little brain") come to the fore when implicit information about movements is learned. These latter structures hook stimuli relatively directly to responses, allowing one to shift from first gear to second as soon as the engine is revving fast enough, to smile when meeting someone, and to lock the door when leaving home. One hallmark of such automatic behaviors is that we usually are not aware that we have done them, even immediately afterward.

However, most of the time one needs to adjust what one does to the specific circumstances at hand. For a golf swing, one needs to adjust how hard to hit the ball to fit the distance it needs to travel, and of course one needs to aim properly (which will require integrating various sorts of information, including factors such as the direction and force of the wind). Thus, the implicit information one stores via imagery may in fact need to be retrieved, at least in part, via imagery and integrated with current circumstances.

CONCLUSIONS

Mental imagery and implicit memory affect each other and together affect behavior. On one hand, implicit memories often affect imagery, and in this sense, imagery is a mental application of implicit memory. On the other hand, implicit memories can be affected by imagery; in this sense, imagery plays a role in forming implicit memories. In this chapter, we focused on mental practice as a prime example of the relationship between imagery and implicit memory. In mental practice, implicit memory and imagery processes interact: The accurate generation, maintenance, manipulation, and integration of imagery during mental practice hone the implicit, procedural memories that help to give rise to this imagery in the first place, and honed implicit memory in turn alters imagery. This interaction culminates in improved physical performance, examples of which have been documented across a striking range of activities.

The circumstances in which mental practice is effective, or is most effective, make sense in light of this interaction between imagery and implicit memory. For example, mental practice has larger effects for more cognitively complex activities, as one would expect if mental practice operates by refining implicit memories. Recommendations for mental practice also flow logically from this perspective. Procedures that improve the quality of relevant implicit memories and mental images will increase the positive effects of mental practice. For example, careful observation of skilled behavior will lead to better implicit memory, better imagery, and therefore more effective mental practice.

Imitation, we argue, is a key mechanism of mental practice because it bridges observation and action. Just as we can imitate perceived others, we also can imitate imagined others—or imitate images of ourselves performing an action. The imagined models that we imitate rely on information stored implicitly, and our imitations—be they of real or imagined models—feed back to affect our implicitly stored information.

Finally, although mental practice is the most researched instance of how imagery and implicit memory interact to affect behavior, other possible examples exist. In particular, research suggests that mental imagery can be used to alter implicit stereotypes (Blair, Ma, & Lenton, 2001) and attitudes (Akalis, Nannapaneni, & Banaji, 2006). As psychologists continue to explore the intersection between imagery and implicit memory, we expect many additional examples of theoretical and practical significance to emerge from these efforts.

ACKNOWLEDGMENTS

Preparation of this chapter was supported by National Science Foundation grant REC-0411725 and National Institutes of Health grant 2 R01 MH060734-05A1.

NOTES

1. This claim is consistent with Pylyshyn's (1981, 2003) notions about "tacit knowledge," but we are claiming that such knowledge guides imagery—as opposed to being a substitute for it. For a detailed discussion of the relevant issues, see Kosslyn et al. (2006).

2. For an amazing video of high-voltage cable inspection, see http://www.youtube.com/results?search_query=High+Voltage+Cable+Inspection.
3. One of the most revealing details of Yue and Cole's (1992) study is that significant strength gains (20%) were also found in the contralateral, untrained finger. This finding strongly suggests that mental training affected the psychomotor processes that control finger movement rather than the peripheral nervous system or muscular activity that implement such commands.
4. This idea is a based on one originally proposed by Nick Humphreys (personal communication, September 2000) to account for placebo effects; he bears no responsibility either for our misunderstanding his theory or for our application of it.
5. For evidence that the mere observation of an act can affect the subsequent performance of that act, see Brass, Bekkering, Wohlschläger, and Prinz, 2000; Brass, Bekkering, and Prinz, 2001; Brass, Zysset, and Cramon, 2001; Castiello, Lusher, Mari, Edwards, and Humphreys, 2002; Edwards, Humpreys, and Castiello, 2003.
6. The motor imagery literature in many ways parallels the visual imagery literature. At first, researchers claimed that the primary motor area (which controls fine movements) was not activated, only the higher-level areas that program movements. Later studies revealed that even the primary motor area is indeed activated during motor imagery (e.g., Roth et al., 1996; Schnitzler, Salenius, Salmelin, Jousmaki, & Hari, 1997; compare the review in Jeannerod, 2001, with that in Jeannerod & Decety, 1995). Indeed, Ersland et al. (1996) went so far as to ask a man who had his right arm amputated to imagine moving the fingers of his right hand; fMRI revealed that the primary motor cortex that would have controlled those fingers was active during this task, even though his hand was no longer present.
7. In fact, when mental practice is occasionally supplemented with actual practice, some researchers report that participants improve as much—or even more—than with only physical practice (e.g., see Richardson, 1967; Weinberg, 1982). However, this pattern does not always hold up (e.g., Meyers, Schleser, Cooke, & Cuvillier, 1979). Clearly, the effects of mental practice not only vary for different sports (as we would expect, given their different requirements) but also depend on exactly what is done (cf. Feltz & Landers, 1983).

REFERENCES

Akalis, S., Nannapaneni, J., & Banaji, M. (2006, January). *Do-it-yourself mental makeovers: How self-generated thoughts shift implicit attitudes.* Poster presented at the Society for Personality and Social Psychology, Palm Springs, CA.

Barr, K., & Hall, C. (1992). The use of imagery by rowers. *International Journal of Sport Psychology, 23,* 243–261.

Berthoz, A. (1996). The role of inhibition in the hierarchical gating of executed and imagined movements. *Cognitive Brain Research, 3,* 101–113.

Bird, E. I. (1984). EMG quantification of mental rehearsal. *Perceptual and Motor Skills, 59,* 899–906.

Bird, E. I., & Wilson, V. E. (1988). The effects of physical practice upon psychophysiological response during mental rehearsal of novice conductors. *Journal of Mental Imagery, 12,* 51–63.

Blair, I. V., Ma, J. E., & Lenton, A. P. (2001). Imagining stereotypes away: The moderation of implicit stereotypes through mental imagery. *Journal of Personality and Social Psychology, 81,* 828–841.

Brass, M., Bekkering, H., & Prinz, W. (2001). Movement observation affects movement execution in a simple response task. *Acta Psychologia, 106,* 3–22.

Brass, M., Bekkering, H., Wohlschläger, A., & Prinz, W. (2000). Compatibility between observed and executed finger movements: Comparing symbolic, spatial and imitative cues. *Brain and Cognition, 44,* 124–143.

Brass, M., Zysset, S., & Cramon, D.Y. (2001). The inhibition of imitative response tendencies. *NeuroImage, 14,* 1416–1423.

Calmels, C., Berthoumieux, C., & d'Arripe-Longueville, F. (2004). Effects of an imagery training program on selective attention of national softball players. *Sport Psychologist, 18,* 272–296.

Caramazza, A., McCloskey, M., & Green, B. (1981). Naive beliefs in "sophisticated" subjects: Misconceptions about trajectories of objects. *Cognition, 9,* 117–123.

Carpenter, W. B. (1894). *Principles of mental physiology.* New York: Appleton.

Carroll, W. R., & Bandura, A. (1982). The role of visual monitoring in observational learning of action patterns: Making the unobservable observable. *Journal of Motor Behavior, 14,* 153–167.

Castiello, U., Lusher, D., Mari, M., Edwards, M. G., & Humphreys, G. W. (2002). Observing a human or a robotic hand grasping an object: Differential motor priming effects. In W. Prinz & B. Hommel (Eds.), *Attention and performance XIX*. Oxford, England: Oxford University Press.

Clark, L. V. (1960). Effect of mental practice on the development of a certain motor skill. *Research Quarterly of the American Association for Health, Physical Education, and Recreation, 31*, 560–569.

Corbin, C. (1972). Mental practice. In W. Morgan (Ed.), *Ergo-genic aids and muscular performance* (pp. 94–118). New York: Academic Press.

Cramer, S. C., Orr, E. L. R., Cohen, M. J., & Lacourse, M. G. (2007). Effects of motor imagery training after chronic, complete spinal cord injury. *Experimental Brain Research, 177*, 233–242.

Crammond, D. J. (1997). Motor imagery: Never in your wildest dream. *Trends in Neurosciences, 20*, 54–57.

Decety, J. (1996). Do imagined and executed actions share the same neural substrate? *Cognitive Brain Research, 3*, 87–93.

Decety, J., Grezes, J., Costes, N., Perani, D., Jeannerod, M., Procyk, E., et al. (1997). Brain activity during observation of actions: Influence of action content and subject's strategy. *Brain, 120*, 1763–1777.

Decety, J., Jeannerod, M., & Prablanc, C. (1989). The timing of mentally represented actions. *Behavioural Brain Research, 34*, 35–42.

Dominey, P., Decety, J., Broussolle, E., Chazot, G., & Jeannerod, M. (1995). Motor imagery of a lateralized sequential task is asymmetrically slowed in hemi-Parkinson's patients. *Neuropsychologia, 33*, 727–741.

Driskell, J. E., Copper, C., & Moran, A. (1994). Does mental practice enhance performance? *Journal of Applied Psychology, 79*, 481–492.

Druckman, D., & Swets, J. A. (1988). *Enhancing human performance: Issues, theories, and techniques*. Washington, DC: National Academy Press.

Edwards, M. G., Humphreys, G. W., & Castiello, U. (2003). Motor facilitation following action observation: A behavioural study in prehensile action. *Brain and Cognition, 53*, 495–502.

Ersland, L., Rosen, G., Lundervold, A., Smievoll, A. I., Tillung, T., Sundberg, H., et al. (1996). Phantom limb imaginary fingertapping causes primary motor cortex activation: An fMRI study. *Neuroreport, 8*, 207–210.

Evans, L., Jones, L., & Mullen, R. (2004). An imagery intervention during the competitive season with an elite rugby union player. *Sport Psychologist, 18*, 252–271.

Fadiga, L., Buccino, G., Craighero, L., Fogassi, L., Gallese, V., & Pavesi, G. (1999). Corticospinal excitability is specifically modulated by motor imagery: A magnetic stimulation study. *Neuropsychologia, 37*, 147–158.

Fadiga, L., Craighero, L., & Olivier, E. (2005). Human motor cortex excitability during the perception of others' action. *Current Opinion in Neurobiology, 15*, 213–218.

Feltz, D. L., & Landers, D. M. (1983). The effects of mental practice on motor skill learning and performance: A meta-analysis. *Journal of Sport Psychology, 5*, 25–57

Fenker, R. M., & Lambiotte, J. G. (1987). A performance enhancement program for a college football team: One incredible season. *Sport Psychologist, 1*, 224–236.

Field, T. M., Woodson, R., Greenberg, R., & Cohen, D. (1982). Discrimination and imitation of facial expressions by neonates. *Science, 218*, 179–181.

Fischer, C. A. (1995). The effects of a 2-hr mental practice preperformance routine on the anxiety levels and performance of equestrian jumpers (Doctoral dissertation, California School of Professional Psychology). *Dissertation Abstracts International, 55*, 3012.

Fourkas, A. D., Avenanti, A., Urgesi, C., & Aglioti, S. M. (2006). Corticospinal facilitation during first and third person imagery. *Experimental Brain Research, 168*, 143–151.

Frak, V., Paulignan, Y., & Jeannerod, M. (2001). Orientation of the opposition axis in mentally simulated grasping. *Experimental Brain Research, 136*, 120–127.

Gallese, V., Fadiga, L., Fogassi, L., & Rizzolatti, G. (1996). Action recognition in the premotor cortex. *Brain, 119*, 593–609.

Ganis, G., Thompson, W. L., & Kosslyn, S. M. (2004). Brain areas underlying visual mental imagery and visual perception: An fMRI study. *Cognitive Brain Research, 20*, 226–241.

Gassner, G. J. (1997). Comparison of three different types of imagery on performance outcome in strength-related tasks with collegiate male athletes. *Dissertation Abstracts International, 58*, 797 (UMI No. AAT 9724230).

Gentilucci, M., Fogassi, L., Luppino, G., Matelli, M., Camarda, R., & Rizzolatti, G. (1988). Functional organization of inferior area 6 in the macaque monkey. I. Somatotopy and the control of proximal movements. *Experimental Brain Research, 71,* 475–490.

Goebel, R., Khorram-Sefat, D., Muckli, L., Hacker, H., & Singer, W. (1998). The constructive nature of vision: direct evidence from functional magnetic resonance imaging studies of apparent motion and motion imagery. *European Journal of Neuroscience, 10,* 1563–1573.

Gordon, S., Weinberg, R., & Jackson, A. (1994). Effect of internal and external imagery on cricket performance. *Journal of Sport Behavior, 17,* 60–75.

Grady, D. (2003, November 18). No longer joined, boys face tough journey. *The New York Times.* Retrieved May 20, 2007 from http://query.nytimes.com/gst/fullpage.html?res=9D02E1D61138F93BA25752C1A9659C8B63

Grafton, S. T., Arbib, M. A., Fadiga, L., & Rizzolatti, G. (1996). Localization of grasp representations in humans by positron emission tomography. *Experimental Brain Research, 112,* 103–111.

Gray, S. W. (1990). Effect of visuomotor rehearsal with videotaped modeling on racquetball performance of beginning players. *Perceptual and Motor Skills, 70,* 379–385.

Grèzes, J., Armony, J. L., Rowe, J., & Passingham, R. E. (2003). Activations related to "mirror" and "canonical" neurones in the human brain: An fMRI study. *NeuroImage, 18,* 928–937.

Grèzes, J., & Decety, J. (2001). Functional anatomy of execution, mental simulation, observation, and verb generation of actions: A meta-analysis. *Human Brain Mapping, 12,* 1–19.

Grossman, E. D., & Blake, R. (2001). Brain activity evoked by inverted and imagined biological motion. *Vision Research, 41,* 1475–1482.

Grouios, G. (1992a). Mental practice: A review. *Journal of Sport Behavior, 15,* 42–59.

Grouios, G. (1992b). The effect of mental practice on diving performance. *International Journal of Sport Psychology, 23,* 60–69.

Hale, B. D. (1982). The effects of internal and external imagery on muscular and ocular concomitants. *Journal of Sport Psychology, 4,* 379–387.

Hale, B. D. (1994). Imagery perspectives and learning in sports performance. In A. A. Sheikh & E. R. Korn (Eds.), *Imagery in sports and physical performance* (pp. 75–96). New York: Baywood.

Hashimoto, R., & Rothwell, J. C. (1999). Dynamic changes in corticospinal excitability during motor imagery. *Experimental Brain Research, 125,* 75–81.

Hemery, D. P. (1988). Psycho-social factors in the development of sports highest achievers (Doctoral dissertation, Boston University). *Dissertation Abstracts International, 49,* 782.

Hird, J. S., Landers, D. M., Thomas, J. R., & Horan, J. J. (1991). Physical practice is superior to mental practice in enhancing cognitive and motor task performance. *Journal of Sport & Exercise Psychology, 13,* 281–293.

Jackson, P., Lafleur, M., Malouin, F., Richards, C., & Doyon, J. (2003). Functional cerebral reorganization following motor sequence learning through mental practice with motor imagery. *Neuroimage, 20,* 1171–1180

Jacobson, E. (1932). Electrophysiology of mental activities. *American Journal of Psychology, 44,* 677–694.

Jeannerod, M. (2001). Neural simulation of action: A unifying mechanism for motor cognition. *NeuroImage, 14,* S103–S109.

Jeannerod, M., & Decety, J. (1995). Mental motor imagery: A window into the representational stages of action. *Current Opinion in Neurolobiology, 5,* 727–732.

Jeannerod, M., & Frak, V. (1999). Mental imaging of motor activity in humans. *Current Opinion in Neurobiology, 9,* 735–739.

Johnson, S. H. (2000). Thinking ahead: the case of motor imagery in prospective judgment of prehension. *Cognition, 74,* 33–70.

Johnston, J. E. (1971). *Effects of imagery on learning the volleyball pass* (Doctoral dissertation, Temple University). *Dissertation Abstracts International, 32,* 772 (UPI No. AAT 7119985).

Jones, L., & Stuth, G. (1997). The uses of mental imagery in athletics: An overview. *Applied & Preventive Psychology, 6,* 101–115.

Kelsey, I. B. (1961). Effects of mental practice and physical practice upon muscular endurance. *Research Quarterly, 32,* 47–54.

Kosslyn, S. M. (1980). *Image and mind.* Cambridge, MA: Harvard University Press.

Kosslyn, S. M. (1994). *Image and brain: The resolution of the imagery debate.* Cambridge, MA: MIT Press.

Kosslyn, S. M., Thompson, W. L., & Ganis, G. (2006). *The case for mental imagery.* New York: Oxford University Press.

Kosslyn, S. M., Thompson, W. L., Wraga, M., & Alpert, N. M. (2001). Imagining rotation by endogenous and exogenous forces: Distinct neural mechanisms for different strategies. *Neuroreport, 12,* 2519–2525.

Lacourse, M. G., Orr, E. L. R., Cramer, S. C., & Cohen, M. J. (2005). Brain activation during execution and motor imagery of novel and skilled sequential hand movements. *NeuroImage, 27,* 505–519.

Lafleur, M. F., Jackson, P. L., Malouin, F., Richards, C. L., Evans, A. C., & Doyon, J. (2002). Motor learning produces parallel dynamic functional changes during the execution and imagination of sequential foot movements. *NeuroImage, 16,* 142–157.

Lejeune, M., Decker, C., & Sanchez, X. (1994). Mental rehearsal in table tennis performance. *Perceptual and Motor Skills, 79,* 627–641.

McBride, E. R., & Rothstein, A. L. (1979). Mental and physical practice and the learning and retention of open and closed skills. *Perceptual and Motor Skills, 49,* 359–365.

McCloskey, M., Caramazza, A., & Green, B. (1980). Curvilinear motion in the absence of external forces: Naïve beliefs about the motion of objects. *Science, 210,* 1139–1141.

McCloskey, M., & Kohl, D. (1983). Naive physics: The curvilinear impetus principle and its role in interactions with moving objects. *Journal of Experimental Psychology: Learning, Memory, and Cognition, 9,* 146–156.

McFadden, S. R. (1983). The relative effectiveness of two types of imagery rehearsal applied as mental preparation strategies to improve athletic performance (Doctoral dissertation, University of Toronto). *Dissertation Abstracts International, 44,* 920.

Mendoza, D., & Wichman, H. (1978). Inner darts: Effects of mental practice on performance of dart throwing. *Perceptual and Motor Skills, 47,* 1195–1199.

Meyers, A. W., Schleser, R., Cooke, C. J., & Cuvillier, C. (1979). Cognitive contributions to the development of gymnastics skills. *Cognitive Therapy and Research, 3,* 75–85.

Millard, M., Mahoney, C., & Wardrop, J. (2001). A preliminary study of mental and physical practice on the kayak wet exit skill. *Perceptual and Motor Skills, 92,* 977–984.

Mills, K. D., Munroe, K. J., & Hall, C. R. (2000–2001). The relationship between imagery and self-efficacy in competitive athletes. *Imagination, Cognition and Personality, 20,* 33–39.

Mishkin, M., & Appenzeller, T. (1987). The anatomy of memory. *Scientific American, 256,* 80–89.

Paivio, A. (1971). *Imagery and verbal processes.* New York: Holt, Rinehart, and Winston.

Paivio, A. (1986). *Mental representations: A dual coding approach.* Oxford, England: Oxford University Press.

Palmer, R. (1971). *The effects of directed and undirected mental practice on the acquisition of a gymnastic skill.* Unpublished master's thesis, University of Iowa, Iowa City.

Park, Y. D. (1993). The effect of mental rehearsal and relaxation techniques on the academic performance and tae kwon do skills of urban public school students (Doctoral dissertation, Texas Southern University). *Dissertation Abstracts International, 53,* 3141.

Parsons, L. M. (1994). Temporal and kinematic properties of motor behavior reflected in mentally simulated actions. *Journal of Experimental Psychology: Human Perception and Performance, 20,* 709–730.

Parsons, L. M., & Fox, P. T. (1998). The neural basis of implicit movements used in recognizing hand shape. *Cognitive Neuropsychology, 15,* 583–615.

Pascual-Leone, A., Walsh, V., & Rothwell, J. (2000). Transcranial magnetic stimulation in cognitive neuroscience—virtual lesion, chronometry, and functional connectivity. *Current Opinion in Neurobiology, 10,* 232–237.

Perrett, D. I., Mistlin, A. J., Harries, M. H., & Chitty, A. J. (1990). Understanding the visual appearance and consequence of hand actions. In M. A. Goodale (Ed.), *Vision and action: The control of grasping* (pp. 163–180). Norwood, NJ: Ablex.

Porro, C. A., Francescato, M. P., Cettolo, V., Diamond, M. E., Baraldi, P., Zuiani, C., et al. (1996). Primary motor and sensory cortex activation during motor performance and motor imagery: A functional magnetic resonance imaging study. *Journal of Neuroscience, 16,* 7688–7698.

Powell, G. E. (1973). Negative and positive mental practice in motor skill acquisition. *Perceptual and Motor Skills, 37,* 312.

Prather, D. C. (1973). Prompted mental practice as a flight simulator. *Journal of Applied Psychology, 57,* 353–355.

Pylyshyn, Z. W. (1981). The imagery debate: Analogue media versus tacit knowledge. *Psychological Review, 88,* 16–45.

Pylyshyn, Z. W. (2003). Return of the mental image: Are there really pictures in the head? *Trends in Cognitive Science, 7,* 113–118.

Rahahleh, W., & Al-Khayyat, O. (2001). The effect of mental practice on placement and speed of serving in tennis. *Dirasat: Educational Sciences, 28,* 35–50.

Richardson, A. (1967). Mental practice: A review and discussion, Part I. *Research Quarterly, 38,* 95–107.

Riley, E., & Start, K. B. (1960). The effect of the spacing of mental and physical practices on the acquisition of a physical skill. *Australian Journal of Physical Education, 20,* 13–16.

Rizzolatti, G., Camarda, R., Fogassi, L., Gentilucci, M., Luppino, G., & Matelli, M. (1988). Functional organization of inferior area 6 in the macaque monkey. II. Area F5 and the control of distal movements. *Experimental Brain Research, 71,* 491–507.

Rizzolatti, G., & Craighero, L. (2004). The mirror-neuron system. *Annual Review of Neuroscience, 27,* 169–192.

Rizzolatti, G., Fadiga, L., Matelli, M., Bettinardi, V., Paulesu, E., Perani, D., et al. (1996). Localization of grasp representations in humans by PET: 1. Observation versus execution. *Experimental Brain Research, 111,* 246–252.

Rodgers, W., Hall, C., & Buckolz, E. (1991). The effect of an imagery training program on imagery ability, imagery use, and figure skating performance. *Journal of Applied Sport Psychology, 3,* 109–125.

Romero, K., & Silvestri, L. (1990). The role of mental practice in the acquisition and performance of motor skills. *Journal of Instructional Psychology, 17,* 218–221.

Ross, J. S., Tkach, J., Ruggieri, P. M., Lieber, M., & Lapresto, E. (2003). The mind's eye: Functional MR imaging evaluation of golf motor imagery. *American Journal of Neuroradiology, 24,* 1036–1044.

Roth, R., Decety, J., Raybaudi, M., Massarelli, R., Delon-Martin, C., Segebarth, C., et al. (1996). Possible involvement of primary motor cortex in mentally simulated movement: A functional magnetic resonance imaging study. *Neuroreport, 7,* 1280–1284.

Ruby, P., & Decety, J. (2001). Effect of subjective perspective taking during simulation of action: A PET investigation of agency. *Nature Neuroscience, 4,* 546–550.

Rushall, B. S., & Lippman, L. G. (1998). The role of imagery in physical performance. *International Journal of Sport Psychology, 29,* 57–72.

Salmon, J., Hall, C., & Haslam, I. (1994). The use of imagery by soccer players. *Journal of Applied Sport Psychology, 6,* 116–133.

Sanders, C. W., Sadoski, M., Bramson, R., Wiprud, R., & van Walsum, K. (2004). Comparing the effects of physical practice and mental imagery rehearsal on learning basic surgical skills by medical students. *American Journal of Obstetrics and Gynecology, 191,* 1811–1814.

Schacter, D. L. (1987). Implicit memory: History and current status. *Journal of Experimental Psychology: Learning, Memory, and Cognition, 13,* 501–518.

Schacter, D. L. (1996). *Searching for memory: The brain, the mind, and the past.* New York: Basic Books.

Schnitzler, A., Salenius, S., Salmelin, R., Jousmaki, V., & Hari, R. (1997). Involvement of primary motor cortex in motor imagery: A neuromagnetic study. *NeuroImage, 6,* 201–208.

Sekiyama, K. (1982). Kinesthetic aspects of mental representations in the identification of left and right hands. *Perception and Psychophysics, 32,* 89–95.

Sekiyama, K. (1983). Mental and physical movements of hands: Kinesthetic information preserved in representational systems. *Japanese Psychological Research, 25,* 95–102.

Slotnick, S. D., Thompson, W. L., & Kosslyn, S. M. (2005). Visual mental imagery induces retinotopically organized activation of early visual areas. *Cerebral Cortex, 15,* 1570–1583.

Smith, D. (1987). Conditions that facilitate the development of sport imagery training. *Sport Psychologist, 1,* 237–247.

Squire, L. R. (1992). Declarative and nondeclarative memory: Multiple brain systems supporting learning and memory. *Journal of Cognitive Neuroscience, 4,* 232–243.

Stebbins, R. J. (1968). A comparison of the effects of physical and mental practice in learning a motor skill, *Research Quarterly, 39,* 714–720.

Suinn, R. M. (1980). Psychology and sports performance: Principles and applications. In R. Suinn (Ed.), *Psychology in sports: Methods and applications* (pp. 26–36). New York: Macmillan.

Suinn, R. M. (1984). Visual motor behavior rehearsal: The basic technique. *Scandinavian Journal of Behaviour Therapy, 13,* 131–142.

Suinn, R. M. (1985). Imagery rehearsal applications to performance enhancement. *The Behavior Therapist, 8,* 155–159.

Suinn, R. M. (1994). Visualization in sports. In A. Sheikh & E. Korn (Eds.), *Imagery in sports* (pp. 23–41). Amityville, NY: Baywood.

Suinn, R. M. (1997). Mental practice in sport psychology: Where have we been, where do we go? *Clinical Psychology: Science and Practice, 4,* 189–207.

Taktek, K. (2004). The effects of mental imagery on the acquisition of motor skills and performance: A literature review with theoretical implications. *Journal of Mental Imagery, 28,* 79–114.

Theiler, A. M., & Lippman, L. G. (1995). Effects of mental practice and modeling on guitar and vocal performance. *Journal of General Psychology, 122,* 329–343.

Trussell, E. M. (1952). *Mental practice as a factor in the learning of a complex motor skill.* Unpublished master's thesis, University of California at Berkeley.

Ungerleider, S., & Golding, J. M. (1991). Mental practice among Olympic athletes. *Perceptual and Motor Skills, 72,* 1007–1017.

Vieilledent, S., Kosslyn, S. M., Berthoz, A., & Giraudo, M. D. (2003). Does mental simulation of following a path improve navigation performance without vision? *Cognitive Brain Research, 16,* 238–249.

Washburn, M. F. (1916). *Movement and mental imagery.* Boston: Houghton.

Weinberg, R. (1982). The relationship between mental preparation strategies and motor performance: A review and critique. *Quest, 33,* 195–221

Whetstone, T. S. (1993). Effects of mental practice on the acquisition of critical psychomotor skills in recruit police officers (Doctoral dissertation, University of Illinois at Urbana-Champaign). *Dissertation Abstracts International, 54,* 1961.

Wiegardt, P. A. (1998). The effect of visual imagery perspective on the learning, retention, and transfer of a complex field hockey skill. *Dissertation Abstracts International, 58,* 4597 (UMI No. AAT 9820301).

Wohldmann, E. L., Healy, A. F., & Bourne, L. E. (2007). Pushing the limits of imagination: Mental practice for learning sequences. *Journal of Experimental Psychology: Learning, Memory, and Cognition, 33,* 254–261.

Wollman, N., Hill, J., & Lipsitz, T. (1985). Effects of imagery on track and bowling performance in naturalistic settings. *Perceptual and Motor Skills, 60,* 986–986.

Woolfolk, R. L., Parrish, M. W., & Murphy, S. M. (1985). The effects of positive and negative imagery on motor skill performance. *Cognitive Therapy and Research, 9,* 335–341.

Wraga, M. J., Thompson, W. L., Alpert, N. M., & Kosslyn, S. M. (2003). Implicit transfer of motor strategies in mental rotation. *Brain and Cognition, 52,* 135–143.

Yamamoto, K., & Inomata, K. (1982). Effect of mental rehearsal with part and whole demonstration models on acquisition of backstroke swimming skills. *Perceptual and Motor Skills, 54,* 1067–1070.

Yue, G. H., & Cole, K. J. (1992). Strength increases from the motor program: Comparison of training with maximal voluntary and imagined muscle contractions. *Journal of Neurophysiology, 67,* 1114–1123.

Yue, G. H., Wilson, S. L., Cole, K. J., & Darling, W. G. (1996). Imagined muscle contraction training increases voluntary neural drive to muscle. *Journal of Psychophysiology, 10,* 198–208.

4 "Thou Shalt Not Make Unto Thee Any Graven Image": The Distance Dependence of Representation

Elinor Amit, Daniel Algom, Yaacov Trope, and Nira Liberman

INTRODUCTION

The prohibition in the Bible against pictorial representations of God is as famous as it is poorly understood. After all, why is it forbidden to depict God in pictures, but it is not forbidden to depict God in words (cf. Halbertal & Margalit, 1992)? God has been richly represented in written or oral narratives in and out of the Bible. If so, why is it permitted to write about God's hand or face, while it is strictly forbidden to provide a drawing of the hand or the face? In a similar vein, God can be heard, but not seen "for man may not see Me and live" (Exodus, 33:20). Again, it is the visual image that is banned. Portrayals in words are not only endorsed, but actively sought. One can listen to (indeed, should follow) God's words and one is encouraged to sing/write God's virtues. In the tradition of Islam, the prohibition against pictorial representation extends beyond God to such a major prophet as Muhammad. The ban on pictorial depiction also is common in the political realm. Kings of Persia would speak to their subjects from behind a screen and were never seen. The reverse asymmetry is also well known in modern politics: Pictures of the king/dictator are distributed everywhere, but one is discouraged to write/talk about the ruler (beyond the simplest banalities) (again, see Halbertal & Margalit, 1992, for a discussion of the biblical prohibition).

Regardless of the interpretation of the biblical prohibition or some time-honored political exploits, it is clear that pictures and words have been used as different ways of representation from time immemorial. What is the essence of this difference between pictures and words? One clue comes precisely from the representation of God. In monotheistic religions, God is transcendental. God is immeasurably remote and secluded from humans and their pursuits. Is the picture-word divide associated with this infinite distance? Can pictorial representation violate the inaccessibly great remoteness of God? Does the violation result from the concrete, contextual way that pictures construe their referents? If so, words are well suited to represent God because they convey information in a more generic, decontextualized, even categorical fashion.

These observations already highlight the association between imagination and mental simulation on the one hand and the picture-word contrast in mental representation on the other hand. Imagination and mental simulation differ with pictorial and verbal representations. Although the picture-word divide is subsumed under a variety of terms and concepts (as we show throughout this chapter), common to virtually all theories is the perceptual quality and imaginability of the former. Pictures are always imaginable, whereas words sometimes are (concrete terms) and sometimes are not (abstract terms). Even when imaginable, mental simulation based on words (sequentially processed symbols that stand for referents) differs from that based on pictures (spatial icons processed in a parallel fashion). We elucidate the respective processes and theoretical notions in our discussions and relate them to developments in cognitive psychology and social cognition.

In this chapter, we elucidate the idea of a distance-related difference between pictures and words and augment it through novel empirical observations. In our approach, an essential difference between pictures and words is their association with different values of psychological distance. We argue that the disparate ways that pictures and words transcribe event information makes them singularly potent means of conveying proximal and distant data, respectively. Construal-level theory (CLT) explicates the levels of construal employed by humans to represent events and makes the association of those levels with psychological distance pellucid (Liberman, Trope, & Stephan, 2007; Trope & Liberman, 2003). The picture-word distinction thus becomes a natural derivative of CLT.

Construal-level theory proposes that objects or events can be mentally represented at multiple levels. High-level construals are abstract representations that extract the gist of event information. They are general, goal-oriented, decontextualized, and coherent. Low-level construals are concrete representations. They are goal irrelevant and include contextual, incidental features of the referent object or event (see also Libby & Eibach, Chapter 24, this volume). CLT thus builds on social cognitive theories that have distinguished between local and global representations (Gasper & Clore, 2002); gist and verbatim memory (Reyna & Brainerd, 1995); means and ends in goal hierarchies (Carver & Scheier, 2000; Vallacher & Wegner, 1987); concrete and abstract representations of action (Semin & Fiedler, 1988); the ingroup versus the outgroup (e.g., Linville, 1982; Park & Judd, 1990); behavior identification and trait inferences (Trope, 1986); and specific and general traits (Hampson, John, & Goldberg, 1986).

One factor that determines the level of construal of an object or event is psychological distance. The greater the distance, the more likely events are to be represented on a high level of construal. Near objects, in contrast, are usually represented at a low level of construal. People tend to construct distal events on a higher level because less is known (or remembered) about such events. Also of importance, high-level construal bypasses incidental changes over time and space that the referent object might undergo. The type of representation of the event affects judgments, predictions, and choices regarding the event.

An object can be represented by its picture or by its name. Contrasting the two types of representations, words are exemplars of high-level construal. Each word is actually a fairly wide category; hence, a word provides generic meaning in a relatively abstract fashion. By contrast, pictures are low-level construals. Vital and irrelevant features are sometimes provided equal prominence in pictures. Pictures are contextualized concrete representations, and hence they denote smaller categories than words.

Given the association between level of construal and psychological distance in CLT, an interesting hypothesis concerning pictures and words can be derived. Because pictures are low-construal representations and words are high-construal representations, the former are associated with smaller values of distance than are the latter. Moreover, the hypothesis states that people preferentially use pictures to represent proximal events and words to represent distal events (cf. Coulmas, 2003).

Therefore, in the special case of pictures and words, the two modes of construal have crystallized into dedicated means of representation. Distal events are more likely to be represented verbally, whereas proximal events are more likely to be represented pictorially. Conversely, pictures convey a sense of closeness to the referent event more than do words.

Study of the picture-word contrast enriches the network of ideas associated with CLT itself. CLT-induced research to date has mainly addressed levels of construal of concepts. Accommodating the picture-word distinction is conducive to the examination of perceptual processes as well. Perceptual processes dominate with pictures but are virtually absent with words; one can succinctly portray the respective mental processes by saying that pictures are mainly perceived, whereas words are cognized. Consequently, one focus of the present chapter is the examination of differences between perceptual and higher-level organization processes employed by people to represent events in their lives.

LEVEL OF CONSTRUAL AND PSYCHOLOGICAL DISTANCE

Research conducted in the framework of CLT has investigated the association between level of construal and psychological distance. For example, Liberman, Sagristano, and Trope (2002) tested the effect of temporal distance on categorization of items. Note that categorization is a mental activity that entails the collection of different stimuli (objects, events) under the same rubric; creating fewer categories for a given set of stimuli signals deeper mental organization. In other words, the fewer the number of categories, the higher the level of construal. People were presented with a list of "things to do in New York City when a friend comes to visit." The main manipulation was the time of the forthcoming visit: immediate (in a few days) or in the future (in a couple of weeks or months). The task for the participant was to reduce the list items (e.g., Statue of Liberty, Brooklyn Bridge, various monuments) into a few categories. Liberman et al. (2002) found that people in the distant time condition produced fewer categories than did those in the near time condition. Clearly, distal events were more highly organized and abstracted than proximal ones.

Other studies conducted within the framework of CLT have shown that people respond to temporally more distant objects in terms of their primary rather than secondary features. For example, Trope and Liberman (2000) asked participants to judge the attractiveness of a radio-clock planned to be bought "tomorrow" or in "a year from now." The main component of the product was the radio, with the clock as an added feature. Trope and Liberman found, as expected, that a product with a good-quality radio (main feature) but a poor-quality clock (secondary feature) was rated more attractive than one with a poor-quality radio and a good clock. Notably, this difference was amplified with time. The former product was rated more attractive in the future time frame than in the immediate one. With time, the essence of an object gains in importance, whereas the reverse holds for nonessential features.

The concept of psychological distance is not limited to the temporal dimension. Other embodiments of distance create the same respective levels of construal. In a study by Fujita, Henderson, Eng, Trope, and Liberman (2006), spatial distance was manipulated. Two groups of students viewed the same short video recording (of student interaction in classroom), but one group was told that the event was filmed at a close location (in their own campus), whereas another was told that the event was filmed at a distal location (in a campus abroad). Written descriptions of the event by students in the two groups revealed that those at the spatially remote condition used more abstract language than did those at the spatially proximal condition. Further dimensions of distance (e.g., social, hypothetical) yielded similar results (Bar-Anan, Liberman, Trope, & Algom, 2007).

Psychological distance (in its various senses) has been shown to influence level of construal, but the reverse influence, that of level of construal on distance, has also been demonstrated. Thus, Liberman, Trope, McCrae, and Sherman (2007) have shown an effect of construal level on temporal distance, and Wakslak, Trope, Liberman, and Alony (2006) did the same for the distance dimension of hypotheticality. Clearly, the association between level of construal and psychological distance is bidirectional (cf. Stephan, Liberman, & Trope, 2007).

These and other CLT studies demonstrated that features of high construal are associated with distal objects or events, whereas features of low construal are associated with proximal objects or events. Because words are inherently high construal and pictures are inherently low construal, we expect words to be associated with distal events and pictures to be associated with proximal events.

HIGH- AND LOW-LEVEL CONSTRUAL VERSUS WORDS AND PICTURES

Consider Table 4.1. The pair of left-hand columns provides the attributes associated with different levels of construal according to CLT (see Trope and Liberman, 2003). The right-hand half of Table 4.1 presents the attributes of pictures and words culled from pertinent research in cognitive psychology. The parallelism between the two halves of Table 4.1 is interpretative. It is the subject

TABLE 4.1

**Construal of Far and Near Events (Trope & Liberman, 2003) and
Attributes of Words and Pictures Uncovered in Studies of
Cognitive Psychology**

Construal Level		Modes of Representation	
High Construal	**Low Construal**	**Words**	**Pictures**
Abstract	Concrete	Abstract[a]	Concrete[a]
Simple	Complex	Simple[b]	Highly distinctive[b]
Structured coherent	Unstructured incoherent	Generalized[c]	Context bound[c]
Decontextualized	Contextualized	Primary, core[c]	Peripheral[c]
Primary, core	Secondary, surface	Arbitrary[a]	Analogous to the world[a]
Goal relevant	Goal irrelevant		
Superordinate	Subordinate		

[a] Paivio (1986), Glaser (1992).
[b] Mintzer & Snodgrass (1999).
[c] Durso & Johnson (1979).

of the present chapter. Table 4.1 demonstrates that words are high-level construal par excellence, whereas pictures are singular examples of low-level construal.

Why have two systems of representation evolved in humans? Arguably, pictures and words serve different cognitive functions. Words preserve the essential properties of stimuli across momentary changes in appearance and through changes in space and time. They function somewhat like perceptual constancies (Rock, 1983), abstracting the stimulus into its basic, invariant properties. Words have evolved to represent distal events because, with distance, one needs to preserve the essential, invariant properties of the referent event. If you plan to buy a car next year, many particular features of the car (e.g., color, seat, type of radio) are relatively unimportant and irrelevant at that stage. Pictures, by contrast, preserve the object in minute detail for immediate use. Words transcend the here and now, pictures instantiate the present. Indeed, the association of pictures with small distance and words with great distance might be overgeneralized by people. Even when the available information is comparable, people prefer to represent distal events verbally and proximal events through pictures.

According to CLT, proximal and distal events are processed in a different manner. We extend this idea to apply to words and pictures as generic means of representation. We propose that words typically serve to represent objects that are distal in time, space, society, or culture, whereas pictures serve to represent objects that are proximal along the various dimensions of distance. This distance-medium association carries several implications. First, words comprise a higher level of construal than do pictures. Thus, when people categorize a given set of items as words or as pictures, they produce fewer categories with the former. Because each word is a category, it already comprises an organization of data. Again, words are cognized, whereas pictures are mainly perceived. Second, cognitive processing is most efficient when there is a congruency between psychological distance and medium. Incongruity between medium and distance takes a toll on cognitive processing. The distance-medium association is automatic and reflexive to the extent that people react optimally to pictures in a proximal position (spatially, temporally, or culturally) and to words in a distal position but react in a suboptimal fashion to the reverse arrangement. Third, the distance-medium association dictates preferences. People tend to use pictures to represent proximal events but tend to use words to represent more distant events. Finally, the distance-medium association extends into memory to govern the dating of past events. This is not a new principle, but its implications for memory retrieval are of great importance. Thus, pictures are better at engendering memories for recent events, words for distant events. The reverse also holds: People tend to think of recent events in pictures but of more distant events in words. The next section presents several novel experiments testing these predictions.

ILLUSTRATIVE DISTANCE-MEDIUM RESEARCH

CATEGORIZATION OF THE SAME OBJECTS AS PICTURES VERSUS WORDS

The first study, tailored after Liberman et al. (2002), was designed to test the idea that words are high construal whereas pictures are low construal. In the study by Liberman et al., participants were asked to create categories from a pool of items associated with a specific event (e.g., "things to do in New York City when a friend comes to visit"). There were several events. In each case, the event was near (e.g., the friend comes tomorrow) or distal (the friend comes in several months). Liberman et al. found that people generated more categories in the near future condition than in the distal future condition, thereby revealing higher-level construal of distal events. A twist in the procedure rendered the experiment a study on the association between distance and medium. The current participants were asked to think about three events (adapted from Liberman et al., 2002): a camping trip, moving an apartment, and a yard sale. For each scenario, we presented a set of items in two forms, one of words and the other of pictures. Presented with a set of items, the participant was asked to classify the items into as few categories as she or he found comfortable. One group of participants was asked to categorize the words, and another group was asked to categorize the pictures. The results showed that, for each event, participants created fewer categories for words than for pictures of the same objects. In fact, there were almost twice as many categories created for the pictures than for the words. These results support the idea that words are high-level construal, whereas pictures are exemplars of low-level construal. Startlingly, the current results with pictures and words also reproduced the Liberman et al. results with words only at different time frames.

SPEEDED CLASSIFICATION OF OBJECTS REPRESENTED AS PICTURES AND WORDS

Social Distance

According to our hypothesis, cognitive processing is more efficient when medium and distance are congruent (i.e., pictures represent proximal objects and words represent distal objects) than when they are incongruent (pictures represent distal objects and words represent proximal objects). The following experiments tested this prediction with various embodiments of psychological distance (Bar-Anan et al., 2007). The dimension of distance tested in this experiment was social distance.

The participants were presented with objects that belonged in their own culture (proximal condition), and with objects that did not belong to their culture (distal condition). For our Israeli participants, the socially proximal objects were the Israeli shekel, a soccer ball, and the Knesset building. The socially distal objects were an American dollar, a football, and the Tower of Pisa. Each object was presented either as a picture or as a word. In each block, there were two stimulus items, one proximal and one distal (e.g., an Israeli shekel and a dollar). Each of the four objects thus produced (a picture of a shekel, the word SHEKEL, a picture of a dollar, the word DOLLAR) was presented several times in a random order. On each trial, a single stimulus appeared, and the participant's task was to decide, while timed, whether the object was a shekel or a dollar, regardless of the medium of presentation (picture or word). The participant responded by pressing one of a pair of lateralized keys standing for the respective stimuli.

The most revealing outcome of this experiment was that participants responded differently to the same objects depending on the distance of the objects from their social milieu and on the mode of appearance. When the objects belonged to the observer's cultural sphere, pictorial representations yielded faster classification responses than verbal ones. When the objects belonged in another culture, however, verbal representations held an advantage over pictorial ones. Thus, participants responded faster to the picture of an Israeli shekel than to the word SHEKEL, but they responded faster to the word DOLLAR than to the picture of a U.S. dollar.

These results show an influence of the distance-medium association on mental organization. Socially proximal objects (whether perceived pictorially or in written form) are more familiar than socially distal objects. One might then expect more efficient processing, expressed in faster responses to familiar than less-familiar objects. Yet, familiarity did not explain the results. Rather, the interaction of distance-medium did, such that congruent stimuli (proximal pictures or distal words) were better processed than were incongruent stimuli (distal pictures or proximal words). Thus, the distance-medium association modified the effect of familiarity.

Temporal Distance

We designed another study to generalize the results obtained with social distance. Obtaining similar results with stimuli separated in time can provide converging evidence to support the claim that medium is associated with distance. The same paradigm was used. Participants were presented with ancient items (a carriage, a quill pen, and an oil lamp) and parallel modern items (a car, a Pilot pen, and a lamp). In each block, there were two stimulus items, one proximal and one distal (e.g., a car and a carriage). On each trial, a single stimulus appeared, and the participant's task was to decide, while timed, whether the object was a car or a carriage, regardless of the medium of presentation (picture or word).

The results showed that responses were faster to pictures of modern objects than to pictures of ancient objects, but that subjects were faster to respond to words denoting ancient objects than to words denoting modern objects. These findings further support the hypothesis that pictures are associated with proximity and words with distance. The results demonstrate that the relation between medium and distance is not limited to social distance but extends to temporal distance. Notably, as in the previous study, the distance-medium association superseded the effect of familiarity, such that congruent stimuli (proximal pictures and distal words) were better processed than incongruent stimuli (distal pictures and proximal words).

Spatial Distance

The spatial distance experiment tested our hypothesis with stimuli defined by the most natural depiction of distance, spatial layout. In addition to providing converging evidence, spatial distance affords a further bonus. The *same* stimulus can be presented in both a close and a far-off position. To create a feeling of distance, we made use of a pair of vertically oriented converging straight lines (emulating the Ponzo illusion). These lines served to place the target stimuli, presented as an outline of drawings and words, in a near (bottom) or a distal (top) position. As in the previous experiments, two stimulus items appeared in each block. In the first block, the stimuli were a bird and a pear; in the second block, they were an ice cream and a lamp. Again, the task for the participant was to classify the objects while ignoring location and medium of presentation.

The results showed that responses were faster to proximal pictures than to distal pictures and were faster to distal words than to proximal words. Thus, spatial distance had an opposite effect on pictures and words: Proximity improved the processing of pictures, whereas distance improved the processing of words. In other tests of the distance-medium hypothesis, the objects standing for proximal and distal values are different. Only spatial distance permits the use of the same objects at the two positions, thereby controlling for all extraneous variables (e.g., familiarity, likeableness). The results of this experiment show that it is distance alone that instantiates the differential processing of pictures and words.

SPEEDED CATEGORIZATION OF OBJECTS REPRESENTED AS PICTURES AND WORDS: SPATIAL DISTANCE

In the speeded tasks reported, participants were asked to classify objects. In the next experiment, we changed the task to that of speeded categorization. The stimulus objects belonged to two groups:

clothes (tie, dress, pant, and jacket) and animals (lion, bird, camel, and elephant). The items were presented as words and as outline drawings. As in the previous experiment, the items were placed at the ends of two converging straight lines, either in the top end ("distal"), or in the bottom end ("proximal"). On each trial, a single stimulus appeared, and the participant's task was to categorize the item as either a piece of clothing or an animal and to ignore the medium of representation and location of the objects. We predicted that categorization would be faster for congruent stimuli (i.e., proximal pictures or distal words) than for incongruent stimuli (distal pictures or proximal words).

The results indicated that categorization of pictures was generally faster than that of words. However, this main effect was modified by the interaction between medium and distance, such that categorization was faster for near pictures than for distal pictures and was faster for distal words than for proximal words. The results of the current study strongly support the notion that the distance-medium association is task independent. A change in task did not affect the fundamental association between medium and distance. This strengthens our confidence in the robustness of this particular mental organization. Note that the change from identification to categorization effected in this study is a substantive one. Categorization entails quite extensive semantic processing, the placing of different objects under a common rubric. Nevertheless, the distance-medium bond remained intact.

EFFECT OF DISTANCE ON MEDIUM PREFERENCES

In the previous studies, medium (picture, word) and distance (close, distal) were manipulated jointly. They each affected performance in tasks of speeded classification and in tasks of speeded and non-speeded categorization. However, most revealing in the results were not the main effects of medium and distance but rather their interaction. Medium and distance interacted in a particular way to affect cognitive processing. In this study, we tested the relationship between distance and medium themselves. We manipulated psychological distance and observed its influence on people's favored medium. We predicted that pictures would be the preferred medium of representation for proximal events, whereas words would be the preferred medium of representation for distal events.

Distance was manipulated socially and geographically by referring in the experimental cover story to students in either one's own university or at another university. Favorite medium was tested by the amount of space that the participant devoted to text or to pictures on the computer screen. The experiment was presented as a computerized "blind date" project—creating a site for one's own university or for another university. Initially, equal-size text and picture boxes were under the participant's control, such that the participant decided their final size (more space for text or more space for picture) on the "member card." We predicted that participants would allocate *relatively* more space to text than to pictures when the candidates were from another university.

We found that participants indeed devoted more space to text than to pictures for another university's site, but that this difference almost vanished for one's own university site. Although the space allocation for picture and text did not fully reverse across distance, these findings demonstrate that distance is a potent determinant of the preferred medium of representation. This experiment revealed the causal effect of distance on medium. Can the reverse causal chain also be demonstrated? This was attempted in the next experiment.

EFFECT OF MEDIUM ON MEMORY RETRIEVAL

We tested how medium influences the dating of events in memory. In an experiment by Semin and Smith (1999), participants were presented with words that were either trait terms (abstract stimuli) or verbs (concrete stimuli). For each stimulus, participants were asked the date or time elapsed since an associated event occurred. Semin and Smith (1999) found that abstract cues (traits) elicited more remote memories than concrete cues (verbs). In this study, we used the Semin and Smith (1999) task but presented different stimuli. The participants were presented with words and pictures. Following

Rosch's (1975) taxonomy of categories, there were three different levels of abstraction for words: superordinate (e.g., food, animal, furniture); basic (e.g., fruit, dog, chair); or subordinate (e.g., apple, bulldog, kitchen table). Notably, we also presented pictures. The participants were asked to recall an occasion when the presented item appeared in their life and to briefly describe it. They were then asked to specify the date on which the event occurred and rate how long ago it happened (on a scale ranging from 1 [recently] to 7 [long time ago]). We predicted that the more abstract cues would elicit more distant memories. In particular, we predicted that a picture of an object would elicit more recently dated memories than would the name of the same object. We found that words (from all levels of abstraction) elicited memories that were older by more than 400 days than did pictures. Moreover, the most concrete word cues, those at a subordinate level, elicited even older memories than did the pictures. These findings suggest that medium affects the temporal distance of the memories.

In summary, the theoretical framework of CLT and the novel empirical observations support the idea that an essential difference between pictures and words is the level at which these alternative representations are construed. According to the present theory, pictures and words are specific cases of low- and high-level construal, respectively. Consequently, they carry the gamut of distinctive characteristics associated with these two types of mental organization. A potent diagnostic feature is the connection with psychological distance: People tend to construct proximal events at a lower level than they do distal events. Pictures and words exemplify these propensities and indeed amplify them at the boundary. Conversely, the presentation of pictures and words conveys differing values of psychological distance. These ideas predict an array of novel intriguing empirical observations with pictures and words.

How does the current framework of ideas and data fit with those on picture-word processing as pursued in cognitive psychology? The processing of pictures and words has been studied quite extensively within cognitive psychology. The following selective review reveals a rich network of potentially important connections. CLT can provide a conceptual umbrella to unify a substantial portion of the sundry data that have been collected. Conversely, research and ideas from mainstream cognitive psychology can inform CLT research and, in particular, the current conceptualization of the difference between pictures and words.

WORDS AND PICTURES AS HIGH- AND LOW-CONSTRUAL REPRESENTATIONS: INSIGHTS FROM PICTURE-WORD PROCESSING IN COGNITION RESEARCH

A renewed look at Eleanor Rosch's (1975; Rosch, Mervis, Gray, Johnson, & Boyes-Braem, 1976) famous scheme of natural categories can serve as a convenient point of departure. This fresh scrutiny reveals that Rosch's taxonomy mainly applies to words—and much less to pictures—as vehicles to represent categories. Words have larger category width than do pictures. Larger category width is in turn compatible with construal at a higher level and indeed might enable such a construal in the first place.

ROSCH'S TAXONOMY: LARGER CATEGORY WIDTH FOR WORDS THAN FOR PICTURES

According to Rosch, people categorize natural objects at three levels that differ in category width. The *superordinate level* comprises objects collected under an abstract rule. An example of this level is the category of "furniture." The *basic level* entails the classifications of everyday life. It includes classes of objects that share a great number of perceptual and functional features. An example of this level is "chair." Presented with an object and asked to name it, people typically respond by using a basic-level term. Finally, the *subordinate level* is the most specific or least inclusive category. An example for an item at this level is "kitchen chair."

It is sometimes overlooked that Rosch's classification mainly applies to words. There cannot be a pictorial representation of "furniture." It is arguable whether there exist pictures to represent categories at the basic level. Consider the basic-level term *chair*. Even the most impoverished outline drawing of a chair is specific to an extent that might compromise the attempt to represent this basic-level concept pictorially. Note that people might well rely on images when thinking about concepts or objects at a basic level (or at a superordinate level). Philosopher David Hume made this point forcefully in his *Enquiry* (1739/1951). However, this underlying cognitive process of individuation actually accentuates the difference between the particularity of the picture-image and the generality of a word. Each word is a category (including words that denote concepts at a subordinate level), a feature that enables a higher level of construal with words than with pictures. Pictures are more concrete and contextualized than words, features that are compatible with a lower level of construal.

The last point is notable. It means that even the words denoting subordinate concepts in Rosch's scheme entail fairly wide categories. It also means that these terms cannot be fully represented as pictures. The subordinate level in Rosch's taxonomy is the most concrete level possible, yet it is still a fairly wide category. Consider the subordinate term SPORTCAR. *Any* outline drawing would reveal details such as the number of doors, size, shape, color, insignia, or plate—information that is not conveyed by the word SPORTCAR. A subordinate word also fails to capture the excessive concreteness of a picture. The upshot is that all of Rosch's categories include discriminably different objects that cannot be represented by a picture. Language does not assign a word to each specific example of the endless variety of states of nature. Pictures, by contrast, are more concrete and, under certain circumstances, can even function as singular representations. In those cases, pictures can perhaps be conceived as zero-width categories.

This CLT-inspired review of Rosch's taxonomy is important for several reasons. Three stand out. First, uncritical acceptance of the taxonomy has fostered the notion that it applies universally. Rosch experimented with pictures herself, further encouraging the notion of picture-word comparability. Our analysis shows that the taxonomy actually applies to words, and hence, that pictures and words are qualitatively different representations. Second, our analysis reinforces the idea that pictures and words are not fully interchangeable means of representation. Indeed, a main point of the CLT conceptualization is picture-word incommensurability from a psychological point of view. Third, the concept of category width is elaborated and applied to pictures and words.

If, following Hume and many modern-day psychologists (e.g., Johnson-Laird, 1983; Logan, 1988; Medin & Schaffer, 1978), people think about concepts or categories of objects by retrieving a special exemplar, then this process should be faster with pictures than with words. The reason is that a picture already *is* or is very close to the sought exemplar. Retrieval is more time consuming with words due to the wider width of the associated category. Consequently, tasks that entail semantic processing (notably, categorization) should be faster with pictures than with words. Tasks that do not entail semantic processing (e.g., naming, identification) should not hold a similar advantage and may actually be faster with words than with pictures due to the highly overlearned graphemes-to-phonemes mappings.

NAMING AND CATEGORIZING WITH WORDS AND PICTURES

An object can be construed at a high or at a low level; as a special case, it can be (re)presented by a word or by a picture. Now, consider the following fundamental results from cognitive psychology (Glaser, 1992; Smith & Magee, 1980): When people are asked to name an object, they are faster to do so when it is a word than when it is a picture. However, when people are asked to categorize the same object (e.g., to decide whether it is a piece of furniture or a fruit), they do so faster with its picture than with its verbal name. Finally, when a picture and a word appear in tandem (e.g., the word is superimposed on the picture), the word interferes with the picture in tasks of naming. Thus, people *name* the picture faster in congruent combinations (the word is the name of the picture) than in incongruent combinations (word and picture mismatch). However, when the task is changed to that of categorization, pictures interfere with word performance.

How can this naming-categorization difference be explained? First, consider naming. A widely accepted account implicates differential semantic processing of pictures and words (Glaser, 1992).

To name (read) a word, one does not have to engage the semantic system but can use the direct route between the graphemes seen and the phonemes spoken. This mode likely dominates in the standard laboratory task of speeded naming of words presented briefly for view. Each word activates its vocal expression in a direct way. Clearly, words can be named in a meaningless manner. A ready example is the ability to name (read) a word in a foreign, unfamiliar language. In contradistinction, pictures cannot be named without semantic involvement. One cannot name a picture without engaging its meaning. There does not exist a direct route between pictorial and articulatory features. This mandatory semantic processing with pictures is time consuming, hence the advantage of words in naming.

Next, let us consider categorization with pictures and words. Categorization, unlike naming, is a semantic task with both pictures and words because it entails the collection of discriminably different objects in the same class under a common name. However, the genuinely semantic nature of pictures affords them an advantage over words in such processing, hence the faster categorization of pictures.

Based on the current theoretical framework and experiments, we propose an alternative account for the advantage of pictures over words in categorization. Our account is based on the semantic underpinning of words and pictures. The pertinent differences are cognitively interpretable. Pictures are species of low-construal representations, whereas words are species of high-construal representations. Underlying this difference is the larger category width of words. Representing something by a word is tantamount to conferring on it at least a modicum of high-order meaning; in effect, the event is thereby categorized into a meaningful concept. Representing the same thing by a picture accomplishes less semantic work because less categorization is involved. On the other hand, pictures entail a larger amount of perceptual processing than do words.

Therefore, the task of categorizing words and pictures presents people with decisions to make with respect to stimulus items that differ in category width. One must code the presented items as concepts; otherwise, categorization is impossible. People think of concepts by retrieving specific exemplars (images). Because this process of retrieval is done more readily with pictures than with words, categorization is easier with pictures than with words. The low level of construal with pictures coupled with the propensity to retrieve concepts at precisely those levels conspire to produce the good categorization performance observed routinely with pictures.

CAVEAT: PICTURES AND WORDS ARE SPECIAL CASES OF LOW- AND HIGH-LEVEL CONSTRUAL

Let us issue a few caveats before proceeding. Pictures and words comprise examples of low- and high-level construal, respectively. Recognizing their membership in these CLT-defined classes advances our understanding of their sundry functions and processing characteristics. However, one ought to realize that the picture-word contrast is a highly specific one in the generic low- and high-construal distinction.

Consider pictures first. Pictures are unique members in the class of low-level construal in that they lack a linguistic component. Many other instances of low-level construal entail long, often rich, verbal depictions. A picture, though, is language blind, which explains the frequent use of pictures in places in which familiarity with (a particular) language is not expected (e.g., airports, tourist attractions, museums). Inevitably, a picture represents the referent event in a concrete (often, retinal-image-like) fashion. Task-relevant and task-irrelevant details sometimes are given equal exposure. A picture does often allude to its main referent and can impart meaning (DeLoache, Pierroutsakos, & Uttal, 2003; DeLoache, Pierroutsakos, Uttal, Rosengren, & Gottlieb, 1998), but not in the abstract, unambiguous way that language does. Indeed, language is often employed to disambiguate the message carried in an image.

The upshot is that pictures entail perceptual or quasi-perceptual processes that are missing in other low-construal representations. CLT research to date has not focused on perceptual processes;

the low- versus high-construal divide has not hitherto entailed perception as a classification principle. Perceptual analysis is a major feature of picture processing to the extent that some investigators maintain that "recognizing pictures comprises essentially the same cognitive processes as perceiving the objects themselves" (Glaser, 1992, p. 62; see also Gibson, 1980; but consult DeLoache et al., 1998, or Ittelson, 1996, for a more moderate view). Regardless of what other processes they undergo, pictures are foremost perceived.

Consider now the word anchor of the picture-word contrast. By this anchor we usually mean a single word that is the accepted name of the referent object or event. This word comprises a higher-level construal of the object than does a picture of the same object. The reason is that a name is the end product of a deeper semantic analysis of the referent object than that associated with a picture. A word bestows a meaning on the object that is more abstract and poignant than its picture can be. Nevertheless, the names associated with the picture-word contrast comprise special cases of high-level construal. Most instances of high-level construal entail deeply elaborated depictions, not single nouns or adjectives. A single word—a name—is a high-level construal when considered in the context of being compared to a kindred picture.

In sum, the perception-semanticity continuum is not critical when comparing instances of high- and low-level construal in general. However, it is of importance when comparing pictorial and verbal means of representations—themselves special instances of low- and high-level construal. This contrast can enrich the level of construal continuum itself. Novel developments within CLT (Liberman, Trope & Stephan, 2007) indeed develop the notion of zero distance (at which perception dominates) and contrast it with some positive value of distance (at which higher levels of construal are relevant). Along these lines, we turn next to a further discussion of the picture-word difference.

ICONS, INDEXES, AND SYMBOLS

What then is the basic difference between pictures and words? According to philosopher C. S. Pierce (cf. Hartshorne & Weiss, 1965), there are three types of representations. The first is called *icon*. The representational quality of icons is based on physical similarity between the representation and the object. A representation is an icon if it is "like that thing (it represents) and used as a sign of it" (pp. 143–144). Pictures are icons. They are representations based on physical similarity to the object denoted. The second type is called *index*. Its representational quality is based on a causal relationship with the object being represented (e.g., metonymy). The third type is called *symbol*. The representational quality of a symbol is based on convention or law, hence the relation with the object denoted is arbitrary. The representational quality of words and of language in general is based on such an arbitrary assignment. The names of objects or events are symbols. Therefore, according to Pierce's influential scheme, pictures and words comprise qualitatively different representations. Pictures represent the referent objects in an analogous manner by virtue of similarity. Pictures are not arbitrary representations; they are fairly unique—almost as unique indeed as the objects denoted sometimes—and have few alternatives. Words, by contrast, are arbitrary representations established by convention.

Goodman (1976; see also DeLoache et al., 1998) has challenged Pierce's classification and argued that convention-based components in pictures are actually larger than is usually recognized. However, Goodman (1976) also acknowledges that pictures hold a more analogous and hence less-arbitrary relationship with their referents than do words. On the analogue-convention continuum, pictures are closer to the former end than are words. Thus, the processing of pictures (icons) entails a larger perceptual component than does the processing of words (symbols). Although this view is widely held, an important implication is not widely recognized. A trivial stipulation for perception is exposure to the object; otherwise, the stimuli do not impinge on the sensory surface. This stipulation does not hold when processing *pictures* of objects. Nevertheless, the semiperceptual processes associated with pictures might well impart a feeling of proximity. Because such components are missing from word processes, feelings of proximity are not generally conveyed by words.

In summary, people tend to construe distal events at a higher level than they do proximal events. The reverse also holds. A higher level of construal tends to be associated with events at a distance (in a spatial, temporal, or cultural sense). Because pictures and words are low- and high-level representations themselves, they also act according to these same rules. However, in the special case of pictures and words, a further mechanism may be involved to augment their function as markers of psychological distance. Pictures often carry a quasi-perceptual quality that is weaker or nonexistent with words. This difference acts to reinforce the distance-medium association above and beyond the impetus provided by differential levels of construal.

Conceiving words and pictures as instances of high- and low-level construal entails further bonuses. It enables deeper glimpses into further dynamic processes of cognition and the drawing of intriguing predictions. High-level construal means, among other things, tolerance to momentary, incidental changes in the focal object or event. It is the gist of the event that is preserved. Low-level construal is, on the other hand, much less forgiving when alterations occur. The implications for cognitive organization of these features are considerable. Because a word is high-level construal, it is able to function as a better conveyor of information than a picture. A picture might be too unique a vehicle to convey useful information. It is these implications that we discuss next.

PICTURES AND WORDS IN PRIMING AND MEMORY: SOME EVIDENCE

In experiments within the priming paradigm (see Neely, 1991, for a review), two stimuli are presented in a sequence, the prime and the target. The task for the participant is to respond to the target. It is typically found that responses to the target are facilitated by a related prime, even though this stimulus does not require a response. How do pictures and words function as primes? In a study by Durso and Johnson (1979), participants named a picture (target) preceded by itself or by a word that was the picture's name (primes). In other conditions, participants named a word (target) preceded by itself or by a pictorial representation of the word (primes). The results showed that word primes facilitated the subsequent naming of the target *regardless* of the modality of the target (i.e., picture or word). By contrast, picture primes facilitated the naming of subsequent picture targets but not of word targets. Efficient naming of a word was not facilitated by having been exposed to a pictorial representation of that word prior to its naming. The authors concluded that pictures differ qualitatively from words. Pictures are like "words in context—they generate ... specific representations. ... [In contrast, a] word ... activates ... a large set of semantic features" (Durso & Johnson, 1979, p. 457).

Therefore, words were better conveyors of semantic information than were pictures. Because pictures are context-bound representations, the benefit from prior exposure of pictures was confined to those pictures themselves. Due to their higher level of construal, words were able to survive surface changes and serve as potent conveyors of meaning and semantic organization. The same resistance to change, even in surface characteristics, affects memory for pictures. Memory for words, by contrast, withstands such changes successfully. In this domain, too, stimuli of low- and high-level construal carry cognitive consequences.

Mintzer and Snodgrass (1999) probed memory for concepts presented in different contexts. In the study phase, participants were presented with common objects as either pictures (e.g., the picture of a dog) or as words (the word DOG). On a subsequent recognition test, the studied (old) stimuli were presented to the participants in either the same form (e.g., the studied picture of the dog tested as a picture) or in a different form (e.g., the studied picture of the dog tested as the word DOG). New nonstudied items were presented as well. Participants were then instructed to respond "old" to any item that had been presented in the study even if that item appeared in a different form; otherwise, they were asked to respond "new" to any nonstudied item. The results showed that changing the form of an item between study and test took a toll on memory performance. Notably, the cost of form change was appreciable for pictures but not for words. Studied words survived changes in their form during test, such that memory was hardly affected. Studied pictures, by contrast, were vulnerable to changes in appearance.

Mintzer and Snodgrass (1999) explained the results by the enhanced distinctiveness of pictures in comparison with words. Pictures form distinctive stimuli, so changes in their appearance are highly noticeable. Words are less discriminable from one another, so a change in form does not impair memory (cf. Snodgrass, 1984; Snodgrass & McCullough, 1986). We question the authors' account as a full or major explanation of the results. We maintain that the picture-word difference would have remained the same even with the differences in discriminability removed (but see Arieh & Algom, 2002, for qualifications). One can create word stimuli that are as distinct perceptually as pictures, yet the latter only will suffer a change cost. In our account, the underlying reason for the word-picture contrast is the different construal of words and pictures as means of representation. Words are larger categories than pictures and hence are also more abstract than pictures. It is the context-bound nature of pictures that makes them distinctive cognitively and exacts a heavy price on any change in this mode of representation.

DUAL-CODING THEORY

How does the current conception fare with the one formulation in the cognitive psychology literature that is explicitly devoted to exploring the differences in processing between pictures and words?

According to Paivio's dual-coding theory (Paivio, 1971, 1986), there are two separate cognitive systems. One is specialized for representing information conveyed by spatial, nonverbal objects, and the other is specialized for representing words and language information (see also Kosslyn & Moulton, Chapter 3, this volume). Words are initially represented by the verbal system, and scenes and pictures are initially represented by the nonverbal or imagery system. In subsequent processing, each type of stimulus can be coded by the other system as well, hence the possibility of dual coding. The theory does not posit mutually exclusive processing of words and pictures. On the contrary, each stimulus can be encoded and processed by each of the two systems. The major explanatory variable in the theory is the imaginability of the input. Pictures are readily imaginable. Concrete words are also easily imaginable; therefore, such words are likely to be encoded by the image system as well as by the verbal system. In contrast, abstract words are likely to be encoded by the verbal system only. This difference explains the superiority in memory of concrete over abstract words and, often, of pictures over words.

The concrete-abstract distinction in dual-coding theory is well taken. It is somewhat analogous to the high- versus low-construal distinction at the base of CLT. There are some minor differences, though. The concrete-abstract distinction in dual-coding theory is orthogonal to the picture-word distinction as a means of representation. Words can be as concrete as pictures (although pictures cannot be as abstract as some words). When concreteness (or abstractness) is comparable, then processing is comparable. We agree in principle but maintain that, in practice, a word is always higher construed than is a picture.

Concrete words, such as the word TABLE, and pictures, such as a drawing of your table, are close relatives in dual-coding theory. Both stimuli are dual coded by both systems. Consequently, comparable performance is expected with such stimuli. In the current approach, there is a difference between the word TABLE and the picture of a table, although admittedly both items are highly imaginable. The reason is that the word TABLE encompasses a larger category (innumerable individual tables, including your desk) than does the picture of a table. As a result, pictures are categorized better than words (including concrete, readily imaginable words), are less-valuable primes, are more vulnerable to incidental changes, and impart a sense of proximity. All of these features are either difficult to account for or ignored in dual-coding theory.

CONCLUDING REMARKS

The marriage between CLT and the picture-word contrast as studied in cognitive psychology is a good one, but as in most marriages, the partners do not fit perfectly. Pictures and words have served humans to represent their environment, their past, and their future, from time immemorial. We are now beginning to understand the common and different functions of these tools. CLT greatly sustains this quest to understand the psychological underpinnings of pictures and words and helps us to predict when they are likely to be used and what associations they engender beyond their explicit contents. Conversely, research on cognition with words and pictures helps one to appreciate the variegated nature of the differences that exist among instances of low- and high-level construal. Perceptual processes dominate with some but not with other representations. Cognition research also shows stimuli of low and high construal in action; it shows how they shape cognitive processing in tasks of naming, categorization, priming, and memory.

An essential contribution of CLT is its integration of the word-picture contrast into mainstream psychological theorizing. Major differences between words and pictures thus become a natural derivative of substantive theory. A chief contribution is the association of the two means of representation with level of construal. The association explains how words and pictures function at deep layers of cognition and how the two representations have evolved to satisfy their differing goals. Another major contribution is the association with psychological distance. This association is missing from routine research in cognitive psychology. It explains when pictures and words are likely to appear and the way that they in turn affect the observer. The network of CLT variables connecting to pictures and words results in a general conclusion of considerable import: Pictures and words are *not* interchangeable means of representation.

Nevertheless, pictures and words are unique species of low- and high-level construal. Unlike many other low-level representations, pictures entail perceptual or perception-like processing. These processes enhance the feeling of closeness to the referent object beyond that engendered by low construal per se. Words, needless to say, lack such perceptual processing. Unlike many instances of high-level construal, a single word stands for the name of an object in the context of the picture-word contrast. This word is high construal in this context, although richer and more extensive verbal depictions might be low construal in a more general context.

Finally, research in cognition adds dynamic detail to the CLT distinction between levels of construal. For example, the advantage of pictures in classification or the advantage of words in priming are not immediately obvious effects of construal level. Cognitive research and theory show them to be quite natural outcomes of such construal. A fuller understanding of the picture-word divide remains a daunting task, but harnessing CLT into this mission makes it look more manageable.

ACKNOWLEDGMENTS

Preparation of this chapter was supported by Israel Science Foundation grant (ISF 221-0607) and a Tel-Aviv University Research Authority grant to Daniel Algom, grant 1R01MH59030-01A1 to Yaacov Trope, and a United States-Israel Binational Science Foundation Grant 2001057 to Nira Liberman and Yaacov Trope.

We wish to thank Yaniv Mama and Shirley Melamed for assistance with the experiments.

REFERENCES

Arieh, Y., & Algom, D. (2002). Processing picture-word stimuli: The contingent nature of picture and of word superiority. *Journal of Experimental Psychology: Learning, Memory, and Cognition, 26*, 259–274.

Bar-Anan, Y., Liberman, N., Trope, Y., & Algom, D. (2007). Automatic processing of psychological distance: Evidence from a Stroop task. *Journal of Experimental Psychology: General, 136*, 610–622.

Carver, C. S., & Scheier, M. F. (2000). Scaling back goals and recalibration of the affect system are processes in normal adaptive self-regulation: Understanding 'response shift' phenomena. *Social Science & Medicine, 50*, 1715–1722.

Coulmas, F. (2003). *Writing systems.* Cambridge: Cambridge University Press.

DeLoache, J. S., Pierroutsakos, S. L., & Uttal, D. H. (2003). The origins of pictorial competence. *Current Directions in Psychological Science, 12*, 114–118.

DeLoache, J. S., Pierroutsakos, S. L., Uttal, D. H., Rosengren, K. S., & Gottlieb, A. (1998). Grasping the nature of pictures. *Psychological Science, 9*, 205–210.

Durso, F. T., & Johnson, M. K. (1979). Facilitation in naming and categorization repeated pictures and words. *Journal of Experimental Psychology: Human Learning and Memory, 5*, 449–459.

Fujita, K. F., Henderson, M. D., Eng, J., Trope, Y., & Liberman, N. (2006). Spatial distance and mental construal of social events. *Psychological Science, 17*, 278–282.

Gasper, K., & Clore, G. L. (2002). Attending the big picture: Mood and global vs. local processing of visual information. *Psychological Science, 13,* 34–40.

Gibson, C. P. (1980). Binocular disparity and head-up displays. *Human Factors, 22*, 435–444.

Glaser, W. R. (1992). Picture naming. *Cognition, 42*, 61–105.

Goodman, N. D. (1976). *Languages of art: An approach to a theory of symbols.* Indianapolis, IN: Hackett.

Halbertal, M., & Margalit, A. (1992). *Idolatry.* Cambridge, MA: Harvard University Press.

Hampson, S. E., John, O. P., & Goldberg, L. P. (1986). Category breadth and hierarchial structure in personality: Studies of asymmetries in judgments of trait implications. *Journal of Personality and Social Psychology, 51,* 37–54.

Hartshorne, C., & Weiss, P. (1965–1967). *Collected papers of Charles Sanders Pierce.* Cambridge, MA: Harvard University Press.

Hume, D. (1951). *Enquiry*: A treatise of human nature (L. A. Selby-Bigge, Ed.), Oxford, England: Clarendon Press. (Original work published 1739)

Ittelson, W. H. (1996). Visual perception of markings. *Psychonomic Bulletin and Review, 3*, 171–187.

Johnson-Laird, P. N. (1983). *Mental models: Towards a cognitive science of language, inference, and consciousness.* Cambridge, MA: Harvard University Press.

Liberman, N., Sagristano, M. D., & Trope, Y. (2002). The effect of temporal distance on level of mental construal. *Journal of Experimental Social Psychology, 38*, 523–534.

Liberman, N., Trope, Y., McCrae, S. M., & Sherman, S. J. (2007). The effect of level of construal on the temporal distance of activity enactment. *Journal of Experimental Social Psychology, 43*, 143–149.

Liberman, N., Trope, Y., & Stephan, E. (2007). Psychological distance. In: E. T. Higgins & A. W. Kruglanski (Eds.), *Social psychology: A handbook of basic principles* (Vol. 2, pp. 353–383). New York: Guilford Press.

Linville, P. W. (1982). The complexity-extremity effect and age-based stereotyping. *Journal of Personality and Social Psychology, 46,* 193–211.

Logan, G. D. (1988). Toward an instance theory of automatization. *Psychological Review*, 95, 492–527.

Medin, D. L., & Schaffer, M. M. (1978). Context theory of classification learning. *Psychological Review, 85*, 207–238.

Mintzer, M. Z., & Snodgrass, J. G. (1999). The picture superiority effect: Support for the distinctiveness model. *American Journal of Psychology, 112*, 113–146.

Neely, J. H. (1991). Semantic priming effects in visual word recognition: A selective review of current findings and theories. In D. Besner & G. W. Humphreys (Eds.), *Basic processes in reading and visual word recognition* (pp. 264–333). Hillsdale, NJ: Erlbaum.

Paivio, A. (1971). *Imagery and verbal processes.* Oxford, England: Holt, Rinehard & Winston.

Paivio, A. (1986). *Mental representations.* New York: Oxford University Press.

Park, B., & Judd, C. M. (1990). Measures and models of perceived group variability. *Journal of Personality and Social Psychology, 59,* 173–191.

Reyna, V. F., & Brainerd, C. T. (1995). Fuzzy-trace theory: An interim synthesis. *Learning and Individual Differences, 7,* 1–75.

Rock, I. (1983). *The logic of perception.* Cambridge, MA: MIT Press.

Rosch, E. (1975). Cognitive representations of semantic categories. *Journal of Experimental Psychology: General, 104*, 192–233.

Rosch, E., Mervis, C. B., Gray, W. D., Johnson, D. M., & Boyes-Braem, P. (1976). Basic objects in natural categories. *Cognitive Psychology, 8*, 382–439.

Semin, G. R., & Fiedler, K. (1988). The cognitive functions of linguistic categories in describing persons: Social cognition and language. *Journal of Personality and Social Psychology, 54,* 558–568.

Semin, G. R., & Smith, E. R. (1999). Revisiting the past and back to the future: Memory systems and the linguistic representation of social events. *Journal of Personality and Social Psychology, 76,* 877–892.

Smith, M. C., & Magee, L. E. (1980). Tracing the time course of picture-word processing. *Journal of Experimental Psychology: General*, *109*, 373–392.

Snodgrass, J. G. (1984). Concepts and their surface representations. *Journal of Verbal Learning and Verbal Behavior, 23*, 3–24.

Snodgrass, J. G., & McCullough, B. (1986). The role of visual similarity in picture categorization. *Journal of Experimental Psychology: Learning, Memory and Cognition, 112*, 147–154.

Stephan, E., Liberman, N., & Trope, Y. (2007). *Politeness and its relation to psychological distancing.* Manuscript submitted for publication.

Trope, Y. (1986). Self-assessment and self-enhancement in achievement motivation. In R. M. Sorrentino & E. T. Higgins (Eds.), *Handbook of motivation and cognition: Foundations of social behavior* (Vol. 1, pp. 350–378). New York: Guilford.

Trope, Y., & Liberman, N. (2000). Temporal construal and time dependent changes in preference. *Journal of Personality and Social Psychology, 79*, 876–889.

Trope, Y., & Liberman, N. (2003). Temporal construal. *Psychological Review, 110*, 403–421.

Wakslak, S. J., Trope, Y., Liberman, N., & Alony, R. (2006). Seeing the forest when entry is unlikely: Probability and the mental representation of events. *Journal of Experimental Psychology: General, 135*, 641–653.

Wallacher, R. R., & Wegner, D. M. (1989). What do people think they're doing? Action identification and human behavior. *Psychological Review, 94*, 3–15.

5 Implementation Intentions: The Mental Representations and Cognitive Procedures of If-Then Planning

Tanya S. Faude-Koivisto, Daniela Wuerz, and Peter M. Gollwitzer

INTRODUCTION

The cognitive processes that support and maintain goal pursuit have become a central issue among researchers studying self-regulation and motivation (Gollwitzer & Bargh, 1994; Oettingen & Gollwitzer, 2001; Shah & Kruglanski, 2000; Sorrentino & Higgins, 1986). Two key notions in self-regulation research on goals are the model of action phases (Gollwitzer, 1990; Heckhausen, 1991; Heckhausen & Gollwitzer, 1987) and the concept of implementation intentions (Gollwitzer, 1993, 1996) as both address the complex interaction of cognitive and motivational processes. The model of action phases posits distinct consecutive stages of goal pursuit an individual has to successfully navigate to attain a goal and implies that self-regulation within each stage is facilitated by developing the respective mindset. On the other hand, implementation intentions (a concept stimulated by the action-phase model) are specific self-regulatory tools aimed at helping individuals plan and initiate goal-directed actions. A further self-regulatory process that has been identified to foster goal attainment is mental simulation (Escalas & Luce, 2003, 2004; Greitemeyer & Wuerz, 2006; Pham & Taylor, 1999; Phillips & Baumgartner, 2002; Taylor & Pham, 1999). However, so far the cognitive processes associated with mental simulation have not been studied within the framework of the model of action phases or in comparison to implementation intentions.

The focus of this chapter is on expanding the existing theoretical and empirical framework of both the theoretical model of action phases and the concept of implementation intentions in two consecutive steps. First, implementation intentions and mental simulations (as two distinct self-regulatory tools) are contrasted in regard to their mode of cognitive functioning within the planning stage of goal pursuit. Second, basic cognitive properties of implementation intentions postulated to date are challenged and advanced in the light of the preceding comparison.

THE MODEL OF ACTION PHASES AND RELATED MIND-SETS

The model of action phases, providing a first comprehensive account of goal attainment, posits four different consecutive action phases of goal pursuit: the predecisional phase, the preactional phase, the actional phase, and the postactional phase (Gollwitzer, 1990; Heckhausen, 1991; Heckhausen & Gollwitzer, 1987). In particular, the theory assumes that each phase is characterized by a distinct task that must be accomplished. The main task individuals have to solve in the first, predecisional phase, is to set a goal by making the best-possible choice between different wishes they entertain. To achieve this selection or prioritization, they weigh the pros and cons of their wishes on the basis of desirability and feasibility. Once a wish has been given the highest preference, individuals are ready to make a commitment to realize this wish (i.e., form a goal intention). If the perceived feasibility of realizing this wish is high and this expectation becomes activated (Oettingen, Pak, & Schnetter, 2001; Oettingen & Kappes, Chapter 26, this volume), people indeed form a strong goal intention. In the second, preactional phase, the main task is to plan the implementation of the chosen goal. Having formed a goal intention creates a feeling of commitment, prompting people to start planning and implementing respective goal-directed actions for goal attainment. Accordingly, individuals in this phase address questions of when and where to start acting, how to act, and how long to act. The transition from the preactional phase to the third, actional, phase is marked by action initiation. Individuals in the actional phase finally engage in activities to achieve their goals. Here, it becomes important to shield ongoing goal-directed activities from becoming derailed by distractions, difficulties, and hindrances. In the final, postactional phase, individuals have to solve the final task of evaluating the success of goal attainment.

The model of action phases implies that undertaking the four distinct tasks described activate congruent *mind-sets* (i.e., phase-typical cognitive procedures that promote successful task completion; Gollwitzer, 1990; see also Galinsky & Kray, 2004). So far, a body of research has theoretically and empirically distinguished between *deliberative* and *implemental* mind-sets, that is, differences in cognitive processes when an individual is choosing a goal as compared to planning the attainment of a goal (summaries by Gollwitzer, 1990; Gollwitzer & Bayer, 1999; Gollwitzer, Fujita, & Oettingen, 2004).

Deliberative and Implemental Mind-Sets: Empirical Support

Research on the features of deliberative and implemental mind-sets has primarily looked at differences in regard to two cognitive procedures: cognitive tuning and biased inferences. Several studies exploring differences between the two mind-sets in cognitive tuning used the thought-sampling technique to demonstrate that a deliberative mind-set produces thoughts about expectancy-value issues, that is, thoughts focusing on aspects of goal feasibility and desirability (Heckhausen & Gollwitzer, 1987; Puca & Schmalt, 2001; Taylor & Gollwitzer, 1995). On the other hand, thoughts of individuals in an implemental mind-set are focused on the when, where, and how of goal implementation. Using a cued-recall task, Gollwitzer, Heckhausen, and Steller (1990) found in addition that individuals in deliberative mind-sets process information on expectancy-value issues more effectively than individuals in implemental mind-sets, while individuals in implemental mind-sets process information on goal implementation more effectively than individuals in deliberative mind-sets. These findings suggest that cognitive tuning in deliberative and implemental mind-sets is task congruous, that is, it is tuned toward thought contents that allow choosing between goals versus implementing a chosen goal, respectively.

Further, research on biased information processing suggests that individuals in a deliberative mind-set analyze information more impartially as their task is to choose between different wishes (i.e., they need to decide which wish is to be turned into a binding goal). Individuals in an implemental mind-set, on the other hand, tend to analyze information in a more partial way as they tend to look for information that justifies the goal choices made and thus supports goal implementation. Deliberating on one's wishes seems to activate even-handed processing of information that should benefit a good goal decision, while planning the implementation of a chosen goal, on the other hand, seems to activate partial processing of information to help defend the goal decision and protect it from questioning one's goal commitment (Armor & Taylor, 2003; Gagne & Lydon, 2001; Gollwitzer & Kinney, 1989; Taylor & Gollwitzer, 1995).

DELIBERATIVE AND IMPLEMENTAL MIND-SETS: OPEN-MINDEDNESS TO INFORMATION

A further-suggested difference between deliberative and implemental mind-sets is openness to information. Gollwitzer (1990) argued that due to the different tasks associated with deliberative and implemental mind-sets (i.e., making a goal decision vs. implementing a chosen goal), individuals in a deliberative mind-set should be particularly open to any available information that might help them with the decision-making process (referred to as "general open-mindedness to information"). When assessing desirability and feasibility, it seems beneficial to approach different pieces of information with a general open-mindedness because it is initially unclear which pieces of information are particularly relevant to the decision to be made. In contrast, individuals in an implemental mind-set are primarily concerned with information about the when, where, and how of goal implementation. They process information more selectively, focusing on goal-relevant stimuli, while ignoring goal-irrelevant stimuli. As a result, a deliberative mind-set is associated with open-mindedness to information and an implemental mind-set with more closed-minded processing of information.

The suggested differences in open-mindedness between deliberative and implemental mind-sets have been investigated by Fujita, Gollwitzer, and Oettingen (2007). In three studies, a deliberative mind-set led to superior recognition memory for incidental information than an implemental mind-set. For example, in Study 3, participants were either assigned to the deliberative mind-set, the implemental mind-set, or a control condition. After the mind-set manipulation, all participants had to perform a computerized concentration test. Randomly during the test, participants were presented with incidental words (e.g., bone, every, flag, always). After filling out various questionnaires, participants were asked to perform a surprise computerized recognition memory test containing the initially presented incidental words. Participants in the deliberative mind-set performed significantly better on the recognition memory test than those in the implemental mind-set and the control conditions, indicating that deliberative mind-sets are marked by more open-minded processing of available information than implemental mind-sets. As in all mind-set research, the Fujita et al. studies used unrelated tasks to instigate deliberative versus implemental mind-sets (i.e., deliberating the pros and cons of an unresolved personal problem vs. planning out the implementation of a chosen personal project, respectively). So, all of the incidental words were unrelated to the mind-set induction, and the findings can be confidently interpreted as mind-set effects rather than mere task-set effects.

IMPLEMENTATION INTENTIONS: A STRATEGY FOR EFFECTIVE SELF-REGULATION OF GOAL PURSUIT

A development in intention-behavior relations is Gollwitzer's (1993, 1996, 1999) concept of implementation intentions, a concept stimulated by the action-phases model. Implementation intentions are if-then plans aimed at helping people overcome self-regulatory problems in goal striving by successfully achieving the task they are confronted with in the preactional phase of goal pursuit—preparing the execution of actions that are instrumental to attaining the chosen goal. This form of planning is assumed to increase the likelihood of attaining one's objectives compared to the formation of a mere goal intention.

Whereas goal intentions specify what one wants to achieve (e.g., "I intend to reach Z!"), implementation intentions specify in advance when, where, and how one intends to achieve it (e.g., "If situation X occurs, then I will initiate goal-directed behavior Y!"). Forming an implementation intention first involves the identification of a response that will promote goal attainment (i.e., is instrumental) and second the anticipation of a critical situation (i.e., a particular place, object, person, or point in time; but also a critical inner state such as being irritated; Achtziger, Gollwitzer, & Sheeran, 2008) to initiate that response. Finally, the specified cue is linked to the response in an if-then format. For instance, an implementation intention formed to reach the goal "to pursue a healthy lifestyle" would involve an appropriate behavior (i.e., "choosing green tea") and a suitable situational context (i.e., "being asked for one's order at a restaurant") and take the format of "If I am having dinner at a restaurant and I'm asked for my order of drinks, then I will choose green tea."

A wealth of research has demonstrated the beneficial effects of implementation intentions as a self-regulatory tool in goal attainment. For example, Gollwitzer and Schaal (1998) observed that participants who had formed an implementation intention in addition to a goal intention were able to solve more arithmetic problems despite being distracted by simultaneously shown film clips of advertisements, compared to participants who had only formed a goal intention. Implementation intentions have been shown to be effective in promoting infrequently performed behaviors (e.g., cancer screening; Sheeran & Orbell, 2000) and daily-performed behaviors (e.g., supplement use; Sheeran & Orbell, 1999), no matter whether self-report or objective measures of performance were taken (e.g., Gollwitzer & Brandstätter, 1997; Milne, Orbell, & Sheeran, 2002). The effects on goal attainment were shown among students, the general public, and clinical samples (e.g., Brandstätter, Lengfelder, & Gollwitzer, 2001; Lengfelder & Gollwitzer, 2001; Orbell, Hodgkins, & Sheeran, 1997). To this end, a meta-analysis of 94 independent studies reported a medium-to-large effect size of implementation intentions (Gollwitzer & Sheeran, 2006), and this was on top of the medium effect of goal intentions on goal attainment.

So far, two processes have been proposed to explain why implementation intentions benefit goal achievement, relating either to the anticipated situation (i.e., the if-part) or the goal-directed behavior (i.e., the then-part). As forming implementation intentions implies the *selection* of a critical future situation (i.e., a great opportunity, a difficult situation), the mental representation of this situation is assumed to become highly activated and hence more accessible (Gollwitzer, 1993, 1996, 1999). Forming an implementation intention involves the selection of a situation that is ripe for action, thereby rendering the critical situation salient. This idea implies that people process information about the critical situation in a highly proficient manner (Gollwitzer, 1993; Achtziger, Bayer & Gollwitzer, 2008; Webb & Sheeran, 2006). Therefore, compared to those who merely form a respective goal intention, people who form implementation intentions are assumed to exhibit increased sensitivity to the critical cue. Various experiments (for a summary, see Gollwitzer, 1999) demonstrated that participants holding implementation intentions were more likely to detect (e.g., Steller, 1992), remember (e.g., Gottschaldt, 1926; Witkin, 1950), and attend (e.g., Achtziger, Bayer & Gollwitzer, 2008) to the critical situation compared to participants who had only formed goal intentions.

Implementation intentions have also been shown to benefit action initiation through processes of *automatization* (Gollwitzer, 1993, 1996). Gollwitzer (1993) argued that forming an implementation intention (i.e., linking a critical situation to an intended behavior in the form of an if-then plan) is a conscious act of will that effectively delegates control of behavior from the self to specified situational cues that directly elicit action (also described as strategic "delegation of control to situational cues"). Forming an if-then plan means that the person commits himself or herself in advance to acting as soon as certain contextual constraints are satisfied. Once the specified situation is encountered, action initiation should proceed swiftly and effortlessly, without requiring the person's conscious intent. Thus, the execution of a behavior specified in an implementation intention is assumed to exhibit features of automaticity such as immediacy, efficiency, and no conscious intent (Bargh, 1992, 1994; Moors & De Houwer, 2006). The postulated automation of action initiation has been supported by the results of various experiments that tested immediacy (e.g., Gollwitzer & Brandstätter, 1997, Experiment 3; Webb & Sheeran, 2006); efficiency (e.g., Brandstätter et al., 2001; Lengfelder & Gollwitzer, 2001); and the absence of conscious intent (e.g., Bayer, Achtziger, Gollwitzer, & Moskowitz, in press; Sheeran, Webb, & Gollwitzer, 2005; overview by Gollwitzer & Sheeran, 2006). In sum, the facilitating effects of implementation intentions appear to be associated with enhanced accessibility of good opportunities to act (if-component) and with the automation of goal-directed responding (then-component).

MENTAL SIMULATION AND IMPLEMENTATION INTENTIONS: TWO DISTINCT SELF-REGULATION TECHNIQUES FOR GOAL STRIVING

In addition to implementation intentions, there are other self-regulation techniques that lead to successful goal attainment, namely, mental simulations. Conceptually different from implementation intentions (i.e., linkages of cues and responses in an if-then format), mental simulations can best be described as "imitative mental representations of some event or a series of events" (Taylor & Schneider, 1989). When planning via mental simulation, a desired end state is approached through exploration of possible paths to goal attainment. Taylor, Pham, Rivkin, and Armor (1998) call such mental simulations process simulations, that is, the process of goal attainment is imagined step by step. Similar to implementation intentions, the effects of mental simulation have been found to promote goal attainment in many different domains, such as academic achievement (Pham & Taylor, 1999; Taylor & Pham, 1999), improving health-related behavior (Greitemeyer & Wuerz, 2006), and facilitating behavioral intentions in the consumer domain (Escalas & Luce, 2003, 2004; Phillips & Baumgartner, 2002). Why do process-focused mental simulations benefit goal achievement? Several studies have demonstrated that the beneficial effects of mental simulation on the achievement of desired outcomes is linked to enhanced levels of planning, that is, action plan formation (Escalas & Luce, 2003, 2004; Rivkin & Taylor, 1999). Thus, both mental simulation and implementation intentions further goal attainment through enhanced planning of goal-directed actions.

However, the way in which mental simulations benefit the planning process should differ from that furthered by implementation intentions. The planning process associated with a mental simulation is marked by exploration of possible means or paths to a goal (Oettingen, 2000; Oyserman & James, Chapter 25, this volume), while the formation of an implementation intention leads to the selection of a critical situation, which is then linked to a goal-directed response. No research to date has compared the two self-regulation tools against each other to detect differences and commonalities. Addressing this question will help us to better understand the various ways in which people can self-regulate goal striving by planning.

In this section, we introduce four studies that compare the cognitive functioning of two distinct self-regulation tools: implementation intentions versus mental simulations. The first set of studies (Studies 1 and 2) explores differences in mind-sets induced by if-then plans versus mental simulation. The second set of studies (Studies 3 and 4) builds on the initial results and investigates activation levels of the underlying mental representations implicated by the different planning techniques.

RESEARCH ON MIND-SETS INDUCED BY IMPLEMENTATION INTENTIONS VERSUS MENTAL SIMULATION

Does mental simulation versus forming an if-then plan activate different mind-sets? If-then plans and mental simulations have thus far been considered as self-regulatory techniques that further goal attainment in the preactional phase through enhanced planning of goal-directed activities. The mind-set associated with this stage of the model of action phases is an implemental mind-set (Gollwitzer, 1990). However, we postulate that an individual can switch on an explorative mind-set in the preactional phase when performing mental simulations. Empirical support for this assumption is provided by research on hindsight bias and counterfactual priming, which suggests that inducing a mental simulation mind-set results in generating and considering additional alternatives (Galinsky & Kray, 2004; Hirt, Kardes, & Markman, 2004; Hirt & Markman, 1995; Kahneman & Tversky, 1982; Markman, Lindberg, Kray, & Galinsky, 2007; Wong, Galinsky, & Kray, Chapter 11, this volume). For example, Markman et al. (2007) found that activating a mental simulation mind-set through additive counterfactual thinking enhanced performance on creative generation tasks and lead to more expansive information processing with broader conceptual attention. As mentioned, finding and considering alternatives should be associated with an open-minded processing of information.

On the other hand, several studies have demonstrated that forming if-then plans tunes individuals' thoughts into the when, where, and how of goal implementation, a feature associated with an implemental mind-set (Fujita et al., 2007; Gollwitzer & Bayer, 1999; Taylor & Gollwitzer, 1995). Fujita et al. (2007) further argued that implemental less so than deliberative mind-sets are associated with openness to available information. An implemental mind-set, then again, is associated with filtering of information and selective processing of stimuli (e.g., Gollwitzer, 1990; Kuhl, 1984). Therefore, Studies 1 and 2 were aimed at testing two assumptions: Mental simulation induces an explorative mind-set associated with a more open-minded processing of information (i.e., considering various means for a given goal), whereas forming if-then plans induces an implemental mind-set associated with a more closed-minded processing of information (i.e., focusing on one particular means to a given goal).

To measure breadth of information processing, we asked participants to generate alternatives of situational opportunities and goal-directed responses. Situational cues and goal-directed responses are both considered as means to a goal and represent the two parts of an implementation intention, that is, the if-part and the then-part. The structure of an if-then plan was reflected in our studies, such that Study 1 targeted the anticipated situation specified in the if-component of the implementation intention, and Study 2 targeted the critical response specified in the then-component. The second study further included a cognitive load condition to (a) replicate previous findings showing that implementation intentions operate efficiently (e.g., Brandstätter et al., 2001, Studies 2 and 3) and (b) explore the effect of cognitive load on mental simulation.

In Study 1, undergraduate students were asked to adopt the goal "to do well in school" (Wuerz, Gollwitzer, & Greitemeyer, 2007). Next, half of the participants listened to a tape-recorded mental simulation, describing three different scenarios beneficial to the given goal (i.e., reading a textbook and marking passages in it with a highlighter, taking notes on a notepad in a lecture, writing an essay on a laptop). Participants were instructed to visualize the described scenarios as vividly as possible. In sum, the three scenarios contained a total of five critical situational cues (i.e., highlighter, textbook, notepad, laptop, lecture). The other half of the participants were asked to adopt five implementation intentions in the service of the adopted goal. The assigned if-then plans contained the same five situational cues described as elements of the if-part of the plans (e.g., "If I sit in front of my textbook, then I will read every passage very carefully"). Finally, participants in the mental simulation and implementation intention conditions were seated in front of a computer and presented with the five situational cues. For each stimulus, they were asked to come up with as many alternatives as possible during a time period of 3 min. At the same time, we measured the time of stimulus onset (i.e., the presentation of the situational cues on the computer screen) to the moment when participants first pressed a key on the keyboard to start typing in alternatives. Hence, our dependent variables consisted of the mean number of generated alternatives to the presented stimuli and mean reaction times.

Mental simulation participants created more possible alternatives for the presented situational cues than implementation intention participants. However, after presentation of the situational cues, implementation intention participants started typing in alternatives to the cues more quickly than did mental simulation participants. The conclusions of the reported results are twofold. First, the explorative mind-set induced by mental simulation seems to enhance open-mindedness in the sense of making it easier to generate alternatives to presented situational cues (see also Wong et al., Chapter 11, this volume). On the other hand, forming if-then plans seems to lead to a more closed-minded processing of information, as indicated by producing fewer alternatives. Second, we observed that if-then plans not only lead to an overall narrower focus but also lead to a stronger focus on the situation specified beforehand, indicated by implementation intention participants' shorter reaction times between stimulus onset (i.e., presentation of the situational cues) and their initial response (i.e., starting to type in alternatives for the presented cues). Overall, these results suggest that mental simulation seems to create an exploratory mind-set with associated open-mindedness, while if-then plans lead to an implemental mind-set with a more closed-minded focus on the situations specified in the if-part of the implementation intentions.

Study 2 targeted the then-component of an implementation intention (Wuerz et al., 2007). Besides replicating the previous results, we wanted to demonstrate that mental simulation leads to finding more possible goal-directed actions. Furthermore, we examined whether mental simulation would be affected by cognitive load. The procedure of this study was very similar to the previous one with the exception that participants had to generate their own mental simulations or implementation intentions (as opposed to listening to a prerecorded mental simulation or adopting assigned if-then plans). The goal given to participants was "to study effectively for an upcoming exam." Mental simulation participants were asked to visualize three different self-generated scenarios of studying for an exam. To this end, mental simulation participants were provided with three general examples of scenarios they could visualize (e.g., summarizing passages of a textbook) but were then prompted to come up with their own scenarios. They were told to visualize each scenario for at least 1 min. After each visualization, participants had to briefly summarize the content of their visualization. Accordingly, participants in the implementation intention condition were first provided with the same three examples of studying as mental simulation participants and were then asked to generate three different if-then plans related to this goal. Specifically, they were asked to specify when, where, and how they would study. Implementation intention participants specified, for instance, "If I sit at home at my desk, then I will read my textbook carefully."

After the experimental manipulation, all participants were presented with three of the situational cues they had previously specified (e.g., textbook, desk, lecture material) on a computer screen. For each presented cue, they were asked to generate as many goal-directed responses (i.e., behaviors they considered as beneficial for the given goal in that particular situation) as possible. For example, if "desk" was one of the previously generated situations of a particular participant, the participant might have generated "writing, reading, concentrating" as different kinds of behaviors related to studying that the participant thought of performing at a desk (i.e., goal-related responses). The situational cues presented to participants differed for each participant as they were chosen from their individually created materials. As soon as they started working on the computer task, half of the participants in each condition were put under cognitive load by asking them to count the number of vowels presented to them over headphones.

Mental simulation participants generated more possible action words related to presented situational cues (i.e., the cues that were selected from the individual mental simulations or implementation intentions) than implementation intention participants. However, this effect was moderated by cognitive load: Mental simulation participants generated a higher number of action words than if-then plan participants only under cognitive load, while under no load both groups performed equally well. Evidently, the open-mindedness associated with the explorative mind-set activated by mental simulations was enhanced by the depletion of resources. The generation of more action words under no load than under load by if-then plan participants, on the other hand, indicates that the closed-mindedness associated with the activated implemental mind-set was enhanced by the load manipulation. It appears, then, that the explorative mind-set effects associated with mental simulation (open-mindedness) versus the implemental mind-set effects associated with forming implementation intentions (closed-mindedness) are enhanced when cognitive resources become scarce. As habitual behavioral and cognitive orientations are commonly unaffected by load, we take this finding to mean that the habitual cognitive orientation of the explorative mind-set associated with mental simulations is open-mindedness, whereas the habitual cognitive orientation of the implemental mind-set associated with forming implementation intentions is closed-mindedness.

RESEARCH ON THE ACTIVATION OF MENTAL REPRESENTATIONS BY IMPLEMENTATION INTENTIONS VERSUS MENTAL SIMULATIONS

In Studies 3 and 4, we compared the activation of the mental representations that underlie if-then plans and mental simulations. As indirect measures have become the norm to measure construct activation (e.g., Kruglanski et al., 2002; Marsh & Landau, 1995; Shah & Kruglanski, 2000), we used a lexical decision task. Specifically, we compared the activation of the mental representation of critical situational stimuli and goal-directed responses when mentally simulating or forming if-then plans. Study 3 focused on the if-component of an implementation intention, assessing the mental representation of the specified situation, whereas Study 4 focused on its then-component, assessing the mental representation of the goal-directed response. In both studies, assigned if-then plans and mental simulations were used to ensure that heightened accessibility would not be muddled by semantic relatedness between words.

On their arrival at the laboratory, Study 3 participants were asked to adopt the goal "to do well in school." Next, mental simulation participants had to listen to a tape-recorded mental simulation describing three scenarios beneficial to the given goal (i.e., highlighting important passages in a textbook with a highlighter, writing an essay on a laptop, writing notes on a notepad during class). Hence, the mental simulation contained a total of five critical situational cues (i.e., textbook, highlighter, laptop, essay, notepad). Implementation intention participants were asked to adopt two if-then plans related to the goal, each plan containing one of the five situational cues mentioned (e.g., "If I have a highlighter in my hand, then I will underline important passages in my lecture materials"). Implementation intention participants were presented with the remaining situational cues (i.e., the situational cues that were not contained in their if-then plans) through a "spelling test" to ensure equal exposure to the stimuli across conditions. This test contained the three situational cues plus misspelled words, and participants were asked to correct any misspelled words. Finally, all participants were seated in front of a computer screen to perform a lexical decision task that contained the five situational cues (i.e., textbook, highlighter, laptop, essay, notepad), five matched neutral words, and ten nonwords.

The lexical decision task yielded faster reaction times to critical situational cues for implementation intention participants than for mental simulation. Assuming that faster latencies reflect more activation (e.g., Anderson, 1983; Ratcliff & McKoon, 1978), this result indicates that forming implementation intentions leads to higher activation levels for the situation words than mentally simulating. Additional analyses demonstrated that, among implementation intention participants, only those situation words that were part of an if-then plan showed higher activation levels, but not the situation words that were presented in the spelling test. Mental simulation participants demonstrated equal activation levels for all five situation words, but their overall activation levels were lower than those of implementation intention participants. Thus, implementation intention participants seemed to focus on the two situational cues contained in their implementation intentions, while mental simulation participants focused on all five situation words equally strongly.

The aim of Study 4 was to replicate these findings with regard to the then-component of an implementation intention. This time, we used the goal "to lead a healthy lifestyle." One half of the participants had to perform a mental simulation describing three different goal-directed actions related to the goal (i.e., climbing the stairs, cooking a healthy meal, exercising in the gym). The other half of the participants had to adopt three if-then plans containing the three goal-directed actions of the mental simulation in the then-part of the plan (e.g., "If I enter a multistory building, then I will climb the stairs instead of taking the elevator"). Next, participants had to perform a lexical decision task containing the three critical action words, three matched neutral words, and six nonwords.

Results of the lexical decision task indicated that participants who had formed if-then plans responded faster to the action words describing the target response than to the words describing a neutral response. On the other hand, mental simulation participants reacted only slightly faster to target words compared to neutral words. Thus, the results of the present study indicate that forming if-then plans also leads to a higher activation of the target response contained in the then-component (and not just to a heightened activation of the situational cue specified in the if-component, as observed in the previous study).

In sum, the findings of Studies 3 and 4 presented suggest that forming if-then plans leads not only to higher activation of specified situational cues, but also to higher activation of a previously specified behavioral response, as is observed for mental simulations that contain these situations and responses.

IMPLEMENTATION INTENTIONS AS MENTAL CONSTRUCTS: RECENT FINDINGS

The last two studies presented in the preceding section primarily addressed the question of whether implementation intentions and mental simulations are associated with different activation levels of the mental representations of relevant situations and responses. These results thus provide new insights about the basic cognitive properties that may underlie the beneficial effects of implementation intention formation per se. According to the present findings, formation of implementation intentions (i.e., if-then linkage of specified situations and goal-directed behaviors) leads to higher activation of the mental representations of both of an if-then plan's components (i.e., the situation and the goal-directed behavior) in comparison to the mental representation of respective components that have only been mentally simulated.

As mentioned, two component processes have so far been postulated and empirically supported to explain implementation intentions' effectiveness: heightened accessibility of the specified situation and automatic initiation of the goal-directed behavior. In other words, only one component of if-then plans, that is the specified situation, has been referred to and investigated on a cognitive level. Yet, the question of how the goal-directed behavior (i.e., the then-component) is mentally represented has received no theoretical analysis or empirical attention. Rather, hitherto research on the then-component of an implementation intention has been limited to a behavioral level, investigating the features of goal-directed behavior when being triggered by the specified situation. That is, the specified behavior within an implementation intention has been merely conceptualized as an automatic response to the stimulus cue without consideration of potential intervening mental processes.

Hence, the results reported above not only contribute to evidence that forming an if-then plan enhances activation of the if-component, but also constitute first evidence of the mental representation and heightened activation of the plan's then-component on implementation intention formation. It therefore seems plausible to argue that (a) two cognitive processes—the heightened activation of the if-component and then-component, respectively—underlie the beneficial effects of implementation intention formation; and (b) on formation of an implementation intention (i.e., linking the specified situation to the goal-directed response) both components (the if-component and the then-component) become activated at the same time. However, these conclusions are premature particularly as activation levels of the if-component and the then-component of implementation intentions were measured in two separate studies, and in each study, the if-then plans were formed in the service of a different goal.

Therefore, the following line of research (Faude, 2005) attempted a critical, more specific test of the hypothesis of the coactivation of implementation intentions' two components. Specifically, the following assumptions were made regarding the anticipated situation and the goal-directed behavior as elements of an implementation intention: (a) Both components are mentally represented as knowledge structures and become simultaneously highly activated on formation of the if-then plan; and (b) the heightened accessibility of both elements is a result of their superior status due to having been linked in an "if-then" format and the functional relation between the two components. Three studies tested these assumptions using lexical decision latencies to assess levels of activation.

FORMING IF-THEN PLANS: ACTIVATION OF BOTH COMPONENTS?

It was determined that the best method to preliminarily investigate the mental representation of implementation intentions' dual components was to compare the accessibility of the anticipated situation and the goal-directed behavior between participants who had been asked to form if-then plans (experimental condition) and participants who had been equally exposed to the situation and behavior words but had not formed a plan (yoked control condition). Based on Gollwitzer's (1993,

1996) argument that the selection of an implementation intention's particular component leads to heightened activation, Study 1 used self-generated if-then plans.

Experimental participants were first asked to generate two self-relevant goals in given domains by completing the sentence "I want to …" (e.g., "I want to improve my relationship" as an interpersonal goal). After generation of each goal, participants were asked to list four behaviors (e.g., "forgive") they thought of as beneficial for achieving their goal and then were asked to generate relevant situations (e.g., "conversation") in which they wanted to carry out the behaviors they had listed before. Finally, they were asked to form implementation intentions (four per goal) by formulating an "If … , then …" plan using the previously generated behaviors and situations (e.g., "If I am disappointed in a conversation, then I will forgive!"). Control participants were yoked to experimental participants by being exposed to the situation and behavior words that the respective experimental participant had generated beforehand, this by asking them to work on word lists.

Next, a lexical decision was administered to measure the accessibility of implementation intentions' components. The lexical decision included the critical words (i.e., previously generated situations and goal-directed responses) and nonwords. Hence, the words used in the lexical decision task differed for each participant in the experimental condition. Within the yoked control condition, the words in the lexical decision task corresponded to the materials of the participant in the implementation intention condition to which they were yoked.

Participants who had generated if-then plans responded significantly faster to situation words and behavior words than participants in the yoked control condition who had not formed plans. Applying the standard assumption that faster latencies reflect more activation (e.g., Anderson, 1983; Ratcliff & McKoon, 1978), the present findings indicate that linking a specified situation to a goal-directed behavior in an if-then format (i.e., forming an implementation intention) leads to enhanced activation of the mental representation of both components of the plan (i.e., the specified situation *and* the goal-directed behavior).

COMPONENTS OF IF-THEN PLANS: COACTIVATION DUE TO THEIR FUNCTIONAL RELATION AND SUPERIOR STATUS

The reasons behind conducting Study 2 were multifold. First, the aim was to replicate the findings of Study 1 by introducing assigned (vs. self-generated) implementation intentions. Introducing assigned plans allowed for testing of the hypothesis that the heightened accessibility of implementation intentions' components is due to the superior status of the anticipated situation and the goal-directed behavior on linking in an if-then format and not due to a generation effect of the components. Second, to further investigate the superior status hypothesis, Study 2 used the same basic design as Study 1 but was augmented in the following ways: An equifinal goal plan structure was used that included one goal only and six implementation intentions. According to conventional goal architecture, lateral relations within a goal system are assumed to be primarily inhibitory (Kruglanski et al., 2002; Shah, Kruglanski, & Friedman, 2003). Introducing several lateral relations on a mean level allows for conservative testing of the accessibility of the mental representation of the plans' components. Further, a "goal-only" condition was added in which participants were assigned the same goal intention as participants in the implementation intention condition but were not assigned any plan. This allowed for addressing the question of whether holding a goal intention only might suffice to activate certain goal-facilitating situations and behaviors without the need of forming specific plans. Third, to provide more direct support for the argument that heightened activation of implementation intentions' components is based on a functional (and not merely semantic) relation between these components, semantically unrelated words were chosen for the if-parts and then-parts of the plans to be assigned.

The materials consisted of one goal intention (i.e., "becoming socially integrated") plus six corresponding if-then plans (e.g., "If I am at the gym, then I will introduce myself to a fellow student."). Each if-then plan contained two critical words for the lexical decision task that corresponded to the situation (e.g., "gym") and the goal-directed behavior (e.g., "introduce"). After assigning the goal to participants in the plan condition and goal-only condition, participants in the plan condition were asked to adopt the six plans by reading them and then filling in respective blanks (e.g., "If I am at the _____, then I will _____ myself."). Participants in the goal-only and control condition were presented with a word list that contained the situation and behavior words of the implementation intentions to ensure equal encoding of the critical words to be used in the lexical decision task across conditions. Finally the identical lexical decision task was introduced to all three conditions.

Forming assigned implementation intentions led to heightened activation of both its components (i.e., the specified situation and the goal-directed behavior), as indicated by shorter mean response times to the situation and behavior words for participants who had formed if-then plans (i.e., implementation intention condition) compared to participants who had not (i.e., goal-only and control participants). Further, response times to the critical words did not differ between the goal-only and the control conditions, and comparing response latencies between the different plans in the implementation intention condition revealed no significant differences.

Demonstrating the robustness of the previous findings (i.e., simultaneous activation of both components of if-then plans on having formed an implementation intention), this result was hereinafter referred to as the "plan activation effect." In particular, the results offer evidence that this effect is functional rather than semantic (as only semantically unrelated words were used). In addition, activation of if-then plans' components was found to be attributable to neither a generation effect of the components (as assigned implementation intentions were used) nor a goal activation effect (as reaction times between the goal-only condition and the control condition did not differ), indicating that the plan activation effect is a result of the superior status of the components of implementation intentions. The superior status is further supported by the fact that the plan activation effect was found within an equifinal goal system of one goal with several potentially reciprocal inhibiting, lateral relations on a means level (i.e., six implementation intentions). The one-goal, six-plans structure did not attenuate the response latency advantage of the specified situations and the goal-directed behaviors.

AUTOMATICITY IN PLAN ACTIVATION

The aim of Study 3 was to investigate if the effect of plan activation is based on a consciously controlled process (i.e., requiring cognitive resources) or rather due to an automatic process that is characterized by its crucial features of immediacy, efficiency (i.e., not requiring much cognitive resources), and lack of conscious intent (Bargh, 1994, 1996, 1997; Bargh & Chartrand, 1999; Logan, 1992; Shiffrin & Schneider, 1977). The findings of the two previous studies can so far be interpreted as the plan activation process displaying two characteristics of automaticity, namely, the lack of conscious intent (as the measure of activation consisted of an indirect measure, i.e., lexical decision) and immediacy (as higher activation of if-then plans' components could be observed from the onset of activation measurement). However, thus far it is unclear if the cognitive advantage of implementation intentions' components is contingent on the amount of available cognitive resources.

To address the question of automaticity in if-then plan activation, the lexical decision task in Study 3 was administered under mental load, and activation levels of if-then plans' components were compared between implementation intentions and goal-only subjects. Based on the design of Study 2, in Study 3 high levels of cognitive load were induced by presenting the target words in the lexical decision with a background pattern (following Park, Hertzog, Kidder, Morrell, & Mayhorn, 1997). The dual task consisted of participants having to remember how many different background patterns they saw simultaneously while making lexical decisions.

As predicted, a higher activation of implementation intentions' components was also found under conditions of high cognitive load, as indicated by shorter mean response times to the situation and behavior words in the implementation intention condition compared to the goal-only condition.[1] Evidently, the plan activation effect is based on an automatic process that does not require cognitive resources. Taken together, the results of Study 3 (a) closely replicate the plan activation effect (i.e., coactivation of both implementation intentions' components on formation of such plans) found in Studies 1 and 2 and (b) show that this effect appears to fulfill the three criteria of automaticity: immediacy, lack of conscious intent, and efficiency (i.e., not requiring cognitive resources; Bargh, 1994, 1996, 1997; Bargh & Chartrand, 1999; Logan, 1992).

CONCLUSIONS AND IMPLICATIONS

This chapter had two primary objectives. First, it contrasted implementation intentions and mental simulations (i.e., two planning strategies shown to enhance goal attainment) with respect to the associated mind-sets (i.e., implemental vs. explorative mind-set, respectively). Second, the mental representations activated by mental simulations versus implementation intentions were mapped out by investigating the mental representation of the critical situations and behaviors entailed.

At the outset of the chapter, the so far theoretical and empirical association of deliberative and implemental mind-sets with distinct action phases (i.e., the predecisional and the preactional phases, respectively) was questioned (Wuerz et al., 2007). According to the model of action phases, choosing a goal (in the predecisional phase) activates a deliberative mind-set, whereas planning the implementation of a goal (in the preactional phase) always activates an implemental mind-set. In contrast, we proposed a more flexible approach to the question of type of mind-set in the preactional phase. We postulated that becoming involved with planning the implementation of a chosen goal induces either an implemental or an explorative mind-set, depending on which planning technique (i.e., implementation intentions or mental simulations) is used. The results of two studies were consistent with this supposition.

In Studies 1 and 2, open- versus closed-minded information processing (as characteristic of differential mind-sets) for participants in a mental simulation condition or an implementation intention condition were investigated by having to generate different means to a goal (i.e., situational opportunities in Study 1 and goal-directed responses in Study 2). In both studies, participants in the mental simulation condition came up with more means compared to participants in the implementation intention condition. These results indicate that mental simulation induces an explorative mind-set (see also Markman et al., 2007; Wong et al., Chapter 11, this volume) associated with open-mindedness (a cognitive feature previously solely associated with the predecisional phase), whereas implementation intentions induce an implemental mind-set associated with closed-mindedness (so far the only cognitive feature associated with the preactional phase). Hence, according to these findings, an explorative and an implemental mind-set can be activated within the preactional phase of goal pursuit depending on what planning strategy (i.e., mental simulations or implementation intentions, respectively) an individual chooses to apply.

In addition, in Studies 1 and 2, reaction times from stimulus onset (i.e., appearance of situational cues on the computer screen to which participants were asked either to find alternative situations or to generate corresponding goal-directed behaviors) to the participants' initial pressing of the keyboard when generating means (i.e., situational opportunities or goal-directed responses) were measured. Implementation intention participants responded faster to the presented materials than did mental simulation participants. This finding was first of all interpreted as evidence of a stronger focus on previously specified means as part of forming implementation intentions as compared to engaging in mental simulations. Second, this result was construed as a possible indicator of the basic cognitive processes (i.e., activation levels of mental representations) that underlie the differential mind-sets induced by implementation intentions and mental simulations, respectively. To address this question, two further studies measured activation levels of implementation intentions' and mental simulations' respective mental representations via a lexical decision task. Forming implementation intentions was found to result in heightened activation of the mental representation of situational cues (Study 3) and behavioral responses (Study 4), compared to mental simulation participants. This result was interpreted as evidence that differential activation levels of the mental representations of implementation intentions and mental simulations underlie the distinct information-processing modes that these two self-regulation tools trigger (i.e., closed- versus open-mindedness, respectively).

The second line of research (Faude, 2005) presented in this chapter marks the first direct attempt to map out implementation intentions as knowledge structures (i.e., as cognitive representations of a specified situation and a goal-directed behavior linked in an if-then format) and the first direct test of simultaneous activation of the mental representation of both components of implementation intentions (i.e., the situational cue and the goal-directed response) on formation of such plans. In three studies, forming implementation intentions led to shorter response times on a lexical decision task for situation and behavior words (i.e., the if-components and then-components of the previously formed if-then plans), relative to neutral words and relative to a condition in which only a goal intention was activated. Implicating that the formation of an implementation intention (i.e., linking a situational cue and a goal-directed response in an if-then format) leads to a heightened coactivation of the mental representation of both its components, this finding was termed the plan activation effect.

Specifically, in Study 1, self-generation of if-then plans was found to result in heightened activation of both components (i.e., the cue and the response) compared to a condition in which no plans were generated. Studies 2 and 3 replicated the plan activation effect with assigned implementation intentions implying that the heightened activation is a result of a superior status of the if-component and then-component (as part of an if-then plan) and not due to a generation effect of the components. The superior status of the components of if-then plans was further supported by Studies 2 and 3, in which it was demonstrated that (a) assigning (i.e., activating) a goal intention only, without corresponding plans, did not suffice to activate certain goal-facilitating situations and behaviors (rather, plan activation was contingent on assignment of implementation intentions in addition to an underlying goal intention); and that (b) the plan activation effect could be obtained under conditions of several plans competing for resources in the face of a shared goal. In addition, Studies 2 and 3 provided evidence that forming implementation intentions leads to heightened activation of the specified situation and the goal-directed behavior as a result of their functional relation (i.e., having been linked in an if-then format) rather than due to their semantic relation. Last, the results of Study 3 demonstrated that the plan activation effect could be reliably obtained under conditions of high cognitive load, implying that the activation of implementation intentions' components on forming an if-then plan is due to an automatic process that does not require cognitive resources.

Together, these three studies demonstrate the following cognitive features of the mental representation of the anticipated situation and the goal-directed behavior as components of an implementation intention: (a) Both elements are cognitively represented as knowledge structures; (b) the formation of an implementation intention (i.e., linking the cue and the response in an if-then format) enhances the coactivation of both components, thereby demonstrating a plan activation effect; (c) the heightened accessibility of implementation intentions' components is a result of an automatic process due to their superior status and a functional relation between the components due to having been linked in an if-then format. The originality of these findings resides in the fact that they provide initial insights into the most basic processes by which implementation intentions promote goal attainment.

PLANNING VIA IMPLEMENTATION INTENTIONS VERSUS MENTAL SIMULATIONS

If implementation intentions and mental simulations both represent effective planning techniques that foster goal attainment, when is it advisable to use one or the other? Do both strategies lead to the same outcome (i.e., reaching one's goals) and are therefore interchangeable depending on, for example, a person's random or personal preference? Or, does the effectiveness of each planning strategy vary depending on the respective circumstances (e.g., temporal) after having set a goal? The personal preference argument seems plausible in light of research on individual differences in mind-set activation. For example, Hirt et al. (2004) found that the manipulation of a mental simulation mind-set is less successful in individuals with a high need for closure (i.e., the desire to establish a definite opinion about topics; Kruglanski & Webster, 1996). This suggests that individuals high in need for closure—if given the choice between planning via if-then plans or mental simulation—would lean toward forming implementation intentions rather than mental simulation as the former creates an implemental mind-set associated with closed-mindedness, whereas the latter creates an explorative mind-set associated with open-mindedness.

However, based on the differences we found in information processing (i.e., closed- vs. open-mindedness) between if-then planners and mental simulators, we also speculate about the differential effectiveness of if-then planning versus mental simulation depending on the kind of goal striving at issue. An explorative mind-set associated with mental simulation might be beneficial at the outset of striving for a chosen goal as it allows for an exploration of the best ways to achieve a desired goal. Openness to information on possible means should thus also be very helpful in the face of novel or complex goals (i.e., whenever a detailed elaboration of the problem space is needed; see Oettingen & Kappes, Chapter 26, this volume). However, once a decision about the best path toward a goal has been made, the planning of goal-directed action should benefit more from thoughts about when, where, and how to take the chosen path as it is done by forming implementation intentions. In other words, in the preactional phase individuals might benefit from an explorative mind-set associated with mental simulation at the onset of planning goal-directed actions and when the implementation of novel and complex goals is demanded, but when it comes to finalizing one's plans, formation of implementation intentions seems to be the preferred strategy as the associated implemental mind-set provides the necessary closed-mindedness.

Imagine that you adopted the goal to lead a healthy lifestyle and so far have not paid a lot of attention to your health. When trying to achieve this goal, you would initially benefit from an explorative mind-set that allows you to imagine possible options on how to go about it (e.g., exercise more, eat more vegetables, drink more water, get more sleep). Therefore, mentally simulating different courses of action toward goal attainment would give you a good idea of what routes are available and most likely beneficial to you (e.g., your professional duties might not allow you to get more sleep, but you could easily exercise more). Once you are clear on your options on how to achieve your goal, your planning process would then benefit from forming implementation intentions as this would enable you to focus and decide on how to exactly implement your chosen course of action (i.e., exercise more by taking the stairs instead of the elevator or going to your gym in the evenings). That is, you can now further ensure goal achievement by forming an implementation intention that links an anticipated cue with an identified response in an if-then format (e.g., "If I find myself standing in front of an elevator, then I will choose to walk up the stairs"). As a positive side effect, making such if-then plans frees cognitive capacity for other endeavors as the initiation of the preselected response does not necessitate conscious intent. Taken together, we suggest that mental simulation and implementation intentions benefit the process of goal striving at different points in time of striving for a chosen goal, and this is particularly true for novel and complex goals. An important avenue for future research will be to systematically explore this assumption. This could be done by experimentally manipulating the order of mental simulation and forming implementation intentions and assessing the amount and quality of attainment of simple versus complex goals. Alternatively, field studies using time-sampling methodologies could obtain people's planning-related thoughts and then determine whether those individuals who most successfully attained their goals first engaged in mental simulations and only thereafter formed implementation intentions and whether this is particularly true for goals that are novel and complex.

In conclusion, this chapter highlights insights into motivational phenomena (i.e., goals and their means) that follow from a cognitive perspective on motivation (Gollwitzer & Bargh, 1996; Kruglanski, 1996; Shah & Kruglanski, 2000; Shah et al., 2003). Investigating the cognitive processes (i.e., mind-sets and mental representations) related to forming implementation intentions and engaging in mental simulations allows for an understanding of how these two self-regulation techniques of goal striving promote goal attainment. The findings afford new empirical and theoretical insights into the current understanding of (a) the beneficial effects of planning on goal striving in general and (b) the functioning of mental simulations and implementation intentions in particular. Besides the primary significance of the present research to understanding the functioning of mental simulations and implementation intentions, it has vast implications for the understanding of successful striving for chosen goals.

NOTE

1. A load manipulation check revealed a decrease in accuracy performance and an increase in overall latencies on the lexical decision task in Study 3 compared to Study 2, as well as no differential effects between the plan condition and the goal-only condition in Study 3 on accuracy of performance. Therefore, even though the study did not include a control condition to directly test the cognitive load manipulation, a sufficient and equal cognitive load manipulation is assumed for the plan and goal-only condition in Study 3 (for details, see Faude, 2005).

REFERENCES

Achtziger, A., Bayer, U. C., & Gollwitzer, P. M. (2008). Comitting to implementation intentions: Attention and memory effects for selected situational cues. (Submitted.)

Achtziger, A., Gollwitzer, P. M., & Sheeran, P. (2008). Implementation intentions and shielding goal striving from unwanted thoughts and feelings. *Personality and Social Psychology Bulletin, 34,* 381–393.

Anderson, J. R. (1983). *The architecture of cognition.* Cambridge, MA: Harvard University Press.

Armor, D. A., & Taylor, S. E. (2003). The effects of mindset on behavior: Self-regulation in deliberative and implemental frames of mind. *Personality and Social Psychology Bulletin, 29,* 86–95.

Bargh, J. A. (1992). The ecology of automaticity: Towards establishing the conditions needed to produce automatic processing effects. *American Journal of Psychology, 105,* 181–199.

Bargh, J. A. (1994). The four horsemen of automaticity: Awareness, efficiency, intention, and control in social interaction. In R. S. Wyer, Jr. & T. K. Srull (Eds.), *Handbook of social cognition* (2nd ed., pp. 1–40). Hillsdale, NJ: Erlbaum.

Bargh, J. A. (1996). Principles of automaticity. In E. T. Higgins & A.. Kruglanski (Eds.), *Social psychology: Handbook of basic principles* (pp. 169–183). New York: Guilford Press.

Bargh, J. A. (1997). The automaticity of everyday life. In R. S. Wyer Jr. (Ed.), *The automaticity of everyday life: Advances in social cognition* (Vol. 10, pp. 1–61). Mahwah, NJ: Erlbaum.

Bargh, J. A., & Chartrand, T. L. (1999). The unbearable automaticity of being. *American Psychologist, 54,* 462–479.

Bayer, U. C., Achtziger, A., Gollwitzer, P. M., & Moskowitz, G. B. (in press). Responding to subliminal cues: Do if-then plans facilitate action preparation and initiation without conscious intent? *Social Cognition.*

Brandstätter, V., Lengfelder, A., & Gollwitzer, P. M. (2001). Implementation intentions and efficient action initiation. *Journal of Personality and Social Psychology, 81,* 946–960.

Escalas, J. E., & Luce, M. F. (2003). Process versus outcome thought-focus and advertising. *Journal of Consumer Psychology, 13,* 246–54.

Escalas, J. E., & Luce, M. F. (2004). Understanding the effects of process-focused versus outcome-focused thought in response to advertising. *Journal of Consumer Research, 31,* 274–285.

Faude, T. S. (2005). *The mental representation of plans.* Unpublished doctoral dissertation, University of Konstanz, Germany.

Fujita, K., Gollwitzer, P. M., & Oettingen, G. (2007). Mindsets and pre-conscious open-mindedness to incidental information. *Journal of Experimental Social Psychology, 43,* 48–61.

Gagne, F. M., & Lydon, J. E. (2001). Mind-set and close relationships: When bias leads to (in)accurate predictions. *Journal of Personality and Social Psychology, 81,* 85–96.

Galinsky, A. D., & Kray, L. J. (2004). From thinking about what might have been to sharing what we know: The effects of counterfactual mind-sets on information sharing in groups. *Journal of Experimental Social Psychology, 40,* 606–618.

Gollwitzer, P. M. (1990). Action phases and mindsets. In E. T. Higgins & R. M. Sorrentino (Eds.), *Handbook of motivation and cognition: Foundations of social behavior* (Vol. 2, pp. 51–92). New York: Guilford Press.

Gollwitzer, P. M. (1993). Goal achievement: The role of intentions. In W. Stroebe & M. Hewstone (Eds.), *European review of social psychology* (Vol. 4, pp. 141–185). New York: Wiley.

Gollwitzer, P. M. (1996). The volitional benefits of planning. In P. M.. Gollwitzer & J. A. Bargh (Eds.), *The psychology of action: Linking cognition and motivation to behavior* (pp. 287–312). New York: Guilford Press.

Gollwitzer, P. M. (1999). Implementation intentions: Strong effects of simple plans. *American Psychologist, 54*, 493–503.

Gollwitzer, P. M., & Bargh, J. A. (1994). *The psychology of action: Linking cognition and motivation to behavior.* New York: Guilford Press.

Gollwitzer, P. M., & Bayer, U. C. (1999). Deliberative and implemental mind-sets in the control of action. In S. Chaiken & Y. Trope (Eds.), *Dual-process theories in social psychology* (pp. 403–422). New York: Guilford Press.

Gollwitzer, P. M., & Brandstätter, V. (1997). Implementation intentions and effective goal pursuit. *Journal of Personality and Social Psychology, 73*, 186–199.

Gollwitzer, P. M., Fujita, K., & Oettingen, G. (2004). Planning and the implementation of goals. In R. Baumeister & K. Vohs (Eds.), *Handbook of self-regulation research* (pp. 211–228). New York: Guilford Press.

Gollwitzer, P. M., Heckhausen, H., & Steller, B. (1990). Deliberative and implemental mind-sets: Cognitive tuning toward congruous thoughts and information. *Journal of Personality and Social Psychology, 59*, 1119–1127.

Gollwitzer, P. M., & Kinney, R. F. (1989). Effects of deliberative and implemental mind-sets on illusion of control. *Journal of Personality and Social Psychology, 56*, 531–542.

Gollwitzer, P. M., & Schaal, B. (1998). Metacognition in action: The importance of implementation intentions. *Personality and Social Psychology Review, 2*, 124–136.

Gollwitzer, P. M., & Sheeran, P. (2006). Implementation intentions and goal achievement: A meta-analysis of effects and processes. *Advances in Experimental Social Psychology, 38*, 69–119.

Gottschaldt, K. (1926). Ueber den Einfluss der Erfahrung auf die Wahrnehmung von Figuren: 1. Ueber den Einfluss gehaeufter Einpraegung von Figuren auf ihre Sichtbarkeit in umfassenden Konfigurationen. *Psychologische Forschung, 8*, 261–317.

Greitemeyer, T., & Wuerz, D. (2006). Mental simulation and the achievement of health goals: The role of goal difficulty. *Imagination, Cognition, and Personality, 25*, 239–251.

Heckhausen, H. (1991). *Motivation and action.* Heidelberg: Springer-Verlag.

Heckhausen, H., & Gollwitzer, P. M. (1987). Thought contents and cognitive functioning in motivational versus volitional states of mind. *Motivation and Emotion, 11,* 101–120.

Hirt, E. R., Kardes, F. R., & Markman, K. D. (2004). Activating a mental simulation mind-set through generation of alternatives: Implications for debiasing in related and unrelated domains. *Journal of Experimental Social Psychology, 40*, 374–383.

Hirt, E. R., & Markman, K. D. (1995). Multiple explanations: A consider-an-alternative strategy for debiasing judgments. *Journal of Personality and Social Psychology, 36*, 384–409.

Kahneman, D., & Tversky, A. (1982). The simulation heuristic. In D. Kahneman, P. Slovic, & A. Tversky (Eds.), *Judgment under uncertainty: Heuristics and biases* (pp. 201–208). Cambridge, England: Cambridge University Press.

Kruglanski, A. W. (1996). Goals as knowledge structures. In P. M. Gollwitzer & J. A. Bargh (Eds.), *The psychology of action: Linking cognition and motivation to behavior* (pp. 599–618). New York: Guilford Press.

Kruglanski, A. W., Shah, J. Y., Fishbach, A., Friedman, A., Young Chun, W., & Sleeth-Keppler, D. (2002). A theory of goal-systems. *Advances in Experimental Social Psychology, 34*, 331–378.

Kruglanski, A. W., & Webster, D. M. (1996). Motivated closing of the mind: "Seizing" and "freezing." *Psychological Review, 103*, 263–283.

Kuhl, J. (1984). Volitional aspects of achievement motivation and learned helplessness: Toward a comprehensive theory of action control. In B. A. Maher (Ed.), *Progress in experimental personality research* (Vol. 13, pp. 99–171). New York: Academic Press.

Lengfelder, A., & Gollwitzer, P. M. (2001). Reflective and reflexive action control in patients with frontal lobe lesions. *Neuropsychology, 15*, 80–100.

Logan, G. D. (1992). Attention and preattention in theories of automaticity. *American Journal of Psychology, 105*, 317–339.

Markman, K. D., Lindberg, M. J., Kray, L. J., & Galinsky, A. D. (2007). Implications of counterfactual structure for creative generation and analytical problem solving. *Personality and Social Psychology Bulletin, 33*, 312–324.

Marsh, R. L., & Landau, J. D. (1995). Item availability in cryptomnesia: Assessing its role in two paradigms of unconscious plagiarism. *Journal of Experimental Psychology: Learning, Memory, and Cognition, 21*, 1568–1582.

Milne, S., Orbell, S., & Sheeran, P. (2002). Combining motivational and volitional interventions to promote exercise participation: Protection motivation theory and implementation intentions. *British Journal of Health Psychology, 7*, 163–184.

Moors, A., & De Houwer, J. (2006). Automaticity: A theoretical and conceptual analysis. *Psychological Bulletin, 132*, 297–326.

Oettingen, G. (2000). Expectancy effects on behavior depend on self-regulatory thought. *Social Cognition, 18*, 101–129.

Oettingen, G., & Gollwitzer, P. M. (2001). Goal setting and goal striving. In A. Tesser & N. Schwarz (Eds.), *Blackwell handbook in social psychology: Intraindividual processes* (Vol. 1, pp. 329–347). Oxford, England: Blackwell.

Oettingen, G., Pak, H., & Schnetter, K. (2001). Self-regulation of goal setting: Turning free fantasies about the future into binding goals. *Journal of Personality and Social Psychology, 80*, 736–753.

Orbell, S., Hodgkins, S., & Sheeran, P. (1997). Implementation intentions and the theory of planned behavior. *Personality and Social Psychology Bulletin, 23*, 945–954.

Park, D. C., Hertzog, C., Kidder, D. P., Morrell, R. W., & Mayhorn, C. B. (1997). Effect of age on event-based and time-based prospective memory. *Psychology and Aging, 12*, 314–327.

Pham, L. P., & Taylor, S. E. (1999). From thought to action: Effects of process-versus outcome-based mental simulations on performance. *Personality and Social Psychology Bulletin, 25*, 250–260.

Phillips, D. M., & Baumgartner, H. (2002). The role of consumption emotions in the satisfaction response. *Journal of Consumer Psychology, 13*, 243–252.

Puca, R. M., & Schmalt, H. D. (2001). The influence of the achievement motive on spontaneous thoughts in pre- and post-decisional action phases. *Personality and Social Psychology Bulletin, 27*, 302–308.

Ratcliff, R., & McKoon, G. (1978). Priming in item recognition: Evidence for the propositional structure of sentences. *Journal of Verbal Learning and Verbal Behavior, 17*, 403–417.

Rivkin, I. A., & Taylor, S. E. (1999). The effects of mental simulation on coping with controllable stressful events. *Personality and Social Psychology Bulletin, 25*, 1451–1462.

Shah, J., & Kruglanski, A. (2000). Aspects of goal networks: Implications for self-regulation. In M. Boekaerts, P. Pintrich, & M. Zeidner (Eds.), *Handbook of self-regulation* (pp. 85–110). San Diego, CA: Academic Press.

Shah, J. Y., Kruglanski, A. W., & Friedman, A. (2003). Goal systems theory: Integrating the cognitive and motivation aspects of self-regulation. In S. Spencer, S. Fein, M. Zanna, & J. Olson (Eds.), *Motivated social perception: The Ontario symposium* (pp. 247–275). Mahwah, NJ: Erlbaum.

Sheeran, P., & Orbell, S. (1999). Implementation intentions and repeated behavior: Augmenting the predictive validity of the theory of planned behavior. *European Journal of Social Psychology, 29*, 349–369.

Sheeran, P., & Orbell, S. (2000). Using implementation intentions to increase attendance for cervical cancer screening. *Health Psychology, 19*, 283–289.

Sheeran, P., Webb, T. L., & Gollwitzer, P. M. (2005). The interplay between goal intentions and implementation intentions. *Personality and Social Psychology Bulletin, 31*, 87–98.

Shiffrin, R. M., & Schneider, W. (1977). Controlled and automatic human information processing: II. Perceptual learning, automatic attending, and a general theory. *Psychological Review, 84*, 127–190.

Sorrentino, R. M., & Higgins, E. T. (1986). *Handbook of motivation and cognition (Vol. 1): Foundations of social behavior.* New York: Guilford Press.

Steller, B. (1992). *Vorsaetze und die Wahrnehmung guenstiger Gelegenheiten.* Munich: Tuduv Verlagsgesellschaft.

Taylor, S. E., & Gollwitzer, P. M. (1995). Effects of mindset on positive illusions. *Journal of Personality and Social Psychology. 69*, 213–226.

Taylor, S. E., & Pham, L. B. (1999). The effect of mental simulation on goal-directed performance. *Imagination, Cognition, and Personality, 18*, 253–268.

Taylor, S. E., Pham, L. B., Rivkin, I. D., & Armor, D.A. (1998). Harnessing the imagination: Mental simulation, self-regulation, and coping. *American Psychologist, 53*, 429–439.

Taylor, S. E., & Schneider, S. K. (1989). Coping and the simulation of events. *Social Cognition, 7,* 174–194.

Webb, T. L., & Sheeran, P. (2006). Does changing behavioral intentions engender behavior change? A meta-analysis of the experimental evidence. *Psychological Bulletin, 132,* 249–268.

Witkin, H. A. (1950). Individual differences in ease of perception of embedded figures. *Journal of Personality, 19,* 1–15.

Wuerz, D., Gollwitzer, P. M., & Greitemeyer, T. (2007). *Mental simulation and implementation intentions: Initiating different mind-sets.* Unpublished manuscript.

Section II

Mental Simulation and Memory

6 False Memories: The Role of Plausibility and Autobiographical Belief

Daniel M. Bernstein, Ryan D. Godfrey, and Elizabeth F. Loftus

On the other side of the dungeon, he perceived an inscription, the white letters of which were still visible on the green wall; "'Oh God",' he read, "'preserve my memory!" Oh yes,' he cried, 'that was my only prayer at last; I no longer begged for liberty, but memory ...'

Dumas, 1844/1997, *The Count of Monte Cristo*, p. 848

INTRODUCTION

False memories can reveal much about the structure and function of memory (Brainerd & Reyna, 2005; Schacter, 2001), especially how we organize details from past and present sources to form a coherent autobiography (Conway & Pleydell-Pearce, 2000). False memories, or memories for experiences that never occurred, abound in our autobiographies. Although the past several decades have seen a great deal of research on false memories, relatively little is known about the underlying mechanisms that cause them. In this chapter, we first review recent findings on false memories. We then propose several ideas about potential mechanisms associated with false memories and present new experimental data that bear on those mechanisms.

What do we know about false memories? We know that false memories *do* occur and are quite common. Looking into one's own past, it is easy to recall a time when two friends had two distinctly different versions of the same event. Most false memories are harmless (e.g., "I visited the Grand Canyon in my youth," when in truth I did not); however, some may have devastating consequences. For example, an eyewitness misidentifies a suspect, thereby leading to the wrongful conviction and imprisonment of an innocent person (see Cutler & Penrod, 1995; Doyle, 2005; Loftus, 1979). After examining these cases, no one would ask whether false memories occur. Rather, a better question to ask is *how* and *why* do false memories occur? Recent laboratory-based studies have helped answer these important questions.

Various techniques have been used to increase people's belief that they experienced a particular event in their past. For example, Loftus and Pickrell (1995) developed the following procedure for planting false memories in participants: First, they confirmed with parents of participants that the subjects had never experienced a particular event in their childhood such as getting lost in a shopping mall for an extended time. Next, the researchers obtained from the parents three true memories for childhood events that had occurred. Finally, the researchers asked participants to discuss their memories for these four events. Three of the events were true and one (shopping mall) was false for every subject tested. Over three successive interviews using these four events, 25% of the participants came to believe that they had been lost in a shopping mall as a child. Hyman, Husband, and Billings (1995) used a similar procedure to suggest falsely to participants that they had spilled a punch bowl at a wedding. Here also, about 25% of the participants came to believe, wholly or partially, that this event had occurred in their childhood.

In other work, Garry, Manning, Loftus, and Sherman (1996) asked participants about a variety of childhood experiences, such as breaking a window with one's hand. Later, some participants were asked to "Imagine that it is after school, and you are playing in the house. You hear a strange noise outside, so you run to the window to see what made the noise. As you are running, your feet catch on something, and you trip and fall." These participants were then asked to imagine breaking the window with their hand, cutting themselves and bleeding. This simple imagination exercise increased participants' confidence that they had broken a window with their hand as a child. Other work involving "imagination inflation" has shown how imagination can lead to the creation of false memories (see Goff & Roediger, 1998; Seamon, Philbin, & Harrison, 2006). Similar findings have emerged using even subtler techniques. For example, explaining how particular events might have occurred in one's life (Sharman, Manning, & Garry, 2005) or writing a biographical sketch (from a third-person perspective) for a fictional adolescent (Nourkova, Bernstein, & Loftus, 2004) increased one's confidence that these events personally occurred in one's own adolescence.

In other work, Wade, Garry, Read, and Lindsay (2002) obtained family photographs of their experimental participants as young children and inserted these photographs into a picture depicting a hot air balloon ride. This manipulation made it appear as though participants had actually gone on a hot air balloon as a child when in fact they had not (this fact was confirmed by the subjects' parents). After seeing a photo of themselves and a family member riding in a hot air balloon, nearly half the participants increased their belief that they had ridden in a hot air balloon as children. More recent studies involving the effects of photographs and imagination on memory have shown that simply seeing yearbook-type photographs of one's entire class is sufficient to increase people's confidence that they got in trouble for hiding toy slime in their teacher's desk (Lindsay, Hagen, Read, Wade, & Garry, 2004). In addition, photographs that depict violence and destruction can also change people's memory for news events, making people falsely remember more negative details about the events (Garry, Strange, Bernstein, & Kinzett, 2007; Sacchi, Agnoli, & Loftus, 2007). For example, Garry et al. asked participants to read a newspaper story of a hurricane hitting a coastal town. Accompanying this story was a photograph. Participants saw either a picture of a village before or after the hurricane struck. Those who saw the photograph of the village *after* the hurricane struck were far more likely to report having read information describing death and injury in the initial newspaper story, although no such mention of death and injury existed in the story. These studies suggest that various techniques can increase people's confidence in individual details for events as well as entire events that never occurred (see also Bodner & Richardson-Champion, 2007; Hannigan & Reinitz, 2001; Pezdek & Lam, 2007; Wade et al., 2007).

One possible explanation for how these procedures produce a false memory involves source monitoring (Johnson, Hashtroudi, & Lindsay, 1993). False memories may arise from participants' inability to attribute their present processing experience to the correct source in their past, that is, to suggestion, imagination, or false feedback (Garry & Polaschek, 2000; Johnson et al., 1993). Participants who imagine having had an experience (like breaking a window and getting cut) may have a feeling of familiarity when tested about that item later. They may misattribute this feeling to early childhood experience rather than to the more recent act of imagination.

Another theory called *fuzzy-trace theory* distinguishes between two types of memory traces: verbatim and gist. Verbatim-based memories store sensory information and are typically linked to detailed recollection of past experiences, while gist-based memories store semantic information and are linked to familiarity (Brainerd & Reyna, 2002; see also Mandler, 1980). Both memory traces can produce accurate as well as false memories; however, accurate memory is more often associated with verbatim traces, while false memory is more often associated with gist traces.

It is now commonly accepted that false memories can and do occur (Brainerd & Reyna, 2005). However, it is still unclear exactly how and why false memories emerge. Mazzoni, Loftus, and Kirsch (2001) proposed a three-step model for the development of false memories. According to the model, (a) an event comes to be seen as plausible in the culture of the remitter (plausibility); (b) one obtains a personal belief that the event likely occurred to him or her (autobiographical belief);

and (c) one interprets thoughts and images about the event as actual memories (autobiographical memory). Mazzoni and colleagues have since added a step to their model in which an event comes to be seen as personally plausible before one comes to believe that the event likely occurred to them (Scoboria, Mazzoni, Kirsch, & Relyea, 2004). The present work focuses on the mechanisms underlying plausibility and autobiographical belief.

We hypothesize that the probability that an individual comes to believe that an event is generally plausible and that it likely occurred in their remote past depends, in part, on the ease with which the event is processed. Researchers have typically defined ease of processing as speed and speed of processing as fluency because processing speed is easily measured with reaction time. However, fluency can also be the integration, coherence, or well-formedness of perceptual detail or the perception of ease independent of the speed of processing (Whittlesea & Leboe, 2003). Fluency can be enhanced by different stimulus variables, such as repetition, clarity, and presentation duration. When people are unaware of the source of their fluency, they may mistake that fluency for familiarity. Put another way, when people experience fluent processing of some material, they sometimes mistakenly believe that the material is familiar to them.

For example, Jacoby and Whitehouse (1989) found that when viewing words in a recognition test, subjects unaware of subliminal repetition prime words misattributed the enhanced fluency of test words to a prior exposure of the test words. Thus, they developed a false memory for having experienced the words in the past, although these illusions of familiarity arose from brief and subliminal exposure to the repetition primes. Subjects have also been shown to misattribute fluency to various cognitive, perceptual, and affective judgments, including memory, belief, clarity, liking, fame, and even beauty (see Bernstein, 2005; Briñol, Petty, & Tormala, 2006; Clore, 1992; Kelley & Lindsay, 1993; Sanna & Schwarz, 2006; Sanna, Schwarz, & Kennedy, Chapter 13, this volume; Unkelbach, 2006; Winkielman, Schwarz, Reber, & Fazendeiro, 2003). These experiments show that sometimes an increase in fluency leads people to think they like something more, to think a made-up name is actually that of a famous person, and that something is beautiful. We operationalize fluency as the speed, ease, and accuracy with which a person processes a stimulus.

Researchers have argued that increasing one's belief that an event is generally plausible helps to make people believe that the event was personally experienced (Hyman & Loftus, 1998; Pezdek, Finger, & Hodge, 1997; Smeets, Merckelbach, Horselenberg, & Jelicic, 2005). Also, the more plausible the event seems generally, the more likely it is that a person will come to believe that it occurred in the past. Once belief in the general event is instilled (plausibility), it can then be transformed into an autobiographical belief and memory through a variety of suggestive techniques, including imagination, suggestive stories, and dream interpretation (Garry et al., 1996; Lynn, Barnes, & Matthews, Chapter 7, this volume; Mazzoni, Loftus, Seitz, & Lynn, 1999; see also Mazzoni & Kirsch, 2003). All of these techniques serve to increase the fluency with which the event is later processed. For processing fluency to increase plausibility and autobiographical belief, we hypothesize that the individual must be unaware of the actual source of the fluency. After all, if the person is aware of the actual source, he or she will not misattribute it to an actual memory from the past. We argue that a single, general process underlies both plausibility and autobiographical belief. The current work aims to clarify the path of false memory formation. Although our focus here is on plausibility and autobiographical belief, we hypothesize that both of these processes (and the creation of complete false memories) occur, in part, through the misattribution of processing fluency.

Consider the following experimental paradigm: Participants see a sentence with one word scrambled, and their task is to unscramble that word (e.g., "broke a *nwidwo* playing ball"). Most participants will quickly recognize that the scrambled word is "window." Participants are then asked to indicate how likely it is that in their childhood they had the experience "broke a window playing ball." Several studies using this procedure have revealed that unscrambling a word enhances the perception that the experience did in fact occur (Bernstein, Whittlesea, & Loftus, 2002; Kronlund & Bernstein, 2006). But why? The idea here is that participants use the intact portions of the event to help them unscramble the anagram. At first, participants' processing of the word *nwidwo* is dysfluent. However, when they successfully unscramble the word to form window, they experience a rush of meaning and fluent processing, akin to an "aha" experience. They may then misattribute this enhancement of fluency as familiarity for experiencing the event in their childhood.

This manipulation bears directly on an intriguing observation in cognitive psychology called the *revelation effect* (Watkins & Peynircioglu, 1990). The revelation effect refers to the tendency for participants to claim that an item is "old" in a recognition task if the target word itself is somehow degraded or obscured and then revealed (*rednelb* for blender) or if the target word is preceded by an anagram (*rednelb*—raindrop). This effect has traditionally been regarded as idiosyncratic to episodic memory (Frigo, Reas, & LeCompte, 1999; Hockley & Niewiadomski, 2001; Luo, 1993; Mulligan & Lozito, 2006; Watkins & Peynircioglu, 1990; Westerman & Greene, 1996). Bernstein et al. (2002) replicated this finding with judgments of childhood history (e.g., "Hit your finger with a *mharme* [hammer]"). They also obtained similar effects for general knowledge statements ("heaviest internal organ"—*velir* [liver]). Unscrambling an anagram served to increase participants' confidence that the life events had indeed occurred in their childhood and that the general knowledge statements were true.

The present work explores the processes responsible for making life events feel generally plausible and part of one's own autobiographical past—the first two stages in Mazzoni et al.'s (2001) model of false memory formation. In Experiment 1, we explore the formation of plausibility. In Experiments 2 and 3, we investigate the formation of autobiographical belief. The thread running throughout the experiments reported here is that belief in the general plausibility of life events and in the likelihood that the events occurred in one's own past depends, in part, on the misattribution of familiarity.

EXPERIMENT 1: PLAUSIBILITY

Experiment 1 had two goals. First, we wished to replicate and extend the revelation effect that Bernstein et al. (2002) obtained for general knowledge and childhood experiences. In our previous work, we showed that unscrambling key words in the context of answering trivia questions or remembering life events increased confidence that the answer was true or that the events occurred in one's own childhood. We wondered whether a revelation effect would also occur if, instead of attempting to remember their own childhood, participants estimated the likelihood that the events occurred in *another person's* childhood; in this case, the other person was the "average" North American. It is not obvious that the revelation effect would occur in these circumstances given that nearly all demonstrations of the effect involve episodic memory judgments. Estimating the likelihood that life events occurred in another person's childhood is clearly not an episodic memory judgment according to Tulving's (1972, 1983) episodic-semantic classification of memory. If we observe a revelation effect for judgments of another person's childhood, this would extend the boundary conditions of the effect to yet another nonepisodic judgment.

Our second aim in Experiment 1 was to show that such increases in the general plausibility of various life events may occur, in part, through the misattribution of familiarity. We attempted to create familiarity for certain items in Experiment 1 by first training participants on "unconstrained items" that contained an anagram. Unconstrained items are those that lack contextual detail that might aid in solving the anagram in the context of a life event: "saw a rpaead [parade]." In previous work, we failed to obtain any revelation effects without this type of training procedure (Bernstein et al., 2002; Bernstein, Godfrey, Davison, & Loftus, 2004). Next, we presented unconstrained items at test along with some highly "constrained" critical items: "witnessed a solar lecsiep [eclipse]." These constrained items are much easier to solve than the unconstrained items because they provide context. However, the result of pairing unconstrained and constrained test items is that the training items and the unconstrained test items lead participants to expect that unscrambling anagrams is difficult. Thus, when they encounter a constrained anagram, they should experience it as surprisingly easy to unscramble. In turn, if participants fail to realize that this ease of processing is due to the contextual detail contained in the phrase, they may interpret processing fluency as familiarity and misattribute this familiarity to the general plausibility of the event.

We calculated two means for each participant. First, we obtained the mean plausibility rating for intact items; that mean was 4.42 on an 8-point scale. Next, we obtained the mean plausibility rating for all correctly unscrambled anagrams. Participants correctly unscrambled 99% of the items, and the mean rating for plausibility for those items was significantly higher, at 4.60. Between these two means, 0.18 ± 0.16 was the mean difference.[1] Thus, solving an anagram embedded within a life event description increased participants' belief that the event was likely to occur in the average North American childhood.

It is unclear exactly how this increase in plausibility arises. One possibility is that participants use their own childhood experience as a gauge to determine what likely occurs in the average child's life (see Rogers, Kuiper, & Kirker, 1977). While this might be true, it is unclear why participants would choose only the events for which they had to unscramble words to be likely candidates of the average childhood. Another, perhaps better, alternative stresses the importance of processing fluency and familiarity in the formation of plausibility. The fact that anagrams increase the plausibility of life events indicates that the way in which the item is processed is what is crucial to the plausibility effect. While some theorists might argue that subjective ease (i.e., fluency) arising from successfully unscrambling anagrams is sufficient to produce the enhanced plausibility that we observed in Experiment 1 (Sanna, Schwarz, & Kennedy, Chapter 13, this volume), we suggest that plausibility arises partly through the misattribution of familiarity. To graphically represent these two alternatives, fluency can affect plausibility directly (fluency → plausibility) or indirectly via familiarity (fluency → familiarity → plausibility). We favor the latter path for reasons that we now outline.

What people experience on completing an anagram within the context of a life event ("broke a nwidwo [window] playing ball") is an unexpected rush of meaning and fluency (Bernstein et al., 2002). This unexpected fluency in turn leads to the perception of discrepancy between one's initial expectation of how difficult it will be to unscramble the word and the subsequent rush of meaning that they experience on successfully unscrambling the word. This perception of discrepancy is interpreted by participants as a feeling of familiarity, a process that Whittlesea and Williams (2000) call "discrepancy attribution." Participants seek to attribute this feeling of familiarity to a source. In the present experiment, we argue that participants mistakenly attribute familiarity to the general plausibility of the life event in question rather than to the fact that they just unscrambled the word (see Bernstein et al., 2002, 2004).

In sum, Experiment 1 extends the boundary conditions of the revelation effect to include plausibility judgments about childhood life experiences. The fact that unscrambling can also increase plausibility ratings for general knowledge statements leads us to posit that illusory plausibility arises, in part, through the misattribution of familiarity. Although familiarity misattribution provides a mechanism to explain how events come to be regarded as plausible, it is also possible that fluency exerts a direct effect on plausibility. We cannot at present distinguish between these two alternatives. We now turn to the role of familiarity misattribution in the formation of false autobiographical belief. The next two experiments address this stage of the process.

EXPERIMENTS 2 AND 3: AUTOBIOGRAPHICAL BELIEF

There is substantial evidence suggesting that exposure to misinformation after an event hinders one's ability to accurately remember the details of the event (Ayers & Reder, 1998; Loftus, Miller, & Burns, 1978). Moreover, people sometimes combine details from postevent misinformation with their memory of the original event, resulting in a "blended" memory (Loftus, 1977). So, a blue car that was seen is later described as green, and some subjects will remember it as bluish-green. We wondered whether prior experience with words or phrases that later appear in the context of life events might influence participants' confidence that the events had occurred in their childhood. There is ample reason to think that prior exposure would affect belief about one's past. For instance, many judgments are influenced by prior experience with words, phrases, and names, including judgments of recognition and truth (Bernstein, 2005; Hasher, Goldstein, & Toppino, 1977; Kelley & Lindsay, 1993); perceptual duration (Witherspoon & Allan, 1985); perceptual clarity (Whittlesea, Jacoby, & Girard, 1990); and fame (Jacoby, Woloshyn & Kelley, 1989). Fluency and familiarity appear to be involved in each of these illusory judgments. If the mechanism responsible for illusory plausibility is familiarity, as we have argued, then we might expect that prior exposure to key words would increase the fluency with which those words are later processed in the context of life events. Consequently, this increased fluency could lead to a feeling of familiarity and increase one's belief that the events occurred in one's own childhood. To be more concrete, suppose that a person is exposed to the word *window* on a list of words or a photograph of a window. Shortly thereafter, the person is asked whether they ever broke a window playing ball. Would prior exposure to window increase fluency, and would that make people more likely to think they had, as a child, broken a window playing ball? Experiments 2 and 3 explore this idea.

EXPERIMENT 2: FORCED CONFABULATION

Drivdahl and Zaragoza (2001) developed a useful technique involving forced confabulation to increase confidence for events that were never experienced. They asked participants to view a film depicting a bank robbery. Participants then read a narrative of the event that contained several misleading suggestions in addition to several questions designed to elicit perceptual elaboration of details for events that were never seen in the film. For example, a participant might be asked to answer specific questions about the location or physical appearance of a suggested but false event ("Was the ring that the thief stole in a box?"). This "forced confabulation" significantly increased false memory for such fictitious details.

We wondered whether a procedure similar to forced confabulation would increase participants' confidence for a variety of childhood events, presumably through the misattribution of familiarity. In the present experiment, participants imagined a series of life events in detail and then answered a question about each event. For example, participants might imagine "broke a window playing ball" and then answer whether the window was broken in many pieces, one long crack, or with a hole through it. These same events later appeared on a life events inventory along with new events. We hypothesized that imagining the events and answering questions about them would increase one's confidence that the imagined events were from their own childhood.

This did not occur. Participants were no more likely to believe that old items were part of their childhood in comparison to new items ($M = 4.26$ vs. 4.24, respectively; Mean difference = 0.02 ± 0.34). Thus, previously imagining life events and answering a question about each event did not increase participants' belief that these events had occurred in their childhood. Judging from the magnitude of the confidence interval, one possible reason for our failure to detect a difference in our conditions might be a lack of statistical power. We think this is unlikely for reasons that will become apparent later. Another, perhaps better, explanation for our failure to increase confidence for previously seen events is that those events were in fact processed more fluently than new events, but participants realized the source of the fluency. When and if participants realize why some items feel familiar and others do not, they will likely attribute the familiarity to its true source, in this case the imagination exercise they performed during training. This raises the question of why techniques like imagination inflation and forced confabulation have been found to work at all (e.g., Drivdahl & Zaragoza, 2001; Mazzoni & Memon, 2003).

Two important factors that are present in many imagination inflation studies are the use of a time delay (up to 1 week) between imagination and testing and the use of very few (up to six) critical, imagined items in relation to many noncritical items. These factors may obscure the imagination exercise, thereby making imagination a less-obvious source of the familiarity that it produces. As Garry and Polaschek (2000) have argued, imagination inflation works largely because participants fail to realize that imagination creates familiarity for the critical items. In the present experiment, participants imagined 24 of the 48 events on the Life Events Inventory. This may have been too many. By having participants vividly imagine half of the test items as well as answering questions about them, the source of the fluency may have been transparent. Thus, in Experiment 3, we attempted to obscure the source of familiarity for some items and make it more obvious for others.

EXPERIMENT 3: VOWEL COUNTING AND VIVIDNESS

In contrast to Experiment 2, in which participants encountered the same life events in the exposure and test phases, in Experiment 3 participants rated key words (e.g., "eclipse") in terms of either their number of vowels or their vividness. The main question was whether either type of experience would affect participants' subsequent processing of those words if they appeared in the context of life events (e.g., "witnessed a solar eclipse") either a short time after the initial exposure or 1 week later.

There is good reason to think that previous experience with words would facilitate and prime later processing of those words (cf. Jacoby & Dallas, 1981; Kolers, 1976), and that longer delays between encoding and retrieval impairs memory (Ebbinghaus, 1885/1964). Moreover, the type of initial processing that one performs affects how well one later remembers, with deeper processing leading to better memory (Craik & Lockhart, 1972).

We hypothesized that processing words by counting their vowels (a shallow task) or rating their vividness (an elaborate task) would enhance the fluency with which participants subsequently processed those words in comparison to new words by mistaking that fluency as evidence that they experienced particular life events in their childhood. In addition, we were interested in whether the attribution to one's childhood would be affected by participants' memory for the particular words that they rated in terms of vividness or for which they counted vowels.

During an exposure phase, participants counted vowels or visualized words or short phrases (e.g., hammer, laughed hard). For visualization, participants spent 3 to 5 s creating a vivid picture of the item in their minds. Participants then completed a distractor task, after which they completed a Life Events Inventory. Participants returned a week later to complete another Life Events Inventory. Each of these Life Events Inventories contained items that participants had seen before in the exposure phase in addition to new items. Finally, participants completed a recognition test.

Six means were calculated for each participant. There were no differences between old items that had been seen during the exposure phase and new items (Old $M = 4.11$; New $M = 4.07$; Difference $= 0.04 \pm 0.16$). Moreover, the 1-week delay had no effect on confidence ratings (Time 1 $M = 4.07$; Time 2 $M = 4.12$; Difference $= 0.05 \pm 0.20$). Finally, there was no interaction between prior exposure and delay (Interaction $= -0.11 \pm 0.54$).

To analyze recognition performance, the probability that participants recognized words from the exposure phase alone was calculated, as well as from the exposure phase and the two test phases combined. As expected, participants had better recognition for words they had visualized during the exposure phase and from the exposure phase and test phases combined ($M = 0.42$ and 0.16, respectively) than after counting vowels in words ($M = 0.31$ and 0.11, respectively).

These results suggest that prior exposure to words or phrases that later appear in the context of life events has little effect on beliefs that such events derived from childhood. Although we did not measure fluency directly, we can only infer that prior exposure to words increased the fluency with which the words were later processed in the context of life events (see Kolers, 1976, for evidence that prior exposure to words can facilitate reading those words even 1 year later). It is possible that participants recognized the source of the fluency if they had previously visualized those words. However, it is unlikely that participants realized the source of fluency when they had only counted vowels in those words. Indeed, counting vowels could have been such a shallow processing task that it failed to act as a prime at all. The recognition data clearly show that participants were better at remembering words they had previously visualized than words for which they had simply counted vowels. So, our processing manipulation worked as we had intended. These results indicate that fluency per se is likely insufficient to cause people to believe that an event occurred in their child-hood (autobiographical belief).[2]

GENERAL DISCUSSION

To summarize, we showed that unscrambling an anagram in the context of a life event (e.g., broke a nwidwo [window] playing ball) increased participants' belief that the event occurred in the average North American childhood (Experiment 1). In other work, we have shown that unscrambling anagrams also increases confidence in one's own childhood autobiographical belief (Bernstein et al., 2002, 2004). However, visualizing a phrase (e.g., broke a window playing ball) and then answering a question about it (e.g., Was the window broken in many pieces, one long crack, or with a hole through it?) had no effect on participants' confidence that the event occurred in their own childhood (Experiment 2). Also, visualizing or counting the number of vowels in a series of key words or phrases (e.g., window) had no effect on participants' autobiographical confidence when they later encountered those key words or phrases in the context of childhood life events (e.g., broke a window playing ball, Experiment 3). Thus, unscrambling words increases one's confidence in childhood biography and autobiography, but prior elaboration of and exposure to entire life events, key words, or phrases had no direct effect on one's childhood autobiographical belief.

This data pattern is puzzling. There is ample evidence in the literature that various manipulations can lead to false autobiographical belief and memory. These manipulations include imagination inflation, anagram unscrambling, forced confabulation, suggestion, and misinformation, to name but a few. The real puzzle here is why these manipulations produce false autobiographical belief and memory, while prior exposure to key words or phrases does not. We have now conducted over 10 experiments to test the effect of prior exposure on false autobiographical belief and memory. In no case have we obtained a significant effect. We must therefore conclude that prior exposure in and of itself does not produce false autobiographical belief and memory, at least with this experimental paradigm.

Adding to this puzzle, we obtained evidence in two previous experiments that elaborate prior exposure can interact with anagram unscrambling to produce false autobiographical belief (Bernstein et al., 2004; Experiment 2 and 3). In these previous experiments, during an exposure phase, participants visualized key words or generated sentences using key words (e.g., window: He saw the bird through the window). Later, in the test phase, participants encountered these words either intact or as anagrams in the context of life events (e.g., broke a nwidwo playing ball). When participants had to unscramble the key words, they were more likely to claim that these events had occurred in their childhood. This prior exposure by anagram unscrambling interaction disappeared, however, when participants counted vowels in the key words during the exposure phase (Bernstein et al., 2004, Experiment 1) or when they generated childhood events using the key words during the exposure phase (Bernstein et al., 2004, Experiment 4).

There are at least two reasons why the vowel counting and the childhood event generation manipulations did not interact with anagram unscrambling in our previous work: (a) Vowel counting is too shallow a processing task to render a lasting memory trace (see note 2); (b) generating a childhood event with a key word or phrase, although an elaborate processing task, provides participants with a likely (and correct) source to explain the familiarity that they experience when they encounter those key words and phrases in the context of childhood life events. Once again, in none of these four experiments from our previous work did prior exposure directly produce false autobiographical belief. Thus, we conclude that elaborate prior exposure can interact with other manipulations, such as anagram unscrambling, to produce false autobiographical belief; however, this elaborate prior exposure must be obscured as a source that would otherwise explain the familiarity that participants likely experience for target life events (see Clore, 1992). Finally, prior exposure does not *directly* produce false autobiographical belief.

So, what are we to make of our puzzle? Memory is inherently a reconstructive process (Bartlett, 1932). As such, memory encodes experiences in preparation for future action (see Schacter & Addis, 2007). Sometimes this encoding is faulty, leading people to misremember both the details of past events and entire past events. The precise mechanism responsible for false memory is unknown; however, memory errors come in different shades. It is therefore likely that there is no single mechanism subserving all false memories. We next turn to a brief discussion of two mechanisms that may underlie false memory: binding and familiarity misattribution.

BINDING

To the extent that the details of an encoded experience are bound together, the person will correctly remember the original experience. This idea helps explain false memory for details of an event. However, it does not explain rich false memories or memories for entire events that are false (Loftus & Bernstein, 2005). The binding problem pertains to how the brain combines sensory information at encoding to permit us to represent an experience (Roskies, 1999). For example, seeing a red fire engine zoom by with sirens blaring in the rain is a complex sensory experience. Each of the sensory details of this experience (e.g., red large moving object making loud noise while water pelts one's skin) must be combined to faithfully capture the event. Our brain appears to execute this process seamlessly. This apparent ease is misleading, however, for we often misremember the details of experience.

But, what about mistakenly remembering an *entire* experience that never happened? Such rich false memories cannot be the result of binding errors, especially when the details of these memories never occurred. Researchers have identified the integral role that suggestion and imagination play in the formation of false memories (Garry & Polaschek, 2000; Johnson & Raye, 1981; Lynn et al., Chapter 7, this volume). Merely imagining an experience, and imbuing it with sensory details, is often sufficient to render the entire experience and its details indistinguishable from a real memory.

Where the concept of binding may pertain to rich false memories is in one's failure to adequately tag an experience as imagined or otherwise false. Imagining the details of an experience, such as witnessing a solar eclipse or listening to a friend's detailed recollection of her own experience of witnessing a solar eclipse, may be bound faithfully in one's memory. However, if the imaginer or the listener fails to correctly tag this experience as imagined or as belonging to one's friend, then the experience is apt to become part of one's own autobiography (Marsh & Bower, 1993; Nourkova et al., 2004). Such gist-based encoding, although highly adaptive for later remembering and performance, leaves memory vulnerable to error (see Brainerd & Reyna, 2002; Mandler, 1980; Schacter & Addis, 2007).

FAMILIARITY MISATTRIBUTION

Prior experience facilitates and primes subsequent processing of the same experience. This priming leads to fluent processing, which in turn may be interpreted as familiarity. What does one do with this familiarity? To the extent that the correct source of the familiarity is obscured, misattribution ensues.

What leads an individual to believe that a particular life event occurred in their childhood? It cannot be pure fluency because if it were, then we would expect to see an increase in confidence for old items versus new items (an old/new effect) in the studies that involved all intact test items (Experiments 2 and 3). What we observed instead in the present study and in our previous work was that prior exposure to key words had no direct effect on subsequent confidence ratings. Thus, prior exposure by itself is insufficient to cause a later increase in autobiographical belief despite the increased fluency that typically accompanies words that have been seen before.

The paradox posed by our current and previous results is that unscrambling words increases childhood confidence, while prior exposure to words has no direct effect on childhood confidence. One might expect the opposite pattern of results for several reasons. First, the mere act of unscrambling a word embedded within a life event should have no effect on one's confidence that the event occurred in one's childhood. Yet, it does. Second, prior exposure has been shown to influence a variety of judgments, including recognition and truth (Begg, Anas, & Farinacci, 1992), fame (Jacoby et al., 1989), and perceptual duration (Witherspoon & Allan, 1985). The key is to make the context of the test judgment sufficiently different from that of the prior exposure so participants do not discount the fluency. If participants realize that the increased fluency is due to recent prior exposure, they will likely discount it by attributing the fluency to the recent exposure (Jacoby & Whitehouse, 1989). If, however, participants fail to make this connection or if prior exposure appears irrelevant to the present judgment (see Bernstein, 2005), then they will misattribute the fluency. Thus, we contend that participants simply fail to see the connection between unscrambling words and autobiographical belief (leading to misattribution of familiarity), whereas participants do see the connection between prior exposure to words and phrases and autobiographical belief (leading to discounting of familiarity).

One way to conceptualize the effects of unscrambling and prior exposure on autobiographical belief is that the fluency derived from the active unscrambling of anagrams produces a different phenomenological experience than does the more passive experience of being exposed to key words. Although passive exposure may enhance processing fluency, the fluency associated with the active production of a response via unscrambling anagrams may lead people to infer incorrectly that the reason it was so easy to unscramble the anagram was because it came from one's own memory (an illusion of familiarity).

If this account is correct, then the absence of the old/new effect that we observed in several other studies is likely the result of fluency discounting. In contrast, the revelation effect for plausibility and autobiographical belief occurs because participants fail to realize that unscrambling anagrams is a legitimate source of fluency. This failure to make the connection between unscrambling the anagram and the aha that participants experience on successfully unscrambling it results in a mistaken belief that the event in question occurred in one's own (autobiographical belief) or another person's childhood (plausibility). Schooler and Dougal (2007) have proposed a theory that accounts for some of our findings. According to their theory, discovering the solution to an anagram produces an aha that is mistaken for remembering. By this account, we would not expect to find increased confidence in our studies involving a simple old/new paradigm (Experiments 2 and 3) because there is no self-discovery or aha. In revelation studies, on the other hand, in which participants must unscramble words, there is the opportunity for self-discovery: Successful unscrambling produces an aha that can be mistaken for remembering. The notion of self-discovery thus accounts nicely for the absence of the old/new effect that was observed in Experiments 2 and 3.

CONCLUSION

We designed the present experiments to explore possible mechanisms underlying the formation of plausibility and autobiographical belief, the first two stages in Mazzoni et al.'s (2001) model of false memory formation. We have tried to show that familiarity and its subsequent attribution to a source is one likely mechanism. Other work has investigated the roles of familiarity and recollection in false memory (e.g., Roediger & McDermott, 1995), often using Tulving's (1985) remember versus know distinction. However, much of this work has been done using recognition and recall of words presented earlier in the study. The present work focused instead on memory for childhood autobiographical events. In this way, our work departs from many studies on false memory and offers a mechanism (familiarity misattribution) that might also explain how entire autobiographical events come to be viewed as both plausible and likely to have occurred in one's own childhood (see also Conway & Pleydell-Pearce, 2000). Future work, possibly using methods similar to those presented here, should aim to assess the role of familiarity in the formation of false autobiographical memory (see Mazzoni & Kirsch, 2003; Scoboria et al., 2004, for discussion). We suspect that autobiographi-

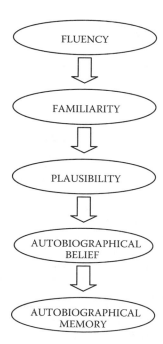

FIGURE 6.1   Hypothesized steps in false memory formation.

cal memory, just like plausibility and autobiographical belief, relies in part on evaluations and attributions of fluency and familiarity (see Figure 6.1).

NOTES

1. When we report $x + y$, x refers to a mean difference between conditions, and y refers to the 95% confidence interval. We report no hypothesis tests; rather, we consider effects "real" if the mean difference plus or minus the confidence interval excludes zero. Such effects are also significant using traditional null hypothesis significance testing (see Loftus & Masson, 1996).
2. We ran an additional experiment ($N = 51$) involving vowel counting of words or phrases, as was done in this experiment, and vowel counting of words embedded within the same life event that appeared approximately 30 min later at test. For example, participants may have counted vowels in the underlined word, "wedding" or "Participated in a wedding" and later rated how likely they were to have "Participated in a wedding" as a child. Once again, on a 1–8 scale, old events containing words that appeared alone prior ($M = 4.20$, SEM [standard error of the mean] $= 0.10$) and old events that appeared as full sentences prior ($M = 4.25$, $SEM = 0.10$) were no more likely to be judged as autobiographical experiences than were new events ($M = 4.28$, $SEM = 0.10$).

REFERENCES

Ayers, M. S., & Reder, L. M. (1998). A theoretical review of the misinformation effect: Predictions from an activation-based memory model, *Psychonomic Bulletin & Review*, 5, 1–21.

Bartlett, F. C. (1932). *Remembering: A study in experimental and social psychology*. Cambridge, England: Cambridge University Press.

Begg, I. M., Anas, A., & Farinacci, S. (1992). Dissociation of processes in belief: Source recollection, statement familiarity, and the illusion of truth. *Journal of Experimental Psychology: General*, 121, 446–458.

Bernstein, D. M. (2005). Making sense of memory. *Canadian Journal of Experimental Psychology*, 59, 199–208.

Bernstein, D. M., Godfrey, R., Davison, A., & Loftus, E. F. (2004). Conditions affecting the revelation effect for autobiographical memory. *Memory & Cognition*, 32, 455–462.

Bernstein, D. M., Whittlesea, B. W. A., & Loftus, E. F. (2002). Increasing confidence in remote autobiographical memory and general knowledge: Extensions of the revelation effect. *Memory & Cognition, 30*, 432–438.

Bodner, G., & Richardson-Champion, D. D. (2007). Remembering is in the details: Effects of test-list context on memory for an event. *Memory, 15*, 718–729.

Brainerd, C. J., & Reyna, V. F. (2002). Fuzzy-trace theory and false memory. *Current Directions in Psychological Science, 11*, 164–168.

Brainerd, C. J., & Reyna, V. F. (2005). *The science of false memory.* New York: Oxford University Press.

Briñol, P., Petty, R. E., & Tormala, Z. L. (2006). The meaning of subjective ease and its malleability. *Psychological Science, 17*, 200–206.

Clore, G. L. (1992). Cognitive phenomenology: Feelings and the construction of judgment. In L. L. Martin & A. Tesser (Eds.), *The construction of social judgments* (pp. 133–163). Hillsdale, NJ: Erlbaum.

Conway, M. A., & Pleydell-Pearce, C. W. (2000). The construction of autobiographical memories in the self memory system. *Psychological Review, 107*, 261–288.

Craik, F. I. M., & Lockhart, R. S. (1972). Levels of processing: A framework for memory research. *Journal of Verbal Learning and Verbal Behavior, 11*, 671–684.

Cutler, B. L., & Penrod, S. D. (1995). *Mistaken identification.* New York: Cambridge University Press.

Doyle, J. M. (2005). *True witness.* New York: Palgrave Macmillan.

Drivdahl, S. B., & Zaragoza, M. S. (2001). The role of perceptual elaboration and individual differences in the creation of false memories for suggested events. *Applied Cognitive Psychology, 15*, 265–281.

Dumas, A. (1997). *The count of Monte Cristo.* Ware, Hertfordshire: Wordsworth Editions. (Original work published 1844)

Ebbinghaus, H. E. (1964). *Memory: A contribution to experimental psychology.* New York: Dover. (Original work published 1885)

Frigo, L. C., Reas, D. L., & LeCompte, D. C. (1999). Revelation without presentation: Counterfeit study list yields robust revelation effect. *Memory & Cognition, 27*, 339–343.

Garry, M., Manning, C. G., Loftus, E. F., & Sherman, S. J. (1996). Imagination inflation: Imagining a childhood event inflates confidence that it occurred. *Psychonomic Bulletin and Review, 3*, 208–214.

Garry, M., & Polaschek, D. L. L. (2000). Imagination and memory. *Current Directions in Psychological Science, 9*, 6–10.

Garry, M., Strange, D., Bernstein, D. M., & Kinzett, D. (2007). Photographs can distort memory for the news. *Applied Cognitive Psychology, 21*, 995–1004.

Goff, L. M., & Roediger, H. L., III. (1998). Imagination inflation for action events: Repeated imaginings lead to illusory recollections. *Memory & Cognition, 26*, 20–33.

Hannigan, S. L., & Reinitz, M. T. (2001). A demonstration and comparison of two types of inference-based memory errors. *Journal of Experimental Psychology: Learning, Memory and Cognition, 27*, 931–940.

Hasher, L., Goldstein, D., & Toppino, T. (1977). Frequency and the conference of referential validity. *Journal of Verbal Learning and Verbal Behavior, 16*, 107–112.

Hockley, W. E., & Niewiadomski, M. W. (2001). Interrupting recognition memory: Tests of a criterion-change account of the revelation effect. *Memory & Cognition, 29*, 1176–1184.

Hyman, I. E., & Loftus, E. F. (1998). Errors in autobiographical memories. *Clinical Psychology Review, 18*, 933–947.

Hyman, I. E., Husband, T. H., & Billings, J. F. (1995). False memories of childhood experiences. *Applied Cognitive Psychology, 9*, 181–197.

Jacoby, L. L., & Dallas, M. (1981). On the relationship between autobiographical memory and perceptual learning. *Journal of Experimental Psychology: General, 110*, 306–340.

Jacoby, L. L., & Whitehouse, K. (1989). An illusion of memory: False recognition influenced by unconscious perception. *Journal of Experimental Psychology: General, 118*, 126–135.

Jacoby, L. L., Woloshyn, V., & Kelley, C. (1989). Becoming famous without being recognized: Unconscious influences of memory produced by dividing attention. *Journal of Experimental Psychology: General, 118*, 115–125.

Johnson, M. K., & Raye, C. L. (1981). Reality monitoring. *Psychological Review, 88*, 67–85.

Johnson, M. K., Hashtroudi, S., & Lindsay, D. S. (1993). Source monitoring. *Psychological Bulletin, 114*, 3–28.

Kelley, C. M., & Lindsay, D. S. (1993). Remembering mistaken for knowing: Ease of retrieval as a basis for confidence in answers to general knowledge questions. *Journal of Memory and Language, 32*, 1–24.

Kolers, P. A. (1976). Reading a year later. *Journal of Experimental Psychology: Human Learning and Memory, 2,* 554–565.

Kronlund, A., & Bernstein, D. M. (2006). Unscrambling words increases brand name recognition and preference. *Applied Cognitive Psychology, 20,* 681–687.

Lindsay, D. S., Hagen, L., Read, J. D., Wade, K. A., & Garry, M. (2004). True photographs and false memories. *Psychological Science, 15,* 149–154.

Loftus, E. F. (1977). Shifting human color memory. *Memory & Cognition, 5,* 696–699.

Loftus, E.F. (1979). *Eyewitness testimony.* Cambridge, MA: Harvard University Press.

Loftus, E. F., & Bernstein, D. M. (2005). Rich false memories: The royal road to success. In A. Healy (Ed.). *Experimental cognitive psychology and its applications: Festschrift in honor of Lyle Bourne, Walter Kintsch, and Thomas Landauer* (pp. 101–113). Washington, DC: American Psychological Association Press.

Loftus, E. F., Miller, D. G., & Burns, H. J. (1978). Semantic integration of verbal information into a visual memory. *Journal of Experimental Psychology: Human Learning and Memory, 4,* 19–31.

Loftus, E. F., & Pickrell, J. E. (1995). The formation of false memories. *Psychiatric Annals, 25,* 720–725.

Loftus, G. R., & Masson, M. E. J. (1996). Using confidence intervals in within-subject designs. *Psychonomic Bulletin & Review, 1,* 476–490.

Luo, C. R. (1993). Enhanced feeling of recognition: Effects of identifying and manipulating test items on recognition memory. *Journal of Experimental Psychology: Learning, Memory & Cognition, 19,* 405–413.

Mandler, G. (1980). Recognizing: The judgment of previous occurrence. *Psychological Review, 87,* 252–271.

Marsh, R. L., & Bower, G. H. (1993). Eliciting cryptomnesia: Unconscious plagiarism in a puzzle task. *Journal of Experimental Psychology: Learning, Memory, and Cognition, 19,* 673–688.

Mazzoni, G., & Kirsch, I. (2003). Autobiographical memories and beliefs: A preliminary metacognitive model. In T. Perfect & B. Schwartz (Eds.), *Applied metacognition* (pp. 121–145). Cambridge, UK: Cambridge University Press.

Mazzoni, G., Loftus, E. F., & Kirsch, I. (2001). Changing beliefs about implausible autobiographical events: A little plausibility goes a long way. *Journal of Experimental Psychology: Applied, 7,* 51–59.

Mazzoni, G., Loftus, E. F., Seitz, A., & Lynn, S. J. (1999). Changing beliefs and memories through dream interpretation. *Applied Cognitive Psychology, 13,* 125–144.

Mazzoni, G., & Memon, A. (2003). Imagination can create false autobiographical memories. *Psychological Science, 14,* 186–188.

Mulligan, N. W., & Lozito, J. P. (2006). An asymmetry between memory encoding and retrieval: Revelation, generation, and transfer-appropriate processing. *Psychological Science, 17,* 7–11.

Nourkova, V. V, Bernstein, D. M., & Loftus, E. F. (2004). Biography becomes autobiography: Distorting the subjective past. *American Journal of Psychology, 117,* 65–80.

Pezdek, K., & Lam, S. (2007). What research paradigms have cognitive psychologists used to study "false memory," and what are the implications of these choices? *Consciousness & Cognition, 16,* 2–17.

Pezdek, K., Finger, K., & Hodge, D. (1997). Planting false childhood memories. *Psychological Science, 8,* 437–441.

Roediger, H. L., III, & McDermott, K. B. (1995). False perceptions about false memories. *Journal of Experimental Psychology: Learning, Memory and Cognition, 22,* 803–814.

Rogers, T. B., Kuiper, N. A., & Kirker, W. S. (1977). Self-reference and the encoding of personal information. *Journal of Personality and Social Psychology, 35,* 677–688.

Roskies, A. L. (1999). The binding problem. *Neuron, 24,* 7–9.

Sacchi, D. L. M., Agnoli, F., & Loftus, E. F. (2007). Changing history: Doctored photographs affect memory for past public events. *Applied Cognitive Psychology, 21,* 1005–1022.

Sanna, L. J., & Schwarz, N. (2006). Metacognitive experiences and human judgment. *Current Directions in Psychological Science, 15,* 172–176.

Schacter, D. L. (2001). *The seven sins of memory: How the mind forgets and remembers.* Boston: Houghton Mifflin.

Schacter, D. L., & Addis, D. R. (2007). The cognitive neuroscience of constructive memory: Remembering the past and imagining the future. *Philosophical Transactions of the Royal Society (B), 362,* 773–786.

Schooler, J. W., & Dougal, S. (2007). Discovery misattribution. *Journal of Experimental Psychology: General, 136,* 577–592.

Scoboria, A., Mazzoni, G., Kirsch, I., & Relyea, M. (2004). Plausibility and belief in autobiographical memory. *Applied Cognitive Psychology, 18,* 791–807.

Seamon, J. G., Philbin, M. M., & Harrison, L. G. (2006). Do you remember proposing marriage to the Pepsi machine? False recollections from a campus walk. *Psychonomic Bulletin and Review, 13*, 752–756.

Sharman, S. J., Manning, C. G., & Garry, M. (2005). Explain this: Explaining childhood events inflates confidence for those events. *Applied Cognitive Psychology, 19*, 67–74.

Smeets, T., Merckelbach, H., Horselenberg, R., & Jelicic, M. (2005). Trying to recollect past events: Confidence, beliefs and memories. *Clinical Psychology Review, 25*, 917–934.

Tulving, E. (1972). Episodic and semantic memory. In E. Tulving & W. Donaldson (Eds.), *Organization of memory* (pp. 381–403). New York: Academic Press.

Tulving, E. (1983). *Elements of episodic memory*. New York: Oxford University Press.

Tulving, E. (1985). Memory and consciousness. *Canadian Psychologist, 26*, 1–12.

Unkelbach, C. (2006). The learned interpretation of cognitive fluency. *Psychological Science, 17*, 339–345.

Wade, K. A., Garry, M., Read, J. D., & Lindsay, D. S. (2002). A picture is worth a thousand lies: Using false photographs to create false childhood memories. *Psychonomic Bulletin & Review, 9*, 597–603.

Wade, K. A., Sharman, S. J., Garry, M., Memon, A., Mazzoni, G., Merckelbach, H., et al. (2007). False claims about false memory research. *Consciousness and Cognition, 16*, 18–28.

Watkins, M. J., & Peynircioglu, Z. F. (1990). The revelation effect: When disguising items induces recognition. *Journal of Experimental Psychology: Learning, Memory and Cognition, 16*, 1012–1020.

Westerman, D. L., & Greene, R. L. (1996). On the generality of the revelation effect. *Journal of Experimental Psychology: Learning, Memory and Cognition, 22*, 1147–1153.

Whittlesea, B. W. A., Jacoby, L. L., & Girard, K. (1990). Illusions of immediate memory: Evidence of an attributional basis for feelings of familiarity and perceptual quality. *Journal of Memory and Language, 29*, 716–732.

Whittlesea, B. W. A., & Leboe, J. P. (2003). Two fluency heuristics (and how to tell them apart). *Journal of Memory & Language, 49*, 62–79.

Whittlesea, B. W. A., & Williams, L. D. (2000). The source of feelings of familiarity: The discrepancy-attribution hypothesis. *Journal of Experimental Psychology: Learning, Memory and Cognition, 26*, 547–565.

Winkielman, P., Schwarz, N., Reber, R., & Fazendeiro, T. A. (2003). Cognitive and affective consequences of visual fluency: When seeing is easy on the mind. In L. M. Scott & R. Batra (Eds.), *Persuasive imagery: A consumer response perspective* (pp. 75–89). Mahwah, NJ: Erlbaum.

Witherspoon, D., & Allan, L. G. (1985). The effects of a prior presentation on temporal judgments in a perceptual identification task. *Memory and Cognition, 13*, 101–111.

7 Hypnosis and Memory: From Bernheim to the Present

Steven Jay Lynn, Abigail Matthews, and Sean Barnes

INTRODUCTION

Hypnosis has long been a flash point of contention in the larger and long-standing controversy about whether therapeutic procedures can create false memories (see also Bernstein, Godfrey, & Loftus, Chapter 6, this volume). By the late 19th century, the controversy was brewing, stirring concerns about suggestive techniques and pseudomemories that mirror contemporary concerns. Freud's idea that traumatic memories, like those reported by his now-famous patient Bertha Pappenheim, could be repressed and forgotten were dogged by criticisms that hypnosis and other suggestive techniques that were used to elicit traumatic memories were more likely to create than to uncover them (Powell & Boer, 1994). Close examination of Freud's writings reveals that he had often used highly suggestive procedures to elicit the memories of traumatic experiences and "childhood seductions" from his patients. Moreover, Freud had failed to consider alternative explanations for the evidence he presented when first claiming that the recovered memories of sexual abuse were real (Pintar & Lynn, in press).

By the end of the 19th century, the phenomenon of false (pseudo) memory creation was well documented by Freud's contemporaries. Bernheim (1889/1973), for example, used hypnosis to create perceptions and memories that he dubbed "retroactive hallucinations." Janet (1894) was one of the first therapists to realize that hypnosis could be used to uncover traumatic memories and images and substitute less-traumatic images in their stead. Janet reported the famous case of Justine, who developed a morbid fear of death after she helped her mother—a nurse—treat dying patients. Justine became haunted by intrusive images of naked corpses who died of cholera and, with Janet's help, used hypnosis to gradually transform the image of the naked corpses to clothed people, including a Chinese general Justine had actually seen. Justine's hysterical seizures that accompanied the unbidden images of naked corpses ceased after she was able to produce a comic image of the general dancing.

In the case of his patient Marie, Janet went beyond transforming images to actually creating false memories to neutralize traumatic memories. Janet used hypnosis to recover Marie's memory of a highly troubling incident in which she observed a child with a facial deformity. To counteract the lingering effects of this image, Janet suggested to Marie that the boy who frightened her did not actually have any unusual facial features. Marie's symptoms disappeared when she accepted the "reality" of the implanted memory.

The community of 19th century hypnosis researchers and practitioners was well acquainted with the apparent power of suggestion to permanently alter memory (Pintar & Lynn, in press). Bernheim (1891/1973) reported that he suggested to a patient that she went to the bathroom four times, and on her last visit she fell and hit her nose. The patient reported remembering having gone to the bathroom four times because of diarrhea and having fallen on the fourth visit, hitting nose. The striking aspect of this memory is that it was impossible for Bernheim to shake her belief that this memory was false. As Bernheim stated, "She persists in her statement, saying that she had not been dreaming, that she was perfectly conscious of getting up, that all the patients were asleep;—and she remains convinced that the occurrence was genuine" (pp. 164–165).

Bernheim (1889) also created a false memory of a horrific rape and demonstrated his subject's willingness to discuss the traumatic event with a representative of the law (Rosen, Sageman, & Loftus, 2003). Still, as our discussion of hypnotic pseudomemories unfolds, it will become apparent that questions can be raised about the extent that expressed conviction in suggested events reflects social compliance versus "believed-in" memories.

Concerns about hypnosis and the pliability of memory remained dormant for the better part of a century and did little to dissuade clinicians from the belief that mental healing follows the recovery of repressed or dissociated traumatic memories. Indeed, memory recovery became not only the cornerstone of psychoanalysis and Janet and Bernheim's treatments, but also of recovered memory therapists during the last decades of the 20th century. Even though Freud came to substitute free association methods for hypnosis, modern psychodynamic therapists still consider hypnosis a viable tool for uncovering memories, unconscious phenomena, and personality dynamics (Fromm & Nash, 1997; Orne, Dinges, & Bloom, 1995).

As late as 1980, many researchers believed that there was something special about hypnosis. For example, Hayward and Ashworth (1980) reported that hypnosis can "induce a mental state which facilitates recall and enables the subject to produce more information than he would be able to provide in the so-called waking state" (p. 471). Not surprisingly, hypnosis for memory recovery gradually seeped into mainstream psychotherapy, well beyond the purview of psychoanalysis. Yapko (1994) conducted a survey of over 850 psychotherapists in private practice; the survey revealed the following high rates of endorsement of beliefs concerning hypnosis as a vehicle for memory enhancement: (a) 75% believed that "Hypnosis enables people to accurately remember things they otherwise could not"; (b) 47% felt that "Therapists can have greater faith in details of a traumatic event when obtained hypnotically than otherwise"; (c) 31% felt that "When someone has a memory of a trauma while in hypnosis, it objectively must actually have occurred"; (d) for 54%, "Hypnosis can be used to recover memories of actual events as far back as birth"; and (e) 19% believed that "Hypnotically obtained memories are more accurate than simply just remembering" (p. 35).

In 1995, Poole, Lindsay, Memon, and Bull reported that at least 25% of licensed doctoral-level psychologists surveyed in the United States and Great Britain indicated that they (a) use two or more techniques such as hypnosis and guided imagery to facilitate recall of repressed memories; (b) consider memory recovery an important part of treatment; and (c) can identify patients with repressed or otherwise unavailable memories as early as the first session (see Polusny & Follette, 1996, for similar findings).

In that same year, the American Society of Clinical Hypnosis (ASCH) issued guidelines for clinical hypnosis aimed at memory improvement or recovery (Hammond et al., 1995). Although the guidelines acknowledged the possibility that hypnosis could create pseudomemories, they suggested that when therapists used nonleading procedures, hypnosis posed no special risk for false memories.

The rosy view of hypnosis in the eye of clinicians is perhaps understandable in light of prevailing popular beliefs about hypnosis and memory recovery. For instance, Whitehouse, Orne, Orne, and Dinges (1991) found that 93% of college-age subjects reported that hypnosis enhances memory retrieval. More than a decade later, Green (2003) reported that, on average, college students were in reasonably close agreement with the statement that "Hypnosis can make subjects remember things that they could not normally remember" (rated 5.42 on a 7-point scale of agreement).

As a counterpoint to these optimistic assessments, the reputation of hypnosis was sullied by a number of developments. First, hypnosis and memory recovery procedures, in general, were implicated in a virtual explosion of cases of dissociative identity disorder (DID, formerly known as multiple personality disorder) that critics contended were produced by iatrogenic psychotherapy techniques (see Lilienfeld et al., 1999). The number of cases of reported DID began to rise during the 1970s and by 1986 had increased to nearly 6000. At the turn of the 21st century, the number of reported cases of DID, although difficult to accurately determine, has been estimated at 40,000. Lawsuits against therapists for malpractice in "creating" rather than "discovering" multiple personalities paralleled the increase in the diagnosis of DID, and hypnosis was frequently at the center of contention.

Second, courts across the United States became increasingly skeptical of hypnosis as expert opinion suggested that hypnotically elicited testimony is unreliable. By the late 1970s (Orne, 1979), a growing number of reports of the memory-bending effects of hypnosis began to appear. For example, Timm (1981) noted that several hypnotized subjects reported in a most convincing fashion that the mock assassin they were attempting to identify was unkempt and wearing a khaki-colored army jacket and gloves. In reality, the person was immaculately groomed, had a blue formal jacket, and was not wearing gloves. Clearly, participants' prior conceptions about what assassins look like affected their responses. Beyond such anecdotes, a steady stream of studies that cast doubt on the reliability of hypnotically augmented recall appeared in the 1980s.

By 1994, the courts in most of the 40 cases reportable used the Daubert standard to reject scientifically unsound evidence and contended that suggestibility effects justified the exclusion of hypnotically elicited testimony (Underwager & Wakefield, 1998). At present, only a few states (e.g., Wyoming, Tennessee) hold that hypnotically elicited testimony is generally admissible, although some states admit such testimony (subject to cross-examination) when certain procedural safeguards are followed.

Clearly, a vast divide separated scientific opinion regarding false memory risk from both public opinion and some clinicians who continued to use hypnosis to promote memory recovery. Seeking a practical resolution to the disparate views of clinicians and researchers, beginning in the 1990s professional societies, including divisions and task forces of the American Psychological Association (APA, 1995) and the Canadian Psychiatric Association (CPA, 1996), increasingly have recommended against the use of hypnosis for memory retrieval. The American Medical Association has suggested that hypnosis be used only for investigative purposes in forensic contexts. Surveys of the use of hypnosis have not been conducted in recent years, but it is likely that many clinicians have become wary of using hypnosis to recover memories, if for no other reason than sidestepping potential litigation.

Fortunately, clinicians and the courts can consult the sizable corpus of findings regarding the effects of hypnosis, suggestion, and suggestibility on memory that we review in the remainder of this chapter. In the course of our discussion, we examine the accuracy of hypnotically elicited memories; confidence in such memories; the role of expectancies in producing pseudomemories; the strength, persistence, and reversibility of false memories; and criticisms of extant research leveled by proponents of the use of hypnosis for memory recovery.

ACCURATE VERSUS INACCURATE MEMORIES

There is little disagreement among cognitive scientists that memory is a fallible construction—an unwinding narrative based on current beliefs, feelings, expectations, images, and guesses about past events (Lynn & McConkey, 1998). It is by now commonplace to say that many ordinary memories are an admixture of accurate and inaccurate recollections. Accordingly, any evaluation of hypnosis must consider both accurate and inaccurate memories and compare hypnotic with nonhypnotic recall.

Two major reviews summarized much of the research conducted through the mid-1990s. Erdelyi (1994) reviewed 34 studies published before 1988 and concluded that recall tests for high-sense stimuli such as poetry and meaningful pictures almost always produce hypermnesia or enhancement of memory. However, recognition tests for high sense and recognition and recall tests for low-sense stimuli such as nonsense syllables or word lists failed to show evidence of hypnotic hypermnesia. Erdelyi argued that a problem in interpreting these results is that even when hypnosis results in greater recall, there is an attendant increase in incorrect information. Hence, without controlling for response criteria, it is not possible to evaluate recall levels.

Several studies conducted after Erdelyi's review addressed this concern. In two studies (Dinges et al., 1992; Whitehouse, Dinges, Orne, & Orne, 1988) that evaluated hypermnesia with response productivity controlled by means of a forced-choice recall procedure, hypnosis did not produce enhanced recall beyond nonhypnotic hypermnesia. In one of the studies (Dinges et al., 1992), hypnosis not only failed to enhance retrieval of correct items, but also increased the production of incorrect information. Relatedly, a study by Dywan and Bowers (1983) found that subjects who were hypnotized reported twice as many items and three times as many errors as nonhypnotic controls.

In a meta-analysis of 24 studies, Steblay and Bothwell (1994) found evidence for superior recall in hypnosis in response to nonleading questions when a delay of at least 24 hr between event and recall attempt was imposed. However, the authors concluded that this finding must be tempered by three considerations: (a) Leading questions even in the delay condition reduced the effect size and eliminated group differences; (b) the confidence intervals for these effect sizes were quite large and encompassed zero, suggesting considerable unaccounted for variability; and (c) any benefit for hypnosis was limited to delays of 1 to 2 days. Even a 1-week delay reverses the effect to favor control subjects. Moreover, Steblay and Bothwell (1994) reported that, relative to waking conditions, hypnosis produces more recall errors, more intrusions of uncued errors, and higher levels of memories for false information relative to nonhypnotic methods. Later reviews (Kebble & Wagstaff, 1998; Orne, Whitehouse, Dinges, & Orne, 1996; Wagstaff, in press) have confirmed the conclusion that hypnosis does not offer recall advantages beyond waking conditions and can result in an increase of accurate memories that is at times more than compensated for by an increase in inaccurate memories.

That said, hypnosis does not always evoke more information or increased error rates (Sanders & Simmons, 1983; Sheehan, 1988a; Sheehan & Tilden, 1983), bolstering Erdelyi's (1994) conclusion that "no hypnosis-specific effect on memory has been observed" (p. 383). In many studies in which no differences are discerned between hypnotic and nonhypnotic conditions, highly suggestive and misleading questions or procedures are used in control as well as hypnotic conditions (e.g., Barnier & McConkey, 1992; Lynn, Rhue, Myers, & Weekes, 1994; McConkey et al., 1990; Neuschatz, Lynn, Benoit, & Fite, 2003; Spanos & Bures, 1993–1994; Spanos, Burgess, Burgess, Samuels, & Blois, 1999; Spanos, Gwynn, Comer, Baltruweit, & deGroh, 1989; Terrance, Matheson, Allard, & Schnarr, 2000; Weekes, Lynn, Green, & Brentar, 1992).

The types of procedures range from the suggestion of a specific event shortly after birth (Spanos et al., 1999; Terrance et al., 2000), to the suggestive Deese/Roediger and McDermott (DRM) paradigm (Neuschatz et al., 2003), misleading information that a purse snatching offender wore a scarf (Barnier & McConkey, 1992), and the suggestion that the participant was awakened during the night by a loud noise (Weekes et al., 1992). In contrast, when researchers do not provide leading or misleading suggestions, differences between hypnotic and nonhypnotic procedures often emerge, such that hypnosis compromises recall (e.g., Burgess & Kirsch, 1999; Krackow, Lynn, & Payne, 2005–2006; Scoboria, Mazzoni, Kirsch, & Milling, 2002).

Researchers have also addressed the question of whether hypnosis potentiates the effects of leading questions (in terms of inaccurate information). Here, the evidence is decidedly, or perhaps we should say "undecidedly," mixed. Three studies have found that hypnosis did indeed potentiate the effects of leading questions (Putnam, 1979; Scoboria et al., 2002; Zelig & Beidleman, 1981), whereas in four other studies (Linton & Sheehan, 1994; Scoboria, Mazzoni, & Kirsch, 2006; Sheehan, Garnett, & Robertson, 1993; Sheehan & Linton, 1993), this was not the case.

Interestingly, only two studies have independently manipulated the effects of hypnotic induction and misleading questions. In the first study, Scoboria and his associates (2002) determined that hypnosis and misleading questions independently decreased the accuracy of memory reports and decreased "don't know" responses. Moreover, the effects of misleading questions surpassed the effects of hypnosis, with the two effects being additive. In a second study (Scoboria et al., 2006), only misleading questions reduced accuracy and don't know responses. That is, the research failed to replicate the negative effect of hypnosis on memory reports. The reason for this nonreplication may be that the latter study, unlike the first study, was conducted on a group rather than an individual basis, thus diluting the effects of hypnosis on memory. Although the evidence is mixed, it is clear that misleading questions, which are often an integral part of the "hypnotic" intervention, may both account for effects previously attributed to hypnosis and obscure the ability to find differential effects for hypnosis in studies that include leading procedures in nonhypnotic conditions.

THE QUESTION OF CONFIDENCE

The confidence expressed by a witness is the single most important factor in persuading subject-jurors that a witness correctly identified the culprit (Wells & Bradfield, 1998). Accordingly, in forensic situations, a central question is whether hypnosis can increase confidence in inaccurate as well as accurate memories (Steblay & Bothwell, 1994), thereby having the potential to distort testimony.

A substantial body of evidence has accumulated regarding the effects of hypnosis on the confidence of eyewitnesses or people asked to recall specific events. More than two thirds of the studies that have examined confidence in recollections have shown inflated confidence rates for hypnotically elicited memories. More specifically, 23 studies have shown that hypnosis either increases confidence relative to a nonhypnotic group or participants confidently report hypnotic pseudomemories of events they earlier denied occurred while they were not hypnotized (Bryant & Barnier, 1999; Burgess & Kirsch, 1999; Dinges et al., 1992; Dywan & Bowers, 1983; Green & Lynn, 2005; Laurence, 1982; Laurence & Perry, 1983; McConkey & Kinoshita, 1988; Nogrady, McConkey, & Perry, 1985; Rainer, 1984; Scoboria et al., 2002; Sheehan & Grigg, 1985; Sheehan, Grigg, & McCann, 1984; Sheehan & Tilden, 1983, 1984, 1986; Spanos, Quigley, Gwynn, Glatt, & Perlini, 1991; Wagstaff, 1981; Wagstaff, Traverse, & Milner, 1982; Whitehouse et al., 1988, 1991; Zelig & Beidleman, 1981).

Researchers have assessed confidence in a variety of ways, including explicit self-report measures of confidence in specific memories (e.g., Dinges et al., 1992), shifts from don't know to know (e.g., Scoboria et al., 2006), and willingness to change answers when given an opportunity to do so (Green & Lynn, 2005). Little information is available regarding the interrelation among such measures and precisely how they relate to more real-world forensic and clinical situations, but the consilience of the evidence indicates that hypnosis can augment confidence ranging from a very small to a great extent.

Still, not all studies have found evidence for enhanced confidence. Nine published studies have found no difference in confidence expressed in hypnotic versus nonhypnotic situations. However, in five of the studies (Putnam, 1979; Ready, Bothwell, & Brigham, 1997; Sanders & Simmons, 1983; Scoboria et al., 2002; Yuille & McEwan, 1985), hypnosis produced more errors or less-accurate information on some or all measures, and in all of the remaining studies (Gregg & Mingay, 1987; Mingay, 1986; Scoboria et al., 2006; Spanos et al., 1989), with one exception, there were no differences in memory accuracy across hypnotic and nonhypnotic conditions.

In the single study in which differences surfaced (Terrance et al., 2000): (a) nearly half of hypnotic and nonhypnotic participants expressed a high degree of certainty in the reality of their recovered memories of a suggested event the day after birth (presumed to be inaccurate); and (b) the nonhypnotic participants who participated in guided imagery were slightly but significantly more likely (90%) to report infancy experiences than were hypnotic participants (76%). In all likelihood, the reason why this difference was apparent is that in the guided imagery group, the researchers informed participants that both high and low hypnotizable individuals could respond to the procedures (a detail not mentioned in the hypnosis condition), both clouding any difference between the hypnosis and imagery contexts and arguably creating more positive and universal expectancies for responding.

In summary, the majority of studies find evidence for increased confidence in hypnotic participants compared to nonhypnotic participants. However, with only one exception, when there is no problem with increased confidence in recollections, there is either no superiority for hypnotically enhanced recall, or hypnosis diminishes the yield of accurate information. That said, only the three studies we consider next have assessed confidence in recollections in terms of the breakdown of testimony in a cross-examination situation with arguably high forensic relevance.

HYPNOSIS AND CROSS-EXAMINATION

In the first study, Spanos et al. (1989) determined that hypnotizable individuals[1] who viewed a videotape of a crime misattributed a substantial number of suggested characteristics to the offender and frequently misidentified a mug shot of the offender. Hypnotic and nonhypnotic interrogations with leading questions produced equivalent effects across the two conditions. Afterward, participants were subjected to cross-examination, and the hypnotized and nonhypnotized subjects were equally likely to "break down" during questioning and disavow their earlier misattributions and misidentifications. However, of the eight subjects who selected a mug shot during interrogation, fully 50% maintained their selection during cross-examination. In contrast, only one of the control subjects (no hypnosis, imagery, no leading questions) selected the mug shot during interrogation, and that individual did not maintain the selection during cross-examination. Spanos et al. did not report an analysis from this comparison, but it appears as if the rates of misidentification differ between hypnotic and control subjects. The general finding that hypnotized subjects did not differ from subjects who received guided imagery and leading questions is not at all surprising in that both guided imagery and leading questions have been shown to produce pseudomemories.

In the second study, all subjects were hypnotized and cross-examined under three conditions: (a) stringent forensic cross-examination that implied participants were careless or dishonest during their testimony; (b) benign cross-examination in which participants were informed they would be asked a few questions, and earlier misidentifications were implied to be honest mistakes; and (c) participants were informed they had a hidden part (i.e., hidden observer) that can always distinguish between suggestions and reality. The investigators hypothesized that the last condition would legitimize the reversal of earlier testimony. The researchers found that subjects in the stringent cross-examination were more resistant to cross-examination than subjects in both the benign and hidden observer treatments.

In a third study, Spanos, Quigley et al. (1991) reported that hypnosis inflated participant confidence. That is, compared to nonhypnotized individuals, hypnotized subjects were more confident of their identifications of mug shots. Moreover, subjects who underwent a hypnosis interrogation and were then prepared for cross-examination (i.e., told to tell the truth but to be polite but firm and not let the prosecutor plant doubts in their mind) expressed higher certainty in their mug shot identifications than subjects who were not prepared. In contrast, preparation did not influence nonhypnotized subjects' certainty of identifications: Prepared and nonprepared individuals responded equivalently.

All subjects were subjected to cross-examinations of their earlier testimony. Hypnotized subjects were neither more nor less likely to break down under cross-examination than nonhypnotized subjects. But, the fact bears emphasis that across conditions, 37 of the 78 subjects evaluated (47%) did *not* break down in the face of both direct examination and cross-examination. In fact, fully 73% of people who were prepared for cross-examination did not break down under cross-examination. In contrast, 86% of individuals who were not prepared by lawyers to withstand cross-examination did break down and reversed their earlier testimony.

In short, the combination of hypnosis and routine trial preparation to withstand cross-examination resulted in a high rate of certainty and resistance to changing mug shot identifications while testifying. Combined, the research on accuracy, confidence, and hypnosis suggest that Steblay and Bothwell (1994) were right to conclude, "Hypnosis is not necessarily a source of accurate information; at worst it may be a source of inaccurate information provided with confident testimony" (p. 649).

THE SOCIAL-COGNITIVE MODEL AND THE ROLE OF EXPECTANCIES

The results we have reviewed are entirely consistent with a social-cognitive model of hypnosis. An abundance of literature indicates that expectancies are influential determinants of memories (Hirt, Lynn, Payne, Krackow, & McCrae, 1999). According to the sociocognitive perspective, hypnosis does not involve a special or unique altered state of consciousness, and that hypnotic experience and behavior are similar to other complex social behaviors. For example, hypnotized subjects strive to fulfill role demands and behave in a manner consistent with their expectancies (e.g., Barber, 1969; Coe & Sarbin, 1991; Lynn, Kirsch, & Hallquist, in press; Spanos, 1986). As far as memory goes, widely held prehypnotic attitudes and beliefs that hypnosis facilitates recall, as well as suggestions that directly state or imply that hypnosis involves an altered state or trance, generate expectancies that hypnotic and posthypnotic recall will be improved.

Because many individuals expect that hypnosis will increase the volume and accuracy of their memories, it increases motivation to search for memories and report imagined events or guesses as real memories (Scoboria et al., 2006). After all, if participants believe that hypnotic recollections are akin to memories produced following ingestion of a "truth serum," then it is understandable that they would conclude with confidence that their remembrances are accurate. Moreover, by encouraging imagination, relaxation, and the complete experience of suggestions, hypnotic situations discourage critical evaluation of suggested events and memories and lower report criteria for "memories." Hence, it is not surprising that people frequently recall more information with confidence in hypnotic than in many nonhypnotic contexts.

Considerable evidence indicates that hypnotic procedures can increase participant's rapport with the experimenter (see Lynn & Rhue, 1991). Individuals may accord suggestions for enhanced recall greater weight when the experimenter or interrogator is well liked or perceived to be a credible authority. Consistent with the important role that sociocognitive theorists ascribe to social influence, Sheehan, Green, and Truesdale (1992) found that poor rapport between hypnotist and subject appreciably decreased the pseudomemory rate.

A sociocognitive account of memory and hypnosis assumes that memory distortions are not unique to hypnosis. When research controls for attitudes, expectancies, suggestive influences, and motivation to report memories, differences between hypnotic and nonhypnotic conditions in memory accuracy and confidence should be minimal or nonexistent. As our review indicates, this is the case.

According to the sociocognitive model, people who respond to hypnotic suggestions (so-called high- and medium-suggestible individuals) would be especially prone to develop positive response expectations. Indeed, research indicates that high- and medium-suggestible individuals typically produce more pseudomemories than do low-suggestible individuals (see Lynn & Nash, 1994; Terrance et al., 2000). In some studies, medium-suggestible people perform comparably to highly suggestible individuals (Neuschatz et al., 2003; Sheehan, Statham, & Jamieson, 1991b; Terrance et al., 2000), and in other studies, medium-suggestible people display less pseudomemory than highly suggestible individuals but more than low-suggestible subjects (Sheehan, Statham, & Jamieson, 1991a).

Interestingly, high-suggestible subjects exhibit pseudomemories to a greater extent than low-suggestible people in nonhypnotized as well as hypnotized conditions (McConkey, Labelle, Bibb, & Bryant, 1990; Sheehan, Statham, Jamieson, & Ferguson, 1991; Spanos et al., 1989). This suggests that pseudomemory responding is associated with a general suggestibility or compliance factor that transcends the hypnotic situation. However, a retrospective analysis (Orne et al., 1996) of results from several studies of hypnotically influenced memories indicates that even low-suggestible subjects can be vulnerable to false memories in hypnotic conditions. The fact that many medium-suggestible persons, who represent the modal subjects in the population, and even some low-suggestible individuals report pseudomemories indicates that the effect may be much more pervasive than certain writers have contended (e.g., Brown, 1995).

According to the sociocognitive perspective, it follows that prehypnotic instructions and induced expectancies should affect the rate of pseudomemories. Not surprisingly, the available evidence supports this contention. The role of expectancies is particularly apparent in studies of hypnotic age regression. Whereas hypnosis does not accurately reinstate memories from the recent past, the same can be said for experiences from the distant past. Nash (1987) reviewed more than 60 years of research on hypnotic age regression (a technique in which a subject is asked to respond to specific hypnotic suggestions to think, feel, or act like a child at a particular age). He concluded that the behaviors and experiences of age-regressed adults were often different from those of actual children. No matter how compelling "age-regressed experiences" appear to observers, they reflect participants' expectancies, beliefs, assumptions, and fantasies about childhood; they rarely, if ever, represent literal reinstatements of childhood experiences, behaviors, and feelings.

In an impressive demonstration of the power of expectancy information, Spanos, Burgess, Burgess, Samuels, and Blois (1999) showed that it is possible to structure expectations to elicit complex, vivid, and detailed memories of the day after birth by providing participants with a plausible rationale for the recall of such memories. Fully 78% of participants who were age regressed reported memories of infancy. Nearly half (49%) of those persons who reported infancy memories classified them as real memories. Interestingly, persons who were not hypnotized (95%) were slightly more likely to report infancy experiences compared to hypnotized persons (79%). Cognitive scientists (see Malinoski, Lynn, & Sivec, 1998) are in general agreement that memories earlier than age 2 are unlikely to be accurate.

In a similar study, Terrance et al. (2000) led participants to believe they had experienced a "cold water treatment" shortly after birth by administering age regression suggestions in the context of hypnosis and guided imagery and by engendering expectations that the body records all events that can be accessed. Participants in the expectancy condition failed to differ from participants in both the hypnosis and the guided imagery conditions. More than two thirds of participants (68%) in the expectancy condition produced a day-after-birth memory compared with 90% of individuals in the guided imagery condition and 76% of participants in the hypnosis condition. Only 8% of control participants, provided with no special rationale, responded comparably. We noted that the guided imagery condition contained especially strong demands for early memory reports. Accordingly, strong expectancies for memory production, created by highly suggestive procedures, can minimize differences between hypnotic and nonhypnotic procedures.

Studies of even earlier "memories"—that is, memories of suggested past lives—also reveal the potentially important role of expectancies in the genesis of false memories. Spanos, Menary, Gabora, DuBreuil, and Dewhirst (1991) conducted a series of hypnotic regression experiments and found that highly hypnotizable participants often enacted past-life identities when instructed to do so. The memories of past lives and the credibility of the past life experiences reported by participants were strongly influenced by preexisting beliefs about reincarnation, as well as expectations regarding the nature of past-life experiences transmitted by the hypnotist to the participant, including whether abuse, for example, was likely to have occurred in a past life.

Studies conducted apart from the context of age regression confirmed the role of prehypnotic and hypnotic expectances in pseudomemory formation. McCann and Sheehan (1988, Study 1) found that when subjects were informed that hypnotic effects would persist following the termination of the hypnotic procedures, the pseudomemory rate was 70%. However, when the hypnosis and waking treatments were clearly differentiated, the pseudomemory rate dropped to 20%. Grabowski, Roese, and Thomas (1991) determined that subjects who expected hypnosis scored higher on a memory test than subjects with no expectation of hypnosis. However, this increase in memory reports came from an increase in errors associated with providing more information. Marmelstein and Lynn (1999) found that participants led to believe they could recall memories back to the first week of life were more confident in their ability to specify when the remembered event occurred and reported more detailed memories than participants who received no specific expectancy information. Lynn et al. (1994) reported that subjects who developed pseudomemories believed that the hypnotist was more likely to expect them to believe the suggested event occurred in reality than were subjects who did not report pseudomemories.

Information provided after hypnosis also can affect the formation of pseudomemories. McCann and Sheehan (1988) demonstrated that when participants viewed incontrovertible videotape evidence regarding a video of a robbery they observed, the pseudomemory rates decreased substantially.

Pseudomemory reports also vary with respect to the nature of the event and the expectancy of its actual occurrence. Memory is the end product of decision and inferential processes: Pseudomemories result when participants mistakenly decide that a suggested event occurred when in fact it did not. Such mistakes are more likely to occur when people imagine and reflect on suggested events, which likely enhances their accessibility, plausibility, and self-relevance (Anderson & Sechler, 1986; Hirt & Markman, 1995; Markman & McMullen, 2003). According to the principle of discrepancy detection (Hall, Loftus, & Tousignant, 1984), misleading information is most likely to bias participants when they do not detect discrepancies between postevent information and memory for an original event (p. 135). That is, bias is most likely to occur when the suggested event is consistent with individuals' expectancies, beliefs, and self-concept regarding what "could" or "did" happen in a particular situation.

In keeping with this hypothesis, events (e.g., phone ringing in the room) that are publicly verifiable, memorable, and in the person's direct field of experience are associated with relatively low hypnotic pseudomemory rates (0–25%). Suggestions for such events are not likely to bias subjects because they can easily detect a discrepancy between what is suggested and what they "know" occurred in reality. In contrast, when events have a high base rate of occurrence (and a concomitant high expectation of future occurrence) in everyday life and are not particularly distinctive or memorable (e.g., door slamming during sleep or in the hallway the previous week; car backfiring), pseudomemory rates ranging from 39% to 81% are reported (see Lynn, Myers, & Malinoski, 1997; Weekes, Lynn, & Myers, 1996). Simply stated, people are likely to report that a suggested event occurred when it is not very memorable and plausibly could have occurred as described.

Studies that inform or warn participants about the possibility of pseudomemory formation during hypnosis shed additional light on the contribution of expectancies. Green, Lynn, and Malinoski (1998) provided some subjects with prehypnotic information that memory is imperfect and people are capable of filling in gaps in memory. These subjects reported fewer suggested memories during hypnosis than did participants who received no such warnings. However, an analysis of those persons who accepted the suggestion showed that 75% of the warned versus 58% of the unwarned persons stated immediately after hypnosis that the suggested event occurred in reality. Comparing pseudomemory rates across all participants, regardless of whether they passed or failed the noise suggestion, 28% of warned participants versus 44% of unwarned participants reported pseudomemories after hypnosis. Warned and unwarned participants were equally confident in their false memories. In short, warnings minimized memory distortions during but not after hypnosis.

In another warning study, Burgess and Kirsch (1999) showed highly suggestible and low-suggestible students slides of 40 line drawings. Highly suggestible students given memory enhancement expectancy information displayed an increase in errors during hypnosis and retained these false memories after hypnosis. However, this effect was mitigated during hypnosis and eliminated after hypnosis among students who were warned that it might occur.

Just as the effects of expectancies are not apparent in studies with especially low base rates of pseudomemories, the same is true in studies with especially high base rates of false memories. Neuschatz et al. (2003) warned participants about the fallibility of memory before, during, and after hypnosis. A control group of subjects who were not hypnotized received the same warnings on three parallel occasions. The researchers used the DRM paradigm (Roediger & McDermott, 1995), which produces high rates of false recognition of nonpresented words thematically related to items that are on lists of words studied. Under these circumstances, participants (a) exhibited a high rate of false recognitions (>0.70) and (b) were very confident in their remembrances, independent of their recognition accuracy and level of hypnotic suggestibility (medium vs. high), whether or not they were hypnotized, and even when they received memory warnings. In a follow-up study (Lynn et al., 2000) using the DRM paradigm, it made no difference at all whether participants received or did not receive warnings on measures of recall as well as recognition. In summary, although induced expectancies play an influential role in hypnotic pseudomemories, the base rate and nature of suggested and target events also affect the pseudomemory rate.

THE PERSISTENCE AND REVERSIBILITY OF PSEUDOMEMORIES

Our discussion raises questions about the strength, persistence, and reversibility of hypnotically elicited pseudomemories. According to the sociocognitive model of hypnosis, memory reports should be sensitive to a wide range of social and contextual influences. The data generally fall in line with this prediction. Murrey, Cross, and Whipple (1992) offered a monetary award to subjects able to distinguish real memories and suggested false memories. Subjects given monetary incentives to report accurately were less likely to report pseudomemories than subjects not given monetary incentives. However, even when participants were provided with a monetary incentive, 40% of the participants who initially reported pseudomemories did not change their reports.

Spanos and McLean (1986) were the first researchers to incorporate the hidden observer procedure into a study of hypnotic pseudomemories, much like the Spanos et al. (1989) study reviewed earlier. Initially, almost 82% (9/11) of subjects who accepted a false memory suggestion to hear a noise in the night that awakened them (they earlier stated that they had slept through the entire night) reported pseudomemories. Subjects were then administered the following hidden observer instructions:

> During deep hypnosis people often confuse reality with things that were only imagined. The hypnotized part of a person's mind accepts suggestions so completely that what was suggested actually seems to have been happening. ... Yet at the same time that you are experiencing suggestions, there is some other part of your mind, a hidden part, that knows what is really going on. ... The hidden part can always distinguish what was suggested from what really happened. (p. 157)

With this instructional set, all but 2 subjects reversed their responding and reported that the noises had only been suggested to them. When the experimenter instructed subjects that she wished to shift from the hidden part back to the hypnotized part, subjects again reported pseudomemories.

However, a number of other studies suggest that it may not be so easy to reverse pseudomemories. Two studies by Weekes, Lynn, Brentar, Myers, and Green (Lynn et al., 1994; Weekes et al., 1992) employed a nonhypnotic manipulation that informed subjects that they can successfully distinguish between fantasy and reality through the use of "deep concentration." Unlike Spanos and McLean's (1986) hidden observer manipulation, the deep concentration manipulation failed to reverse subjects' pseudomemory reports. Unlike the deep concentration instructions, the hidden observer instructions provided clear demands for memory reversal while simultaneously permitting subjects to remain in the role of a responsive hypnotized subject.

Accordingly, in a third study, Green, Lynn, and Malinoski (1998) attempted a close replication of Spanos and McLean's (1986) procedures by using their instructions and assessing hidden observer responses during hypnosis as they did. Even though Green et al. closely followed the procedure of Spanos and McLean, they were once again unable to show that most individuals who report pseudomemories reverse them in response to shifting demand characteristics: Only 22% of persons who initially showed pseudomemories reversed their reports under hidden observer instructions.

Although the reasons for the failure to replicate Spanos and his colleagues' findings are unclear, it appears that pseudomemory reports can be obdurate and recalcitrant to modification. This conclusion is reinforced by Bryant and Barnier's (1999) research, which tested participants in two experiments for recall of their second birthday. In Study 1, all of the highly suggestible hypnosis participants who reported a birthday memory during hypnosis (58%) maintained their reported memory, even after they were told that reliable scientific evidence has demonstrated that immature neurological development precludes accurate recall of events at 2 years of age. However, less than half (38.5%) of the highly suggestible participants who were tested in a nonhypnotic condition and reported a memory of their second birthday maintained their memory after they were provided with scientific evidence regarding early memories. In Study 2, all subjects who reported a memory following hypnosis maintained their belief in the reported memories in the face of challenging information. Whereas low-suggestible participants instructed to fake hypnosis (simulators) reported less confidence with each report of their pseudomemories, highly suggestible non-simulating participants maintained their belief in their reported memory across three assessment periods.

Green and Lynn (2005) asked hypnotized and relaxed subjects to estimate the dates of international news events. After individuals dated the events, their responses were purportedly reviewed, and they were told that they had made at least one error in their estimates and were given an opportunity to change their responses. Hypnotized subjects (16.6%) changed fewer of their estimates than relaxed subjects (24.2%), providing evidence that hypnosis crystallized memories to a small extent, yet greater than relaxation.

Several studies have examined the perseverance of false memories in the face of changes in the experimental context. McConkey et al. (1990) found that on immediate testing, approximately 50% of hypnotizable subjects reported pseudomemory. However, when contacted by telephone at home 4–24 hr later by an experimenter unaffiliated with the earlier session, the rate decreased dramatically to 2.5%. Barnier and McConkey (1992) replicated the finding that the overall pseudomemory rate declined from 60% for a false suggestion that a thief depicted in a series of slides was wearing a scarf to 10% when the experimental context shifted to imply to subjects that the experiment had ended. Similarly, the pseudomemory rate for a false suggestion that he had been carrying a bouquet of flowers dropped from 27% to 3%.

Subjects, however, were tested not only in a different context, after the experiment was apparently over, but also after they were told that some of the slides did not depict what was suggested—implying that they had been misled. Accordingly, the context and information provided were confounded. A close analysis of subjects' responses, as determined by a videotaped interview, showed that they were confused by the highly leading suggestions that implied that they saw things that were clearly not in the tape they had just seen. The authors noted that caution should be exercised in interpreting the findings because it is not clear whether subjects altered their reports because of the change in the experimenter's manner or as a result of the new information that she gave them.

In a study that eliminated the confound, Marmelstein and Lynn (1999) retested earliest memories of participants after the study was completed and after they were fully debriefed. Two weeks later, another experimenter, unaffiliated with the initial hypnosis session, contacted participants. Immediately after hypnosis, nearly two thirds of participants reported memories from 2 years of age or younger. More than half of the participants reported memories that dated from 18 months or younger, more than 40% of the participants recalled events dated from 1 year of age or younger, and 20% of the participants reported memories from 6 months or younger. Even when participants were contacted at home after they were debriefed, 37% of them reported that their earliest memory was from 2 years of age or younger, and a quarter continued to claim recall from 18 months or younger. Taken together, the research we have reviewed implies that at least some hypnotic pseudomemories are not merely the product of response bias but may reflect genuine, or at least enduring, alterations in memories.

CRITICISMS OF RESEARCH

The research we have reviewed notwithstanding, there remain vocal advocates of the use of hypnosis for memory recovery (Brown, Scheflin, & Hammond, 1998). These individuals have advanced a number of incisive criticisms of many extant studies, including the argument that many are flawed because they are (a) based on sterile laboratory research that uses personally irrelevant stimuli far removed from real-life, emotionally laden events; (b) employ relatively short retention intervals, often testing subjects on the same day they are exposed to laboratory stimuli; (c) rely solely on forced-choice recall test procedures that are "predisposed to produce biased, unreliable data" (p. 299); and (d) test for hypnotically created memories during hypnosis instead of following hypnosis (p. 330).

A study (Krackow et al., 2005–2006) addressed these criticisms by evaluating emotional real-life memories of the death of Princess Diana, first 3 days after her death and then after an 11- to

12-week period. Only participants who initially reported an emotional reaction to her death and provided complete narratives of their recollections were included in the data analyses. Task-motivated subjects, simply instructed to do their best to recall the details of her death, and subjects in whom the initial context of recall was reinstated were more consistent in their recall of events than subjects who were hypnotized to augment their recall.

To assess the criticism that hypnosis studies are devoid of emotional meaning, Lynn and his colleagues (Lynn, Myers et al., 1997) reviewed seven studies that compared hypnotic versus non-hypnotic memory in the face of relatively emotionally arousing stimuli (e.g., films of shop accidents, depictions of fatal stabbings, a mock assassination, an actual murder videotaped serendipitously). The studies yielded an unambiguous conclusion: Hypnosis does not improve recall of emotionally arousing events, and arousal level does not mediate hypnotic recall.

CONCLUSIONS

Our review confirms what Bernheim, Janet, and others appreciated more than 100 years ago: Hypnosis can produce false, yet believed-in memories. Today, however, we have a much better understanding of the role of expectancies, individual differences, and contextual factors in pseudo-memory formation. Janet and Bernheim fully recognized the healing potential of hypnosis, which contemporary research suggests should be kept in mind, even as extreme caution about the use of hypnosis for purposes of memory recovery and in forensic situations is warranted. Indeed, hypnosis can play an important role as an adjunctive procedure in a variety of situations, including the treatment of pain, medical conditions, habit problems (e.g., smoking, obesity), anxiety, and depression (see Lynn & Kirsch, 2006).

Our review also supports the skeptical eye that many courts across the United States and other countries have turned toward hypnosis. Even though a variety of suggestive procedures, including misleading questions, may have a deleterious effect on memory that equals or even surpasses that of hypnosis, it neither justifies the use of hypnosis as a recall-enhancement procedure nor implies that hypnotically elicited testimony should be placed before the bar. Still, researchers have much to learn about the relative contribution and potential interaction of expectancies, suggestibility, imagination, and response criteria to pseudomemory reports, both within and apart from the context of hypnosis. Studies that examine hypnotic pseudomemories in naturalistic and forensically relevant, emotion-laden contexts are necessary to better determine the generalizability of findings to the "real world." However, the confluence of evidence indicates that hypnosis is at best a risky and at worst a hazardous recall enhancement procedure.

NOTE

1. Hypnotizability, alternatively termed *hypnotic suggestibility*, is determined by participants' responses to imaginative suggestions (e.g., hallucinations, arm levitation, challenges to resist suggestions) that follow a "hypnotic" induction (i.e., suggestions to experience hypnosis). In experimental studies, hypnotic suggestibility is typically determined by the number of suggestions that participants pass on a standardized scale of hypnotic responsiveness. Approximately 15–20% of participants will test as highly suggestible (pass 9 of 12 suggestions), 15–20% of participants will test as low or nonsuggestible (pass 0–3 suggestions), and the remainder of the participants will test as medium suggestible (4–8 suggestions, 60–70%).

REFERENCES

American Psychological Association, Division 17 Committee on Women, Division 4 Trauma and Gender Issues Committee. (1995, July 25). *Psychotherapy guidelines for working with clients who may have an abuse or trauma history.* Washington, DC: American Psychological Association.

Anderson, C. A., & Sechler, E. S. (1986). Effects of explanation and counterexplanation on the development and use of social theories. *Journal of Personality and Social Psychology, 50,* 24–34.

Barber, T. X. (1969). *Hypnosis: A scientific approach.* New York: Van Nostrand.

Barnier, A. J., & McConkey, K. M. (1992). Reports of real and false memories: The relevance of hypnosis, hypnotizability, and the context of memory test. *Journal of Abnormal Psychology, 101,* 521–527.

Bernheim, H. (1889). *Suggestive therapeutics: A treatise on the nature and uses of hypnotism.* New York: Putnam.

Bernheim, H. (1891/1973). *Hypnotisme, suggestion, psychotherapie; etudes nouvelles.* Paris: Octave Duin. (Trans. Aronson, New York)

Brown, D. (1995). Pseudomemories: The standard of science and the standard of care in trauma treatment. *American Journal of Clinical Hypnosis, 37,* 1–24.

Brown, D., Scheflin, A. W., & Hammond, D. C. (1998). *Memory, trauma treatment, and the law.* New York: Norton.

Bryant, R. A., & Barnier, A. J. (1999). Eliciting autobiographical pseudomemories: The relevance of hypnosis, hypnotizability, and attributions. *International Journal of Clinical and Experimental Hypnosis, 47*(4), 1999.

Burgess, C., & Kirsch, I. (1999). Expectancy information as a moderator of the effects of hypnosis on memory. *Contemporary Hypnosis, 16,* 22–31.

Canadian Psychiatric Association. (1996, March 25). Position statement: Adult recovered memories of childhood sexual abuse. *Canadian Journal of Psychiatry, 41,* 305–306.

Coe, W. C., & Sarbin, T. R. (1991). Role theory: Hypnosis from a dramaturgical and narrational perspective. In S. J. Lynn & J. W. Rhue (Eds.), *Dissociation: Clinical and theoretical perspectives* (pp. 303–323). New York: Guilford.

Dinges, D. F., Whitehouse, W. G., Orne, E. C., Powell, J. W., Orne, M. T., & Erdelyi, M. H. (1992). Evaluating hypnotic memory enhancement (hypermnesia and reminiscence) using multi-trial forced recall. *Journal of Experimental Psychology: Learning, Memory, and Cognition, 18,* 1139–1147.

Dywan, J., & Bowers, K. S. (1983). The use of hypnosis to enhance recall. *Science, 222,* 184–185.

Erdelyi, M. (1994). Hypnotic hypermnesia: The empty set of hypermnesia. *International Journal of Clinical and Experimental Hypnosis, 42,* 379–390.

Fromm, E., & Nash, M. R. (1997). *Psychoanalysis and hypnosis. Mental Health Library Series, Monograph 5.* Madison, CT: International Universities Press.

Grabowski, K. L., Roese, N. J., & Thomas, M. R. (1991). The role of expectancy in hypnotic hypermnesia: A brief communication. *International Journal of Clinical and Experimental Hypnosis, 34,* 193–197.

Green, J. P. (2003). Beliefs about hypnosis: Popular beliefs, misconceptions, and the importance of experience. *International Journal of Clinical and Experimental Hypnosis, 51,* 369–381.

Green, J. P., & Lynn, S. J. (2005). Hypnosis vs. relaxation: Accuracy and confidence in dating international news events. *Applied Cognitive Psychology, 19,* 679–691.

Green, J. P., Lynn, S. J., & Malinoski, P. (1998). Hypnotic pseudomemories, prehypnotic warnings, and the malleability of suggested memories. *Applied Cognitive Psychology, 12,* 431–444.

Gregg, V. H., & Mingay, D. J. (1987). Influence of hypnosis on riskiness and discriminability in recognition memory for faces. *British Journal of Experimental and Clinical Hypnosis, 42*(2), 65–75.

Hall, D. F., Loftus, E. F., & Tousignant, J. P. (1984). Postevent information and changes in recognition for a natural event. In G. Wells and E. Loftus (Eds.), *Eyewitness testimony: Psychological perspectives* (pp. 124–141). Cambridge, England: Cambridge University Press.

Hammond, D. C., Garver, R. B., Mutter, C. B., Crasilneck, H. B., Frischholz, E., Gravitz, M. A., et al. (1995). *Clinical hypnosis and memory: Guidelines for clinicians and for forensic hypnosis.* Des Plaines, IL: American Society of Clinical Hypnosis Press.

Hayward, L., & Ashworth, A. (1980). Some problems of evidence obtained by hypnosis. *Criminal Law Review,* 469–485.

Hirt, E. R., Lynn, S. J., Payne, D. G., Krackow, E., & McCrea, S. M. (1999). Expectancies and memory: Inferring the past from what must have been. In I. Kirsch (Ed.), *How expectancies shape experience* (pp. 93–124). Washington, DC: American Psychological Association.

Hirt, E. R., & Markman, K. D. (1995). Multiple explanation: A consider-an-alternative strategy for debiasing judgments. *Journal of Personality and Social Psychology, 69,* 1069–1086.

Janet, P. (1894). Histoire d'une idee fixe. *Revue Philosophique, 37*(1), 121–163.

Kebble, M. R., & Wagstaff, G. (1998). Hypnotic interviewing: The best way to interview eyewitnesses? *Behavioral Sciences and the Law, 16,* 115–129.

Krackow, E., Lynn, S. J., & Payne, D. G. (2005–2006). The death of Princess Diana: The effects of memory enhancement procedures on flashbulb memories. *Imagination, Cognition, and Personality, 25*(3), 197–219.

Laurence, J.-R. (1982). *Memory creation in hypnosis.* Unpublished doctoral dissertation. Concordia University, Montreal Canada.

Laurence, J.-R., & Perry, C. (1983). Hypnotically created memory among highly hypnotizable participants. *Science, 222,* 523–524.

Lilienfeld, S., Lynn, S. J., Kirsch, I., Chaves, J., Sarbin, T., Ganaway, G., et al. (1999). Dissociative identity disorder and the sociocognitive model: Recalling the lessons of the past. *Psychological Bulletin, 125,* 507–523.

Linton, C. P., & Sheehan, P. W. (1994). The relationship between interrogative suggestibility and susceptibility to hypnosis. *Australian Journal of Clinical and Experimental Hypnosis, 22*(1), 53–64.

Loftus, E. F. (1993). The reality of repressed memories. *American Psychologist, 48,* 518–537.

Lynn, S. J., & Kirsch, I. (2006). *Essentials of clinical hypnosis: An evidence-based approach.* Washington, DC: American Psychological Association.

Lynn, S. J., Kirsch, I., & Hallquist, M. (in press). Social cognitive theories of hypnosis. In M. R. Nash & A. Barinier (Eds.), *The Oxford handbook of hypnosis.* New York/United Kingdom: Oxford University Press.

Lynn, S. J., Lock, T. G., Myers, B., & Payne, D. G. (1997). Recalling the unrecallable: Should hypnosis be used to recover memories in psychotherapy? *Current Directions in Psychological Science, 6,* 79–83.

Lynn, S. J., & McConkey, K. M. (1998). *Truth in memory.* New York: Guilford Press.

Lynn, S. J., Myers, B., & Malinoski, P. (1997). Hypnosis, pseudomemories, and clinical guidelines: A sociocognitive perspective. *NATO ASI series: Series A: Life Sciences, 291,* 305–336.

Lynn, S. J., & Nash, M. R. (1994). Truth in memory: Ramifications for psychotherapy and hypnotherapy. *American Journal of Clinical Hypnosis, 36,* 194–208.

Lynn, S. J., & Rhue, J. W. (1991). *Theories of hypnosis.* New York: Guilford.

Lynn, S. J., Rhue, J. W., Myers, B., & Weekes, J. W. (1994). Pseudomemory and hypnosis: Real versus simulating subjects. *International Journal of Clinical and Experimental Hypnosis, 52,* 118–129.

Malinoski, P., Lynn, S. J., & Sivec, H. (1998). The assessment, validity, and determinants of early memory reports: A critical review. In S. J. Lynn & K. McConkey (Eds.), *Truth in memory.* New York: Guilford.

Markman, K. D., & McMullen, M. N. (2003). A reflection and evaluation model of comparative thinking. *Personality and Social Psychology Review, 7,* 244–267.

Marmelstein, L., & Lynn, S. J. (1999). Expectancies, group, and hypnotic influences on early autobiographical memory reports. *International Journal of Clinical and Experimental Hypnosis, 47,* 301–319.

McCann, T., & Sheehan, P. W. (1988). Hypnotically created pseudomemories: Sampling their conditions among hypnotizable participants. *Journal of Personality and Social Psychology, 54,* 339–346.

McConkey, K. M., & Kinoshita, S. (1988). The influence of hypnosis on memory after 1 day and 1 week. *Journal of Abnormal Psychology, 97,* 48–53.

McConkey, K. M., Labelle, L., Bibb, B. C., & Bryant, R. A. (1990). Hypnosis and suggested pseudomemory: The relevance of test context. *Australian Journal of Psychology, 42,* 197–206.

Mingay, D. J. (1986). Hypnosis and memory for incidentally learned scenes. *British Journal of Experimental and Clinical Hypnosis, 3*(3), 173–183.

Murrey, G. J., Cross, H. J., & Whipple, J. (1992). Hypnotically created pseudomemories: Further investigation into the "memory distortion or response bias" question. *Journal of Abnormal Psychology, 101,* 75–77.

Nash, M. R. (1987). What, if anything, is age regressed about hypnotic age regression? A review of the empirical literature. *Psychological Bulletin, 102,* 42–52.

Neuschatz, J., Lynn, S. J., Benoit, G., & Fite, R. (2003). Hypnosis and memory illusions: An investigation using the Deese/Roediger paradigm. *Imagination, Cognition and Personality, 22,* 3–12.

Nogrady, H., McConkey, K. M., & Perry, C. (1985). Enhancing visual memory: Trying hypnosis, trying imagination, and trying again. *Journal of Abnormal Psychology, 94,* 195–204.

Orne, E. C., Whitehouse, W. G., Dinges, D. F., & Orne, M. T. (1996). Memory liabilities associated with hypnosis: Does low hypnotizability confer immunity? *International Journal of Clinical and Experimental Hypnosis, 44,* 354–369.

Orne, M. T. (1979). The use and misuse of hypnosis in court. *International Journal of Clinical and Experimental Hypnosis, 27,* 311–341.

Orne, M. T., Dinges, D. F., & Bloom, P. B. (1995). Hypnosis. In H. I. Kaplan and B. J. Sadock (Eds.), *Comprehensive textbook of psychiatry VI* (6th ed., pp. 1807–1821). Baltimore: Williams & Wilkins.

Pintar, J., & Lynn, S. J. (in press). *A brief history of hypnosis.* New York: Blackwell.

Polusny, M. A., & Follette, V. M. (1996). Remembering childhood sexual abuse: A national survey of psychologists' clinical practices, beliefs, and personal experiences. *Professional Psychology: Research and Practice, 27,* 41–52.

Poole, D. A., Lindsay, D. S., Memon, A., & Bull, R. (1995). Psychotherapy and the recovery of memories of childhood sexual abuse: U.S. and British practitioners' opinions, practices, and experiences. *Journal of Consulting and Clinical Psychology, 68,* 426–437.

Powell, R. A., & Boer, D. P. (1994). Did Freud mislead patients to confabulate memories of abuse? *Psychological Reports, 74,* 1283–1298.

Putnam, W. H. (1979). Hypnosis and distortions in eyewitness memory. *International Journal of Clinical and Experimental Hypnosis, 28,* 437–488.

Rainer, D. D. (1984). *Eyewitness testimony: Does hypnosis enhance accuracy, distortion and confidence?* Unpublished doctoral dissertation, University of Wyoming, Laramie.

Ready, D. J., Bothwell, R. K., & Brigham, J. C. (1997). The effects of hypnosis, context reinstatement, and anxiety on eyewitness memory. *International Journal of Clinical and Experimental Hypnosis, 45,* 55–68.

Rosen, G. M., Sageman, M., & Loftus, E. (2003). A historical note on false traumatic memories. *Journal of Clinical Psychology, 60,* 137–139.

Sanders, G. S., & Simmons, W. L. (1983). Use of hypnosis to enhance eyewitness accuracy: Does it work? *Journal of Applied Psychology, 68,* 70–77.

Scoboria, A., Mazzoni, G., & Kirsch, I. (2006). Effects of misleading questions and hypnotic memory refreshment on memory reports: A signal detection analysis. *International Journal of Clinical and Experimental Hypnosis, 54,* 340–359.

Scoboria, A., Mazzoni, G., Kirsch, I., & Milling, L. S. (2002). Immediate and persistent effect of misleading questions and hypnosis on memory reports. *Journal of Experimental Psychology: Applied, 8,* 26–32.

Sheehan, P. (1988). Confidence and memory in hypnosis. In H. M. Pettinati (Ed.), *Hypnosis and memory* (pp. 95–127). New York: Guilford.

Sheehan, P. W., Garnett, M., & Robertson, R. (1993). The effects of cue level, hypnotizability, and state instruction on responses to leading questions. *International Journal of Clinical and Experimental Hypnosis, 41,* 287–304.

Sheehan, P. W., Green, V., & Truesdale, P. (1992). Influence of rapport on hypnotically induced pseudomemory. *Journal of Abnormal Psychology, 101,* 690–700.

Sheehan, P. W., & Grigg, L. (1985). Hypnosis, memory, and the acceptance of an implausible cognitive set. *British Journal of Experimental and Clinical Hypnosis, 3,* 5–12.

Sheehan, P. W., Grigg, L., & McCann, T. (1984). Memory distortion following exposure to false information in hypnosis. *Journal of Abnormal Psychology, 93,* 259–265.

Sheehan, P. W., & Linton, C. P. (1993). Parameters influencing response to leading questions. *Australian Journal of Clinical and Experimental Hypnosis, 21*(2), 1–14.

Sheehan, P. W., Statham, D., & Jamieson, G. A. (1991a). Pseudomemory effects and their relationship to level of susceptibility to hypnosis and state instruction. *Journal of Personality and Social Psychology, 60,* 130–137.

Sheehan, P. W., Statham, D., & Jamieson, G. A. (1991b). Pseudomemory effects of time in the hypnotic setting. *Journal of Abnormal Psychology, 100,* 39–44.

Sheehan, P. W., Statham, D., Jamieson, G. A., & Ferguson, S. R. (1991). Ambiguity in suggestion and the occurrence of pseudomemory in the hypnotic setting. *Australian Journal of Clinical and Experimental Hypnosis, 19,* 1–18.

Sheehan, P. W., & Tilden, J. (1983). Effects of suggestibility and hypnosis on accurate and distorted retrieval from memory. *Journal of Experimental Psychology: Learning, Memory, and Cognition, 9,* 293–293.

Sheehan, P. W., & Tilden, J. (1984). Real and simulated occurrences of memory distortion in hypnosis. *Journal of Abnormal Psychology, 93,* 47–57.

Sheehan, P. W., & Tilden, J. (1986). The consistency of occurrences of memory distortion following hypnotic induction. *International Journal of Clinical and Experimental Hypnosis, 34,* 122–137.

Spanos, N. P. (1986). Hypnotic behavior: A social-psychological interpretation of amnesia, analgesia, and "trance logic." *Behavioral and Brain Sciences, 9,* 449–467.

Spanos, N. P., & Bures, E. (1993–1994). Pseudomemory responding in hypnotic, task-motivated and simulating subjects: Memory distortion or reporting bias. *Imagination, Cognition, and Personality, 13,* 303–310.

Spanos, N. P., Burgess, C. A., Burgess, M. F., Samuels, C., & Blois, W. O. (1999). Creating false memories of infancy with hypnotic and non-hypnotic procedures. *Applied Cognitive Psychology, 13*, 201–218.

Spanos, N. P., Gwynn, M. I., Comer, S. L., Baltruweit, W. J., & deGroh, M. (1989). Are hypnotically induced pseudomemories resistant to cross-examination? *Law and Human Behavior, 13*, 271–289.

Spanos, N. P., & McLean, J. (1986). Hypnotically created pseudomemories: Memory distortions or reporting biases? *British Journal of Experimental and Clinical Hypnosis, 3*, 155–159.

Spanos, N. P., Menary, E., Gabora, N. J., DuBreuil, S. C., & Dewhirst, B. (1991). Secondary identity enactments during hypnotic past-life regression: A sociocognitive perspective. *Journal of Personality and Social Psychology, 61*, 308–320.

Spanos, N. P., Quigley, C. A., Gwynn, R. I., Glatt, R. L., & Perlini, A. H. (1991). Hypnotic interrogation, pretrial preparation, and witness testimony during direct and cross-examination. *Law and Human Behavior, 15*, 639–653.

Steblay, N. M., & Bothwell, R. K. (1994). Evidence for hypnotically refreshed testimony: The view from the laboratory. *Law and Human Behavior, 18*, 635–651.

Terrance, C. A., Matheson, K., Allard, C., & Schnarr, J. A. (2000). The role of expectation and memory-retrieval techniques in the construction of beliefs about past events. *Applied Cognitive Psychology, 14*, 361–377.

Timm, H. W. (1981). The effect of forensic hypnosis techniques on eyewitness recall and recognition. *Journal of Police Science and Administration, 9*, 188–194.

Underwager, R., & Wakefield, H. (1998). Recovered memories in the courtroom. In S. J. Lynn, & K. M. McConkey (Eds.), *Truth in memory* (pp. 394–436). New York: Guilford.

Wagstaff, G. (1981). The circle-touch test: Trance-logic, dissociation or demand characteristics? *Contemporary Hypnosis, 14*(1), 16–21.

Wagstaff, G., Traverse, J., & Milner, S. (1982). Hypnosis and eyewitness memory—Two experimental analogues. *Social and Occupational Medicine, 10*, 894–895.

Wagstaff, G. (in press). Hypnosis and the law: Examining the stereotypes. *Criminal Justice and Behavior: An International Journal.*

Weekes, J. R., Lynn, S. J., Green, J. P., & Brentar, J. T. (1992). Pseudomemory in hypnotized and task-motivated participants. *Journal of Abnormal Psychology, 101*, 356–360.

Weekes, J. R., Lynn, S. J., & Myers, B. (1996). *Pseudomemories and hypnosis: The effects of base-rates and event distinctiveness.* Unpublished manuscript, Ohio University, Athens, OH.

Wells, G., & Bradfield, A. L. (1998). "Good," you identified the suspect": Feedback to eyewitnesses distorts their reports of the witnessing experience. *Journal of Applied Psychology, 83*, 360–376.

Whitehouse, W. G., Dinges, D. F., Orne, E. C., & Orne, M. T. (1988). Hypnotic hyperamnesia: Enhanced memory accessibility or report bias? *Journal of Abnormal Psychology, 97*, 289–295.

Whitehouse, W., Orne, E. C., Orne, M. T., & Dinges, D. F. (1991). Distinguishing the source of memories reported prior waking and hypnotic recall attempts. *Applied Cognitive Psychology, 5*, 51–59.

Yapko, M. D. (1994). Suggestibility and repressed memories of abuse: A survey of psychotherapists' beliefs. *American Journal of Clinical Hypnosis, 36*, 194–208.

Yuille, J. C., & McEwan, N. H. (1985). The use of hypnosis as an aid to eyewitness memory. *Journal of Applied Psychology, 70*, 389–400.

Zelig, M., & Beidleman, W. B. (1981). The investigative use of hypnosis: A word of caution. *International Journal of Clinical and Experimental Hypnosis, 29*, 401–412.

8 Episodic Future Thought: Remembering the Past to Imagine the Future

Karl K. Szpunar and Kathleen B. McDermott

INTRODUCTION

Imagine for a moment attending a party for next New Years' Eve. Take 10 s or so to generate a specific mental scene for this upcoming party. Chances are that you can "see" some pretty specific details: You can identify some of the guests, you envision clothes, and you can imagine a configuration of people intermingling in a specific setting—potentially one you know very well. How is it that we are able to envision the future in such a specific way? That question forms the topic of this chapter. Specifically, we examine the capacity for episodic future thought (Atance & O'Neill, 2001) and consider the possibility that recollection of the past is a fundamental component of envisioning the future.

We begin by reviewing the development of the concept of episodic memory and the hypothesis forwarded by Tulving and colleagues that episodic future thought and recollection of the past are tightly intertwined. We consider evidence for this claim from neuropsychological patients with amnesia, from the child development literature, from other special populations, and from neuroimaging. We conclude by considering some of the differences between remembering and episodic future thought (for a related discussion, see Van Boven, Kane, & McGraw, Chapter 9, this volume).

THE CONCEPT OF EPISODIC MEMORY: FROM EVENT MEMORY TO AUTONOETIC CONSCIOUSNESS

Episodic memory, or the ability to remember events from one's personal past (Tulving, 1983, 2002), has a relatively short empirical history. In fact, before 1972 the distinction between episodic memory and semantic memory (declarative knowledge devoid of a sense of reexperiencing the past) had not been acknowledged in the psychological literature (Tulving, 1972). The episodic/semantic distinction has since been embraced by the field, and there now exists a great deal of evidence to suggest that episodic memory represents a dissociable system of the human brain, characterized by its unique function and properties (Schacter & Tulving, 1994; Sherry & Schacter, 1987; Tulving, 1984, 1985a).

At the time of its original conception (Tulving, 1972), episodic memory was framed in terms of the then-prevailing information-processing approach to the study of human memory; that is, the assumption was that processing of event-specific information proceeds through successive stages (i.e., input, storage, output). There was only a vague acknowledgment of the importance of conscious awareness during retrieval. Since then, the concept of episodic memory has been considerably refined, specifically with regard to the conscious awareness associated with reexperiencing the past (Gardiner, 1988; Rajaram, 1993; Tulving, 1985b). In fact, Tulving and his colleagues now consider episodic memory to be one aspect of a more general system that is used for mental time travel (for a recent review, see Szpunar & McDermott, 2008b).

This most recent conceptualization is best captured by the concept of autonoetic consciousness, which is the ability to "both mentally represent and become aware of subjective experiences in the past, present, and future" and is thought to enable "mental time travel in the personal, subjective way that is the hallmark of retrieval from episodic memory" (Wheeler, Stuss, & Tulving, 1997, p. 331). The idea, initially delineated by Tulving (1985b), is roughly that humans possess the ability to mentally represent their personal past and future (see also Suddendorf & Corballis, 1997; Tulving, 2005). That is, just as we can vividly recollect our personal past, we can also, with a seemingly equal level of vividness and efficacy, travel forward in time to preexperience our personal future (Atance & O'Neill, 2001; Buckner & Carroll, 2007; Dudai & Carruthers, 2005; Schacter & Addis, 2007; Szpunar & McDermott, 2007; but see also Van Boven et al., Chapter 9, this volume, for a somewhat different perspective).

Recently, psychologists have directed more empirical attention to understanding the relation between remembering the past and simulating the future. The emerging consensus appears to be that the ability to simulate personal future events relies on the ability to remember the past. Corballis (2003; Suddendorf & Corballis, 1997) posited that in simulating the future we recursively sample elements of remembered events (e.g., people, places, objects, etc.) to help generate a virtually unlimited number of potential future scenarios. According to this view, episodic memory represents an inherently constructive system that enables people to simulate both their personal past and future (Schacter & Addis, 2007).

An implication of this suggestion is that there should be considerable overlap in the psychological and neural processes involved in remembering the past and simulating the future. Next, we discuss an emerging set of empirical findings in support of this hypothesis. Specifically, it has been shown that personal past and future thought can be selectively impaired in patient populations typically associated with deficits of episodic memory (e.g., Addis, Wong, & Schacter, in press; D'Argembeau, Raffard, & Van der Linden, in press; Klein, Loftus, & Kihlstrom, 2002; Tulving, 1985b; Williams et al., 1996), that personal past and future thought emerge together in ontogenetic development (e.g., Busby & Suddendorf, 2005; Suddendorf & Busby, 2005), and that both share common neural correlates (Addis, Wong, & Schacter, 2007; Okuda et al., 2003; Szpunar, Watson, & McDermott, 2007) traditionally associated solely with remembering the past (Maguire, 2001).

METHOD OF ASSESSMENT

Before considering the data, we introduce some background with regard to the method by which episodic future thought is typically assessed. Generally, participants are required to mentally generate hypothetical future scenarios (e.g., I am with my close friends, and we are enjoying a night out at our favorite restaurant ...) in response to word cues (e.g., restaurant) or event cues (e.g., New Year's Eve). To ensure that participants are able to produce detailed mental images, researchers explain to participants that their simulations need not necessarily be related to the cues themselves. That is, participants are encouraged to elaborate on the first event that comes to mind.

Following event generation, participants are asked to rate their mental images on a variety of phenomenological characteristics (e.g., vividness). These ratings are typically completed on a trial-by-trial basis, but participants may also be asked to provide such ratings only after all events have been imagined (see Szpunar et al., 2007). Finally, to compare the likeness of episodic future thought to episodic memory, researchers ensure that participants remember (and rate) an equal number of specific events as they imagine.

AMNESIA

The suggestion that remembering the past and simulating the future may share many component processes was first proposed to the field of psychology by Tulving (1985b), who observed in amne-

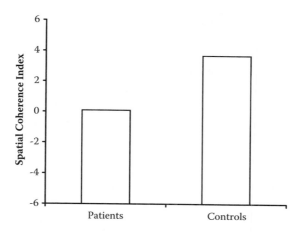

FIGURE 8.1   Average patient and control participant ratings of spatial coherence for mental images of novel future events. Spatial coherence index score ranged between −6 (totally fragmented) to +6 (completely integrated). (Adapted from "Patients With Hippocampal Amnesia Cannot Imagine New Experiences," by D. Hassabis, D. Kumaran, D. S. Vann, and E. A. Maguire, 2007, *Proceedings of the National Academy of Sciences of the United States of America, 104,* 1726–1731.)

sic patient K. C. a complementary inability to perform either task. Patient K. C. became amnesic following brain trauma to his frontal and medial temporal lobes. When asked to report on his personal past or future (e.g., What did you do yesterday? What will you do tomorrow?), patient KC would say that his mind was blank. Furthermore, when asked to compare the phenomenological experience of remembering his past and simulating his future, K. C. would report that both were associated with "the same kind of blankness" (Tulving, 1985b, p. 4).

A more in-depth analysis relating personal past and future thought in amnesia was subsequently reported by Klein, Loftus, and Kihlstrom (2002). Klein et al. studied patient D. B., who had become amnesic following an anoxic episode. As had Tulving (1985b), Klein et al. examined the extent to which patient D. B. was able to remember the personal past and simulate personal future events. Importantly, Klein et al. also asked patient D. B. to think about the past and future from an impersonal perspective (e.g., discuss a general concern for the world in the past/next few decades). As with patient K. C., patient D. B. possessed a profound inability to think about the personal past and future. However, D. B. performed at normal levels (relative to control participants) when thinking about the past and future in a nonpersonal manner. This particular pattern of data highlights the specific (episodic) nature of deficit observed in such patients.

Hassabis, Kumaran, Vann, and Maguire (2007) examined the ability of 5 amnesic patients, with brain damage limited to the hippocampal region, and 10 age-matched control participants to mentally construct novel future scenarios. Relative to control participants, the mental images generated by amnesic patients were particularly deficient in terms of spatial coherence. For instance, when cued to generate a novel future event occurring in the context of an exotic beach, one patient was only able to imagine the sky, whereas control participants conjured highly detailed and integrated scenarios (see Figure 8.1). Hassabis et al. suggested that both remembering the past and simulating the future rely on an intact medial temporal lobe system (particularly the hippocampus), which is believed to be integral to binding together basic elements from memory into a coherent mental image (Cohen et al., 1999; Eichenbaum, 2001; Miller, 2007).

It is important to note that the above-mentioned case reports represent but a few of hundreds of reported cases on amnesia. Thus, a great deal of caution must be exercised in considering such data, at least until they are further corroborated by future investigations. Nonetheless, these studies present an intriguing case for the hypothesis that mentally simulating the future relies on remembering the past, and confidence is gained when considering converging lines of evidence. Next, we turn our attention to studies relating past and future thought in aging and development.

AGING AND DEVELOPMENT

Research involving young children and older adults has recently noted a close coupling of the ability to mentally simulate the personal past and future. With regard to younger children, an extensive body of literature indicates that the ability to mentally reexperience a past event does not emerge until approximately the age of 4 years (Szpunar & McDermott, 2008b; Wheeler, 2000a, 2000b; Wheeler et al., 1997). Although children under the age of 4 are able to report on past events (Bauer & Werenka, 1995; Howe & Courage, 1993), their ability to do so is based largely on knowing about the semantic contents of those events and not on reexperiencing the spatial and temporal details associated with those contents (Gopnik & Graf, 1988; O'Neill & Gopnik, 1991; Wimmer, Hogrefe, & Perner, 1988).

Developmental psychologists have begun to consider that the emergence of the ability to simulate personal future events may coincide with the emergence of the ability to vividly recollect the past. In one study, Hudson, Shapiro, and Sosa (1995) reported that the ability to plan for specific future events gradually improves between the ages of 3 and 5 years. Although we believe it important to differentiate between episodic future thought and planning, this development of planning strategies may emerge as a result of the development of episodic future thought. More recently, Busby and Suddendorf (2005) examined the ability of children aged between 3 and 5 years to report on both personal past (e.g., What did you do yesterday?) and future events (e.g., What will you do tomorrow?). The authors found that although 3-year-olds had difficulty with remembering the past and simulating the future, 4- and 5-year-olds were proficient at both tasks (see Figure 8.2).

One common criticism of studies relating past and future thought in children emerges from the reliance of experimental procedures on verbal protocols. Although research suggests that time-related terms appear within children's speech by the age of 3 (e.g., Veneziano & Sinclair, 1995), such terms are often implemented inaccurately (Clark, 1973). Hence, based on studies employing the use of verbal protocols, it remains uncertain whether children under the age of 4 lack the ability for mental time travel, or rather the ability to describe the experience. Confidence is gained, however, through the use of nonverbal tasks.

Suddendorf and Busby (2005) recently conducted an experiment in which they presented children (ages 3 to 5) with what they call the "rooms task." The experiment required that children initially visit one room, which either contained an empty puzzle board (experimental group) or not

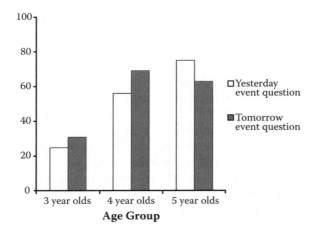

FIGURE 8.2 Percentage of 3-, 4-, and 5-year-old children producing correct answers in response to remembering the past and simulating the future. (Adapted from "Recalling Yesterday and Predicting Tomorrow," by J. Busby and T. Suddendorf, 2005, *Cognitive Development, 20,* 362–372.)

(control group). The children were then momentarily taken to a second room, where they played with other unrelated toys. Finally, the children were told that they would return to the first room, and that they could take one of four toys back with them (one of which was a puzzle set). The critical observation was whether the children in the experimental group would be more likely to take the puzzle set back to the first room. The authors found that this was the case for both 4- and 5-year-old children but not for 3-year-olds. A similar set of findings, using various nonverbal tasks, has been reported (Atance & Meltzoff, 2005; Atance & O'Neill, 2005). In general, it appears that the ability for children to mentally consider a state that they are not currently experiencing does not emerge until approximately 4 years of age (see also Saxe, Chapter 17, this volume).

As with young children, it has been well documented that aging is accompanied by declines in episodic memory function (Craik & Salthouse, 2000). For instance, Levine, Svoboda, Hay, Winocur, and Moscovitch (2002) have shown that, relative to younger participants, older adults recall fewer episodic details when remembering events from their past. Addis et al. (in press) have reported that this episodic deficit extends to mental simulations of the future. In their experiment, participants (both young and old) were asked to generate personal past and future events in response to a series of word cues (e.g., dress). Addis et al. found that the verbal protocols of older adults were characterized by a lack of episodic detail for remembered events and simulated future scenarios. The authors argued that this complementary deficit supports the hypothesis that the contents of memory are regularly sampled in constructing novel future scenarios (D'Argembeau & Van der Linden, 2004, 2006; Schacter & Addis, 2007; Szpunar & McDermott, in press-a). As discussed next, a similar pattern of deficit has been reported using various clinical populations.

CLINICAL POPULATIONS

As with most empirical analyses of episodic memory, research on patients with depression (Evans, Williams, O'Loughlin, & Howells, 1992; Williams, 1996; Williams & Broadbent, 1986; Williams & Dritschel, 1988) and schizophrenia (Danion et al., 2005; Feinstein, Goldberg, Nowlin, & Weinberger, 1998; Riutort, Cuervo, Danion, Peretti, & Salame, 2003; Wood, Brewin, & McLeod, 2006) has focused on the recollection of past events. In general, both patient groups typically produce impoverished and unspecified accounts of their personal past. Williams et al. (1996) extended such findings for patients with depression to include a decreased level of specificity associated with simulating personal future events. Specifically, patients with depression and nondepressed control participants were required to generate personal past and future scenarios in response to a variety of sentence cues (e.g., imagine an event that would make you feel proud). Patients with depression generated memories and mental images of the future that were less specific than those of control participants. Furthermore, the specificity associated with past and future thought was highly correlated within participants ($r = 0.57$). That is, participants (depressed or control) who remembered vivid memories were more likely to generate vivid mental images of the future. This pattern of data (also reported by Addis et al., 2008) further corroborates the hypothesis that common component processes mediate mental simulations of the personal past and future.

A study by D'Argembeau et al. (2008) has reported a similar pattern of data using patients with schizophrenia. In general, it appears that subject populations known to be limited in their ability to remember specific events from their past also possess a complementary inability to mentally simulate personal future events. Next, we consider evidence from brain imaging. If the ability to simulate the future does rely on the ability to remember the past, then simulating the future should engage neural correlates normally associated with remembering the past. Indeed, this appears to be the case.

EVIDENCE FROM BRAIN IMAGING

Functional neuroimaging techniques, such as positron emission tomography (PET) and functional magnetic resonance imaging (fMRI), allow neuroscientists to examine brain activity associated

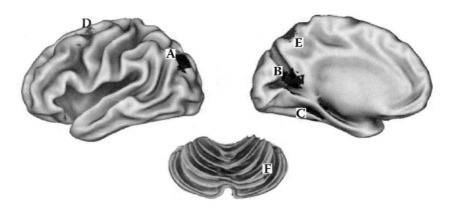

FIGURE 8.3 Brain regions exhibiting similarities (A–C) and differences (D–F) during remembering the past and simulating the future. Regions showing similarities appear within A, superior occipital cortex; B, posterior cingulate cortex; and C, medial temporal lobes. Regions showing differences appear within D, lateral premotor cortex; E, medial posterior parietal cortex; and F, right posterior cerebellum.

with mental activity. When participants in a research study engage in a given cognitive task, PET or fMRI can provide information about the level of cerebral blood flow (PET) or blood oxygenation level (fMRI) in the particular parts of the brain involved in performing the task.

In the typical design of a neuroimaging study, brain activity associated with two tasks is contrasted with the hope of isolating the brain regions that are important for the cognitive process of interest. In most cases, researchers attempt to contrast a pair of tasks that are similar to one another but vary in one key way. For instance, to identify the brain regions that are important for episodic memory, the tasks contrasted might both require the retrieval of a personal memory, but only one requires the recollection of a specific time and place. For example, requiring a person to remember a specific feature of her first day of high school (a task that would place clear demands on episodic memory) might be compared with requiring the person to retrieve the name of the high school she attended. Both tasks require the retrieval of a personal memory, but naming the high school does not involve recollecting experiences at a specific time and place in the past.

In an fMRI study, Szpunar et al. (2007) set out to identify brain regions that might be important for representing oneself in time and then to examine those regions to see whether they are similarly engaged by past and future thought. To accomplish this goal, Szpunar et al. asked study participants to perform a set of three tasks while lying in a scanner. In two of these tasks, participants viewed a series of event cues (e.g., birthday party) and were asked to envision either a personal memory of that kind of event or one that might take place in the future. Brain activity common to both tasks (past and future) was contrasted with that observed during a third task. This task involved similar processes, such as mental construction of lifelike scenarios, but did not involve representing oneself in time. The specific control task required participants to imagine former U.S. president Bill Clinton.

As can be seen in Figure 8.3, several regions in the brain's posterior cortex (A–C) were similarly engaged during personal past and future thought but not during the control task. These regions were located in the occipital cortex, the posterior cingulate cortex, and the medial temporal lobes. Previous research had shown that these regions are consistently engaged during autobiographical memory retrieval (Maguire, 2001; Svoboda, McKinnon, & Levine, 2006). Szpunar et al. (2007) hypothesized that asking participants to envision a personal future scenario likely required similar processes. That is, to effectively generate a plausible image of the future, participants reactivate contextual associations from memory (cf. Bar, 2004, 2007; Bar & Aminoff, 2003). Postexperiment questionnaires indicated that participants did tend to imagine future scenarios in the context of familiar settings and people.

Hypotheses based on exploratory research, such as identifying the neural relation of past and future thought, are significantly strengthened if the results can be replicated. Indeed, Addis et al. (2007) have presented a similar set of data. In their study, participants were given cue words (e.g., car) and asked to remember a past event or to envision themselves in the future. Once the event was "in mind," they were to press a button and then to keep thinking about the event. Relative to baseline tasks that involved sentence generation and imagery, thinking about past and future episodes led to equivalent activity in a set of posterior cortical regions consistently implicated in episodic memory (e.g., medial temporal lobes, posterior parietal cortex) and similar to those reported by Szpunar et al. (2007; see also Okuda et al., 2003, for a relevant study conducted using PET). In sum, brain regions known to be important for remembering the past appear to play an important role in simulating future events.

DIFFERENTIATING PAST AND FUTURE

Thus far, we have considered evidence from clinical, aging, and healthy human populations corroborating the hypothesis that personal past and future thought are closely related and involve similar processes. One issue that has yet to receive much attention is how the human mind/brain is able to distinguish between the experience of remembering the past and that of simulating the future.

Indeed, a similar issue—the differentiation of memory from imagination—has long been a topic of philosophical and psychological debate. In general, memories are characterized by greater sensory detail than are images of imagination (e.g., Hume, 1739/1978; Johnson & Raye, 1981), including those based on mentally projecting oneself into the future (D'Argembeau & Van der Linden, 2004, 2006; Szpunar & McDermott, 2008a; Van Boven et al., Chapter 9, this volume). Some images based on imagination can be more vivid than some memories, however, and yet we are consistently able to distinguish memory from imagination (see Brewer, 1995, for a more in depth discussion).

An alternative possibility, proposed by Hume and others (e.g., Earle, 1956; Johnson, Foley, Suengas, & Raye, 1988), is that images of imagination (including those projected into the future) are consciously experienced as requiring more construction than remembering (see also Sanna, Schwarz, & Kennedy, Chapter 13, this volume). In relation to the present topic of discussion, remembering the personal past requires reconstructing an event that has already taken place (with constructive processes contributing, too), but imagining a future event requires actively and continuously constructing a new scenario. The future event has not yet taken place, so it is up to the individual to decide where the event is taking place, who is there, and what they are doing.

Consider again the neural relation between personal past and future thought. Neither Addis et al. (2007) nor Szpunar et al. (2007) found a single region of the brain that was preferentially engaged as participants remembered past events relative to future events. However, Addis et al. did report greater hippocampal activity associated with simulating the future. The authors argued that although remembering the past and simulating the future both involve sampling the contents of memory, those contents must be bound in novel ways when simulating the future (see also Corballis, 2003).

Furthermore, Szpunar et al. (2007) also reported various brain regions that consistently showed activity differences in favor of simulating the future relative to remembering the past. These regions appeared within lateral premotor cortex, medial posterior parietal cortex, and posterior cerebellum (see Figure 8.3; D–F). Szpunar et al. noted that similar regions have been identified in studies that require participants to mentally simulate motor movements (e.g., Beilock & Lyons, Chapter 2, this volume; Decety & Grezes, 2006; Decety & Stevens, Chapter 1, this volume; Grezes & Decety, 2001). The authors suggested that these regions are preferentially engaged in simulating the future because stored action representations must be combined in novel ways based on the nature of the scenario participants conjure (e.g., What am I doing today after I eat breakfast?).

Based on these preliminary reports, it appears as though it may be the degree of generative and consciously constructive processing that serves to distinguish remembering the past and simulating the future. Of course, future research will need to test these claims.

SUMMARY

In this chapter, we have examined the hypothesis that the ability to simulate one's future is related to one's ability to remember the past. Based on our review of the preliminary data, we believe that the following statements generally support this hypothesis: (a) Those who lack the ability to remember their past appear also to be unable to think about themselves in the future; and (b) brain regions known to play an important role in remembering one's past become similarly engaged as people simulate personal future events.

Episodic memory has been the subject of experimental interest for over 35 years. Until recently, the focus of this research has been unequivocally directed toward understanding how humans represent their personal past. At the same time, there has been surprisingly little inquiry into our ability to mentally represent the future (for an exception, see Amit, Algom, Trope, & Liberman, Chapter 4, this volume). We believe that the coming years will see an increase in the number of studies of how the brain enables us to mentally represent future thought and how future thought may be related to and distinguished from memory.

Importantly, there will also be a need for future research to consider the nature in which episodic future thought is conceptualized and how the concept is assessed. Until now, there has been little consideration of how episodic future thought is differentiated from related concepts such as imagination and daydreaming (for a review, see Klinger, Chapter 15, this volume). For instance, does mentally projecting an imaginary event into the future make it any different from imagining it in the present? We suspect it might, but the nature of this supposed difference remains an empirical question.

As discussed in this chapter, a general method for examining episodic future thought now exists by which participants generate mental images and rate their phenomenological characteristics. Whether the study of episodic future thought might expand beyond a reliance on subjective introspection is yet to be seen. Experimenter analyses of verbal protocols (e.g., D'Argembeau & Van der Linden, 2004) and neuroimaging data represent steps toward a more objective understanding of the concept.

REFERENCES

Addis, D. R., Wong, A. T., & Schacter, D. L. (2007). Remembering the past and imagining the future: Common and distinct neural substrates during event construction and elaboration. *Neuropsychologia, 45,* 1363–1377.

Addis, D. R., Wong, A. T., & Schacter, D. L. (2008). Age-related changes in the episodic simulation of future events. *Psychological Science, 19,* 33–41.

Atance, C. M., & Meltzoff, A. N. (2005). My future self: Young children's ability to anticipate and explain future states. *Cognitive Development, 20,* 341–361.

Atance, C. M., & O'Neill, D. K. (2001). Episodic future thinking. *Trends in Cognitive Sciences, 5,* 533–539.

Atance, C. M., & O'Neill, D. K. (2005). The emergence of episodic future thinking in humans. *Learning and Motivation, 36,* 126–144.

Bar, M. (2004). Visual objects in context. *Nature Reviews Neuroscience, 5,* 617–629.

Bar, M. (2007). The proactive brain: Using analogies and associations to generate predictions. *Trends in Cognitive Sciences, 11,* 280–289.

Bar, M., & Aminoff, E. (2003). Cortical analysis of context. *Neuron, 38,* 347–358.

Bauer, P. J., & Werenka, S. S. (1995). One- to two-year olds' recall of events: The more expressed, the more impressed. *Journal of Experimental Child Psychology, 59,* 475–496.

Brewer, W. F. (1995). What is recollective memory? In D. Rubin (Ed.), *Remembering our past: Studies in autobiographical memory* (pp. 19–66). Cambridge, England: Cambridge University Press.

Buckner, R. L., & Carroll, D. C. (2007). Self-projection and the brain. *Trends in Cognitive Sciences, 11*, 49–57.

Busby, J., & Suddendorf, T. (2005). Recalling yesterday and predicting tomorrow. *Cognitive Development, 20*, 362–372.

Clark, E. V. (1973). On the acquisition of "before" and "after." *Journal of Verbal Learning and Verbal Behavior, 10*, 266–275.

Cohen, N. J., Ryan, J., Hunt, C., Romine, L., Wszalek, T., & Nash, C. (1999). Hippocampal system and declarative (relational) memory: Summarizing the data from functional neuroimaging studies. *Hippocampus, 9*, 83–98.

Corballis, M. C. (2003). Recursion as the key to the human mind. In K. Sterelny & J. Fitness (Eds.), *From mating to mentality: Evaluating evolutionary psychology* (pp. 155–171). New York: Psychology Press.

Craik, F. I. M., & Salthouse, T. A. (Eds.). (2000). *Handbook of aging and cognition* (2nd ed.). Hillsdale, NJ: Erlbaum.

D'Argembeau, A., Raffard, S., & Van der Linden, M. (2008). Remembering the past and imagining the future in schizophrenia. *Journal of Abnormal Psychology, 117*, 247–251.

D'Argembeau, A., & Van der Linden, M. (2004). Phenomenal characteristics associated with projecting oneself back into the past and forward into the future: Influence of valence and temporal distance. *Consciousness and Cognition, 13*, 844–858.

D'Argembeau, A., & Van der Linden, M. (2006). Individual differences in the phenomenology of mental time travel: The effect of vivid imagery and emotion regulation. *Consciousness and Cognition, 15*, 342–350.

Danion, J. M., Cuervo, C., Piolino, P., Huron, C., Riutort, M., Peretti, C. S., et al. (2005). Conscious recollection in autobiographical memory: An investigation in schizophrenia. *Consciousness and Cognition, 14*, 535–547.

Decety, J., & Grezes, J. (2006). The power of simulation: Imagining one's own and other's behavior. *Brain Research, 1079*, 4–14.

Dudai, Y., & Carruthers, M. (2005). The Janus face of mnemosyne. *Nature, 434*, 823–824.

Earle, W. (1956). Memory. *Review of Metaphysics, 10*, 3–27.

Eichenbaum, H. (2001). The hippocampus and declarative memory: Cognitive mechanisms and neural codes. *Behavioral Brain Research, 127*, 199–207.

Evans, J., Williams, J. M. G., O'Loughlin, S., & Howells, K. (1992). Autobiographical memory and problem-solving strategies of parasuicide patients. *Psychological Medicine, 22*, 399–405.

Feinstein, A., Goldberg, T. E., Nowlin, B., & Weinberger, D. R. (1998). Types and characteristics of remote memory impairment in schizophrenia. *Schizophrenia Research, 30*, 155–163.

Gardiner, J. M. (1988). Functional aspects of recollective experience. *Memory & Cognition, 16*, 309–313.

Gopnik, A., & Graf, P. (1988). Knowing how you know: Young children's ability to identify and remember the sources of their beliefs. *Child Development, 59*, 1366–1371.

Grezes, J., & Decety, J. (2001). Functional anatomy of execution, mental simulation, observation, and verb generation of actions: A meta-analysis. *Human Brain Mapping, 12*, 1–19.

Hassabis, D., Kumaran, D., Vann, D. S., & Maguire, E. A. (2007). Patients with hippocampal amnesia cannot imagine new experiences. *Proceedings of the National Academy of Sciences of the United States of America, 104*, 1726–1731.

Howe, M. L., & Courage, M. L. (1993). On resolving the enigma of infantile amnesia. *Psychological Bulletin, 113*, 305–326.

Hudson, J. A., Shapiro, L. R., & Sosa, B. B. (1995). Planning in the real world: Preschool children's scripts and plans for familiar events. *Child Development, 66*, 984–998.

Hume, D. (1739/1978). *A treatise of human nature* (2nd ed.). Oxford, England: Clarendon Press.

Johnson, M. K., Foley, M. A., Suengas, A. G., & Raye, C. L. (1988). Phenomenal characteristics of memories for perceived and imagined autobiographical events. *Journal of Experimental Psychology: General, 117*, 371–376.

Johnson, M. K., & Raye, C. L. (1981). Reality monitoring. *Psychological Review, 88*, 67–85.

Klein, S. B., Loftus, J., & Kihlstrom, J. F. (2002). Memory and temporal experience: The effects of episodic memory loss on an amnesic patient's ability to remember the past and imagine the future. *Social Cognition, 20*, 353–379.

Levine, B., Svoboda, E., Hay, J. F., Winocur, G., & Moscovitch, M. (2002). Aging and autobiographical memory: Dissociating episodic from semantic retrieval. *Psychology and Aging, 17*, 677–689.

Maguire, E. A. (2001). Neuroimaging studies of autobiographical memory. *Philosophical Transactions of the Royal Society of London: B, 356,* 1441–1451.

Miller, G. (2007). A surprising connection between memory and imagination. *Science, 315,* 312.

Okuda, J., Fujii, T., Ohtake, H., Tsukiura, T., Tanji, K., Suzuki, K., et al. (2003). Thinking of the future and past: The roles of the frontal pole and the medial temporal lobes. *NeuroImage, 19,* 1369–1380.

O'Neill, D. K., & Gopnik, A. (1991). Young children's ability to identify the sources of their beliefs. *Developmental Psychology, 27,* 134–147.

Rajaram, S. (1993). Remembering and knowing: Two means of access to the personal past. *Memory & Cognition, 21,* 89–102.

Riutort, M., Cuervo, C., Danion, J. M., Peretti, C. S., & Salame, P. (2003). Reduced levels of specific autobiographical memories in schizophrenia. *Psychiatry Research, 117,* 35–45.

Roediger, H. L., & McDermott, K. B. (1995). Creating false memories: Remembering words not presented in lists. *Journal of Experimental Psychology: Learning, Memory, and Cognition, 21,* 803–814.

Schacter, D. L., & Addis, D. R. (2007). The cognitive neuroscience of constructive memory: Remembering the past and imagining the future. *Philosophical Transactions of the Royal Society of London: B, 362,* 773–786.

Schacter, D. L., & Tulving, E. (1994). What are the memory systems of 1994? In D. L. Schacter & E. Tulving (Eds.), *Memory systems 1994.* Cambridge, MA: MIT Press.

Sherry, D. L., & Schacter, D. L. (1987). The evolution of multiple memory systems. *Psychological Review, 94,* 439–454.

Suddendorf, T., & Busby, J. (2005). Making decisions with the future in mind: Developmental and comparative identification of mental time travel. *Learning and Motivation, 36,* 110–125.

Suddendorf, T., & Corballis, M. C. (1997). Mental time travel and the evolution of the human mind. *Genetic, Social, and General Psychology Monographs, 123,* 133–167.

Svoboda, E., McKinnon, M. C., & Levine, B. (2006). The functional neuroanatomy of autobiographical memory: A meta-analysis. *Neuropsychologia, 44,* 2189–2208.

Szpunar, K. K., & McDermott, K. B. (2007). Remembering the past to imagine the future. *Cerebrum, February.*

Szpunar, K. K., & McDermott, K. B. (2008a). Episodic future thought and its relation to remembering: Evidence from ratings of subjective experience. *Consciousness and Cognition, 17,* 330–334.

Szpunar, K. K., & McDermott, K. B. (2008b). Episodic memory: An evolving concept. In D. Sweat, R. Menzel, H. Eichenbaum, & H. L. Roediger III (Eds.), *Learning and memory: A comprehensive reference.* Elsevier.

Szpunar, K. K., Watson, J. M., & McDermott, K. B. (2007). Neural substrates of envisioning the future. *Proceedings of the National Academy of Sciences of the United States of America, 104,* 642–647.

Tulving, E. (1972). Episodic and semantic memory. In E. Tulving & W. Donaldson (Eds.), *Organization of memory* (pp. 381–403). New York: Academic Press.

Tulving, E. (1983). *Elements of episodic memory.* New York: Oxford University Press.

Tulving, E. (1984). Relations among components and processes of memory. *Behavioral Brain Science, 7,* 257–268.

Tulving, E. (1985a). How many memory systems are there? *American Psychologist, 40,* 385–398.

Tulving, E. (1985b). Memory and consciousness. *Canadian Psychology, 26,* 1–12.

Tulving, E. (2002). Episodic memory: From mind to brain. *Annual Review of Psychology, 53,* 1–25.

Tulving, E. (2005). Episodic memory and autonoesis: Uniquely human? In H. S. Terrace & J. Metcalfe (Eds.), *The missing link in cognition: Origins of self-reflective consciousness* (pp. 3–56). New York: Oxford University Press.

Veneziano, E., & Sinclair, H. (1995). Functional changes in early child language: The appearance of references to the past and of explanations. *Journal of Child Language, 22,* 557–581.

Wheeler, M. A. (2000a). Episodic memory and autonoetic consciousness. In E. Tulving & F. I. M. Craik (Eds.), *Oxford handbook of memory* (pp. 597–608). New York: Oxford University Press.

Wheeler, M. A. (2000b). Varieties of consciousness and memory. In E. Tulving (Ed.), *Memory, consciousness, and the brain: The Tallinn Conference* (pp. 188–199). Philadelphia: Psychology Press.

Wheeler, M. A., Stuss, D. T., & Tulving, E. (1997). Toward a theory of episodic memory: The frontal lobes and autonoetic consciousness. *Psychological Bulletin, 121,* 331–354.

Williams, J. M. G. (1996). The specificity of autobiographical memory in depression. In D. Rubin (Ed.), *Remembering our past: Studies in autobiographical memory* (pp. 271–296). Cambridge, England: Cambridge University Press.

Williams, J. M. G., & Broadbent, K. (1986). Autobiographical memory in suicide attempters. *Journal of Abnormal Psychology, 94*, 144–149.

Williams, J. M. G., & Dritschel, B. (1988). Emotional disturbance and the specificity of autobiographical memory. *Cognition and Emotion, 2*, 221–234.

Williams, J. M. G., Ellis, N. C., Tyers, C., Healy, H., Rose, G., & MacLeod, A. K. (1996). The specificity of autobiographical memory and imaginability of the future. *Memory and Cognition, 24*, 116–125.

Wimmer, H., Hogrefe, G.-J., & Perner, J. (1988). Children's understanding of information access as a source of knowledge. *Child Development, 59*, 386–396.

Wood, N., Brewin, C. R., & McLeod, H. J. (2006). Autobiographical memory deficits in schizophrenia. *Cognition and Emotion, 20*, 336–347.

9 Temporally Asymmetric Constraints on Mental Simulation: Retrospection Is More Constrained Than Prospection

Leaf Van Boven, Joanne Kane, and A. Peter McGraw

INTRODUCTION

"A long time ago, in a galaxy far, far away ..." So read the opening lines of each of the *Star Wars* films, which have captured the fascination of science fiction fans for more than 30 years. Among the many captivating features of *Star Wars*—the Jawas, Darth Vader, and the mysterious "force"—fans' fantasies were also engaged by the supposition that a futuristic society with space travel, intelligent androids, and multicultural alien life existed not in the future, as we might expect, but in the past. Technologically fantastic worlds are supposed to take place not in the past but in the future—like *1984* (published in 1949) or *2001: A Space Odyssey* (released in 1968). Futuristic fantasies framed in the past tense are puzzling; they linger in the mind as we try to reconcile the notion of a fantastically "futuristic" past with the suspicion that our ancestors were inventing wheels and hunting woolly mammoths rather than flying X-wing spacecraft and battling with light sabers.

In this chapter, we explore whether the peculiarity of contemplating a futuristically fantastical past might reflect an important facet of mental simulation in the past versus future tense (in addition to being good science fiction). We hypothesize that past tense mental simulation (retrospection) feels different and is more constrained—more subject to "reality checks"—than is future tense mental simulation (prospection). We also hypothesize that temporally asymmetric constraints on retrospection render it phenomenologically different from prospection (i.e., more effortful and difficult) and lead retrospection to yield predictably different outcomes from those that follow from prospection.

To illustrate the temporally asymmetric constraints on mental simulation, we invite readers to try a thought experiment (or, better yet, administer a thought experiment in a between-persons fashion to indulgent friends or family members). Mentally simulate a first-class tropical vacation in the British Virgin Islands that either took place 2 years in the past or will take place 2 years in the future. How does it feel to retrospect versus prospect? How does the simulated vacation seem different in the past versus future?

We suspect that both retrospective and prospective simulations will involve a good number of realistic details—sandy beaches, sunny days, and warm waters. But, we suspect that compared with the future tense simulations, the past tense simulations will also include contextual details of the past that actually was: those persistent love handles, needing to squeeze in the vacation between winter professional conferences, the financial constraints that would have reined in the tropical adventure, and so on. Even though the retrospective vacation may be as detailed as the prospective vacation, the retrospective details may be more realistic, informed by the past that was, than the prospective details. The prospective details may therefore be more prototypical and extreme (e.g., clear blue skies *every* day of the trip). More generally, we argue that the greater constraints on retrospection than prospection reflect a general temporal asymmetry in retrospection and prospection.

The possibility that retrospection is more constrained than prospection has important theoretical implications because most theories regarding time's effect on thinking, feeling, and deciding are agnostic with respect to tense. These theories include the effect of time on discounting future outcomes (e.g., Harris & Laibson, 2001; Loewenstein, 1992); self-control (Metcalfe & Mischel, 1999); memory decay (Schacter, 1996), construal level (Amit, Algom, Trope, & Liberman, Chapter 4, this volume; Trope & Liberman, 2003); and predictions of adaptation to emotional events (Dunn, Forrin, & Ashton-James, Chapter 22, this volume; Gilbert, Gill, & Wilson, 2002; Gilbert, Pinel, Wilson, Blumberg, & Wheatley, 1998). In each case, people are thought to respond differently to events that are close and far in time (see also Perunovic & Wilson, Chapter 23, this volume).

Although previous theories provide many insights into temporal *distance's* effect on feeling, thinking, and behaving, they provide limited insight into temporal *tense's* effects on feeling, thinking, and behaving. To the degree that there exist temporal asymmetries in retrospection and prospection—and we suggest that there are—existing theories of temporal distance are descriptively incomplete and in need of reexamination and revision. In this chapter, we offer a simple principle about temporal asymmetries in mental simulation—that reality considerations constrain retrospection more than prospection—that we hope will guide theoretical refinement and empirical study.

In this chapter, we review previous work from diverse research domains supporting the hypothesis that reality considerations tend to constrain retrospection more than prospection. We then explore preliminary evidence implying that these everyday differences are mirrored in different subjective experiences and outcomes associated with retrospection and prospection. We conclude with a discussion of theoretical implications and potential moderators of temporally asymmetric constraints on mental simulation.

EVERYDAY DIFFERENCES BETWEEN RETROSPECTION AND PROSPECTION

Relative to our personal pasts and futures, the present is vanishingly brief. Not surprisingly, then, people spend a great deal of time and psychic energy engaged in mental time travel, looking back to the past and forward to the future (Atance & O'Neill, 2001; Johnson & Sherman, 1990; Szpunar & McDermott, Chapter 8, this volume; Tulving, 2002). Given the frequency with which people mentally travel in time, it is somewhat surprising to consider the paucity of research directly comparing mental processes associated with retrospection and prospection (for exceptions, see D'Argembeau & Van der Linden, 2004; Newby-Clark & Ross, 2003; Van Boven & Ashworth, 2007). In this section, we make indirect tense comparisons by reviewing research that separately examined retrospection and prospection.

Our brief and selective review of retrospection and prospection research implies that people's thoughts in everyday life about the past tend to be more constrained by reality concerns than are their thoughts about the future. People regularly engage in retrospective "reality monitoring," that is, thinking about whether their mental representations are of real or imagined past events (Johnson & Raye, 1981). In prospection, by contrast, people engage in less reality monitoring, imagining futures that are less linked to reality considerations.

It may seem mundane, given that the past has happened and the future has not, to point out that past tense mental simulation is more constrained by reality than future tense mental simulation. Notice, however, that people are perfectly capable of mentally simulating a past that did *not* happen, as when thinking about what might have been. And, people are perfectly capable of thinking about a future that actually will happen, especially when they are about to experience events they have experienced previously.[1] As we review, however, people's (blatantly) imaginative acts appear to be more constrained by reality in the past tense than in the future tense.

RETROSPECTION: LOOKING BACK

People tend to think about the past in two ways. People can engage in "remembering," thinking about a past that actually happened. Or, they can engage in counterfactual thinking about a past that could have happened but did not. It might seem that remembering is more constrained by reality than counterfactual thinking. As we will see, however, even when people think counterfactually about the past, they do so in close adherence to reality.

Remembering Realistically

Research makes clear that memory is reconstructive, and therefore departs regularly from veridicality. People do not store memories on a neural hard drive and then later retrieve them (subject to memory degradation). Rather, people reconstruct memories, making educated guesses about what must have happened (Bernstein, Godfrey, & Loftus, Chapter 6, this volume; Loftus, 1979; Loftus & Palmer, 1973; Neisser & Harsch, 1992; Schacter, 1996; Schooler, Gerhard, & Loftus, 1986).

Although memories are not always accurate records of experience, the phenomenology of memory—what it *feels* like to remember—is that remembering is closely tied to and constrained by reality (Alba & Hasher, 1983; Johnson & Raye, 1981; Kunda, 1990). When looking back, people continuously ask whether they remember an event that actually happened or are imagining an event that did not actually happen. This process of reality monitoring is among the most important metacognitive tasks people perform (Johnson & Raye, 1981; Johnson & Sherman, 1990) and may pervade the qualitative characteristics of retrospection. Indeed, people would be reluctant to refer to their retrospective thoughts as "memories" to the degree that those thoughts felt like products of creative imagination rather than veridical representations of reality. Regardless of the factual accuracy of memories, then, the habitual phenomenology of remembering is characterized by the pursuit of factually accurate memories. People remember in a way that attends closely to what feels like objective reality.

Counterfactual Constraints

Imaginative thoughts about the past that purposefully stray from reality are counterfactuals—thoughts that are counter to the facts. Counterfactual thoughts entail the imagination of a past that clearly did not happen: a gold medal rather than a silver one (Medvec, Madey, & Gilovich, 1995), an uneventful drive home rather than a tragic accident (Kahneman & Tversky, 1982), or a courageous moment of asking a secret crush on a date rather than failing to "seize the moment" (Gilovich & Medvec, 1994). Because counterfactuals are blatant departures from reality, people do not monitor reality in terms of asking whether the counterfactual events actually occurred. The potential freedom from reality might seem to allow counterfactual thoughts to stray toward the fantastical, as when a humdrum academic imagines a counterfactual career as a professional bike racer.

Yet, an intriguing observation about the nature of counterfactuals is that they tend to stick surprisingly close to the past that actually happened (Kahneman & Miller, 1986; Roese, 1997). Counterfactual thinking usually involves minimal departures from reality, the smallest mental mutation of specific attributes that would have produced a different outcome. Counterfactual thinking about history that strays too far from reality may seem implausible or illegitimate, a violation of a "minimal rewrite rule" (Tetlock & Belkin, 1996).

Individuals' reactions to the following scenario from Kahneman and Tversky (1982) nicely illustrate the reality constraints on counterfactual thinking:

> Mr. Crane and Mr. Tees were scheduled to leave the airport on different flights, at the same time. They traveled from town in the same limousine, were caught in a traffic jam, and arrived at the airport 30 min after the scheduled departure time of their flights. Mr. Crane is told that his flight left on time. Mr. Tees is told that his flight was delayed, and just left 5 min ago.

When discussing why nearly all (96%) participants thought that Mr. Tees would be more upset than Mr. Crane, Kahneman and Tverksy noted:

> There is an Alice-in-Wonderland quality to such examples, with their odd mixture of fantasy and reality. If Mr. Crane is capable of imagining unicorns—and we suspect he is—why does he find it relatively difficult to imagine himself avoiding a 30-minute delay, as we suggest he does? Evidently, *there are constraints on the freedom of fantasy.* (pp. 203–204, emphasis added)

These constraints on the "freedom of fantasy" illustrate that even when retrospective thought departs blatantly from reality, looking back is nevertheless reined in by reality checks. That is, imaginative thinking in the past tense seems habitually confined to events that realistically could have happened.

Summary

Our brief (and selective) review of mental simulation in the past tense suggests that in everyday life, retrospection adheres closely to the tenures of reality (for more extensive reviews of the counterfactual thinking literature, in this volume see Byrne & Girotto, Chapter 10; Markman, Karadogan, Lindberg, & Zell, Chapter 12; Wong, Galinsky, & Kray, Chapter 11). Even though acts of memory can be scientifically established as reconstructive, they nevertheless have the phenomenal quality of being veridical. Even counterfactual thoughts that depart blatantly from reality tend not to stray too far from reality. Retrospective thoughts are thus habitually subject to reality checks, whether those thoughts are explicitly tied with or depart from reality. As elaborated in this chapter, we suggest that the mental practice of reality checking retrospection generally constrains the practice of past tense mental simulation.

Prospection: Looking Forth

The future is inherently uncertain. Unlike past events, which people usually perceive as having either happened or not, there tends to be more uncertainty when people look forth to the future (Grant & Tybout, 2007; Mitchell, Russo, & Pennington, 1989). People's prospective thoughts can nevertheless be roughly categorized into thoughts about future events they believe will (probably) happen and thoughts about future events they believe will (probably) not happen, just as people tend to retrospect about events that did and did not happen. We hypothesize that regardless of whether people prospect about probable or improbable events, they tend to worry less about the kind of reality checks that constrain retrospection. This habitual freedom from reality constraints characterizes various kinds of mental simulation in the future tense.

Planning Fallaciously

Planning to implement future tasks is arguably a kind of prospective thought quite likely to be shaped and constrained by reality concerns. Given their importance for budgeting time, money, and other resources, plans for the future seemingly should be highly constrained by future-oriented considerations of reality. Before firmly committing to a February 1 deadline for a chapter draft, authors might ask themselves whether they will actually finish a draft by that date or whether they are thinking too wishfully about how they will get it done in time. It seems plausible (and advisable), in other words, to check their plans for the future against reality just as they monitor how realistic their memories are.

As it happens, people's plans about the future are unrealistically optimistic and show an almost wanton disregard for information about previous task completion times (Buehler, Griffin, & Mac-Donald, 1997; Buehler, Griffin, & Ross, 1994). People are overly optimistic about how much time they will need to complete tasks like filing taxes or holiday shopping, even when they accurately recall how much time was required to complete similar tasks in the past (Buehler et al., 1997). When planning for the future, people behave as though there were more than 24 hr in a day (Zauberman & Lynch, 2005).

One reason why people's plans are unrealistically optimistic is that their plans focus primarily on the event under consideration, neglecting to consider the full range of experiences that are likely to interfere with their plans (Lam, Buehler, McFarland, Ross, & Cheung, 2005). This neglect of relevant experiences occurs even though people can readily retrieve information about previous task completion times. Indeed, one way to reduce the planning fallacy is by directing people to think explicitly about future task details (Kruger & Evans, 2004). When planning for the future, then, people think about when they would *like* to (Buehler et al., 1997) and *intend* to complete a task (Koehler & Poon, 2006). People do not consider how long similar tasks took in the past or think about the task's subcomponents.

To the degree that planning fallacy type thoughts characterize prospection, people may habitually fail to think about reality constraints and plausibility constraints on plans for the future. The juxtaposition of the experience of remembering, which is highly constrained by reality, and the experience of planning, which is apparently not as constrained by reality, illustrates how retrospection may be more constrained than prospection.

Imagining Focally

Just as people can engage in counterfactual thoughts about events that could have happened (but did not), they can engage in prospective thoughts about events that might happen (but probably will not). In fact, imaginative thoughts of a future that probably will not happen are commonly studied when participants are asked to predict how they would behave or feel in unlikely hypothetical situations. A recurrent theme in studies of behavioral and affective forecasting is that people tend to focus on salient attributes of hypothetical situations to the neglect of mundane but influential attributes. Thus, people expect that living in California would make them happier than living in the Midwest because they focus on salient attributes about better weather to the neglect of more commonplace similarities between the two locales (Schkade & Kahneman, 1998). And when people predict whether they will take the high road when they face moral dilemmas in the future, they focus on what they would ideally like to do (e.g., donate to charity) to the neglect of what they and others have done in the past (e.g., kept their money to themselves; Epley & Dunning, 2000).

As with the planning fallacy, then, people imagine hypothetical futures by focusing on central attributes to the neglect of peripheral attributes such as the contextual details of future realities. Indeed, manipulations designed to "defocalize" people's thoughts about hypothetical futures cause individuals to make less extreme, more accurate forecasts about how they would behave and feel in those future situations (Epley & Dunning, 2000; Wilson, Wheatley, Meyers, Gilbert, & Axsom, 2000). Because mental simulations of the past are generally more mixed in terms of valence, we predict that when thinking about the past people naturally make less extreme and more accurate estimates of what experiences (both actual and counterfactual) were like.

Summary

The research on planning and imagination implies that prospection is habitually less constrained by reality checks than retrospection. More generally, people think about the future from what has been termed an "inside" rather than an "outside" perspective (Kahneman & Lovallo, 1993). Whereas an inside perspective focuses on salient attributes, intentions, and desires, an outside perspective includes previous experiences, base rates, and other information outside of one's immediate self (Buehler et al., 1994; Griffin & Tversky, 1992; Kahneman & Tversky, 1972). By thinking about the future from an inside perspective, prospection is relatively free of the contextual details of reality compared with retrospection.

LOOKING BACK AND FORTH

We hypothesize that the habitual ways in which reality checks constrain thoughts about the past more than thoughts about the future influence mental simulation in the past and future tense generally. That is, mental simulation in the past tense is more constrained by "reality checks" than is mental simulation in the future tense. Previous researchers have speculated about the possibility of such temporally asymmetric constraints on mental simulation (Johnson & Sherman, 1990), although their focus was on the ways in which thoughts about the past and future are similarly rather than differentially constrained. We agree that looking back and looking forth are constrained by reality in similar ways. However, we suggest that looking back is constrained to a greater degree than looking forth.

The potential of temporally asymmetric constraints on mental simulation raises two related questions. First, does the temporal asymmetry of reality constraint on mental simulation have implications for the phenomenology of mental simulation in the past versus future tense? That is, does the mental simulation of future events *feel* different from the mental simulation of past events? Second, does the temporal asymmetry of reality constraints on mental simulation have implications for the output of mental simulation in the past versus future tense? That is, do people make different judgments of events that they simulate in the past tense compared with events simulated in the future tense? Preliminary evidence from our own and others' labs, which is summarized in Table 9.1, suggests that the answer to both questions is "yes."

TEMPORALLY ASYMMETRIC PHENOMENOLOGY

If reality constrains retrospection more than prospection, mental simulation in the past tense should feel relatively less imaginative than mental simulation in the future tense. Mentally simulating the past, with its greater emphasis on adherence to realistic events, should also feel more mentally effortful than mentally simulating the future, with its emphasis on creative imagination.

We have obtained preliminary evidence that thinking about personal events from the past feels more difficult than thinking about personal events in one's future (Kane, Van Boven, & McGraw, 2008). We asked participants to describe either their last or their next visit to the dentist. We presumed that participants were familiar with dentist visits, could realistically predict what would occur during dentist visits, and so could plausibly use detailed personal memories of dentist visits to think about both their last and next dentist visits. We did not predict differences in whether participants would consult their memories when writing their descriptions, but in how participants would use their memories. When describing past visits to the dentist, we hypothesized that participants would consider their memories as factual representations, which they should faithfully render through their descriptions. In describing future visits, on the other hand, we hypothesized that participants would feel less of a need to adhere strictly to the precise details of the visits they recalled and would think more flexibly and creatively about the visits they described. Consistent with these hypotheses, participants reported that thinking about past dentist visits was more cognitively difficult than thinking about future dentist visits (cf. Sanna, Schwarz, & Kennedy, Chapter 13, this volume).

One reason why retrospective mental simulation may feel more difficult than prospective mental simulation is that retrospection is relatively less imaginative than prospection. Consistent with this possibility are the results of a study in which university students thought about attending a party either 1 month in the past or 1 month in the future, depending on random assignment to condition (Kane et al., 2008). Participants were asked to report how much, while thinking about attending the party, they relied on their memories of previous parties they had attended and how much they relied on imagination about what attending a party would be like. Participants reported that mentally simulating a past tense party was relatively less imaginative than mentally simulating a future tense party, but that mentally simulating a past tense party was equally based on personal memories as was mentally simulating a future tense party.[2] This pattern highlights that although mental simulation in both the past and future tense is somewhat constrained by memories of reality (Johnson & Sherman, 1990), mental simulation in the past tense is also less imaginative.

Other research focused particularly on counterfactual thinking is supportive of our hypothesis that mentally simulating future events engenders more creative thinking, whereas mentally simulating past events engenders more careful reality checking and, perhaps, more analytical thinking. Previous research has distinguished between "additive structures," which may be thought of as decreasing reality constraints through the addition of counterfactual elements, and "subtractive structures," which may maintain or increase constraints on reality by removing counterfactual elements (Roese & Olson, 1993). Additive structures seem to increase creativity, whereas subtractive structures seem to improve analytical problem solving (Markman, Lindberg, Kray, & Galinsky, 2007; Wong et al., Chapter 11, this volume). Consistent with our characterization of future tense mental simulation as more imaginative than past tense simulation, we suspect that prospection tends to be more additive compared with retrospection.

One extension of the tendency to think less imaginatively about past than future events is that people may be less likely to mentally simulate past events in a personally involving, episodic way compared with their mental simulation of future tense events. Mental simulations of the future may be characterized by "prefactual" thinking, akin to preexperiencing the event, rather than "evaluative" thinking, or evaluating the event against reality (Markman & McMullen, 2003). To the extent that people think about future events in a more imaginative way, with less emphasis on memory-based details, they should be more inclined during mental simulation to feel as though they are actually experiencing future than past events.

In one demonstration of this difference, participants contemplated listening to an annoying noise—the disharmonic sound of an analog telephone modem connecting to an Internet service provider, either in the future or in the past (Van Boven & Ashworth, 2007, Study 5). Participants who contemplated the future annoying noise, compared with those who contemplated the past annoying noise, agreed more strongly with statements such as, "It feels as though I am actually listening to the noise right now." Moreover, this tendency to simulate the future annoying noise in a more involving way than a past annoying noise statistically mediated the tendency to report more intense emotions in the "here and now" when contemplating the future annoying noise than when contemplating the past annoying noise.

This temporal asymmetry in thinking about events in an involving, first-person way was similarly demonstrated in another study in which participants were asked either to imagine a birthday they would have 5 years in the future or a birthday they had 5 years in the past (Pronin & Ross, 2006, Study 5). Participants rated how much their simulated behavior on that day was based on the situation (e.g., "it depends who else was there"), which often involve first-person perspectives seen from the mind's eye, versus being based on traits (e.g., "calm or serious"), which tend to be associated with third-person perspectives, as though looking in on the self (see also Libby & Eibach, Chapter 24, this volume). Participants generally reported less situationally based behavior seen from inside the mind's eye during retrospection than during prospection about their birthday. Together, these studies, summarized in the top portion of Table 9.1, demonstrate that mental simulation in the past tense is phenomenologically different from mental simulation in the future tense. Thoughts about past events feel more difficult, less imaginative, and less personally involving than thoughts about future events.

TEMPORALLY ASYMMETRIC JUDGMENTAL OUTCOMES

If the temporal asymmetries in how it feels to engage in retrospective versus prospective mental simulation reflect genuine differences in reality constraints, then retrospective mental simulations should yield different outcomes than prospective mental simulations. More specifically, if retrospective mental simulations are more adherent to the details of a realistic past, then judgmental

TABLE 9.1

Research Comparing Retrospection and Prospection That Suggests Temporally Asymmetric Constraints on Mental Simulation

Research Domain	Participants' (Ps) Task	Principal Findings
Judgmental Phenomenology		
Subjective ease	P's described either their last or next trip to the dentist.	Retrospection felt more difficult than prospection.
Imaginative thought	P's reported how much they used imagination and memory details when describing past or future parties.	Thinking about a past party was less imaginative than thinking about a future tense party, but thinking about past and future parties was equally based on memory.
Personal involvement (Van Boven & Ashworth, 2007)	P's reported how experientially involved they were in contemplating a future or past emotional experience.	Participants were less experientially involved in thinking about a past than a future emotional experience.
First- versus third-person visual perspective (Pronin & Ross, 2006)	P's thought about past or future birthday parties and reported their visual perspective.	Future parties were seen from an involving first-person perspective more than were past parties.
Judgmental Outcomes		
Action identification	P's chose between abstract and concrete identifications of past or future actions.	Past actions were identified more concretely than future actions.
Contextual details (D'Argembeau & Van der Linden, 2004)	P's described autobiographical past or future experiences and rated their mental representations.	P's indicated that mental representations of past events contained more contextual details than representations of future events.
Event prototypicality	P's drew pictures and wrote descriptions of hypothetical tropical vacations in the past or future.	Raters judged past vacations as less proto-typical. Descriptions of past vacations included more idiosyncratic details.
Event similarity	P's wrote descriptions of three hypothetical homeless people they imagined having met in the past year or would meet in the upcoming year.	P's rated the homeless people they imagined having met as less similar to each other than the homeless people they imagined meeting in the past.
Event alternatives (Bavelas, 1973)	P's listed alternatives to future or past vacation itineraries taken by someone else.	P's listed less-varied itineraries for past than future vacations.
Event alternatives (Caruso, Seo, & Gilbert, 2007)	P's listed alternatives to watching a movie in the future or past.	P's listed fewer alternatives to watching a past than a future movie.
Affective intensity (D'Argembeau & Van der Linden, 2004)	P's described autobiographical past or future experiences and rated their mental representations.	P's judged past experiences as less affectively intense than future experiences.
Affective intensity (Van Boven & Ashworth, 2007)	P's judged how intense their affective reactions would be or had been to emotional events.	P's judged past experiences as less affectively intense than future experiences.
Likelihood (Hanko & Gilovich, 2007)	P's judged the likelihood of uncertain past or future events.	P's judged uncertain future events as more likely than past events.
Motivated reasoning (Newby-Clark & Ross, 2003)	P's described autobiographical days in the past or future.	P's described realistically affectively mixed events from the past but uniformly positive events in the future.

Note: Unless otherwise specified, the data come from Kane, Van Boven, and McGraw, 2008.

biases that result from a relative neglect of realistic contextual details should be diminished when people engage in retrospective versus prospective mental simulation. For instance, people's tendency to simulate events in a prototypical fashion should be diminished when those mental simulations also include contextual details. Similarly, people's tendency to judge the likelihood of a particular event by focusing on that event to the neglect or exclusion of other possible events (Rottenstreich & Tversky, 1997; Tversky & Koehler, 1994) should be diminished when people judge the likelihood of events having occurred in the past. Preliminary evidence summarized in the bottom portion of Table 9.1 is supportive of these predictions.

Abstraction and Contextual Detail

When people think about temporally distant future events, they tend to do so abstractly (Trope & Liberman, 2003; see also Amit et al., Chapter 4, this volume), and across temporal distances, most people tend to think about events abstractly rather than concretely (Vallacher & Wegner, 1987). For instance, most people identify "making a list" in abstract terms of "getting organized" rather than in concrete terms of "writing things down," and this tendency increases linearly over future temporal distance (Pennington & Roese, 2003, Study 3).

Our hypothesis implies that people are more constrained by the details of reality when they engage in retrospection than prospection. Thus, temporal perspective should moderate this tendency toward abstraction, and people should engage in relatively more concrete retrospection than prospection.

To test this possibility, we (Kane et al., 2008) asked participants to contemplate various actions in one of four temporal perspectives: 1 year past, 1 week past, 1 week hence, and 1 year hence. Accompanying the actions was a relatively concrete description of the action and a relatively abstract description of the action, as in the example of identifying list-making as getting organized (abstract) versus writing things down (concrete; Vallacher & Wegner, 1987). Participants chose whether each action was better identified by the concrete or abstract description. Overall, participants tended to identify actions abstractly (65%). More important, the degree to which participants identified actions abstractly decreased as the temporal frame moved from distant-future actions (76% 1 year hence) to near-future actions (70% 1 week hence) and from near-past actions (65% 1 week past) to distant-past actions (59% 1 year past).

A related prediction is that mental representations of past events should contain more realistic contextual details of time and place than should mental representations of future events. If reality concerns constrain retrospection more than prospection, then those constraints should leave cognitive traces. Support for this possibility comes from a study in which participants were asked to think back to two events (one positive, one negative) they experienced in the recent past (between 1 and 12 months ago) and in the distant past (between 5 and 10 years ago; D'Argembeau & Van der Linden, 2004). Participants were also asked to think forward to two events (one positive, one negative) that might reasonably happen to them in the near future (between 1 and 12 months) and in the distant future (in 5 to 10 years). Participants rated their mental representations of past experiences as including more contextual details, including specific dates, times of day, and locations. Together, these studies imply that people retrospect on past events at lower contextually detailed levels of identification compared to prospection.

Prototypicality, Similarity, and Variety

People's mental representations of common, everyday events can incorporate, to varying degrees, prototypes or scripts of how those events occur and nonprototypical contextual details about how those events might occur (Colcombe & Wyer, 2002). A family meal, for instance, has a prototypical script: hands washed, salad served, followed by main course and desserts. The mentally represented family meal can also include contextual details: Caesar salad or mixed greens? Spaghetti or stir-fry?

Chocolate cake or ice cream? An implication of the possibility that reality concerns constrain retrospection more than prospection is that past tense mental simulations should adhere less to shared scripts than future tense mental simulations. Mental simulations of past family meals, for instance, should deviate from the socially shared "family meal" script more than mental simulations of future family meals.

We tested this prediction in a study conducted during late winter and early spring in which participants were asked to imagine that they took a tropical beach vacation to a fancy resort either 1 year ago or 2 year in the future (Kane et al., 2008). Participants were asked to spend a few minutes drawing a sketch of their imagined vacation. We then randomly paired drawings of past tense vacations with drawings of future tense vacations. Several coders who were blind to condition viewed each pair and rated which drawing was more prototypical—which drawing more closely followed the prevailing prototypical beach vacation with a bright sun, sandy beach, and palm tree. As expected, drawings of future vacations were rated as more prototypical compared with drawings of past vacations. Just as descriptions of alien life-forms draw heavily from familiar creatures (Ward, 1994), it seems that in the past, at least, hypothetical vacations draw heavily from familiar ones.

We conceptually replicated this pattern in a study in which participants (all university students) were asked to imagine either that they had attended three parties in the past month or would attend three parties in the next month (Kane et al., 2008). We presumed that most, if not all, participants had personal experience with college parties and could therefore draw on a wealth of personal memories to mentally simulate attending parties in both the past and future tense. After writing brief descriptions of these three parties, participants rated how similar their descriptions were to the "typical" party experience. As predicted, participants rated the three past parties as less typical than the three future parties.

One implication of people's tendency to think about past events in a less-prototypical way than future events is that mental representations of past events should be less similar to each other than mental representations of future events. If people think about future events in a way that follows the prototype more closely than people's thoughts about past events, then their representations of future events should be less discrepant from each other than their representations of past events. That is, mental simulations of future events should tend to be cut from the same prototypical mental cloth to a greater degree than should mental simulations of past events.

We obtained support for this possibility from a study in which participants were asked to imagine three encounters with homeless people that occurred either in the past year or in the upcoming year (Kane et al., 2008). Consistent with our reasoning, participants rated the three homeless people that they imagined encountering in the future as more similar to each other than they rated the three homeless people that they imagined having encountered in the past year.

Relatedly, when participants were asked to think about alternative ways they could spend their time rather than watching a movie, they generated more alternatives to viewing a movie in the future than to having viewed a movie in the past (Caruso, Seo, & Gilbert, 2008). Also, when participants were asked to describe a vacation itinerary that a protagonist either had taken in the past or would take in the future, participants wrote more varied itineraries for the future trip than for the past trip (Bavelas, 1973). Participants treated the past as relatively fixed, possibly constrained by reality concerns, compared with the future. In sum, research from various sources indicates that people simulate past tense events less prototypically, less similarly, and less variably than they simulate future tense events.

Affective Extremity

An extension of the idea that people think about past events less prototypically than future events is that people may think about emotional events in the past in a less extreme fashion compared with their thoughts about emotional events in the future. This is because the prototype of emotional events tends to be highly affective (e.g., Gilbert, Morewedge, Risen, & Wilson, 2004). People tend to expect the best of good events and the worst of bad events (Schkade & Kahneman, 1998; Wilson et al., 2000). Because the prototypical affective experience tends to be relatively extreme (see Dunn et al., Chapter 22, this volume), people's actual affective experiences tend to be more moderate than they anticipate. To the degree that mental simulations of affective experiences follow the realistically mundane details of past experience, people should think about emotional experiences as less extreme in retrospect than in prospect.

Preliminary support for this prediction comes from three sources. First, studies comparing on-line reports of emotion with temporally distant estimates of emotions experienced during vacations found that people expected to enjoy their vacations more than they recalled having enjoyed their vacations, although the statistical significance of these comparisons was not reported in the original articles (Mitchell, Thompson, Peterson, & Cronk, 1997; Wirtz, Kruger, Napa Scollon, & Diener, 2003). Second, when thinking about both good and bad events from one's personal past and personal future, participants anticipated that future events would be more intense than they recalled past events having been (D'Argembeau & Van der Linden, 2004). Finally, in research on the emotional consequences of mental time travel for affective experience in the "here and now," participants consistently predicted that they would experience more intense reactions to future emotional events than they "recalled" having experienced during previous emotional events (Van Boven & Ashworth, 2007).

Likelihood

Usually when people predict the likelihood of a given event, they do so based on support for the focal event, neglecting to consider fully the support for the nonfocal event (Rottenstreich & Tversky, 1997; Tversky & Koehler, 1994). For instance, people's estimates of the likelihood that a randomly selected San Franciscan would vote in favor of a Democratic candidate is largely influenced by the evidence consistent with the focal event (e.g., easily accessible examples of San Franciscan Democrats) and insufficiently influenced by evidence consistent with nonfocal events (e.g., the recently wealthy San Franciscans who may favor Republican tax cuts). Such focalism is one reason why people tend to be overconfident: They focus more on why a given event might happen than on why the event might not happen (Koriat, Lichtenstein, & Fischoff, 1980). One consequence of thinking about realistic contextual details is that it encourages people to think about nonfocal events. Such increased thought about nonfocal events can influence people's judgments of the likelihood of focal events.

If people think about past tense events in a way that adheres more to contextual details of reality, then the tendency to focus on the target event should be reduced when thinking about past tense events compared with future tense events. People should therefore judge the likelihood of events in the past tense as less likely than events in the future. This is because people may be more inclined to incorporate information about nonfocal events into "postdictions"—estimates of likelihood in the past tense—than they are to incorporate nonfocal information into predictions.

For example, students who imagined taking a molecular biology exam during the previous semester might judge it to be less likely that they would have aced the exam than students who imagined taking a molecular biology exam during the following semester (Hanko & Gilovich, 2007). We propose that students mentally simulating their preparation for a difficult exam during the previous semester would be more likely to consider all the other (nonfocal) activities in which they were involved at the time (other challenging courses, work, extracurricular activities on campus, etc.), whereas students mentally simulating their preparation for a difficult exam during the following semester would be less likely to consider these nonfocal activities and the ways in which they would interfere with studying.

Such temporally asymmetric likelihood judgments are confirmed by a recent series of studies suggesting that people judge focal events to be more likely in the future tense than in the past tense (Hanko & Gilovich, 2007). In one study, participants judged it more likely that a university student would engage in a variety of activities in the following week than that she had engaged in those same activities over the past week. In another study, people judged it more likely that their peers would endorse a particular political stance if they thought their peers would be surveyed in the near future than if they thought their peers had been surveyed in the near past.

Motivated Reasoning

We have thus far focused on the cognitive consequences of relatively constrained retrospection versus prospection. This temporally asymmetric constraint can also influence the outcomes of motivated reasoning in the past versus future tense. When people remember their pasts, they often do so in a motivated fashion, reconstructing themselves in a favorable light. Importantly, however, even though people reconstruct their pasts motivationally, they also reconstruct realistically (Kunda, 1990). The desires underlying motivated reasoning must also therefore contend with objective (and observable) facts. As we have seen, however, such reality concerns tend to constrain retrospection more than prospection.

One implication of the temporally asymmetric constraints is that people should have more rosy, optimistic views about their futures compared with more realistic, mixed views about their pasts. Specifically, people's retrospections should contain a realistic mixture of the ups and downs of everyday life than their prospections. This prediction was confirmed in a series of studies that examined people's thoughts about negative and positive events in their personal pasts and futures (Newby-Clark & Ross, 2003). In one study, people tended spontaneously to anticipate uniformly positive future events but to recall more affectively mixed events (Newby-Clark & Ross, 2003, Study 1). In two other studies, people took longer to generate future negative events than future positive events, suggesting the relative inaccessibility of negative future events; in contrast, there was no difference in the time taken to generate past negative and past positive events (Newby-Clark & Ross, 2003, Studies 2 and 3). Thus, negative events in the future tense seem to be less comparatively accessible than negative events in the past, consistent with our notion that retrospective mental simulation, with its adherence to a life actually lived, is a more realistic reflection of the ups and downs of daily life than is prospective mental simulation.

SUMMARY

The varied research reviewed here and summarized in the bottom portion of Table 9.1 points to temporally asymmetric constraints on mental simulation. These constraints make retrospection feel different than prospection—more cognitively effortful, detailed, and contextually situated. These temporally asymmetric constraints also produce different judgmental outcomes of retrospection versus prospection. Looking back to the past seems less prototypical, less extreme, less likely, and less rosy than looking forward to the future. Habitual differences in thinking about the past in a more constrained and realistic manner appear to shape the way that people mentally simulate the past and future.

DISCUSSION

Mental time travel is central to the psychological science of mental simulation. People routinely travel back in time, thinking about pasts that actually were and might have been. They also travel forward in time, imagining futures that probably will and probably will not occur. In this chapter, we explored whether there might be systematic differences in the way people generally mentally simulate pasts and futures. Our brief review of the research on retrospection, both to actual and imagined pasts, implied that retrospection is subject to reality checks, as people monitor whether their memories reflect real events and their counterfactual thoughts reflect plausible events. In contrast, our review of the research on prospection, both to futures that probably will and probably will not happen, implied that prospection is less subject to reality checks and tends to neglect the many and varied contextual details of future realities.

Contrasting the literatures on looking back and on looking forth suggested that reality concerns might generally constrain people's retrospective thoughts more than their prospective thoughts. This possibility is supported by a host of recent studies on various types of judgments from various labs. Retrospection appears to feel more constrained than prospection. And retrospection appears to yield different judgmental outcomes than prospection.

Assuming for the time being that retrospection does feel different and yields different outcomes than prospection, three important questions present themselves. The first is whether asymmetric reality constraints are an underlying process shaping retrospection and prospection or an indicator of some alternative underlying process. The second question is whether, and in what ways, theories of psychological distance should be modified to accommodate temporally asymmetric constraints. The third question focuses on identifying some potentially important moderators of temporally asymmetric constraints. We consider each question in turn.

ALTERNATIVE TENSE TENDENCIES

Are asymmetric reality constraints the best way to think about how retrospection and prospection feel different and yield different outcomes? Might some other temporally asymmetric process provide an explanation for the results reviewed here? If there are alternative judgmental tendencies that differ by tense, what might they be?

One possibility is that retrospection tends to rely more on systematic, deliberative "rational" processing, whereas prospection relies on more heuristical, associative, "experiential," or intuitive" processing (Epstein, 2003; Kahneman, 2003; see also Dunn et al., Chapter 22, this volume). Indeed, many of the reviewed findings indicate that prospection is more heuristic than retrospection. Our interpretation, however, is that concerns about reality constrain processing such that past tense mental simulation is more systematic than future tense mental simulation. That is, reality constraints signal to the information-processing system that "experiential" judgment outcomes are insufficiently accurate and thereby prompt more careful information processing (Kahneman, 2003).

Another possibility is that people's goals for the future are primed more by future tense mental simulation than by past tense simulation, and that this differential goal salience explains many of the differences summarized here. Goals probably do differ by tense—indeed, what does it mean to have a present goal for one's past?—and these different goals probably do contribute to some of the present findings, as when people expect their futures to be rosier than were their pasts. But it is unclear why increased goal salience would yield prospective outcomes that are more prototypical and likely, as appears to be the case. Nevertheless, investigating whether rational processing or differential goals coincide and contribute to differential reality constraints is an important question for future research.

BROADER THEORETICAL IMPLICATIONS

Theories of temporal psychological distance typically assume, explicitly or implicitly, temporal symmetry. That is, the judgmental and behavioral effects of being temporally close to or far from an event operate similarly in retrospect and in prospect (see Perunovic & Wilson, Chapter 23, this volume). However, the research reviewed here suggests that these theories are descriptively incomplete.

Construal-level theory, for instance, posits that people construe temporally distant events at a higher, more abstract level than temporally proximate events, and that "the same general principles hold for other distance dimensions, including temporal distance from past events" (Trope & Liberman, 2003, p. 403). However, the preliminary results reported here suggest that people generally construe past events at a lower level than future events. If these results hold up to further empirical scrutiny, the general claim that temporal distance is positively associated with level of construal should be modified to reflect these temporal asymmetries. That is, level of construal may increase less steeply when that distance increases toward the past than toward the future.

Research on affective forecasting implies another set of ideas that may require modification to accommodate temporal asymmetries. Although researchers of affective forecasting note that "it may be that some of the same factors that produce the impact bias in prospect … also produce an impact bias in retrospect" (Wilson, Meyers, & Gilbert, 2003, p. 425), our results imply that people may be more likely to exhibit errors when predicting future affective reactions than when post-dicting previous affective reactions. Looking back, people appear less likely to remember having experienced extreme emotions compared with when they look forward (Caruso, Gilbert, & Wilson, 2007; Dunn et al., Chapter 22, this volume; Van Boven & Ashworth, 2007).

POTENTIAL MODERATORS

Future research may profit from the investigation of variables that moderate the temporal asymmetries we have described. One potential moderator is age. It may be that the tendency to think about the past and future asymmetrically is more common among young adults and middle-aged individuals who have more of their lives both ahead of them and behind them compared with the very young and very old. Young children, eager to feasibly navigate everyday life, may be more inclined to attend to the "how" questions of life, thinking about both the future and past at more concrete levels. More elderly individuals, in contrast, may find themselves in more of a reflective mode, attending to the "why" questions of life (Libby & Eibach, Chapter 24, this volume) and therefore be particularly inclined to construe both the past and the future at relatively high levels.

Another potential moderator is self-relevance. All of the preliminary experiments we have reviewed in this chapter involve highly self-relevant experiences. Participants were asked to describe events such as birthday parties, vacations, and movie screenings—all of which are likely to be extremely familiar to the college students who participated. In this chapter, we have argued that individuals are more likely to insert contextual details into descriptions of past events than descriptions of future events; we suspect that this tendency is due to the fact that individuals consult their personal pasts and attempt to fit even hypothetical or counterfactual events into the past life they recall experiencing. If a past event is presented as having been experienced by another person, individuals may not consult their personal past experience or conduct reality checks against it. As a result, we suggest that individuals may be less likely to include contextual details when describing past events experienced by another person.

CONCLUSION

A constellation of research findings supports the general, tentative hypothesis described in this chapter: Reality checks constrain mental simulation in the past tense more than mental simulation in the future tense. We argue that temporally asymmetric constraints in imagining hypothetical and real events are important to developing more descriptive psychological theory and to achieving a more accurate understanding of mental simulation in everyday life. Fittingly, when we look forward to future research, we expect that there is a great deal of exciting and important work to be done by looking both back and forth.

ACKNOWLEDGMENT

This research was supported by National Science Foundation grant 0552120. For helpful comments, we thank the Judgment Emotion Decision and Intuition lab at the University of Colorado, Boulder.

NOTES

1. Both participants in psychology experiments and professional science fiction writers seem somewhat constrained by reality even when engaging in totally imaginative tasks, like describing alien creatures (Ward, 1994). We are not suggesting that prospection is totally free of realistic considerations, just that it is less constrained by reality than retrospection.
2. Asking participants to consider the extent to which they relied on memories of previous parties when describing a previous party might create experimental demand. Notice, however, that there is actually *no* significant difference between self-reported reliance on memories between the two conditions. Instead, people report relying more on imagination in the future tense than in the past tense.

REFERENCES

Alba, J., & Hasher, L. (1983). Is memory schematic? *Psychological Bulletin, 93*, 203–231.

Atance, C. M., & O'Neill, D. K. (2001). Episodic future thinking. *Trends in Cognitive Science, 5*(12), 533–539.

Bavelas, J. B. (1973). Effects of temporal context of information. *Psychological Reports, 32*(June), 695–698.

Buehler, R., Griffin, D., & MacDonald, H. (1997). The role of motivated reasoning in optimistic time predictions. *Personality and Social Psychology Bulletin, 23*, 238–247.

Buehler, R., Griffin, D., & Ross, M. (1994). Exploring the "planning fallacy": Why people underestimate their task completion times. *Journal of Personality and Social Psychology, 67*, 366–381.

Caruso, E. M., Gilbert, D. T., & Wilson, T. D. (2008). A wrinkle in time: Asymmetric valuation of past and future events. *Psychological Science, 19*, 796–801.

Caruso, E. M., Seo, A. A., & Gilbert, D. T. (2006). *Asymmetric generation of alternatives to past and future events.* Unpublished manuscript.

Colcombe, S. J., & Wyer, R. S. (2002). The role of prototypes in the mental representation of temporally related events. *Cognitive Psychology, 44*, 67–103.

D'Argembeau, A., & Van der Linden, M. (2004). Phenomenal characteristics associated with projecting oneself back into the past and forward into the future: Influence of valence and temporal distance. *Consciousness and Cognition, 13*, 844–858.

Epley, N., & Dunning, D. (2000). Feeling "holier than thou": Are self-serving assessments produced by errors in self- or social prediction? *Journal of Personality and Social Psychology, 79*, 861–875.

Epstein, S. (2003). Cognitive-experiential self-theory of personality. In Millon, T. & Lerner, M. J. (Eds.), *Comprehensive handbook of psychology, volume 5: Personality and social psychology* (pp. 159–184). Hoboken, NJ: Wiley.

Gilbert, D. T., Gill, M. J., & Wilson, T. D. (2002). The future is now: Temporal correction in affective forecasting. *Organizational Behavior and Human Decision Processes, 88*, 430–444.

Gilbert, D. T., Morewedge, C. K., Risen, J. L., & Wilson, T. D. (2004). Looking forward to looking backward. *Psychological Science, 15*, 346–350.

Gilbert, D. T., Pinel, E. C., Wilson, T. D., Blumberg, S. J., & Wheatley, T. P. (1998). Immune neglect: A source of durability bias in affective forecasting. *Journal of Personality and Social Psychology, 75*, 617–638.

Gilovich, T., & Medvec, V. H. (1994). The temporal pattern to the experience of regret. *Journal of Personality and Social Psychology, 67*, 357–365.

Grant, S. J., & Tybout, A. M. (2008). The effects of temporal frame on new product evaluation: The role of uncertainty. *Journal of Consumer Research, 34*, 897–913.

Griffin, D., & Tversky, A. (1992). The weighing of evidence and the determinants of confidence. *Cognitive Psychology, 24*, 411–435.

Hanko, K., & Gilovich, T. (2007). *When the future is more probable than the past.* Paper presented at the Society for Personality and Social Psychology.

Harris, C., & Laibson, D. (2001). Dynamic choices of hyperbolic consumers. *Econometrica, 69*(4), 935–957.

Johnson, M. K., & Raye, C. L. (1981). Reality monitoring. *Psychological Review, 88*, 67–85.

Johnson, M. K., & Sherman, S. J. (1990). Constructing and reconstructing the past and the future in the present. In E. T. Higgins & R. M. Sorrentino (Eds.), *Handbook of motivation and cognition: Foundations of social behavior* (Vol. 2, pp. 482–526). New York: Guilford Press.

Kahneman, D. (2003). A perspective on judgment and choice: Mapping bounded rationality. *American Psychologist, 58*, 697–720.

Kahneman, D., & Lovallo, D. (1993). Timid choices and bold forecast. A cognitive perspective on risk taking. *Management Science, 39*, 17–31.

Kahneman, D., & Miller, D. T. (1986). Norm theory: Comparing reality to its alternatives. *Psychological Review, 93*, 136–153.

Kahneman, D., & Tversky, A. (1972). Subjective probability: A judgment of representativeness. *Cognitive Psychology, 3*, 430–454.

Kahneman, D., & Tversky, A. (1982). The simulation heuristic. In D. Kahneman, P. Slovic, & A. Tversky (Eds.), *Judgment under uncertainty: Heuristics and biases* (pp. 201–208). Cambridge, England: Cambridge University Press.

Kane, J., Van Boven, L., & McGraw, A. P. (2007). *Temporally asymmetric thinking: Past tense thinking is more constrained than future tense thinking.* Unpublished manuscript, University of Colorado, Boulder.

Koehler, D. J., & Poon, C. S. (2006). Self-predictions overweight strength of current intentions. *Journal of Experimental Social Psychology, 42*, 517–524.

Koriat, A., Lichtenstein, S., & Fischoff, B. (1980). Reasons for overconfidence. *Journal of Experimental Psychology: Human Learning and Memory, 6*, 107–118.

Kruger, J., & Evans, M. (2004). If you don't want to be late, enumerate: Unpacking reduces the planning fallacy. *Journal of Experimental Social Psychology, 40*, 586–598.

Kunda, Z. (1990). The case for motivated reasoning. *Psychological Bulletin, 108*, 480–498.

Lam, K. C., Buehler, R., McFarland, C., Ross, M., & Cheung, I. (2005). Cultural differences in affective forecasting: The role of focalism. *Personality and Social Psychology Bulletin, 31*, 1296–1309.

Loewenstein, G. (Ed.). (1992). *Choice over time.* New York: Russell Sage Foundation.

Loftus, E. F. (1979). The malleability of human memory. *American Scientist, 67*, 313–320.

Loftus, E. F., & Palmer, J. C. (1973). Reconstruction of automobile destruction: An example of the interaction between language and memory. *Journal of Verbal Learning and Verbal Behavior, 13*, 585–589.

Markman, K. D., Lindberg, M. J., Kray, L. J., & Galinsky, A. D. (2007). Implications of counterfactual structure for creative generation and analytical problem solving. *Personality and Social Psychology Bulletin, 33*, 312–324.

Markman, K. D., & McMullen, M. N. (2003). A reflection and evaluation model of comparative thinking. *Personality and Social Psychology Review, 7*, 244–267.

McGraw, A. P., Mellers, B. A., & Tetlock, P. E. (2005). Expectations and emotions of Olympic athletes. *Journal of Experimental Social Psychology, 41*, 438–446.

Medvec, V. H., Madey, S. F., & Gilovich, T. (1995). When less is more: Counterfactual thinking and satisfaction among Olympic medalists. *Journal of Personality and Social Psychology, 69*, 603–610.

Metcalfe, J., & Mischel, W. (1999). A hot/cool-system analysis of delay of gratification: Dynamics of willpower. *Psychological Review, 106*, 3–19.

Mitchell, D. J., Russo, J. E., & Pennington, N. (1989). Back to the future: Temporal perspective in the explanation of events. *Journal of Behavioral Decision Making, 2*, 25–38.

Mitchell, T. R., Thompson, L., Peterson, E., & Cronk, R. (1997). Temporal adjustments in the evaluation of events: The "rosy view." *Journal of Experimental Social Psychology, 33*, 421–448.

Neisser, U., & Harsch, N. (1992). Phantom flashbulbs: False recollections of hearing the news about Challenger. In E. Winograd & U. Neisser (Eds.), *Affect and accuracy in recall: Studies of "flashbulb" memories* (4th ed.). New York: Cambridge University Press.

Newby-Clark, I. R., & Ross, M. (2003). Conceiving the past and future. *Personality and Social Psychology Bulletin, 20*, 807–818.

Pennington, G. L., & Roese, N. J. (2003). Regulatory focus and temporal distance. *Journal of Experimental Social Psychology, 39*, 563–576.

Pronin, E., & Ross, L. (2006). Temporal differences in trait self-ascription: When the self is seen as an other. *Journal of Personality and Social Psychology, 90*, 197–209.

Roese, N. J. (1997). Counterfactual thinking. *Psychological Bulletin, 121*, 133–148.

Roese, N. J., & Olson, J. M. (1993). The structure of counterfactual thought. *Personality and Social Psychology Bulletin, 19*, 312–319.

Rottenstreich, Y., & Tversky, A. (1997). Unpacking, repacking, and anchoring: Advances in support theory. *Psychological Review, 104*, 406–415.

Schacter, D. L. (1996). *Searching for memory: The brain, the mind, and the past.* New York: Basic Books.

Schkade, D. A., & Kahneman, D. (1998). Does living in California make people happy? A focusing illusion in judgments of life satisfaction. *Psychological Science, 9*, 340–346.

Schooler, J. W., Gerhard, D., & Loftus, E. F. (1986). Qualities of the unreal. *Journal of Experimental Psychology: Learning, Memory, and Cognition, 12*, 171–181.

Tetlock, P., & Belkin, A. (1996). *Counterfactual thought experiments in world politics: Logical, methodological, and psychological perspectives.* Princeton, NJ: Princeton University Press.

Trope, Y., & Liberman, N. (2003). Temporal construal. *Psychological Review, 110*, 403–421.

Tulving, E. (2002). Episodic memory: From mind to brain. *Annual Review of Psychology, 53*(1), 1–25.

Tversky, A., & Koehler, D. J. (1994). Support theory: A nonextensional representation of subjective probability. *Psychological Review, 101*, 547–567.

Vallacher, R. R., & Wegner, D. M. (1987). What do people think they're doing? Action identification and human behavior. *Psychological Review, 94*, 3–15.

Van Boven, L., & Ashworth, L. (2007). Looking forward, looking back: Anticipation is more evocative than retrospection. *Journal of Experimental Psychology: General, 136*, 289–300.

Ward, T. B. (1994). Structured imagination: The role of category structure in exemplar generation. *Cognitive Psychology, 27*, 1–40.

Wilson, T. D., Meyers, J., & Gilbert, D. T. (2003). "How happy was I, anyway?" A retrospective impact bias. *Social Cognition, 21*, 421–446.

Wilson, T. D., Wheatley, T., Meyers, J. M., Gilbert, D. T., & Axsom, D. (2000). Focalism: A source of the durability bias in affective forecasting. *Journal of Personality and Social Psychology, 78*, 821–836.

Wirtz, D., Kruger, J., Napa Scollon, C., & Diener, E. (2003). What to do on spring break? The role of predicted, on-line, and remembered experience in future choice. *Psychological Science, 14*, 520–524.

Zauberman, G., & Lynch, J. G. (2005). Resource slack and propensity to discount delayed investments of time versus money. *Journal of Experimental Psychology: General, 134*, 23–37.

Section III

Counterfactual Thinking:
Simulating the Past

10 Cognitive Processes in Counterfactual Thinking

Ruth M. J. Byrne and Vittorio Girotto

INTRODUCTION

One of the extraordinary achievements of human cognition is that people are able to consider and reason about facts, as they remember or understand them, and they are also able to consider and reason about hypothetical possibilities. The ability to think hypothetically is fundamental to reasoning and decision making. People often think about hypothetical alternative possibilities when they imagine the future, such as, "If I arrange a reasonable mortgage, I could buy a small apartment in the center of the city." These thoughts about future alternatives may assist people in planning and predicting. But, people also tend to think about hypothetical alternative possibilities when they remember the past, such as, "If I had bought property before prices increased, I would have been able to afford a larger house." These *counterfactual* alternatives may help them to work out the causes of outcomes (e.g., Roese & Olson, 1995). Thinking about counterfactual alternatives may also help people to prepare for the future by informing them about how to prevent bad outcomes (McMullen & Markman, 2002; Roese, 1997; in this volume, see also Markman, Karadogan, Lindberg, & Zell, Chapter 12).

Considerable research has been directed at understanding how people think about what might have been (Mandel, Hilton, & Catellani, 2005). Consider the following scenario:

> Anna, an undergraduate at your university, was asked to participate in a game by a research assistant, who told her, "In order to win two chocolates, you have to mentally multiply either two 1-digit numbers or two 2-digit numbers in 30 seconds. If you fail, you do not receive the chocolates. The two multiplication problems are contained in two sealed envelopes. Let us call them envelope A and envelope B. Of course, we do not know which envelope contains the 1-digit multiplication problem and which one contains the 2-digit multiplication problem." Anna agreed to participate. She chose envelope A. It contained the 2-digit multiplication problem. She failed. Things would have been better for Anna, if …

Studies using scenarios such as the one outlined (adapted from Girotto, Ferrante, Pighin, & Gonzalez, 2007) have provided considerable information about how people think about what might have been. People's counterfactual thoughts have consequences for their experience of emotions such as regret, relief, and guilt and their judgments of cause, responsibility, and blame (Roese, 1997). What cognitive processes underlie the way people think about counterfactual alternatives? One clue comes from what people change about the facts of the situation when they imagine a counterfactual alternative. For example, most people tend to focus on exceptional events rather than routine ones (Kahneman & Miller, 1986; Kahneman & Tversky, 1982b). Moreover, individuals tend to focus on actions rather than inactions (Byrne & McEleney, 2000; Kahneman & Tversky, 1982a) and on controllable rather than uncontrollable actions and events (Girotto, Legrenzi, & Rizzo, 1991; see also Markman, Gavanski, Sherman, & McMullen, 1995; McCloy & Byrne, 2000). Moreover, they tend to focus on aspects of the facts that are in the foreground and have been explicitly represented in their mental representation of the facts (Byrne 2005; Kahneman & Tversky, 1982b; Legrenzi,

Girotto, & Johnson-Laird, 1993). These commonalities suggest that there may be fault lines in reality, junctures that individuals readily identify as mutable in their mental representation of the facts (Kahneman & Tversky, 1982b; see also Hofstadter, 1985).

We suggest that the cognitive processes that underlie the ability people have to imagine counterfactual alternatives are the same processes that guide an individual's mental representation of possibilities (Byrne, 2002). We propose that the possibilities that people think about are guided by the small set of principles that also govern how they generate inferences about counterfactual possibilities, such as, "If Anna had chosen envelope B, she would have won the chocolates" (Byrne, 2005). In this chapter, we examine some recent evidence that indicates that context influences the sorts of possibilities people think about. First, we describe an example of the effect of context on the inferences that individuals tend to make from counterfactual conditionals. Next, we describe an example of the effect of context on the sorts of features that individuals focus on when they simulate counterfactual alternatives.

COUNTERFACTUAL CONDITIONALS

Consider a conditional in the indicative mood such as, "If Anna chooses envelope B, she wins the chocolates." In general, people tend to think about true possibilities but not false possibilities (Johnson-Laird & Byrne, 2002). Thus, they understand the indicative conditional by thinking about the possibility that is true given the assertion "Anna chooses envelope B, and she wins the chocolates," but they do not think about the possibility that is ruled out as false by the assertion "Anna chooses envelope B and does not win the chocolates." There is growing experimental evidence to support this "principle of truth." For example, it has been shown that individuals fall prey to "illusory" inferences when they do not consider false possibilities. Illusory inferences can be illustrated by the following example (from Johnson-Laird, Legrenzi, Girotto and Legrenzi, 2000): Consider the following two sentences: "If there is an A, there is a C or else if there is a B, there is a C" and "There is an A and a C." Can the two sentences be true at the same time? Almost all participants in experiments say that they can, but this answer is an illusion. If the second sentence is true, then both of the conditionals in the first sentence are true. It follows that the first sentence (an exclusive disjunction) is false. People may find illusory inferences difficult to resist because they tend to think about true possibilities rather than false possibilities.

People also tend to think about few possibilities rather than many possibilities. The indicative conditional, "If Anna chooses envelope B, she wins the chocolates," is consistent with several true possibilities, including "Anna chooses envelope B, and she wins the chocolates" and "Anna does not choose envelope B, and she does not win the chocolates." But, people do not tend to think of all of the true possibilities, perhaps because of the constraints of working memory (Johnson-Laird & Byrne, 1991). Instead, they tend to think about a single possibility corresponding to the topic mentioned in the assertion, such as, "Anna chooses envelope B, and she wins the chocolates" (Johnson-Laird, Byrne, & Schaeken, 1992).

When people think about what might have been, they think about things that they suppose or know to be false, but they temporarily suppose them to be true. For example, they may think, "If only Anna had chosen envelope B, she would have won the chocolates." The conditional is in the subjunctive mood, which can serve as a linguistic cue to think about different possibilities (Byrne, 2005). People think about two possibilities to mentally represent this counterfactual conditional. They think about the facts, "Anna did not choose envelope B, and she did not win the chocolates," and they think about the conjecture, "Anna chose envelope B, and she won the chocolates." They keep track of the facts and the counterfactual possibilities (Byrne, 2005; Johnson-Laird & Byrne, 1991). In fact, individuals who have read a counterfactual conditional such as "If Anna had chosen envelope B, then she would have won the chocolates" incorrectly report that they had previously read sentences that expressed the presupposed facts, that is, "Anna did not choose envelope B," and "Anna did not win the chocolates" (Fillenbaum, 1974; see also Thompson & Byrne, 2002).

There is an important difference between the mental representation of an indicative conditional about a hypothetical situation, "If Anna chose envelope B, she won the chocolates," and a counterfactual conditional about what might have been, "If Anna had chosen envelope B, she would have won the chocolates." People think about a *single* possibility when they understand the indicative conditional "Anna chose envelope B and she won the chocolates," but they think about *two* possibilities when they understand the counterfactual, the conjecture "Anna chose envelope B, and she won the chocolates" and the facts "Anna did not choose envelope B, and she did not win the chocolates" (Byrne & Tasso, 1999). Empirical support for the proposition that people think about more possibilities to understand what might have been includes evidence that people can readily make inferences from counterfactual conditionals that they find difficult to make from indicative conditionals. A comparison of two inferences, the *modus ponens* and *modus tollens* inferences, illustrates the difference.

The *modus ponens* inference has the logical form, if A then B, A, therefore B. The *modus tollens* inference has the logical form, if A then B, not B, therefore not A. Logicians consider both inferences to be valid from a standard indicative conditional (Jeffrey, 1981). Many psychological experiments have shown that individuals can make the *modus ponens* inference far more readily than the *modus tollens* one (Evans, Newstead, & Byrne, 1993). Why does this difference in inferential difficulty occur? One way to make an inference is to think about the possibilities that are true given the premises and to examine whether the conclusion is true when the premises are true (Johnson-Laird & Byrne, 2002). When people understand the conditional, "If Anna chose envelope B, she won the chocolates," they think about the possibility that "She chose envelope B, and she won the chocolates." When they understand a second premise, such as, "She chose envelope B," they can match it to the possibility they have thought about for the conditional and make the inference "She won the chocolates." The *modus ponens* inference is made readily from an indicative conditional because the information in the second premise matches directly the initial possibility that individuals think about when they understand the conditional. It is equally easy to make the inference from the counterfactual conditional given that individuals have also mentally represented the conjecture, "She chose envelope B, and she won the chocolates."

Consider now the *modus tollens* inference from the conditional, "If Anna chose envelope B, then she won the chocolates," and the second premise, "She did not win the chocolates." People find it hard to make the inference from the indicative conditional. In experiments, only about half of all participants draw this inference, whereas the other half say that nothing follows from the premises. The source of the difficulty may be that the information in the second premise does not match the possibility that people thought about initially when they understood the conditional. To make the inference, people need to think not only about the possibility "She chose envelope B, and she won the chocolates," but also about the other true possibilities, such as, "She did not choose envelope B, and she did not win the chocolates." They must "flesh out" their initial representation to think about other possibilities. In contrast, the *modus tollens* inference can be made readily from the counterfactual conditional, "If Anna had chosen envelope B, then she would have won the chocolates" (Byrne & Tasso, 1999; Thompson & Byrne, 2002). For the counterfactual conditional, people think about both possibilities from the outset, the conjecture, "She chose envelope B, and she won the chocolates," and also the presupposed facts, "She did not choose envelope B, and she did not win the chocolates." The information in the second premise matches the information they have represented from the outset when they understood the counterfactual.

The principles that guide the possibilities that people think about include the principle of truth (that people think about true possibilities) and the principle of parsimony (that people think about few possibilities). They also include the principle of counterfactual possibilities: People keep track of the epistemic status of the possibilities they think about, for example, that a possibility corresponds to the presupposed facts, or that a possibility is a false possibility temporarily supposed to be true (Johnson-Laird & Byrne, 2002). The same principles help to explain both how people make rational inferences about counterfactual possibilities and how they create such imagined alternatives (Byrne,

2005). The relation between the inferences people draw and the counterfactual alternatives they imagine is illustrated by a recent study to which we now turn that compares inferences derived from imagined counterfactual alternatives to inferences derived from given counterfactual alternatives.

CONTEXT MATTERS

Sometimes, counterfactuals are created in situations in which the facts are known. For example, suppose you witness the selection by Anna of envelope A and her failure to win the chocolates. You know the facts of the situation, and you create a mental alternative, "If Anna had chosen envelope B, she would have won." However, other counterfactuals are created when the facts are unknown. For example, you might say, "If Paul Newman had won an Oscar for *Cool Hand Luke*, it would have been well deserved," even though you may not know whether Paul Newman won the Oscar (Byrne, 2005). Does knowing the facts or not affect the inferences people draw from counterfactual conditionals? Recent evidence suggests that it does.

A study by Caren Frosch examined whether people draw different inferences from counterfactual conditionals when they are based on known facts versus presupposed facts (Byrne & Frosch, 2007). Consider the conditional, "If Jane had taken the newer drug, she would have won the race." How is this assertion understood? We suggest that people think both about the possibility corresponding to the conjecture, "Jane took the newer drug, and she won the race," as well as the facts that a speaker uttering the counterfactual may have presupposed, namely, "Jane did not take the newer drug, and she did not win the race." We may call these conditionals "presupposed facts" counterfactuals (Byrne & Frosch, 2007). Individuals do not know which facts actually occurred, but they may tend to assume that certain facts are presupposed by a speaker who utters the counterfactual. They may make a mental note that one possibility corresponds to the conjecture, whereas the other corresponds to the presupposed facts.

Now suppose you were told the following story about Jane (from Byrne & Frosch, 2007, adapted from Boninger, Gleicher, & Strathman, 1994; McCloy & Byrne, 2002):

> Jane is a runner, and since the age of eight she has competed in the sprint races in local track and field events. Up through school, she had won every race in which she had competed. It was at the age of 13 that she began to dream about the Olympics. At the age of 18, before starting college, she decides to give the Olympics one all-out shot. She makes the Irish Olympic team for the 400-meter race.
>
> On the day before the 400-meter race, in a freak accident during training, she sprains her left ankle. Although there is no break or fracture, when she tries to run, the pain is excruciating. Her trainer tells her about many advances in pain-killing medications and assures her that she will still be able to participate. He recommends that she choose between two drugs, both legal according to Olympic guidelines. One is a well-known painkiller that has been proved effective but also has some serious side effects, including temporary nausea and drowsiness. The other painkiller is a newer and less-well-known drug. Although the research suggests that the newer drug might be a more effective painkiller, its side effects are not yet known because it has not been widely used.
>
> After considerable thought, she elects to go with the more well-known drug. On the day of the race, although there is no pain in her ankle, she already begins to feel the nausea and finds herself fighting off fatigue. She finishes in fourth place, only 1/10 of a second from a bronze medal, 4/10 from a silver, and 5/10 from a gold medal.
>
> After the event, she learns that some athletes in other events who were suffering from similar injuries used the other, newer drug. They felt no pain and experienced no side effects.
>
> Imagine that in the days and weeks following the race Jane thinks, "If only." How do you think she completed this thought?

Consider now the assertion, "If Jane had taken the newer drug, she would have won the race." How is this assertion understood? We suggest that people think both about the possibility corresponding to the conjecture, "Jane took the newer drug, and she won the race," as well as the facts that they know to be the case given the story, specifically, "Jane did not take the newer drug, and she did not win the race." We may call these conditionals "known facts" counterfactuals. In this case, individuals may make a mental note that one possibility corresponds to the conjecture, whereas the other corresponds to the actual known facts.

Do people draw the same inferences from presupposed-facts counterfactuals and from known-facts counterfactuals? We tested the question by asking three groups of participants to draw inferences from conditionals. In the control group, participants made inferences from standard indicative conditionals (e.g., "If Jane took the newer drug, she won the race") in the presupposed-facts experimental group, participants made inferences from a counterfactual conditional presented by itself (e.g., "If Jane had taken the newer drug, she would have won the race"), and in the known-facts experimental group, participants made inferences from the same counterfactual after first reading the story and completing the "if only" question.

We expected that participants in the known-facts group would draw different inferences compared to those in the presupposed-facts group. In particular, we expected that participants in the known-facts group might find it difficult to discount the facts and would thus be less inclined to set aside their appreciation of the facts that, "She did not take the new drug, and she did not win." Hence, we predicted that they would find it harder to draw inferences that relied on the possibility corresponding to the conjecture, "She took the newer drug, and she won the race." Accordingly, we predicted that they would make fewer of the *modus ponens* inferences from "She took the newer drug" to "She won the race." The results corroborated this prediction. We found that participants made fewer *modus ponens* inferences from the known-facts counterfactual (49%) as compared to the presupposed-facts counterfactual (86%) and the indicative conditional (80%).

Unexpectedly, the experiment also showed that people were reluctant to draw inferences even based on the presupposed facts (i.e., "She did not take the new drug, and she did not win the race") in the known-facts condition compared to the presupposed-facts condition. They made fewer of the *modus tollens* inferences from "She did not win the race" to "She did not take the new drug" based on the known-facts counterfactual (45%) and the indicative conditional (58%) as compared to the presupposed-facts counterfactual (81%). Perhaps the construction of the counterfactual conjecture, "If she had taken the other drug" made it difficult for them to draw inferences based solely on the facts. There are several different interpretations of a conditional, each of which supports different sorts of inferences (Johnson-Laird & Byrne, 2002). Participants' interpretation of the conditional appears to be changed by their reading of the story, an interpretation that no longer supports a *modus ponens* or *modus tollens* inference (Byrne & Frosch, 2007).

The results of this experiment illustrate some of the features of the relation between inferences drawn from counterfactual conditionals and the creation of counterfactual alternatives, and they show that context influences the inferences that people draw from counterfactuals. Knowledge of the facts affects the inferences that people are willing to make when they reason about counterfactual possibilities. The cognitive processes that underlie the way people draw inferences from counterfactual conditionals may share a lot in common with the cognitive processes that underlie the way people imagine counterfactual alternatives, and it is to the imagination of counterfactual alternatives that we now turn.

IMAGINED COUNTERFACTUAL ALTERNATIVES

When people think about how a bad outcome could have turned out differently given a scenario to read, they typically change the protagonist's controllable actions, such as, "If only Anna had chosen the other envelope" (Girotto et al., 1991). But, do people change the same things when they think about something that happened to them as compared to when they think about something that happened to someone they have read about? Many studies have focused on how people think about what might have been when they read fictional stories, with the implicit assumption that the findings generalize well to how people think about their own experiences (for a review, see Byrne, 2002). However, a recent set of findings casts doubt on that assumption (Girotto et al., 2007).

It is well known that an individual's perspective or role may affect their inferences and choices (for a review, see Hertwig & Ortman, 2001) as well as corresponding neural activations (e.g., Ruby & Decety, 2004). An individual's perspective could affect the construction of counterfactual alternatives as well (Girotto et al., 2007). One reason to posit a difference between readers and actors in their mental simulations is the difference in the information that is available and salient to readers as opposed to actors. Readers of Anna's story undo her choice because it easily evokes the alternative in which she chooses the other envelope. However, actors have more information available to them regarding numerous features of the problem-solving phase (e.g., the difficulty of the selected task, its time limit; see also McGill, 1989). These features relate to the salient part of the actors' experience, and modifying each of them leads to the construction of an alternative in which they solve the chosen problem. Thus, actors may tend to focus on problem features in their "if only" thoughts more often than readers (Girotto et al., 2007).

Do readers and actors create the same counterfactual alternatives? A study designed to test this question employed two groups of participants. One group read the version of Anna's story outlined earlier about a participant who chose between two envelopes to win chocolates (the "reader" condition). The participants' task was to generate at least one modification to the story so that things would have been better for Anna. A second group was invited to take part in a game in which they faced the same choice as Anna (the "actor" condition). The experimenter arranged the content of the envelopes in such a way that the chosen envelope always contained the difficult problem. Participants were then informed that they had failed and were asked to generate at least one way in which things could have been better for them. When readers thought about how the outcome could have been different, the majority of them (76%) focused on Anna's choice (e.g., "If Anna had chosen the other envelope"; Girotto et al., 2007, Study 1). But, when actors thought about how the outcome could have been different, the majority (70%) focused on problem features (e.g., "If I had had more time" or "If I had had a pen").

The finding that actors and readers construct different counterfactual alternatives (i.e., the "role effect") is robust. In another study, before asking the counterfactual question, the experimenter opened the envelope that the actor had not selected and showed that it contained an easy problem (e.g., 3 × 7). Although actors were made aware that the alternative choice would have produced a positive outcome, they modified problem features (Girotto et al., 2007, Study 2). The effect also does not depend on the nature of the choice. Actors constructed counterfactuals that focused on problem features when they made a blind choice by selecting one envelope without knowing whether it contained an easy or a difficult problem. Yet, they continued to focus on problem features even when they made an informed choice by deliberately selecting the envelope containing the more difficult (but more rewarding) problem (Girotto et al., 2007, Study 4). The effect could be attributed to motivational factors: Actors constructed problem feature counterfactuals because, unlike readers, they were motivated to avoid self-blame for their wrong choice (Elster, 1999; Gilbert, Morewedge, Risen, & Wilson, 2004). However, this interpretation cannot explain why actors focused on problem features in the blind choice condition in which they could not blame themselves for selecting the envelope with the difficult problem. Moreover, the motivational interpretation cannot explain the finding that actors modified problem features even in a condition in which the experimenter, rather than themselves, chose the envelope with the problem (Girotto et al., 2007, Study 7).

CONTEXT MATTERS

Why do actors focus on different features in their counterfactual thoughts compared to readers? A recent series of studies shows that the context in which individuals acquire information matters (Pighin, Byrne, Ferrante, Gonzalez, & Girotto, 2007). In one study, we investigated the counterfactual alternatives produced by observers, that is, individuals who were present during the sequence of events that led an actor to experience the negative outcome. Unlike readers—but like actors—observers can gather direct information about the events producing the outcome, that is, not only the actors' choice but also the features of the problem-solving phase (e.g., the perceived shortness of time available for the task, the lack of pen and paper). Because they see the actor's experience with the events, observers are likely to form the same mental representation of reality as the actor does. In other words, unlike readers, observers are likely to have "cognitive empathy" for the actor and to focus on the elements that are salient for the actor. Therefore, if the role effect depends on the differential availability and salience of information to actors and readers, then observers should focus on problem features just as actors do. Note that observers do not share actors' involvement in the situation and their affective evaluation of the resulting negative outcome. Therefore, if the role effect depends on motivational factors, then observers should not construct the same counterfactuals as actors do. Instead, they should undo the actor's choice, just as readers undo the protagonist's choice.

One study employed three groups of participants. Participants in the "readers" group read the version of Anna's story as outlined earlier, and those in the "actors" group took part in the situation. Participants in the "observers" group sat next to an actor (a confederate) and witnessed the actor carrying out the task. At the end of the game, the confederate left the room, and participants were required to generate at least one way in which things could have been better for the player (see Pighin et al., 2008, Study 1). As predicted, observers behaved just like actors did. Specifically, observers (80%) focused on problem features to the same extent that actors did (92%). Readers, by contrast, tended to focus on the envelope choice (60%).

If context matters, is it simply because it provides more information? Do actors and observers merely have more information about the problem-solving phase to focus on in their "if only" thoughts? As it turns out, information quantity is not the answer. In another experiment, we compared the counterfactuals produced by actors, standard readers, and readers who read a version of Anna's story enriched by information about her behavior during the problem-solving phase:

It's a two-digit, two numbers multiplication: 68 × 76. Anna carefully observes the numbers, she concentrates, and she begins to solve the multiplication problem. She keeps her eyes on the paper for some time. She moves her right index finger ahead and back on the paper nearby the numbers about which she is reasoning. At the same time, she uses her left-hand fingers to count numbers. Suddenly, her left hand stops. The research assistant watches the timer. Anna continues to move her right index finger on the numbers indicated in the paper, and she mumbles numbers looking at the sky. Then, she continues to count on her left hand. At that moment, the research assistant says: "Time is up, I'm sorry. Do you have an answer?" Anna answers, "No," and she doesn't win anything.

Once again, most actors (91%) focused on problem features, and most standard readers (75%) focused on the envelope choice. Importantly, however, the majority of the "well-informed" readers (72%) also focused on the choice of the envelope. Thus, enriching the description of the problem-solving phase was not sufficient to ensure that readers focused on it (Pighin et al., 2008, Study 5).

These experiments demonstrate that context matters. Unlike readers, observers have direct experience of the events experienced by the actor, and thus they construct mental representations and alternatives to reality similar to those constructed by the actor. In sum, the way in which people acquire information about the facts affects the way that they think about alternatives to them.

CONCLUSIONS

People may rely on similar cognitive processes to make inferences about counterfactual possibilities as they do to imagine counterfactual alternatives (Byrne, 2005). The cognitive processes may be ones that construct mental representations of possibilities and that operate on representations of possibilities. A small set of principles may guide the sorts of possibilities that people think about. For example, they tend to think about few possibilities and true possibilities; they tend to think about counterfactual possibilities by thinking about the presupposed facts and also about an imagined alternative, presumed not to correspond to the facts but temporarily conjectured to be true (Johnson-Laird and Byrne, 2002). In this chapter, we have suggested that the cognitive processes that underlie making inferences from counterfactual conditionals and those that underlie imagining counterfactual alternatives may be sensitive to context. That is, the way in which individuals acquire information affects both they way they reason from counterfactual conditionals and they way they create counterfactual alternatives.

The finding that individuals make different inferences from counterfactual conditionals when they are presented in the context of a story that makes clear what the facts are has implications for understanding human reasoning (Byrne & Frosch, 2007). Individuals who are given a story that describes an antecedent and an outcome and then are required to make inferences from a counterfactual conditional that conjectures the opposite antecedent and the opposite outcome generate fewer inferences than do individuals who are given the counterfactual conditional without the contextual information. Their interpretation of a counterfactual conditional, such as, "If the runner had taken the other drug, she would have won the race," appears to change even to the extent that they are no longer prepared to make simple inferences from it, such as the inference from "she took the other drug" to the conclusion "she won the race." Their knowledge of the reality based on the story, that the runner did not in fact take the other drug and did not in fact win the race, appears to be difficult to set aside. Equally, their own construction of the counterfactual conjecture, "If she had taken the other drug," appears to make it hard for them to draw inferences based solely on the facts, such as the inference from "she did not win the race" to "she did not take the other drug."

In addition, the finding that in some cases actors and readers imagine different counterfactual alternatives has widespread implications for understanding the human imagination (Girotto et al., 2007). Readers of a scenario that describes a protagonist's choice to tackle a given problem and the ineffective attempts to solve it focus on the protagonist's choice of envelope. Yet, actors who make the same choice and face the same negative outcome as that depicted in the scenario focus on the features of the problem-solving task itself. This finding calls into question the tendency in many previous studies on counterfactual thinking to rely on scenarios in which participants acquired information in their role as readers (see also Girotto et al., 1991, p. 126; Markman et al., 1995, for a discussion of this point). Instead, it highlights the importance of relying on "in vivo" procedures (see also Gilbert et al., 2004). The discovery of a difference in what actors and readers imagine does not imply that acting and nonacting individuals always imagine different counterfactual alternatives. Observers of another individual's actions produce the same types of "if only" thoughts as generated by the acting individual (Pighin et al., 2008). The observation of an acting individual leads the nonacting individual to construct similar mental representations and similar alternatives to reality as the acting individual does. In all, these findings confirm the extraordinary ability of humans to simulate another individual's mental states.

ACKNOWLEDGMENTS

We thank Keith Markman for his comments on a previous version of this chapter. We are grateful to Caren Frosh for her collaboration on the counterfactual inferences studies and Donatella Ferrante, Michel Gonzalez, and Stefania Pighin for their collaboration in the role effects studies. We thank Caren Frosch and Ilaria Camozzo for their help in experiments on role effects in counterfactual thinking. Preparation of this chapter was funded in part by a Government of Ireland research projects grant from the Irish Research Council for Humanities and Social Sciences to Ruth Byrne and by a COFIN (2005117840_003) grant from the Italian Ministry of Universities to Vittorio Girotto.

REFERENCES

Boninger, D. S., Gleicher, F., & Strathman, A. (1994). Counterfactual thinking: From what might have been to what may be. *Journal of Personality and Social Psychology, 67,* 297–307.

Byrne, R. M. J. (2002). Counterfactual thinking and mental models. *Trends in Cognitive Sciences, 6,* 426–431.

Byrne, R. M. J. (2005). *The rational imagination: How people create alternatives to reality.* Cambridge, MA: MIT Press.

Byrne, R. M. J., & Frosch, C. (2007). *Context effects in counterfactual inferences.* Manuscript submitted for publication.

Byrne, R. M. J., & McEleney, (2000). Counterfactual thinking about actions and failures to act. *Journal of Experimental Psychology: Learning, Memory, & Cognition, 26,* 1318–1331.

Byrne, R. M. J., & Tasso, A. (1999). Deductive reasoning with factual, possible and counterfactual conditionals. *Memory & Cognition, 27*(4), 726–740.

Elster, J. (1999). *Alchemies of mind.* Cambridge, England: Cambridge University Press.

Evans, J. St. B. T., Newstead, S., & Byrne, R. M. J. (1993). *Human reasoning: The psychology of deduction.* Hove: Erlbaum.

Gilbert, D. T., Morewedge, C. K., Risen, J. L., & Wilson, T. D. (2004). Looking forward to looking backward. The misprediction of regret. *Psychological Science, 15,* 346–350.

Girotto, V., Ferrante, D., Pighin, S., & Gonzalez, M. (2007). Post-decisional counterfactual thinking by actors and readers. *Psychological Science, 18,* 510–515.

Girotto, V., Legrenzi, P., & Rizzo, A. (1991). Counterfactual thinking: The role of event controllability. *Acta Psychologica, 78,* 111–133.

Fillenbaum, S. (1974). Information amplified: Memory for counterfactual conditionals. *Journal of Experimental Psychology, 102,* 44–49.

Hertwig, R., & Ortmann, A. (2001). Experimental practices in economics: A methodological challenge for psychologists? *Brain and Behavioral Sciences, 24,* 383–403.

Hofstadter, D. R. (1985). *Metamagical themas: Questing for the essence of mind and pattern.* London: Penguin.

Jeffrey, R. (1981). *Formal logic: Its scope and limits* (2nd ed.). New York: McGraw-Hill.

Johnson-Laird, P. N., & Byrne, R. M. J. (1991). *Deduction.* Hillsdale, NJ: Erlbaum.

Johnson-Laird, P. N., & Byrne, R. M. J. (2002). Conditionals: A theory of meaning, pragmatics, and inference. *Psychological Review, 109,* 646–678.

Johnson-Laird, P. N., Byrne, R. M. J., & Schaeken, W. (1992). Propositional reasoning by model. *Psychological Review, 99,* 418–439.

Johnson-Laird, P. N., Legrenzi, P., Girotto, V., & Legrenzi, M. (2000). Illusions in reasoning about consistency. *Science, 288,* 531–532.

Kahneman, D., & Miller, D. (1986). Norm theory: Comparing reality to its alternatives. *Psychological Review, 93,* 136–153.

Kahneman, D., & Tversky, A. (1982a). The psychology of preferences. *Scientific American, 246,* 160–173.

Kahneman, D., & Tversky, A. (1982b). The simulation heuristic. In D. Kahneman, P. Slovic, & A. Tversky (Eds.), *Judgment under uncertainty: Heuristics and biases* (pp. 201–211). Cambridge, England: Cambridge University Press.

Legrenzi, P., Girotto, V., & Johnson-Laird, P. N. (1993). Focussing in reasoning and decision-making. *Cognition, 49,* 37–66.

Mandel, D. R., Hilton, D. J., & Catellani, P. (2005). *The psychology of counterfactual thinking.* London: Routledge.

Markman, K. D., Gavanski, I., Sherman, S. J., & McMullen, M. N. (1995). The impact of perceived control on the imagination of better and worse possible worlds. *Personality and Social Psychology Bulletin, 21,* 588–595.

McCloy, R., & Byrne, R. M. J. (2000). Counterfactual thinking about controllable events. *Memory & Cognition, 28,* 1071–1078.

McCloy, R., & Byrne, R. M. J. (2002). Semifactual "even if" thinking. *Thinking and Reasoning, 8,* 41–67.

McMullen, M. N., & Markman, K. D. (2002). Affective impact of close counterfactuals: Implications of possible futures for possible pasts. *Journal of Experimental Social Psychology, 38,* 64–70.

Pighin, S., Byrne, R. M. J., Ferrante, D., Gonzalez, M., & Girotto, V. (2007). *Cognitive empathy and the imagination of counterfactual alternatives.* Manuscript submitted for publication.

Roese, N. J. (1997). Counterfactual thinking. *Psychological Bulletin, 121,* 133–148.

Roese, N. J., & Olson, J. M. (1995). *What might have been: The social psychology of counterfactual thinking.* Mahwah, NJ: Erlbaum.

Ruby, P., & Decety, J. (2004). How would *you* feel versus how do you think *she* would feel? A neuroimaging study of perspective-taking with social emotions. *Journal of Cognitive Neuroscience, 16,* 988–999.

Thompson, V. A., & Byrne, R. M. J. (2002). Reasoning counterfactually: Making inferences about things that didn't happen. *Journal of Experimental Psychology: Learning, Memory, and Cognition, 28,* 1154–1170.

11 The Counterfactual Mind-Set: A Decade of Research

Elaine M. Wong, Adam D. Galinsky, and Laura J. Kray

INTRODUCTION

Imagine you are at a concert of one of your favorite bands. Seating is on a first come, first serve basis. At the concert, the announcer reveals that a trip to Hawaii will be given to a lucky fan, and that the winner will be determined by the seat number currently occupied. Now imagine you see a person move seats because his view of the stage is partially obstructed. Shortly after they change seats, the winning seat number is announced. It turns out that the winning seat was the seat from which that person *had just moved*. If you are like the hundreds of individuals who have participated in our experiments using this scenario, you would instantly and spontaneously conjure up thoughts such as, "If only he had not moved, he would have won," and empathically appreciate his poignant sense of disappointment and regret (Kahneman & Miller, 1986).

Indeed, whenever individuals muse about how reality might have turned out differently or consider what almost was, they are engaging in counterfactual thinking. Thoughts of "if only" and "what if" are signposts for counterfactual musings, and their presence in mental life is both pervasive and predictable. They are not only ubiquitous, but also serve a critical role in cognitive functioning. Beyond the meditations of daydreamers and artists conjuring up imaginary worlds, they are essential tools in effective problem solving and social functioning. The process of simulating and considering alternative worlds transforms cognitive processes and reorients how an individual engages and plays with subsequent information (see also Byrne & Girotto, Chapter 10, this volume). In this chapter, we summarize a decade of research showing that thinking counterfactually activates a particular mind-set that guides perception of others, and problem solving.

THE NATURE OF COUNTERFACTUAL THOUGHTS

Although the ability to undo events and construct possible worlds is theoretically unlimited, in reality, when and how counterfactuals are constructed is fairly predictable. The commencement of counterfactual thinking is often initiated when an event *nearly* occurred (Kahneman & Miller, 1986; Roese & Olson, 1997). For example, missing a plane by 5 min tends to evoke more counterfactuals than missing a plane by an hour. In addition to near misses, abnormal events tend to produce counterfactual thoughts. Kahneman and Tversky (1982) used a skiing metaphor to describe the laws governing mutability: Just as it is easier to ski downhill than uphill, it is easier to mutate abnormal (routine-violating) events back to normality than to go from normality to exceptionality. For example, it is easier to undo missing one's flight when a new, atypical route to the airport was taken than after taking one's usual route. Finally, negative and unexpected or surprising events increase the production of counterfactual thoughts (Roese & Hur, 1997; Roese & Olson, 1997; Sanna & Turley, 1996). When we have a need to change or understand the world, counterfactuals are readily available cognitive tools to deal with an uncertain and disquieting environment.

Constructing a counterfactual thought implicitly involves laying out a causal chain of events in a sequence of actions and mutating one step in the process to construct an alternate reality. To the extent that a mutation to an initial event undoes the occurrence of subsequent events, that initial event is seen as causally connected to what happened later (Wells, Taylor, & Turtle, 1987). Thus, running a counterfactual simulation in one's head is the mental equivalent of conducting an experiment. Like the experimental process, counterfactual thinking involves a logical consideration of relationships and causal associations between events (Einhorn & Hogarth, 1986; Mandel & Lehman, 1996; Wells & Gavanski, 1989).

Counterfactuals also involve a comparison between reality and what might have been. This comparison process highlights that counterfactuals come in two different flavors; they are classified according to the direction of this comparison. *Upward counterfactuals* are thoughts about how events could have turned out better, and they tend to intensify negative feelings such as regret, remorse, and disappointment. *Downward counterfactuals*, on the other hand, compare reality to worse possible outcomes and tend to intensify feelings such as joy or surprise at one's good fortune and sometimes guilt or relief that one avoided a disastrous alternative reality (e.g., Markman, Gavanski, Sherman, & McMullen, 1993; Roese, 1994; Sanna, 1996). As detailed in this chapter, upward and downward counterfactuals not only differ in their direction of comparison but also serve distinct functions.

FUNCTIONS OF COUNTERFACTUAL THINKING

Evidence that counterfactuals are an integral part of normal cognitive functions comes from findings that counterfactual thinking is impaired in a variety of disorders. For example, patients with schizophrenia show difficulty in articulating counterfactual thoughts, and this diminished ability to engage in counterfactual thinking partially explains their impaired social functioning (Hooker, Roese, & Park, 2000). Similarly, patients with Parkinson's disease spontaneously generate fewer counterfactuals and perform worse on a counterfactual inference test compared to matched controls (McNamara, Durso, Brown, & Lynch, 2003). The research on both Parkinson's disease and schizophrenia suggests that the ability to construct and make counterfactual inferences is a barometer of frontal lobe capacity. In fact, scores on counterfactual generation and counterfactual inference measures correlate with performance on tests traditionally linked to both frontal lobe functioning and tests of pragmatic communication skills (McNamara et al., 2003).

Counterfactuals are also deeply connected to a core human capacity: the ability to create and find meaning in events and the world (Galinsky, Liljenquist, Kray, & Roese, 2005). Simply considering the alternative paths one's life may have traveled imbue that life with a greater sense of meaning and significance.

Counterfactuals serve both an affective and preparative function. The direction of counterfactual thinking determines whether affect or problem solving is benefited from mental simulation. Upward counterfactual thoughts depress mood but enhance subsequent performance, whereas downward counterfactuals elevate mood but depress later task engagement and performance. Thus, upward counterfactuals produce short-term pain in the service of long-term learning, whereas downward counterfactuals are an immediate balm but do not motivate the self toward improvement (but for exceptions, see Markman, Karadogan, Lindberg, & Zell, Chapter 12, this volume; Markman & McMullen, 2003). Roese (1994) found that directing participants to construct counterfactual thoughts after one anagram task led to better performance on a subsequent anagram task, and it did so by helping to specify the necessary conditions to avoid replication of previous errors. Also, knowing that a task is going to be repeated has been shown to increase the production of upward counterfactual thoughts (Markman et al., 1993). This link from upward counterfactual generation to forming appropriate behavioral intentions is impaired in schizophrenics, further highlighting how upward counterfactual thoughts help individuals learn from experience to effectively regulate their social behavior (Roese, Park, Smallman, & Gibson, 2007). Through the rearview mirror of the upward alternative past, counterfactuals create road maps for the future (for a more extensive review of the affective and preparative consequences of counterfactual thinking, see Markman et al., Chapter 12, this volume).

An interesting context for exploring the functions of counterfactual mind-sets is the bargaining table. Galinsky, Seiden, Kim, and Medvec (2002) found that the more upward counterfactual thoughts negotiators generated in one negotiation, the longer they spent preparing for subsequent negotiations. However, such thoughts also reduced the extent to which negotiators subsequently made first offers, despite the fact that strategic behavior confers a bargaining advantage (Galinsky & Mussweiler, 2001). In a follow-up investigation, Kray and Gelfand (in press) observed that gender moderates whether the affective versus preparative function of counterfactuals prevails following the acceptance of a first offer. Consistent with the observation that women are stereotypically disadvantaged in the competitive negotiation arena (Kray, Thompson, & Galinsky, 2001), women tended to experience relief, which is associated with downward counterfactual thoughts, when their negotiation ended abruptly after they made a first offer. In contrast, men's reactions followed the pattern observed by Galinsky et al., with a heightened sense of regret that they did not make a more extreme opening offer. These findings suggest that counterfactuals serve multiple purposes—affective and preparative—that sometimes conflict with one another (Markman et al., 1993).

THE COUNTERFACTUAL MIND-SET

The preceding section detailed how counterfactuals help individuals prepare for the future (in this volume, see also Carroll & Shepperd, Chapter 28; Zeelenberg & Pieters, Chapter 27). This research has demonstrated that generating counterfactual thoughts in one domain (i.e., anagram tasks, negotiations) affects subsequent behavior in that exact same domain. But, given its ubiquity and its functional nature, considering counterfactual possibilities may alter thinking and affect subsequent information processing in completely unrelated domains as well. Our research over the past 10 years, summarized in Figure 11.1, has explored how thinking counterfactually serves as a prime

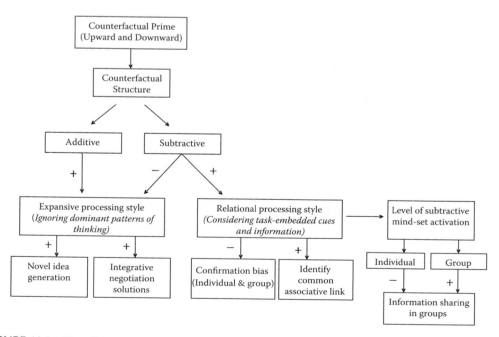

FIGURE 11.1 The effect of counterfactual mind-sets on processing styles, creativity, and decision making.

by activating a particular mind-set that carries through to affect later perceptions of others and problem solving.

PERSON PERCEPTION

The discovery that counterfactual thinking activates a mind-set was a serendipitous finding. Galinsky, Moskowitz, and Skurnik (2000) had set out to test whether behaviors and events that naturally led people to generate counterfactual thoughts would produce spontaneous trait inferences. As a result, they expected that counterfactual events would influence subsequent judgments through activation of a trait construct. Specifically, they predicted that downward and upward counterfactuals from one context would activate different types of trait constructs (e.g., adventurous for downward counterfactuals and reckless for upward counterfactuals) and thus have differential effects on person perception judgments in an unrelated context.

They tested this prediction by leading participants to spontaneously generate upward or downward counterfactuals and examined how counterfactual activation carried over to perceptions of a protagonist in a subsequent, unrelated scenario. Specifically, participants were first asked to read one of four scenarios much like the example at the beginning of the chapter. Each scenario described the actions of Jane, a woman who was attending a rock concert. At this concert, an individual wins a trip to Hawaii. Half of the scenarios describe counterfactual events. In the downward counterfactual scenario, Jane wins the trip to Hawaii when the new seat she had just switched to (to get a better view of the stage) is chosen. In the upward counterfactual scenario, Jane loses the trip to Hawaii when the seat that she had just switched from wins the trip. In the noncounterfactual scenarios, Jane does not change seats, and either wins or loses the trip. After considering the likely thoughts going through Jane's mind, participants read the infamous scenario about a person named Donald.

The "Donald scenario" (Higgins, Rholes, & Jones, 1977) was created to be ambiguous so that he could be perceived as reckless or adventurous and is explicit in mentioning the negative outcomes of his behavior (e.g., risking death and injury). Contrary to Galinsky and his colleagues' predictions, the upward and downward counterfactual manipulations produced the exact same effect on judgments of Donald. Specifically, they found that participants exposed to a counterfactual event (either upward or downward) characterized him as more reckless than did participants who were not exposed to a counterfactual event. Apparently, reading a previous counterfactual scenario did not activate a particular trait construct but rather led participants to use mental simulation to evaluate Donald by considering the different potential outcomes of his behavior. A follow-up study demonstrated that when salient negative alternatives were removed from the scenario, Donald was judged as more adventurous by those exposed to the counterfactual event. Because the counterfactual primes seem to lead participants to focus on the salient potential outcomes of the target, Galinsky et al. (2000) concluded that counterfactuals activate "a mental simulation mind-set that leads people to consider alternatives" (p. 252; see also Hirt & Markman, 1995).

The phrase *counterfactual mind-set* was used because processes of thought, as opposed to the content of thoughts, appeared to be driving the effects. Gollwitzer, Heckhausen, and Steller (1990) defined mind-sets in line with those of the Würzburg school, who posited that mind-sets are a cluster of cognitive processes that are well learned because they serve a functional purpose and suggested that mind-sets can tune information processing, attention, and thought production.

PROBLEM SOLVING

Having found that thinking counterfactually in one context can alter information processing in a later context, the next step was to find more direct evidence for this process and to extend the effects of counterfactual mind-sets to behavioral outcomes. The initial investigations primarily focused on decision-making accuracy at both the individual and group levels because the prosperity of many groups and organizations depends on the ability to make effective decisions and to coordinate and integrate diverse ideas and insights. Biased decision making and lack of information sharing often have tragic consequences, from the ill-conceived Bay of Pigs invasion of 1961, to the explosion of the space shuttle *Challenger* in 1986, to the September 11, 2001, terrorist attacks and the failure beforehand to detect a pattern in the terrorist's activities. Could counterfactual mind-sets reduce or sometimes exacerbate a number of decision-making biases? Several articles from our labs have explored this question and in doing so have offered substantial insights into the nature of the counterfactual mind-set.

Information Search

Building off the notion that counterfactuals prime a mental simulation mind-set in which alternatives are considered, Galinsky and Moskowitz (2000) argued that counterfactual mind-sets could lead people to consider alternatives that are the converse, reverse, or inverse of a focal hypothesis. As a result, they predicted that exposure to a counterfactual prime should decrease individuals' tendencies to search for evidence that confirms one's hypothesis and to neglect information that disconfirms it (Pyszczynski & Greenberg, 1987; Snyder & Swann, 1978).

To test this idea, Galinsky and Moskowitz (2000) told participants they were gong to conduct an interview to determine whether the interviewee was an extrovert. They were given 25 questions they could ask to investigate their hypothesis and were told to select 12 of the 25. Ten questions were designed to elicit hypothesis-confirming responses of extroversion (e.g., "What do you like about parties?"), 10 questions were designed to elicit hypothesis-disconfirming answers of introversion (e.g., "What factors make it hard for you to open up to people?"), and 5 questions were designed to yield responses that were neither hypothesis confirming nor disconfirming. They found that participants who read the rock concert scenario in which Jane moved seats (i.e., a counterfactual) asked more questions designed to elicit hypothesis-disconfirming answers (i.e., introvert questions) and fewer questions designed to elicit hypothesis-confirming responses (i.e., extrovert questions) than did participants who did not hold a counterfactual mind-set. Importantly, these results were not affected by the direction of the counterfactual. By stimulating people to simulate alternatives, prior generation of counterfactual thoughts led participants to actively engage in a search for disconfirmatory evidence.

Kray and Galinsky (2003) extended these findings to group decision-making accuracy and examined the underlying processes by which counterfactual primes have their effect. These processes were examined by presenting participants with actual data from the space shuttle *Challenger* accident, although the data were disguised by having groups play the role of a race car team (the Carter Racing case; Brittain & Sitkin, 1986). The team had to decide whether to race in an event that was marked by exceedingly cold temperatures, and there was ambiguity about whether engine failure was magnified in cold temperatures. Participants were given a chart that only contained information about the air temperature when the car experienced engine failure and did not include any information on races that did not experience any problems. Thus, the chart was essentially inconclusive and ultimately misleading. Most individuals initially favor the decision to race, and it is only through a search for additional information regarding the temperature in all the races that that this initial preference can be changed. In support of their predictions, Kray and Galinsky found that groups exposed to the counterfactual prime were more likely to make the correct decision not to race than were those who were not exposed to the counterfactual prime. Mediation analyses indicated that counterfactual primes increased the number of counterfactual thoughts, which in turn increased the search for disconfirmatory information that ultimately increased decision-making accuracy.

Although the bulk of this discussion has centered on the positive effects of counterfactual mind-sets on decision-making processes, there are situations in which these mind-sets can lead to suboptimal information search. Galinsky and Moskowitz (2000, Study 2) activated a counterfactual mind-set and subsequently had participants complete the Wason card-selection task (Wason &

Johnson-Laird, 1972). In this task, participants are shown four cards: E, K, 4, and 7, and they are told that, "If a card has a vowel on one side, then it has an even number on the other side." Their task is to select only those cards that need to be turned over to find out whether a statement is true or false, in this case E and 7. They predicted that because counterfactual mind-sets increase awareness of alternatives, participants exposed to counterfactual primes might be more likely to assume that the statement is bidirectional and therefore make errors of commission by selecting the card that affirms the consequent (i.e., selecting the 4 card). In support of this claim, participants exposed to the counterfactual event were more likely to affirm the consequent than were those exposed to the noncounterfactual event, thereby demonstrating one way in which information search may hinder effective decision making.

In summary, the finding that counterfactual mind-sets increase the tendency to search for disconfirmatory information demonstrates one route by which counterfactual mind-sets enhance decision-making processes. The results suggest that counterfactual mind-sets increase the search for disconfirmatory information without increasing the search for irrelevant information (Galinsky & Moskowitz, 2000) or simply seeking additional information (Kray & Galinsky, 2003). As such, counterfactual mind-sets appear to focus attention and search on critical information.

Information Sharing

Beyond increasing decision-making accuracy through the search for additional information, counterfactual mind-sets have also been shown to increase decision-making accuracy through their effects on the sharing of unique information among group members. Group discussions are typically characterized by a focus on commonly shared information to the relative detriment of uniquely held information (Larson, Foster-Fishman, & Keys, 1994; Stasser & Stewart, 1992), and even when unique information is presented, it tends to receive less attention (Larson et al., 1994). Prior research has shown that norms that promote critical thinking (Postmes, Spears, & Cihangir, 2001) and a problem-solving orientation (Stasser & Stewart, 1992) lead groups to focus on critical, unshared information. Drawing on this research, if counterfactual mind-set instantiation leads people to seek out and be receptive to task-relevant information as it did in the Carter racing case, then that mind-set should help groups identify unshared information that may be critical to decision-making accuracy.

Galinsky and Kray (2004) tested this prediction using a hidden profile task in which the correct answer can only be determined through the identification of unshared information. Specifically, after manipulating the counterfactual mind-set using the rock concert scenario, they had participants complete Stasser and Stewart's (1992) murder mystery task, in which groups are told that they are investigating a homicide. Galinsky and Kray found that groups exposed to the counterfactual event were more likely to identify the correct suspect than were those who were exposed to the noncounterfactual scenario. In addition, groups exposed to the counterfactual scenario were more likely to discuss unshared information than were those exposed to the noncounterfactual scenario, suggesting that counterfactual mind-sets increased discussion of unique information that ultimately enhanced decision-making accuracy. Moreover, a follow-up study replicated these findings and found that group members exposed to the counterfactual scenario also had an increased awareness that their other group members had different information, indicating that counterfactual mind-sets enhanced participants' understanding of the task structure.

A natural question arising from this work is whether counterfactual mind-sets must be present in all group members or simply in one or two group members to benefit group decision making. Drawing on Postmes et al. (2001), who demonstrated that group norms for critical thinking carried over to group but not to individual decision-making tasks, Liljenquist, Galinsky, and Kray (2004) explored whether counterfactual mind-sets would only benefit decision-making accuracy when activated at the group level. In the Kray and Galinsky (2003) and Galinsky and Kray (2004) research, the counterfactual mind-set was activated through group discussion, and these authors suggested that counterfactual thinking is like sending people down a "rabbit hole" of possibilities. This metaphor is useful for articulating why activating a mind-set at the group level facilitates group performance and information sharing but could debilitate it when activated at the individual level. When groups collectively construct the counterfactual thoughts, they plunge down one rabbit hole together. However, when each individual privately constructs counterfactual thoughts, they are in essence heading down separate holes, creating isolated silos. In this way, the process of counterfactual generation at the group level creates synergistic coordination, which refers to increased information sharing, increased reception to others' ideas, and increased ability to coordinate and integrate this information. Conversely, when counterfactuals are activated at the individual level, group members may be unable to effectively share their thoughts and coordinate their information.

To test their prediction, Liljenquist et al. (2004) used the same counterfactual manipulation and murder mystery task as Galinsky and Kray (2004). They found that groups who read the counterfactual scenario as a group performed better than did those who read the counterfactual scenario individually. Moreover, reading the counterfactual scenario as a group as opposed to individually also increased the number of unique and shared clues that were mentioned and repeated by group members and the degree to which group members coordinated and integrated this information. These findings lend support to the claim that counterfactual primes at the group level increased synergistic coordination, which in turn increased groups' decision-making accuracy.

In sum, Galinsky and Kray (2004) and Liljenquist et al. (2004) highlight another path through which counterfactual mind-sets affect group decision making. When counterfactuals are primed at the group level, groups share unique information and thereby increase the probability that the correct solution will be identified. But, counterfactuals activated at the individual level can impair subsequent group processes; without the prior experience of constructing if-then linkages collectively, these inwardly focused individuals will often fail to coordinate their behavior with other group members.

Creativity

Although the research detailed highlights the benefits of counterfactual mind-sets for tasks with one correct answer (i.e., convergent tasks), the question remains regarding whether counterfactual mind-sets benefit creative tasks. Galinsky and Moskowitz (2000, Experiment 1) first examined the effects of counterfactual primes on a creative association task (i.e., insight task) by having participants complete the Duncker candle problem (Duncker, 1945), in which participants are shown three objects: a small candle, a full book of matches, and a box filled with thumbtacks. They are then asked to affix the candle to a wall such that it will burn properly and not drip wax onto the floor. The correct solution requires people to realize that the box may function not only as a container but also as a platform. The tacks can be dumped out of the box and the box tacked to the wall to support the candle. Participants tend to focus on the typical, singular function of the box as container and thereby fail to see the novel use for it that is required to solve the problem. Yet, activating a counterfactual mind-set resulted in dramatic improvement in solution rate (56%) relative to a baseline condition (6%; Galinsky & Moskowitz, 2000, Experiment 1).

Although Galinsky and Moskowitz's (2000) findings, as well as the research on problem solving, demonstrate the powerful effects of counterfactual mind-sets on convergent tasks and creative association tasks, the effects of counterfactual mind-sets on divergent tasks (Anastasi, 1982) that require dispersed as opposed to focused attention remained unexplored. To address this gap, Kray, Galinsky, and Wong (2006) set out to examine the effects of counterfactual mind-sets on two types of creativity tasks: those that require creative associations (e.g., insight tasks, remote associations tasks) versus those that require the novel generation of ideas (e.g., naming new products, brainstorming). In so doing, the underlying processing style that drives the performance effects of counterfactual mind-sets could be more precisely identified.

PROCESSING STYLES AND COUNTERFACTUAL MIND-SETS

Building on the idea that counterfactual mind-sets are cognitive orientations that facilitate mental simulations and the consideration of alternatives, Kray et al. (2006) initially predicted that the mind-set should benefit performance on novel generation tasks as well as associative creative tasks. However, initial studies only found support for a facilitative effect on the latter type of task, leading them to look more carefully at the mental states that counterfactual primes activate.

In a series of experiments, Kray et al. (2006) found that counterfactual mind-sets increase preferences for critical thinking, structure, and rule-based decision making. Specifically, in two studies they manipulated exposure to counterfactual scenarios and found that participants who were exposed to scenarios evoking counterfactuals rated themselves higher on analytic thought and executive thinking (preference for tasks with a clearly defined structure and guidelines from which to solve problems and build; O'Hara & Sternberg, 2001) measures than did those exposed to noncounterfactual scenarios.

Based on the mental state characteristic of the counterfactual mind-set, it was concluded that counterfactual mind-sets are "a structured form of thought involving a consideration of relationships and the associations between a set of stimuli" (Kray et al., 2006, pp. 33–34). That is, counterfactuals appear to activate a mode of thinking that they termed a *relational processing style*. Because counterfactuals involve a consideration of both reality and what might have been, they are inherently relational in nature: Constructing counterfactual thoughts in one context produces a counterfactual mind-set characterized by a tendency to process information relationally in subsequent contexts. As a result, counterfactual mind-sets create phenomenological experiences of and preferences for structured thought, promote lay conceptions of analytic thought—defined as "an examination of a complex, its elements and their relations" (Merriam-Webster, 2006)—and promote structured imagination (i.e., the tendency to build on existing knowledge structures; Ward, 1994).

As such, Kray et al. (2006) predicted that counterfactual mind-sets would only have a positive effect on creative tasks that require associations between stimuli and would have a detrimental effect on creative tasks that require novel generation of ideas that are hindered by relying on salient associations. Because the mind-set focuses people on building off of associations, people may become trapped in established patterns and examples and therefore be unable to generate novel ideas or "think outside the box."

To test this prediction, Kray et al. (2006) first examined the effects of these mind-sets on analytic thought. They demonstrated that counterfactual mind-set participants performed better on Law School Admission Test (LSAT) problems that assess one's ability to understand and apply rules, determine relationships between concepts, analyze situations and draw conclusions, and apply logic to ambiguous or complex situations (Princeton Review, 2005). Counterfactual mind-sets also benefited performance on a well-established association task, the Remote Associates Test (RAT; Mednick, Mednick, & Mednick, 1964). This test requires identifying a unique association among three distinct words. For example, the common link for the words "sore, shoulder, sweat" is "cold." Similar to the effects observed on the Duncker candle problem (Galinsky & Moskowitz, 2000), by increasing the consideration of the relationships between task stimuli, counterfactual mind-sets improved performance on the RAT.

Conversely, however, counterfactual activation had negative effects on novel idea generation. In one study, participants were asked to generate names for new products (e.g., pasta) and were given several examples. Although all participants were told to ignore the examples, those in the counterfactual mind-set generated product labels that (a) linguistically resembled the examples and (b) created names that were rated as less creative yet more descriptive of the actual product than did those who were in the noncounterfactual mind-set. A follow-up study further supported the idea that counterfactual mind-sets lead individuals to structure their imagination around salient associations. Participants were asked to draw an imaginary animal from another planet (Ward, 1994). Those in the counterfactual mind-set structured their drawings around existing knowledge (e.g., general attributes of science fiction creatures) and took local context into account to a greater degree than did those in the baseline conditions. Moreover, coding of their drawings indicated that those in a counterfactual mind-set included fewer sensory atypicalities (e.g., three eyes) and descriptions than did those who were in a noncounterfactual mind-set. Together, these studies illustrate the detrimental effect of counterfactual mind-sets on thinking outside of the box.

THE MODERATING IMPACT OF COUNTERFACTUAL STRUCTURE

In every study exploring the role of counterfactual mind-sets, the effects were never moderated by counterfactual direction (upward and downward). However, counterfactual thoughts not only differ in their direction but also with regard to their structure. The structure of a counterfactual can be categorized as either additive, which refers to the addition of antecedent elements to reconstruct reality, or subtractive, which refers to the subtraction of antecedent elements when reconstructing reality (Roese & Olson, 1993). For instance, an individual who does poorly on a math exam and considers "If only I had brought my calculator, I would have done better" has generated an additive counterfactual. Conversely, the statement "If only I had not had a beer last night, I would have done better" has generated a subtractive counterfactual. Roese (1994) argued that additive counterfactuals might be more creative than subtractive counterfactuals because the former create new antecedent elements that were not initially present.

In considering the moderating role of counterfactual structure, Markman, Lindberg, Kray, and Galinsky (2007) noted that virtually all of the mind-set research had primarily manipulated counterfactual activation through the rock concert scenarios, which may have elicited mostly subtractive counterfactuals and thereby activated a relational processing style in which people consider the associations and relationships among stimuli. In other words, people in this mind-set essentially "think within the box." Drawing on Roese's (1994) assertion that additive counterfactuals are more creative, Markman et al. suggested that additive counterfactuals may activate an "expansive processing style that broadens conceptual attention" (Markman et al., 2007, p. 312), leading people to generate novel ideas and to think outside the box. Consequently, they predicted that additive counterfactual mind-sets would enhance performance on idea-generation tasks, while subtractive counterfactual mind-sets would enhance performance on association tasks.

To test this prediction, they first reanalyzed the data from Kray et al. (2006) to illustrate that the types of counterfactuals generated in the rock concert scenario tend to have a subtractive structure. Next, they demonstrated that regardless of the direction of the counterfactual prime, participants who generated subtractive counterfactuals performed better on association tasks (the RAT and a syllogism task) that require people to make connections among a set of stimuli or information than did those who generated additive counterfactuals or no counterfactuals (control condition). Conversely, in two additional studies that examined the effects of counterfactual structure on novel idea generation (employing a Scattergories task and a generate-uses-for-a-brick task), they found that participants who generated additive counterfactuals performed better—their work was rated as more novel—than did those who generated subtractive counterfactuals or no counterfactuals. More recently, Kray, Galinsky, and Markman (2007) demonstrated that negotiators who generated additive counterfactuals about a past negotiation were subsequently more likely to create an integrative deal than negotiators who generated subtractive counterfactuals. By adding hypothetical elements to the past, an expansive processing style is invoked that aids in creative generation (cf. Guilford, 1950).

In summary, this body of research not only provides insights into the effects of counterfactual mind-sets on creativity, but also deepens our understanding of the nature of the counterfactual mind-set. Whereas the direction of the counterfactual thought does not appear to affect decision making or creative performance, the structure of the counterfactual thought appears to activate distinct processing styles that differentially affect analytic and creative performance. Subtractive counterfactual mind-sets activate a relational processing style in which people consider the associations and relationships among stimuli and facilitate creative associations and information search and sharing at both the individual and group levels (but information sharing is only increased when the subtractive counterfactual mind-set is created at the group and not the individual level). In contrast, additive counterfactual mind-sets activate an expansive processing style that broadens conceptual attention and facilitates performance on idea generation tasks (see Figure 11.1).

IMAGINING POSSIBLE RESEARCH DIRECTIONS

This chapter has highlighted the wide-ranging and robust effects of counterfactual mind-sets on person perception, decision making, and creative performance at both the individual and group levels. Specifically, counterfactual mind-sets, activated through subtractive counterfactuals, elicit a relational processing style that typically benefits decision-making accuracy and performance on creative association tasks, whereas counterfactual mind-sets that emerge from additive counterfactuals elicit an expansive processing style that improves novel idea generation.

We propose that future research be directed toward two main areas. First, although great strides have been made in understanding how counterfactual mind-sets are linked with creativity, future research should delve further into the multifaceted nature of creativity to better understand when and how counterfactual mind-sets affect innovation. Second, an important issue for future research to address is how counterfactual mind-sets affect these outcomes in organizational settings because, as researchers have pointed out, "to survive and succeed, firms must innovate" (Cummings & Oldham, 1997, p. 22).

BROADENING THE EXAMINATION OF COUNTERFACTUALS AND CREATIVITY

In much of the counterfactual research discussed so far in this chapter, creativity has largely been conceptualized in terms of creative associations among stimuli and novel idea generation. This focus is limited, however, in that it only addresses a narrow definition of creativity. According to Guilford (1950), creative work should demonstrate fluency, flexibility, novelty, synthesis, analysis, reorganization and redefinition, complexity, and elaboration. Thus, future research should examine how counterfactuals affect additional facets of creativity. For instance, in examining fluency, typically operationalized as the number of ideas generated, because additive counterfactuals are associated with expansive processing styles we might expect individuals in this mind-set to demonstrate more between-category fluency (i.e., more categories of ideas generated, less depth). In contrast, because subtractive counterfactuals are associated with relational processing styles, individuals in this mind-set may demonstrate more within-category fluency (i.e., fewer categories of ideas but greater depth).

Beyond broadening our conceptualization and measurement of creativity, it is important to consider other aspects of creative processes as well. For example, innovation is considered to be the combination of two processes: (a) creativity, or the generation of new ideas, and (b) implementation, or the actual introduction of the change (Flynn & Chatman, 2001). Based on previous research, we might expect that counterfactual mind-sets will have different effects on each part of the innovation process. Because expansive processing styles are related to novel idea generation, encouraging people to consider additive counterfactuals may be critical to this stage of creativity, whereas subtractive counterfactuals may facilitate implementation when critical thinking and assessment of ideas become important. A more complete understanding of how counterfactual mind-sets influence various stages of creative processes will aid the prescriptive application of counterfactual mind-set research.

COUNTERFACTUALS AND CREATIVITY IN PRACTICE

Another important question to address is when and how counterfactual mind-sets are activated in naturally occurring groups. Research on performance-enhancing behaviors, such as feedback seeking, suggests that individuals refrain from such behaviors out of concern for how it will affect others' impressions of them (Ashford & Northcraft, 1992). Thus, individuals may refrain from sharing their counterfactual thoughts with others out of fear that voicing how things could have been better might affect others' impressions of their competency. In contrast to this concern, Wong (2007) found that communication of upward counterfactual thoughts was positively perceived by others. In addition, participants who heard someone communicate an upward counterfactual were more motivated and performed better on a similar task. Thus, the preparative functions of upward counterfactuals seemed to be passed on from the communicator to the receiver.

The role of personality in generating and responding to counterfactuals is another avenue for future research. Previous research suggests that personality traits are linked to the generation of specific types of counterfactuals. For example, optimists (versus pessimists) are more likely to generate downward counterfactuals than upward counterfactuals (Kasimatis & Wells, 1995; see also Sanna, 1996). Given that the direction of the counterfactual thoughts did not affect decision-making accuracy or creativity in any of the reviewed literature whereas structure of the counterfactual thoughts did affect creativity, future research should identify personality orientations that might predict the generation of other specific types of counterfactuals, such as additive versus subtractive. Roese, Hur, and Pennington (1999) presented data suggesting that regulatory focus is one individual difference that determines counterfactual structure. Additive counterfactuals are more prevalent following missed opportunities or failed attempts that represent promotion failures (Roese & Olson, 1993), whereas subtractive counterfactuals follow sudden accidents or attacks (Catellani & Milesi, 2001; Kahneman & Tversky, 1982). Given that a promotion focus has been shown to facilitate both creative associations and creative generation relative to a prevention focus (Friedman & Förster, 2001), and we have shown that additive counterfactuals facilitate creative generation whereas subtractive counterfactuals facilitate creative associations, future research should explore how the relationship between regulatory focus and counterfactual structure interact to affect creativity.

Another individual difference that may prove to be an important moderator of the type of counterfactual that individuals spontaneously generate is implicit beliefs about the malleability versus fixedness of ability in a given domain. In their highly influential work on implicit beliefs, Dweck and Leggett (1988) distinguished between entity theorists, who believe that people's abilities in life are relatively fixed, and incremental theorists, who believe that people can improve their abilities through hard work and persistence. Within the negotiation arena, incremental negotiators have been shown to achieve better outcomes than entity theorists (Kray & Haselhuhn, 2007), in part because incremental theorists are willing to persist to overcome obstacles to succeed whereas entity theorists' willingness to persevere hinges on their belief that they will ultimately prevail. In a follow-up investigation, Wong, Haselhuhn, and Kray (2008) identified the construction of counterfactual thoughts as a potential driver of this effect. Specifically, the greater willingness of incremental theorists to pursue a task in the interest of learning appears to promote the generation of upward counterfactuals, with this preparative function promoting future success.

At the organizational level, one way to encourage counterfactual thinking may be through organizational cultures that promote psychological safety, which is defined as "a shared belief that the team is safe for interpersonal risk taking" (Edmondson, 1999, p. 354). Edmondson found that psychological safety within a team was positively related to team learning behaviors, including seeking feedback and discussing errors. Because acknowledging that an outcome might have been better often implies culpability for a personal error (Morris & Moore, 2000), it is likely that organizational cultures that value psychological safety may be more likely to promote the construction and communication of upward counterfactual thoughts.

CONCLUSION

In this chapter, we began by discussing the pervasive human tendency to engage in counterfactual thinking. We first explored the nature of counterfactual thoughts and reviewed their functions.

Second, we reviewed the research on counterfactual mind-sets, demonstrating their systematic effects on cognitive and behavioral outcomes, including decision-making accuracy and creativity. Finally, we elaborated on a number of unanswered questions about counterfactual thinking, encouraging researchers to broadly examine the relationship between counterfactuals and creativity in organizational settings at multiple levels of analysis. Mental simulation is the foundation of imagination, and considering or even hearing about what might have been can lead people to see a different world (see also Byrne & Girotto, Chapter 10, this volume). Counterfactuals not only consider what was almost possible but also create new possibilities on time's horizon.

REFERENCES

Anastasi, A. (1982). *Psychological testing.* New York: Macmillan.

Ashford, S. J., & Northcraft, G. B. (1992). Conveying more (or less) than we realize: The role of impression-management in feedback-seeking. *Organizational Behavior and Human Decision Processes, 53,* 310–334.

Brittain, J., & Sitkin, S. (1986). *Carter racing.* Northwestern University: Dispute Resolution Research Center Exercises.

Catellani, P., & Milesi, P. (2001). Counterfactuals and roles: Mock victims' and perpetrators' accounts of judicial cases. *European Journal of Social Psychology, 31,* 247–264.

Cummings, A., & Oldham, G. R. (1997). Enhancing creativity: Managing work contexts for the high potential employee. *California Management Review, 40,* 22–38.

Duncker, K. (1945). On problem solving. *Psychological Monographs, 58*(5, Whole No. 270).

Dweck, C. S., & Leggett, E. L. (1988). A social-cognitive approach to motivation and personality. *Psychological Review, 95,* 256–273.

Edmondson, A. (1999). Psychological safety and learning behavior in work teams. *Administrative Science Quarterly, 44,* 350–383.

Einhorn H. J., & Hogarth, R. M. (1986). Judging probable cause. *Psychological Bulletin, 99,* 3–19.

Flynn, F. J., & Chatman, J. A. (2001). Strong cultures and innovation: Oxymoron or opportunity? In C. L. Cooper, S. Cartwright, & P. C. Earley (Eds.), *International handbook of organizational culture and climate* (pp. 263–287). Sussex, England: Wiley.

Friedman, R. S., & Förster, J. (2001). The effects of promotion and prevention cues on creativity. *Journal of Personality and Social Psychology, 81,* 1001–1013.

Galinsky, A. D., & Kray, L. J. (2004). From thinking about what might have been to sharing what we know: The effects of counterfactual mind-sets on information sharing in groups. *Journal of Experimental Social Psychology, 40,* 606–618.

Galinsky, A. D., Liljenquist, K. A., Kray, L. J., & Roese, N. J. (2005). Finding meaning from mutability: Making sense and deriving significance through counterfactual thinking. In D. R. Mandel, D. J. Hilton, and P. Catellani (Eds.), *The psychology of counterfactual thinking* (pp. 110–125). New York: Routledge.

Galinsky, A. D., & Moskowitz, G. B. (2000). Counterfactuals as behavioral primes: Priming the simulation heuristic and consideration of alternatives. *Journal of Experimental Social Psychology, 36,* 257–383.

Galinsky, A. D., Moskowitz, G. B., & Skurnik, I. (2000). Counterfactuals as self-generated primes: The effect of prior counterfactual activation on person perception judgments. *Social Cognition, 18,* 252–280.

Galinsky, A. D., & Mussweiler, T. (2001). First offers as anchors: The role of perspective-taking and negotiator focus. *Journal of Personality and Social Psychology, 81,* 657–669.

Galinsky, A. D., Seiden, V., Kim, P. H., & Medvec, V. H. (2002). The dissatisfaction of having your first offer accepted: The role of counterfactual thinking in negotiations. *Personality and Social Psychology Bulletin, 28,* 271–283.

Gollwitzer, P. M., Heckhausen, H., & Steller, B. (1990). Deliberative versus implemental mind-sets: Cognitive tuning toward congruous thoughts and information. *Journal of Personality and Social Psychology, 59,* 1119–1127.

Guilford, J. P. (1950). Creativity. *American Psychologist, 5,* 444–454.

Higgins, E. T., Rholes, W. S., & Jones, C. R. (1977). Category accessibility and impression formation. *Journal of Experimental Social Psychology, 13,* 141–154.

Hirt, E. R., & Markman, K. D. (1995). Multiple explanation: A consider-an-alternative strategy for debiasing judgments. *Journal of Personality and Social Psychology, 69,* 1069–1086.

Hooker, C., Roese, N. J., & Park, S. (2000). Impoverished counterfactual thinking is associated with schizo-phrenia. *Psychiatry: Interpersonal and Biological Processes, 63,* 326–335.

Kahneman, D., & Miller, D. T. (1986). Norm theory: Comparing reality to its alternatives. *Psychological Review, 93,* 136–153.

Kahneman, D., & Tversky, A. (1982). The simulation heuristic. In D. Kahneman, P. Slovic, & A. Tversky (Eds.), *Judgment under uncertainty: Heuristics and biases* (pp. 201–208). New York: Cambridge University Press.

Kasimatis, M., & Wells, G. L. (1995). Individual differences in counterfactual thinking. In N. J. Roese and J. M. Olson (Eds.), *The social psychology of counterfactual thinking* (pp. 81–101). Hillsdale, NJ: Erlbaum.

Kray, L. J., & Galinsky, A. D. (2003). The debiasing effect of counterfactual mind-sets: Increasing the search for disconfirmatory information in group decisions. *Organizational Behavior and Human Decision Processes, 91,* 69–81.

Kray, L. J., Galinsky, A. D., & Markman, K. D. (2007). *Adding versus subtracting what might have been: The impact of counterfactual thinking on integrative negotiations.* Working paper, University of California.

Kray, L. J., Galinsky, A. D., & Wong, E. M. (2006). Thinking inside the box: The relational processing style elicited by counterfactual mind-sets. *Journal of Personality and Social Psychology, 91,* 33–48.

Kray, L. J., & Gelfand, M. (in press). Relief versus regret: The impact of gender on reactions to having one's first offer accepted. *Social Cognition.*

Kray, L. J., & Haselhuhn, M. P. (2007). Implicit negotiation beliefs and performance: Longitudinal and exper-imental evidence. *Journal of Personality and Social Psychology, 93,* 49–64.

Kray, L. J., Thompson, L, & Galinsky, A. D. (2001). Battle of the sexes: Gender stereotype confirmation and reactance in negotiations. *Journal of Personality and Social Psychology, 80,* 942–958.

Larson, J. R., Foster-Fishman, P. G., & Keys, C. B. (1994). Discussion of shared and unshared information in decision-making groups. *Journal of Personality and Social Psychology, 67,* 446–461.

Liljenquist, K. A., Galinsky, A. D., & Kray, L. J. (2004). Exploring the rabbit hole of possibilities by myself or with my group: The benefits and liabilities of activating counterfactual mind-sets for information shar-ing and group coordination. *Journal of Behavioral Decision Making, 17,* 263–279.

Mandel, D. R., & Lehman, D. R. (1996). Counterfactual thinking and ascriptions of cause and preventability. *Journal of Personality and Social Psychology, 71,* 450–463.

Markman, K. D., Gavanski, I., Sherman, S. J., & McMullen, M. N. (1993). The mental simulation of better and worse possible worlds. *Journal of Experimental Social Psychology, 29,* 87–109.

Markman, K. D., Lindberg, M. J., Kray, L. J., & Galinsky, A. D. (2007). Implications of counterfactual struc-ture for creative generation and analytical problem solving. *Personality and Social Psychology Bul-letin, 33,* 312–324.

Markman, K. D., & McMullen, M. N. (2003). A reflection and evaluation model of comparative thinking. *Personality and Social Psychology Review, 7,* 244–267.

McNamara, P., Durso, R., Brown, A., & Lynch, A. (2003). Counterfactual cognitive deficit in persons with Parkinson's disease. *Journal of Neurology, Neurosurgery, and Psychiatry, 74,* 1065–1070.

Mednick, M. T., Mednick, S. A., & Mednick, E. V. (1964). Incubation of creative performance and specific associative priming. *Journal of Abnormal and Social Psychology, 69,* 84–88.

Merriam-Webster. (2006). *Merriam-Webster online dictionary.* Retrieved definition of "analysis" April 11, 2006 from http://www.m-w.com/cgi-bin/dictionary?book=Dictionary&va=analysis.

Morris, M. W., & Moore, P. C. (2000). The lessons we (don't) learn: Counterfactual thinking and organiza-tional accountability after a close call. *Administrative Science Quarterly, 45,* 737–765.

O'Hara, L. A., & Sternberg, R. J. (2001). It doesn't hurt to ask: Effects of instructions to be creative, practical, or analytical on essay-writing performance and their interaction with students' thinking styles. *Creativ-ity Research Journal, 13,* 197–210.

Postmes, T., Spears, R., & Cihangir, S. (2001). Quality of decision making and group norms. *Journal of Per-sonality and Social Psychology, 80,* 918–930.

Princeton Review. (2005). *The LSAT in detail.* Retrieved May 3, 2006 from http://www.princetonreview.com/law/testprep/testprep.asp?TPRPAGE=87&TYPE=LSAT-SECTIONS.

Pyszczynski, T., & Greenberg, J. (1987). Toward an integration of cognitive and motivational perspectives on social inference: A biased hypothesis-testing model. In L. Berkowitz (Ed.), *Advances in experimental social psychology* (Vol. 20, pp. 297–340). New York: Academic Press.

Roese, N. J. 1994. The functional basis of counterfactual thinking. *Journal of Personality and Social Psychol-ogy, 66,* 805–818.

Roese, N. J., & Hur, T. (1997). Affective determinants of counterfactual thinking. *Social Cognition, 15,* 274–290.

Roese, N. J., Hur, T., & Pennington, G. L. (1999). Counterfactual thinking and regulatory focus: Implications for action versus inaction and sufficiency versus necessity. *Journal of Personality and Social Psychology, 77,* 1109–1120.

Roese, N. J., & Olson, J.M. (1993). The structure of counterfactual thought. *Personality and Social Psychology Bulletin, 19,* 312–319.

Roese, N. J., & Olson, J. M. (1997). Counterfactual thinking: The intersection of affect and function. In M. P. Zanna (Ed.), *Advances in experimental social psychology* (Vol. 29, pp. 1–59). New York: Academic Press.

Roese, N. J., Park, S., Smallman, R., & Gibson, C. (2007). Schizophrenia involves impairment in the activation of intentions by counterfactual thinking. *Schizophrenia Research* June 27 [Epub ahead of print].

Sanna, L. J. (1996). Defensive pessimism, optimism, and simulating alternatives: Some ups and downs of prefactual and counterfactual thinking. *Journal of Personality and Social Psychology, 71,* 1020–1036.

Sanna, L. J., & Turley, K. J. (1996). Antecedents to spontaneous counterfactual thinking: Effects of expectancy violation and outcome valence. *Personality and Social Psychology Bulletin, 22,* 906–919.

Snyder, M., & Swann, W. B. (1978). Hypotheses testing processes in social interaction. *Journal of Personality and Social Psychology, 36,* 1202–1212.

Stasser, G., & Stewart, D. (1992). Discovery of hidden profiles by decision making groups: Solving a problem versus making a judgment. *Journal of Personality and Social Psychology, 63,* 426–434.

Ward, T. B. (1994). Structured imagination: The role of category structure in exemplar generation. *Cognitive Psychology, 27,* 1–40.

Wason, P. C., & Johnson-Laird, P. N. (1972). *Psychology of reasoning.* Cambridge, MA: Harvard University Press.

Wells, G. L., & Gavanski, I. (1989). Mental simulation of causality. *Journal of Personality and Social Psychology, 56,* 161–169.

Wells, G. L., Taylor, B. R., & Turtle, J. W. (1987). The undoing of scenarios. *Journal of Personality and Social Psychology, 53,* 421–430.

Wong, E. M. (2007). Narrating near-histories: The effects of counterfactual communication on motivation and performance. *Management and Organisational History. Special issue on Counterfactual History, 2,* 351–370.

Wong, E. M., Haselhuhn, M. P., & Kray, L. J. (2008). *Learning from the past by looking toward the future: implicit negotiation beliefs and counterfactual generation.* Working paper, Northwestern University.

12 Counterfactual Thinking: Function and Dysfunction

Keith D. Markman, Figen Karadogan,
Matthew J. Lindberg, and Ethan Zell

Counterfactual thinking—the capacity to reflect on what would, could, or should have been if events had transpired differently—is a pervasive, yet seemingly paradoxical human tendency. On the one hand, counterfactual thoughts can be comforting and inspiring (Carroll & Shepperd, Chapter 28), but on the other they can be anxiety provoking and depressing (Zeelenberg & Pieters, Chapter 27). Likewise, such thoughts can illuminate pathways toward better future outcomes (Wong, Galinsky, & Kray, Chapter 11), yet they can also promote confusion and lead us astray (Sanna, Schwarz, & Kennedy, Chapter 13). The first part of this chapter focuses on work that supports the prevailing zeitgeist in the counterfactual thinking literature: Counterfactual thinking is beneficial. The second part of the chapter, however, strikes a more cautionary tone by reviewing work that describes some deleterious consequences of counterfactual thinking. We conclude by offering a tentative reconciliation of these conflicting perspectives and suggesting directions for future research.

THE FUNCTIONAL SIDE OF COUNTERFACTUAL THINKING

With every mistake, we must surely be learning …

The Beatles, While My Guitar Gently Weeps, 1968

SIMULATION DIRECTION

Early research on counterfactual thinking examined the cognitive rules that govern the availability of various counterfactuals (see also Byrne & Girotto, Chapter 10, this volume; Roese & Olson, 1995a). For example, research showed that people are more likely to imagine what might have been different about exceptional (i.e., surprising or unexpected) events than about normal events (Kahneman & Miller, 1986). In addition, counterfactual thinking was shown to influence both social judgments and feelings, including regret, victim compensation, and event causality (e.g., Landman, 1987; D. T. Miller & McFarland, 1986; Wells & Gavanski, 1989).

In addition to understanding the cognitive rules that govern counterfactual thinking, researchers also came to believe that a full understanding of counterfactual thinking processes requires consideration of how they might serve people's motives and goal states: What are the costs and benefits of imagining what could have been? Borrowing a theoretical distinction drawn in the social comparison literature between upward and downward comparisons (e.g., Collins, 1996; Taylor, Buunk, & Aspinwall, 1990; Wood, 1989), researchers (e.g., Markman, Gavanski, Sherman, and McMullen, 1993; McMullen, Markman, & Gavanski, 1995; Roese, 1994) classified counterfactuals on the basis of their direction of comparison. Specifically, *upward counterfactuals* construct imagined alternatives that improve on reality, whereas *downward counterfactuals* construct alternatives that worsen reality. In turn, possible functions of upward and downward counterfactual thoughts were identified. One is the affective function (e.g., McMullen, 1997; Roese, 1997; Taylor & Schneider, 1989), by which a given outcome is judged more favorably to the extent that a less-desirable alternative is salient. In this way, downward counterfactuals can enhance coping and well-being by highlighting how the outcome could easily have been worse. A second is the preparative function. Although upward counterfactuals may devalue the actual outcome and make one feel worse (e.g., Johnson, 1986; Landman, 1987; Mellers, Schwartz, Ho, & Ritov, 1997), simulating routes to better realities may help individuals improve on their outcomes in the future (Johnson & Sherman, 1990; Karniol & Ross, 1996; Markman & McMullen, 2003; for a related distinction, see Folkman & Lazarus, 1980).

Roese (e.g., 1994, 1997) has been particularly explicit about specifying the mechanisms underlying the preparative function. According to Roese, counterfactual thoughts may lead to causal inferences. For example, if Tom fails an exam and then realizes that he would have passed if he had read the textbook chapters more carefully, he has identified a causally potent antecedent action that may trigger an expectancy regarding the consequences of taking that action in the future. This realization should then heighten intentions to perform that action and thereby influence the manifestation of that action. Subsequent performance will be enhanced to the extent that the initial causal inference was at least partly correct (Parks, Sanna, & Posey, 2003; Roese & Olson, 1995b; Segura & Morris, 2005).

SIMULATION MODE

The first wave of research on counterfactual thinking assumed that *contrast-based* reactions to counterfactual generation—by which judgments are displaced away from the counterfactual standard—were the default: Upward counterfactuals elicit negative affect, whereas downward counterfactuals elicit positive affect (e.g., Larsen, McGraw, Mellers, & Cacioppo, 2004; Markman et al., 1993; Medvec, Madey, & Gilovich, 1995; Sanna, 1996; Wohl & Enzle, 2003; and a point still maintained by Roese, Sanna, & Galinsky, 2005). However, a second wave of work (e.g., Boninger, Gleicher, & Strathman, 1994; Landman & Petty, 2000; Markman, Elizaga, Ratcliff, & McMullen, 2007; Markman & Tetlock, 2000; McMullen, 1997; McMullen & Markman, 2000, 2002; McMullen et al., 1995; Sanna, 1997; Sanna & Meier, 2000; Teigen, 2005; Tetlock, 1998; Wayment, 2004) indicated that *assimilation-based* reactions to counterfactual generation—by which judgments are pulled toward the counterfactual standard—are also common, meaning that upward counterfactuals can also elicit positive affect, and downward counterfactuals can also elicit negative affect. Markman and McMullen (2003; see also Markman & McMullen, 2005; Markman, Ratcliff, Mizoguchi, Elizaga, & McMullen, 2007) developed a process model, the reflection and evaluation model (REM) of comparative thinking, that accounts for the elicitation of assimilative and contrastive responses to upward and downward counterfactuals, as well as the motivational and behavioral consequences of such responses. At the heart of the model is the assertion that two psychologically distinct modes of mental simulation operate during comparative thinking. The first of these modes is *reflection*, wherein one vividly simulates that information about the comparison standard is true of, or is part of, one's self-construal or present standing, and the second is *evaluation*, whereby the outcome of a mental simulation run is used as a reference point against which to evaluate oneself or one's present standing.

Figure 12.1 depicts the interaction between simulation direction and simulation mode. To illustrate, consider the student who receives a B on an exam but realizes that an A was easily attainable with some additional studying. In the case of upward evaluation, the student switches attention between the outcome (a grade of B) and the counterfactual standard (a grade of A). According to the REM, the dual focus ("I got a B ... I could have gotten an A but instead I got a B") instigates evaluative processing that encourages using the comparison standard as a reference point (Mussweiler, 2003; Oettingen, Pak, & Schnetter, 2001; Pham & Taylor, 1999). In the case of upward reflection, however, the student's attention is only focused on the counterfactual. The single focus (see also Oettingen & Kappes, Chapter 26, this volume) instigates reflective processing in which the student

Mode

Direction	Reflection	Evaluation
Upward	Positive Affect	Negative Affect
Downward	Negative Affect	Positive Affect

FIGURE 12.1 The interaction between simulation direction and simulation mode.

temporarily experiences the counterfactual as if it were real ("What if I had actually gotten an A?"). Phenomenologically, reflection "transports" the student into the counterfactual world (Green & Brock, 2000; Green & Donahue, Chapter 16, this volume). Likewise, consider the case of a driver who pulls away from the curb without carefully checking rear- and side-view mirrors and subsequently slams on the brakes as a large truck whizzes by. In the case of downward evaluation, the driver compares the counterfactual standard to the outcome ("I was fortunate not to have been hit by that truck"), whereas in the case of downward reflection, the driver only focuses on the counterfactual ("I nearly got hit by that truck").

AFFECT AND MOTIVATION

The REM asserts that both upward and downward counterfactuals can have an energizing effect on subsequent behavior. A key assumption is that the initial impetus to act, or disinclination to change the status quo, is rendered by recognizing one's internal affective state following counterfactual generation. Drawing on Schwarz and Clore's (1983) feelings-as-information perspective (see also Martin, Ward, Achee, & Wyer, 1993), the REM posits that counterfactuals that elicit negative affect should encourage greater persistence than should counterfactuals that elicit positive affect. Moreover, any useful causal inferences that are derived from contemplation of the counterfactual will suggest specific behaviors that the individual might perform in the future (Roese, 1997). Thus, upward evaluation is more likely than upward reflection to heighten motivation. Conversely, the REM posits that downward reflection should heighten motivation, whereas downward evaluation should engender complacency. According to the model, the negative affect elicited by downward reflection raises an individual's awareness of the possibility that a negative goal-state may be attained (see also Lockwood, Jordan, & Kunda, 2002; Wayment, 2004), whereas the positive affect elicited by downward evaluation suggests that a negative goal state has been successfully avoided.

An Empirical Test

To provide evidence for basic REM predictions regarding affect, motivation, and behavior, Markman, McMullen, and Elizaga (2008) had participants complete an initial set of anagrams and then gave them performance feedback. To manipulate simulation direction, participants were instructed to "think about how something different could have happened rather than what actually happened." Those assigned to the upward counterfactual condition were told, "Think about how your performance on the anagrams might have turned out better than it actually did," whereas those assigned to the downward counterfactual condition were told, "Think about how your performance on the anagrams might have turned out worse than it actually did." Simulation *mode* was then manipulated. Evaluative mode instructions directed participants: "Think about your actual performance on the anagrams compared to how you might have performed better (worse). Vividly evaluate your performance in comparison to how you might have performed better (worse)"; whereas reflective mode instructions directed participants: "Vividly imagine what might have been. Imagine how your performance on the anagrams might have been better (worse)." Participants then described these thoughts in writing and indicated their current mood. Subsequently, participants were given as much time as they liked to complete a second set of anagrams, and both persistence and performance on this second set were measured.

The general prediction was that upward evaluation would enhance motivation and performance to a greater extent than would upward reflection, whereas downward reflection would enhance motivation and performance to a greater extent than would downward evaluation. In addition, Markman et al. (2008) sought to examine the psychological mechanisms by which counterfactual thinking exerts effects on motivation and behavior. According to the REM, negative affect mediates the relationship between counterfactual thinking and persistence. Thus, upward evaluation should elicit more persistence than upward reflection because upward evaluation evokes negative affect, whereas downward reflection should elicit more persistence than downward evaluation because downward reflection evokes negative affect. Furthermore, however, it was posited that the mechanisms by which counterfactual thinking affects performance would differ for upward and downward counterfactuals. For both types of counterfactuals, it was predicted that persistence would enhance performance through affect. Notably, however, prior theorizing (e.g., Markman et al., 1993; Roese, 1997) contends that upward counterfactuals prepare for the future by suggesting specific courses of action (e.g., "If I had studied harder, I would have received a better grade; therefore, I will study harder next time"), whereas downward counterfactuals suggest no such specific routes to better performance and thus are not involved in future preparation. Thus, Markman et al. (2008) predicted that when upward counterfactuals were generated, evaluative processing would affect performance by dual mechanisms: (a) indirectly, vis-à-vis affect and enhanced persistence, and (b) directly, by eliciting useful inferences. On the other hand, it was predicted that when downward counterfactuals were generated, reflective processing would affect performance by a single mechanism: indirectly, vis-à-vis affect and persistence.

Results

Consistent with predictions, upward evaluation enhanced motivation and performance to a greater extent than did upward reflection, whereas downward reflection enhanced motivation and performance to a greater extent than did downward evaluation Separate analyses were then performed on the upward and downward counterfactual thinking groups.

First examined was the prediction that affect would mediate the relationship between mode and motivation in the upward counterfactual condition. Mode predicted affect, $p = .002$, and (Set 2) persistence, $p < .001$, and when persistence was regressed on affect and mode, affect remained significantly related to persistence, $p < .001$, and mode remained significantly related to persistence, $p = .007$. Providing evidence for mediation, the relationship between mode and persistence was significantly reduced when affect was included as a mediator. Analyses were then conducted to determine how each of the study variables contributed to (Set 2) performance. As expected, persistence was significantly related to performance, $p = .05$, but mode *also* exerted a significant and independent effect on performance, $p = .05$.

To further understand which aspects of upward evaluative processing influenced performance, the counterfactuals were coded for evidence of useful inferences. An example of a counterfactual that received a "not at all useful" code was, "Easily finding the unscrambled words amidst the jumble and writing down multiple correct answers," and an example of a counterfactual that received a "quite useful" code was, "I can discover more words by finding commonly used words within the letters and then seeing if a prefix or suffix can be added. I also can try to find common letter combinations." Analyses indicated that whereas upward evaluation elicited more useful inferences than did upward reflection, downward reflection and evaluation did not differ in this regard.

Two separate regressions were performed to determine whether inference scores in the upward counterfactual condition were associated with persistence and performance. First, when inference scores were allowed to predict persistence while controlling for affect, the analysis revealed a marginally significant positive association between the usefulness of the inferences and subsequent persistence on the anagram task, $p = .10$. Second, when inference scores were allowed to predict performance while controlling for affect and persistence, the analysis revealed a significant positive association between the usefulness of the inferences and subsequent performance on the anagram task, $p = .05$. Thus, the usefulness of the inferences derived from upward evaluative processing accounted for enhanced performance above and beyond the influence of persistence vis-à-vis affect.

Second, in the downward counterfactual condition, mode predicted affect, $p = .02$, and persistence, $p = .003$; affect was significantly related to persistence, $p = .001$; and demonstrating mediation once again, the path from mode to persistence became nonsignificant when affect was included as a mediator, $p = .06$. Next, performance was regressed on mode, affect, and persistence. As expected, persistence was significantly related to performance, $p = .05$. In contrast to the analyses conducted in the upward counterfactual condition, however, mode did not exert a significant effect on performance when affect and persistence were controlled, $p = .38$. Rather, mode was found to indirectly affect performance through its influence on persistence (vis-à-vis affect).

THE MODERATING ROLE OF REGULATORY FOCUS

The REM also posits that the consequences of counterfactual generation should be moderated by whether individuals are focused on either promotion or prevention goals (see also Hur, 2000; Pennington & Roese, 2002; Roese, Hur, & Pennington, 1999). According to regulatory focus theory (Higgins, 1998), promotion-oriented individuals are focused on growth, advancement, and accomplishment and thus tend to pursue strategies aimed at approaching desirable outcomes. On the other hand, prevention-oriented individuals are focused on protection, safety, and responsibility and thus tend to pursue strategies aimed at avoiding undesirable outcomes. Thus, a promotion focus should encourage the development of strategies (e.g., putting more effort into schoolwork) that focus on achieving outcomes that are more favorable than the actual outcome, whereas a prevention focus should encourage the development of strategies (e.g., checking all rearview and side mirrors before pulling out of a parking space) that attempt to avoid outcomes that are less favorable than the actual outcome.

Research has shown that the manner in which an object is chosen can affect the object's perceived value (e.g., Camacho, Higgins, & Luger, 2003; Higgins, Idson, Freitas, Spiegel, & Molden, 2003), a finding that has been termed the *regulatory fit effect* (e.g., Higgins, 2000, 2005). According to regulatory fit theory, when people engage in decisions or choices with strategies that sustain their orientation, they "feel right" about what they are doing, and this "feeling right" experience then transfers to subsequent choices, decisions, and evaluations. For example, Avnet and Higgins (2003) found that participants offered more of their own money to buy the same chosen book light when the choice strategy they used fit their regulatory orientation than when it did not fit, and Higgins et al. (2003) found that participants assigned a price up to 40% higher for the same chosen coffee mug when their choice strategy fit their regulatory orientation than when it did not fit.

Regulatory fit theory also predicts that motivational strength will be enhanced when the manner in which people work toward a goal sustains (rather than disrupts) their regulatory orientation, and that this enhanced motivational strength should in turn improve efforts at goal attainment. Spiegel, Grant-Pillow, and Higgins (2004) applied this notion to the domain of mental simulation. These researchers hypothesized that people with a promotion focus who develop approach-oriented plans should perform better at a task than people with a promotion focus who develop avoidance-oriented plans, whereas people with a prevention focus who develop avoidance-oriented plans should perform better at a task than people with a prevention focus who develop approach-related plans. In support, Spiegel et al. (2004, Experiment 1) found that participants with regulatory fit between their predominant regulatory focus and the type of plans they mentally simulated were 50% more likely to turn in a report on time than participants without regulatory fit.

In a similar vein, Markman, McMullen, Elizaga, and Mizoguchi (2006) posited that counterfactuals should enhance motivational strength to the extent that there is regulatory fit between the counterfactual and the predominant regulatory focus. The initial formulation of the REM (Markman & McMullen, 2003) predicted that upward counterfactuals should be more associated with promotion concerns, whereas downward counterfactuals (and downward reflection in particular) should be more associated with prevention concerns. In a refinement of this prediction, however, Markman et al. (2006) hypothesized that upward evaluation might be associated with both a promotion *and* a prevention focus. Roese (1997) characterized upward counterfactual thoughts as being "part of a virtual, rather than an actual, process of avoidance behavior" (p. 135), and Mandel and colleagues (e.g., Mandel, 2003; Mandel & Lehman, 1996) provided evidence that upward counterfactual thoughts are most commonly directed toward how an outcome could have been avoided and prevented. Thus, upward evaluation may focus one on how an actual negative outcome can be avoided in the future while also suggesting means by which one can approach a relatively more favorable future outcome.

Overall, Markman et al. (2006) hypothesized that whereas upward reflection provides a good regulatory fit with promotion focus because it gives rise to the eager simulation and development of approach-oriented plans (Spiegel et al., 2004), upward evaluation provides a good regulatory fit with both promotion and prevention foci because it focuses the individual on both the approach-related plans associated with the attainment of a desired end state (i.e., the counterfactual outcome) and the avoidance-related plans associated with the prevention of an undesired end state (i.e., the actual outcome). Thus, upward evaluation and upward reflection should both be motivating in a promotion context, whereas upward evaluation should be more motivating than upward reflection in a prevention context. Second, they hypothesized that downward reflection provides a good regulatory fit with prevention focus because it focuses the individual on the vigilant simulation and development of avoidance-related plans, whereas downward evaluation should not be motivating in any context as it merely focuses the individual on feeling better about the present state of affairs. Thus, whereas neither downward reflection nor downward evaluation should be motivating in a promotion context, downward reflection should be more motivating than downward evaluation in a prevention context.

Like Markman et al. (2008), participants completed an initial set of anagrams, received performance feedback, generated either upward or downward counterfactuals about their performance, and then engaged in either reflection or evaluation. Participants then completed a second set of anagrams, and the incentive for completing these was framed either in terms of gaining or not gaining an extra dollar for the promotion focus (from a starting point of $4) or in terms of losing or not losing a dollar for the prevention focus (from a starting point of $5; see Shah, Higgins, & Friedman, 1998). Consistent with predictions, (a) upward counterfactual thinking elicited a larger increase in persistence than did downward counterfactual thinking under promotion framing; (b) upward evaluation elicited a larger increase in persistence than did upward reflection under prevention framing; and (c) downward reflection elicited a larger increase in persistence than did downward evaluation under prevention framing (see Figures 12.2 and 12.3).

These results have intriguing implications for decision making because they suggest that the generation of counterfactuals enhances the likelihood that individuals will choose courses of action that fit with their preferred (chronically or contextually determined) orientation—eagerness means for promotion, vigilance means for prevention. To illustrate, a promotion-oriented student who is seeking strategies for improving class performance would best be served by generating upward counterfactuals because they fit with the student's habitual orientation. Not only should the student be more likely to select promotion-oriented strategies (e.g., studying over a longer period of time, asking more questions in class), but also the student should pursue such strategies with greater vigor

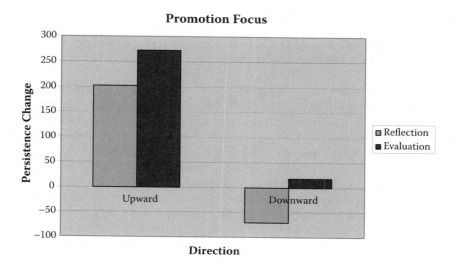

FIGURE 12.2 Persistence change under promotion focus as a function of simulation direction and simulation mode.

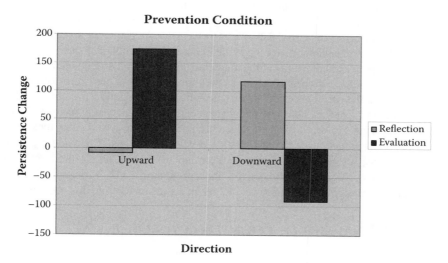

FIGURE 12.3 Persistence change under prevention focus as a function of simulation direction and simulation mode.

because the experience of regulatory fit enhances engagement strength. On the other hand, a prevention-oriented student would be well served by generating either upward evaluative or downward reflective counterfactuals. In addition to enhancing the likelihood of selecting prevention-oriented strategies (e.g., getting more sleep, socializing less), regulatory fit should also enhance the strength of the student's engagement in such strategies.

THE SENSE-MAKING FUNCTION OF COUNTERFACTUAL THINKING

In addition to the preparative and affective functions afforded by counterfactual thinking, Galinsky, Liljenquist, Kray, and Roese (2005) have speculated that counterfactual *mutability* (i.e., the ability to alter or change multiple aspects of reality to create new and imagined realities) serves a more general sense-making function. According to these authors:

Mutability provides the cognitive raw materials with which the sense-making process can construct alternative worlds juxtaposed against reality. The fact that alternative pasts existed, but one path ultimately prevailed, makes the particular features of one's life all the more extraordinary, all the more significant, and thus all the more meaningful. (p. 114)

Sense-making cognitions can be triggered by either downward or upward counterfactuals. For instance, a clear instance of downward reflection is the near-death experience (e.g., vividly imagining perishing in one of the World Trade Center towers on September 11, 2001). Interestingly, however, switching to an evaluative mode of thinking can help ascribe significance to the event as well as to the individual's life as a whole: That an individual came so close to death and "defied the odds" (i.e., downward evaluation; they could have died but did not) makes the fact that they survived all the more impressive and gives rise to a sense of fate or determinism, facilitating a psychological conversion from "what might have been" to "what was meant to be." Conversely, a number of individuals were reportedly visiting the World Trade Center for the first time in their lives on the morning of September 11, 2001, and thus easily could not have been (and "should not have been") killed during the attacks (i.e., an upward evaluative counterfactual). As Galinsky et al. (2005) noted, "Whether lives were lost or saved due to the pairing of routine-violating behaviors and this unexpected attack, in both cases one may sense a mysterious force conjoining this pairing, rendering fate as a compelling explanation" (p. 116).

In a study designed to provide empirical support for the notion that mutability can trigger sense-making cognitions that imbue improbable events with greater meaning, Lindberg and Markman (2008) had participants read an account of a 1942 football game played between heavily favored Boston College and Holy Cross in which Holy Cross prevailed, 55–12. After the game, the dejected Boston College players decided not to spend a planned evening at the Coconut Grove nightclub. Half of the participants then learned that 500 people died in a fire at the nightclub that evening. Participants who read about the fire indicated that Holy Cross's improbable victory was more fated and predetermined than did those who did not read about the fire. This effect is intriguing because, logically, an event (i.e., the fire) that transpires after a target event (i.e., Holy Cross's victory) cannot retrospectively increase the chances of the target event occurring. However, through some combination of motivated sense making and magical thinking, such a posttarget event can apparently give rise to feelings of fate and predetermination (for related discussions, see Brickman, Ryan, & Wortman, 1975; McClure, Hilton, & Sutton, 2007; Spellman, Kincannon, & Stose, 2005; Tykocinski, Pick, & Kedmi, 2002). Research is currently being conducted to explore the cognitive and motivational mechanisms underlying this phenomenon.

THE DYSFUNCTIONAL SIDE OF COUNTERFACTUAL THINKING

You can spend your time alone re-digesting past regrets, oh
or you can come to terms and realize
you're the only one who cannot forgive yourself, oh
makes much more sense to live in the present tense

Pearl Jam, Present Tense, 1996

Although lab research employing problem-solving tasks has provided clear evidence for the performance-enhancing effects of counterfactual thinking (e.g., Markman, Lindberg, Kray, & Galinsky, 2007; Roese, 1994; Wong et al., Chapter 11, this volume), it is also important to consider data that indicate more "dysfunctional" responses. The second part of this chapter explores the potentially dysfunctional implications of downward and upward counterfactual thinking.

DOWNWARD COUNTERFACTUALS

In addition to the complacency-inducing influence of downward counterfactuals, such counterfactuals can also lower personal expectations and standards. Markman, Mizoguchi, and McMullen

(2008) speculated that even when counterfactuals elicit clear contrastive effects on outcome evaluations, expectations regarding future outcomes may still assimilate to the counterfactual standard. In other words, counterfactual generation may shift the standard by which future outcomes are evaluated. Thus, although upward counterfactual thinking (e.g., "I got a B ... if only I had gotten an A") may elicit negative outcome evaluations via contrast, the standard by which future outcomes are evaluated may be elevated—the individual now perceives oneself as a potential A student. Similarly, although downward counterfactual thinking (e.g., "At least I didn't get a C") may elicit positive outcome evaluations via contrast, the standard by which future outcomes are evaluated may be lowered—the individual now perceives oneself as a C student who was fortunate to have obtained a B. Markman et al. (2008) examined this possibility within the context of the Abu Ghraib prison scandal.

The Abu Ghraib Study

In January 2004, an internal criminal investigation was launched by the U.S. Army in response to accounts of abuse and torture of prisoners that had allegedly occurred in the Abu Ghraib prison in Iraq. The acts were committed by personnel of the 372nd Military Police Company, Central Intelligence Agency (CIA) officers, and contractors involved in the occupation of Iraq. Reports of the abuse, as well as graphic pictures showing American military personnel in the act of abusing prisoners, came to public attention when a *60 Minutes* news report broke the story on April 28. Ultimately, the Department of Defense removed 17 soldiers and officers from duty, and 7 soldiers were charged with dereliction of duty, maltreatment, aggravated assault, and battery.

Arguably, the resulting political scandal damaged the credibility of the United States and its allies with regard to their ongoing military operations in the Iraq War. In an effort to lessen the rising tide of criticism being leveled against the Bush administration, a number of individuals, some employed by newspaper, radio, and television media and others by the U.S. government itself, drew a comparison in public statements between American treatment of Iraqi prisoners at Abu Ghraib and the even more severe treatment these prisoners "would have" received if former Iraqi president Saddam Hussein had still been in power. For instance, during a U.S. Senate Armed Services Committee hearing on the treatment of Iraqi prisoners, Senator James Inhofe (R, Oklahoma) remarked:

> I have to say that when we talk about the treatment of these prisoners that I would guess that these prisoners wake up every morning thanking Allah that Saddam Hussein is not in charge of these prisons. When he was in charge, they would take electric drills and drill holes through hands, they would cut their tongues out, they would cut their ears off. We've seen accounts of lowering their bodies into vats of acid. All of these things were taking place. (Washingtonpost.com, 2004)

To examine the possible deleterious consequences of considering the "it would have been worse under Saddam" argument, Markman et al. (2008) asked study participants to read a packet of materials that began with a paragraph describing a *60 Minutes* television broadcast from April 2004 that showed photographs of the "abuse and humiliation of Iraqi prisoners" by a small group of U.S. soldiers at Abu Ghraib prison in Iraq. After reading this paragraph, participants in the control condition were prompted to describe their reaction to the event in writing. In a downward counterfactual condition, participants read an additional paragraph that described how thousands of political prisoners had been tortured and executed at Abu Ghraib during Saddam Hussein's tenure as Iraqi president and were prompted to "make an argument that being at Abu Ghraib under Saddam's control would be worse than being there under U.S. control." On the other hand, participants in an upward counterfactual condition read a paragraph that described the ethical treatment of Iraqi prisoners by a small contingent of Danish soldiers in a military prison based in the city of Al Quma and were prompted to "make an argument that the ethical standards employed by the Danish in their treatment of Iraqi prisoners were better than the standards employed by the U.S. in treating Iraqi prisoners."

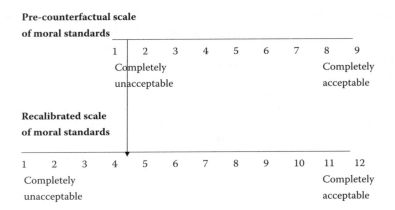

FIGURE 12.4   How comparison to a counterfactual reference point recalibrates a scale of moral standards.

Participants then responded to items (on a 7-point scale) that assessed their feelings toward the events that transpired at Abu Ghraib (e.g., "I am morally outraged by the events that took place at Abu Ghraib"), as well as their attitudes (on a 7-point scale) toward how the United States should treat prisoners of war in the future (e.g. "In future conflicts, to what extent should the U.S. employ interrogation tactics that include the use of torture?"). Consistent with the notion that counterfactual thinking can elicit shifting standards, it was predicted that in comparison to generating upward counterfactuals or no counterfactuals at all, generating downward counterfactuals would lead participants to feel better about Abu Ghraib, thereby evidencing contrast, but would also lower ethical standards regarding how the United States should treat prisoners of war in the future, thereby evidencing assimilation.

As predicted, participants in the downward condition indicated feeling better about the treatment of prisoners at Abu Ghraib ($M = 3.38$) than did participants in either the control condition ($M = 2.50$) or the upward condition ($M = 1.85$). On the other hand, and consistent with the predicted standard-lowering assimilation effect, participants in the downward condition indicated lower standards with respect to human rights ($M = 3.44$) than did participants in either the control condition ($M = 4.34$) or the upward condition ($M = 5.60$). Thus, considering how the treatment of Iraqi prisoners at Abu Ghraib could have been worse had the effect of lowering participants' standards regarding how the United States should treat their prisoners of war in the future.

This effect is consistent with the types of shifting standards models proposed by Biernat and others (e.g., Biernat, 2005; Biernat & Manis, 2007; Parducci, 1963; Upshaw, 1962), which assume that when called on to render judgments along subjective rating scales, individuals fix the end-points of the rating scale to reflect the expected distribution of targets on the judgment dimension. As depicted in Figure 12.4, consideration of the downward (i.e., "it would have been worse under Saddam") counterfactual may lead individuals to recalibrate their scales of moral standards and enhance the relative standing of a range of behaviors that they may have previously deemed unethical. In this way, behaviors that seriously violate default standards of moral behavior may come to be seen as relatively benign in light of the new standard and thereby lower expectations regarding how the United States should treat prisoners of war in the future.

The consequences of the argument that it would have been worse are insidious. Although it is likely that individuals understand the intent of the argument—to mitigate the harsh criticism that has been directed against the American soldiers and the Bush administration more generally—they may be less aware of the subtle yet significant effect that the promulgation of such an argument can have on lowering personal standards. Just as exposure to violence can desensitize subsequent reactions to violence (e.g., Geen, 1991), consistent and chronic exposure to downward counterfactual arguments of this kind may have a numbing or dampening effect on the likelihood of expressing negative attitudes toward human rights violations in the future. In other words, the consideration of such arguments might have the effect over time of raising thresholds for expressing moral outrage.

UPWARD COUNTERFACTUALS

As we have described, currently prevailing models of counterfactual thinking (e.g., Markman & McMullen, 2003; Roese, 1997; Sanna, 2000; Tykocinski & Steinberg, 2005) suggest that although upward counterfactuals may devalue actual outcomes and elicit feelings of disappointment and regret, by simulating routes to imagined better realities one may learn to improve on outcomes in the future. Other researchers, however, argue that regret is an emotion that ultimately yields greater costs than benefits for the individual. For instance, in a study about reactions to miscarriages, Callender, Brown, Tata, and Regan (2007) found a positive association between upward counterfactual thoughts and anxiety and no relationship between counterfactual thinking and positive outcomes. Furthermore, individuals who ruminate on their regrets are more likely to report reduced life satisfaction and to experience difficulty coping with negative life events (e.g., Lecci, Okun, & Karoly, 1994; Schwartz et al., 2002).

Counterfactual Thinking and Self-Blame

Naturalistic studies have also documented a pervasive tendency among individuals who have encountered negative, unexpected events such as sexual assault, spinal cord injury, and traumatic loss of a spouse or child to blame themselves (e.g., Arata, 1999; Branscombe, Wohl, Owen, Allison, & N'gbala, 2003; Davis, Lehman, Silver, Wortman, & Ellard, 1996; Janoff-Bulman, 1979; A. K. Miller, Markman, & Handley, 2007). Self-blame among sexual assault victims is associated with distress (Arata, 1999), and a large-scale review of causal attributions following traumatic life events found that self-blame was 5.2 times more likely to be associated with poor outcomes than all other attribution categories (Hall, French, & Marteau, 2003). According to Hall et al., "When the consequences of events are severe, any potential benefit conferred by self-blame may be outweighed by the severity of consequences of making these attributions" (p. 526).

Critically for the present analysis, a host of studies have demonstrated a clear connection between the generation of counterfactuals and subsequent imputations of self- and other blame (e.g., Branscombe, Owen, Garstka, & Coleman, 1996; Catellani, Alberici, & Milesi, 2004; Davis et al., 1996; Goldinger, Kleider, Azuma, & Beike, 2003; Mandel & Dhami, 2005; McGill & Tenbrunsel, 2008; Nario-Redmond & Branscombe, 1996; Turley, Sanna, & Reiter, 1995; Zeelenberg, van der Plight, & de Vries, 2000). By generating "if only" inferences (e.g., "if only I had not gone to that party") in an effort to understand how a negative experience might have been prevented, an individual may identify multiple counterfactual instances when the event may not have occurred had they behaved differently (Connolly & Zeelenberg, 2002). Yet, as Sherman and McConnell (1995) cautioned, counterfactuals that improve on past negative outcomes may be dysfunctional insofar as they lead to incorrect causal inferences, overwhelming negative affect, and disproportionate self-blame. Discussing rape victims, they argued that, "It is clearly irrational for one to take blame for behaviors that in foresight would not have reduced the probability of the event's occurrence," and, "the despair … that can result from this kind of counterfactual thinking can be devastating" (p. 213; see also Gilovich, 1983; D. T. Miller & Gunasegaram, 1990; Sherman & McConnell, 1996). Moreover, D. T. Miller and Turnbull (1990) noted that counterfactuals can lead to misplaced sympathies in which "innocent" bystanders who are not the direct target of an attack are afforded greater sympathy than are the intended victims.

Depression

Recent work suggests that upward counterfactual thinking may be less functional for individuals suffering from depression. Markman and Miller (2006) grouped participants according to nondepressed, mild-to-moderately depressed, and severely depressed symptom categories and asked them to describe negative academic events and make upward counterfactuals about those events. According to the results, moderate depressives were particularly likely to engage in controllable counterfactual thinking (i.e., to generate counterfactuals about objectively controllable aspects of events; see also Markman & Weary, 1998). However, although nondepressives experienced a boost in retrospective control perceptions (e.g., "I believe that I was in control of the events that led to the academic outcome"), to the extent that they engaged in controllable counterfactual thinking, moderate depressives did not experience a concomitant boost in retrospective control perceptions following controllable counterfactual thinking. In a way, then, such individuals were merely "spinning their wheels" by devoting inordinate attention to how they could have prevented an outcome without experiencing any clear psychological benefit from doing so. Finally, the results suggest that severe depressives might best be served by avoiding upward counterfactual generation entirely. The counterfactuals they generated were clearly dysfunctional in nature—more uncontrollable and more characterological (cf. Janoff-Bulman, 1979)—and to the extent that they did engage in controllable counterfactual thinking, their subsequent retrospective control perceptions actually decreased. Moreover, the controllable counterfactuals generated by severe depressives were typically less reasonable and feasible (e.g., "I could have memorized all of the chapters") than were those generated by individuals experiencing less-severe depression levels, a thought process that should in theory only serve to exacerbate self-blame and worsen depressive symptoms.

Future and Lost Opportunities

There is ample evidence to indicate that counterfactuals have short-term beneficial effects on problem solving and performance (e.g., Parks et al., 2003; Roese, 1994; Wong et al., Chapter 11, this volume), and that negative affect mediates relationships between counterfactual thinking and both persistence and performance (Markman et al., 2008; McMullen & Markman, 2000). However, Roese and Summerville (2005) argued for a more general *opportunity principle*, suggesting that opportunity breeds regret, and that feelings of disappointment and dissatisfaction are strongest when the chances for corrective action are clearest. Specifically, Roese and Summerville (2005) noted that, "By opportunity, we mean an open rather than a closed door to further action in the service of correction, advancement, and betterment, defined in terms of the individual's perception of situational features or personal talents that enable such pursuit" (p. 1273).

To provide evidence for the opportunity principle, Roese and Summerville (2005) described a study conducted by Markman et al. (1993) in which participants played a computer-simulated blackjack game. In this study, participants who believed they would be playing again generated a greater proportion of upward to downward counterfactuals in comparison to those who believed they would only be playing once (see also Gilbert & Ebert, 2002; Linder, Cooper, & Jones, 1967). On the basis of this and other studies, we agree that regret, or, inferences derived from acknowledging how one could have made a better choice or decision, spur corrective action in the short run. Thus, the opportunity principle is sensible for those events that are (or are perceived to be) repeatable in the foreseeable future. However, it is unclear whether regret has long-term beneficial consequences for nonrepeatable events.

First, it is important to note that regret and counterfactual thinking are not the same. Rather, the former is an emotional response elicited by the latter—an explicit comparison between factual reality and an imagined better reality. Interestingly, Roese (1997) argued for a dissociation between counterfactual thinking and its emotional consequences. Specifically, he noted that, "Under normal conditions … most individuals seem adept at inhibiting counterfactual ruminations before they become chronically debilitating, thereby canceling the negative affect deriving from contrast effects, while preserving the inferential benefits deriving from the causal-inference mechanism" (p. 144; see also Taylor, 1991). However, if it is indeed the case that negative affect is typically minimized over time, and that it is the inferences derived from counterfactual thinking that ultimately benefit the individual, then it would seem that the experience of intense, long-term regret would not ultimately benefit the individual and thereby reflects a failure of the minimization system.

Second, there is insufficient empirical evidence for the functionality of long-term regrets. Roese and Summerville (2005) performed a meta-analysis on nine published journal articles and found that education was the most commonly reported life regret, accounting for 32.2% of all reported regrets. According to Roese and Summerville, this finding supports the opportunity principle because, "Education is open to continual modification throughout life. ... You can always go back to school" (p. 1274). In our view, however, this line of reasoning is questionable because windows of opportunity are often quite bounded and finite. Courses end, college ends, and interpersonal relationships are often irrevocably terminated, at which point the present and the future are shunted to the past, and the possibility for corrective action is lost. Thus, we believe that when older individuals indicate that their greatest life regrets center around lost educational opportunities, what they are actually ruing are *lost* opportunities. They will never have the opportunity to be 19 years old again, attend college, and make educational decisions that might impact their choice of career or general intellectual development.

In support of this supposition, Beike, Markman, and Karadogan (2008; see also Karadogan & Markman, in press) asked 68 individuals, ranging in age from 40 to 73, to indicate the extent (on a scale of 1 = low opportunity to 7 = high opportunity) to which they felt that they would have future opportunities to better or improve themselves in each of 12 life domains: education, career, romance, parenting, self, leisure, finance, family, health, friends, spirituality, and community (i.e., the most frequently reported life regret domains in Roese and Summerville's meta-analysis). If Roese and Summerville are correct in assuming that education is a domain in which individuals see high opportunities for future improvement, then education should come out near the top of the list in terms of high-opportunity ratings. However, the data indicated exactly the opposite. Whereas spirituality ($M = 5.5$) and self ($M = 4.9$) were perceived as offering the highest opportunity for future improvement, career ($M = 3.7$) and education ($M = 3.7$) were perceived as offering the lowest opportunity for future improvement. In our view, these data suggest that education is not the most frequently reported life regret because individuals believe that they will have opportunities to take corrective action in this domain. Rather, we would argue that it is the most frequently regretted life domain precisely because it represents a lost opportunity (see also Wrosch & Heckhausen, 2002).

Beike et al. (2008) also experimentally manipulated perceived opportunity in two separate studies to examine whether greater regret was felt when opportunity was perceived as high versus low. One study employed a scenario vignette about a hypothetical individual, and a second study asked participants to recall their own negative life events. In both studies, participants who considered nonrepeatable negative events felt more regret than did those who considered repeatable negative events, findings that once again run contrary to Roese and Summerville's (2005) framework.

Rumination and State Orientation

Recent work in the clinical literature (e.g., Ehlers & Clark, 2000; El Leithy, Brown, & Robbins, 2006; Watkins & Baracaia, 2002) has noted that although counterfactual thinking following negative events may further emotional processing and understanding, there are circumstances under which the balance of costs and benefits can shift such that a preoccupation with what might have been can actually contribute to the development and maintenance of traumatic stress reactions and what Lyubomirsky and Nolen-Hoeksema (1993) term "ruminative responses to depressed mood." One of the critical challenges facing the counterfactual thinking literature will be to define conditions under which counterfactuals serve an adaptive function as opposed to when they merely perpetuate a negative mood state.

A promising research avenue draws on Kuhl's (1994) distinction between action and state orientation. According to Watkins and Baracaia's (2002) analysis, rumination is a mode of thinking that reflects a state orientation characterized by a preoccupation with simulating alternative plans and by the evaluation of past successes and failures that tend to work against the initiation of new actions (in this volume, see also Faude, Wuerz, & Gollwitzer, Chapter 5; Oettingen & Kappes, Chapter 26). On the other hand, action orientation is characterized by action planning and effective self-monitoring. Importantly, Watkins and Baracaia reported data indicating that inducing an action orientation in a sample of depressed individuals who had initially tended to respond with a state orientation improved problem-solving performance (see also McElroy & Dowd, 2007; Seta, McElroy, & Seta, 2001).

In light of these findings, what would constitute an adaptive response to a negative and non-repeatable event? According to recent work (e.g., Koole & Jostmann, 2004; Kuhl, 2000), under stressful conditions action-oriented individuals mobilize central executive systems and engage in downregulation of negative affect, and to the extent that downregulation is successful (e.g., via downward counterfactual thinking, distraction, etc.) action-oriented individuals display mood improvements and facilitated self-regulation. On the other hand, state-oriented individuals respond to stressful situations by engaging in ineffective forms of affect regulation that result in persistent negative affect, negative rumination, and inhibited self-regulation. Thus, action-oriented individuals appear better equipped to deal with negative and nonrepeatable events than do state-oriented individuals because the former have the capacity to minimize their negative affect even though they have been stripped of their ability to initiate future ameliorative action. Nevertheless, the picture remains far from rosy. Individuals who are depressed, traumatized, or state oriented are vulnerable to persistent and perhaps even tormenting counterfactual thoughts. And, although action-oriented individuals may be able to buffer their immediate affective reactions, it is likely that many of them still suffer from wistful (Gilovich, Medvec, & Kahneman, 1998) and perhaps gnawing feelings of regret stemming from opportunities lost and foreclosed (Beike et al., 2008).

CONCLUSION

A substantial body of research indicates that counterfactual thinking can be beneficial (e.g., Grieve, Houston, Dupuis, & Eddy, 1999; Markman, Lindberg, et al., 2007; Nasco & Marsh, 1999; Sanna, 1998). On the other hand, real-world instances of dysfunctional counterfactual thinking are abundant. Although much work is needed to uncover the conditions under which counterfactual thinking may be more or less functional, we suggest that repeatability is a critical moderator. Counterfactual thinking appears to be beneficial for potentially repeatable events because it can spur corrective action and reduce the intensity of felt regret. However, research also indicates that an earmark of healthy cognitive functioning is a system that effectively downregulates negative emotional experiences while preserving useful inferential benefits (e.g., Kuhl, 1994; Roese, 1997; Watkins & Baracaia, 2002). To the extent that this system breaks down during the consideration of long-term, nonrepeatable events, the result may be depressive rumination (Lyubomirsky & Nolen-Hoeksema, 1993) that perpetuates a self-defeating cycle of self-blame. Overall, we believe that the proposition that counterfactual thinking and the concomitant emotion of regret are beneficial for the individual requires additional research to establish boundary conditions on what is currently seen as a general principle (e.g., Roese, 2005; Zeelenberg, 1999).

REFERENCES

Arata, C. M. (1999). Coping with rape: The roles of prior sexual abuse and attributions of blame. *Journal of Interpersonal Violence, 14*, 62–78.

Avnet, T., & Higgins, E. T. (2003). Locomotion, assessment, and regulatory fit: Value transfer from "how" to "what." *Journal of Experimental Social Psychology, 39*, 525–530.

The Beatles. (1968). While my guitar gently weeps. *The Beatles.* Apple Records, United Kingdom. Vinyl.

Beike, D. R., Markman, K. D., & Karadogan, F. (2008). What people really regret are lost opportunities. Unpublished manuscript.

Biernat, M. (2005). *Standards and expectancies: Contrast and assimilation in judgments of self and others.* New York: Psychology Press.

Biernat, M., & Manis, M. (2007). Stereotypes and shifting standards: Assimilation and contrast in social judgment. In D. Stapel & J. Suls (Eds.), *Assimilation and contrast in social psychology* (pp. 75–97). New York: Psychology Press.

Boninger, D. S., Gleicher, F., & Strathman, A. J. (1994). Counterfactual thinking: From what might have been to what may be. *Journal of Personality and Social Psychology, 67,* 297–307.

Branscombe, N. R., Owen, S., Garstka, T. A., & Coleman, J. (1996). Rape and accident counterfactuals: Who might have done otherwise and would it have changed the outcome? *Journal of Applied Social Psychology, 26,* 1042–1067.

Branscombe, N. R., Wohl, M. J. A., Owen, S., Allison, J. A., & N'gbala, A. (2003). Counterfactual thinking, blame assignment, and well-being in rape victims. *Journal of Applied Social Psychology, 25,* 265–273.

Brickman, P., Ryan, K., & Wortman, C. B. (1975). Causal chains: Attribution of responsibility as a function of immediate and prior causes. *Journal of Personality and Social Psychology, 32,* 1060–1067.

Callender, G., Brown, G. P., Tata, P., & Regan, L. (2007). Counterfactual thinking and psychological distress following recurrent miscarriage. *Journal of Reproductive and Infant Psychology, 25,* 51–65.

Camacho, C. J., Higgins, E. T., & Luger, L. (2003). Moral value transfer from regulatory fit: What feels right is right and what feels wrong is wrong. *Journal of Personality and Social Psychology, 84,* 498–510.

Catellani, P., Alberici, I. A., & Milesi, P. (2004). Counterfactual thinking and stereotypes: The nonconformity effect. *European Journal of Social Psychology, 34,* 421–436.

Collins, R. L. (1996). For better or worse: The impact of upward social comparison on self-evaluations. *Psychological Bulletin, 119,* 51–69.

Connolly, T., & Zeelenberg, M. (2002). Regret and decision making. *Current Directions in Psychological Science, 11,* 212–216.

Davis, C. G., Lehman, D. R., Silver, R. C., Wortman, C. B., & Ellard, J. (1996). Self-blame following a traumatic event: The role of perceived avoidability. *Personality and Social Psychology Bulletin, 22,* 557–567.

Ehlers, A., & Clark, D. M. (2000). A cognitive model of posttraumatic stress disorder. *Behaviour Research and Therapy, 38,* 319–345.

El Leithy, S., Brown, G. P., & Robbins, I. (2006). Counterfactual thinking and posttraumatic stress reactions. *Journal of Abnormal Psychology, 115,* 629–635.

Folkman, S., & Lazarus, R. S. (1980). An analysis of coping in a middle-aged community sample. *Journal of Health and Social Behavior, 21,* 219–239.

Galinsky, A. D., Liljenquist, K. A., Kray, L. J., & Roese, N. J. (2005). Finding meaning from mutability: Making sense and deriving significance through counterfactual thinking. In D. R. Mandel, D. J. Hilton, & P. Catellani (Eds.), *The psychology of counterfactual thinking* (pp. 110–125). London: Routledge.

Geen, R. G. (1991). Social motivation. *Annual Review of Psychology, 42,* 377–399.

Gilbert, D. T., & Ebert, J. E. J. (2002). Decisions and revisions: The affective forecasting of changeable outcomes. *Journal of Personality and Social Psychology, 82,* 503–514.

Gilovich, T. (1983). Biased evaluation and persistence in gambling. *Journal of Personality and Social Psychology, 67,* 1110–1126.

Gilovich, T., Medvec, V. H., & Kahneman, D. (1998). Varieties of regret: A debate and partial resolution. *Psychological Review, 105,* 602–605.

Goldinger, S. D., Kleider, H. M., Azuma, T., & Beike, D. R. (2003). "Blaming the victim" under memory load. *Psychological Science, 14,* 81–85.

Green, M. C., & Brock, T. C. (2000). The role of transportation in the persuasiveness of public narratives. *Journal of Personality and Social Psychology, 79,* 701–721.

Grieve, F. G., Houston, D. A., Dupuis, S. E., & Eddy, D. (1999). Counterfactual production and achievement orientation in competitive athletic settings. *Journal of Applied Social Psychology, 29,* 2177–2202.

Hall, S., French, D. P., & Marteau, T. M. (2003). Causal attributions following serious unexpected negative events: A systematic review. *Journal of Social and Clinical Psychology, 22,* 515–536.

Higgins, E. T. (1998). Promotion and prevention: Regulatory focus as a motivational principle. In M. P. Zanna (Ed.), *Advances in experimental social psychology* (Vol. 30, pp. 1–46). San Diego, CA: Academic Press.

Higgins, E. T. (2000). Making a good decision: Value from fit. *American Psychologist, 55,* 1217–1230.

Higgins, E. T. (2005). Value from regulatory fit. *Current Directions in Psychological Science, 14,* 209–213.

Higgins, E. T., Idson, L. C., Freitas, A. L., Spiegel, S., & Molden, D. C. (2003). Transfer of value from fit. *Journal of Personality and Social Psychology, 84,* 1140–1153.

Hur, T. (2000). Counterfactual thinking and regulatory focus: Upward versus downward counterfactuals and promotion versus prevention. *Dissertation Abstracts International, 60,* 6422B.

Janoff-Bulman, R. (1979). Characterological versus behavioral self-blame: Inquiries into depression and rape. *Journal of Personality and Social Psychology, 37,* 1789–1809.

Johnson, J. T. (1986). The knowledge of what might have been: Affective and attributional consequences of near outcomes. *Personality and Social Psychology Bulletin, 12,* 51–62.

Johnson, M. K., & Sherman, S.J. (1990). Constructing and reconstructing the past and future in the present. In E. T. Higgins & R. M. Sorrentino (Eds.), *Handbook of motivation and cognition: Foundations of social behavior* (Vol. 2, pp. 482–526). New York: Guilford.

Kahneman, D., & Miller, D. T. (1986). Norm theory: Comparing reality to its alternatives. *Psychological Review, 93,* 136–153.

Karadogan, F., & Markman, K. D. (in press). The psychology of regret and counterfactual thinking: Issues and controversies. *Social and Personality Psychology Compass.*

Karniol, R., & Ross, M. (1996). The motivational impact of temporal focus: Thinking about the future and the past. *Annual Review of Psychology, 47,* 593–620.

Koole, S. L., & Jostmann, N. B. (2004). Getting a grip on your feelings: Effects of action orientation and external demands on intuitive affect regulation. *Journal of Personality and Social Psychology, 87,* 974–990.

Kuhl, J. (1994). A theory of action and state orientations. In J. Kuhl & J. Beckmann (Eds.), *Volition and personality: Action- and state-oriented modes of control* (pp. 9–46). Gottingen, Germany: Hogrefe & Huber.

Kuhl, J. (2000). A functional-design approach to motivation and self-regulation: The dynamics of personality systems interactions. In M. Boekaerts, P. R. Pintrich, & M. Zeidner (Eds.), *Handbook of self-regulation* (pp. 111–169). San Diego, CA: Academic Press.

Landman, J. (1987). Regret and elation following action and inaction. *Personality and Social Psychology Bulletin, 13,* 524–536.

Landman, J., & Petty, R. (2000). "It could have been you": How states exploit counterfactual thought to market lotteries. *Psychology and Marketing, 17,* 299–321.

Larsen, J. T., McGraw, A. P., Mellers, B. A., & Cacioppo, J. T. (2004). The agony of victory and the thrill of defeat: Mixed emotional reactions to disappointing wins and relieving losses. *Psychological Science, 15,* 325–220.

Lecci, L., Okun, M. A., & Karoly, P. (1994). Life regrets and current goals as predictors of psychological adjustment. *Journal of Personality and Social Psychology, 66,* 731–741.

Lindberg, M. J., & Markman, K. D. (2008). [Counterfactual thinking as magical thinking: When what happens tomorrow makes today seem pre-determined.] Unpublished data.

Linder, D. E., Cooper, J., & Jones, E. E. (1967). Decision freedom as a determinant of the role of incentive magnitude in attitude change. *Journal of Personality and Social Psychology, 6,* 245–254.

Lockwood, P., Jordan, C. H., & Kunda, Z. (2002). Motivation by positive or negative role models: Regulatory focus determines who will best inspire us. *Journal of Personality and Social Psychology, 83,* 854–864.

Lyubomirsky, S., & Nolen-Hoeksema, S. (1993). Self-perpetuating properties of dysphoric rumination. *Journal of Personality and Social Psychology, 65,* 339–349.

Mandel, D. R. (2003). Judgment dissociation theory: An analysis of differences in causal, counterfactual, and covariational reasoning. *Journal of Experimental Psychology: General, 132,* 419–434.

Mandel, D.R., & Dhami, M.K. (2005). "What I did" versus "What I might have done": Effect of factual and counterfactual thinking on blame, guilt, and shame in prisoners. *Journal of Experimental Social Psychology, 41,* 627–635.

Mandel, D. R., & Lehman, D. R. (1996). Counterfactual thinking and ascriptions of cause and preventability. *Journal of Personality and Social Psychology, 71,* 450–463.

Markman, K. D., Elizaga, R. A., Ratcliff, J. J., & McMullen, M. N. (2007). The interplay between counterfactual reasoning and feedback dynamics in producing inferences about the self. *Thinking and Reasoning, 13,* 188–206.

Markman, K. D., Gavanski, I., Sherman, S. J., & McMullen, M. N. (1993). The mental simulation of better and worse possible worlds. *Journal of Experimental Social Psychology, 29,* 87–109.

Markman, K. D., Lindberg, M. J., Kray, L. J., & Galinsky, A. D. (2007). Implications of counterfactual structure for creative generation and analytical problem solving. *Personality and Social Psychology Bulletin, 33,* 312–324.

Markman, K. D., & McMullen, M. N. (2003). A reflection and evaluation model of comparative thinking. *Personality and Social Psychology Review, 7,* 244–267.

Markman, K. D., & McMullen, M. N. (2005). Reflective and evaluative modes of mental simulation. In D. R. Mandel, D. J. Hilton, & P. Catellani (Eds.), *The psychology of counterfactual thinking* (pp. 77–93). London: Routledge.

Markman, K. D., McMullen, M. N., & Elizaga, R. A. (2008). Counterfactual thinking, persistence, and performance: A test of the reflection and evaluation model. *Journal of Experimental Social Psychology, 44,* 421–428.

Markman, K. D., McMullen, M. N., Elizaga, R. A., & Mizoguchi, N. (2006). Counterfactual thinking and regulatory fit. *Judgment and Decision Making, 1,* 98–107.

Markman, K. D., & Miller, A. K. (2006). Depression, control, and counterfactual thinking: Functional for whom? *Journal of Social and Clinical Psychology, 25,* 210–227.

Markman, K. D., Mizoguchi, N., & McMullen, M. N. (2008). "It would have been worse under Saddam": Implications of counterfactual thinking for the ethical treatment of prisoners of war. *Journal of Experimental Social Psychology, 44,* 650–654.

Markman, K. D., Ratcliff, J. J., Mizoguchi, N., Elizaga, R. A., & McMullen, M. N. (2007). Assimilation and contrast in counterfactual thinking and other mental simulation-based comparison processes. In D. A. Stapel & J. Suls (Eds.), *Assimilation and contrast in social psychology* (pp. 187–206). New York: Psychology Press.

Markman, K. D., & Tetlock, P. E. (2000). The loser who nearly won and the winner who nearly lost. *Personality and Social Psychology Bulletin, 26,* 1213–1224.

Markman, K. D., & Weary, G. (1998). Control motivation, depression, and counterfactual thought. In M. Kofta, G. Weary, & G. Sedek (Eds.), *Personal control in action: Cognitive and motivational mechanisms* (pp. 363–390). New York: Plenum.

Martin, L. L., Ward, D. W., Achee, J. W., & Wyer, R. S. (1993). Mood as input: People have to interpret the motivational implications of their moods. *Journal of Personality and Social Psychology, 64,* 317–326.

McClure, J., Hilton, D. J., & Sutton, R. M. (2007). Judgments of voluntary and physical causes in causal chains: Probabilistic and social functionalist criteria for attributions. *European Journal of Social Psychology, 37,* 879–901.

McElroy, T., & Dowd, K. (2007). Action orientation, consistency, and feelings of regret. *Judgment and Decision Making, 2,* 333–341.

McGill, A. L., & Tenbrunsel, A. E. (2000). Mutability and propensity in causal selection. *Journal of Personality and Social Psychology, 79,* 677–689.

McMullen, M. N. (1997). Affective contrast and assimilation in counterfactual thinking. *Journal of Experimental Social Psychology, 33,* 77–100.

McMullen, M. N., & Markman, K. D. (2000). Downward counterfactuals and motivation: The "wake-up call" and the "Pangloss effect." *Personality and Social Psychology Bulletin, 26,* 575–584.

McMullen, M. N., & Markman, K. D. (2002). Affect and close counterfactuals: Implications of possible futures for possible pasts. *Journal of Experimental Social Psychology, 38,* 64–70.

McMullen, M. N., Markman, K. D., & Gavanski, I. (1995). Living in neither the best nor worst of all possible worlds: Antecedents and consequences of upward and downward counterfactual thinking. In N. J. Roese & J. M. Olson (Eds.), *What might have been: The social psychology of counterfactual thinking* (pp. 133–167). Hillsdale, NJ: Erlbaum.

Medvec, V. H., Madey, S. F., & Gilovich, T. (1995). When less is more: Counterfactual thinking and satisfaction among Olympic medalists. *Journal of Personality and Social Psychology, 69,* 603–610.

Mellers, B. A., Schwartz, A., Ho, K., & Ritov, I. (1997). Decision affect theory: Emotional reactions to the outcomes of risky options. *Psychological Science, 8,* 423–429.

Miller, A. K., Markman, K. D., & Handley, I. M. (2007). Self-blame among sexual assault victims prospectively predicts revictimization: A perceived sociolegal context model of risk. *Basic and Applied Social Psychology, 29,* 129–136.

Miller, D. T., & Gunasegaram, S. (1990). Temporal order and the perceived mutability of events: Implications for blame assignment. *Journal of Personality and Social Psychology, 59,* 1111–1118.

Miller, D. T., & McFarland, C. (1986). Counterfactual thinking and victim compensation: A test of norm theory. *Personality and Social Psychology Bulletin, 12,* 513–519.

Miller, D. T., & Turnbull, W. (1990). The counterfactual fallacy: Confusing what might have been with what ought to have been. *Social Justice Research, 4,* 1–19.

Mussweiler, T. (2008). Comparison processes in social judgment: Mechanisms and consequences. *Psychological Review, 110,* 472–489.

Nario-Redmond, M. R., & Branscombe, N. R. (1996). It could have been better and it might have been worse: Implications for blame assignment in rape cases. *Basic and Applied Social Psychology, 18,* 347–366.

Nasco, S. A., & Marsh, K. L. (1999). Gaining control through counterfactual thinking. *Personality and Social Psychology Bulletin, 25,* 556–568.

Oettingen, G., Pak, H., & Schnetter, K. (2001). Self-regulation of goal setting: Turning free fantasies about the future into binding goals. *Journal of Personality and Social Psychology, 80,* 736–753.

Parducci, A. (1963). Range-frequency compromise in judgment. *Psychological Monographs, 77*(Whole No. 565), 1–29.

Parks, C. D., Sanna, L. J., & Posey, D. C. (2003). Retrospection in social dilemmas: How thinking about the past affects future cooperation. *Journal of Personality and Social Psychology, 84,* 988–996.

Pearl Jam. (1996). Present tense. *No code.* Sony, New York, NY.

Pennington, G. L., & Roese, N. J. (2002). Regulatory focus and mental simulation. In S. J. Spencer, M. P. Zanna, & J. M. Olson (Eds.), *Motivated social perception: The Ontario Symposium* (Vol. 9, pp. 277–298). Hillsdale, NJ: Erlbaum.

Pham, L. B., & Taylor, S. E. (1999). From thought to action: Effects of process- versus outcome-based mental simulations on performance. *Personality and Social Psychology Bulletin, 25,* 250–260.

Roese, N. J. (1994). The functional basis of counterfactual thinking. *Journal of Personality and Social Psychology, 66,* 805–818.

Roese, N. J. (1997). Counterfactual thinking. *Psychological Bulletin, 121,* 133–148.

Roese, N. J. (2005). *If only: How to turn regret into opportunity.* New York: Broadway Books.

Roese, N. J., Hur, T., & Pennington, G. L. (1999). Counterfactual thinking and regulatory focus: Implications for action versus inaction and sufficiency versus necessity. *Journal of Personality and Social Psychology, 77,* 1109–1120.

Roese, N. J., & Olson, J. M. (1995a). Counterfactual thinking: A critical overview. In N. J. Roese & J. M. Olson (Eds.), *What might have been: The social psychology of counterfactual thinking* (pp. 1–55) Hillsdale, NJ: Erlbaum.

Roese, N. J., & Olson, J. M. (1995b). Functions of counterfactual thought. In N. J. Roese & J. M. Olson (Eds.), *What might have been: The social psychology of counterfactual thinking* (pp. 169–197) Hillsdale, NJ: Erlbaum.

Roese, N. J., Sanna, L. J., & Galinsky, A. D. (2005). The mechanics of imagination: Automaticity and control in counterfactual thinking. In R. R. Hassin, J. S. Uleman, & J. A. Bargh (Eds.), *The new unconscious* (pp. 138–170). New York: Oxford University Press.

Roese, N. J., & Summerville, A. (2005). What we regret most ... and why. *Personality and Social Psychology Bulletin, 31,* 1273–1285.

Sanna, L. J. (1996). Defensive pessimism, optimism, and simulating alternatives: Some ups and downs of prefactual and counterfactual thinking. *Journal of Personality and Social Psychology, 71,* 1020–1036.

Sanna, L. J. (1997). Self-efficacy and counterfactual thinking: Up the creek with and without a paddle. *Personality and Social Psychology Bulletin, 23,* 654–666.

Sanna, L. J. (1998). Defensive pessimism and optimism: The bittersweet influence of mood on performance and prefactual and counterfactual thinking. *Cognition and Emotion, 12,* 635–665.

Sanna, L. J. (2000). Mental simulation, affect, and personality: A conceptual framework. *Current Directions in Psychological Science, 9,* 168–173.

Sanna, L. J., & Meier, S. M. (2000). Looking for clouds in a silver lining: Self-esteem, mental simulations, and temporal confidence changes. *Journal of Research in Personality, 34,* 236–251.

Schwartz, B., Ward, A., Monterosso, J., Lyubomirsky, S., White, K., & Lehman, D. (2002). Maximizing versus satisficing: Happiness is a matter of choice. *Journal of Personality and Social Psychology, 83,* 1178–1197.

Schwarz, N., & Clore, G. L. (1983). Mood, misattribution, and judgments of well-being: Informative and directive functions of affective states. *Journal of Personality and Social Psychology, 45,* 513–523.

Segura, S., & Morris, M. W. (2005). Scenario simulations in learning: Forms and functions at the individual and organizational levels. In D. R. Mandel, D. J. Hilton, & P. Catellani (Eds.), *The psychology of counterfactual thinking* (pp. 94–109). London: Routledge.

Seta, J. J., McElroy, T., & Seta, C. E. (2001). To do or not to do: Desirability and consistency mediate judgments of regret. *Journal of Personality and Social Psychology, 80,* 861–870.

Shah, J., Higgins, E. T., & Friedman, R. (1998). Performance incentives and means: How regulatory focus influences goal attainment. *Journal of Personality and Social Psychology, 74*, 285–293.

Sherman, S. J., & McConnell, A. R. (1995). Dysfunctional implications of counterfactual thinking: When alternatives to reality fail us. In N. J. Roese & J. M. Olson (Eds.), *What might have been: The social psychology of counterfactual thinking* (pp. 199–231). Mahwah, NJ: Erlbaum.

Sherman, S. J., & McConnell, A. R. (1996). The role of counterfactual thinking in reasoning. *Applied Cognitive Psychology, 10*, 113–124.

Spellman, B. A., Kincannon, A. P., & Stose, S. J. (2005). The relation between counterfactual and causal reasoning. In D. R. Mandel, D. J. Hilton, & P. Catellani (Eds.), *The psychology of counterfactual thinking* (pp. 28–43). London: Routledge.

Spiegel, S., Grant-Pillow, H., & Higgins, E. T. (2004). How regulatory fit enhances motivational strength during goal pursuit. *European Journal of Social Psychology, 34*, 39–54.

Taylor, S. E. (1991). Asymmetrical effects of positive and negative events: The mobilization-minimization hypothesis. *Psychological Bulletin, 110*, 67–85.

Taylor, S. E., Buunk, B. P., & Aspinwall, L. G. (1990). Social comparison, stress, and coping. *Personality and Social Psychology Bulletin, 16*, 74–89.

Taylor, S. E., & Schneider, S. K. (1989). Coping and the simulation of events. *Social Cognition, 7*, 174–194.

Teigen, K. H. (2005). When a small difference makes a big difference: Counterfactual thinking and luck. In D. R. Mandel, D. J. Hilton, & P. Catellani (Eds.), *The psychology of counterfactual thinking* (pp. 129–146). London: Routledge.

Tetlock, P. E. (1998). Close-call counterfactuals and belief system defense: I was not almost wrong but I was almost right. *Journal of Personality and Social Psychology, 75*, 639–652.

Turley, K. J., Sanna, L. J., & Reiter, R. L. (1995). Counterfactual thinking and perceptions of rape. *Basic and Applied Social Psychology, 17*, 285–303.

Tykocinski, O. E., Pick, D., & Kedmi, D. (2002). Retroactive pessimism: A different kind of hindsight bias. *European Journal of Social Psychology, 32*, 577–588.

Tykocinski, O. E., & Steinberg, N. (2005). Coping with disappointing outcomes: Retroactive pessimism and motivated inhibition of counterfactuals. *Journal of Experimental Social Psychology, 41*, 551–558.

Upshaw, H. S. (1962). Own attitude as an anchor in equal-appearing intervals. *Journal of Abnormal and Social Psychology, 64*, 85–96.

Washingtonpost.com. (2004, May 11). Transcript: Taguba, Cambone on Abu Ghraib report. Retrieved August 15, 2006 from http://www.washingtonpost.com/ac2/wp-dyn/A17812–2004May11

Watkins, E., & Baracaia, S. (2002). Rumination and social problem solving in depression. *Behaviour Research and Therapy, 40*, 1179–1189.

Wayment, H. A. (2004). It could have been me: Vicarious victims and disaster-focused distress. *Personality and Social Psychology Bulletin, 30*, 515–528.

Wells, G. L., & Gavanski, I. (1989). Mental simulation of causality. *Journal of Personality and Social Psychology, 56*, 161–169.

Wohl, M. J. A., & Enzle, M. E. (2003). The effects of near wins and near losses on self-perceived personal luck and subsequent gambling behavior. *Journal of Experimental Social Psychology, 39*, 184–191.

Wood, J. V. (1989). Theory and research concerning social comparisons of personal attributes. *Psychological Bulletin, 106*, 231–248.

Wrosch, C., & Heckhausen, J. (2002). Perceived control of life regrets: Good for young and bad for old adults. *Psychology and Aging, 17*, 340–350.

Zeelenberg, M. (1999). The use of crying over spilled milk: A note on the rationality and functionality of regret. *Philosophical Psychology, 13*, 326–340.

Zeelenberg, M., van der Plight, J., & de Vries, N. K. (2000). Attributions of responsibility and affective reactions to decision outcomes. *Acta Psychologica, 104*, 303–315.

Section IV

Alternatives and Alternate Selves

13 It's Hard to Imagine: Mental Simulation, Metacognitive Experiences, and the Success of Debiasing

Lawrence J. Sanna, Norbert Schwarz, and Lindsay A. Kennedy

You cannot depend on your judgment
when your imagination is out of focus.

Mark Twain's Notebook, 1898

INTRODUCTION

Mental simulation plays a critical role in many life domains. The chapters in this volume give testament to this importance, from thinking about possible futures (e.g., Dunn, Forrin, & Ashton-James, Chapter 22; Oyserman & James, Chapter 25) to revisiting past events (e.g., Bernstein, Godfrey, & Loftus, Chapter 6; Lynn, Barnes, & Matthews, Chapter 7), and from taking others' perspectives (e.g., Epley & Caruso, Chapter 20; Saxe, Chapter 17) to planning one's own course of action (e.g., Carroll & Shepperd, Chapter 28; Zeelenberg & Pieters, Chapter 27) or undoing the outcomes of past actions (e.g., Byrne & Girotto, Chapter 10; Markman, Karadogan, Lindberg, & Zell, Chapter 12) and so on. Throughout, mental simulation can profoundly influence how people think and feel about an issue, with important consequences for motivation and behavior. Not surprisingly, psychologists have attempted to harness the power of mental simulation in various ways, often with considerable success. For example, helping people to see things from another's perspective can increase empathy (e.g., Batson, Chapter 18), having people imagine desirable or undesirable aspects of possible futures can facilitate behavior change (e.g., Oettingen & Kappes, Chapter 26), and imagining circumstances conducive to goal enactment can increase the likelihood of actual enactment later (e.g., Faude, Wuerz, & Gollwitzer, Chapter 5).

Similarly, judgment and decision-making researchers have attempted to harness mental simulation in the service of good judgment. This chapter reviews some of the lessons learned from this endeavor. We first summarize widely shared assumptions about the emergence and attenuation of judgmental biases. These assumptions focus on what people think about and on how motivated they are to get it right. A growing body of research illustrates, however, that we cannot understand the emergence and attenuation of bias without paying attention to the metacognitive experiences that accompany thinking. Experiences like the ease or difficulty with which information can be retrieved or thoughts can be generated are informative in their own right and qualify the implications of thought content. We review relevant experiments and summarize a model that conceptualizes the interplay of declarative and experiential information in the emergence and attenuation of bias (see also Sanna & Schwarz, 2006; Schwarz, Sanna, Skurnik, & Yoon, 2007). The chapter concludes with a discussion of the role of metacognitive experiences in other domains of mental simulation.

EMERGENCE AND ATTENUATION OF BIAS

People's judgments often fall short of normative ideals and exhibit numerous biases and shortcomings (for reviews, see Gilovich, Griffin, & Kahneman, 2002; Nisbett & Ross, 1980). Presumably, these biases arise because people focus narrowly on some select features of the issue and fail to take a wider range of information into account. For example, people are overconfident about future success because they focus on behaviors that will lead to success and fail to consider variables that may impede success (e.g., Koriat, Lichtenstein, & Fischhoff, 1980). Similarly, after learning about the outcome of an event, people assume that they "knew it all along" because they focus on outcome-congruent knowledge and fail to consider variables that may have given rise to alternative outcomes (e.g., Fischhoff, 1975). When asked to predict the time by which a task will be completed, people's estimates are too optimistic because they focus on goal-directed behaviors and fail to consider variables that may impede progress (e.g., Buehler, Griffin, & Ross, 1994). Given the emphasis on thought content, the strength of these and other biases is assumed to increase with the number of focal thoughts and to decrease with the number of alternatives that are considered. From this perspective, any strategy that succeeds in encouraging people to consider information about alternatives should attenuate the respective biases—and the more so, the more alternatives people actually consider (see Larrick, 2004).

Accordingly, one of the most widely recommended debiasing strategies encourages people to "consider the opposite" or to counterargue their initial response by asking themselves, "What are some reasons that my initial judgment might be wrong?" (Larrick, 2004, p. 323; see also Fischhoff, 1982; Hirt & Markman, 1995; Lord, Lepper, & Preston, 1984; Soll & Klayman, 2004). Empirically, this content-focused strategy meets with mixed success and can profoundly backfire, as the examples that we review will illustrate. The empirical complexities derive from the interplay of thought content and metacognitive experiences. Thinking about an issue's focal aspects only results in bias when focal aspects come to mind easily; conversely, thinking about alternative aspects only attenuates bias when alternative aspects come to mind easily. In contrast, when recall or thought generation is experienced as difficult, people's conclusions are opposite to the implications of accessible thought content, reversing the otherwise observed influences. We first illustrate how people's judgments are influenced by metacognitive experiences with representative findings and then present an integrative process model.

THE CASE OF HINDSIGHT BIAS

Hindsight bias (Fischhoff, 1975; Fischhoff & Beyth, 1975) refers to people's exaggerated sense of event inevitability once outcomes are known, relative to foresight estimates when outcomes are unknown—after the fact, people routinely assume that they "knew it all along." Most theories of hindsight bias share the presumption that the bias will be greater when many rather than few reasons for the known outcome come to mind (for reviews, see Christensen-Szalanski & Willham, 1991; Guilbault, Bryant, Posavac, & Brockway, 2004; Hawkins & Hastie, 1990). Conversely, thinking about alternative outcomes in an attempt "to convince oneself that it might have turned out otherwise" (Fischhoff, 1982, p. 343) is one of the most frequently recommended debiasing strategies. But, as we describe in the following sections, these content-focused notions fail to account for all of the available data.

ACCESSIBILITY EXPERIENCES

Sanna, Schwarz, and Small (2002, Experiment 1) examined the role of accessible thought content and metacognitive accessibility experiences in producing and reducing hindsight bias.

Their participants read a story of a battle in the British-Gurkha war (adapted from Fischhoff, 1975), which they were told the British won. Some were asked to list either 2 or 10 thoughts

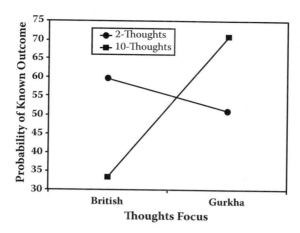

FIGURE 13.1 Mean probability of known outcome in percentages. All participants were told that the British won. British focus thus represents the known outcome, whereas Gurkha focus represents the alternative outcome. (Adapted from "Accessibility Experiences and the Hindsight Bias: I Knew It All Along Versus It Could Never Have Happened," by L. J. Sanna, N. Schwarz, and E. M. Small, 2002, *Memory & Cognition, 30,* 1288–1296, Experiment 1.)

supporting this outcome, whereas others were asked to list either 2 or 10 thoughts supporting the alternative outcome. If only thought content mattered, hindsight bias should be greater when participants list 10 rather than 2 thoughts supporting a British victory (the known outcome); conversely, hindsight bias should be lesser when they list 10 rather than 2 thoughts supporting a Gurkha victory (the alternative outcome). However, exactly the opposite happened (see Figure 13.1): Listing more thoughts favoring the known outcome, which participants experienced as difficult, decreased hindsight bias, whereas listing more thoughts favoring alternative outcomes, likewise experienced as difficult, increased hindsight bias (see also Sanna, Schwarz, & Stocker, 2002). These results are incompatible with theories focused on thought content but follow directly from a metacognitive, experiential perspective.

The observed pattern is not due to some methodological quirk when listing more thoughts. One could wonder, for example, whether the quality of thoughts deteriorated as more were listed, leaving those in the 10-thought conditions with poorer sets of reasons. If so, differences in the quality of generated thoughts may have produced the obtained pattern and not people's metacognitive experiences. But, this is not the case. Sanna, Schwarz, and Small (2002, Experiment 2) asked all participants to list five thoughts, holding thought content constant. Subjective experiences of difficulty were varied instead by asking some participants to contract the corrugator muscle during thoughts listing, resulting in a furrowed brow, which conveys a sense of mental effort paralleling difficult thoughts listing (e.g., Strack & Neumann, 2000). Replicating the prior pattern, participants listing five thoughts favoring a British victory (the known outcome) considered a British victory less likely when furrowing brows than when they did not. Conversely, participants listing five thoughts favoring a Gurkha victory (the alternative outcome) considered a British victory more likely when furrowing their brows than when they did not.

FLUENCY, FAMILIARITY, AND SURPRISE

Familiar information is easier to process than novel information, as reflected in faster response times. Presumably informed by this correct observation, people also draw the reverse inference and conclude from experienced ease of processing that the processed information must be familiar. They even do so when the fluency of processing is solely due to variables unrelated to actual familiarity, like high figure-ground contrast, an easy-to-read print font, a rhyming presentation format, long exposure times, or preceding semantic primes (for reviews, see Jacoby, Kelley, & Dywan, 1989; Schwarz, 2004; Winkielman, Schwarz, Fazendeiro, & Reber, 2003). Hence, numerous normatively irrelevant variables can influence perceivers' subjective sense of familiarity with important consequences (for a review, see Schwarz et al., 2007).

Exploring the role of processing fluency in the emergence of hindsight bias, Werth and Strack (2003) exposed participants to general knowledge questions and answers (e.g., "How high is the Eiffel tower?" "300 m") and asked them to report what they would have answered had they not been given the solutions. Questions and answers were presented in colors that were either easy or difficult to read against a background. Participants believed more strongly that they "knew" the correct answer all along when the material was easy rather than difficult to read—after all, the answer would not feel "familiar" had they not known it earlier.

Harley, Carlsen, and Loftus (2004) identified a visual hindsight bias that is also driven by processing fluency. Participants were asked to identify degraded photos of celebrity faces as they were resolved to full clarity, and then they predicted how others would perform at this task. Having just seen the faces, participants mistook their own processing fluency to mean that naive observers would identify the faces earlier, or that others "saw the faces all along." Fluent processing of outcomes thus increases hindsight bias, whereas disfluent processing of outcomes decreases hindsight bias—and even small changes in variables like readability of the print font can be sufficient to affect our beliefs about prior knowledge.

Much as feelings of familiarity increase hindsight bias, feelings of surprise decrease hindsight bias—after all, outcomes would not be surprising if one "knew it all along." In general, high surprise indicates that outcomes deviate from expectations, whereas low surprise indicates that outcomes are consistent with expectations. Across several studies, Ofir and Mazursky (1997; Mazursky & Ofir, 1990) demonstrated that hindsight bias occurs following outcomes that elicit low or moderate levels of surprise. When the outcomes are highly surprising, however, people infer that they were unexpected—or why else would they react with surprise? The opposite holds when alternatives seem surprising or unsurprising. What complicates the role of surprise in the emergence of hindsight bias is that initial high surprise may also elicit greater attempts to make sense of outcomes, resulting in more hindsight bias after some time has passed (Pezzo & Pezzo, 2007). We return to these temporal trajectories later in our "Naive Theories" section on page 204.

METACOGNITIVE MODEL OF BIASING AND DEBIASING

Figure 13.2 depicts a general model of judgmental biasing and debiasing (see also Sanna & Schwarz, 2007; Schwarz et al., 2007). In short, we propose that to fully understand when biases may occur and how they might be attenuated, one must consider (a) declarative information (accessible thought content); (b) accompanying metacognitive experiences; (c) perceived informational value; and (d) naive theories used to interpret the experiences.

We suggest that judgments are always a joint function of thought content—accessible declarative information—and accompanying metacognitive experiences (the top oval in Figure 13.2). As a default, people consider their metacognitive experiences relevant to what they are thinking about—or else, why would they be having these experiences now while thinking about this issue? Hence, people draw on their metacognitive experiences as a source of information that qualifies the implications of accessible thought content (lower left-hand oval).[1] What exactly people conclude from their metacognitive experiences depends on the nature of the experience (ease of thought generation or recall, processing fluency, surprise, and so on) and the particular naive theory of mental processes that is applied. Conversely, if the informational value of the metacognitive experience to the judgment at hand is discredited (e.g., Sanna & Schwarz, 2003), judgments are based solely on declarative information (lower right-hand oval). Each of these components and their operation are described in more detail in the following sections.

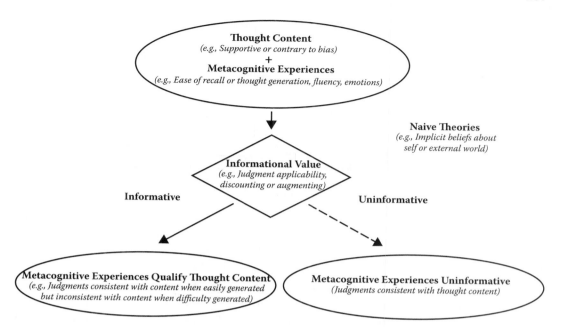

FIGURE 13.2 Metacognitive model of biasing and debiasing. Solid arrows indicate the default path (i.e., metacognitive experiences are informative and qualify judgments); dashed arrow indicates the path where metacognitive experiences are rendered uninformative to the judgment at hand. (Adapted from "Metacognitive Experiences and Hindsight Bias: It's Not Just the Thought (Content) That Counts!" by L. J. Sanna and N. Schwarz, 2007, *Social Cognition, 25*, 185–202, and "Metacognitive Experiences and the Intricacies of Setting People Straight: Implications for Debiasing and Public Information Campaigns," by N. Schwarz, L. J. Sanna, I. Skurnik, and C. Yoon, 2007, *Advances in Experimental Social Psychology, 39*, 127–161.)

APPLICATIONS TO OTHER BIASES

Consistent support for this model comes from a study that took advantage of a real-world event, students' first exam in a psychology class (Sanna & Schwarz, 2004). In a between-subjects design, students made a variety of judgments either 28 days or a few minutes before their exam or right after they received their grades. In addition, students listed either 0 (control), 3, or 12 thoughts about succeeding or failing on the exam, as we describe next. Manipulation checks and pilot testing indicated that listing 3 thoughts was experienced as easy, whereas listing 12 thoughts was experienced as difficult irrespective of whether thoughts were about success or failure.

Confidence Changes

People usually become less confident in their possible success when events draw near than they are at a more distant time. For example, several studies have demonstrated that students become significantly less confident in their eventual success as the time to take an exam approaches (Gilovich, Kerr, & Medvec, 1993; Sanna, 1999; Shepperd, Ouellette, & Fernandez, 1996). Job seekers are also more muted in their first salary estimates when asked just before entering the market than they are years in advance, and patients are less confident in results when about to receive feedback from medical tests than they are immediately after the test is taken, and so on (for reviews, see Carroll & Shepperd, Chapter 28; Carroll, Sweeny, & Shepperd, 2006). Such confidence shifts over time have even been observed in the forecasts of professional market analysts (for a review, see Kadous, Krische, & Sedor, 2006).

As depicted on the left in Figure 13.3, the confidence of participants who listed no thoughts (control condition) replicated this familiar pattern. These participants reported lower confidence in

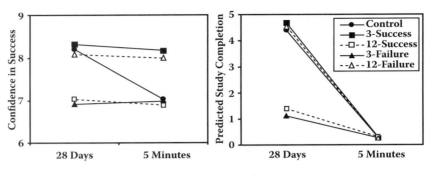

FIGURE 13.3 Confidence changes (confidence in success) and planning fallacy (predicted study completion). Confidence in success is depicted on scale ranging from 0 to 10. Predicted study completion is depicted in days. (Adapted from "Integrating Temporal Biases: The Interplay of Focal Thoughts and Accessibility Experiences," by L. J. Sanna and N. Schwarz, 2004, *Psychological Science, 15,* 474–481.)

their likely success when asked right before taking the exam than they did 28 days earlier. However, when asked to generate thoughts implying success (3 success, 12 failure), participants' confidence in success was just as high 5 min before the exam as it was 28 days prior. Conversely, when asked to generate thoughts implying failure (3 failure, 12 success), participants' confidence in success was just as low 28 days before the exam as it was at exam time. This pattern bears directly on the effectiveness of potential debiasing strategies (see also Hirt, Kardes, & Markman, 2004). Thoughts about success and failure seem to account for distal confidence and proximal pessimism, respectively—but only when they are easy to generate. When students listed 12 thoughts, which they found difficult, this pattern reversed. In short, confidence changes are a joint function of thought content and metacognitive experiences.

Planning Fallacy

People are notoriously overoptimistic when predicting task completion times, believing they will finish tasks sooner than they actually do (Buehler et al., 1994; Kahneman & Tversky, 1979). This planning fallacy has been observed for a variety of activities, including household chores, holiday shopping, and various laboratory tasks (Buehler et al., 1994; Kruger & Evans, 2004; Sanna, Parks, Chang, & Carter, 2005). Incentives worsen the planning fallacy as people expecting tax refunds or other monetary rewards for speedy completion are even more optimistic than those who have no incentives (Buehler, Griffin, & MacDonald, 1997). This bias presumably reflects a focus on mentally simulating acts that facilitate task completion at the expense of hurdles that impair it. Accordingly, planning fallacies might be lessened when attention is drawn to reasons for slow progress (Newby-Clark, Ross, Buehler, Koehler, & Griffin, 2000).

As depicted on the right in Figure 13.3, at 28 days before the exam, control participants predicted that they would complete their preparation 4.4 days prior to the exam, although their peers who responded only 5 min prior to the exam reported that they were not done until 0.3 days before. This replicates the standard finding. Control participants' early optimism matched the optimism of those who generated 3 success thoughts 28 days before the exam, whereas those who generated 3 failure thoughts provided more realistic estimates, attenuating the planning fallacy. More important, 28 days before the exam, listing 12 failure thoughts failed to lessen the planning fallacy, whereas listing 12 success thoughts, ironically, did lessen it. Once again, listing few success- (failure-) related thoughts, an easy task, was functionally equivalent to listing many failure- (success-) related thoughts, a difficult task, suggesting that metacognitive experiences are one critical factor in producing and reducing the planning fallacy.[2]

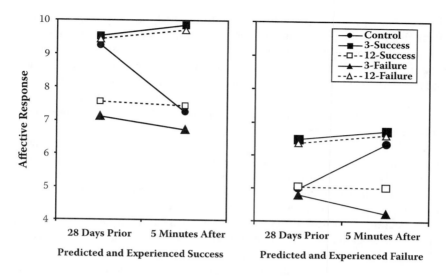

FIGURE 13.4 Impact bias in affective forecasting. Predicted and experienced affective responses, scored in a positive affect direction, are depicted on a scale ranging from 0 to 10. (Adapted from "Integrating Temporal Biases: The Interplay of Focal Thoughts and Accessibility Experiences," by L. J. Sanna and N. Schwarz, 2004, *Psychological Science, 15,* 474–481.)

Impact Bias

As a final example, *impact bias* refers to the fact that people predict that their emotional reactions to events will be more intense than actually turns out to be the case. Overpredicting future emotional impact is one of the most prevalent biases in affective forecasting (for a review, see Wilson & Gilbert, 2003). For example, voters and students thought they would be happier or sadder after their preferred candidates or teams won or lost, respectively, yet no differences in actual happiness (sadness) were observed between supporters of winners and losers when asked afterward (Wilson, Wheatley, Meyers, Gilbert, & Axom, 2000; see also Loewenstein & Schkade, 1999).

Impact bias can presumably be attenuated by getting people to consider other things that may also be happening when the event is actually experienced (Wilson et al., 2000). As depicted on the right in Figure 13.4, when predicting reactions to success, generating thoughts about failure 28 days before the exam lessened the outcome's anticipated impact to a level equal to those who had just received their grades and were actually experiencing success—but only when thoughts were easy to generate in the 3-failure condition. In fact, generating 12 thoughts about success, experienced as difficult, was just as likely to debias the impact bias. Likewise, depicted on the left in Figure 13.4, when predicting reactions to failure, generating thoughts implying success 28 days prior to the exam lessened the outcome's anticipated impact to a level equal to those who were actually experiencing failure—but again only when thought generation was easy (2-success). Generating 12 thoughts about failure, experienced as difficult, was just as likely to debias the impact bias. Again, the production and reduction of impact bias appears, at least in part, to be a joint function of thought content and people's metacognitive experiences.

INFORMATIONAL VALUE

As we noted, people by default draw on both declarative as well as experiential information, resulting in the interaction of thought content and metacognitive experiences shown in Figure 13.2. However, the impact of any source of information is a function of its perceived informational value.

In the case of metacognitive experiences, people do not find their experiences informative when they attribute them to sources unrelated to the judgment at hand, such as background music (e.g., Schwarz et al., 1991), presentation format (e.g., Wänke, Bless, & Biller, 1996), or other context variables (for reviews, see Schwarz, 1998, 2004). Similarly, attributions to internal sources, such as one's own lack of knowledge, can render metacognitive experiences uninformative for judgments unrelated to one's knowledge (Schwarz, 1998). Whenever metacognitive experiences are considered uninformative for the judgment, they do not qualify the implications of thought content (dashed arrow from diamond in Figure 13.2).

Sanna and Schwarz (2003) provided direct evidence for this in a study of hindsight bias in the 2000 U.S. presidential election. Participants were asked to predict the outcome of the popular vote 1 day prior to the November 7 election. Following an extended court battle over disputed election outcomes in Florida, the Democratic candidate Gore conceded the election on December 13, 2000. On December 14, participants were asked to recall their preelection predictions, made on November 6. The actual election result was that Gore-Lieberman led Bush-Cheney by a small difference of 0.32%. Prior to the election, participants had predicted a clear victory for Gore-Lieberman, with a lead of 4.71%. After the election, participants who were merely asked to recall their preelection prediction recalled that they did predict a Gore-Lieberman win, but at a much smaller margin of 0.58%. This replicates the typical hindsight bias effect.

Participants who were asked to list 12 ways in which Gore-Lieberman could have won the election before recalling their predictions concluded that they never expected them to win by a large margin (0.61%)—even though they had predicted a large margin of victory for Gore-Lieberman over Bush-Cheney prior to the election (5.26%). Most important here, when we first asked other participants how much they know about politics before making judgments, they attributed their difficulty of generating 12 thoughts to their own lack of political expertise, rendering their metacognitive experiences uninformative with regard to Gore-Lieberman's preelection likelihood of winning. In this case, participants drew on the content of their thoughts despite their difficulty and concluded that Gore-Lieberman could have won instead—even to the extent of overestimating the margin of victory they predicted for Gore-Lieberman prior to the election (7.52%). A parallel study, using the outcome of a football game as the content domain, produced comparable results (see Sanna & Schwarz, 2003).

Similar augmenting and discounting effects are observed when misattribution manipulations are applied to feelings of surprise and familiarity. For example, Müller and Stahlberg (2007) conducted a series of studies in which participants were asked to predict color and number sequences with either surprising or unsurprising outcomes. As anticipated, high surprise led to inferences that outcomes were not inevitable. However, once feelings of surprise were attributed to a source other than the outcome itself, like varying task demands (e.g., cognitive load), feelings of surprise no longer affected hindsight inevitability estimates. In addition, people may not infer low familiarity from low processing fluency when the experience is attributed to interference from another source (e.g., like noise next door), whereas high processing fluency may seem particularly informative under these conditions (for reviews of relevant findings from diverse domains, see Kelley & Rhodes, 2002; Schwarz, 2004).

Naive Theories

A growing body of research indicates that the specific inferences drawn from a given metacognitive experience depend on the naive theories of mental processes that people bring to bear on the task (for reviews, see Schwarz, 2004; Schwarz et al., 2007). These naive theories can relate to the self or the external world. Our hindsight bias findings (Sanna & Schwarz, 2003; Sanna, Schwarz, & Small, 2002; Sanna, Schwarz, & Stocker, 2002; see also Sanna & Chang, 2003) are compatible with a common naive theory at the heart of Tversky and Kahneman's (1973) availability heuristic: When there are many (few) examples or reasons, it is easy (difficult) to bring some to mind. Applying this naive theory, people infer from the experienced ease or difficulty that there are many or few reasons of the sought-after type, giving rise to the effects that we reviewed. For the same reason, ease of thought generation may increase confidence in thought content, whereas difficulty of thought generation may decrease confidence in thought content (Tormala, Petty, & Briñol, 2002).

But, people also hold a variety of other naive theories about the difficulty of recall and thought generation. Hence, the meaning of metacognitive experiences is malleable and theory driven (see Petty, Briñol, Tormala, & Wegener, 2007; Schwarz et al., 2007; Wilson & Brekke, 1994). One naive theory holds that recent events are easier to recall than distant events, making ease of recall a cue for temporal distance (Sanna, Chang, & Carter, 2004; Schwarz, Cho, & Xu, 2005; see also Perunovic & Wilson, Chapter 23, this volume). Other naive theories hold that important events are easier to recall than unimportant ones, and that thought generation is easier when one has high rather than low expertise, making ease a cue for importance and expertise (e.g., Schwarz et al., 2005). Drawing on these naive theories, people may consider ease of thought generation more informative, and difficulty less informative, when the event is distant rather than recent, unimportant rather than important, and when they lack rather than have domain expertise or confidence. Hence, different naive theories of mental processes suggest variables that may moderate the magnitude of various biases and their debiasing by influencing the inferences drawn from metacognitive experiences.

Particularly intriguing possibilities involve potential changes in the inferences people may draw from metacognitive experiences as time passes. For example, suppose that initial exposure to outcome information elicits feelings of high surprise, and this curtails hindsight bias (e.g., Ofir & Mazursky, 1997). But, surprising events can also elicit more explanatory activity than unsurprising events (see Pezzo & Pezzo, 2007). When plausible explanations for outcomes later come to mind easily (or another person provides explanations), hindsight bias may then creep in—"I was surprised, but I should have expected this." With the passage of time, initial surprise may fade from memory, consistent with the idea that subjective experiences are not well represented, quickly fade over time, and need to be reconstructed on the basis of episodic information or naive theories (for a review, see Robinson & Clore, 2002). Thus, a variable that attenuates, and sometimes even reverses, hindsight bias at the time of initial exposure to outcome information may set in motion processes that later result in increased hindsight bias. Naive theories about the meaning of metacognitive experiences may further change the conclusions that people draw from those experiences at different points in time.

We suggest that such temporal shifts may be particularly likely when outcomes are especially important, striking, or impactful. At first, the shock of the outcome elicits a strong sense of surprise, and events appear to have been very unpredictable. However, as people strive to make sense out of what happened, the search for explanations makes potential causes highly accessible, which may result in the conclusion that the event could have been foreseen and, in fact, might have been prevented. As one example, public discourse following the 9/11 terror attacks is consistent with this conjecture (for a review, see Wirtz, 2006). Media coverage may further change the metacognitive experiences that are associated with event outcomes through frequent repetition of key event scenes. This could affect metacognitive experiences by rendering events highly accessible and fluent or by providing explanations for why the events happened the way they did. The result of all this could be far-reaching implications for public opinion, calls for relevant policy, and individual coping strategies. To date, little is known about temporal trajectories in people's metacognitive experiences, but this may be an especially promising avenue for future research.

WHAT HAVE WE LEARNED?

In combination, the reviewed research highlights that the production and reduction of bias is a function of the joint influence of the content of people's mental simulations and their accompanying metacognitive experiences. First, focal thoughts give rise to bias when they are easy to bring to mind. This is usually the case when people are left to their own devices as they truncate the search process early (Bodenhausen & Wyer, 1987) before any difficulty is experienced. For example, judgments of control participants, who did not list any thoughts, converged with the judgments of participants who listed three focal thoughts (see Figures 13.3 and 13.4). Second, focal thoughts attenuate or eliminate bias when they are difficult to bring to mind. Hence, bias is more likely to arise when people generate few rather than many focal thoughts, in contrast to what content-focused models would predict. Third, conversely, thoughts about alternatives attenuate or eliminate bias when they come to mind easily but, fourth, increase bias when they are difficult to bring to mind.

Our model can thus account for the findings of previous content-focused theories as well as make novel and unique predictions. Specifically, the model converges with content-based models by predicting thought-content congruent judgments (a) when thought generation or recall is experienced as easy or (b) when the relevance of the metacognitive experience to the judgment at hand is discredited. It differs from content-based models by predicting (c) that easily generated or recalled thoughts are more influential when the experience is considered informative than when it is not. And most important, it (d) makes predictions that are opposite to the predictions of thought-content-based models when thought generation or recall is difficult. As a result, one of the most frequently recommended debiasing strategies of mentally simulating alternatives, or "considering the opposite," may only be effective when people do not try too hard to follow it—and it may backfire when people are overly zealous in protecting themselves against bias, as we also elaborate next.

IMPLICATIONS AND CONJECTURES

The interplay of experiential and declarative information in mental simulation has implications that go beyond the reviewed biases and methods designed to reduce them. In this section, we offer a few more conjectures and suggestions for future research.

Several chapters in this volume address the dynamics of counterfactual thinking and the related issue of regret (e.g., Markman et al., Chapter 12; Wong, Galinsky, & Kray, Chapter 11; Zeelenberg & Pieters, Chapter 27). Researchers in these areas have long assumed that people's reactions to thoughts about "what might have been" are influenced by how easily these thoughts come to mind (see Kahneman & Miller, 1986). In practice, however, the extent to which participants engage in counterfactual thinking is often assessed only by counting the numbers of counterfactual thoughts generated (Sanna & Turley-Ames, 2000), with little attention given to the ease or difficulty with which those thoughts were brought to mind. For example, many researchers who assess numbers of counterfactuals conclude that upward counterfactuals—thoughts about better alternatives—routinely increase people's preparation for the future (Markman, Gavanski, Sherman, & McMullen, 1993; Roese, 1994; Sanna, Turley-Ames, & Meier, 1999). However, as our chapter illustrates, metacognitive experiences may be a more important determinant of people's reactions to thinking about counterfactual alternatives than the number of counterfactuals per se.

As numerous social cognition studies demonstrated (for a review, see Bodenhausen & Wyer, 1987), people often truncate information search as soon as "enough" information has come to mind to form a judgment. Similarly, they may truncate the search for counterfactuals before any difficulty of thought generation is experienced, ensuring that the counterfactuals they did generate were experienced as easy. As our research on hindsight bias illustrates (for reviews, see Sanna & Schwarz, 2006, 2007), however, when people find counterfactuals surprising, disfluent, or difficult to generate, they draw inferences that are opposite to the implications of their thought content. Accordingly, prior research that focused solely on the number of counterfactuals generated may have missed an important irony: Counterfactual thinking may be least effective when it is most needed. The more important the outcome, and the higher people's motivation to understand what went wrong, the more counterfactuals people may try to generate, resulting in the experience that counterfactuals are difficult to bring to mind. This may leave people less able to learn from past mistakes and unlikely to take steps to improve. It is also possible that people high in need for closure (Kruglanski & Webster, 1996) or need for cognition (Cacioppo & Petty, 1982) would be more apt to generate many alternatives and, ironically, be more prone to various biases. These and other possibilities in which people may be overly zealous in generating alternatives could be explored in future research.

The effects of taking another person's perspective are also influenced by people's metacognitive experiences. For example, Caruso, Epley, and Bazerman (2006, Experiment 2), using analogous manipulations to our debiasing research (e.g., Sanna, Schwarz, & Small, 2002), asked participants to list either 3 or 10 personal contributions to a group project. Those asked to list 3 contributions found this to be easy and inferred that they contributed more to the group project, whereas those who were asked to list 10 contributions inferred that they contributed less to the group project—even though they listed objectively more contributions—because they found this latter task to be experientially difficult. Once these conclusions were drawn, participants who thought they contributed more showed decreased enjoyment and less desire for future collaboration when asked to take another's perspective (see also Epley & Caruso, Chapter 20, this volume). Moreover, people also give relatively more weight to metacognitive experiences in judgments of self than in judgments of others, presuming that "people view subjective ease as more diagnostic for self-judgments than for most other-judgments" (Caruso, 2008, p. 151), a generally correct naive theory of mental processes. But, when people's subjective experiences for self are rendered nondiagnostic to the judgment at hand, people rely on the content of their thoughts rather than metacognitive experiences, just as they generally do when making other judgments (Caruso, 2008).

CODA

Several decades of psychological research have now shown that people's judgments are susceptible to an ever-growing number of systematic biases that influence decision accuracy across a wide variety of contexts. Much effort has correspondingly been placed on identifying debiasing strategies. Sometimes, these strategies have been successful, sometimes not. The main objective of our chapter was to illustrate how people's metacognitive experiences are a critical, but relatively understudied, variable that determines when debiasing will be a success. Taking into account these issues not only may further our knowledge of people's judgment and decision making but, paraphrasing the words of Mark Twain with which we opened this chapter, perhaps may also help us to more fully understand how to bring people's judgments back into focus.

NOTES

1. Several other of lines of research have similarly shown that the default process is that people presume that any thoughts that come to mind, or feelings they have, while thinking about X are in fact "about" X—or else why would they have these thoughts or feelings at this point in time? Hence, people are likely to find their metacognitive experiences informative by default unless their attention is drawn to influences that call their informational value into question for the judgment (for reviews, see Clore et al., 2001; Higgins, 1998; Schwarz & Clore, 2007).
2. The fact that no impact of the thoughts-listing manipulations were observed 5 min prior to the exam most likely simply reflects that actual study completion times were now known at that point.

ACKNOWLEDGMENT

We thank editors Bill Klein and Keith Markman and the Imagination, Goals, and Affect (IGoA, or ego) laboratory group members at the University of North Carolina at Chapel Hill for comments on this chapter.

REFERENCES

Buehler, R., Griffin, D., & MacDonald, H. (1997). The role of motivated reasoning in optimistic time predictions. *Personality and Social Psychology Bulletin, 23*, 238–247.

Buehler, R., Griffin, D., & Ross, M. (1994). Exploring the "planning fallacy": Why people underestimate their task completion times. *Journal of Personality and Social Psychology, 67,* 366–381.

Bodenhausen, G. V., & Wyer, R. S. (1987). Social cognition and social reality: Information acquisition and use in the laboratory and the real world. In H. J. Hippler, N. Schwarz, & S. Sudman (Eds.), *Social information processing and survey methodology* (pp. 6–41). New York: Springer-Verlag.

Cacioppo, J. T., & Petty, R. E. (1982). The need for cognition. *Journal of Personality and Social Psychology, 42,* 116–131.

Carroll, P., Sweeny, K., & Shepperd, J. A. (2006). Forsaking optimism. *Review of General Psychology, 10,* 56–73.

Caruso, E. M. (2008). Use of experienced retrieval ease in self and social judgments. *Journal of Experimental Social Psychology, 44,* 148–155.

Caruso, E. M., Epley, N., & Bazerman, M. H. (2006). The costs and benefits of undoing egocentric responsibility assessments in groups. *Journal of Personality and Social Psychology, 91,* 857–871.

Christensen-Szalanski, J. J. J., & Willham, C. F. (1991). The hindsight bias: A meta-analysis. *Organizational Behavior and Human Decision Processes, 48,* 147–168.

Clemens, S. L. (1898). Mark Twain quotations, newspaper collections, and related resources. Retrieved January 8, 2007, from http://www.twainquotes.com/Judgment.html

Clore, G. L., Wyer, R. S., Dienes, B., Gasper, K., Gohm, C. L., & Isbell, L. (2001). Affective feelings as feedback: Some cognitive consequences. In L. L. Martin & G. L. Clore (Eds.), *Theories of mood and cognition: A user's handbook* (pp. 27–62). Mahwah, NJ: Erlbaum.

Fischhoff, B. (1975). Hindsight ≠ foresight: The effect of outcome knowledge on judgments under uncertainty. *Journal of Experimental Psychology: Human Perception and Performance, 1,* 288–299.

Fischhoff, B. (1982). Debiasing. In D. Kahneman, P. Slovic, & A. Tversky (Eds.), *Judgment under uncertainty: Heuristics and biases* (pp. 422–444). New York: Cambridge University Press.

Fischhoff, B., & Beyth, R. (1975). I knew it would happen. Remembered probabilities of once-future things. *Organizational Behavior and Human Performance, 13,* 1–16.

Gilovich, T., Griffin, D., & Kahneman, D. (2002). *Heuristics and biases: The psychology of intuitive judgment.* New York: Cambridge University Press.

Gilovich, T., Kerr, M., & Medvec, V. H. (1993). Effect of temporal perspective on subjective confidence. *Journal of Personality and Social Psychology, 64,* 552–560.

Guilbault, R. L., Bryant, F. B., Posavac, E. J., & Brockway, J. H. (2004). A meta-analysis of research on hindsight bias. *Basic and Applied Social Psychology, 26,* 103–117.

Harley, E. M., Carlsen, K. A., & Loftus, G. R. (2004). The "saw-it-all-along" effect: Demonstrations of visual hindsight bias. *Journal of Experimental Psychology: Learning, Memory, and Cognition, 30,* 960–968.

Hawkins, S. A., & Hastie, R. (1990). Hindsight: Biased judgments of past events after the outcomes are known. *Psychological Bulletin, 107,* 311–327.

Higgins, E. T. (1998). The aboutness principle: A pervasive influence on human inference. *Social Cognition, 16,* 173–198.

Hirt, E. R., Kardes, F. R., & Markman, K. D. (2004). Activating a mental simulation mindset through generation of alternatives: Implications for debiasing in related and unrelated domains. *Journal of Experimental Social Psychology, 40,* 374–383.

Hirt, E. R., & Markman, K. D. (1995). Multiple explanation: A consider-an-alternative strategy for debiasing judgments. *Journal of Personality and Social Psychology, 69,* 1069–1086.

Jacoby, L. L., Kelley, C. M., & Dywan, J. (1989). Memory attributions. In H. L. Roediger & F. I. M. Craik (Eds.), *Varieties of memory and consciousness: Essays in honour of Endel Tulving* (pp. 391–422). Hillsdale, NJ: Erlbaum.

Kadous, K., Krische, S. D., & Sedor, L. M. (2006). Using counter-explanation to limit analysts' forecast optimism. *The Accounting Review, 81,* 377–397.

Kahneman, D., & Miller, D. T. (1986). Norm theory: Comparing reality to its alternatives. *Psychological Review, 93,* 136–153.

Kahneman, D., & Tversky, A. (1979). Intuitive prediction: Biases and corrective procedures. *Management Science, 12,* 313–327.

Kelley, C. M., & Rhodes, M. G. (2002). Making sense and nonsense of experience: Attributions in memory and judgment. *The Psychology of Learning and Motivation, 41,* 293–320.

Koriat, A., Lichtenstein, S., & Fischhoff, B. (1980). Reasons for overconfidence. *Journal of Experimental Psychology: Human Learning & Memory, 6,* 107–118.

Kruger, J., & Evans, M. (2004). If you don't want to be late, enumerate: Unpacking reduces the planning fallacy. *Journal of Experimental and Social Psychology, 40*, 586–598.

Kruglanski, A. W., & Webster, D. M. (1996). Motivated closing of the mind: Seizing and freezing. *Psychological Review, 103*, 263–283.

Larrick, R. P. (2004). Debiasing. In D. J. Koehler & N. Harvey (Eds.), *Blackwell handbook of judgment and decision making* (pp. 316–337). Oxford, England: Blackwell.

Loewenstein, G. F., & Schkade, D. (1999). Wouldn't it be nice? Predicting future feelings. In D. Kahneman, E. Diener, & N. Schwarz (Eds.), *Well-being: The foundations of hedonic psychology* (pp. 85–105). New York: Russell Sage Foundation.

Lord, C. G., Lepper, M. R., & Preston, E. (1984). Considering the opposite: A corrective strategy for social judgment. *Journal of Personality and Social Psychology, 47*, 1231–1243.

Markman, K. D., Gavanski, I., Sherman, S. J., & McMullen, M. N. (1993). The mental simulation of better and worse possible worlds. *Journal of Experimental Social Psychology, 29*, 87–109.

Mazursky, D., & Ofir, C. (1990). "I could never have expected it to happen": The reversal of the hindsight bias. *Organizational Behavior and Human Decision Processes, 46*, 20–33.

Müller, P. A., & Stahlberg, D. (2007). The role of surprise in hindsight bias: A cognitive model of reduced and reversed hindsight bias. *Social Cognition, 25*, 165–184.

Newby-Clark, I. R., Ross, M., Buehler, R., Koehler, D. J., & Griffin, D. (2000). People focus on optimistic scenarios and disregard pessimistic scenarios while predicting task completion times. *Journal of Experimental Psychology: Applied, 6*, 171–182.

Nisbett, R. E., & Ross, L. (1980). *Human inference: Strategies and shortcomings of social judgment.* New York: Prentice Hall.

Ofir, C., & Mazursky, D. (1997). Does a surprising outcome reinforce or reverse the hindsight bias? *Organizational Behavior and Human Decision Processes, 69*, 51–57.

Petty, R. E., Briñol, P., Tormala, Z. L., & Wegener, D. T. (2007). The role of metacognition in social judgment. In A. W. Kruglanski & E. T. Higgins (Eds.), *Social psychology: Handbook of basic principles* (2nd ed., pp. 254–284). New York: Guilford Press.

Pezzo, M. V., & Pezzo, S. P. (2007). Making sense after failure: A motivated model of hindsight bias. *Social Cognition, 25*, 147–164.

Robinson, M. D., & Clore, G. L. (2002). Belief and feeling: Evidence for an accessibility model of emotional self-report. *Psychological Bulletin, 128*, 934–960.

Roese, N. J. (1994). The functional basis of counterfactual thinking. *Journal of Personality and Social Psychology, 66*, 805–818.

Sanna, L. J. (1999). Mental simulations, affect, and subjective confidence: Timing is everything. *Psychological Science, 10*, 339–345.

Sanna, L. J., & Chang, E. C. (2003). The past is not what it used to be: Optimists' use of retroactive pessimism to diminish the sting of failure. *Journal of Research in Personality, 37*, 388–404.

Sanna, L. J., Chang, E. C., & Carter, S. E. (2004). All our troubles seem so far away: Temporal pattern to accessible alternatives and retrospective team appraisals. *Personality and Social Psychology Bulletin, 30*, 1359–1371.

Sanna, L. J., Parks, C. D., Chang, E. C., & Carter, S. E. (2005). The hourglass is half full or half empty: Temporal framing and the group planning fallacy. *Group Dynamics, 9*, 173–188.

Sanna, L. J., & Schwarz, N. (2003). Debiasing the hindsight bias: The role of accessibility experiences and (mis)attributions. *Journal of Experimental Social Psychology, 39*, 287–295.

Sanna, L. J., & Schwarz, N. (2004). Integrating temporal biases: The interplay of focal thoughts and accessibility experiences. *Psychological Science, 15*, 474–481.

Sanna, L. J., & Schwarz, N. (2006). Metacognitive experiences and human judgment: The case of hindsight bias and its debiasing. *Current Directions in Psychological Science, 15*, 172–176.

Sanna, L. J., & Schwarz, N. (2007). Metacognitive experiences and hindsight bias: It's not just the thought (content) that counts! *Social Cognition, 25*, 185–202.

Sanna, L. J., Schwarz, N., & Small, E. M. (2002). Accessibility experiences and the hindsight bias: I knew it all along versus it could never have happened. *Memory & Cognition, 30*, 1288–1296.

Sanna, L. J., Schwarz, N., & Stocker, S. L. (2002). When debiasing backfires: Accessible content and accessibility experiences in debiasing hindsight. *Journal of Experimental Psychology: Learning, Memory, and Cognition, 28*, 497–502.

Sanna, L. J., & Turley-Ames, K. J. (2000). Counterfactual intensity. *European Journal of Social Psychology, 30*, 273–296.

Sanna, L. J., Turley-Ames, K. J., & Meier, S. (1999). Mood, self-esteem, and simulated alternatives: Thought-provoking affective influences on counterfactual direction. *Journal of Personality and Social Psychology, 76,* 543–558.

Schwarz, N. (1998). Accessible content and accessibility experiences: The interplay of declarative and experiential information in judgment. *Personality and Social Psychology Review, 2,* 87–99.

Schwarz, N. (2004). Metacognitive experiences in consumer judgment and decision making. *Journal of Consumer Psychology, 14,* 332–348.

Schwarz, N., Bless, H., Strack, F., Klumpp, G., Rittenauer-Schatka, H., & Simons, A. (1991). Ease of retrieval as information: Another look at the availability heuristic. *Journal of Personality and Social Psychology, 61,* 195–202.

Schwarz, N., Cho, H., & Xu, J. (2005, July). *Diverging inferences from identical inputs: The role of naive theories.* Paper presented at the European Association of Experimental Social Psychology, Würzburg, Germany.

Schwarz, N., & Clore, G. L. (2007). Feelings and phenomenal experiences. In A. W. Kruglanski & E. T. Higgins (Eds.), *Social psychology: Handbook of basic principles* (2nd ed. pp. 385–407). New York: Guilford Press.

Schwarz, N., Sanna, L. J., Skurnik, I., & Yoon, C. (2007). Metacognitive experiences and the intricacies of setting people straight: Implications for debiasing and public information campaigns. *Advances in Experimental Social Psychology, 39,* 127–161.

Shepperd, J. A., Ouellette, J. A., & Fernandez, J. K. (1996). Abandoning unrealistic optimism: Performance estimates and the temporal proximity of self-relevant feedback. *Journal of Personality and Social Psychology, 70,* 844–855.

Soll, J. B., & Klayman, J. (2004). Overconfidence in interval estimates. *Journal of Experimental Psychology: Learning, Memory, and Cognition, 30,* 299–314.

Strack, F., & Neumann, R. (2000). Furrowing the brow may undermine perceived fame: The role of facial feedback in judgments of celebrity. *Personality and Social Psychology Bulletin, 26,* 762–768.

Tormala, Z. L., Petty, R. E., & Briñol, P. (2002). Ease of retrieval effects in persuasion: The roles of elaboration and thought confidence. *Personality and Social Psychology Bulletin, 28,* 1700–1712.

Tversky, A., & Kahneman, D. (1973). Availability: A heuristic for judging frequency and probability. *Cognitive Psychology, 5,* 207–232.

Wänke, M., Bless, H., & Biller, B. (1996). Subjective experiences versus content of information in the construction of attitude judgments. *Personality and Social Psychology Bulletin, 22,* 1105–1113.

Werth, L., & Strack, F. (2003). An inferential approach to the knew-it-all-along phenomenon. *Memory, 11,* 411–419.

Wilson, T. D., & Brekke, N. (1994). Mental contamination and mental correction: Unwanted influences on judgments and evaluations. *Psychological Bulletin, 116,* 117–142.

Wilson, T. D., & Gilbert, D. T. (2003). Affective forecasting. *Advances in Experimental Social Psychology, 35,* 345–411.

Wilson, T. D., Wheatley, T., Meyers, J. M., Gilbert, D. T., & Axom, D. (2000). Focalism: A source of durability bias in affective forecasting. *Journal of Personality and Social Psychology, 78,* 821–836.

Winkielman, P., Schwarz, N., Fazendeiro, T., & Reber, R. (2003). The hedonic marking of processing fluency: Implications for evaluative judgment. In J. Musch & K. C. Klauer (Eds.), *The psychology of evaluation: Affective processes in cognition and emotion* (pp. 189–217). Mahwah, NJ: Erlbaum.

Wirtz, J. J. (2006). Responding to surprise. *Annual Review of Political Science, 9,* 45–65.

14 Children's Imaginary Companions: What Is It Like to Have an Invisible Friend?

Marjorie Taylor, Alison B. Shawber, and Anne M. Mannering

INTRODUCTION

The creation of an imaginary companion is only one of many forms that fantasy production takes during the preschool years, but we think it is particularly intriguing. Children as young as 2 or 3 talk to their imaginary companions and listen to what they have to say, showing that the capacity to love and derive comfort from an imaginary other does not require a lengthy history or extensive experience with interpersonal interactions. However, adult observers often do not know what to make of this type of play. While they might admire or be amused by children's descriptions of the lives and characteristics of imaginary companions, they quickly become concerned when children seem too caught up in the fantasy. Despite research showing that imaginary companions are common and tend to be associated with positive characteristics such as the ability to take the perspective of another person (D. Singer & Singer, 1990; Taylor & Carlson, 1997), it can be unnerving to see a child smile toward empty space and whisper to an invisible friend. Does the child really believe there is someone sitting there? In this chapter, we discuss the extent that children are aware of the make-believe status of their imaginary companions and other issues related to how invisible friends are experienced by young children.

WHAT COUNTS AS AN IMAGINARY COMPANION? THE SPECIAL CASE OF INVISIBLE FRIENDS

In one of the first widely read articles on the subject, Svendsen (1934) defined an imaginary companion as

> an invisible character, named and referred to in conversation with other persons or played with directly for a period of time, at least several months, having an air of reality for the child but no apparent objective basis. This excludes that type of imaginative play in which an object is personified, or in which the child himself assumes the role of some person in his environment. (p. 988)

Although this definition is still the one most often cited, researchers have tended to broaden their investigations to include one or both of the types of play Svendsen explicitly excluded—the personification of objects and the impersonation of imagined characters. In particular, the distinction between invisible friends and personified objects is usually collapsed, with both referred to as imaginary companions (Bouldin & Pratt, 2001; Hoff, 2005a, 2005b; Taylor, Cartwright & Carlson, 1993); but see Gleason and Hohmann (2006) and Gleason, Sebanc, and Hartup (2000). More recently, the enactment of a role on a regular basis (referred to here as having a *pretend identity*) is sometimes included as a related type of pretend play in research investigating children's creation of imaginary companions (Mathur & Smith, 2007; Taylor, Carlson, Maring, Gerow, & Charley, 2004).

There are pros and cons to the inclusion of personified objects and pretend identities, along with invisible friends, in research on imaginary companions. According to Harris (2000), all these pretend activities are similar in that they involve role play; the child imagines the thoughts, actions, and emotions of a person or creature. Within role play, Harris makes distinctions based on the vehicle for the imagined character: (a) an object as the vehicle (i.e., a personified object); (b) nothing as the vehicle (i.e., an invisible friend); or (c) the self as the vehicle (i.e., a pretend identity). There is empirical support for Harris's conceptual analysis in studies that showed similarities in the characteristics of children who have invisible friends, personified objects, and pretend identities. For example, Taylor and Carlson (1997) found that children who engaged in any of the three types of role play scored higher on a theory of mind task (see also Saxe, Chapter 17, this volume) than children who did not engage in role play.[1] Similarly, Shawber and Taylor (2007) found that children with invisible friends, personified objects, and pretend identities shared abilities (e.g., the capacity to generate an imaginary conversation on a play phone) and personalities (e.g., lack of shyness) that distinguished them from other children.

Clearly, all three types of role play are important to consider to gain a full understanding of children's imaginative activities; however, it is important not to lose sight of the differences between these types of play. In this chapter, we break with the current trend of inclusiveness to focus on the experiences that are unique to children with invisible friends. By doing so, we are not arguing for the exclusion of personified objects as a type of imaginary companion. Pretense involving the animation of toys can be elaborate, vivid, and important to young children. We consider the capacity to endow a physical object with personal and emotional significance to be fascinating in its own right. In our role play research, we also include questions about pretend identities because the enactment of a role can be an intense preoccupation for some children, especially preschool boys (Carlson & Taylor, 2005).

However, interactions with invisible friends have some characteristics that make them especially interesting. In our view, there is more discontinuity between play with invisible friends and everyday play behaviors than there is for other types of role play. Most children have favorite toys, dolls, and stuffed animals with which they interact and personify (e.g., having a tea party with dolls). Similarly, most children engage in at least some role play in which they pretend to be doctors, teachers, or superheroes in social games of pretending. At what point do these types of play become elaborated and consistent enough to be referred to as having an imaginary companion or a pretend identity? This is a difficult methodological problem that confronts all researchers in this area. After all, identifying a child as having an imaginary companion begins to lose meaning when every teddy bear becomes a candidate. The inclusion of personified objects is one reason why current estimates for the prevalence of imaginary companions are as high as 65% (D. Singer & Singer, 1990; Taylor et al. 2004).

In contrast, a child's daily interactions with an invisible friend do not blend so smoothly with other play activities. This is a striking type of behavior that nevertheless is fairly common; by age 7 years, about 37% of children have had an invisible friend (Taylor et al., 2004). In most cases, we suspect that children come up with the idea of creating an invisible friend on their own. Whereas parents and other adults routinely animate objects and act out roles in play with young children, it is less common for children to observe adults interacting with invisible others. Furthermore, invisible friends raise interesting questions about exactly what the child is experiencing. When a child looks into the face of a teddy bear, there is some perceptual support for the experience of a friend, but what about the child who looks into the space occupied by an invisible friend? When a child holds and talks to a bear, there is some perceptual support for deriving comfort from the softness of the fur, but the comfort derived from an invisible friend is more unambiguously cerebral. What exactly are children experiencing when they interact with their invisible friends?

SEEING, HEARING, AND TOUCHING AN INVISIBLE FRIEND

One question concerning children's experiences of invisible friends is whether children visualize or think of them as having particular physical appearances. The answer to this question is yes. Although there are some counterexamples, the majority of children with invisible friends promptly provide physical descriptions on request, often complete with idiosyncratic details (e.g., brown toe-nails, purple hair, glasses, etc.). They also are happy to draw pictures of them (Taylor, Carlson, & Gerow, 2001). In one study, children who were reinterviewed 7 months after the initial interview provided descriptions of the invisible friends that were as stable as their descriptions of real friends (Taylor et al., 1993). In some cases, the child's sense of what the invisible friend looks like can be retained for years. For example, one 4-year-old girl who described and drew her invisible friend Elfie Welfie as a tiny person with tie-dye-colored hair described and drew Elfie Welfie the same way when she was 6 years old.

In addition to describing physical appearances of their invisible friends, children sometimes mention other types of sensory experiences (e.g., "Sometimes I tap her on the shoulder, and she pops up like a horse"; "I don't like him to take up too much space in my bed"; "I like the way Pajama Sam talks"; "One day I touched him, and he said, 'Hey don't touch me; what are you and what's your name?'"). Moreover, when asked explicitly about whether they can see, hear, or touch their imaginary companions, the majority of children say yes (Mannering, 2006; Taylor et al., 1993).

Children's descriptions suggest that many children have visual, auditory, and tactile images of their invisible friends. One might also ask if children with invisible friends tend to have more vivid imagery in general than other children or a greater tendency to use imagery habitually. Self-report data tend to support this hypothesis. Adults who report having had imaginary companions as children also report more vivid and colorful night dreams and more daily use of imagery (Dierker, Davis, & Sanders, 1995; Gleason, Jarudi, & Cheek, 2003). In developmental research, Bouldin and Pratt (2001; Bouldin, 2006) found that children with imaginary companions were more likely to report experiencing visual images and to report that their images sometimes seemed so real that they could almost see or hear them. Although Bouldin found that children with and without imaginary companions did not differ in the amount of pretend games they played while alone, more children with imaginary companions reported that they could almost see the people and places that were part of the theme of the pretend game.

These studies suggest that children with invisible friends (and perhaps children with personified objects) have more vivid imagery than other children, but there is an important limitation to this interpretation of the results. In all these studies, imagery ability or vividness was measured by self-report. A growing number of studies with adults have failed to find any relation between self-report and behavioral measures of either visual imagery (Ernest, 1977; Kozhevnikov, Hegarty, & Mayer, 2002; Lequerica, Rapport, Bradley, Telmer, & Whitman, 2002) or auditory imagery (Aleman, Böcker, Koen, & de Haan, 2001; Halpern, 1988). Thus, children's reports of imagery use and vividness might not predict actual behavioral performance on imagery tasks.

To our knowledge, there have been three behavioral studies comparing imagery processes in children with and without imaginary companions. For two of these studies (Fernyhough, Bland, Meins, & Coltheart, 2007; Pearson et al., 2001), the goal was to explore the continuum between normal and pathological hallucinatory experiences from a developmental perspective. Children with and without imaginary companions listened to a meaningless sample of speech sounds and wrote down or told the experimenter any words that they heard (Jumbled Speech task). Pearson et al. tested 212 children aged 9 to 11 years, including 20 children who reported having imaginary companions. (The authors did not specify whether the imaginary companions were invisible or also included personified objects.) They found that the children with imaginary companions reported hearing words in the ambiguous auditory stimulus more often than the children who did not have imaginary companions. Fernyhough et al. replicated this result with a younger sample of 80 children aged 4 to 8 years, including 37 children who reported having imaginary companions (78% were invisible friends). The results of these studies were interpreted as suggesting that interacting with an imaginary companion might be similar in some respects to having an auditory hallucination.

In contrast, in a behavioral study of visual and auditory imagery processes, Mannering (2006) found no relation between 5-year-old children's imagery and their report of having invisible friends. In a series of trials, children were asked to form visual images of two animals and report which one was larger. In this type of task, participants who take longer to make their decision when the animals are similar in size (e.g., a cat vs. a dog) than when the animals are very different in size (e.g., a cat vs. a mouse) are assumed to be using visual imagery (Kosslyn, Margolis, Barrett, Goldknopf, & Daly, 1990; Kosslyn & Moulton, Chapter 3, this volume; McGonigle & Chalmers, 1984). Similarly, children in this study were given auditory imagery tasks in which reaction time was used as an index of imagery use. For example, children were asked to mentally "turn up the volume" of a soft animal sound until it was as loud as a second one. When the animal sounds were very different in volume (a bee buzzing turned up to the volume of a lion roaring), it was expected to take more time to complete the task than when the sounds were similar in volume (a cow mooing turned up to the volume of a lion roaring). Both the auditory and visual imagery tasks elicited patterns of performance that reflected the use of imagery, but individual differences in imagery use were not related to having an invisible friend.

In addition to reaction time data, Mannering (2006) asked children about their use of visual and auditory images using a procedure based on the Berkley Puppet Interview (Measelle, Ablow, Cowan, & Cowan, 1998). For a series of trials, two puppets made opposing statements (e.g., Iggy: "I made a picture of the animals in my head"; Ziggy: "I didn't make a picture of the animals in my head"), and then the puppets asked the child, "How about you?" Children's self-reports of imagery use were unrelated to their reaction time patterns for either imagery task. Mannering also found no differences between children with and without invisible friends in their self-report of imagery use. Overall, these results suggest that children with invisible friends do not necessarily use imagery differently in their everyday life than other children. In summary, although we do not doubt that children have mental images of their invisible friends, it is not clear that more generally their use of imagery differs from that of other children.

IS AN INVISIBLE FRIEND EXPERIENCED AS AN EXTENSION OF THE SELF OR AS AN AUTONOMOUS AGENT?

The notion that invisible friends are extensions of the self often appears in psychodynamic interpretations of case studies and other writings on this topic (Bach, 1971; Benson, 1980; Nagera, 1969). This is a complex and interesting idea, but the testable predictions that follow from it are not entirely obvious. One possibility is that children might explicitly describe an invisible friend as their twin or, more implicitly, as looking and acting exactly like the children themselves. On the other hand, an extension of the self could be an invisible friend who embodies characteristics that are an exaggeration or even the opposite of the child's—a better, worse, or split version of the self. We have collected a few explicit "twin" and "opposite-to-the-self" descriptions (e.g., "He has pink fingernails, and he looks like all me; he looks like the whole self of me"; "Digger was my twin"), but they are not common (2% of a sample of 341 invisible friends). In addition, although the content of children's descriptions can be a source of information about concerns related to the self and the diverse functions served by this type of play (Harter & Chao, 1992; Hoff, 2005b), post hoc accounts generated by comparing the characteristics of the child and the invisible friend are not very satisfying.

Another way to explore the self/other question is to examine the extent that children describe the invisible friend as controlled by the self or as an autonomous agent. The autonomous agent experience is most easily identified when children express frustration or even anger at the words or actions of an invisible friend. At first, it seems counterintuitive that children might experience their invisible friends this way because it is reasonable to assume that children have complete control of invisible friends. In fact, some researchers have suggested that control over the actions and words of another individual is at the root of the appeal of this type of fantasy (Benson & Pryor, 1973). However, in a study by Taylor, Carlson, and Shawber (2007), about a third of 46 children described their invisible friends as disobedient, bossy, argumentative, or unpredictable. Children complained that they came and went on their own schedule (rather than according to the child's wishes) and did not always want to play what the child wanted to play. They talked too loudly, did not share, or did not do as they were told. It is possible that this study underestimates the amount of independent behavior because it focused on negativity in the children's descriptions. Hoff (2005a) provided some positive descriptions that also suggest some degree of perceived autonomy. For example, some children in her study reported that their invisible friends taught them new things ("he can teach me about where he was before, when he didn't know who I am") (p. 175).

According to Taylor, Hodges, and Kohanyi (2003; see also Myers & Hodges, Chapter 19, this volume), there is precedent for this type of experience in research with adult fiction writers, who frequently describe autonomy in their characters, a phenomenon Taylor et al. refer to as the *illusion of independent agency*. The illusion of independent agency occurs when a fictional character is experienced by the person who created it as having independent thoughts, words, desires, or actions (i.e., as having a mind and will of its own). Taylor et al. (2003) found evidence of this illusion in 92% of a sample of 50 adult fiction writers who were asked to describe the process of creative writing and their relationships with the characters in their novels (also see Watkins, 1990).

Perhaps someone who pretends a lot—a child who regularly plays with an invisible friend or an adult who day after day thinks about the world of a novel—could be described as developing expertise in the domain of fantasy such that the process of imagining the companion or the fictional world is automatized until it is no longer consciously experienced (in this volume, see also Green & Donahue, Chapter 16; Klinger, Chapter 15). As the person readies him- or herself for the imaginative act, the fantasy characters present themselves automatically. Their words and actions begin to be perceived, listened to, and recorded rather than consciously created. As a result, the imagined characters are experienced as speaking and acting independently. When children experience the illusion of independent agency with invisible friends, they are likely not to conceptualize (at least not consciously) the friend as part of the self.[2]

DOES THE CHILD HAVE A PERSONAL RELATIONSHIP WITH THE INVISIBLE FRIEND, OR IS IT A VEHICLE FOR STORYTELLING?

This chapter is focused primarily on cognitive questions related to children's experience of invisible friends, but emotional support is clearly an important function of this type of role play (for discussion of the emotional significance of imaginary companions, see Hoff, 2005b; D. Singer & Singer, 1990; Taylor, 1999). In fact, an early and still popular hypothesis about imaginary companions is that they provide companionship to lonely or otherwise socially challenged children (Ames & Learned, 1946; Manosevitz, Prentice, & Wilson, 1973; Nagera, 1969; Svendsen, 1934). In support of this social-deficit view, there is evidence that first-born children and only children are somewhat more likely to have imaginary companions than children with siblings (Hurlock & Burstein, 1932). However, children who have imaginary companions are not the shy loners that is suggested by this account. They are actually less shy (Mauro, 1991; Shawber & Taylor, 2007; Wingfield, 1948), less fearful and anxious in social situations, and smile and laugh more in social interactions (J. L. Singer & Singer, 1981) than children who do not have imaginary companions. In addition, Gleason (2004) found that children with imaginary companions had just as many reciprocal friendships and were nominated by their peers as well liked as frequently as their classmates who did not have imaginary companions.

The most recent research suggests that children with imaginary companions tend to be outgoing, sociable individuals with a particular interest in interpersonal interaction that is reflected in their pretend play. Children's exploration of friendship in imaginary relationships seems to be particularly evident in the case of play with invisible friends. Gleason (2002) found that children with invisible friends have friendship schemas that are more developmentally advanced than children with personified objects or children who do not have any type of imaginary companion. In addition, Gleason, Sebanc, and Hartup (2000) found that children tend to have "horizontal" relationships with invisible friends (egalitarian and peer-like), whereas relationships with personified objects tend be vertical (nurturing and parent-like) (also see Gleason & Hohmann, 2006).

Taken together, these results suggest that children develop personal relationships with their imaginary companions that are likely to involve imaginary conversations and face-to-face interactions. Thus, it is not surprising that parents frequently report that they have observed their children talking to invisible friends and reacting to what they have to say. We have also observed such face-to-face interactions in the lab. While being interviewed about their invisible friends, children sometimes consult with them, ask them questions, or reprimand them ("Will you stop it! How many times have I told you not to do that?"). Not all children interact with their invisible friends in the lab, but most children report having face-to-face interactions with them much like they would with a real friend (e.g., playing various games together, arguing, telling jokes, etc.).

However, personal interactions are not the only way that invisible friends are experienced by young children. Many parents in our studies reported that their children have conversations with them about the friends' lives and activities. In the lab, we have also heard children tell stories about the imaginary social worlds of the invisible friend (friends, family members, and pets), imaginary places where they live, and the ongoing events that happen there. Thus, having an invisible friend is not just about needing or wanting an extra companion. Invisible friends may also provide a vehicle for communicating a narrative (cf. Libby & Eibach, Chapter 24, this volume). Just as adult fiction writers sometimes develop personal relationships with the characters in their novels, children appear sometimes to use their invisible friends as the main characters in stories that are told to parents and other family members.

The narrative function of imaginary companions has received much less attention than companionship, possibly due to the influence of thinking about imaginary companions in terms of social deficit. However, Gleason (2005) has recently developed a procedure to investigate the extent to which children use imaginary companions as a vehicle for personal interaction versus a vehicle for storytelling. In her study, parents collected regular diary observations of their children over a period of several weeks. There are limitations in the interpretation of these data; for example, parents might have more opportunities to hear stories about an imaginary companion's exploits than to observe the child interacting with it. However, the results thus far suggest that storytelling is a particularly common activity for children who have invisible friends.

Research by Trionfi and Reese (2005) explored an implication of children's use of imaginary companions as a vehicle for narrative. They were interested in the extent that having an imaginary companion might facilitate children's narrative ability because children have the sole knowledge about their imaginary companion's lives and communicate this information to parents. In support of this hypothesis, children with imaginary companions (20 children with invisible friends and 3 children with personified objects) were found to have better narrative skills than children without imaginary companions. Even after controlling for children's language ability and birth order, having an imaginary companion uniquely predicted children's narrative skills. This finding suggests that the narrative function of imaginary companions is a promising topic for future research. More specifically, research on individual differences in the balance between companionship and narrative types of experiences might lead to a better understanding of the social and cognitive correlates of having an invisible friend.

DO CHILDREN BELIEVE THEIR IMAGINARY FRIENDS ARE REAL?

Children often have intense emotional relationships with their invisible friends; they claim to love them and sometimes to get angry or sad when the pretend friend does something the child does not like. They can become very involved in the fantasy and make demands on their invisible friend's behavior (e.g., insisting that a place be set at the family dinner table; making sure that the TV is turned on whenever the family goes out so that the invisible friend will not be lonely; having a separate car seat in the family car so that the invisible friend will be safe). It is no wonder that parents and others sometimes worry that their children do not have a firm grasp of reality.

The question of how well children understand the distinction between fantasy and reality crops up in other contexts as well as those associated with invisible friends. For example, children can become genuinely afraid when engaged in scary pretend play, which has sometimes been interpreted as evidence of confusion between fantasy and reality (Bourchier & Davis, 2000a; DiLalla & Watson, 1988). Maintaining the boundary between what is real and what is pretend might be especially difficult when fantasy or pretend play arouses strong emotion in young children. However, the child who retreats from a scary game of monster may be akin to the adult who walks out of a movie that crosses the line of what the adult experiences as pleasurable arousal of fear (Harris, 2000; Lillard, 1994; Taylor, 1999). Thus, an emotional response to a pretend entity is not a reliable indication of confusion about whether the pretend entity has somehow become real for the child.

A case can be made that young children are actually surprisingly adept in their ability to negotiate the boundary between fantasy and reality (Woolley, 1997). For the most part 3- and 4-year-old children are proficient in their early understanding of the words *real* and *pretend*. They are able to answer questions about the differences between real and pretend entities, and they understand that imagining is a private mental process occurring in a person's mind (Bretherton & Beeghley, 1982; Estes, Wellman, & Woolley, 1989; Flavell, Flavell, & Green, 1987; Sharon & Woolley, 2004; Wellman & Estes, 1986), although they tend to restrict pretend to physical actions (Lillard, 1993). In addition, young children are skillful at classifying objects as pretend or real (Bourchier & Davis, 2000b; Harris, Brown, Marriott, Whittall, & Harmer, 1991) and realize that knowledge reflects reality more accurately than imagination, and that objects they have been asked to imagine do not really exist (Golomb & Galasso, 1995; Woolley & Wellman, 1993). They understand pretend actions and statements and act accordingly (Harris & Kavanaugh, 1993). In fact, when an adult play partner acts in ways that violate the fantasy-reality boundary (e.g., taking a real bite out of a play dough cookie during a pretend picnic), 3- and 4-year-olds react strongly to these transgressions ("Oh, you took a real bite. Now your teeth are all pink. How does it taste? … Yuck, do you always eat that play dough?") (Golomb & Kuersten, 1996, p. 208). Their surprise is evidence that, although they were engrossed in the game of pretense, they had not lost track of the fact that play dough is not an edible substance.

Studies that have examined the possibility that children with invisible friends differ from other children in their understanding of the fantasy/reality distinction have reported mixed results. Sharon and Woolley (2004) found that children with high fantasy orientation, which was partially determined by the presence of an imaginary companion (the percentages of invisible friends and personified objects were not reported), were better at categorizing real and fantastical entities than low-fantasy-oriented children (also see J. L. Singer & Singer, 1981). Researchers have also found no differences between high- and low-fantasy children on the ability to distinguish real and fantasy events (Carrick & Quas, 2006; Dierker & Sanders, 1996; Taylor et al., 1993). However, high-fantasy children were more likely to believe in a novel fantasy figure, the Candy Witch (Woolley, Boerger, & Markman, 2004). Furthermore, Bouldin and Pratt (2001) found that children with imaginary companions (it is not reported whether invisible friends and personified objects were both included) were more likely than other children to believe there might really be a monster after a shadow of a monster was briefly projected on a tent wall.

More specifically, do children with invisible friends understand that their friends are completely make-believe? Interviews with parents and children provide convincing evidence that almost all children are well aware that their invisible friends are pretend. For this chapter, we reviewed the interviews of 86 children (mean age = 5 years; 50 girls, 36 boys) who were categorized as having invisible friends in three recent studies (25.8% of the overall sample of 333 children). Table 14.1

TABLE 14.1

Examples of Invisible Friends

Child	Invisible Friend
Boy, 4 years, 2 months	*Jackson the Ghost:* A ghost who can turn into an elephant or giraffe; can do magic, disappear, and reappear; shows up when he wants to.
Boy, 5 years, 2 months	*Ellen:* A boy who wears a blue shirt with black stripes, can do flips, likes to scare people, and sometimes wakes the child up when he's sleeping.
Girl, 5 years	*Angelina:* A 79-year-old big sister who looks like an angel and a ghost. Angelina has a boyfriend named Jeff and "can fly and shrink into a parrot and go onto my head."
Girl, 4 years	*Bunsen:* A 10-foot tall, gray-haired 5-year-old boy who is the child's best friend and playmate; sometimes Bunsen does not share.
Boy, 5 years, 3 months	*Clover:* An alien astronaut who is really smart, has a clover stuck on his head, and can fly, jump real high, and shoot out anything.
Girl, 5 years, 5 months	*MacKenzie:* A 5-year-old girl with red hair and a journal who cannot talk and has to do sign language and came to live with the child when MacKenzie's parents died. The child said, "when it's bedtime, we dream and she knows what I'm dreaming about because she's an expert."
Boy, 4 years, 8 months	*Chip Bag:* A 6-year-old boy with a round face who walks with bags on his feet, helps the child when he's in trouble, and loves playing with sticks.

provides examples of the invisible friends described by these children. Our goal was to examine the transcripts of the interviews carefully for any indications that the children were confused about the pretend status of their invisible friends (also see Taylor & Mottweller, in press).

In these studies, the children and the parents were interviewed separately, their responses were compared, and follow-up interviews were conducted as necessary. This procedure helps resolve interpretive difficulties. For example, when a child describes a pretend friend that is not mentioned by the parent, it is important to check with the parent to determine if the child misunderstood that question and described a real friend instead of a pretend one. When a child says he or she does not have a pretend friend but the parent provides a description of one, we reinterviewed the child (in the same session) to ask specifically about the pretend friend named by the parent.

When asked if they had a pretend friend, 66 of the 86 children (76.7%) said "yes" and immediately named the pretend friend. One might argue that a child who says yes when asked if he or she has a pretend friend shows some understanding that the friend is not real. However, we also carefully examined the entire transcripts for any signs that the children were confused about the fantasy status of the friend. Instead of confusion, we found that many of the children (39.5% from the entire sample of 86) provided spontaneous comments at some point during the interview that explicitly pointed out the pretend status of their invisible friends (see Table 14.2). It was rare for children to say anything that suggested they thought their pretend friends were real. Of the 66 children who immediately identified a pretend friend, this happened twice. One child described a vivid invisible friend named Yosa, a little boy who was always there at his side and, in fact, was present at the time of the interview. This child referred to Yosa as a pretend friend and said that he had "made him up," but he also said, "Sometimes he turns real, and he talks real so everybody can hear him." Similarly, a second child described her friend Emma as pretend but commented, "She's actually real to me, but she's invisible to my mom and sister."

In the sample of 86 children, 20 did not initially tell us about a pretend friend. There are a number of reasons why this might happen (e.g., the child does not want to talk about it with the experimenter, has a different label for the friend such as "fake friend," "house ghost," etc.), but one possibility is that the child does not think of the friend as pretend. However, the follow-up interviews for 18 of the 20 children did not show any evidence of confusion about the pretend status of their invisible friend. Fifteen of these children did not initially mention the invisible friend because

TABLE 14.2

Children's Statements About the Pretend Status of Their Invisible Friends

Experimenter: When you want to play with (friend's name), how do you get him/her to show up? Examples of child responses:

"Sometimes I call George in my imagination and he just says 'coming' in my imagination." (5-year-old girl)

"I just imagination." (4-year-old girl)

"I just make him show up." (5–year-old girl)

"She does not talk because she's not a real baby." (4-year-old)

"I think about her, and then I just start playing with her as soon as she shows up." (5-year-old girl)

Experimenter: How did you meet (friend's name)? Examples of child responses:

"I didn't. I made it up." (4-year-old girl)

"I just made him up in my head." (5-year-old boy)

"She's just my imaginary friend." (5-year-old girl)

"It's just pretend." (5-year-old girl)

"Her is a fake animal." (4-year-old girl)

"It's really just because it's pretend." (4-year-old girl)

"In one of my dreams." (5-year-old girl)

"In my imagination." (4-year-old girl)

"He's not in real life." (4-year-old boy)

"I found out the way to go to Sillyland, and that's how I met her." (4-year-old girl; this child later explained that Sillyland is "where all my pretend friends live.")

Experimenter: Where is he/she when he is not with you? Examples of child responses:

"She pretends that she's real by herself and with her parents and with her brother and with her pet." (4-year-old girl)

"He goes into my head." (5-year-old boy)

"I pretend they're real, but they're not." (4-year-old girl)

"He goes in my mind and the world in my mind is called Neoland, I mean Pokemon Land; I have two lands in my mind." (5-year-old boy)

Note: Examples from Taylor & Mottweiler (in press).

---

they described another friend or the invisible friend was from the past. In one case, the child did not initially tell us about the pretend friend because of embarrassment; however, this child described the invisible friend in the follow-up interview. For two of the children, there was no apparent reason why they did not mention the invisible friends named by the parents, but neither showed any evidence of confusion in the follow-up interviews.

The remaining 2 children were the only ones from the sample of 86 who showed significant signs of confusion about their invisible friends. In one case, the child said "no" when asked if she had a pretend friend, but her mother reported that the child had many pretend friends called "Sailor Scouts" (characters in a Japanese animation movie). When asked why the child did not mention the Sailor Scouts during the original interview, the parent said that the child "sometimes won't admit that they are pretend." In the follow-up interview with the child, she described Phoenix (a made-up Sailor Scout that is not actually one of the characters in the movie) who was "really beautiful and good at defending." The child said that she met Phoenix when "we were walking, and we bonked heads and became friends." Overall, our impression was that this child did not seem completely clear about the fantasy status of the invisible friend.

Finally, we describe the one case in our sample in which the child consistently and repeatedly insisted that her invisible friend was real. When initially asked if she had a pretend friend, this child paused and replied, "There's a real friend that I have, but she's invisible" and went on to describe a little girl named Carly who she met one day when she saw Carly walking on the sidewalk ("I only can see her; nobody else"). Carly did not like where she was living, so she moved into the child's house. The child described Carly's physical appearance (e.g., "Her body is orange, and her tummy is kind of skinny, her hands are black, she looks kind of weird"); habits (e.g., "she always sleeps in late"); personality (e.g., "She always be's funny sometimes … she always makes up stories that are really funny, and I like it because they make me laugh a lot"). Repeatedly, the child stressed that her friend was invisible but real ("She is really really invisible, and I can really hear her when she talks"; "She makes projects for me … invisible ones I can see"). At one point during the interview, the child looked to her left, laughed, and said "Carly just told a joke to you." The experimenter asked if Carly was in the room, and the child said "No, she told me on our invisible cell phones." The child's mother also provided extensive information about Carly and reported that her daughter played with or talked to Carly almost every day. She said that she felt some discomfort about Carly because "I like to deal with things I can see, and I can't see Carly. [The child] really thinks that she's real."

If children tended to experience their pretend friends as real, we would expect many more children to provide the type of description and commentary that we observed in this case. Instead, the child's account of a colorful invisible girl with a cell phone stands out in marked contrast to what usually happens when we ask children about their pretend friends—the exception that proves the rule. Despite children's detailed descriptions and emotional attachments to their invisible friends, the vast majority of them understand that invisible friends are pretend. More generally, we agree with Harris's (2000) claim that in many ways children's pretend play tends to demonstrate their knowledge of reality rather than any confusion about it.

CONCLUSION

Imaginary friends come in all shapes, sizes, ages, genders, and species. They vary as much as the children who create them, defying the attempts of researchers to make generalizations about what imaginary companions are like and what it means to have one. Invisible friends are particularly fascinating because they are designed by the children themselves and are potentially a source of information about children's concerns and interests, as well as their developing imaginations.

Research investigating children's creation of invisible friends tends to provide counterintuitive results that challenge stereotypic beliefs about the nature of this type of play. Children with invisible friends tend to be particularly sociable individuals who enjoy the company of others and are somewhat advanced in social understanding. When no one is around to play with, they make someone up. An invisible friend can serve a variety of functions (see Hoff, 2005a; Taylor, 1999), but an important part of the experience is companionship. Children have face-to-face interactions with invisible friends and develop personal relationships with them. It is interesting, however, that although children clearly seem to be using imagery in these interactions, more generally their imagery skills do not differ from those of other children.

It is also interesting that the invisible friends are often described as independent and sometimes difficult. Although it is reasonable to assume that a made-up friend would not suffer from the moodiness, stubbornness, and other flaws of real friends, invisible friends can be experienced as unruly and argumentative to the point of causing frustration and annoyance. We consider this experience to be not unlike the reports of adult fiction writers, who sometimes have difficulty controlling a character. Children also are like fiction writers in that they sometimes use invisible friends as a vehicle for telling stories to their parents and other family members. Finally, although children tend to report being able to see and hear their invisible friends, there is very little evidence that these children have problems with the fantasy/reality distinction, and in almost all cases the invisible friends are quite clearly experienced by children as make-believe. In fact, children often take pains to point out to an adult interviewer that it is all just pretend.

NOTES

1. An example of a theory-of-mind task used by Taylor and Carlson (1997) is the unexpected contents false belief, which measures children's understanding that people can hold a false belief about the world (Perner, Leekam & Wimmer, 1987). Children are shown a Band-Aid box and are asked what it contains. After they say "Band-Aids," the experimenter reveals that the box contains a teddy bear instead of Band-Aids, and the children are asked what someone who had not looked inside the box would think was there. Most 3-year-olds say "a teddy bear" because it is difficult for them to appreciate that someone might have a false belief, but most 5-year-olds correctly say "Band-Aids" (in this volume, see also Epley & Caruso, Chapter 20; Saxe, Chapter 17).

2. The issue of autonomy related to imaginary companions has also been raised by researchers who study dissociative disorders in children. One of the differences that has been proposed between pathological and normative experiences with imaginary companions is whether the child is in control of the imaginary companion (Putnam, 1997; Silberg, 1998). However, children with dissociative problems also tend to be confused about whether the imaginary companion is real or imaginary, believe that the imaginary companion can take over the body, feel the need to protect the privacy of the imaginary companion's identity, and often report conflicts between imaginary companions that leave the child confused about how to behave. In research investigating the link between dissociation and having an imaginary companion, Carlson, Tahiroglu, and Taylor (in press) distinguish pathological and nonpathological dissociation and show that having an imaginary companion is linked to the latter.

REFERENCES

Aleman, A., Böcker, K. B. E., Koen, B. E., & de Haan, E. H. F. (2001). Hallucinatory predisposition and vividness of auditory imagery: Self-report and behavioral indices. *Perceptual & Motor Skills, 93*, 268–274.

Ames, L. B., & Learned, J. (1946). Imaginary companions and related phenomena. *Journal of Genetic Psychology, 69*, 147–167.

Bach, S. (1971). Notes on some imaginary companions. *The Psychoanalytic Study of the Child, 26*, 159–171.

Benson, R. M. (1980). Narcissistic guardians: Developmental aspects of transitional objects, imaginary companions, and career fantasies. *Adolescent Psychiatry, 8*, 253–264.

Benson, R. M., & Pryor, D. B. (1973). When friends fall out: Developmental interference with the function of some imaginary companions. *Journal of the American Psychoanalytic Association, 21*, 457–468.

Bouldin, P. (2006). An investigation of the fantasy predisposition and fantasy style of children with imaginary companions. *The Journal of Genetic Psychology, 167*, 17–29.

Bouldin, P., & Pratt, C. (2001). The ability of children with imaginary companions to differentiate between fantasy and reality. *British Journal of Developmental Psychology, 19*, 99–114.

Bourchier, A., & Davis, A. (2000a). Individual and developmental differences in children's understanding of the fantasy-reality distinction. *British Journal of Developmental Psychology, 18*, 353–368.

Bourchier, A., & Davis, A. (2000b). The influence of availability and affect on children's pretence. *British Journal of Developmental Psychology, 18*, 137–156.

Bretherton, I., & Beeghley, M. (1982). Talking about internal states: The acquisition of an explicit theory of mind. *Developmental Psychology, 18*, 906–921.

Carlson, S. M., Tahiroglu, D., & Taylor, M. (in press). Links between dissociation and role play in a non-clinical sample of preschool children. *Journal of Trauma and Dissociation.*

Carlson, S. M., & Taylor, M. (2005). Imaginary companions and impersonated characters: Sex differences in children's fantasy play. *Merrill Palmer Quarterly, 51*, 93–118.

Carrick, N., & Quas, J. A. (2006). Effects of discrete emotions on young children's ability to discern fantasy and reality. *Developmental Psychology, 42*, 1278–1288.

Dierker, L. C., Davis, K. F., & Sanders, B. (1995). The imaginary companion phenomenon: An analysis of personality correlates and developmental antecedents. *Dissociation: Progress in the Dissociative Disorders, 8*, 220–228.

Dierker, L. C., & Sanders, B. (1996). Developmental and individual differences in children's ability to distinguish reality from fantasy. *Imagination, Cognition and Personality, 16*, 25–49.

DiLalla, L. F., & Watson, M. W. (1988). Differentiation of fantasy and reality: Preschoolers' reactions to interruptions in their play. *Developmental Psychology, 24*, 286–291.

Ernest, C. H. (1977). Imagery ability and cognition: A critical review. *Journal of Mental Imagery, 2*, 181–216.

Estes, D., Wellman, H. M., & Woolley, J. D. (1989). Children's understanding of mental phenomena. In H. W. Reese (Ed.), *Advances in child development and behavior* (pp. 41–87). San Diego, CA: Academic Press.

Fernyhough, C., Bland, K., Meins, E., & Coltheart, M. (2007). Imaginary companions and young children's responses to ambiguous auditory stimuli: Implications for typical and atypical development. *Journal of Child Psychology and Psychiatry, 48,* 1094–1101.

Flavell, J. H., Flavell, E. R., & Green, F. L. (1987). Young children's knowledge about the apparent-real and pretend-real distinctions. *Developmental Psychology, 23,* 816–822.

Gleason, T. R. (2002). Social provisions of real and imaginary relationships in early childhood. *Developmental Psychology, 38,* 979–992.

Gleason, T. R. (2004). Imaginary companions and peer acceptance. *International Journal of Behavioral Development, 28,* 204–209.

Gleason, T. R. (2005, April). Talking to a tiger: Children's day-to-day interactions with their imaginary companions. In G. Trionfi & E. Reese (Chairs), *Individual differences in pretense play: Children with and without imaginary companions.* Paper presented at symposium presented at the Biennial Meeting of the Society for Research in Child Development, Atlanta, GA.

Gleason, T. R., & Hohmann, L. M. (2006). Concepts of real and imaginary friendships in early childhood. *Social Development, 15,* 128–144.

Gleason, T. R., Jarudi, R. N., & Cheek, J. M. (2003). Imagination, personality, and imaginary companions. *Social Behavior and Personality, 31,* 721–738.

Gleason, T. R., Sebanc, A. M., & Hartup, W. W. (2000). Imaginary companions of preschool children. *Developmental Psychology, 36,* 419–428.

Golomb, C., & Galasso, L. (1995). Make believe and reality: Explorations of the imaginary realm. *Developmental Psychology, 31,* 800–810.

Golomb, C., & Kuersten, R. (1996). On the transition from pretense play to reality: What are the rules of the game? *British Journal of Developmental Psychology, 14,* 203–217.

Halpern, A. R. (1988). Mental scanning in auditory imagery for songs. *Journal of Experimental Psychology: Learning, Memory, and Cognition, 14,* 434–443.

Harris, P. L. (2000). *The work of the imagination.* Oxford, England: Blackwell Publishers Ltd.

Harris, P. L., Brown, E., Marriott, C., Whittall, S., & Harmer, S. (1991). Monsters, ghosts and witches: Testing the limits of the fantasy-reality distinction in young children. *British Journal of Developmental Psychology, 9,* 105–123.

Harris, P. L., & Kavanaugh, R. D. (1993). Young children's understanding of pretense. *Monographs of the Society for Research in Child Development, 58*(1).

Harter, S., & Chao, C. (1992). The role of competence in children's creation of imaginary friends. *Merrill-Palmer Quarterly, 38,* 350–363.

Hoff, E. V. (2005a). A friend living inside me—the forms and functions of imaginary companions. *Imagination, Cognition and Personality, 24,* 151–189.

Hoff, E. V. (2005b). Imaginary companions, creativity, and self-image in middle childhood. *Creativity Research Journal, 17,* 167–180.

Hurlock, E. B., & Burstein, M. (1932). The imaginary playmate: A questionnaire study. *Journal of Genetic Psychology, 41,* 380–391.

Kosslyn, S. M., Margolis, J. A., Barrett, A. M., Goldknopf, E. J., & Daly, P. F. (1990). Age differences in imagery abilities. *Child Development, 61,* 995–1010.

Kozhevnikov, M., Hegarty, M., & Mayer, R. E. (2002). Revising the visualizer-verbalizer dimension: Evidence for two types of visualizers. *Cognition and Instruction, 20,* 47–77.

Lequerica, A., Rapport, L., Bradley, N. A., Telmer, K., & Whitman, R. D. (2002). Subjective and objective assessment methods of mental imagery control: Construct validation of self-report measures. *Journal of Clinical and Experimental Neuropsychology, 25,* 1103–1116.

Lillard, A. (1993). Young children's conceptualization of pretense: Action or mental representational state? *Child Development, 64,* 372–386.

Lillard, A. (1994). Making sense of pretense. In C. Lewis & P. Mitchell (Eds.), *Children's early understanding of the mind* (pp. 211–234). Hillsdale, NJ: Erlbaum.

Mannering, A. M. (2006). *The development of visual and auditory imagery in young children.* Unpublished doctoral dissertation, University of Oregon.

Manosevitz, M., Prentice, N. M., & Wilson, F. (1973). Individual and family correlates of imaginary companions in preschool children, *Developmental Psychology, 8,* 72–79.

Mathur, R., & Smith, M. C. (2007, March). *"I didn't have anyone to play with, she just appeared": Imaginary companions in an ethnically and grade-diverse sample.* Poster presented at the Biennial Meeting of the Society for Research in Child Development, Boston, MA.

Mauro, J. A. (1991). *The friend that only I can see: A logitudinal investigation of children's imaginary companions.* Unpublished doctoral dissertation, University of Oregon.

McGonigle, B., & Chalmers, M. (1984). The selective impact of question form and input mode on the symbolic distance effect in children. *Journal of Experimental Child Psychology, 37,* 525–554.

Measelle, J. R., Ablow, J. C., Cowan, P. A., & Cowan, C. P. (1998). Assessing young children's views of their academic, social, and emotional lives: An evaluation of the self-perception scales of the Berkeley Puppet Interview. *Child Development, 69,* 1556–1576.

Nagera, H. (1969). The imaginary companion: Its significance for ego development and conflict solution. *Psychoanalytic Study of the Child, 24,* 165–196.

Pearson, D., Burrow, A., Fitzgerald, C., Green, K., Lee, L., & Wise, N. (2001). Auditory hallucinations in normal child populations. *Personality and Individual Differences, 31,* 401–407.

Perner, J., Leekam, S. R., & Wimmer, H. (1987). Three-year-olds' difficulty understanding false beliefs: Representational limitation, lack of knowledge or pragmatic misunderstanding. *British Journal of Developmental Psychology, 5,* 125–137.

Putman, F. W. (1997). *Dissociation in children and adolescents.* New York: Guilford Press.

Sharon, T., & Woolley, J. D. (2004). Do monsters dream? Young children's understanding of the fantasy/reality distinction. *British Journal of Developmental Psychology, 22,* 293–310.

Shawber, A. B., & Taylor, M. (2007, March). *Personality correlates of preschool children's elaborated role play.* Poster presented at the Biennial Meeting of the Society for Research in Child Development, Boston, MA.

Silberg, J. L. (1998). *The dissociative child: Diagnosis, treatment, and management.* Lutherville, MD: The Sidran Press.

Singer, D., & Singer, J. L. (1990). *The house of make-believe: Children's play and developing imagination.* Cambridge, MA: Harvard University Press.

Singer, J. L., & Singer, D. G. (1981). *Television, imagination, and aggression: A study of preschoolers.* Hillsdale, NJ: Erlbaum.

Svendsen, M. (1934). Children's imaginary companions. *Archives of Neurology and Psychiatry, 32,* 985–999.

Taylor, M. (1999). *Imaginary companions and the children who create them.* Oxford, England: Oxford University Press.

Taylor, M., & Carlson, S. M. (1997). The relation between individual differences in fantasy and theory of mind. *Child Development, 68,* 436–455.

Taylor, M., & Mottweiler, C. M. (in press). Imaginary companions: Pretending they are real but knowing they are not. *American Journal of Play.*

Taylor, M., Carlson, S. M., & Gerow, L. (2001). Imaginary companions: Characteristics and correlates. In S. Reifel (Ed.), *Play and culture studies: Theory in context and out* (Vol. 3, pp. 179–198). Westport, CT: Ablex.

Taylor, M., Carlson, S. M., Maring, B., Gerow, L. E., & Charley, C. (2004). The characteristics and correlates of high fantasy in school-aged children: Imaginary companions, impersonation, and social understanding. *Developmental Psychology, 40,* 1173–1187.

Taylor, M., Carlson, S. M., & Shawber, A. B. (2007). Autonomy and control in children's interactions with imaginary companions. In I. Roth (Ed.), *Imaginative minds.* Oxford, England: British Academy and Oxford University Press.

Taylor, M., Cartwright, B. S., & Carlson, S. M. (1993). A developmental investigation of children's imaginary companions. *Developmental Psychology, 29,* 276–285.

Taylor, M., Hodges, S. D., & Kohanyi, A. (2003). The illusion of independent agency: Do adult fiction writers experience their characters as having minds of their own? *Imagination, Cognition and Personality, 22,* 361–38.

Trionfi, G., & Reese, E. (2005, April). Storytelling: Narrative skills of children with and without imaginary companions. In G. Trionfi & E. Reese (Chairs), *Individual differences in pretense play: Children with and without imaginary companions.* Paper presented at symposium presented at the Biennial Meeting of the Society for Research in Child Development, Atlanta, GA.

Watkins, M. (1990). *The development of imaginal dialogues: Invisible guests.* Boston: Sigo Press.

Wellman, H. M., & Estes, D. (1986). Early understanding of mental entities: A reexamination of childhood realism. *Child Development, 57,* 910–923.

Wingfield, R. C. (1948). Bernreuter personality ratings of college students who recall having had imaginary playmates during childhood. *Journal of Psychiatry, 1,* 190–194.

Woolley, J. (1997). Thinking about fantasy: Are children fundamentally different thinkers and believers from adults? *Child Development, 68,* 991–1011.

Woolley, J. D., Boerger, E. A., & Markman, A. B. (2004). A visit from the candy witch: Factors influencing young children's belief in a novel fantastical being. *Developmental Science, 7,* 456–468.

Woolley, J. D., & Wellman, H. M. (1993). Origin and truth: Young children's understanding of imaginary mental representations. *Child Development, 64,* 1–17.

15 Daydreaming and Fantasizing: Thought Flow and Motivation

Eric Klinger

INTRODUCTION

Most people understand the meaning of daydreaming and fantasy intuitively. They have had the experience of reading text and suddenly realizing that while their eyes had traversed half a page their minds had been on something altogether different, perhaps an upcoming business meeting or a romance. They have imagined themselves as an alluring person able to win a coveted partner or as one of unusual strength or agility able to defeat an opponent. They have seen and enjoyed fiction in books and films. They have been told to stop daydreaming and get back to work, or that some belief of theirs is pure fantasy. Most people view their daydreams as very private affairs that they feel less comfortable describing to other people than when they are describing their real experiences (Klinger, Murphy, Ostrem, & Stark-Wroblewski, 2004–2005). That is, they have experienced daydreaming and fantasy as their own perfectly natural states, and they have experienced the limits of social tolerance for them.

From a scientific standpoint, these topics of daydreaming and fantasy are considerably more complex. Daydreaming appears to be an essential component of people's equipment for functioning. Yet, both daydreaming and fantasizing are poorly defined concepts, and they are by no means the same thing.

Everyone agrees that *daydreaming* is a mental process that involves some kind of imaginal activity, but beyond that theorists have offered roughly three ways to define daydreaming. One way, exemplified by Sigmund Freud (1900/1961, 1908/1953) and adopted by innumerable writers since, indeed does overlap with fantasy. That is, daydreaming is mental activity that departs from reality, either as imagining fulfillment of wishes that may not ever be fulfilled or as imagining oneself or others acting in ways that unrealistically violate social norms or physical laws of nature. One may label this kind of thought *fanciful*. Freud's developmental paradigm for wish-fulfilling ideation was the hungry infant's supposed hallucinations of suckling at the absent breast, which in Freud's theory provided the infant with partial gratification.

A second way to define daydreaming was as thinking (or as any mental content) that is unrelated to an ongoing activity (e.g., Singer, 1966, 1975). The reader whose mind drifts away from the content of the reading illustrates this definition.

A third way defines daydreaming as unintended mental content, nonworking, noninstrumental content that comes to mind unbidden and effortlessly—that is, spontaneously (Klinger, 1971). They stand in contrast to deliberate, directed thoughts that one has to serve some purpose, such as solving a problem. In most instances, spontaneous thoughts drift in and out of consciousness with little notice and no attempt to evaluate or harness them. Nevertheless, spontaneous thoughts often feature the same themes as deliberate thoughts. For example, one could think seriously and deliberately about whom to invite to a party, or one could entertain spontaneous images of the future party and its guests. What distinguishes spontaneous thoughts from deliberate thoughts is how they came to be and the extent to which the thinker deliberately directs them. However, deliberate and spontaneous thoughts often intermix in that the person planning the party may slip into a spontaneous daydream of the guests interacting, or the daydreamer may visualize two guests getting into a nasty argument, remember that these two do not get along, and resolve not to invite them both. At that point, the spontaneous thought has yielded an important insight and triggered a planning segment.

Although all three definitions of daydreaming appear to be getting at the same concept—daydreaming—they are, in fact, largely unrelated dimensions of thought. When one samples thoughts by asking participants to note and rate what was in their minds whenever they were beeped, their ratings along these three dimensions are largely uncorrelated with one another (Klinger & Cox, 1987–1988). That is, one can think fancifully about what one is doing right now or think realistically about something else, and either thought may be either spontaneous or deliberate.

With three largely unrelated definitions for the same concept (i.e., daydreaming), there has clearly not been a consensual definition of this phenomenon. It is best to think of the concept as a nontechnical one, a concatenation of different phenomena. For technical purposes, clarity requires stating where a given thought falls on each of these three dimensions—Is it activity-related or unrelated? Deliberate or spontaneous? Realistic or fanciful?—and proceed from there.

However, daydreaming is for most people a category that has meaning and hence needs a definition. My response to this need is to define daydreaming as nonworking thought that is either spontaneous or fanciful. This includes mindwandering—a paradigm of spontaneous thought when it is unrelated to an ongoing activity—and also instances when people decide to daydream about something, such as a tropical beach or a sexual escapade, and then let their minds run undirected into whatever fanciful directions occur to them.

This definition omits consideration of whether the thought is related to an immediate activity, which is an important dimension in its own right but not necessarily indicative of daydreaming. One may, after all, decide to do some deliberate party planning while driving home from work.

Fantasy is an equally complex concept. Its classical definition in psychology was well stated by English and English (1958):

> Imagining a complex object or event in concrete symbols or images, whether or not the object or event exists; or the symbols or images themselves: e.g., a daydream. … [I]t is now distinguished by the fact that, if it represents reality at all, it is whimsical or visionary, not primarily either constructive or reproductive. (p. 203)

That is, one kind of daydream may constitute one form of fantasy, but *fantasy* as currently used implies a departure from concrete reality and is not necessarily a mental process in that it may also be a physical representation such as a work of art or literature. Furthermore, in popular parlance the term is often used as equivalent to a person's misconceptions within contexts such as relationships, organizations, or physical sensations (e.g., a romantic partner, a boss's attitude, a corporate strategy, the experience of pregnancy, etc.). The definition used here, however, follows that of English and English (1958), and this chapter is concerned only with its mental portion—fanciful thought.

What follows, then, is a summary of what science appears to have established about daydreaming and fanciful thought, especially as a part of the human system for keeping on track toward goals.

SOME BASIC PROPERTIES OF DAYDREAMS

The systematic observation and investigation of daydreaming began most clearly with one of Sigmund Freud's disciples, Julien Varendonck, whose 1921 book *The Psychology of Daydreams* laid out in exquisite detail his painstaking introspective observations, meticulously recorded over years, of his own daydream experiences. Varendonck arrived at conclusions about the properties of daydreaming that still appear quite valid (parenthesized references below are to subsequent data consistent with Varendonck's conclusions). For example, (a) daydreams are composed of behavioral fragments already in the daydreamer's repertoire (Griffith's [1935] "pre-established properties" of play); (b) daydreams come in clear segmental units, such that one can delineate the beginning and end of a daydream and also of subunits within it (Klinger, 1971); (c) their content may be playful but is more often a quite sober treatment of serious themes (Klinger, 1977, 1990; Klinger, Barta, & Maxeiner, 1980; Singer, 1966); (d) segments of fantasy are instigated by bursts of affective response, often to some secondary feature of the preceding thought segment; (e) the contents of daydreaming tend to drift, distinguishing it from working thought; (f) although daydreaming is directly or indirectly about daydreamers' serious goal pursuits, it lacks a disciplined focus on working toward a goal—the intervention of "will"—and is more an affectively toned reaction to preceding cues (what I have termed, borrowing Skinner's word, *respondent* activity [Klinger, 1971]) than a proactive attempt at goal attainment (i.e., *operant* activity); (g) daydream segments are free of evaluations of how well they are advancing daydreamers toward their goals and free of attempts to direct the daydreamer's attention back to a problem (Klinger, 1974).

The first substantial research program on daydreaming in the modern scientific-psychological tradition was conducted by Jerome L. Singer, the initial stages of which are brought together in his 1966 book, *Daydreaming: An Introduction to the Experimental Study of Inner Experience*. This groundbreaking book has stimulated a large research literature on daydreaming (e.g., Klinger, 1990, 1999; Singer, 1975), both by Singer and his close research collaborator, John Antrobus, whose joint work actually preceded and fed the 1966 book), their colleagues, and by many others, including Leonard Giambra, Ruth and Steven Gold, Russell Hurlburt, Steven Starker, and Gabriele Oettingen (see Oettingen & Kappes, Chapter 26, this volume). Virtually everything in this research literature that has come afterward owes a debt to Singer's and Antrobus's work. It is worth noting here two key contributions among several of Singer and Antrobus. First, they delineated conditions governing the frequency of daydream ("task-irrelevant") episodes: These declined with greater task-related stimulation, with more complex tasks, and with greater incentives for good task performance, and they increased after emotionally arousing, threatening news (Antrobus, Singer, & Greenberg, 1966; see also Mason et al., 2007). Second, their research produced a major questionnaire to assess individual daydreaming tendencies—the Imaginal Processes Inventory (Huba, Singer, Aneshensel, & Antrobus, 1982; Singer & Antrobus, 1970)—and established three reasonably replicable second-order factors underlying individual differences in these tendencies: positive-constructive daydreaming, guilt and fear of failure daydreaming, and attentional control (Huba, Aneshensel, & Singer, 1981; Huba, Segal, & Singer, 1977; Tanaka & Huba, 1985–1986). Moreover, these scales have been shown to be related to participants' broad personality traits (Zhiyan & Singer, 1997). The implication is clear: Daydreaming is an integral part of each person, and its emotional tone and tempo reflect each person's personal traits.

DIMENSIONS OF THOUGHT FLOW

Four investigations beeped student research participants on a quasi-random schedule as they went about their everyday activities (Klinger, 1978a; Klinger & Cox, 1987–1988; Klinger & Kroll-Mensing, 1995; Klinger & Kroll-Mensing, 1992). At each beep, participants noted their latest thoughts and rated them on a series of scales. These ratings were standardized within participants and then pooled. The results of these investigations were roughly similar. Factor analyses (e.g., Klinger & Cox, 1987–1988) found eight dimensions (factors): (a) visual intensity (visualness, picture-like quality, color); (b) attentiveness to external stimulation (including relation of thought to the external environment); (c) operantness/specificity (directedness vs. spontaneity of the thought segment, and specificity vs. vagueness of content); (d) controllability (sense of being able to modify or stop the thought if one wanted to); (e) auditory intensity (sounds, others talking); (f) strangeness (departure from reality; disjointedness); (g) future time orientation; and (h) past time orientation.

Although these dimensions are almost certainly not exhaustive, they indicate the many ways in which thoughts of all kinds vary. Because these were independent (i.e., uncorrelated, orthogonal) dimensions, they also suggest the huge number of combinations of qualities to be found in different thoughts. The third and sixth of these dimensions correspond, of course, to the dimensions suggested for defining daydreaming. The fact that these dimensions are independent of the others indicates that the characterization of thoughts in general along the other dimensions applies approximately equally to daydreams.

DURATION OF THOUGHT SEGMENTS

A group of participants was also provided with training in estimating the duration of their thoughts (Klinger, 1978b). The median duration of distinct thought segments of all kinds was 5 s; the mean duration was 14 s. These durations were essentially unrelated to other dimensions of the thoughts and hence also unrelated to whether the thought was a daydream. Obviously, some thoughts are considerably longer than this, but many are brief flashes of content. Extrapolating from these figures provides the generalization that people who sleep 8 hr of 24 entertain about 4,000 thoughts of all kinds during the other 16 hr of the day.

PROPORTION OF THOUGHTS THAT ARE DAYDREAMS

As indicated, there are two overlapping classes of thought that are popularly accepted as daydreaming: thought that is predominantly undirected (i.e., spontaneous, respondent thought such as mind-wandering) and thought that is at least partially fanciful. Thoughts that fall into these two classes, taken together, account for about half of all thought samples. It is therefore reasonable to assert that about half of human thought qualifies as daydreaming by one or the other of these definitions, amounting to an estimated average of about 2,000 daydream segments per day.

This rate will vary according to the pressures of task difficulty and the incentives at stake in good performance. However, as Singer (1966) has suggested, there may be a minimum rate of daydreaming (about 10%) across all but the shortest time intervals, even when tasks are maximally demanding and the stakes are enormous.

OTHER FEATURES OF THOUGHT, INCLUDING DAYDREAMS

The thought-sampling results permit some statements about typical and occasional features of thought segments. The most prominent other features of thought segments were their degree of relation to the external world (64% of participants could recall their surroundings "moderately well" or better), their directedness (on average, they contained "some directed thought," but also "some nondirected thought"), their controllability (on average, a sense of "moderate control"), and their visualness (on average, midway between "just a little" and "moderately visual" and between having a "trace of" and "fairly prominent picture elements," with "probably a trace" of color).

On average, the thought samples also contained "just a little" sound and "one or a few words" of others talking. Interior monologues were part of a majority of thought samples, with 74% containing some degree of self-talk. These monologues contained on average "some disconnected things" but were "mostly coherent," and their content departed only slightly from "completely normal" and physically "probably possible." Nevertheless, about 20% of the thought samples can be considered "fanciful" in the sense of departing substantially from physical or social reality. Notably, these characterizations of thought were substantially replicated with a sample of 184 students selected for high or low scores on measures of depression and anxiety (Kroll-Mensing, 1992).

DETERMINANTS OF DAYDREAM CONTENT

What people daydream about (and night dream about) appears to be determined by a confluence of their goals and their encounters with cues that remind them of particular goals. This is only part of the story, in that the content evoked by the interaction of goal and cue mobilizes thoughts and images in the daydreamer's existing repertoire, but it may also enlist the daydreamer's capability to create new content out of old elements or to extrapolate new content from previous experience. This creative process draws on a lifetime of learning and of cultural and familial influences on daydreaming.

The focus here, however, is on goals and goal-related cues as determinants of daydreaming. There is now extensive evidence to support this proposition, and, indeed, the further proposition that when people become committed to pursuing a goal, that commitment sets in motion a powerful processing priority for cues related to that goal. That is, goal-related cues appear to compel individuals to process them first, even at the cost of delaying other processing. Thus, they are recognized quickly, grab attention early, are recalled better, and are likelier to enter conscious thought.

GOALS AND CURRENT CONCERNS AS DETERMINANTS OF COGNITIVE PROCESSING AND DAYDREAM CONTENT

If there are goals, they need to be pursued, and if that pursuit is more than momentary, several things have to happen to make it possible. First, there has to be a prospective memory of each goal, that is, an underlying (i.e., latent, nonconscious) brain process with a tendency to seize on opportunities for advancing toward the goal. Goal pursuits have beginnings and endings. They begin with commitment to that goal and end with goal attainment or, in the case of final failure, disengagement from the goal. In between, there is that latent state, which I have labeled a *current concern*. This concept is a way of saying "having a goal" while also pointing out that having a goal entails a complex, time-binding process to support it. Thus, having a goal entails a covert mental process that persists over the life of the goal pursuit.

There is a growing theory around this construct of current concerns (Klinger, 1971, 1975, 1977, 1990, 1996a, 1996b; Klinger & Cox, 2004). This theory about goals, originally devised to account for daydreaming, has spawned applications in organizational settings (Roberson, 1989; Roberson & Sluss, 2004) and a set of methods for treating excessive alcohol use, such as systematic motivational counseling (Cox & Klinger, 2004b; Schroer, Fuhrmann, & deJong-Meyer, 2004) and attentional retraining (Fadardi & Cox, 2006a, 2006b). It is currently also being extended to correctional settings (Sellen, McMurran, Cox, Theodosi, & Klinger, 2006).

In a nutshell, a current concern (i.e., having a goal) sensitizes the person to respond to cues associated with the goal pursuit. The responses are emotional, perceptual, cognitive, and, if opportunities present themselves, actions directed toward attaining the goal. Its effects are similar to those classically attributed to another construct, mental set or *Einstellung*, but in a much more comprehensive way. In psychological science, a *mental set* is "temporary readiness to perceive, think, or act in a particular way, usually as a result of experimental instructions or an experimental manipulation" (Colman, 2001). Sets may also be longer-term cognitive habits. In contrast, a *current concern* is a state that persists from the onset of commitment to pursuing a particular goal up to attainment of the goal or disengagement from it. However, like a set, it directs perceptual and cognitive activity into particular channels, in this case toward foci and interpretations that are related to the goal pursuit. Thus, while preparing to decorate a house, a person in a gallery is likely to view paintings from the standpoint of their size, color compatibility with the room, and theme, whereas an art student is likely to view them from the standpoint of the techniques that the artist used to produce them. If the decorator decided to enroll in an art class or the student decided to redecorate his or her house, their ways of looking at the paintings are likely to be reversed.

Current concerns are also associated with emotional responding. There is a strong correlation between people's ratings of how much something is related to one of their current concerns and how emotionally arousing it is (e.g., Bock & Klinger, 1986). Furthermore, people's emotions become dependent on the signs of success or failure in the goal pursuit. Loss or failure precipitates a predictable sequence of emotional changes—invigoration, aggression, low mood or depression, and recovery—as the individual gradually disengages from the goal (Klinger, 1975, 1977, 1987a). Thus, commitment to pursuing a goal instates a process that is difficult to end without some psychological pain in the form of disappointment, sadness, or depression.

As subsequent sections describe, daydreams reflect all of these effects of current concerns on cognition and emotion. The evolutionary function of current concerns is presumably to keep organisms on track toward their goals. The result is goal-directed action and, in the absence of action, goal-directed daydreams, dreams, and other thoughts.

EFFECTS OF GOAL PURSUITS AND CURRENT CONCERNS ON ATTENTION AND COGNITION, INCLUDING DAYDREAMS

Initial investigations of this construct assessed participants' concerns, and a few days later asked participants to listen simultaneously to two different but similar 15-min narratives on audiotape, one narrative in each ear. Here and there, at particular time points on the tape, a few words going to one ear had been modified to relate to one of the individual participant's own goals, while simultaneously a few words going to the other ear had been modified to relate to another participant's goals but not, as far as we could determine, to this participant's goals. Participants used a toggle switch to indicate when they switched the ear to which they were paying attention. This told us at any given time to which narrative they were listening. Just after each modified passage, we stopped the tape and asked them what they were thinking about and what they recalled from the tape. The results were very powerful: Participants spent significantly more time listening to passages associated with their own goals than to passages associated with others' goals, recalled those passages about twice as often, and had thought content that (by ratings of blind judges) was related to passages associated with their own goals about twice as often as to the opposite passages (Klinger, 1978b).

A large proportion of those thoughts qualified as daydreams. It is therefore evident that the goal relatedness of the cues we embedded into the tapes triggered daydream content.

EFFECTS OF LOSING GOALS ON DAYDREAMS

If daydream content arises from a person's current concerns, one would expect that the loss of a goal would also eliminate daydreams about attaining that goal. Indeed, clinical treatment for phobic disorders reduces processing priority for cues of the aversive goals (e.g., spiders for spider phobics) that are part of these disorders (see Klinger, 1996b, for a review). Moreover, following prostate surgery, which often impairs sexual potency, patients experienced a reduced rate or loss of sexual fantasies (Bokhour, Clark, Inui, Sillilman, & Talcott, 2001). Presumably, impaired potency leads people to abandon some of their sexual goals, and with the loss of those goals there is a loss of daydreams associated with them.

AUTOMATICITY OF THE EFFECTS: LEXICAL, STROOP, AND SLEEP INVESTIGATIONS

Subsequent studies of both waking and sleeping participants indicated that these effects are apparently nonconscious and automatic rather than attributable to a conscious process, such as deliberately focusing on goal-related stimuli. In fact, goal-related stimuli seem to impose an extra cognitive-processing load even when they are peripheral and participants are consciously ignoring them. When asked to judge as quickly as possible whether a string of letters on a screen constitutes a word, goal-related distractor stimuli but not goal-unrelated distractor stimuli delayed the lexical decisions about the target words (Young, 1987).

This processing priority for goal-related stimuli (or emotionally evocative stimuli, which are usually goal related) has also been shown in at least 16 studies using the so-called emotional and alcohol Stroop procedures (summarized by Cox, Fadardi, & Pothos, 2006). In the Stroop procedures, people are presented with words on a screen and instructed to name the font color of the words as quickly as possible. Participants in these experiments name font colors more slowly when the words or images are related to one of their own goals (or are emotionally evocative stimuli, which are in most cases concern related) than when they are not. This slowing of response suggests that the brain gives processing priority to the goal-related features of the stimulus words, which delays the processing of other features and therefore slows judgments about these other features.

Even when people are asleep, goal-related stimuli influence dream content much more reliably than do other stimuli. One investigation in a sleep laboratory (Hoelscher, Klinger, & Barta, 1981) assessed participants' goals before putting them to sleep in the laboratory on four consecutive nights. While they slept during the last three nights, about six times per night, the experimenters played for them various taped words or phrases related to their different goals or to other participants' goals. Eight seconds after each stimulation, participants were awakened and reported on their dream content. Dream reports resembled the immediately preceding stimuli about three times as often if the stimuli related to participants' own goals than if they related to other people's goals. Comparing dreams to stimuli played after the dreams had already occurred produced little resemblance, regardless of how goal related the stimulus was. Thus, the effect on dream content was clearly produced by the goal relatedness of the stimuli that preceded the dreams.

In a later sleep laboratory investigation (Nikles, Brecht, Klinger, & Bursell, 1998), the experimenters instructed participants before they went to sleep to dream about a particular topic. Sometimes, the topic was related to one of their individual goals, and sometimes it was related to another's goal. The instructions to dream about topics related to participants' own goals significantly influenced dream content, whereas instructions to dream about others' goals did not.

Taken together, these results confirm that goal-related cues get processed cognitively in a way that is substantially automatic and probably inexorable. In other words, goal-related cues—concern-related cues—receive priority in processing, and this processing priority is reflected at each further processing level, right up to thought content and the content of people's daydreams.

MINDWANDERING AS MENTAL DEFAULT: MIND AT "REST" BUT STILL FOCUSED ON GOALS

How is it that goals determine the content of our daydreams? The answer appears to be that daydreams are the residue of blocked goal-directed actions.

Viewed from an evolutionary perspective, goal striving is what sets humans and other animals apart from plants, and successful goal striving is the indispensable condition for their survival. Naturally, successful goal striving must entail some action on the environment. In two investigations, the goals people reported were highly related to their actions in subsequent weeks (Church et al., described in Klinger, 1987b; Roberson, 1989). Recent work (e.g., Bargh, Gollwitzer, Lee-Chai, Barndollar, & Trötschel, 2001; Devine, Sedikides, & Fuhrman, 1989; Shah, 2005) has demonstrated important implicit and priming influences on goal striving when cues are associated with goal pursuits.

However, taking appropriate action toward a goal is not always possible. People take action when there are opportunities to advance goal pursuits and no good reason not to act. But what happens, as is often the case, when the moment is inopportune for action? Then, well-adapted organisms will abort the action—inhibit its outward expression—but the inner process is likely to continue in the form of mental images and thoughts. Spontaneous imagery and thought of this kind are what I theorize to constitute the largest part of daydreaming, such as mindwandering.

Thus, in the absence of reasonable opportunities for action, the mindwandering form of daydreaming may be thought of as the default mode of mental processing. It may also be thought of as the mind at rest, a state that continues into sleep. That is, it is a state that occurs in the absence of directed working thought. However, "rest" is here in quotation marks because the mind apparently remains quite active, continuing to process material related to current concerns. In other words, brains are constituted in such a way that when they are not advancing toward a specific active goal, they lapse into a default mode that continues processing thoughts and images related to the goal. Beyond this, if momentary tasks are easy enough to leave the brain spare processing capacity, it uses that opportunity to work over goals, often goals unrelated to the immediate task—goals that at that moment cannot be pursued.

When I first proposed this concept of daydreaming as a mental default (Klinger, 1971), it was an inference, an informed speculation. Now, however, new evidence by Mason et al. (2007) confirms this view by showing that mindwandering entails activity in pathways associated with the mind at "rest"—that it constitutes the default mode of mental operation in the absence of action and directed thinking. They did this using functional magnetic resonance imaging (fMRI). Earlier work had shown that in the absence of task activity, certain brain areas actually become more active than they are during mental work. These areas have been dubbed a "default network of cortical regions" (Mason et al., 2007, p. 393). Mason et al. demonstrated that in an easy task condition in which participants were assigned well-practiced tasks, the default network[1] became more active than in a condition in which the same tasks were new to the participants and therefore required more mental work. Those well-practiced tasks were also accompanied by more mindwandering (stimulus-independent thought) than the new tasks, thereby establishing a relationship between mindwandering and the default brain network. As we have seen, mindwandering is occupied with current concerns. This indicates that not only is mindwandering the default state of the brain in the absence of action or directed thought, this default state keeps processing the range of a person's more pressing goals.

To corroborate the association between the default brain network and daydreaming, Mason et al. (2007) also asked participants to fill out the self-report Imaginal Processes Inventory (IPI; Singer & Antrobus, 1970), which assesses daydream frequency. Those participants whose default network brain activity showed the most activation during the practiced relative to the novel tasks also tended to report a high level of daydreaming in their everyday lives.

What might be the evolutionary advantage of a default state of mental rest that keeps spontaneously processing goal pursuits? First, while a person is occupied with one task, this system keeps the individual's larger agenda fresher in mind. It thus serves as a kind of reminder mechanism, thereby increasing the likelihood that the other goal pursuits will remain intact and not get lost in the shuffle of pursuing many goals. Second, it provides opportunities for spontaneous, creative problem solving, which sometimes occurs during the default mode. Third, insofar as daydreams often feature future challenges, such as an upcoming job interview or social date, they serve as a form of rehearsal. Fourth, insofar as daydreams often work over stressful past events, they can act as a form of review of one's past behavior from which individuals can gain insight that might improve their future performance.

CONCLUSIONS REGARDING THE EFFECTS OF GOALS ON DAYDREAMING

The full panoply of these results, from those of Singer and Antrobus in the 1960s to the most recent evidence regarding effects of goals on processing and the default cortical network, leads to some clear conclusions:

- Daydream-like activity—unbidden, undirected, drifting—represents a kind of human mental baseline.
- This activity automatically fills in the mental spaces not preempted by directed, working thought.
- This automatic filler is shaped by the individual's current concerns.
- The greater the pressure to focus on particular tasks, the more the undirected activity is crowded out.
- The more the individual has pressing, emotionally laden concerns separate from a task at hand, the harder it is to crowd out the undirected activity.

DAYDREAM CONTENT AND DAYDREAMERS' ACTIONS

DIRECT CORRESPONDENCE OF DAYDREAMS TO ACTIONS

If daydreams happen when goal-directed action cannot, one would expect to find evidence that people's daydreams predict what people do when opportunities to act arise. Although there are very few investigations aimed at testing precisely this hypothesis, a considerable number of studies have provided indirect evidence. For example, investigators have found that the content of people's deviant sexual fantasies are consistent with their sexual behavior. This has been found for sexual inhibition (Bhugra, Rahman, & Bhintade, 2006); paraphilias (Långström & Seto, 2006); molestation (Baumgartner, Scalora, & Huss, 2002); and among murderers, sexual coercion and abuse (Ressler & Burgess, 2004; Ressler et al., 2004). Outside the sexual sphere, Miller, Springer, Tobacyk, and Wells (2004) reported that students' daydreams about future occupations were related to their scores on the Self-Directed Search, a career interest instrument.

NONCORRESPONDENCE OR INVERSE CORRESPONDENCE OF DAYDREAMS TO ACTIONS

Sometimes, the rate of daydreaming about something is unrelated or even inverse to the rate of doing something about it. Early work using picture-story fantasy methods suggested a principle at work here (Klinger, 1971): When the action is of a kind supported by surrounding society, the relationship of fantasy content to action is direct, but when the action is of a kind discouraged or punished by society, the relationship is inverse. When the extent of support for the action varies within a sample, there is likely to be little correspondence between fantasy and action because the relationship will be direct for some people and inverse for others.

For example, Lesser (1957) gave a picture-story test to preadolescent boys and obtained sociometric ratings of their overt aggression. For boys whose mothers were more supportive (above the median) of aggression, the correlation between fantasy and actual aggression was +.43; for boys whose mothers were less supportive of aggression, the correlation was −.41. The two coefficients were significantly different from each other. When the correlation was computed on the whole group, the coefficient was .07. One possible explanation for such findings is that in environments that disapprove of a particular behavior, those most inclined to manifest it are likely to reap the most experience with punishment for it, potentially driving its overt expression below the level of those who may have been less inclined toward it and hence experienced less punishment for it. This assumes, of course, that the punishment contingencies persist at the time the overt behavior is assessed.

These findings become relevant in light of a conclusion by Gellerman and Suddath (2005): "No consistent predictive relationship between violent fantasies and criminally dangerous behavior is reported in the available scientific literature" (p. 484). Support for aggression is highly variable. The relation of environmental support to behavioral expression would also help to explain another recent finding with first-year university students: "Participants who scored higher on the religiosity scale were more likely to report fantasies about heterosexual intercourse but less likely to have participated in heterosexual intercourse" (Nicholas, 2004, p. 37). Perhaps people who scored high on religiosity lived in more restrictive environments than others, which would then produce the inverse relationship described here. Another possibility arises from reactance theory (Brehm, 1972), which posits that restricting choices makes the restricted option more attractive than it would be otherwise. Perhaps living in sexually restrictive environments makes sexual activity especially alluring, which surfaces in fantasy, even while suppressing its expression in action.

DAYDREAM PROPERTIES AND RELATIONSHIP TO GOAL ATTAINMENT

Although daydreams appear heavily influenced by daydreamers' goals, the extent to which daydreamers reach their goals is associated with the relative extent to which their daydreams dwell on the pleasures of goal attainment versus the challenges and steps of reaching those goals. Gabriele Oettingen and her colleagues (e.g., Oettingen & Mayer, 2002; Oettingen, Pak, & Schnetter, 2001) have shown in an extensive program of investigation that daydreamers who include both kinds of elements in their daydreams have on average the best chance of goal attainment and of superior performance (see also Markman & McMullen, 2003). Her research program has employed both correlational and experimental designs and has worked with both subjective responses and observable action outcomes, which renders the results convincing. Because this work is described elsewhere in this volume (Oettingen & Kappes, Chapter 26, this volume), it is not detailed here. There is also evidence that focusing daydreams on happy outcomes to a problem situation is related to later increased depression (Feldman & Hayes, 2005).

It is, however, worth noting an important implication of Oettingen's results: Despite most daydreaming being, by definition, spontaneous and nonworking mental activity, it does almost certainly perform or at least reflect a planning function. That is, daydreams often feature scenarios of future goal-related activities. An important goal may spawn hundreds or thousands of brief daydreams of goal-related actions. Even though these daydreams are spontaneous, unintended thoughts and images, they in effect explore possibilities, develop tactics, and sometimes detect potential mistakes. Gollwitzer and his colleagues have amply demonstrated the utility of people furnishing their intentions with specific plans ("implementation intentions"; see Brandstätter, Lengfelder, & Gollwitzer, 2001; Faude, Wuerz, & Gollwitzer, Chapter 5, this volume; Gollwitzer, 1999; Gollwitzer & Brandstätter, 1997). Accordingly, those daydreamers who incorporate both the motivating pleasurable elements into their daydreams along with the practicalities of reaching their goals are likely to make best use of their daydreaming resources for goal attainment. It may also be, of course, that those daydreamers who have already equipped themselves with the knowledge and skills they need to reach their goals are more likely to incorporate that knowledge into their daydreams, but the experimental designs used by Oettingen et al. suggest that the realistic planning function of daydreams also plays a role.

OTHER FINDINGS REGARDING DAYDREAMING

AGE DIFFERENCES IN DAYDREAMING

At some ill-defined point, children's imaginative play becomes interiorized and takes the form of daydreams (see also Taylor, Shawber, & Mannering, Chapter 14, this volume). In the conventional meaning of daydreams, their frequency and vividness peak during the teens and early twenties and then gradually become less frequent and less vivid (Giambra, 1999–2000a, 2000b; Giambra, 2000; Giambra & Grodsky, 1991–1992). This has been demonstrated repeatedly using both questionnaires and a laboratory procedure in which participants are assigned tasks and report task-unrelated images and thoughts (TUITs) as they occur or within brief time intervals. It has been found using both cross-sectional and longitudinal designs in participants ranging in age from 17 to 95. Contrary to common belief, old age is not associated with more thoughts about the past or distant past; time frames for daydreams remain fairly constant over the life span (Giambra, 1977). Sexual daydreaming gradually declines with age, especially after age 65. It is particularly elevated for young men (Giambra, 1999–2000b; Giambra & Martin, 1977). Problem-solving daydreams become proportionately more common with advancing age (Giambra, 1974).

CONTINUITY OF DAYDREAMS AND NIGHT DREAMS

There is considerable continuity between daydreams and night dreams. As noted, the cuing of dream content by goal-related cues follows a pattern similar to that in daydreaming. They appear to reflect similar themes (Beck, 2002; Nikles et al., 1998) and even seem to share the same 90- to 100-min cycles of fluctuation in vividness (Kripke & Sonnenschein, 1978). Daydreams are more coherent and less bizarre than night dreams (Williams, Merritt, Rittenhouse, & Hobson, 1992), but the differences are a matter of degree.

PRESUMED BENEFITS AND HAZARDS OF DAYDREAMING

Daydreams probably perform important, even central, functions in human life. While a person is absorbed in one particular task, daydreams serve as continual reminders of the rest of the person's agenda. They thereby help people to stay organized. People also gain knowledge by spontaneously reviewing their past experiences in daydreams and by spontaneously rehearsing for future situations. Daydreams appear sometimes to generate creative solutions to difficult problems. They are linked with greater empathy for others. They may be spontaneous but not entirely idle.

However, daydreaming can also become dysfunctional. For example, when people have sustained losses or failures or are fearful of doing so, these reverses to their goal pursuits become prominent in their daydreams. A certain amount of such processing may be important to successfully disengaging from unobtainable goals, but excessively dwelling on depressing or anxiety-arousing topics, which are common in depressed and anxious moods (Butler & Nolen-Hoeksema, 1994; Nolen-Hoeksema, 1987), can deepen and prolong these negative moods (e.g., Nolen-Hoeksema & Morrow, 1993; Nolen-Hoeksema, Morrow, & Fredrickson, 1993).

For many decades, textbooks on mental health warned against daydreaming, especially excessive daydreaming, as something that could propel the daydreamer into various forms of psychopathology, including schizophrenia. Empirical research during the 1960s and 1970s largely refuted these ideas (Klinger, 1990). Although some investigations (Lynn & Rhue, 1988; Rhue & Lynn, 1987) appeared to demonstrate a link between fantasy-proneness (Wilson & Barber, 1981, 1983) and indicators of psychopathology, further analyses of this relationship (Klinger, Henning, & Janssen, 2005) suggest that this relationship is attributable to a confounded assessment instrument (the Inventory of Childhood Memories and Imaginings and its variants; Wilson & Barber, 1981, 1983) rather than to an actual hazard of normal daydreaming. On the other hand, it is no doubt true that insofar as an individual suffers from a mental disorder, the disorder is likely to be reflected in the content of the person's daydreams.

SUMMARY

Daydreams constitute a default form of mental processing while people are awake and not using all of their mental capacity for instrumental work. Their content is determined by the confluence of their current concerns—the latent brain processes that form the substrates for goal pursuits—and goal-related cues, whether external or internal. Because brains give processing priority to cues related to goal pursuits, daydreams compete for attention with tasks at hand. If concerns are particularly pressing and emotionally laden, daydreams may intensify to take the form of worry and rumination. Daydreams are part of a mental process that continues through sleep. They appear to serve a planning function, one consequence of which is that daydreams advance goal pursuits insofar as they include not only desired outcomes but also the challenges and steps on the path to goal attainment. One hazard of this planning function is that sexually or criminally deviant daydreams may maintain motivation and mold action plans for deviant actions. Another hazard is that rumination that is devoid of effective planning and problem solving is likely to deepen and prolong depression. However, normal positive daydreaming is not a risk factor for psychopathology.

NOTE

1. The brain areas most activated during the more mindwandering-intensive time periods were the "bilateral aspects of the mPFC (BAs 6, 8, 9, and 10); bilateral superior frontal gyri (SFG; BAs 8 and 9); the anterior cingulate (BA 10); bilateral aspects of the posterior cingulate (BAs 29 and 30) and precuneus (BAs 7 and 31); the left angular gyrus (BA 39); bilateral aspects of the insula (BA 13); the left superior temporal (BA 22), the right superior temporal (BA 41) and the left middle temporal gyri (BA 19)" (Mason et al., 2007, p. 394). Here, mPFC is the medial prefrontal cortex, and BA indicates Broca's areas.

REFERENCES

Antrobus, J. S., Singer, J. L., & Greenberg, S. (1966). Studies in the stream of consciousness: Experimental enhancement and suppression of spontaneous cognitive processes. *Perceptual and Motor Skills, 23*, 399–417.

Bargh, J. A., Gollwitzer, P. M., Lee-Chai, A., Barndollar, K., & Trötschel, R. (2001). The automated will: Nonconscious activation and pursuit of behavioral goals. *Journal of Personality and Social Psychology, 81*, 1014–1027.

Baumgartner, J. V., Scalora, M. J., & Huss, M. T. (2002). Assessment of the Wilson sex fantasy questionnaire among child molesters and nonsexual forensic offenders. *Sexual Abuse: Journal of Research and Treatment, 14*, 19–30.

Beck, A. T. (2002). Cognitive patterns in dreams and daydreams. *Journal of Cognitive Psychotherapy, 16*, 23–28.

Bhugra, D., Rahman, Q., & Bhintade, R. (2006). Sexual fantasy in gay men in India: A comparison with heterosexual men. *Sexual and Relationship Therapy, 21*, 197–207.

Bock, M., & Klinger, E. (1986). Interaction of emotion and cognition in word recall. *Psychological Research, 48*, 99–106.

Bokhour, B. G., Clark, J. A., Inui, T. S., Silliman, R. A., & Talcott, J. A. (2001). Sexuality after treatment for early prostate cancer: Exploring the meanings of "erectile dysfunction." *Journal of General Internal Medicine, 16*(10), 649–655.

Brandstätter, V., Lengfelder, A., & Gollwitzer, P. M. (2001). Implementation intentions and efficient action initiation. *Journal of Personality and Social Psychology, 81*, 946–960.

Brehm, J. W. (1972). *Responses to loss of freedom: A theory of psychological reactance.* Morristown, NJ: General Learning Press.

Butler, L. D., & Nolen-Hoeksema, S. (1994). Gender differences in responses to depressed mood in a college sample. *Sex Roles, 30*, 331–346.

Colman, A. M. (2001). *A dictionary of psychology.* New York: Oxford University Press. Retrieved September 28, 2007 from http://www.encyclopedia.com/doc/1O87-set.html

Cox, W. M., Fadardi, J. S., & Pothos, E. M. (2006). The addiction-Stroop test: Theoretical considerations and procedural recommendations. *Psychological Bulletin, 132*, 443–476.

Cox, W. M., & Klinger, E. (Eds.) (2004a). *Handbook of motivational counseling.* Chichester, England: Wiley.

Cox, W. M., & Klinger, E. (2004b) Systematic motivational counseling: The Motivational Structure Questionnaire in action. In W. M. Cox & E. Klinger (Eds.), *Handbook of motivational counseling* (pp. 217–237). Chichester, England: Wiley.

Devine, P. G., Sedikides, C., & Fuhrman, R. W. (1989). Goals in social information processing: The case of anticipated interaction. *Journal of Personality and Social Psychology, 56*, 680–690.

English, H. B., & English, A. C. (1958). *A comprehensive dictionary of psychological and psychoanalytical terms: A guide to usage.* New York: McKay.

Fadardi, J. S., & Cox, M. W. (2006a). Alcohol attentional bias: Drinking salience or cognitive impairment? *Psychopharmacology, 185*(2), 169–178.

Fadardi, J. S., & Cox, M. W. (2006b). *Developing and evaluating attention-diversion training for excessive drinkers.* Unpublished report to the Economic and Social Research Council.

Feldman, G., & Hayes, A. (2005). Preparing for problems: A measure of mental anticipatory processes. *Journal of Research in Personality, 39*, 487–516.

Freud, S. (1961). *The interpretation of dreams.* New York: Wiley. (Original work published 1900)

Freud, S. (1953). The relation of the poet to day-dreaming. In *Collected Papers* (Vol. 4). London: Hogarth. (Original work published 1908)

Gellerman, D. M., & Suddath, R. (2005). Violent fantasy, dangerousness, and the duty to warn and protect. *Journal of the American Academy of Psychiatry and the Law, 33*, 484–495.

Giambra, L. M. (1974). Daydreaming across the life span: Late adolescent to senior citizen. *International Journal of Aging and Human Development, 5*, 115–140.

Giambra, L. M. (1977). Daydreaming about the past: The time setting of spontaneous thought intrusions. *Gerontologist, 17*, 35–38.

Giambra, L. M. (1999–2000a). Frequency and intensity of daydreaming: Age changes and age differences from late adolescent to the old-old. *Imagination, Cognition and Personality, 1*, 229–267.

Giambra, L. M. (1999–2000b). The temporal setting, emotions, and imagery of daydreams: Age changes and age differences from late adolescent to the old-old. *Imagination, Cognition and Personality, 19*, 367–413.

Giambra, L. M. (2000). Daydreaming characteristics across the life-span: Age differences and 7 to 20 year longitudinal changes. In R. G. Kunzendorf & B. Wallace (Eds.), *Individual differences in conscious experience* (pp. 147–206). Amsterdam, Netherlands: Benjamins.

Giambra, L. M., & Grodsky, A. (1991–1992). The influence of age on the frequency of spontaneous task-unrelated thought intrusions during reading. *Imagination, Cognition and Personality, 11*, 367–379.

Giambra, L. M., & Martin, C. E. (1977). Sexual daydreams and quantitative aspects of sexual activity: Some relations for males across adulthood. *Archives of Sexual Behavior, 6*, 497–505.

Gollwitzer, P. M. (1999). Implementation intentions: Strong effects of simple plans. *American Psychologist, 54*, 493–503.

Gollwitzer, P. M., & Brandstätter, V. (1997). Implementation intentions and effective goal pursuit. *Journal of Personality and Social Psychology, 73*, 186–199.

Griffiths, R. (1935). *Imagination in early childhood.* London: Kegan Paul.

Hoelscher, T. J., Klinger, E., & Barta, S. G. (1981). Incorporation of concern- and nonconcern-related verbal stimuli into dream content. *Journal of Abnormal Psychology, 49*, 88–91.

Huba, G. J., Aneshensel, C. S., & Singer, J. L. (1981). Development of scales for three second-order factors of inner experience. *Multivariate Behavioral Research, 16*, 181–206.

Huba, G. J., Segal, B., & Singer, J. L. (1977). Consistency of daydreaming styles across samples of college male and female drug and alcohol users. *Journal of Abnormal Psychology, 86*, 99–102.

Huba, G. J., Singer, J. L., Aneshensel, C. S., & Antrobus, J. S. (1982). *Short imaginal processes inventory manual.* Port Huron, MI: Research Psychologists Press.

Klinger, E. (1971). *Structure and functions of fantasy.* New York: Wiley.

Klinger, E. (1974). Utterances to evaluate steps and control attention distinguish operant from respondent thought while thinking out loud. *Bulletin of the Psychonomic Society, 4*, 44–46.

Klinger, E. (1975). Consequences of commitment to and disengagement from incentives. *Psychological Review, 82*, 1–25.

Klinger, E. (1977). *Meaning and void: Inner experience and the incentives in people's lives.* Minneapolis: University of Minnesota Press.

Klinger, E. (1978a). Dimensions of thought and imagery in normal waking states. *Journal of Altered States of Consciousness, 4*, 97–113.

Klinger, E. (1978b). Modes of normal conscious flow. In K. S. Pope & J. L. Singer (Eds.), *The stream of consciousness: Scientific investigations into the flow of human experience* (pp. 225–258). New York: Plenum.

Klinger, E. (1987a). Current concerns and disengagement from incentives. In F. Halisch & J. Kuhl (Eds.), *Motivation, intention and volition* (pp. 337–347). Berlin: Springer.

Klinger, E. (1987b). The Interview Questionnaire technique: Reliability and validity of a mixed idiographic-nomothetic measure of motivation. In J. N. Butcher & C. D. Spielberger (Eds.), *Advances in personality assessment* (Vol. 6, pp. 31–48). Hillsdale, NJ: Erlbaum.

Klinger, E. (1990). *Daydreaming.* Los Angeles: Tarcher.

Klinger, E. (1996a). The contents of thoughts: Interference as the downside of adaptive normal mechanisms in thought flow. In I. G. Sarason, B. R. Sarason, & G. R. Pierce (Eds.), *Cognitive interference: Theories, methods, and findings* (pp. 3–23). Hillsdale, NJ: Erlbaum.

Klinger, E. (1996b). Emotional influences on cognitive processing, with implications for theories of both. In J. A. Bargh & P. M. Gollwitzer (Eds.), *The psychology of action: Linking cognition and motivation to behavior* (pp. 168–189). New York: Guilford.

Klinger, E. (1999). Thought flow: Properties and mechanisms underlying shifts in content. In J. A. Singer & P. Salovey (Eds.), *At play in the fields of consciousness: Essays in honor of Jerome L. Singer* (pp. 29–50). Mahwah, NJ: Erlbaum.

Klinger, E., Barta, S. G., & Maxeiner, M. E. (1980). Motivational correlates of thought content frequency and commitment. *Journal of Personality and Social Psychology, 39*, 1222-1237.

Klinger, E., & Cox, W. M. (1987–1988). Dimensions of thought flow in everyday life. *Imagination, Cognition and Personality, 7*, 105–128.

Klinger, E., & Cox, W. M. (2004) Motivation and the theory of current concerns. In W. M. Cox & E. Klinger (Eds.), *Handbook of motivational counseling* (pp. 3–27). Chichester, England: Wiley.

Klinger, E., Henning, V. R., & Janssen, J. M. (2005, January 21). *Examination of a scale for fantasy-proneness.* Poster presented at the Sixth Annual Meeting of the Society for Personality and Social Psychology, New Orleans, LA.

Klinger, E., & Kroll-Mensing, D. (1995). Idiothetic assessment: Experience sampling and motivational analysis. In J. N. Butcher (Ed.), *Clinical personality assessment: Practical approaches* (pp. 267–277). New York: Oxford University Press.

Klinger, E., Murphy, M. D., Ostrem, J. L., & Stark-Wroblewski, K. (2004–2005). Disclosing daydreams versus real experiences: Attitudes, emotional reactions, and personality correlates. *Imagination, Cognition and Personality, 24*, 101–138.

Kripke, D. F., & Sonnenschein, D. (1978). A biologica rhythm in waking fantasy. In J. L. Singer & K. S. Pope (Eds.), *The stream of consciousness: Scientific investigations into the flow of human experience* (pp. 321–332). New York: Plenum.

Kroll-Mensing, D. (1992). *Differentiating anxiety and depression: An experience sampling analysis.* Unpublished Ph.D. dissertation, University of Minnesota.

Långström, N., & Seto, M. C. (2006). Exhibitionistic and voyeuristic behavior in a Swedish national population survey. *Archives of Sexual Behavior, 35*, 427–435.

Lesser, G. S. (1957). The relationship between overt and fantasy aggression as a function of maternal response to aggression. *Journal of Abnormal and Social Psychology, 55*, 218–221.

Lynn, S. J., & Rhue, J. W. (1988). Fantasy proneness: Hypnosis, developmental antecedents, and psychopathology. *American Psychologist, 43*, 35–44.

Markman, K. D., & McMullen, M. N. (2003). A reflection and evaluation model of comparative thinking. *Personality and Social Psychology Review, 7*, 244.

Mason, M. F., Norton, M. I., Van Horn, J. D., Wegner, D. M., Grafton, S. T., & Macrae, C. N. (2007). Wandering minds: The default network and stimulus-independent thought. *Science, 315*, 393–395.

Miller, M. J., Springer, T. P., Tobacyk, J., & Wells, D. (2004). Congruency between occupational daydreams and SDS scores among college students. *College Student Journal, 38*, 57–60.

Nicholas, L. J. (2004). The association between religiosity, sexual fantasy, participation in sexual acts, sexual enjoyment, exposure, and reaction to sexual materials among black South Africans. *Journal of Sex and Marital Therapy, 30*, 37–42.

Nikles, C. D., II, Brecht, D. L., Klinger, E., & Bursell, A. L. (1998). The effects of current-concern- and nonconcern-related waking suggestions on nocturnal dream content. *Journal of Personality and Social Psychology, 75*, 242–255.

Nolen-Hoeksema, S. (1987). Sex differences in unipolar depression: Evidence and theory. *Psychological Bulletin, 101*, 259–282.

Nolen-Hoeksema, S., & Morrow, J. (1993). Effects of rumination and distraction on naturally occurring depressed mood. *Cognition & Emotion, 7*, 561–570.

Nolen-Hoeksema, S., Morrow, J., & Fredrickson, B. L. (1993). Response styles and the duration of episodes of depressed mood. *Journal of Abnormal Psychology, 102*, 20–28.

Oettingen, G., & Mayer, D. (2002). The motivating function of thinking about the future: Expectations versus fantasies. *Journal of Personality and Social Psychology, 83*, 1198–1212.

Oettingen, G., Pak, H., & Schnetter, K. (2001). Self-regulation of goal-setting: Turning free fantasies about the future into binding goals. *Journal of Personality and Social Psychology, 80*, 736–753.

Ressler, R. K., & Burgess, A. W. (2004). The split reality of murder. In J. H. Campbell & D. DeNevi (Eds.), *Profilers: Leading investigators take you inside the criminal mind* (pp. 83–90). Amherst, NY: Prometheus Books.

Ressler, R., Burgess, A. W., Hartman, C., Douglas, J. E., & McCormack, A. (2004). Murderers who rape and mutilate. In J. H. Campbell & D. DeNevi (Eds.), *Profilers: Leading investigators take you inside the criminal mind* (pp. 61–72). Amherst, NY: Prometheus Books.

Rhue, J. W., & Lynn, S. J. (1987). Fantasy proneness and psychopathology. *Journal of Personality and Social Psychology, 53*, 327–336.

Roberson, L. (1989). Assessing personal work goals in the organizational setting: Development and evaluation of the work concerns inventory. *Organizational Behavior and Human Decision Processes, 44*, 345–367.

Roberson, L., & Sluss, D. M. (2004). Systematic motivational counseling at work: Improving employee performance, satisfaction, and socialization. In W. M. Cox & E. Klinger (Eds.), *Handbook of motivational counseling* (pp. 283–299). Chichester, UK: Wiley.

Schroer, B. M., Fuhrmann, A., & deJong-Meyer, R. (2004). Systematic Motivational Counseling in groups: Clarifying motivational structure during psychotherapy. In W. M. Cox & E. Klinger (Eds.). *Handbook of motivational counseling* (pp. 239–258). Chichester, England: Wiley.

Sellen, J. L., McMurran, M., Cox, W. M., Theodosi, E., & Klinger, E. (2006). The Personal Concerns Inventory (Offender Adaptation): Measuring and enhancing motivation to change. *International Journal of Offender Therapy and Comparative Criminology, 50,* 294–305.

Shah, J. Y. (2005). The automatic pursuit and management of goals. *Current Directions in Psychological Science, 14,* 10–13.

Singer, J. L. (1966). *Daydreaming: An introduction to the experimental study of inner experience.* New York: Random House.

Singer, J. L. (1975). *The inner world of daydreaming.* New York: Harper.

Singer, J. L., & Antrobus, J. S. (1970). *The Imaginal Processes Inventory.* Princeton, NJ: Educational Testing Service.

Tanaka, J. S., & Huba, G. J. (1985–1986). Longitudinal stability of three second-order daydreaming factors. *Imagination, Cognition and Personality, 5,* 231–238.

Varendonck, J. (1921). *The psychology of daydreams.* New York: Macmillan.

Williams, J., Merritt, J., Rittenhouse, C., & Hobson, J. A. (1992). Bizarreness in dreams and fantasies: Implications for the activation-synthesis hypothesis. *Consciousness & Cognition, 1,* 172–185.

Wilson, S. C., & Barber, T. X. (1981). Vivid fantasy and hallucinatory abilities in the life histories of excellent hypnotic subjects ("somnambules"): Preliminary report with female subjects. In E. Klinger (Ed.), *Imagery, Vol. 2: Concepts, results, and applications* (pp. 133–149). New York: Plenum.

Wilson, S. C., & Barber, T. X. (1983). The fantasy-prone personality: Implications for understanding imagery, hypnosis, and parapsychological phenomena. In A. A. Sheikh (Ed.), *Imagery: Current theory, research, and applications* (pp. 340–390). New York: Wiley.

Young, J. (1987). *The role of selective attention in the attitude–behavior relationship.* Doctoral dissertation, University of Minnesota.

Zhiyan, T., & Singer, J. L. (1997). Daydreaming styles, emotionality and the big five personality dimensions. *Imagination, Cognition and Personality, 16*(4), 399–414.

16 Simulated Worlds: Transportation Into Narratives

Melanie C. Green and John K. Donahue

INTRODUCTION

Telling stories is a universal human activity. Effective storytellers can bring about comfort, joy, and excitement. Understanding and learning from stories seems to be a fundamental cognitive process. Indeed, Schank and Abelson (1995) claimed that all knowledge is stories. While this strong claim may be somewhat overstated, the power of the narrative form has been demonstrated in the judgment and decision-making literature with Pennington and Hastie's story model of jury decision making (1988), as well as in the consumer psychology literature (e.g., Adaval & Wyer, 1998; Deighton, Romer, & McQueen, 1989). There is even support from developmental studies for a weaker version of the claim that narratives are a basic mental structure; people in most cultures have an internalized narrative grammar, or understanding of story structure, by age 3 (Mancuso, 1986).

Hearing and telling stories, then, is a form of imaginative experience that most people have beginning in early childhood and continuing throughout the life span. Becoming immersed in story worlds, or transported into a narrative, might be considered a guided form of mental simulation. Rather than imagining one's own possible future or engaging in independent problem solving, a transported individual follows the tracks laid down by an author or storyteller.

The psychological theory of transportation into narrative worlds suggests that becoming immersed in a story can have powerful emotional and persuasive consequences. The theory centers on the experience of readers being transported into a text; in this state, readers' imaginative resources have them feeling removed from their surroundings and completely engaged in the world created by the author (Green & Brock, 2000). We define transportation as an integrative melding of attention, imagery, and feelings, focused on story events.

This chapter describes transportation theory and research, explores how transportation is different from other forms of mental simulation, and discusses the effects of transportation on belief change. The chapter also highlights emerging directions, such as evolutionary perspectives on immersion into narrative worlds, and the effect of transportation on the self.

TRANSPORTATION INTO NARRATIVE WORLDS

Imagine a person immersed in a favorite mystery novel. This person may not hear others enter or leave a room while she is reading. She may stay up late into the night because she does not realize how much time has gone by. Her heart may start beating faster during tense moments in the plot, or she may laugh or cry along with the main characters in the story. She may have a vivid mental image of the appearance of these characters. Being lost in a book, or what we call being transported into a narrative world, can have all of these effects and more.

Transportation has long been used as a metaphor for the narrative experience, as in Emily Dickinson's poem, "There is no frigate like a book." Gerrig (1993) extended this metaphor in his exploration of the cognitive psychology of narratives, and Green and Brock formalized the measurement of transportation with a 15-item self-report transportation scale (Green & Brock, 2000). Example transportation scale items include "I was emotionally involved in the narrative while reading it" and "I could picture myself in the scene of the events described in the narrative." The items tap the cognitive, emotional, and mental imagery components of transportation. Participants answer each item on a scale of 1 (not at all) to 7 (very much). The scale has shown good internal consistency as well as discriminant and convergent validity. Specifically, the scale is correlated with measures of empathy and absorption (discussed separately in the section comparing transportation to other forms of mental simulation) and is distinct from need for cognition. Furthermore, the scale is sensitive to story manipulations (reducing story quality by making the plot more trivial decreases transportation; see Green & Brock, 2000).

Scope of Transportation

Although individuals may become engaged in nonnarrative media (for example, science programs), transportation per se occurs solely or primarily in response to narrative communications. Narratives present a sequence of connected events and characters, typically in a causal chain that moves from beginning to end (e.g., Bruner, 1986; Kreuter et al., 2007). In contrast, nonnarrative persuasive communications present propositions or evidence in support of a claim. Although the empirical work on transportation has most frequently used written narratives (with some forays into studies of films), the mental processes involved in transportation are assumed to take place across a variety of media, including written, spoken, and filmed stories. The truth status of a narrative does not matter for transportation; individuals can be just as easily transported into a fictional narrative as a factual one.

Individuals may also become transported into virtual reality worlds, although virtual reality simulations present unique narrative challenges. Inviting the reader to actually participate in a narrative world, rather than merely providing the feeling of participation, appears to require a looser narrative structure that may be less effective in creating a mental simulation of a particular sequence of events (see Biocca, 2002). The study of transportation into interactive narratives is still in the early stages (although there is a growing body of literature on feelings of "presence" in virtual worlds).

Transportation and Participation

Virtual reality aside, even though readers cannot actually participate in the action of a book or movie, readers often react as if they were part of story events. Gerrig (e.g., Polichak & Gerrig, 2002) refers to these reactions as "participatory responses" or "p-responses." These p-responses can range from relatively automatic and reflexive *as if* responses, in which individuals respond as they would to a real situation (for example, wanting to yell, "Watch out!" when the villain is sneaking up behind the hero) to relatively more complex responses such as problem solving (attempting to gain information from the narrative to predict outcomes) or replotting responses (mentally undoing earlier narrative events to try to change the outcome, much like counterfactual thinking in real life). The kinds of participatory responses that readers have to a narrative can affect their emotional responses, their memory for narrative events, and their real-world judgments.

The Joys of Travel

Transportation is a pleasant state. In their free time, many people seek out compelling novels, exciting television programs, and dramatic films. (Indeed, individuals' anger at being interrupted in the midst of a transporting story is one indication of how valued this experience can be.) However, an examination of the themes of classic stories or best picture winners reveals that individuals are regularly transported into narratives that evoke negative emotions such as fear, sadness, or anger. Although this "pleasure from pain" may seem paradoxical, the enjoyment of a transportation experience does not necessarily stem from the particular emotions evoked by a narrative (although individuals might indeed choose particular narratives for their mood-management effects), but instead from the process of temporarily leaving one's one reality behind (Green, Brock, & Kaufman, 2004).

One aspect of leaving the "real world" behind is a reduction in self-focused attention. Because self-focus can be negative, particularly when individuals evaluate themselves as falling short of their standards (Duval & Wicklund, 1972), transportation into an alternative universe may provide an appealing alternative. For example, Moskalenko and Heine (2003) found that individuals who had received failure feedback (a threat to the self) in a laboratory experiment spent longer watching a television program immediately afterward. Furthermore, they found that in a naturalistic setting, individuals who completed questionnaires immediately after watching television showed lower self-discrepancies than those who completed the questionnaires before watching television. Although these researchers did not measure transportation per se, their findings are consistent with this function of transportation. Stepping into a narrative world appears to go beyond other activities in allowing individuals to distance themselves from self-criticism. Theoretically, such distancing should be especially likely when individuals are not able to change self-discrepancies in other ways (e.g., by improving behavior).

TRANSPORTATION COMPARED TO OTHER FORMS OF MENTAL SIMULATION

Transportation resembles other forms of imagination and likely relies on some of the same basic mental processes as other types of simulation. For example, as discussed in this volume, empathy (e.g., Batson, Chapter 18) and transportation both require understanding other minds (e.g., Epley & Caruso, Chapter 20; Myers & Hodges, Chapter 19; Saxe, Chapter 17), and transporting narratives are a means of evoking vivid mental images. Nonetheless, transportation has distinct characteristics that differentiate it from related processes.

EMPATHY

Transportation has a moderate positive correlation with empathy, as measured by the Interpersonal Reactivity Index (Davis, 1983). Transportation likely relies on some of the same fundamental cognitive processes, such as the ability to take the perspective of another person. A better understanding of the links between empathy for real others in our social world and the ability to put oneself in the shoes of a character, as transported readers do, may be a fruitful direction for future research. For example, are individuals who are more empathically accurate (e.g., Klein & Hodges, 2001) also better at understanding and becoming immersed in stories? (We also discuss studies suggesting the reverse possibility: that reading stories can improve social skills.)

ABSORPTION

Transportation also has a moderate positive correlation with Tellegen's Absorption Scale (1982), which measures a more general tendency to become immersed in a range of experiences. Absorption is associated with susceptibility to hypnosis (e.g., Lynn, Barnes, & Matthews, Chapter 7, this volume) as well as with aspects of openness to experience (particularly imaginative involvement).

FLOW

The subjective experience of being fully engaged in an experience and losing track of time resembles the concept of flow (Csikszentmihalyi, 1990). Flow is a type of optimal experience marked by effortless, deep concentration. In a typical flow experience, the challenge of the activity matches the skills of the individual. Although much of the research on flow focuses on more active pursuits (sports, music), Csikszentmihalyi highlights reading as the most frequent flow activity engaged in by people around the world (see Csikszentmihalyi, 1990, Chapter 6). However, flow is a more general term for absorption or engagement in an activity, and transportation highlights aspects more specific to narrative worlds, such as emotional connections, mental imagery, and potential real-world belief change.

MODES OF PROCESSING

Markman and McMullen (2003; see also Markman, Karadogan, Lindberg, & Zell, Chapter 12, this volume) presented an organizing framework for understanding types of mental simulation. They proposed that a division can be drawn between reflection, an experiential way of thinking that vividly simulates the self in some alternative reality, and evaluation, which involves comparing the self to an external standard. Markman and McMullen's model is explicitly focused on comparative thinking, in which individuals are considering alternatives to a current state. Transportation could be considered a type of reflective thinking during which individuals bring the self into the narrative world.

Epstein's cognitive-experiential self theory (CEST; 1990) is also a broad framework that describes two different processing modes, the cognitive (rational, conscious, and verbal) and the experiential (preconscious, automatic, and emotional; see also Dunn, Forrin, & Ashton-James, Chapter 22, this volume). Transportation shares some common ground with the experiential mode of this theory. The experiential system relies on emotions and encodes reality in terms of concrete images, both of which are characteristic of transported readers. Both CEST and transportation theory suggest that vivid mental images are similar to real experience. The experiential system also emphasizes a holistic approach to information processing rather than an analytical one. This distinction echoes the differences between transportation and elaboration. It also mirrors the reflective/evaluative dichotomy drawn by Markman and McMullen (2003), in which the reflective mode is experiential and the evaluative mode is more cognitive. However, there are also conceptual differences between transportation and the experiential mode. The experiential system is designed to "assess events rapidly and promote immediate decisive action" (p. 168). In contrast, a transported reader may linger over the experience and is not necessarily moved to any particular action. Further, the experiential system is proposed to operate in the background of mental experience, while transportation is consciously experienced and absorbs much of one's mental capacity.

FIRST- VERSUS THIRD-PERSON PERSPECTIVE

Images, and stories themselves, can be experienced from different perspectives. Research on autobiographical memory and imagery perspective suggests that a third-person perspective (for instance, "he" or "she") creates more psychological distance from past selves than a first-person perspective ("I" or "me"; e.g., Libby & Eibach, Chapter 24, this volume; Libby, Eibach, & Gilovich, 2005). However, many fictional works are written from the third-person perspective, and this point of view does not appear to diminish individuals' engagement in these stories. It appears that there is an important difference between mental simulations that directly involve the self (autobiographical memory or simulating one's own future experiences) versus existing narrative worlds that a reader can enter through transportation and identification with characters.

AFFECTIVE FORECASTING

Wilson, Gilbert, Dunn, and their colleagues have presented evidence suggesting that individuals are not particularly good at predicting (or mentally simulating) their future emotional states (e.g., Dunn et al., Chapter 22, this volume; Wilson & Gilbert, 2005). Individuals tend to overestimate the duration and intensity of their future emotions because they fail to take into account other events that will affect their emotional state or the cognitive processes that will act to moderate the emotions. Gilbert has suggested that examining the emotional reactions of another person who is already going through a particular experience (the experiment participant who has already chosen the particular gamble that you are considering; the fellow academic who has already earned or failed to earn tenure) will be a better predictor of one's own emotional reactions than one's own simulation or prediction. Narratives may serve a similar function and might provide a good source of information for predicting future emotional consequences. A direction for future research could be to test the utility of narratives (vs. information from actual persons) in affective forecasting situations.

PSYCHOLOGICAL PROCESSES UNDERLYING TRANSPORTATION

In the preceding section, we outlined how transportation was related to (and distinct from) other forms of mental simulation. In this section, we turn our attention to some of the psychological processes underlying the experience of being transported into a narrative world.

TRANSPORTATION-IMAGERY MODEL

One component of transportation is story-guided visual imagery. The transportation-imagery model (Green & Brock, 2002) highlights the role of visual imagery in transportation-based belief change. According to this model, images take on meaning from their role in a story. The transportation experience links the vivid images with beliefs implied by the story. This linkage may be one basis for the power of narrative-based persuasion. It may be difficult for verbal or statistical arguments to overcome the power of a mental image; even though a person may know rationally that airplane travel is quite safe, the person may not be able to shake the mental picture of a plane crash (similar to the availability heuristic; Tversky & Kahneman, 1974). In addition, over time, recalling the image may reevoke large parts of the original communication, thus reinforcing story-relevant beliefs. An implication of this perspective is that individuals' imagery ability and situations that allow for the formation of rich mental images increase the persuasive power of a story.

AUTOMATICITY OF TRANSPORTATION

The extent to which transportation is under conscious control remains to be determined. Transportation requires some action on the part of the individual (reading, watching, or listening). At a minimum, the recipient must pay attention to the narrative to be transported into it. However, beyond merely comprehending the text, individuals may not be able to force themselves to become involved in a story that they find boring (as any high school English teacher can attest). Removing oneself from a narrative world is easier, though. Even individuals who find themselves inadvertently transported (perhaps by a trashy television program encountered while channel surfing) can likely take themselves out of a narrative world through the use of distraction strategies (e.g., refocusing attention on events going on around them or making a conscious decision to stop watching). Experimentally, transportation can be manipulated by giving individuals instructions to focus on the surface aspects of the story, such as word choice and grammar (Green & Brock, 2000). This surface focus lowers transportation.

NEURAL BASIS OF TRANSPORTATION

Although the study of the neural underpinnings of story immersion is still in its infancy, Mar (2004) provided a summary of related findings, focusing on narrative comprehension and production. Mar noted that data from both imaging and lesion studies suggest that stories activate frontal, temporal, and cingulate areas, the same areas that appear to support working memory and theory of mind processes. Mar provided several examples of fruitful new directions involving neuroscience, including studying differences in brain activity when the text is a rich sensory experience compared to when the text is an abstract representation. Another avenue of research could examine the neuropsychological effects of the reading of a narrative text in contrast to the reading of an expository text (Mar, 2004) to better understand the nature and consequences of transportation.

INFLUENCES ON TRANSPORTATION

Not all narratives or all reading situations create a powerful sense of transportation. Rather, aspects of the individual, the narrative, and the situation can all influence the extent of immersion into a story. Primary influences on transportation include story quality, individual differences in "transportability," the match between reader knowledge and story content, and reader goals. Typical studies investigating this question bring individuals into the lab to read a story and then rate their transportation into it (using the transportation scale described in the section on transportation into narrative worlds; Green & Brock, 2000). Studies might include manipulated differences, such as altering the quality of a story or providing different reading goals, or they might include measured differences, such as preexisting reader familiarity with settings or themes described in the story.

Story Quality

A major influence on the extent of transportation experienced is the quality of the narrative or text. Not surprisingly, well-written and well-structured stories are more transporting. Best sellers or classic texts are rated as more transporting than stories created by psychologists for experiments, for instance (Green & Brock, 2000), and disrupting the logical order of a story has been shown to reduce transportation (Wang & Calder, 2006).

Craftsmanship may also involve the use of stylistic techniques, such as metaphor, irony, or alliteration. Using literary language to defamiliarize the world in this way is known as *foregrounding* (e.g., Miall & Kuiken, 1994). These literary devices make aspects of the familiar world seem new or strange, thus allowing readers to break out of their automatic or customary ways of seeing the world and gain a deeper understanding of the human experience. For example, the phrase "a lofty midnight tunnel of smooth, sinewy branches" from the short story "The Trout" uses alliteration, the repeated "s" sound, to draw the reader's attention to the description of the trees. Texts that use foregrounding are rated as more striking, and readers spend more time reading them (Miall & Kuiken, 1994; van Peer, 1986).

Individual Differences

Some individuals easily and readily leap into narrative worlds, whereas others find that stories do not hold their attention. *Transportability*, or the extent to which individuals readily become deeply transported into stories, can be measured as an individual difference (Dal Cin, Zanna, & Fong, 2004; Green, 1996). This individual difference measure of general or dispositional transportation tendencies predicts depth of actual transportation into later texts and films, as measured by the transportation scale (Green & Brock, 2000). Across studies, there is no consistent gender difference in transportation, although men may be more transported into some kinds of stories and women into others.

Familiarity and Fluency

Preexisting familiarity with an aspect of the narrative world can increase transportation. For example, individuals who reported greater knowledge about the fraternity/sorority system were more transported into a story about a man attending his fraternity reunion. Similarly, individuals who had homosexual friends or family members were more transported into a story that had a homosexual protagonist (Green, 2004). Having common ground with characters or knowing something about a narrative world appears to ease the passage into that world.

Vaughn and colleagues (2007) provided evidence for an even more general influence on transportation. Specifically, these authors suggested that feelings of processing fluency or subjective ease may increase transportation, as long as individuals attribute these feelings to the narrative (see also Sanna, Schwarz, & Kennedy, Chapter 13, this volume). Any factor that creates feelings of ease should enhance transportation. For example, individuals reading a story during the winter season that, itself, is set in wintertime should experience greater ease of processing because winter-related thoughts are chronically accessible during the winter season. These readers should be more transported into the winter narrative than those who read the winter story in the summertime. Vaughn's studies support this hypothesis and have shown similar effects using a misattribution paradigm (Vaughn et al., 2007).

Reader Goals or Prereading Instructions

As noted, goals that focus a reader on surface aspects of the story (e.g., proofreading) can reduce transportation (Green & Brock, 2000). Whether the story was freely chosen might also affect transportation; readers who feel that it was their choice to read or watch a narrative may enjoy it more than those who were compelled to do so by some external force, such as a class assignment or family obligation (cf. Shedlosky-Shoemaker, Brock, & Costabile, 2007).

TRANSPORTATION AND BELIEF CHANGE

The effects of being transported do not end at the borders of the narrative world. Rather, transportation is a key mechanism of narrative-based persuasion.

Transportation may aid in belief change in three ways. First, transportation reduces counterarguing about the issues raised in the story. Individuals transported into a compelling narrative world may not have the cognitive resources to counterargue story implications or may not be motivated to disrupt the enjoyable transportation experience by quibbling with the author's claims (Escalas, 2004; Green & Brock, 2000). Next, transportation may affect beliefs by making narrative events seem more like personal experience. If a reader or viewer feels as if she has been part of narrative events, the lessons implied by those events may seem more powerful (Green, 2004). Finally, attachment to characters may play a critical role in narrative-based belief change. If a viewer likes or identifies with a character (see Bandura, 1986; Singhal, Cody, Rogers, & Sabido, 2003), statements made by the character or implications of events experienced by that character may carry special weight.

FICTION VERSUS NONFICTION

As noted, individuals may be transported into both factual and fictional narratives. Transportation does not depend on whether a narrative reflects real-world truth; rather, individuals appear to seek plausibility rather than strict accuracy in their narratives. Indeed, labeling a story as fiction can be a cue to readers to engage in more immersive, less-critical processing (Green, Garst, & Brock, 2004).

A growing body of research suggests that fictional narratives can often be just as powerful as factual ones in changing beliefs. For example, Strange and Leung (1999) showed that narratives could change readers' beliefs about the causes of students dropping out of high school, regardless of whether those narratives were described as news articles or as fictional stories. Green and Brock (2000) showed changes in both specific and general beliefs related to a story about an attack on a small child at a shopping mall; these changes occurred even when the narrative was clearly described as fiction. Marsh and colleagues (Marsh, Meade, & Roediger, 2003) have shown that individuals learn "false facts" from fiction.

The ability of fiction to persuade is somewhat counterintuitive when viewed against the backdrop of traditional persuasion research; after all, who would alter their worldview in response to a false advertisement? However, the finding that individuals easily entertain and learn from these possible worlds makes more sense when viewed in the context of other forms of mental simulation. Individuals readily imagine possible future outcomes, and these simulated futures can guide their behavior (e.g., in this volume, Oettingen & Kappes, Chapter 26; Oyserman & James, Chapter 25). In the same way, fictional stories may in some sense be a more structured means of considering future or alternative events.

COUNTERFACTUALS

Transportation can lead to other types of mental simulation. For example, transported individuals may generate counterfactual alternatives to an unhappy ending of a story. This counterfactual thinking can enhance the persuasive power of the narrative (Tal-Or, Boninger, Poran, & Gleicher, 2004; see also Gerrig, 1993).

APPLICATIONS OF TRANSPORTATION THEORY

Narratives can be a persuasive force in a variety of domains. Transportation theory has been applied to marketing, health, and political settings. For example, consumer psychology research shows that individuals who mentally simulate experience with products (imagining themselves wearing a pair of running shoes) are transported and thus show reduced critical thinking and a more positive attitude toward the advertisement and the product (Escalas, 2004).

Transportation is also relevant to health communications and may underlie some of the effects observed in entertainment-education, a technique that embeds health messages in stories (radio programs, telenovelas; see Singhal, Cody, Rogers, & Sabido, 2003, and Slater, 2002, for reviews). Researchers and public health officials have used narratives about topics ranging from safe sex to adult education in the hope of changing attitudes and behaviors (Singhal & Rogers, 1999). For instance, after the broadcast of *Acompaname (Come Along With Me)*, a Mexican telenovela (soap opera) focused on family-planning issues, visits to family-planning clinics increased by 32% (Institute for Communication Research, 1981, cited in Slater, 2002). Entertainment-education has been used most often in developing nations, but there is growing interest in the use of narratives for changing health beliefs in the United States. For example, narratives can be used to encourage health screenings and healthy behaviors (e.g., Green, 2006; Kreuter et al., 2007).

Television narratives about controversial contemporary issues such as the death penalty have been shown to reduce resistance to attitude change that stems from prior liberal/conservative ideology (Slater, Rouner, & Long, 2006). On a broader level, over time, transportation may contribute to cultivation effects, in which individuals' beliefs come to reflect the somewhat skewed vision of the world as reflected in television portrayals rather than the real world (e.g., higher crime rates; Shrum, Burroughs, & Rindfleisch, 2005). Transported individuals may be especially likely to integrate televised portrayals into their real lives.

TRANSPORTATION AND SOCIAL SKILLS

The ease with which individuals relate to story characters may be a natural extension of individuals' ability to understand real others in the social world (see Zunshine, 2006). Transportation draws on individuals' natural tendency toward empathy and perspective taking. An intriguing new line of research has explored the possibility that reading narrative fiction may actually help develop these social skills as well. Mar and colleagues (Mar, Oatley, Hirsh, de la Paz, & Peterson, 2006) found that lifetime exposure to fiction was a positive predictor of measures of social ability, such as perceiving the mental states of others. Nonfiction reading (e.g., philosophy, business, self-help), on the other hand, showed no such benefits. These authors suggested that understanding characters in a fictional world provides parallels to understanding real interaction partners. Thus, contrary to the stereotype of "bookworms" as socially awkward, becoming transported into narrative worlds may in fact equip individuals to more successfully navigate real social interactions.

An implication of this research is that the simulations provided by quality fiction may take people beyond the knowledge they could gain through their own self-created simulations of social interactions. These findings raise the interesting question of whether some types of fiction are better than others at improving social ability. In other words, are readers of classic literature preparing themselves for social success to a greater extent than people who pick up a formulaic thriller? Or is the process of engaging in a narrative world—any narrative world—and attempting to understand the people, relationships, and situations presented there sufficient to hone social abilities? Future research should address these important questions.

TRANSPORTATION AND THE SELF

Another potential extension for transportation research is to consider the effects of transportation on the self beyond changing attitudes and beliefs about external objects (see Green, 2005). Just as transportation creates openness to new beliefs and attitudes about the world, it may also allow people to explore new possible selves (Oyserman & James, Chapter 25, this volume). Narratives provide an especially low-risk way of trying on alternative selves. Individuals can imagine what it would be like to be a fighter pilot, a homeless person, or a multimillionaire without actually getting behind the wheel of a plane, sleeping on the streets, or winning the lottery. Characters may also provide role models for desired future selves. To the extent that a story can provide specific pathways to goals (for example, showing how a character overcame a particular obstacle, such as quitting smoking or overcoming prejudice), it may be especially effective in motivating individuals to reach a desired future self and may increase individuals' optimism about their ability to achieve their goals (Klein & Zajac, Chapter 21, this volume).

Stories do not necessarily need to evoke change; they may provide new perspectives that allow increased understanding of one's current self. This function of narratives may be especially valuable when individuals experience life events that evoke extreme emotions (e.g., the death of a loved one, divorce). Oatley (1999), following Scheff (1979), suggested that, theoretically, narratives may provide a middle ground in which emotions are experienced strongly enough for their meaning to be understood but not so intensely that they overwhelm the reader. Narratives provide a safe space for individuals to explore the implications of their emotional experiences. Because the emotions evoked through reading are a result of events happening to characters rather than to the individual, readers may feel freer to express those emotions. A reader who feels sadness for the end of a character's relationship may then be able to link these feelings back to his or her own life.

EVOLUTIONARY APPROACHES TO TRANSPORTATION

Given the influence of stories and transportation in a variety of social domains, it is worthwhile to explore the potential evolutionary basis of transportation and storytelling. While stories have not been a primary focus of evolutionary psychology, some lines of evolutionary theorizing may shed light on how humans developed the capacity for constructing and becoming transported into imagined worlds.

STORIES FROM RELIGIOUS BELIEFS AND THEORY OF MIND

The emergence of stories may have begun with shamanistic or early religious beliefs resulting from an expansion of the concept of theory of mind (Boyer, 2001). For Boyer (2001), religious beliefs are theorized to stem from two constraints: a salience constraint and an inferential constraint. The salience constraint stresses that the belief must be conspicuous: drawing attention to its novelty, often by breaking the laws of nature. The representation is circumscribed to some extent by the inferential constraint: Inferences must be allowed regarding the intention of the object or agent. A storyteller, through an expansive theory of mind, could place himself or herself in the mind of an agent or object. For example, a storyteller could claim that a river has talked to her (salience constraint), and the fact that the river spoke is a sign that the hunting season will not be fruitful this year (inferential constraint). Thus, the storyteller, through an expansive theory of mind, can bring meaning to the community. This meaning-making ability could then be extended to other contexts.

In the prehistoric period, humans may initially have attempted to understand phenomena such as fertility through stories ascribing personality characteristics to unseen characters. Festinger (1983) suggested that those who could bring meaning to the community by discerning supernatural phenomena would become the elite. Perhaps effective storytellers, who could create meaning by telling stories about such subjects as gods in conflict, would have had an advantage in prehistoric society.

Examining the content of literature through the lens of evolutionary psychology, Pinker (1997) argued that the goals of literary characters are Darwinian: either to survive or reproduce. Indeed, Buss (1999) stated that, "It is probably no coincidence that the most successful novels and movies such as *Titanic* and *Gone With the Wind* contain patterns of intrasexual competition, mate choice, romance, and life-threatening hostile forces of nature" (p. 410). An interesting empirical question is whether stories that are more closely linked to issues of survival or reproduction are also more transporting.

FICTION AS AN ADAPTATION TO THE SOCIAL WORLD

Oatley and Mar (2005) hypothesized that fiction is a progression of evolutionary adaptations for attempting to understand the social world, and that these adaptations are reflected in the features of characters offered in contemporary stories. While conceding that fiction is not true, these authors argued that: "Nonetheless it [fiction] is a model, a useful simulation, of selves in the social world. ... [These models are] molded by culture to provide the contexts for oral storytelling and more recently written literature" (p. 180).

Drawing on the work of others, Oatley and Mar (2005) provided a framework to explain the development of language, with preverbal imitation beginning approximately 1.9 million years ago by the human ancestor of *Homo erectus*. Humans continue to possess this imitation ability that permits an understanding of the actions and emotions of another, facilitating narrative's capacity to describe one's actions to the self and to others through language. Dunbar (2004) argued recursion is necessary for narrative, with Oatley and Mar summarizing the three levels of recursion as:

> A conversationalist or story-teller must know (1) that the hearer can know (2) what a person in the story knows (3). We take simulation together with its recursive aspects to be important steps towards the more explicit simulations of fiction, which requires a further increase of abstraction, to depict people who may never have existed or acted in the ways depicted. (p. 184)

Oatley and Mar (2005) maintained that evolution provided the use of mental models of others, the conveyance of conversational narratives, and metaphor; then culture, and more specifically the writers within culture, developed a "theory of character" with more depth. Skilled writers can move beyond a description of external actions of a character in narrative fiction to describe the inner consciousness of the character. In sum, Oatley and Mar stated that a comprehension of a narrative character's inner state likely involves a process related to understanding a real person: an adaptive process like language and metaphor.

TRANSPORTATION INTO IMMORTALITY

Nell (2002) provided another evolutionary rationale for stories. He stated that individuals have to forget their own mortality to function, and that narratives can accomplish the suspension of knowledge of one's mortality because stories have the common element of a protagonist overcoming a challenge involving possible death.

Nell (2002) argued that all cultures have narratives with the same essential structure: a hero's call to adventure, "undergoing a supreme ordeal at the nadir of his journey, and finally re-emerging from the kingdom of dread to redeem the world" (p. 20; see also Campbell, 1949). Nell believed that current narratives involve "domestication" of older narratives so that immortality is "tamed" as hopefulness. He noted the inconsistency that "if all readers were death-defying optimists, the extraction of hope from narrative would be psychologically redundant" (p. 21), and argued that readers of both fictional stories as well as news stories seek hope from a narrative to suspend the fact that death is inescapable. This perspective is consistent with the general tenets of terror management theory (e.g., Greenberg, Pyszczynski, & Solomon, 1986; Solomon, Greenberg, & Pyszczynski, 2007).

SELECTION BENEFITS FROM NARRATIVE

Also from an evolutionary standpoint, the display hypothesis proposes a reason for why art is created. According to this hypothesis, men perform their art in public (e.g., singing) to impress others and gain greater access to women (Miller, 1998). However, the display hypothesis fails to account for the many people who enjoy experiencing art in a solitary manner (Buss, 1999). The psychology of narrative provides a possible answer: The artist may be more attractive because the people who enjoy the art are fully immersed or transported by the quality of the product, resulting in cognitive, affective, and imagery involvement.

Good artistry may affect a reader's judgment of the artist as a potential mate by prompting immersion from physical surroundings and inducing other psychological effects, such as positive emotion or arousal/excitement. Stories and other kinds of art may signal other desirable traits. Psychologists have determined that intelligence and empathy are important to potential mates (Buss & Barnes, 1986). Art, in the form of good literature or storytelling ability, may suggest an intelligent author, and the perspective taking in stories might serve a similar function for displaying empathy. Research by Haselton and Miller (2006) suggests that women desire the benefits of industriousness and creativity to varying degrees because industriousness signals the benefits of a "good dad," while creativity indicates "good genes," genes that will help increase reproductive success. In terms of evolutionary advantage, literary skill or storytelling ability might have been more valued in men because the ability might have indicated good genetic quality. On the other hand, storytelling may also have been useful in gaining resources (for instance, if it were used to persuade others or to gain higher status in a community). Future research should test some of these possible explanations for the development of storytelling skill.

CONCLUSIONS

Transportation into a narrative world is a form of immersive, imaginative engagement in a story. Transportation shares some qualities with other forms of mental simulation—a transported individual entertains possibilities beyond literal reality, forms mental images, and experiences emotional reactions in response to simulated events. However, a key difference between transportation and other forms of mental simulation is the guided nature of the experience. Individuals are not creating their own simulated worlds from scratch, but rather are following along the narrative trails blazed by an author. If the author is skillful, these simulated worlds may be even richer and more detailed than a mental simulation that a person might personally develop. Transportation is also likely to lead to real-world belief change; transported individuals learn from the experiences of characters and may integrate the lessons from story events into their own belief systems.

Transportation theory suggests several exciting areas for future research. Transportation has been explored in the context of health communications, and a future priority would be to uncover what specific aspects of transportation are most conducive to improving societal concerns. Another research direction might address how narratives can help overcome common biases. For example, the affective forecasting literature suggests that individuals overestimate the duration and intensity of their future emotional states, but (transporting) stories may be a means of overcoming these misprediction biases. Furthermore, advances in neuroscience techniques and evolutionary theorizing may provide new insights into the nature and origin of transportation into narrative worlds.

REFERENCES

Adaval, R., & Wyer, R. S., Jr. (1998). The role of narratives in consumer information processing. *Journal of Consumer Psychology, 7,* 207–245.

Bandura, A. (1986). *Social foundations of thought and action: A social cognitive theory.* Englewood Cliffs, NJ: Prentice-Hall.

Biocca, F. (2002). The evolution of interactive media: Toward "being there" in nonlinear narrative worlds. In M. C. Green, J. J. Strange, & T. C. Brock (Eds.), *Narrative impact: Social and cognitive foundations* (pp. 97–130). Mahwah, NJ: Erlbaum.

Boyer, P. (2001). Cultural inheritance tracks and cognitive predispositions: The example of religious concepts. In H. Whitehouse (Ed.), *The debated mind: Evolutionary psychology versus ethnography* (pp. 57–89). New York: Berg.

Bruner, J. (1986). *Actual minds, possible worlds.* Cambridge, MA: Harvard University Press.

Buss, D. M. (1999). *Evolutionary psychology: The new science of the mind.* Boston: Allyn and Bacon.

Buss, D. M., & Barnes, M. (1986). Preferences in human mate selection. *Journal of Personality and Social Psychology, 50,* 559–570.

Campbell, J. (1949). *The hero with a thousand faces.* Princeton, NJ: Princeton University Press.

Csikszentmihalyi, M. (1990). *Flow: The psychology of optimal experience.* New York: Harper and Row.

Dal Cin, S., Zanna, M. P., & Fong, G. T. (2004). Narrative persuasion and overcoming resistance. In E. S. Knowles & J. Linn (Eds.), *Resistance and persuasion* (pp. 175–191). Mahwah, NJ: Erlbaum.

Davis, M. H. (1983). Measuring individual differences in empathy: Evidence for a multidimensional approach. *Journal of Personality and Social Psychology, 44,* 113–126.

Deighton, J., Romer, D., & McQueen, J. (1989). Using drama to persuade. *Journal of Consumer Research, 16,* 335–343.

Dunbar, R. I. M. (2004). *The human story: A new history of mankind's evolution.* London: Faber.

Duval, T. S., & Wicklund, R. A. (1972). *A theory of objective self-awareness.* New York: Academic Press.

Epstein, S. (1990). Cognitive-experiential self-theory. In L. A. Pervin (Ed.), *Handbook of personality: Theory and research* (pp. 165–192). New York: Guilford Press.

Escalas, J. E. (2004). Imagine yourself in the product: Mental simulation, narrative transportation, and persuasion. *Journal of Advertising, 33*(2), 37–48.

Festinger, L. (1983). *The human legacy.* New York: Columbia University.

Gerrig, R. J. (1993). *Experiencing narrative worlds: On the psychological activities of reading.* New Haven, CT: Yale University Press.

Green, M. C. (1996). *Mechanisms of narrative-based belief change.* Unpublished master's thesis, Ohio State University.

Green, M. C. (2004). Transportation into narrative worlds: The role of prior knowledge and perceived realism. *Discourse Processes, 38*(2), 247–266.

Green, M. C. (2005). Transportation into narrative worlds: Implications for the self. In A. Tesser, D. A. Stapel, & J. W. Wood (Eds.), *On building, defending and regulating the self: A psychological perspective* (pp. 53–75). New York: Psychology Press.

Green, M. C. (2006). Narratives and cancer communication. *Journal of Communication,* 56, S163–S183.

Green, M. C., & Brock, T. C. (2000). The role of transportation in the persuasiveness of public narratives. *Journal of Personality and Social Psychology, 79,* 701–721.

Green, M. C., & Brock, T. C. (2002). In the mind's eye: Transportation-imagery model of narrative persuasion. In M. C. Green, J. J. Strange, & T. C. Brock (Eds.), *Narrative impact: Social and cognitive foundations* (pp. 315–341). Mahwah, NJ: Erlbaum.

Green, M. C., Brock, T. C., & Kaufman, G. F. (2004). Understanding media enjoyment: The role of transportation into narrative worlds. *Communication Theory, 14*(4), 311–327.

Green, M. C., Garst, J., & Brock, T. C. (2004). The power of fiction: Persuasion via imagination and narrative. In L. J. Shrum (Ed.), *The psychology of entertainment media: Blurring the lines between entertainment and persuasion* (pp. 161-176). Mahwah, NJ: Erlbaum.

Greenberg, J., Pyszczynski, T., & Solomon, S. (1986). The causes and consequences of a need for self-esteem: A terror management theory. In R. F. Baumeister (Ed.), *Public self and private self* (pp. 189–212). New York: Springer-Verlag.

Haselton, M. G., & Miller, G. F. (2006). Women's fertility across the cycle increases the short-term attractiveness of creative intelligence. *Human Nature, 17,* 50–73.

Institute for Communication Research. (1981). *The social use of commercial television.* Strasbourg, France: Author.

Klein, K. J. K., & Hodges, S. D. (2001). Gender differences, motivation, and empathic accuracy: When it pays to understand. *Personality and Social Psychology Bulletin, 27,* 720–730.

Kreuter, M. W., Green, M. C., Cappella, J. N., Slater, M. D., Wise, M. E., Storey, D., et al. (2007). Narrative communication in cancer prevention and control: A framework to guide research and application. *Annals of Behavioral Medicine, 33*(3), 221–235.

Libby, L. K., Eibach, R. P., & Gilovich, T. (2005). Here's looking at me: The effect of memory perspective on assessments of personal change. *Journal of Personality and Social Psychology, 88*, 50–62.

Mancuso, J. C. (1986). The acquisition and use of narrative grammar structure. In T. R. Sarbin (Ed.), *Narrative psychology: The storied nature of human conduct* (pp. 91–125). New York: Praeger.

Mar, R. A. (2004). The neuropsychology of narrative: Story comprehension, story production and their interrelation. *Neuropsychologia, 42*, 1414–1434.

Mar, R. A., Oatley, K., Hirsh, J., de la Paz, J., & Peterson, J. B. (2006). Bookworms versus nerds: Exposure to fiction versus non-fiction, divergent associations with social ability, and the simulation of fictional social worlds. *Journal of Research in Personality, 40*(5), 694–712.

Markman, K. D., & McMullen, M. N. (2003). A reflection and evaluation model of comparative thinking. *Personality and Social Psychology Review, 7*, 244–267.

Marsh, E. J., Meade, M. L., & Roediger, H. L. (2003). Learning facts from fiction. *Journal of Memory and Language, 49*(4), 519–536.

Miall, D. S., & Kuiken, D. (1994). Foregrounding, defamiliarization, and affect: Response to literary stories. *Poetics, 22*, 389–407.

Miller, G. F. (1998). How mate choice shaped human nature: A review of sexual selection and human evolution. In C. Crawford & D. Krebs (Eds.), *Handbook of evolutionary psychology* (pp. 87–129). Mahwah, NJ: Erlbaum.

Moskalenko, S., & Heine, S. J. (2003). Watching your troubles away: Television viewing as a stimulus for subjective self-awareness. *Personality and Social Psychology Bulletin, 29*, 76–85.

Nell, V. (2002). Mythic structures in narrative: The domestication of immortality. In M. C. Green, J. J. Strange, & T. C. Brock (Eds.), *Narrative impact: Social and cognitive foundations* (pp. 17–37). Mahwah, NJ: Erlbaum.

Oatley, K. (1999). Why fiction may be twice as true as fact: Fiction as cognitive and emotional simulation. *Review of General Psychology, 3*(2), 101–117.

Oatley, K., & Mar, R. A. (2005). Evolutionary pre-adaptation and the idea of character in fiction. *Journal of Cultural and Evolutionary Psychology, 3*, 179–194.

O'Faolain, S. (1980–1982). The trout. In *The collected short stories of Sean O'Faolain* (vol. 1, pp. 383–386). London: Constable.

Pennington, N., & Hastie, R. (1988). Explanation-based decision making: Effects of memory structure on judgment. *Journal of Experimental Psychology: Learning, Memory, and Cognition, 14*, 521–533.

Pinker, S. (1997). *How the mind works.* New York: Norton.

Polichak, J. W., & Gerrig, R. J. (2002). Get up and win! Participatory responses to narratives. In M. C. Green, J. J. Strange, & T. C. Brock (Eds.), *Narrative impact: Social and cognitive foundations* (pp. 71–95). Mahwah, NJ: Erlbaum.

Schank, R. C., & Abelson, R. P. (1995). Knowledge and memory: The real story. In R. S. Wyer, Jr. (Ed.), *Advances in social cognition* (Vol. 8, pp. 1–85). Hillsdale, NJ: Erlbaum.

Scheff, T. J. (1979). *Catharsis in healing, ritual, and drama.* Berkeley: University of California Press.

Shedlosky-Shoemaker, R. A., Brock, T. C., & Costabile, K. A. (2007, January). *The role of choice in film rewatching.* Poster presented at Society for Personality and Social Psychology meeting, Memphis, TN.

Shrum, L. J., Burroughs, J. E., & Rindfleisch, A. (2005). Television's culture of material values. *Journal of Consumer Research, 32*, 473–479.

Singhal, A., Cody, M. J., Rogers, E. M., & Sabido, M. (Eds.). (2003). *Entertainment-education and social change: History, research, and practice.* Mahwah, NJ: Erlbaum.

Singhal, A., & Rogers, E. M. (1999). *Entertainment-education: A communication strategy for social change.* Mahwah, NJ: Erlbaum.

Slater, M. D. (2002). Entertainment education and the persuasive impact of narratives. In M.C. Green, J. J. Strange, & T. C. Brock (Eds.), *Narrative impact: Social and cognitive foundations* (pp. 157–181). Mahwah, NJ: Erlbaum.

Slater, M. Rouner, D., & Long, M. (2006). Television dramas and support for controversial public policies: Effects and mechanisms. *Journal of Communication, 56*, 235–252.

Solomon, S., Greenberg, J., & Pyszczynski, T. (2007). The cultural animal: Twenty years of terror management theory and research. In J. Greenberg, S. L. Koole, & T. Pysczynski (Eds.), *Handbook of experimental existential psychology* (pp. 13–34). New York: Guilford.

Strange, J. J., & Leung, C. C. (1999). How anecdotal accounts in news and in fiction can influence judgments of a social problem's urgency, causes, and cures. *Personality and Social Psychology Bulletin, 25*, 436–449.

Tal-Or, N., Boninger, D. S., Poran, A., & Gleicher, F. (2004). Counterfactual thinking as a mechanism in nar-rative persuasion. *Human Communication Research, 30,* 301–328.

Tellegen, A. (1982). *Brief manual for the Differential Personality Questionnaire.* Unpublished manuscript, University of Minnesota, Minneapolis.

Tversky, A., & Kahneman, D. (1974). Judgment under uncertainty: Heuristics and biases. *Science, 185,* 1124–1131.

Van Peer, W. (1986). *Stylistics and psychology: Investigations of foregrounding.* London: Croom Helm.

Vaughn, L. A., Petkova, Z., Trudeau, L., Hesse, S., McCaffrey, N., Candeloro, L., et al. (2007, January). *Processing fluency and narrative transportation: Effects of accessibility and regulatory fit.* Poster pre-sented at Society for Personality and Social Psychology, Memphis, TN.

Wang, J., & Calder, B. J. (2006). Media transportation and advertising. *Journal of Consumer Research, 33,* 151–162.

Wilson, T. D., & Gilbert, D. T. (2005). Affective forecasting: Knowing what to want. *Current Directions in Psychological Science, 14,* 131–134.

Zunshine, L. (2006). *Why we read fiction: Theory of mind and the novel.* Columbus: Ohio State University Press.

Section V

Perspective Taking:
Simulating Other Minds

17 The Happiness of the Fish: Evidence for a Common Theory of One's Own and Others' Actions

Rebecca Saxe

Chuangtse and Hueitse had strolled onto the bridge over the Hao, when the former observed, "See how the small fish are darting about! That is the happiness of the fish." "You are not a fish yourself," said Hueitse. "How can you know the happiness of the fish?" "And you not being I," retorted Chuangtse, "how can you know that I do not know?"

Chuangtse, ca. 300 B.C.

INTRODUCTION

Through introspection, we feel that we have direct knowledge of the causes and goals of our own actions (cf. Nisbett & Wilson, 1977); understanding someone else's action seems by contrast like a highly abstract—if not semimiraculous entertainment-education–achievement. Simulation theories offer a demystification of the process: Knowledge of others is parasitic on our direct access to ourselves (Gallese, Keysers, & Rizzolatti, 2004; Rizzolatti, Fogassi, & Gallese, 2001). An observer can understand someone else's action using the same cognitive and neural mechanisms that he or she uses to produce his or her own—that is, by running his or her action execution system in a "simulation" mode (Nichols & Stich, 2003).

There is a fundamentally different sense in which we use the same mechanisms to understand others and ourselves. We explain and predict our own actions just like we understand other people's: by using a theory of how human minds work. So, the central simulationist claim that we use the "same mechanisms" for understanding our own and other people's actions may be true in at least two unrelated senses. The confusion arises because of two senses in which a person can "understand her own action" (Gopnik, 1993). In one sense, an actor "understands" all of his or her current, ongoing intentional actions. That is, when the person is acting rationally in pursuit of personal goals, the person has responsibility for his or her actions. However, there is another sense of understanding actions that involves being able to provide verbal reasons for or causes of that action (Malle, 2004). It is in the latter sense, and not the former, that representing and understanding one's own actions depends on a theory of mind.

In the current chapter, I therefore propose that among mechanisms for understanding human action, the cognitively relevant distinction is not between self and other but between action execution and perception on the one hand and action explanation and prediction on the other. Humans possess two distinct cognitive and neural mechanisms for representing actions: the sensorimotor mechanisms for planning, executing, and perceiving goal-directed actions on-line and distinct cognitive mechanisms for explaining and predicting actions in terms of a theory of mind. Both mechanisms can be applied to others' actions and to one's own. Evidence for the first mechanism is provided in other chapters of this book (e.g., Beilock & Lyons, Chapter 2; Decety & Stevens, Chapter 1). I review developmental, social psychological, and neuroscientific evidence for the second mechanism, theories of mind that are used to understand both other people's actions and one's own.

THEORIES APPLY TO SELF AND OTHER: DEVELOPMENTAL EVIDENCE

When the actor has a false belief, action predictions based on a conceptual theory of mind diverge most obviously from predictions based solely on facts about the local environment (Dennett, 1978). For this reason, many studies of theory of mind development require children to make action predictions given a false belief. In one basic design, a child watches while a puppet places a toy in location A. The puppet leaves the scene, and the toy is transferred to location B. The puppet returns, and the child is asked to predict where the puppet will look for the toy. Three-year-olds predict the puppet will look in location B, where the toy actually is; older children predict the puppet will look in location A, where the puppet last saw the toy (Wellman, Cross, & Watson, 2001; Wimmer & Perner, 1983).

The striking feature of this developmental pattern is not that 5-year-olds pass while 3-year-olds fail; performance on most tasks improves with age. What is notable is that the 3-year-olds who fail the false-belief task are not performing at chance or confused by the questions. They make systematic predictions, with high confidence (Ruffman, Garnham, Import, & Connolly, 2001).

These results have been described in terms of the development of a concept of belief (Wimmer & Perner, 1983). According to the mature concept, a belief is a constructed representation of the world. It is supposed to be true, and a determinant of the believer's actions, but having a correct belief depends on having current perceptual access or reliable sources of knowledge; when these are missing, beliefs can be partially or entirely false, causing predictable mistakes in action. By contrast, the younger children's theory of mind does not include a complete understanding of access and reliable sources (O'Neill, 1992) and so does not flexibly accommodate error and misrepresentation (Perner, 1991).

The traditional false-belief task is of course subject to other interpretations. For example, predictions based on false beliefs require children to inhibit the salient true state of affairs so developmental trends in prediction may reflect the development of domain-general inhibitory control (Carlson, Moses, & Claxton, 2004; Leslie, 2000; Moses, 2001). The interpretation of these results in terms of the development of a theory of mind therefore requires support from other methods; one approach is to focus on action explanation (e.g., why did the puppet look for the toy in location A?) (Bartch, Campbell, & Troseth, 2007; Hickling & Wellman, 2001) instead of action prediction.

Development of the ability to explain actions in terms of thought and beliefs is correlated with, and precedes, success in action prediction (Amsterlaw & Wellman, 2006). In general, children who fail to predict future actions based on false beliefs do not explain past actions in terms of false beliefs (Moses, 2001). Instead, they explain actions in terms of desires and other psychological states (Bartch et al., 2007). For example, Goodman et al. (2006) gave children the standard false-belief prediction task but then after the prediction showed children the character looking for the object in the opposite (unpredicted) location. Children were then asked to explain the character's actions. The content of these explanations was theoretically consistent with the child's original answer. The children who predicted that the character would look in the actual location (B) and then saw the character look in the original location (A, the "standard" outcome) explained this action by generating a novel desire (e.g., "well, that's where she wants to look") and not by appeal to the character's false belief. By contrast, children who predicted that the character would look in the original location (A) and then saw the character look in the actual location (B, the "psychic" outcome) explained this action by generating a novel source of access to the true location (e.g., "I think he heard his sister going over there"). Given these results, it would clearly be misleading to claim that 5-year-olds "have" a theory of mind whereas 3-year-olds do not have one (Bloom & German, 2000). The younger children's theory is coherent, but limited.

If children apply their theory of mind to explain and predict their own actions as well as those of others, then the same limitations should appear. Versions of the false-belief task have been developed to explicitly tap children's ability to attribute false beliefs to themselves. On direct tests, 3-year-olds do make the same systematic errors about their own past false beliefs as they make about false beliefs of other people (Gopnik, 1993; Gopnik & Astington, 1988). For example (Gopnik & Astington, 1988), children saw a candy box and then discovered that it was filled with pencils. They were then asked what they thought was in the box when they first saw it. The youngest children reported that they initially thought the box contained pencils and predicted that other people would think the box contained pencils; success on the first- and third-person versions was correlated (see also Epley & Caruso, Chapter 20).

These results are counterintuitive. We might expect children to just remember their previous thoughts and so to have qualitatively different, and better, access to the mental state explanations of their own actions than those of others. But, the evidence suggests that they do not.

In an elegant study, Atance and O'Neill (2004) gave 3-year-olds an opportunity to make plans and act based on a false belief. Then, immediately after the action, the children discovered the true state of affairs and were asked to explain their own immediately past action. On one trial, for example, the child was shown a crayon box and asked to say what she thought was inside. When she said "crayons," the experimenter pointed out a piece of paper and suggested the child retrieve the paper so she could draw with the crayons. Then, the box was opened to reveal candles. The child was asked what she initially thought was in the box, and consistent with prior work (Gopnik & Astington, 1988), most children said "candles." Amazingly, though, when asked to explain why they picked up the piece of paper, these children still failed to refer to their prior belief (saying instead, e.g., "Because there was [sic] no crayons," or "There it was on the floor").

Children's explanations of their own past actions thus show no benefit of direct recall or privileged access. Action understanding does not appear to develop from direct access to the "self" into inferential understanding of "others." The conceptual content is consistent, at a developmental stage, in explanations of both one's own and other people's actions. These results are best understood in terms of a common theory of one's own and other's minds. A similar lesson can be drawn from social psychological evidence in adults, to which I now turn.

SEEING THE SELF AS AN OTHER: SOCIAL PSYCHOLOGICAL EVIDENCE

Like children, adults explain and predict their past, future, and hypothetical actions using the same theory of mind that they use for other people. Because adults' theories are so much more robust than children's, though, the traces of theory use are fairly subtle. Nevertheless, by creating experimental situations in which the true explanation of a behavior is ambiguous (Bem, 1967), social psychologists have found systematic evidence that adults reconstruct the best explanation for their own past behavior from current evidence rather than introspecting and recalling the conscious experience of the event (Nisbett & Wilson, 1977).

Daryl Bem was the best-known advocate, in social psychology, of the view that adults infer the internal reasons for their actions from the externally observable evidence of the actions themselves. Consistent with the current argument, Bem proposed that "an individual's belief and attitude statements and the beliefs and attitudes that an outside observer would attribute to him are often functionally equivalent in that both sets of statements are 'inferences' from the same evidence" (Bem, 1965, p. 200).

Bem's self-perception theory was initially intended to provide an account of "cognitive dissonance" phenomena, in which a person's self-attribution of beliefs and attitudes is influenced by the person's perception of their own actions. One example is "spreading of alternatives": After they are forced to choose between two good options, people subsequently rate the chosen alternative more favorably and derogate the unchosen option (Festinger, 1957). A more counterintuitive instance is the forced compliance effect. After participants comply with a request to do an action that does not fit well with their prior beliefs and attitudes (e.g., describe a boring task as interesting or write a speech for a political position they do not hold), and only if there was apparently little external pressure compelling the action (e.g., they were apparently given a choice whether to act and very little monetary reward for acting), participants changed their reported attitude, claiming that they found the task less boring or that they agreed more with the political position (for a review, see Olson & Stone, 2005). Bem explained these results in terms of self-perception theory. On observing themselves making a choice or voluntarily acting without a reward, participants made the same inference that an outside observer would make: that they must really have preferred the chosen option or found the task interesting.

More recently, social psychologists have directly manipulated the observable consequences of the participants' actions. Again, people's subsequent explanations followed the observable evidence, rather than any direct internal access to the causes of their own behavior. For example, Johansson, Hall, Sikström, and Olsson (2005) showed participants two pictures and asked them to pick the more attractive one. The participants were given the chosen photo and then asked to explain their choice. Through a sleight of hand, the experimenters sometimes gave the participant their actual choice but sometimes gave the opposite picture. In all, participants detected the swap very rarely. Remarkably, the justifications that participants gave for choosing the swapped photograph (which they did not choose) were largely indistinguishable from justifications they gave for choosing the one that they did choose in length, confidence, emotionality, detail, or number of embarrassed laughs. Participants' own explanations appeared to operate much the way an external observer's would, by finding the property of the outcome that could have justified choosing it rather than by recalling the moment of the choice (seconds earlier) and directly reexperiencing those reasons. Similarly, Evans (1989) asked participants to first solve a problem and then retrospectively explain their reasoning processes. Participants made systematic errors in the explanations that were predicted by their theories of reasoning rather than by the actual reasoning they had just completed.

Attributions to past and future selves are not just distorted; they are also qualitatively similar to attributions to other people (Robinson & Clore, 2002; Trope & Lieberman, 2003). For example, other people's actions are ascribed to stable traits, whereas one's own actions are generally seen as variable and situation dependent (Jones & Nisbett, 1972). A past or future self, however, is just like another person in this respect: Past and future selves are characterized in terms of stable traits (both positive and negative) just as often as past or present other people are and significantly more often than the present self (Pronin & Ross, 2006).

In sum, social psychological evidence, like the developmental evidence reviewed, suggests that the mechanisms people use for understanding action are not divided between direct access to the self and inferential understanding of others. Instead, the relevant distinction is that between mechanisms for action execution and theories for action explanation, each of which is applied both to other people and to oneself (in this volume, see also Batson, Chapter 18; Epley & Caruso, Chapter 20; Myers & Hodges, Chapter 19). Functional neuroimaging has begun to offer a third converging line of evidence for the importance of this distinction.

Brain Regions for Theory of Mind: Neuroscientific Evidence

The current section describes brain imaging evidence for three claims: (a) There are brain regions implicated specifically in explaining actions in terms of mental state causes (theory of mind); (b) these brain regions are distinct from those implicated in action execution and action perception; and (c) these same brain regions are used for attributing mental states to oneself. To date, there is much more detailed evidence for the first of these claims than for the second and third; these will be important topics for future research.

The first step toward understanding the neural basis of a higher-level cognitive function, like theory of mind, is to identify candidate brain regions that may be involved in the operation of that function. Some hypotheses may come from lesion studies (e.g., Broca's and Wernicke's areas) or from animal models (e.g., V1). For higher cognitive functions, though, animal models are not available, so hypotheses about region-function links come from early imaging studies using simple subtraction analyses (e.g., for theory of mind, see Gallagher et al., 2000). The logic of subtraction analyses is as follows: (a) Assume that to perform a complex, high-level task, participants must use many interacting cognitive mechanisms (and therefore many brain regions). (b) Most of these mechanisms are used for general aspects of task performance, like perceiving the stimuli and producing the response, but some of the processing corresponds to the cognitive mechanism under investigation—in this case, the representation of a mental state. (c) The goal is therefore to find a second task that demands all of the same general processing, with one key difference—in this case, there is no need to think about mental states.

Following developmental psychology, early neuroimaging investigations of theory of mind used false beliefs conveyed in stories or cartoons (e.g., Gallagher et al., 2000; Saxe & Kanwisher, 2003). A reliable group of brain regions was implicated in the "false-belief" condition (relative to a variety of control conditions, described next), including right and left temporoparietal junction (right and left TPJ), medial parietal cortex (including posterior cingulate and precuneus), and medial prefrontal cortex (MPFC; not including anterior cingulate cortex). Of these regions, the region in the right TPJ appears to be most selectively recruited for thinking about thoughts relative to controls both for the logical demands and for the social content of the task. The closest control condition for the logical demands of the standard false-belief task is the "false-sign" task. In the false-sign task, participants read (or hear) about a sign or map that is constructed, and then the reality changes, rendering the sign or map out of date. For example, a sign is supposed to point to the current location of an ice cream van, but the van moves, and the ice cream man forgets to change the sign; or, a map is made of the locations of all the toys in a room, and then one toy is moved. As in the false-belief task, participants can then be asked about the true state of affairs (where the toy really is) or about the content of the representation (where the toy is in the map). In development, performance on false-signs tasks is highly correlated with performance on false-belief tasks (Sabbagh, Moses, & Shiverick, 2006).

The false-sign task therefore provides an excellent control condition for a subtraction analysis. Any brain region recruited more during false-belief tasks than during false-sign tasks must play a specific role in thinking about people or mental states. Perner, Aichhorn, Kronbichler, Wolfgang, and Laddurner (2006) had participants read four kinds of vignettes describing false beliefs, false signs, outdated photographs (Saxe & Kanwisher, 2003; Zaitchik, 1990), and changes in reality over time. The right TPJ showed a significantly higher response for the false beliefs than for false signs but did not differentiate false signs (which involved the logic of false representations) from temporal change stories (which did not). These results suggest that the role of the right TPJ was specific to social/belief components of the false-belief task rather than the other, more general processing demands of performing the task.

In a study from my own lab, we tested an alternative minimal-pair control task. A standard false-belief task could be solved without considering beliefs by using simple rules (Povinelli & Vonk, 2003; Bloom & German 2000) (e.g., when asked where the puppet thinks the object is, point to the object's location when the puppet was last facing it). While still posing complex demands on spatial and temporal memory, these rules would not refer to beliefs or to any mental or social properties. To investigate the neural mechanisms specific to theory of mind, we (Saxe, Schulz, & Jiang, 2006) therefore induced participants to perform a false-belief task by following a nonsocial stimulus-response rule. The stimuli were short animated films of a girl and a chocolate bar that moved between two boxes. One set of task instructions (the algorithm rule) instructed participants to use the girl's facing direction at the end of the trial (away from the boxes vs. toward the boxes) as an arbitrary cue to attend to the chocolate's first, or last, location. The other set of instructions (the theory of mind rule) asked participants to identify "where the girl thinks the chocolate bar is." For any combination of the girl's position and box location, these two rules generated the same response. When participants used the algorithm rule, only domain-general brain regions (e.g., intraparietal sulcus, inferior frontal gyrus) were recruited. On the other hand, the right TPJ was recruited specifically when participants were thinking about the girl's thoughts.

We have also observed that the right TPJ response is specific to thinking about thoughts relative to thinking about other facts about people. In one study (Saxe & Powell, 2006), we used stories from three conditions, each highlighting a different aspect of reasoning about another person: (a) "Appearance" stories that described representing socially relevant information about a person that is visible from the outside; (b) "bodily sensations" stories that elicited attribution of subjective states that do not include representational content, like hunger and tiredness; and (c) "thoughts" stories that described the contents of another person's thoughts. The right TPJ showed a significantly greater response to the thoughts stories than to the appearance and bodily sensations stories, which did not differ from each other or from fixation. In another study (Saxe & Wexler, 2005), we presented two facts about each character in sequence: the character's social background and the character's belief or desire. The timing of the response in the right TPJ was precisely dependent on the timing of belief information: When the background information was presented for 6 s before a belief was described, the response in the right TPJ was delayed 6 s.

Across studies, then, the right TPJ appears to be recruited whenever the participant is required to think about someone else's belief. Belief attribution can be elicited in at least three different ways: (a) explicitly, when the participant reads a verbal sentence that simply states a character's beliefs (e.g., Saxe & Powell, 2006); (b) by directing participants to consider a character's beliefs in the task instructions (e.g., Saxe et al., 2006); or (c) by asking participants to predict the actions of a character who has an inferable false belief (e.g., Sommer et al., 2007). Action prediction based on true beliefs, however, need not involve any consideration of the character's beliefs (Dennett, 1978). This analysis may explain an apparent contradiction in the literature. Sommer et al. used a nonverbal action prediction task modeled on the developmental psychologists' false-belief task and found more recruitment of right TPJ for false- than for true-belief trials. Apperly et al. (Apperly, Riggs, Simpson, Chiavarino, & Samson, 2006) found that subjects hold on to belief information in this kind of task only while that information is strictly necessary (i.e., when the character is holding a false belief and that belief is relevant for the subject's own task performance). By contrast, using verbal stories and explicit belief statements, Young, Cushman, Hauser, and Saxe (2007) found no difference in the response of right TPJ to true versus false beliefs.

Importantly, the theory of mind brain regions—including the regions in the right and left TPJ and in the medial prefrontal and precuneus—are completely distinct, anatomically, from the brain regions implicated in action execution or action perception (Rizzolatti et al., 2001). Many neuroimaging studies, inspired by simulation theories, have focused on the overlapping activation during action perception and action execution, of ventral premotor cortex, inferior frontal gyrus, and right inferior parietal cortex (e.g., Buccino, Binkofski, & Riggio, 2004; Grezes, Armony, Rowe, & Passingham, 2003; Molnar-Szakacs, Kaplan, Greenfield, & Iacoboni, 2006; Vogt & Thomaschke, 2007). By contrast, the regions implicated in theory of mind have no known role in motor planning or action execution. Instead, these regions are among the latest maturing parts of "association" cortex (Gogtay et al., 2004).

Although the two groups of regions are clearly anatomically segregated, their functional properties have not yet been investigated within a common task. Future work should investigate tasks in which action execution and action explanation are invoked to allow for a direct functional dissociation between these mechanisms.

Research into the neural substrates for explaining one's own past actions is also lacking. The key prediction of the current chapter is that the brain regions that are implicated in theory of mind for others (a) would not be recruited while participants actually acted or reasoned based on a false belief but (b) would be recruited when the same participants subsequently explained those actions in terms of false beliefs. The ideal experimental design would thus be an adult version of that presented by Atance and O'Neil (2004): Participants should be induced to believe and act on one idea, then learn the truth and be asked to explain their previous actions. Nothing like this design has yet been used with neuroimaging.

One related study has been conducted, and the results are promising. Vogeley et al. (2001) had participants read short verbal stories about a protagonist; half of the stories described actions and thoughts in the second person (e.g., "In the morning, when you leave the hotel, the sky is blue and the sun is shining, so you do not expect it to start raining"). Because these stories describe nonactual events and actions, the participants could not directly experience the narrated thoughts and plans; instead, the participants must have interpreted these as the thoughts and actions of a hypothetical self. These stories should therefore recruit the same brain regions as are implicated in theory of mind for others. Just as predicted, these second-person stories elicited a significant response (relative to a scrambled baseline) in the right TPJ. If anything, the stories in the second person elicited a significantly higher response in theory of mind regions than did the same stories in the third person (Vogeley et al., 2001).

CONCLUSIONS

Brain imaging results thus converge with those from both developmental and social psychology, suggesting that a common theory of mind is used for explaining both other people's actions and one's own (in this volume, see also Batson, Chapter 18; Epley & Caruso, Chapter 20; Myers & Hodges, Chapter 19). Theory of mind is therefore an instance of a "common mechanism" for representing actions by the self and others. Nevertheless, the theory of mind is a fundamentally different kind of shared mechanism from those usually envisioned in simulation theory. First, theory of mind is invoked when providing reasons for actions but not when choosing or executing actions. Second, access to the reasons for one's own actions is not qualitatively privileged. The clearest behavioral consequences of theory use result from the theories' limitations; especially in young children, these limitations apply equally to explanations of one's own actions and those of other people. Importantly, though, theory of mind is used in action explanation across a wide range of contexts: for true and false beliefs and when the theory is accurate as well as inaccurate. These "correct" applications of the theory are hard to detect behaviorally and are therefore an important target for future studies using functional neuroimaging.

REFERENCES

Amsterlaw, J., & Wellman, H. M. (2006). Theories of mind in transition: A microgenetic study of the development of false belief understanding. *Journal of Cognition and Development, 7,* 139.

Apperly, I. A., Riggs, K. J., Simpson, A., Chiavarino, C., & Samson, D. (2006). Is belief reasoning automatic? *Psychological Science, 17,* 841–844.

Atance, C. M., & O'Neill, D. K. (2004). Acting and planning on the basis of a false belief: Its effects on 3-year-old children's reasoning about their own false beliefs. *Developmental Psychology, 40,* 953–964.

Bartch, K., Campbell., M. D., & Troseth, G. L. (2007). Why else does Jenny run? Young children's extended psychological explanations. *Journal of Cognition and Development, 8,* 33.

Bem, D. J. (1965). An experimental analysis of self-persuasion. *Journal of Experimental Social Psychology, 1*(3), 199–218.

Bloom, P., & German, T. P. (2000). Two reasons to abandon the false belief task as a test of theory of mind. *Cognition, 77,* 25–31.

Buccino, G., Binkofski, F., & Riggio, L. (2004). The mirror neuron system and action recognition. *Brain and Language, 89,* 370–376.

Carlson, S. M., Moses, L. J., & Claxton, L. J. (2004). Individual differences in executive functioning and theory of mind: An investigation of inhibitory control and planning ability. *Journal of Experimental Child Psychology, 87,* 299–319.

Dennett, D. (1978). Beliefs about beliefs. *Behavioral and Brain Science, 1,* 568–570.

Evans, J. S. B. T. (1989). *Bias in human reasoning: Causes and consequences.* Hove, UK and Hillsdale, NJ: Erlbaum.

Festinger, L. (1957). *A theory of cognitive dissonance.* Stanford, CA: Stanford, University Press.

Gallagher, H. L., Happe, F., Brunswick, N., Fletcher, P. C., Frith, U., & Frith, C. D. (2000). Reading the mind in cartoons and stories: An fMRI study of "theory of mind" in verbal and nonverbal tasks. *Neuropsychologia, 38,* 11–21.

Gallese, V., Keysers, C., & Rizzolatti, G. (2004). A unifying view of the basis of social cognition. *Trends in Cognitive Science, 8,* 396–403.

Gogtay, N., Giedd, J. N., Lusk, L., Hayashi, K. M., Greenstein, D., Vaituzis, A. C., et al. (2004). Dynamic mapping of human cortical development during childhood through early adulthood. *Proceedings of the National Academy of Science of the United States of America, 101,* 8174–8179.

Goodman, N. D., Baker, C. L., Bonawitz, E. B., Mansinghka, V. K., Gopnik, A., Wellman, H., et al. (2006). *Intuitive theories of mind: A rational approach to false belief.* Paper presented at the Proceedings of the 28th Annual Conference of the Cognitive Science Society, Vancouver, Canada. July 2006.

Gopnik, A. (1993). How we know our minds: The illusion of first-person knowledge of intentionality. *Behavioral and Brain Sciences, 16,* 1–14.

Gopnik, A., & Astington, J. W. (1988). Children's understanding of representational change and its relation to the understanding of false belief and the appearance-reality distinction. *Child Development, 59,* 26–37.

Grezes, J., Armony, J. L., Rowe, J., & Passingham, R. E. (2003). Activations related to "mirror" and "canonical" neurones in the human brain: An fMRI study. *Neuroimage, 18,* 928–937.

Hickling, A. K., & Wellman, H. M. (2001). The emergence of children's causal explanations and theories: Evidence from everyday conversation. *Developmental Psychology, 37,* 668–683.

Johansson, P., Hall, L., Sikström, S., & Olsson, A. (2005). Failure to detect mismatches between intention and outcome in a simple decision task. *Science, 210,* 116.

Jones, E. E., & Nisbett, R.E. (1972). The actor and the observer: Divergent perceptions of the cause of behavior. In E. E. Jones, H. H. Kelley, S. Valins, & B. Weiner (Eds.), *Attribution: Perceiving the causes of behavior* (pp. 79–94). Morristown, NJ: General Learning Press.

Leslie, A. (2000). "Theory of mind" as a mechanism of selective attention. In M. Gazzaniga (Ed.), *The new cognitive neurosciences* (2nd ed., pp. 1235–1247). Cambridge, MA: MIT Press.

Malle, B. F. (2004). *How the mind explains behavior: Folk explanations, meaning, and social interaction.* Cambridge, MA: MIT Press.

Molnar-Szakacs, I., Kaplan, J., Greenfield, P. M., & Iacoboni, M. (2006). Observing complex action sequences: The role of the fronto-parietal mirror neuron system. *Neuroimage, 33,* 923–935.

Moses, L. J. (2001). Executive accounts of theory-of-mind development. *Child Development, 72,* 688–690.

Nichols, S., & Stich, S. (2003). *Mindreading: An integrated account of pretence, self-awareness, and understanding of other minds.* New York: Oxford University Press.

Nisbett, R. E., & Wilson, T. D. (1977). The halo effect: Evidence for unconscious alteration of judgments. *Journal of Personality and Social Psychology, 35,* 250–256.

Olson, J., & Stone, J. (2005). The influence of behavior on attitudes. In D. Albarracin, B. Johnson, & M. P. Zanna (Eds.), *The handbook of attitudes* (pp. 223–272): Routledge.

O'Neill, D. K. (1992). Young children's understanding of the role that the sensory experiences play in knowledge acquisition. *Child Development, 63,* 474–491.

Perner, J. (1991). *Understanding the representational mind.* Cambridge, MA: MIT Press.

Perner, J., Aichhorn, M., Kronbichler, M., Wolfgang, S., & Laddurner, G. (2006). Thinking of mental and other representations: The roles of left and right temporo-parietal junction. *Social Neuroscience, 1,* 235–2258.

Povinelli, D. J., & Vonk, J. (2003). Chimpanzee minds: Suspiciously human? *Trends in Cognitive Science, 7,* 157–160.

Pronin, E., & Ross, L. (2006). Temporal differences in trait self-ascription: When the self is seen as an other. *Journal of Personality and Social Psychology, 90,* 197–209.

Rizzolatti, G., Fogassi, L., & Gallese, V. (2001). Neurophysiological mechanisms underlying the understanding and imitation of action. *Nature Reviews Neuroscience, 2,* 661–670.

Robinson, M. D., & Clore, G. L. (2002). Belief and feeling: Evidence for an accessibility model of emotional self-report. *Psychological Bulletin, 128,* 934–960.

Ruffman, T., Garnham, W., Import, A., & Connolly, D. (2001). Does eye gaze indicate implicit knowledge of false belief? Charting transitions in knowledge. *Journal of Experimental Child Psychology, 80,* 201–224.

Sabbagh, M. A., Moses, L. J., & Shiverick, S. (2006). Executive functioning and preschoolers' understanding of false beliefs, false photographs, and false signs. *Child Development, 77*, 1034–1049.

Saxe, R., & Kanwisher, N. (2003). People thinking about thinking people. The role of the temporo-parietal junction in "theory of mind." *Neuroimage, 19*, 1835–1842.

Saxe, R., & Powell, L. J. (2006). It's the thought that counts: Specific brain regions for one component of theory of mind. *Psychological Science, 17*, 692–699.

Saxe, R., Schulz, L., & Jiang, Y. (2006). Reading minds versus following rules: Dissociating theory of mind and executive control in the brain. *Social Neuroscience, 1*, 284–298.

Saxe, R., & Wexler, A. (2005). Making sense of another mind: The role of the right temporo-parietal junction. *Neuropsychologia, 43*, 1391–1399.

Sommer, M., Dohnel, K., Sodian, B., Meinhardt, J., Thoermer, C., & Hajak, G. (2007). Neural correlates of true and false belief reasoning. *Neuroimage, 35*, 1378–1384.

Trope, Y., & Lieberman, N. (2003). Temporal construal. *Psychological Review, 110*, 403–421.

Vogeley, K., Bussfeld, P., Newen, A., Herrmann, S., Happe, F., Falkai, P., et al. (2001). Mind reading: Neural mechanisms of theory of mind and self-perspective. *Neuroimage, 14*, 170–181.

Vogt, S., & Thomaschke, R. (2007). From visuo-motor interactions to imitation learning: Behavioural and brain imaging studies. *Journal of Sports Science, 25*, 497–517.

Wellman, H. M., Cross, D., & Watson, J. (2001). Meta-analysis of theory-of-mind development: The truth about false belief. *Child Development, 72*, 655–684.

Wimmer, H., & Perner, J. (1983). Beliefs about beliefs: representation and constraining function of wrong beliefs in young children's understanding of deception. *Cognition, 13*, 103–128.

Young, L., Cushman, F., Hauser, M., & Saxe, R. (2007). The neural basis of the interaction between theory of mind and moral judgment. *Proceedings of the National Academy of Science of the United States of America, 104*, 8235–8240.

Zaitchik, D. (1990). When representations conflict with reality: The preschooler's problem with false beliefs and "false" photographs. *Cognition, 35*, 41–68.

18 Two Forms of Perspective Taking: Imagining How Another Feels and Imagining How You Would Feel

C. Daniel Batson

INTRODUCTION

Encounter a stranger in need and, sometimes, you will feel empathic concern—an other-oriented emotional response evoked by and congruent with the perceived welfare of that person. What determines whether you will? Perhaps the most common answer among psychologists is that empathic concern is felt when you adopt the perspective of the person in need (see Batson, 1987; Davis, 1994; Stotland, 1969). But in this answer, what is meant by adopting the person's perspective? First, it is an act of imagination. One does not literally take another person's place or look through his or her eyes. One imagines how things look from the other's point of view. Second, it is not the same as perspective taking in the symbolic-interaction tradition (e.g., Mead, 1934). In that tradition, one adopts the perspective of another—often a significant other—to imaginatively see oneself through the other's eyes (and values). The perspective taking that evokes empathic concern involves imaginatively perceiving the other's situation, not oneself.

TWO WAYS OF PERCEIVING THE OTHER'S SITUATION

There are, however, two different ways of perceiving the other's situation, and these are often confused. First, you can imagine how another person sees his or her situation and feels as a result (an *imagine-other perspective*). Second, you can imagine how you would see the situation were you in the other person's position and how you would feel as a result (an *imagine-self perspective*).

IMAGINE-OTHER PERSPECTIVE

What I am calling an imagine-other perspective involves more than simply inferring the other's internal state. Goldie (1999) described it as "imagining the enactment of a narrative from that other person's point of view" (p. 397). Barrett-Lennard (1981) spoke of an "empathic attentional set"—"a process of feeling into, in which Person A opens him- or herself in a deeply responsive way to Person B's feelings and experiencing but without losing awareness that B is a distinct other self" (p. 92). At issue are both a conception of the feelings and thoughts of the other and how one is affected by this conception. It is a process of "responsively knowing" (Barrett-Lennard, 1981, p. 92). One imagines the effect of the situation on the other given the other's needs and desires. The result is not simply understanding, but *sensitive* understanding. It is this form of perspective taking that has been claimed to evoke other-oriented empathic concern (Batson, 1987, 1991).

IMAGINE-SELF PERSPECTIVE

An imagine-self perspective involves, in Adam Smith's (1759/1853) colorful phrase, "changing places in fancy." It has also been called "mental simulation" (Goldman, 1992; Gordon, 1992). Especially when the other's situation is unfamiliar or unclear, imagining how you would feel in that situation may provide a useful, possibly essential, basis for sensitive understanding of the other's plight. It may provide a stepping-stone to imagining how the other is affected by his or her situation and so to empathic concern. But if the other differs from you, then although focusing on how you would think and feel in the other's situation may provide comparative context, it also may prove misleading (Hygge, 1976; Jarymowicz, 1992).

When the other's situation is familiar or clear, imagining how you would feel in that situation may not be needed for sensitive understanding and may even inhibit it (Nickerson, 1999). Hearing that a friend was recently "dumped" by a romantic partner may remind you of your own experience last year when you suffered the same fate. You may get so caught up in reliving your own experience that you fail to appreciate your friend's pain. Especially if you found it easy to rebound, you may contrast your own experience to that of your friend, who is struggling. Rather than sensitive understanding and empathic concern, you may respond with impatience and judgment.

The role of an imagine-self perspective in evoking empathic concern is, then, indirect at best. At times, it serves as a stepping-stone on the way to the imagine-other perspective that evokes empathy. At other times, it may inhibit the adoption of an imagine-other perspective and thereby inhibit empathy.

The distinction between these two forms of perspective taking (imagine-other, imagine-self) has often been ignored in social-psychological discussions of perspective taking. It has been assumed that the psychological process involved and the effects of each form are essentially the same (cf., Aderman, Brehm, & Katz, 1974; Davis, 1994; Davis, Conklin, Smith, & Luce, 1996; Galinsky & Moskowitz, 2000; Lerner, 1980). However, empirical evidence suggests that there is good reason to doubt this assumption. In this chapter, I provide an overview of evidence that reveals important differences between these two perspectives on another's situation. Then, I suggest some implications of this distinction for current social-psychological research on perspective taking by considering some different reasons for adopting another person's perspective.

EMPIRICAL EVIDENCE

EMOTIONAL DIFFERENCES

In his pioneering research on empathy, Stotland (1969) found that both an imagine-other and an imagine-self perspective led to more physiological arousal and self-reported emotion than did simply attending carefully to the other's behavior—an *objective perspective*. (This distinction of both forms of perspective taking from an objective perspective makes clear that each form involves more than focusing attention on the other; an objective perspective is as focused on the other and the other's situation as is either an imagine-other or imagine-self perspective.)

Stotland also found that the physiological and self-report effects of an imagine-other and an imagine-self perspective were not the same. When observing a young man undergo what they thought was a painful diathermy experience, participants asked to adopt an imagine-other perspective showed more vasoconstriction, which Stotland (1969) interpreted as evidence that they "were reacting to the feelings they perceived the model as having at a given moment" (p. 296). In contrast, participants asked to adopt an imagine-self perspective showed more palmar sweat and reported feeling more tension and nervousness, which Stotland interpreted as evidence that their emotional reactions were more self-oriented and "not quite so tied to the experience of the model" (p. 297).

Distinguishing Empathic Concern From Personal Distress

Since the time of Stotland's (1969) research, two distinct emotional reactions to another in need have been identified: empathic concern and personal distress. Factor analyses have shown that in response to another's relatively severe, unexpected distress—especially physical distress or pain—ratings of sympathetic, softhearted, warm, compassionate, tender, and moved typically load highly on one factor, whereas ratings of alarmed, grieved, troubled, distressed, upset, disturbed, worried, and perturbed typically load highly on a second, orthogonal factor (see Batson, 1987). The first factor, labeled *empathic concern*, seems to reflect an other-oriented emotional response congruent with the perceived plight of the person in need; it taps feeling *for* the other. The second factor, labeled *personal distress*, seems to reflect a self-oriented aversive emotional response; it taps *direct* feelings of discomfort evoked by witnessing the plight of the other.

A Complication: Two Types of Distress

Reports of distress at encountering a person in need have also highlighted a measurement problem. The distress adjectives (distressed, upset, grieved, and so on) can be interpreted differently depending on context. When people unexpectedly encounter another experiencing relatively severe physical discomfort or pain, most interpret the adjectives in terms of the direct, personal distress they feel as a result of witnessing the other's suffering. When people encounter another experiencing less-acute psychological discomfort (e.g., sorrow, loneliness), most interpret the adjectives in terms of feelings of distress *for* the person in need (see Batson et al., 1988, 1989, 1991). The latter feelings might be called *empathic distress* because they reflect other-oriented empathic concern, not self-oriented personal distress.

A Test

Linking Stotland's (1969) findings and the distinction between empathic concern (including empathic distress) and personal distress, Batson, Early, and Salvarani (1997) predicted distinct emotional effects of the two perspectives when encountering a person in psychological discomfort. They suggested that an imagine-other perspective would evoke empathic concern, whereas an imagine-self perspective would evoke both empathic concern and personal distress. Symmetry might seem to dictate that an imagine-self perspective evoke only personal distress, not empathic concern, but Batson, Early, and Salvarani (1997) did not expect so neat a pattern. Imagining yourself in a psychologically distressing situation may lead you to feel personal distress or sorrow. It may do more, however. Especially when responding to a situation that is relatively unfamiliar and in which the other's feelings are not obvious, imagining yourself in that situation may be an important source of information about how the other feels (Goldman, 1992; Nickerson, 1999; Van Boven & Lowenstein, 2003). As suggested, this information may serve as a stepping-stone to imagining how the other feels and hence to feelings of empathic concern (including feelings of distress or sorrow *for* the other).

Batson, Early, and Salvarani (1997) tested these predictions by having undergraduate research participants listen to a (bogus) pilot radio interview with Katie Banks, a senior at the university struggling to care for her younger brother and sister after her parents were killed in an auto accident. Participants were randomly assigned to one of three perspective conditions prior to hearing the broadcast—imagine-other, imagine-self, and objective. Listening instructions for participants in the imagine-other condition were as follows:

> While you are listening to this broadcast, try to *imagine how the person being interviewed feels about what has happened and how it has affected his or her life*. Try not to concern yourself with attending to all the information presented. Just concentrate on trying to imagine how the person interviewed in the broadcast feels.

Instructions for participants in the imagine-self condition were as follows:

... try to *imagine how you yourself would feel if you were experiencing what has happened to the person being interviewed and how this experience would affect your life.* Try not to concern yourself with attending to all the information presented. Just concentrate on trying to imagine how you yourself would feel.

The following were the instructions for participants in the objective condition:

... try to *be as objective as possible about what has happened to the person interviewed and how it has affected his or her life.* To remain objective, do not let yourself get caught up in imagining what this person has been through and how he or she feels as a result. Just try to remain objective and detached.

Once they listened to the interview with Katie, participants completed a reaction questionnaire. Part 1 of this questionnaire listed 26 adjectives describing different emotional states, including those found in past research to load on the empathic concern and personal distress factors. Part 2 assessed whether distress reported in Part 1 was direct, personal distress or empathic distress. Instructions explained that a number of the emotions rated in Part 1 could be experienced in different ways. "You can feel *directly distressed*, as you might when you have a bad experience. ... You can be *distressed for* someone else who has a bad experience, as when a person suffers a broken relationship or fails to succeed on a task. Each of these emotions may be described as distress, but they are different types of distress." Participants were then asked to indicate the degree they experienced each of these types of response for four of the distress emotions rated previously: distressed, upset, troubled, and grieved.

Batson et al. (1997) assumed that when responding to Katie's plight, which involved clear distress but not immediate physical pain, an imagine-other perspective would lead to empathic distress for her. They assumed that an imagine-self perspective would lead to a mix of empathic distress and personal distress. Although not all comparisons were statistically reliable, the emotions patterned as predicted. Participants instructed to imagine how Katie felt (imagine-other perspective) reported more empathy than distress and more empathy than did participants instructed to remain objective. When asked about the nature of their distress, these participants reported a relatively high level of empathic distress for Katie and a relatively low level of direct distress. In contrast, participants instructed to imagine how they would feel in Katie's situation (imagine-self perspective) reported high levels of both empathy and distress, more of each than was reported by participants instructed to remain objective. Regarding the nature of their distress, these participants reported high levels of both empathic distress for Katie and direct, personal distress.

These results seem quite consistent with Stotland's (1969) results. Recall that he found an imagine-other perspective produced vasoconstriction, which reflected observers' other-oriented concern evoked by "the feelings they perceived the model as having at a given moment," whereas an imagine-self perspective produced palmar sweat, which reflected a more self-oriented tension "not quite so tied to the experience of the model." These results are also consistent with those of Schoenrade (1981); her participants (who heard about another in psychological distress) reported relatively high empathic concern in an imagine-other condition and high levels of both empathic concern and distress in an imagine-self condition.

COGNITIVE DIFFERENCES

Davis et al. (2004, Experiment 1) used a thought-listing procedure to assess cognitive effects of the two forms of perspective taking. They randomly assigned undergraduate research participants to one of four perspective conditions: imagine-other, imagine-self (instructions in these two conditions were similar to those used by Batson et al., 1997), observe-the-other's-behavior, or watch-naturally. Participants then watched a 150-s video segment of a talk show interview with a woman named Jackie, who had serious kidney problems. As Jackie spoke about her physical weakness and experience with dialysis, she began to cry. After seeing the video, participants were asked to write down all thoughts that had occurred to them as they watched. Davis et al. then coded the thoughts into one of four categories: (a) target-related (imagine Jackie's experiences and reactions; other-oriented emotion felt for Jackie [e.g., sympathy]; positive sentiment for Jackie [e.g., admiration]); (b) self-related (imagine oneself in Jackie's situation; identification of self with her; or recall of past personal experience); (c) distancing (differentiation of self from Jackie; negative assessment of her [e.g., irritation]; focus on Jackie's physical appearance or behavior); and (d) other (self-oriented emotion [e.g., personal distress]; recall of third-party past experience; recall of other information; extraneous thoughts [e.g., lunch]).

Davis et al. (2004) found that participants in the imagine-other condition reported both more target-related thoughts and fewer self-related thoughts than did participants in the imagine-self condition ($p < .01$ for each comparison). This pattern of results, which replicated the pattern found in a preliminary study using the same interview with Jackie, was quite consistent with the results for other-oriented and self-oriented emotions (empathic concern; personal distress) found in the two perspective conditions by Batson et al. (1997). The pattern suggested that in response to Jackie, who presented clear information about her situation and reaction to it, an imagine-self perspective was not required as a stepping-stone to an imagine-other perspective. Rather, an imagine-self perspective seemed to inhibit other-oriented thoughts and feelings.

Participants asked to watch naturally responded much as those asked to imagine Jackie's feelings, which suggests that in response to a sympathetically presented person in clear need, most people naturally adopt an imagine-other perspective. Finally, as might be expected, participants asked to observe Jackie's behavior reported more distancing thoughts than did participants in any of the other three conditions.

Davis et al. (2004) conducted a second experiment and found different results. The difference is instructive. In their second experiment, participants watched a relatively bland video interview in which Lisa, an average student with no particular need, talked about her experiences at college. A new measure of self-related thoughts suggested that participants in both perspective conditions had more self-related thoughts than did participants instructed to remain objective. One ready explanation for the different results is that in Experiment 2, with no clear need or strong reactions, participants who were instructed to imagine Lisa's feelings found they had to imagine themselves in her situation as a stepping-stone, producing more self-related thoughts. This explanation could also account for the lack of difference produced by imagine-other and imagine-self perspectives in an earlier experiment reported by Davis et al. (1996, Experiment 1), which used the same Lisa tape.

NEUROPHYSIOLOGICAL DIFFERENCES

Research reviewed thus far suggests that, when confronted with a person in clear distress, an imagine-other and an imagine-self perspective each produce emotional response, with the former producing other-related thoughts and relatively pure empathic concern (including empathic distress) and the latter producing self-related thoughts and direct personal distress. If this is true, then both perspectives should lead to increased hemodynamic activity in regions of the brain associated with the affective experience of concern, distress, or pain. Further, if these two perspectives are psychologically distinct in the way described, with (a) an imagine-other perspective involving sensitive attention to the plight of other and maintenance of clear self-other differentiation and (b) an imagine-self perspective involving projection of oneself into the other's situation, then the two perspectives should lead to differences in hemodynamic activity in areas associated with self-other differentiation.

Three neuroimaging studies by Jean Decety and colleagues provide data consistent with each of these two predictions. First, Ruby and Decety (2004) had research participants imagine a number of possible life situations that would induce various emotions (e.g., shame, guilt, pride), as well as situations that were emotionally neutral. For example, one emotion-inducing situation was to imagine that someone opens the door of a toilet stall in which you are sitting after you forget to lock the door. Across trials, participants were asked either to imagine how they would feel were they in the situation or to imagine how their mother would feel were she in the situation. One might consider these two conditions to involve an imagine-self perspective and an imagine-(m)other perspective, respectively. (However, note that this imagine-self perspective simply requires participants to imagine themselves in a situation, not to imagine themselves in another person's situation.)

In both the imagine-self and imagine-mother conditions, neuroimagining scans (functional magnetic resonance imaging, fMRI) revealed activation of cortical regions involved in the experience of emotion, such as the amygdala and temporal poles. In addition, in the imagine-mother condition there was increased activation of regions critical for distinguishing the self from the other and for distinguishing self-agency from other-agency. These regions included the right inferior parietal lobule or right temporoparietal junction (TPJ), the ventromedial (and medial) prefrontal cortex, and the posterior cingulate cortex.

This pattern of results is what we would expect if both the imagine-self and imagine-mother conditions produced emotion, the former producing direct distress and the latter producing empathic distress (distress for one's mother). It is also what we would expect if the imagine-mother perspective involved self-other differentiation, whereas the imagine-self perspective did not.

Ruby and Decety's (2004) results parallel those of Singer et al. (2004), with one notable difference. Singer et al. conducted fMRI scans on female participants across four repeated-measures conditions in a 2 × 2 factorial design. Across trials, either participants received painful (self/pain) or not painful (self/no-pain) electrical stimulation to the back of the right hand or they were signaled that their husband or romantic partner, who was sitting beside them with only his hand visible, was receiving painful (partner/pain) or not painful (partner/no-pain) electrical stimulation.

In the self/pain condition but not in the partner/pain condition, Singer et al. (2004) found increased activation of brain regions associated with the actual sensory experience of pain, including the posterior insula/secondary somatosensory cortex, the sensorimotor cortex, and the caudal anterior cingulate cortex (ACC). In both the self/pain and the partner/pain conditions, they found increased activation of brain regions associated with what they called "the affective component of pain," including the anterior insula (AI), the rostral ACC, the cerebellum, and the brain stem. In addition, they found a different pattern of activation in the inferior parietal lobule in the self/pain condition as compared to the partner/pain condition. There was increased activation on the right side in the self/pain condition and increased activation on the left side in the partner/pain condition.

The left-right hemisphere reversal in this inferior parietal pattern compared to the pattern found by Ruby and Decety (2004) may have occurred because action (agency) did not play a role in the Singer et al. (2004) study. Participants and their partners simply awaited stimulation. In addition, the immediacy of the Singer et al. situation may have left little to the imagination. Participants had clear visual cues for what level of simulation was to be given to whom. Consistent with this latter possibility, Singer et al. interpreted activation of the left inferior parietal cortex in the partner/pain condition as activity in the "visual stream" (p. 1159).

Two more recent studies explicitly involved the imagine-self and imagine-other perspectives. Jackson, Brunet, Meltzoff, and Decety (2006) showed participants pictures of people with their hands or feet in painful or nonpainful everyday life situations. The painful situations included, for example, shutting a door on one's finger or setting a heavy object on one's toe. Nonpainful situations paralleled the painful ones (e.g., a hand on the pull of a drawer rather than being caught in the drawer). Across trials, participants were asked to imagine the hand or foot as their own (imagine-self perspective), to imagine it as the hand or foot of a specific but unfamiliar person (imagine-other perspective), and to imagine it as a plastic limb (artificial-limb perspective). In addition to fMRI scans, participants rated the intensity of the pain in each situation. (Participants in the artificial-limb condition rated the amount of damage to the artificial limb.)

Jackson et al. (2006) found that both the imagine-self perspective and the imagine-other perspective produced increased activation of areas involved in the affective experience of pain, including the AI and ACC. In addition, the imagine-self perspective produced higher pain ratings and more extensive activation in the secondary somatosensory cortex, the ACC, and the insula proper. Although both the imagine-self and the imagine-other perspective increased activation in the insula, the imagine-self perspective activated specifically the posterior part, whereas the imagine-other perspective activated specifically the anterior part. And, although both perspectives increased activation in the ACC, the self-perspective selectively activated the part of this region that mediates visceral responses. Similar to Ruby and Decety (2004), the imagine-other perspective uniquely produced increased activity in the posterior cingulate/precuneus and the right TPJ, regions associated with distinguishing self and other.

Reminiscent of Stotland (1969), Jackson et al. (2006) interpreted these results as indicating that the imagine-self perspective not only triggered the affective aspects of pain but was "able to trigger part of the sensory aspects as well" (p. 758). In contrast, the imagine-other perspective produced activation "restricted to the affective component of pain processing" (p. 759), suggesting that whereas the imagine-self perspective produced direct distress, the imagine-other perspective produced empathic distress. They also noted that their results for the imagine-other perspective, especially the increased activity in the posterior cingulate/precuneus and the right TPJ, "strongly suggest that empathy for pain does not rely on a full overlap between Self and Other. ... Self and Other must be distinguished rather than merged" (p. 760).

In the clearest test to date of the neurophysiological effects of the two forms of perspective taking, Lamm, Batson, and Decety (2007) took fMRI scans while research participants observed brief video clips of the faces of patients undergoing a therapeutic treatment in which the patients received painful, aversive sounds. Across trials, participants were instructed either to imagine the feelings of the patient (imagine-other perspective) or to imagine themselves in the patient's situation (imagine-self perspective). As a crosscutting factor, on some trials participants were told that for this patient the treatment had been successful and on other trials that the treatment had not been successful. Participants also rated the intensity and unpleasantness of the imagined pain on each trial. Following the scans, participants again viewed videos in each of the four conditions and were asked to report their emotional response on the empathic concern and personal distress adjectives used by Batson et al. (1997).

Lamm et al. (2007) found that participants reported more empathic concern in the imagine-other conditions and more personal distress in the imagine-self conditions. In addition, consistent with Batson et al.'s (1997) finding that distress reported in the imagine-other condition tended to be empathic distress for the person in need, Lamm et al. found heightened distress accompanied by high empathic concern in the imagine-other condition when the treatment was not effective. Along with the reports of more personal distress in the imagine-self condition, the fMRI scans revealed that only the imagine-self perspective activated areas involved in affective response to threat or pain, including the amygdala, insula, and ACC. Across conditions, self-reported empathic concern for the patients correlated positively with activation of the ACC (medial).

A masking analysis (masking with participant's response when subjected to the aversive sounds themselves) revealed that, regardless of perspective, observation of the painful treatment and first-hand experience of the treatment activated some of the same neural networks. However, this overlap did not include areas that would reflect the sensory experience of pain. Those areas were activated only by first-hand experience of pain. The overlap included areas involved in the motivational-affective dimension of pain, such as the AI, ACC, and the amygdala, as well as areas involved in motor control. This parallel activation by both the imagine-other and the imagine-self perspectives suggests that both empathic distress and direct distress have motivational consequences. Parallel activation of these motivational-affective areas does not, of course, reveal the nature of the motivation associated with either perspective, although other research suggests that empathic distress evokes altruistic motivation and direct distress evokes egoistic motivation (Batson, 1991).

Finally, the different perspective-taking instructions produced activation of distinct regions in the parietal cortex. Imagine-other instructions produced higher activity in the right parietal cortex, whereas imagine-self instructions produced higher activity in the left parietal cortex. As noted, the right parietal cortex or TPJ has been associated with self-other distinctiveness, specifically with the distinction between self-produced actions and actions generated by others (also see Blakemore & Frith, 2003; Jackson & Decety, 2004; Saxe, Chapter 17, this volume).

To summarize, then, recent neuroimaging research has found generally consistent differences between the two forms of perspective taking. Moreover, these differences are much as we would expect based on the assumption that adopting an imagine-other perspective toward another in need produces other-oriented empathic concern, whereas adopting an imagine-self perspective produces, at best, a mixture of other-oriented empathic concern and self-oriented distress.

Of course, it is far too soon to claim strong neuroimaging support. I have interpreted two pieces of evidence as consistent with the idea that an imagine-other perspective evokes empathic concern: (a) activation of motivational-affective areas of distress or pain coupled with (b) lack of activation of sensory areas of pain. Note, however, that empathic concern is a qualitatively different emotion from the one experienced by the person in pain whose feelings are being imagined. Thus, my interpretation is contrary to currently popular views claiming that such evidence indicates direct matching or mirroring (contagion) of the affective state of the person in pain (e.g., Singer et al., 2004). Further research is required to know if the interpretation I am proposing is correct. If it is, then views that claim these studies show matching or mirroring will need to be rethought (for a related discussion, see Decety & Stevens, Chapter 1, this volume).

Also suggestive but not conclusive is neuroimaging evidence of self-other differentiation as opposed to self-other merging. The finding of Lamm et al. (2007; also see Jackson et al., 2006, and Ruby & Decety, 2004) that the imagine-other perspective activates the right inferior parietal lobule (TPJ)—a region associated with distinguishing self from other and self-agency from other agency—supports the idea that this perspective is not associated with self-other merging but with self-other distinctiveness. The finding of Lamm et al. that the imagine-self perspective activates the left inferior parietal lobule—a region associated with self-agency—supports the idea that this perspective may be associated with some loss of self-other differentiation (although in this condition the self may simply have been inserted into the position of the other, which would be substitution rather than merging). Again, however, more research is needed before we adequately understand when right and left parietal activation occurs and what each form of activation means.

MOTIVATIONAL DIFFERENCES

If, as the research I reviewed suggests, an imagine-other perspective evokes relatively pure empathic concern uncontaminated by personal distress, then according to the empathy-altruism hypothesis (Batson, 1987), this perspective should lead to relatively pure altruistic motivation. Indeed, there is much evidence that it does (see Batson, 1991, for a partial review).

In contrast, if an imagine-self perspective evokes a mix of empathy and distress, then this perspective should lead to a mix of altruistic and egoistic motivation. It may enable one to imagine how the other feels and so serve as a stepping-stone to empathic concern and, thereby, to altruistic motivation. But, as noted, this stepping-stone may be slippery. Once focused on one's own feelings, one may erroneously project those feelings onto the other. Moreover, an imagine-self perspective may promote substitution—the observer may lose sight of the other's distress and instead focus on his or her own distress in the other's situation. Such self-focus may in turn evoke egoistic motivation to escape one's personal distress or to improve one's mood (Cialdini et al., 1987; Piliavin, Dovidio, Gaertner, & Clark, 1981).

The combination of motives evoked by an imagine-self perspective may under certain circumstances produce as much or more helping behavior than the purely altruistic motivation evoked by an imagine-other perspective. So, if one wishes to maximize motivation to help, then inducing an imagine-self perspective may, at times, be more effective than inducing an imagine-other perspective. Lending some support to this suggestion, Schoenrade (1981) found not only significantly more helping in her two imagine conditions than in an objective condition, $p < .02$, but also a nonsignificant trend for more helping in an imagine-self than an imagine-other condition. Note, however, that egoistic motivation can be fickle. If its goals can be reached in a less-costly way, it should discourage helping. If one wishes to evoke more reliable motivation for helping, then inducing an imagine-other perspective, with its purer induction of empathic concern, seems advisable.

Batson et al. (2003, Experiment 1) provided some data consistent with this analysis of motivational differences between the two forms of perspective taking. They gave research participants an opportunity to anonymously assign themselves and another participant to tasks, with one task clearly more desirable than the other. As did participants in a no-perspective condition, participants led to imagine themselves "in the place of the other participant" showed a strong bias toward assigning themselves the task with more desirable consequences, suggesting egoistic motivation. In contrast, participants led to "imagine how the other participant likely feels" were more likely to assign the other participant the more desirable consequences. Consistent with the idea that an imagine-other perspective evokes empathic concern that in turn produces altruistic motivation, assignment of the other to the more desirable consequences was significantly positively correlated with self-reported empathic concern in the imagine-other condition.

WHY TAKE ANOTHER PERSON'S PERSPECTIVE?

Implicit in the foregoing analysis and review is one answer to the question of why we might be motivated (or led by others) to take another person's perspective: to evoke empathic concern. But, this is by no means the only reason we might take another person's perspective, as both classic and recent research illustrate. To place the foregoing analysis in context and to make explicit the implications for other research on perspective taking, let me conclude by considering possible reasons and conditions for taking another's perspective.

TO EVOKE EMPATHIC CONCERN

Little more need be said about this reason, except to note that evoking empathic concern is relevant only when another is in need. As we have seen, the form of perspective taking most likely to evoke empathic concern is the responsive, sensitive understanding of the other's feelings and reactions that I have called an imagine-other perspective. When there is sufficient information either through direct communication from the person in need (Katie and Jackie provided ample information about their feelings and thoughts) or through environmental cues (patients wincing in pain at aversive sounds), one may adopt this perspective naturally—as long as there is no basis for antipathy toward the person in need (Batson, Eklund, Chermok, Hoyt, & Ortiz, 2007). In such cases, there may be no need to imagine oneself in the needy person's situation as a stepping-stone (Davis et al., 2004, Experiment 1). At most, an imagine-self perspective may provide interpretative context or serve as an ancillary means to "bring home" the other's plight. At worst, it may inhibit sensitive understanding due to faulty projection, self-absorption, or substitution.

When, however, we have only limited direct information (a friend sits in blank-faced silence after learning of the death of an uncle), we may be forced to rely on an imagine-self perspective as a stepping-stone to help us appreciate how the other is feeling (Davis et al., 1996, 2004, Experiment 2). For this process to produce truly sensitive understanding, we must maintain clear self-other differentiation, adjusting our inferences for known differences between ourselves and the person in need. Simple projection, self-absorption, or substitution will not suffice. Of course, if we have no real information about the other—knowing about the need situation but not about the other's reaction to it or about the other as a person—then we are forced to rely on projection or stereotypes as a best guess (Ames, 2004; Epley & Caruso, Chapter 20, this volume; Mitchell, Macrae, & Banaji,

2006; Myers & Hodges, Chapter 19, this volume; Van Boven & Lowenstein, 2003). Fortunately, when encountering others in need outside the lab, we usually know—or can quickly learn—something about their reactions.

To Reduce Stereotyping and Prejudice

Another specific reason for taking the perspective of another in need—or for encouraging others to do so—is to reduce stereotyping and prejudice. There is evidence that this goal can be reached by inducing either an imagine-other perspective or an imagine-self perspective.

However, different psychological processes seem to be involved in the two cases. Effects of imagining the feelings and reactions of a member of a stigmatized group (an imagine-other perspective) on attitudes toward and action on behalf of the group have been found to be mediated both by situational attributions for the group member's difficulties (Vescio, Sechrist, & Paolucci, 2003) and by empathic concern felt for the group member, including empathic anger toward those mistreating him or her (Batson, Chang, Orr, & Rowland, 2002; Batson, Polycarpou et al., 1997; Dovidio et al., 2004). Effects of imagining oneself in the place of a member of a stigmatized group ("walking a mile in his moccasins") seem to be mediated more by cognitive/perceptual processes such as gaining understanding of why members of the group act as they do ("Hey, if I were treated that way, I'd be angry and suspicious too!" Finlay & Stephan, 2000) and, especially when one has limited information, by projection (Galinsky & Ku, 2004; Galinsky & Moskowitz, 2000).

To Know the Other's Thoughts, Desires, and Intentions

Thinking beyond others in need, there are many occasions when we wish to know someone's thoughts, desires, and intentions. Such knowledge helps us predict that person's behavior, which is especially important if that behavior has consequences for us (e.g., a boss) or if we need to adjust our behavior to it—as when we cooperate or compete (Caruso, Epley, & Bazerman, 2006; Epley & Caruso, Chapter 20, this volume; Epley, Caruso, & Bazerman, 2006). Such knowledge may also help us communicate. It provides a context for interpreting what people say to us (Epley, Keysar, Van Boven, & Gilovich, 2004; Myers & Hodges, Chapter 19, this volume) and for framing what we say back.

The form of perspective taking most useful for gaining this knowledge depends on what information we already have about the other's thoughts, desires, and intentions. Consider three possibilities. First, the other, a third party, or the situation may make it clear what the other thinks and wants. In such cases, imaginative perspective taking of either form is not needed. Second, even though explicit information is lacking, there may be sufficient clues that a little imagination about the other's internal state can make matters clear. In such cases, an imagine-other perspective may be quite useful. Third, as noted, we may have information about the other's situation but little or no information about the other's character or reaction to the situation. In such cases, we may need to resort to imagining how we would react in the situation to guess how the other is reacting (an imagine-self perspective and projection). Cases of this last type have been the focus of much social judgment research, by which it has been found that research participants often engage in egocentric anchoring followed by adjustment (Epley et al., 2004), a form of imagine-self perspective taking.

To Understand the Environment

We see a look of surprise and fear on another person's face, and we want to know what provoked it. In a case like this, our interest is less in knowing the other's internal state than in knowing what is in the environment. We want to know what he or she has seen that we have not. If we cannot simply follow the other's gaze, turn, and see for ourselves, we may try to imagine what we would see from his or her vantage point (an imagine-self perspective). The process may also be reversed. To know where to hide something, we may imagine what we could not see were we in the other's position. It was perspective taking of this kind that interested Piaget (1953)—specifically, the age at which children could accurately infer what could and could not be seen from a perceptual perspective different from their own (see Steins & Wicklund, 1996, for an interesting examination of this inference among adults).

TO UNDERSTAND (EVALUATE) ONESELF

Finally, as noted at the outset, the goal of perspective taking in the symbolic-interaction tradition is to understand and evaluate—even to create—the self. To this end, one adopts the perspective of significant others toward both oneself and the roles one plays. A specific form of imagine-other perspective is involved. One imagines the other's thoughts and feelings about oneself. An imagine-self perspective is irrelevant to achieving this goal.

SUMMARY AND CONCLUSION

This chapter attempts to correct three common misconceptions in recent social-psychological discussions of perspective taking. The most basic misconception is that there is no important psychological difference between imagining another's thoughts and feelings (an imagine-other perspective) and imagining your own thoughts and feelings in the other's situation (an imagine-self perspective). A review of the empirical evidence reveals that there are important emotional, cognitive, neurological, and motivational differences. Claims of no difference come from research situations that provide no or limited information about the person whose perspective one is asked to take, forcing participants to rely on imagining themselves in the other's situation to infer the other's thoughts and feelings.

A second and closely related misconception is that all perspective taking begins with simulation or projection (i.e., an imagine-self perspective) followed by adjustment to correct for known differences between self and other. Once again, evidence for this claim comes from research situations that severely limit information about the other, forcing this form of perspective taking. When more information is available, participants can think about—and can feel for—the other without first thinking about themselves.

The third misconception is that perspective taking relies on self-other merging. This misconception claims that when one takes the perspective of another (whether an imagine-other or an imagine-self perspective) awareness of the difference between self and other is lost, and understanding of the other is assimilated into or replaced by understanding of oneself. This claim is based on the research finding that, following perspective taking, perceptions of the other are more like perceptions of the self, at least if the self is perceived positively. But two people—like two chairs—can be seen as having many common attributes without being seen as one. Emotional, behavioral, and neurological data all indicate that an imagine-other perspective does not produce self-other merging. Whether an imagine-self perspective does is not yet clear.

The most general conclusion to be drawn is that researchers need to recognize the range of reasons for perspective taking as well as the range of information one can have about others and their situations. Whether a given form of perspective taking is useful—or whether any form is useful—depends crucially on these factors. Perspective taking is not one process. Rather, the term applies to a range of tools that can be used to perform a variety of tasks. A hammer and a teaspoon are both tools, but it would be unwise to fail to recognize their differences. The same is true for forms of perspective taking.

ACKNOWLEDGMENT

Thanks to Jean Decety and Nick Epley for helpful comments on a draft.

REFERENCES

Aderman, D., Brehm, S. S., & Katz, L. B. (1974). Empathic observation of an innocent victim: The just world revisited. *Journal of Personality and Social Psychology, 29*, 342–347.

Ames, D. R. (2004). Inside the mind reader's tool kit: Projection and stereotyping in mental inference. *Journal of Personality and Social Psychology, 87*, 340–353.

Barrett-Lennard, G. T. (1981). The empathy cycle: Refinement of a nuclear concept. *Journal of Counseling Psychology, 28*, 91–100.

Batson, C. D. (1987). Prosocial motivation: Is it every truly altruistic? In L. Berkowitz (Ed.), *Advances in experimental social psychology* (Vol. 20, pp. 65–122). New York: Academic Press.

Batson, C. D. (1991). *The altruism question: Toward a social-psychological answer.* Hillsdale, NJ: Erlbaum.

Batson, C. D., Batson, J. G., Griffitt, C. A., Barrientos, S., Brandt, J. R., Sprengelmeyer, P., & Bayly, M. J. (1989). Negative-state relief and the empathy-altruism hypothesis. *Journal of Personality and Social Psychology, 56*, 922–933.

Batson, C. D., Batson, J. G., Slingsby, J. K., Harrell, K. L., Peekna, H. M., & Todd, R. M. (1991). Empathic joy and the empathy-altruism hypothesis. *Journal of Personality and Social Psychology, 61*, 413–426.

Batson, C. D., Chang, J., Orr, R., & Rowland, J. (2002). Empathy, attitudes, and action: Can feeling for a member of a stigmatized group motivate one to help the group? *Personality and Social Psychology Bulletin, 28*, 1656–1666.

Batson, C. D., Dyck, J. L., Brandt, J. R., Batson, J. G., Powell, A. L., McMaster, M. R., et al. (1988). Five studies testing two new egoistic alternatives to the empathy-altruism hypothesis. *Journal of Personality and Social Psychology, 55*, 52–77.

Batson, C. D., Early, S., & Salvarani, G. (1997). Perspective taking: Imagining how another feels versus imagining how you would feel. *Personality and Social Psychology Bulletin, 23*, 751–758.

Batson, C. D., Eklund, J. H., Chermok, V. L., Hoyt, J. L., & Ortiz, B. G. (2007). An additional antecedent of empathic concern: Valuing the welfare of the person in need. *Journal of Personality and Social Psychology, 93*, 65–74.

Batson, C. D., Lishner, D. A., Carpenter, A., Dulin, L., Harjusola-Webb, S., Stocks, E. R., et al. (2003). "… As you would have them do unto you": Does imagining yourself in the other's place stimulate moral action? *Personality and Social Psychology Bulletin, 29*, 1190–1201.

Batson, C. D., Polycarpou, M. P., Harmon-Jones, E., Imhoff, H. J., Mitchener, E. C., Bednar, L. L., et al. (1997). Empathy and attitudes: Can feeling for a member of a stigmatized group improve feelings toward the group? *Journal of Personality and Social Psychology, 72*, 105–118.

Blakemore, S. J., & Frith, C. D. (2003). Self-awareness and action. *Current Opinion in Neurobiology, 13*, 219–224.

Caruso, E. M., Epley, N., & Bazerman, M. H. (2006). The costs and benefits of undoing egocentric responsibility assessments in groups. *Journal of Personality and Social Psychology, 91*, 857–871.

Cialdini, R. B., Schaller, M., Houlihan, D., Arps, K., Fultz, J., & Beaman, A. L. (1987). Empathy-based helping: Is it selflessly or selfishly motivated? *Journal of Personality and Social Psychology, 52*, 749–758.

Davis, M. H. (1994). *Empathy: A social psychological approach.* Madison, WI: Brown and Benchmark.

Davis, M. H., Conklin, L., Smith, A., & Luce, C. (1996). The effect of perspective taking on the cognitive representation of persons: A merging of self and other. *Journal of Personality and Social Psychology, 70*, 713–726.

Davis, M. H., Soderlund, T., Cole, J., Gadol, E., Kute, M., Myers, M., et al. (2004). Cognitions associated with attempts to empathize: How *do* we imagine the perspective of another? *Personality and Social Psychology Bulletin, 30*, 1625–1635.

Dovidio, J. F., ten Vergert, M., Stewart, T. L., Gaertner, S. L., Johnson, J. D., Esses, V. M., et al. (2004). Perspective and prejudice: Antecedents and mediating mechanisms. *Personality and Social Psychology Bulletin, 30*, 1537–1549.

Epley, N., Caruso, E. M., & Bazerman, M. (2006). When perspective taking increases taking: Reactive egoism in social interaction. *Journal of Personality and Social Psychology, 91*, 872–889.

Epley, N., Keysar, B., Van Boven, L., & Gilovich, T. (2004). Perspective taking as egocentric anchoring and adjustment. *Journal of Personality and Social Psychology, 87*, 327–339.

Finlay, K. A., & Stephan, W. G. (2000). Reducing prejudice: The effects of empathy on intergroup attitudes. *Journal of Applied Social Psychology, 30*, 1720–1737.

Galinsky, A. D., & Ku, G. (2004). The effects of perspective-taking on prejudice: The moderating role of self-evaluation. *Personality and Social Psychology Bulletin, 30*, 594–604.

Galinsky, A. D., & Moskowitz, G. B. (2000). Perspective-taking: Decreased stereotype expression, stereotype accessibility, and in-group favoritism. *Journal of Personality and Social Psychology, 78*, 708–724.

Goldie, P. (1999). How we think of others' emotions. *Mind and Language, 14*, 394–423.

Goldman, A. I. (1992). Empathy, mind, and morals. *Proceedings from the American Philosophical Association, 66*, 17–41.

Gordon, R. M. (1992). The simulation theory: Objections and misconceptions. *Mind and Language, 7*, 11–34.

Hygge, S. (1976). Information about the model's unconditioned stimulus and response in vicarious classical conditioning. *Journal of Personality and Social Psychology, 33*, 764–771.

Jackson, P. L., Brunet, E., Meltzoff, A. N., & Decety, J. (2006). Empathy examined through the neural mechanisms involved in imagining how I feel versus how you feel pain. *Neuropsychologia, 44*, 752–761.

Jackson, P. L., & Decety, J. (2004). Motor cognition: A new paradigm to study self-other interactions. *Current Opinion in Neurobiology, 14*, 1–5.

Jarymowicz, M. (1992). Self, we, and other(s): Schemata, distinctiveness, and altruism. In P. M. Oliner, S. P. Oliner, L. Baron, L. A. Blum, D. L. Krebs, & M. Z. Smolenska (Eds.), *Embracing the other: Philosophical, psychological, and historical perspectives on altruism* (pp. 194–212). New York: New York University Press.

Lamm, C., Batson, C. D., & Decety, J. (2007). The neural substrate of human empathy: Effects of perspective-taking and cognitive appraisal. *Journal of Cognitive Neuroscience, 19*, 1–17.

Lerner, M. J. (1980). *The belief in a just world: A fundamental delusion.* New York: Plenum.

Mead, G. H. (1934). *Mind, self, and society.* Chicago: University of Chicago Press.

Mitchell, J. P., Macrae, C. N., & Banaji, M, R. (2006). Dissociable medial prefrontal contributions to judgments of similar and dissimilar others. *Neuron, 50*, 655–663.

Nickerson, R. S. (1999). How we know—and sometimes misjudge—what others know: Imputing one's own knowledge to others. *Psychological Bulletin, 125*, 737–759.

Piaget, J. (1953). *The origins of intelligence in the child.* New York: International Universities Press.

Piliavin, J. A., Dovidio, J. F., Gaertner, S. L., & Clark, R. D., III (1981). *Emergency intervention.* New York: Academic Press.

Ruby, P., & Decety, J. (2004). How would you feel versus how do you think she would feel? A neuroimaging study of perspective taking with social emotions. *Journal of Cognitive Neuroscience, 16*, 988–999.

Schoenrade, P. (1981). *Emotional and motivational distinctions between imagining oneself and imagining another in a need situation.* Unpublished master of arts thesis, University of Kansas.

Singer, T., Seymour, B., O'Doherty, J., Kaube, H., Dolan, R. J., & Frith, C. D. (2004). Empathy for pain involves the affective but not sensory components of pain. *Science, 303*, 1157–1162.

Smith, A. (1853). *The theory of moral sentiments.* London: Alex Murray. (Original work published 1759)

Steins, G., & Wicklund, R. A. (1996). Perspective-taking, conflict, and press: Drawing an *E* on your forehead. *Basic and Applied Social Psychology, 18*, 319–346.

Stotland, E. (1969). Exploratory investigations of empathy. In L. Berkowitz (Ed.), *Advances in experimental social psychology* (Vol. 4, pp. 271–313). New York: Academic Press.

Van Boven, L., & Lowenstein, G. (2003). Social projection of transient drive states. *Personality and Social Psychology Bulletin, 29*, 1159–1168.

Vescio, T. K., Sechrist, G. B., & Paolucci, M. P. (2003). Perspective taking and prejudice reduction: The mediational role of empathy arousal and situational attributions. *European Journal of Social Psychology, 33*, 455–472.

19 Making It Up and Making Do: Simulation, Imagination, and Empathic Accuracy

Michael W. Myers and Sara D. Hodges

INTRODUCTION

How many times have you had a conversation with someone, only to ask yourself as you were leaving, "What *was* she thinking?!" Researchers have also asked this question, and the last 20 years in particular have produced active attempts to identify why some people are better at understanding another person's thoughts and feelings than others. Over time, many terms have been used to describe this ability, such as social insight (Chapin, 1942), cognitive role-taking (Eisenberg, 1986), accurate empathy (Ickes, 1993), everyday mindreading (Ickes, 2003), and simply "empathy" itself (see also Batson, Chapter 18, this volume). However, most recently researchers have gravitated toward the term *empathic accuracy*, which is defined as one's ability to accurately infer the specific content of another person's covert thoughts and feelings (Ickes, 1993). Empathic accuracy is a diabolically difficult task, in large part because one never has direct access to the contents of another person's mind. One cannot "peer" into a friend's head and understand all of his thoughts and feelings. The friend's mind—like the mind of every other person in this world—is simply not available for direct "download" (a modern metaphor for the ancient "other minds" problem). Invariably, mental contents are interpreted, translated, converted, degraded, and otherwise changed during the inference process.

Accurate inferences rely on the motivation and skill to collect a set of cues about the other person's thoughts and feelings—cues that provide an incomplete and ambiguous guide at best. Paired with attention to cues, however, we also argue that mental simulation (through the use of mental representations) and imagination are necessary parts of empathic accuracy as a remedy for this other minds dilemma. In fact, research in the related fields of perspective taking and mental state inference has identified a whole host of "tools" that perceivers use to compensate for their lack of knowledge about another target person (in this volume, see also Epley & Caruso, Chapter 20, and Saxe, Chapter 17). Along with mental simulation, two other commonly used strategies are using the self as a template for understanding the other person (projection) and the use of stereotypes (Ames, 2004; Davis, Conklin, Smith, & Luce, 1996; Epley, Keysar, Van Boven, & Gilovich, 2004).[1] Although these strategies have not been as extensively examined in the specific area of empathic accuracy, we believe that the use of mental representations and these related strategies allow the observer to fill in the gaps in the information about the other person's mental state and may be just as important—perhaps sometimes even more important—than attending to cues from the other person when considering factors that predict empathic accuracy.

In this chapter, we start by providing a brief overview of how researchers have studied empathic accuracy. Next, we describe what we have learned from these studies regarding which factors do and do not predict empathic accuracy. Specifically, we focus on the surprising results that individual difference variables that seem intuitively or theoretically related to empathic accuracy do a remarkably weak job of predicting this ability. Rather, it appears that the most powerful predictors are variables that tap the extent to which an observer can create a complex and fleshed-out representation of the other person. Third, we suggest that conceptualizing accuracy as knowing the exact thoughts of a specific individual at a specific time may constitute a higher standard than is necessary for successfully navigating the majority of everyday social interactions. Fourth, we provide some examples of why people can risk being a little "inaccurate" and rely on what might be construed as a variant of "stereotype accuracy" when inferring other people's thoughts. Finally, we end this chapter by discussing some possible avenues of research that may extend our understanding of mental simulation, imagination, and empathic accuracy.

Our chapter regarding empathic accuracy looks on the bright side (cf. Epley & Caruso, Chapter 20, this volume). Given the obstacle of the other minds problem, we believe that strategies such as stereotypes and simulation—although flawed—help provide observers with some insight into the thoughts and feelings of the other person that they would not normally know. That being said, we readily acknowledge that with more effort, people could probably often do a better job inferring others' thoughts than they do, and that mistakes in inferring others' thoughts often stem from these imperfect strategies. Although participants are better than chance at inferring the thoughts and feelings of another person, none of the empathic accuracy studies cited in this chapter demonstrate that people are even remotely close to what we would consider "expert" or even "good" mind readers. One of the major points of our chapter, however, is that accuracy may not be as functionally important as has been previously thought.

WHITHER ACCURACY: REINCARNATION AFTER CRONBACH

Interest in the accurate perception of others has had a long history of research, dating back to the work of Kohler (1929) and Mead (1934) in the first part of last century and later in the 1940s and 1950s with empathy researchers such as Dymond (1948, 1949). Earlier use of the term *empathy* tended to emphasize the emotional aspect of understanding another person, as illustrated by the origins of the word (from the German word *Einfühlung*), which translates literally as "feeling into" (as in projecting oneself into something else; Hodges & Myers, 2007). In contrast, these theorists emphasized the cognitive ability to understand what another person was thinking or feeling rather than sharing in that feeling. In fact, defining empathy as a cognitive ability to understand or deduce what another person was thinking became the dominant view in the 1940s and 1950s. Unfortunately, the general study of accuracy in person perception took a major hit after several articles by Cronbach criticized the methodology commonly used by these researchers to assess accuracy (Cronbach, 1955; Gage & Cronbach, 1955). Using a series of statistical arguments, Cronbach demonstrated that "accuracy" scores of social perception were actually the aggregate of several different components. One of these components, called *stereotype accuracy* by Cronbach (1955), was defined as one's "accuracy in predicting the generalized other" (p. 179). Cronbach argued that a person could obtain a high accuracy score simply by guessing what most people do most of the time.[2] For example, one could have an accurate idea of how the typical actress would describe herself and use this stereotype to describe Halle Berry relatively well in spite of not knowing her at all. In contrast, Cronbach considered another component, *differential accuracy*, as a true measure of "social sensitivity" because it actually assessed an individual's ability to predict a specific person's response for a particular trait or in a particular situation. In other words, the perceiver is able to successfully identify an individuating profile of traits or other characteristics of a particular person that distinguishes that person from others (Davis & Kraus, 1997). Thus, the validity of these accuracy scores (as measured by the current methodology at that time) was thrown into question because these two components were confounded. Unable to devise new techniques to disentangle these components, many researchers saw the problem as intractable and moved away from the study of the accurate perception of others.

In the last couple of decades, however, research into the accurate inference of the thoughts and feelings of another person has experienced a revival, due in large part to the development of new methodologies for studying empathic accuracy. Because our chapter focuses mainly on studies that have used a particular methodology originally devised by Ickes, Stinson, Bissonnette, and Garcia (1990), we start by providing a brief overview of the technique (for a more thorough review, see Ickes, 2001). Ickes and colleagues' empathic accuracy methodology is based on comparing the actual thoughts and feelings reported by a target person with the inferences of those thoughts and feelings that are provided by another person. To do this, a target person is first videotaped either interacting with another person or talking to the camera. The target person then watches this videotaped interaction and is instructed to stop the tape at any point at which he or she remembered having had a thought or feeling.[3] After stopping the tape, the target person then writes down the content of this thought or feeling. Later, the other person (the "perceiver") also watches the filmed clip. For the perceiver, the tape is stopped at every point at which the target person recorded having a thought or feeling. Paralleling the target person's instructions, the perceiver is instructed to provide a brief description—a best guess—of what the target person was thinking or feeling. In some studies, perceivers play double duty, serving as the conversation partners who originally interacted with the target person in the videotape as well as perceivers (e.g., Ickes et al., 1990; Simpson, Oriña, & Ickes, 2003; Stinson & Ickes, 1992). Other studies use strangers who never met the target person to serve as the perceivers (e.g., Barone et al., 2005; Gesn & Ickes, 1999; Klein & Hodges, 2001; Marangoni, Garcia, Ickes, & Teng, 1995).

After collecting perceivers' inferences, coders then rate the extent to which the perceiver's responses are similar to the target's responses using a 3-point scale ranging from 0 ("the inferred content and actual content are not the same") to 2 ("the inferred content captures the 'gist' of the actual content"). Using a group of three to six raters to code each response, our lab has found an average Cronbach's alpha of .86, which is consistent with the reliabilities reported by Ickes (1993).

One important difference between the original Cronbach trait inference research and empathic accuracy research is that the criterion for trait accuracy can come from several sources, among them what the target person self-reports to be his or her traits, consensus traits attributed to the target by others (who might be "experts" or close friends of the target), or behavioral criteria. In contrast, with empathic accuracy, because of the other minds problem, the target person is always the one who must supply the criterion against which to judge accuracy. Other forms of interpersonal sensitivity that do rely on external indicators, such as the ability to accurately read nonverbal cues, may contribute to empathic accuracy, but they are only a part of the message that has to be read.

Given the relative simplicity of its design, the empathic accuracy methodology has been applied to a variety of interactions and social situations. Different dyadic interactions have included strangers (Ickes et al., 1990), same-sex friends (Stinson & Ickes, 1992), romantic or married partners (Kilpatrick, Bissonnette, & Rusbult, 2002; Simpson, Ickes, & Blackstone, 1995; Simpson et al., 2003), and client-therapist pairs (Barone et al., 2005; Marangoni et al., 1995). Topics discussed in those interactions have included academic problems (Klein & Hodges, 2001), the attractiveness of another person (Simpson et al., 1995), marital problems and divorce (Gesn & Ickes, 1999; Marangoni et al., 1995), and being a first-time mother (Hodges, 2005).

WHAT IS NOT RELATED TO EMPATHIC ACCURACY?

Of the studies cited, the Marangoni et al. (1995) and the Gesn and Ickes (1999) studies were unique because they had their observers infer the thoughts and feelings of several different targets. Both of these studies indicated that participants' accuracy showed consistency across different targets, with cross-target intraclass correlations of .86 and .91, respectively, suggesting that there may be stable differences in empathic accuracy ability. This begs the question that will serve as the next focus of the chapter: If there is reliability in predicting empathic accuracy, what are the consistent factors either within the person or in the situation that affect empathic accuracy?

Among the several studies that have addressed this question, the surprising answer is that traditional, empathy-related constructs generally do not predict empathic accuracy. In the very first published study that used this methodology, Ickes and his colleagues (1990) examined whether self-reported measures of dispositional empathy and empathic accuracy predicted participants' empathic accuracy scores. To assess individual differences in empathy, they used Davis's (1980) Interpersonal Reactivity Index (IRI), which taps four constructs related to empathy: empathic concern, personal distress, perspective taking, and fantasy. They also created a scale to measure self-reported individual differences in empathic accuracy. Neither of these scales significantly predicted empathic accuracy in this study. In fact, two of the subscales on the IRI (perspective taking and fantasy) as well as the self-report empathic accuracy measure were negatively correlated (although not significantly) with empathic accuracy performance. Stinson and Ickes (1992) later partially replicated these results when they again found that higher fantasy subscale scores from Davis's IRI were negatively and significantly correlated with empathic accuracy in dyads consisting of strangers. In unpublished data from our lab, where we collected data on the IRI along with measures of empathic accuracy (e.g., Laurent & Hodges, 2008), we have also found the same inverse relationship between empathic accuracy and perspective taking as found by Ickes et al. (1990).

One possible explanation for these findings is that the IRI only assesses people's self-perceived drive to understand and empathize with others, not necessarily their success in these tasks. As Ickes (1993) pointed out, the discrepancy between self-perceptions of empathy and objective measures of accurately understanding another person's thoughts and feelings may suggest that perceivers lack insight (or metaknowledge) into their own relative level of empathic skill. In fact, people who are particularly weak at empathic accuracy may be the ones who most overestimate how skilled they are in general (Dunning, Johnson, Ehrlinger, & Kruger, 2003; Kruger & Dunning, 1999).

One might suggest that perhaps more proximal measures of an observer's reaction to a particular situation are better predictors of empathic accuracy than individual differences. Research has consistently demonstrated that an "other-oriented" emotion of sympathy, concern, and compassion—what we will call *empathic concern*—can arise when an observer takes the perspective of another person in need (Batson, Early, & Salvarani, 1997; Batson, Sager, et al., 1997). Impressively, feelings of empathic concern can also motivate the observer to help that other person in spite of the fact that this helping can appear to provide no apparent direct benefit to the observer. Thus, it seems plausible that the increased connection and involvement that accompany greater empathic concern may also predict greater empathic accuracy. For example, if empathic concern increases Sam's motivation to help Holly after she lost her dog, he would need to identify *how* he could help her. This would require that Sam have a good understanding of Holly's thoughts and feelings so he could provide the appropriate type of support. However, several studies conducted in our lab (e.g., Hodges & Klein, 2000) suggested that empathic accuracy and empathic concern are orthogonal. In one study, perspective-taking instructions were manipulated between participants (i.e., either imagine how a target person feels or remain as objective as possible), and then participants watched a college woman describing an academic setback. After completing a measure of empathic concern created by Batson, Early et al. (1997), the participants then watched the tape a second time using Ickes's empathic accuracy methodology. Consistent with past findings by Batson and colleagues, taking the perspective of the woman led to greater feelings of empathic concern. However, perspective-taking instructions had no effect on empathic accuracy.

In a second study (Hodges, 2005), we varied the target's similarity with the participants who served as perceivers and examined similarity's effect on empathic concern and empathic accuracy. Past research suggests that perceived similarity—functioning somewhat like perspective taking—can lead to increased feelings of empathic concern (Batson, Lishner, Cook, & Sawyer, 2005; Cialdini, Brown, Lewis, Luce, & Neuberg, 1997). Women who had never been mothers, were pregnant with their first child, or had just given birth to their first child served as three different groups of perceivers. All of the perceivers watched videotapes of targets—who were all new mothers—describing their experiences with their babies. Similar to the Hodges and Klein (2000) study, perceivers first reported their feelings of empathic concern for the target and then watched the videotape a second time, during which they inferred the target's thoughts and feelings. As expected, the results indicated a significant linear trend for empathic concern, with women who had just given birth to their first child reporting the most empathic concern, followed by the pregnant women, and then by those who had never been mothers. In contrast, however, similarity had no effect on empathic accuracy; all three groups were equally—and moderately—accurate in inferring the thoughts and feelings of the new mother.

These two sets of results offer support for the idea that empathic concern and empathic accuracy are separate constructs and that consequently empathic concern is not necessarily a good predictor of empathic accuracy. Thus, individual differences in self-reported empathy (using empirically valid and reliable scales) do not predict empathic accuracy, and other empathy-related constructs evoked by specific interactions do not appear to fare much better.

WHAT IS RELATED TO EMPATHIC ACCURACY?

On the other hand, a number of studies have identified factors that predict empathic accuracy, and we turn to those in this section. The results suggest that the key to effective empathic accuracy is not the extent that a person feels concern for another person, but rather a perceiver's motivation and ability to create a coherent mental representation of the target person. One consistent result is that general intelligence (such as cognitive complexity and high field independence) and, in particular, verbal intelligence of the perceiver positively predict empathic accuracy (Davis & Kraus, 1997; Ickes et al., 1990, 2000, although significant effects in the last study were found only for males). This is consistent with the theory that taking the perspective of another person is a mentally taxing task that requires more than just keen observational skills; it requires considerable motivation and intelligence to construct an understanding of the other person.

Second, it is not surprising to learn that research indicates that people are better at inferring the thoughts and feelings of their friends than those of strangers. This does not appear to occur because friends are more similar to each other or that they are more expressive with each other during the interactions. After controlling for these differences, Stinson and Ickes (1992) still found a significant effect for relationship status on empathic accuracy. They found that the differences were driven by the superior ability of participants to correctly identify the thoughts and feelings of their friends that concerned events and places outside the immediate experimental context—that is, events that could be seen as requiring mental simulation and imagination. Without shared reference points and memories, a stranger serving as an interaction partner could not bring to mind, for example, the past melodrama of how his conversation partner had been treated by an ex-girlfriend when the partner mentioned her name—a history that might provide a rich background for understanding what the partner is thinking or feeling about her in the current context.

The idea that creating a coherent mental representation of another person improves empathic accuracy was supported by the first empathic accuracy study conducted by Ickes et al. (1990). While self-reported measures of empathic ability in this study did not predict empathic accuracy, the researchers did find that the extent to which perceivers made attributions about the stable characteristics and traits of the target (e.g., "This guy is pretty creative," "She is snobbish," "What a weirdo") was positively correlated with empathic accuracy. The authors believed that these results implicated how "both [attribution making and empathic accuracy] may be outcomes or products of a more general epistemic attempt to 'understand' another person" (p. 736).

An overarching theme in these studies is that an empathically accurate perceiver is one who engages in on-line attempts during the interaction to develop a more "fleshed-out" representation of the target person. Furthermore, the components that make up this mental representation do not necessarily derive solely from the immediate interaction. Instead, the perceiver may access schemas of the self, stereotypes, and past experiences to create an impression of the target person that goes beyond what the target person is actually saying or doing in the interaction.

Furthermore, there is evidence to suggest that, as interactions unfold over time, mental constructions such as schemas and simulations may become increasingly more important sources of information for the perceiver than the actual behavior of the target person during the interaction. For example, Gesn and Ickes (1999) found that participants who saw a videotape of the target person played as it was originally filmed were equally mediocre at inferring the target's thoughts and feelings than were participants who saw segments of the video in a randomized order. On closer inspection, however, Gesn and Ickes found that this null effect was due to a significant schema consistency-by-order effect: Participants who saw the tape in its original order were apparently able to construct a mental representation of the target person that they consistently relied on when trying to imagine what that person was thinking or feeling. As long as the target person's thoughts and feelings were highly or moderately consistent with this representation, these participants were more empathically accurate than their counterparts in the randomized-order condition, who were unable to create a coherent mental representation of the target person. However, when the target person had a thought or feeling that was inconsistent with this representation, participants in the original-order condition exhibited significantly worse empathic accuracy because they appeared to erroneously base their inferences on the schema that they had created about the target person rather than the immediate cues present in the interaction. Lacking a well-developed representation about the interaction, participants in the randomized-order condition had to pay more attention to its individual segments. Consequently, they were better able to react to inconsistencies in the target person's behaviors and thoughts when they arose in the interaction. Gesn and Ickes's study suggests that when people can apply a schema or generate a simulation, they will use it to infer others' thoughts and feelings. Given that it is far more common for people to experience an interaction in its correct chronological order than in randomly ordered pieces, the use of these representations should be considered the norm rather than the exception.

Kilpatrick et al.'s (2002) study of empathic accuracy among newly married couples further supports the idea that over time people may increasingly rely on schemas and simulations—that is, internally generated constructs rather than externally cued ones—to infer what another person is thinking or feeling. As part of a larger longitudinal study, couples were brought into the lab three times over the first 3 years of their marriage. Each time, the researchers videotaped the couples interacting with each other. They then ran each member of the couple through the empathic accuracy methodology described in this chapter. Thus, each partner in the couple served as both a perceiver and a target for the study. In addition to empathic accuracy scores, stereotype accuracy scores were computed (see Ickes et al., 1990) by randomly pairing actual thoughts and feelings from one partner with inferences for different thoughts or feelings made by the other partner and rating their similarity. Stated differently, this stereotype empathic accuracy (that Kilpatrick et al. and others have called "baseline" empathic accuracy)[4] represents the accuracy of a perceiver in inferring the thoughts and feelings of a target person in a specific context that is due to chance. This stereotype empathic accuracy score was then subtracted from the total empathic accuracy score to create an "adjusted" empathic accuracy score. Following Cronbach's logic, this adjusted empathic accuracy score represents a "purer" measure of accuracy because it partials out other components that could artificially inflate these scores.

Consistent with their hypotheses, Kilpatrick et al. (2002) found that adjusted empathic accuracy decreased over time. Specifically, couples scored significantly higher at Time 1 than Time 2 or 3. However, were these results due to a decrease in overall unadjusted empathic accuracy, an increase in stereotype empathic accuracy, or both? When they examined these two components, Kilpatrick et al. found a marginally significant decrease of unadjusted empathic accuracy over time as well as a marginally significant increase in stereotype empathic accuracy. The importance of this marginal result lies in the possible meaning that this baseline score may represent. According to Kilpatrick et al.:

> If we assume that partners' "stereotype accuracy," or global understanding of one another's thought
> and feelings, is at least roughly tapped by our measure of baseline accuracy, it is noteworthy that

this index did not decline over time; indeed, from a descriptive point of view, stereotype accuracy increased. (p. 338)

It is as if simulating how a messy kitchen would look to one's returning spouse or retrieving one's script for how the spouse would react to a surprise weekend getaway was as important—or more important—than monitoring the partner's actual reaction when couples tried to understand each other.

While Ickes et al. (1990) originally conceptualized "baseline" accuracy as a form of error, their conclusion that empathic accuracy taps a "general epistemic attempt to 'understand' another person" (p. 736) sounds quite similar to the way this construct was viewed by Kilpatrick and her colleagues. Once again, the results suggest that understanding another person's thoughts and feelings requires the construction and use of mental representations that go beyond the immediate information gathered from the interaction.

We think the important take-home message from the Gesn and Ickes (1999) study, the Kilpatrick et al. (2002) study, and other studies that have found predictors of empathic accuracy is that the use of mental representations appears to have contributed to a better understanding of the target person. Only in those few instances when reality severely deviated from perceivers' imagined understanding did they display major deficits in empathic accuracy.

GOOD ENOUGH ACCURACY

In this chapter, we described Cronbach's distinction between differential accuracy and stereotype accuracy. In our third point of the chapter, we return to this topic and consider how our understanding of these concepts should be reevaluated in light of the research described previously. While there are important differences between differential accuracy and stereotype accuracy, the reality is that people often use generalizations and representations when trying to understand another person. After Cronbach's articles were published, an assumption was made that differential accuracy was the most valid or true measure of social sensitivity. The other components identified by Cronbach, especially stereotype accuracy, were subsequently downgraded to either measurement artifacts or theoretically unimportant constructs. When stereotype accuracy was identified as a theoretically meaningful construct, the implication was that it was an inferior component of accuracy, masquerading as the more valued differential accuracy.

Furthermore, these terms were defined during a time when most person perception research focused on the accurate inference of personality traits, not the specific thoughts and feelings of another person. The meanings of differential accuracy and stereotype accuracy differ slightly when we apply them to the study of empathic accuracy. As highlighted by Kilpatrick et al.'s (2002) work, stereotype empathic accuracy may be a different kind of generalization than previously defined in trait perception. In terms of empathic accuracy, the generalization may be across multiple thoughts and feelings, but all within the same person, whereas in trait accuracy, stereotype accuracy involves a generalization across multiple individuals. Thus, it is important to note the unit of analysis when talking about stereotyping: individuals versus individual thoughts and feelings within the same individual.

Of course, we still think that forms of differential accuracy can play an important role in empathic accuracy. Certainly, stereotype accuracy that generalizes across people can get us in trouble (for example, inferring that one's boss likes being called by her first name just because other people at work like to be called by their first names). In other instances, moment-by-moment differential accuracy may be important for the success of an interaction (e.g., "Uh-oh, I think my teasing is starting to get to her, and I should stop now"). Similarly, if a woman has correctly inferred in the past that her boyfriend will be excited to hear that they are going out for steaks, it would be a major mistake to continue making this same inference right after he announces that he has become a vegetarian.

In support of the importance of differential empathic accuracy, there is ample evidence in the literature to suggest that the ability to effectively gather information about the target person from the specific interaction is associated with better empathic accuracy (Barone et al., 2005; Ickes et al., 1990; Thomas, Fletcher, & Lange, 1997). This is particularly true when people are interacting with strangers and have very little beginning information (Stinson & Ickes, 1992). Thus, people are gathering information and generating impressions, modifying and revising their view of the other person as they incorporate additional information into their mental representations.

MISIMAGINING OTHERS: WOULD YOU KNOW, AND DOES IT MATTER?

Given the challenge of the other minds problem, people likely need to rely on both stereotypes and differentiating information at various times to make accurate, meaningful inferences about what others are thinking or feeling. Even when both are used, we are probably still frequently inaccurate in our inferences about the thoughts of others. Yet, most of us muddle by—how? We think there are three major qualities of everyday social interactions that help explain why errors in empathic accuracy are frequently benign. The first quality, foreshadowed in the previous discussion, is that perceivers generally do not need to have moment-by-moment, thought-by-thought accuracy in their inferences about another person's thoughts and feelings to be socially successful. For example, while Kilpatrick et al. (2002) found that empathic accuracy had an initial boost on accommodative behavior and couple well-being among newlyweds, the effect of empathic accuracy quickly lost strength after the first year of marriage. In other words, being more accurate (or inaccurate) about their spouse's thoughts and feelings did not seem to have long-term benefits for the status of the relationship (whereas other variables clearly do, such as simply being "nice" to each other; e.g., Gottman & Levenson, 1992). Sometimes, being "good enough" works just fine in real life.

Related to the first quality, perceivers may be able to function with relatively accurate stereotypes and simulations of what the other person is thinking even when their moment-by-moment inferences are inaccurate because the target person rarely has access to many of the perceiver's inferences. Thus, the target is frequently unaware of the perceiver's inaccuracies. In everyday interactions, we do not stop to share every inference about the other person's mental state by saying to that person, "So, now, based on what you've been saying and your behavior, I think you're thinking this ... ." Such explicitly stated inferences are of course sometimes made, but outside of Rogerian therapy sessions and empathic accuracy experiments, they occur generally when the target person's thoughts and feelings are the specific focus of discussion or when the perceiver believes his or her comprehension of the interaction is directly impeded without a clarification of the target's mental state. So, if perceivers do not verbalize their inferences, then targets generally do not become aware of inaccurate inferences. Sometimes, the perceiver's behavior may reveal an incorrect inference without the perceiver explicitly stating it, but frequently the perceiver's subsequent behaviors are unrelated or too ambiguous and thus also do not betray incorrect inferences. Finally, empathic inaccuracies about issues that are tangential to the gist of an interaction may not really matter.

Let us use a real-life example from academia that we know actually occurred and nicely illustrates these first two qualities. A graduate student was presenting a poster at a conference when another conferee stopped by to talk to him about his work. The other conferee happened to mention that she would be interviewing at the graduate student's home university in the near future. The graduate student incorrectly assumed that she was a prospective student and, consequently, incorrectly inferred that she was nervous about visiting a place where she did not know anyone. In an attempt to ease her anxiety, the graduate student invited her to stay at his apartment when she visited. In truth, she was a prospective faculty member who was almost certainly expecting to be put up in a hotel during her interview. However, the conversation actually went remarkably smoothly despite this misunderstanding. Why?

First, even with the graduate student's incorrect inference about the reason for the visit, the conversation still could have continued along a path that never exposed the error. For example, instead of inviting the other conferee to stay with him, he could have said something entirely unrelated to his inference that she was an anxious prospective student like, "Well, be sure to bring your umbrella; it's rainy this time of year." Furthermore, many of the graduate student's utterances that were related to the incorrect inference could be ambiguously appropriate for multiple inferences, including either the prospective student or job candidate scenario, such as, "I'm really glad you're visiting, I'll look forward to seeing you again soon."

Notably, the graduate student never explicitly said anything about inferring that the other conferee was a prospective student, and the prospective faculty member never said anything to imply that things were amiss, perhaps because she simply assumed the student was joking about staying with him (we personally think it is pretty funny), or she politely assumed that the student was naive about how job candidates are treated, or (as we have been told is actually the case) she failed to encode that the student was inviting her to stay at his apartment, probably because it deviated so radically from her "script" for how conversations about interview visits go—she never even realized the mistaken inference was made.

Inevitably, there will be times when we are all exposed as having put that proverbial foot in our mouth because we have made and acted on an incorrect inference that is noticed by the other person. This brings us to the third and final quality of everyday interactions that make inaccurate inferences less of a problem than we might initially assume: Even when targets realize that we have made a mistake, most of the time they still tend to be fairly forgiving. They frequently simply correct the perceiver on their misinference ("No, you see, I'm interviewing for a job; I'm almost done with graduate school"), and they move on in the conversation. "Forgive and forget" would seem to be an apt description for the target person's behavior during most everyday interactions. When someone does explode because the other person made the wrong inference, these outbursts may have been triggered by factors within the target person that occurred outside the immediate interaction, perhaps due to the frustration of continued negative interactions with the perceiver ("You never take the time to find out what I really want!") or frustration from some previous event unrelated to the present interaction ("You made some crack about that last week, too; are you suggesting I'm racist?"). Moreover, there are examples of socially disastrous consequences that can occur because an isolated inference about another person's words turns out to be incorrect. Many of us can probably remember instances when someone made a huge social gaffe because he or she thought the other person was joking, when in reality the individual was completely serious. However, if people are relying on imperfect stereotype accuracy and mental simulation as much as we suggest, we think it is notable that these situations do not occur more often.

Like other domains in which people use heuristics, there are times when deleterious consequences follow from empathic inaccuracies. As a general rule, however, we believe that the use of mental simulation and stereotype accuracy typically improves empathic accuracy. First, as we stated at the outset of this chapter, they help solve the other minds problem by allowing us to fill in the gaps of information about the other person that are inaccessible or unavailable to the perceiver. Second, they reduce the amount of effort required in an interaction because the perceiver does not have to spend as much energy detecting subtle (or unreadable) cues provided by the target person throughout the immediate interaction. Finally, even when the use of mental simulation and stereotypes leads to inaccurate perceptions, the consequences are often not nearly as negative as we might fear.

KNOWING THE MINDS OF OTHERS WHO EXIST ONLY IN OUR MINDS

In a more speculative vein, we end this chapter by looking at some parallels between the mundane and important social task of inferring others' thoughts and feelings and the fantasy-oriented endeavor of creating fictional others' thoughts and feelings (see also Green & Donahue, Chapter 16, this volume). Although the latter may be a more elaborated "recreational" version of the former, we believe that both draw on similar strategies: The same skills that allow us to flesh out and make sense of the inaccessible contents of others' minds may also allow us to imagine the minds of others who exist only in our minds.

Much can be learned from fiction writers and their process of creating imaginary characters. Taking a page from research on psychopathology, studying extreme cases of a particular behavior can often provide insight into the general, underlying processes of more typical behavior. Why do we believe that fiction writers engage in a more "extreme" version of everyday perspective taking? For one thing, similar to someone who can accurately understand what another person is thinking or feeling, a good fiction writer is able to create a fully formed and complex mental representation of a fictional character. Fiction writers are then able to use this mental representation to "understand" the unique thoughts and feelings of their character for any situation, including potential future events previously unimagined by the author. Being able to come up with a reasonable answer to the question "What was she thinking?" is as important for promoting smooth social interactions as it is for creating a compelling work of fiction.

Of course, one might point out that there is a fundamental difference between inferring the (independently existing) thoughts of a real person and "knowing" the thoughts of a fictional person who has no thoughts until the author writes them, along the lines of Harold Crick, Will Farrell's character in the movie *Stranger Than Fiction* (2006). Crick discovers that his whole life is being written by an author played by Emma Thompson. However, as preposterous as it may seem to suggest that the fictional character (and not the writer) may direct the plot of the book, there is growing evidence to suggest that fiction writers often view their fictional characters as independent and autonomous entities.

Interviews with authors and comments made by them about the writing process provide anecdotal evidence of writers who feel they have "personal relationships" with their characters and imagined conversations with them. These stories belie the reality that these characters are completely fabricated creations and instead paint them as "peers" whose wills are not easily bent by the wishes of the authors. For example, when J. K. Rowling, the author of the best-selling Harry Potter books, was asked in a National Public Radio interview why she made her main character a boy, she answered that she had tried to make him a girl:

> About 6 months into writing the book, I thought that I am female, and that he is a boy. But it was too late, it was too late to make Harry Harriet. He was very real to me as a boy, and to put him in a dress would have felt like Harry in drag. ... I never write and say "OK, now I need this sort of character." My characters come to me in this sort of mysterious process that no one really understands, they just pop up. (Rowling, 1999)

Studies using more systematic approaches to examine the phenomenon of characters coming to life provide similar evidence. Taylor, Hodges, and Kohanyi (2003; see also Taylor, Shawber, & Mannering, Chapter 14, this volume) recruited writers who varied in their experience and success in fiction writing and interviewed them about the characters in their work. In particular, they were asked about the development of one of their characters and the extent that they experienced a phenomenon that the researchers labeled the *illusion of independent agency* (IIA)—the sense that their characters were independent agents not directly under the author's control but rather have their own thoughts, feelings, and actions. One of the main results that emerged from this study was that the overwhelming majority of the sample (92%) reported experiencing IIA as a writer at least once. In fact, Taylor et al. (2003) reported that the fiction writers appeared to have no problem understanding and providing vivid responses to the questions related to IIA, such as whether they interacted with and heard the voices of their fictional characters. Thus, although fictional characters do not actually exist outside their authors' head, experienced authors have the sensation that they do, and that phenomenon may be what enables authors to apply the same arsenal of skills to their craft as the rest of us do to our everyday interactions.

However, the fact remains that empathic accuracy involves focusing on a real person, while fiction writing is an act of fantasy that focuses on an imaginary person. As a result, during real-world interactions one has an objective standard (i.e., the actual target person) to compare against one's mental simulation and can determine how correct it is, while with fiction writing there is no objective standard against which to evaluate the accuracy of the mental simulation. That said, we hope it has become clear from this chapter that *accuracy* as it has been traditionally defined (i.e., differential accuracy) may not be the last word in understanding the thoughts and feelings of another person. In other words, in spite of being able to measure empathic accuracy against an objective standard in the form of specific thoughts and feelings, "successful" perceivers may not always track 100% on those individual thoughts and feelings. They may instead be generating a "good story." If something akin to stereotype accuracy is more important when we are trying to imagine what another person is thinking, how different is this process from fiction writing? Maybe there are the makings of a fiction writer deep down in all of us.

CONCLUSION

Researchers and laypeople alike continue to be interested in the question, "What makes someone a good mind reader?" so we suspect that the study of empathic accuracy will remain a thriving field for many years to come. After almost 20 years of research, empathic accuracy researchers have been able to provide some tentative (and often-surprising) answers to this question. In spite of theoretical and intuitive reasons to expect a relationship between self-reported measures of dispositional empathy and empathic accuracy, individual differences in self-reported empathic ability and other related constructs have consistently shown to be poor predictors. We do not want to go on record claiming that there is no connection among these constructs; however, the connections do appear to be much more complex than originally thought. One possible reason for this deficit has been mentioned already—perceivers rarely receive explicit feedback from their interaction partner that they have mistakenly inferred the target person's thoughts and feelings. Most of the time, the perceiver's errors are still "close enough" to promote a fluid social interaction, so the target person either does not discover the perceiver's mistake or has no need to make a correction.

In hindsight, perhaps we should be more surprised that we are not asking ourselves, "What was she thinking?" more often. Given the complexity and variety of people's thoughts and the limited resources perceivers have at their disposal to accurately infer those thoughts, it is amazing that people are as successful interacting with each other as they are. In the realm of fiction writing, there are clear examples of authors who are experts in the creation of complex, interesting, and above all, realistic characters, but it might be a challenge to identify even a handful of people in the real world who could be identified as expert mind readers. There may be master forensic scientists or prosecutors out there who are able to reconstruct the specific sequence of thoughts and meta-thoughts of the other person based on a cursory glance at the evidence, but it should be noted that *CSI* is just a TV show and not reality!

Luckily, reality is much more forgiving than a TV show or movie. We do not need mystic levels of empathic accuracy to achieve success interacting with and understanding others. Of course, there may be some professional domains in which empathic accuracy is a key to success. Negotiators and diplomats could surely benefit from knowing how the other side really feels about the proposal on the table. Similarly, generals and coaches who can read their opponents' minds to outmaneuver them should be successful. Those in service occupations who anticipate and deliver their clients' desires will likely see repeat business. The salesperson who can distinguish between an uninterested customer and the one who is simply too shy to ask about prices will do well.

The most accurate perceiver may simply be someone who is (a) motivated and (b) able to create a consistent schema or representation of the other person. Granted, there are many instances when people are still unable to perform these skills, but this is at least a more attainable standard of success for most of us. In the end, we do not need to be experts; we just need to be good enough when it comes to understanding another person.

NOTES

1. One factor that determines which strategy an observer will use is the extent that he or she feels similar to the target person (Ames, 2004). Recent advances in social neuroscience have provided additional evidence for this claim. For example, Mitchell, Macrae, and Banaji (2006) found that making mental state inferences about a similar target was associated with greater activation of the ventral medial prefrontal cortex (an area also implicated in processing information about the self), while making inferences about a dissimilar target led to greater activation of the dorsal medial prefrontal cortex. According to the authors, these results suggest that observers may use simulation when they are making inferences about a similar target but tend to use a different strategy—such as stereotyping—to understand a dissimilar target.
2. It is important to note that Cronbach's argument was based on studies examining personality traits that generalized across people; in the realm of empathic accuracy, generalizations could also be made across thoughts and feelings within a particular person, a point we return to in this chapter.
3. One limitation of the methodology is that it assumes that the targets can both accurately recall and describe their thoughts and feelings. While it is generally agreed that people know their emotional states much better than their self-reported personality traits, people sometimes are unaware that they are expressing emotions that are reliably different from the emotional response they later recounted (Malatesta, Izard, Culver, & Nicolich, 1987; Zebrowitz, 1990).
4. *Stereotype* in this case refers to generalization in general and not specifically to generalizations about a group of people.

ACKNOWLEDGMENTS

We sould like to thank Anna Bell, Stephanie Fackler, Tracy Gagnon, Adam Kramer, Sean Laurent, John Myers, Becca Neel, and Holly Oh for their comments on this work.

REFERENCES

Ames, D. R. (2004). Inside the mind reader's tool kit: Projection and stereotyping in mental state inference. *Journal of Personality and Social Psychology, 87*, 340–353.
Barone, D. V., Hutchings, P. S., Kimmel, H. J., Traub, H. L., Copper, J. T., & Marshall, C. M. (2005). Increasing empathic accuracy through practice and feedback in a clinical interviewing course. *Journal of Social and Clinical Psychology, 24*, 156–171.
Batson, C. D., Early, S., & Salvarani, G. (1997). Perspective taking: Imagining how another feels versus imagining how you would feel. *Personality and Social Psychology Bulletin, 23*, 751–758.
Batson, C. D., Lishner, D. A., Cook, J., & Sawyer, S. (2005). Similarity and nurturance: Two possible sources of empathy for strangers. *Basic and Applied Social Psychology, 27*, 15–25.
Batson, C. D., Sager, K., Garst, E., Kang, M., Rubchinsky, K., & Dawson, K. (1997). Is empathy-induced helping due to self-other merging? *Journal of Personality and Social Psychology, 73*, 495–509.
Chapin, F. S. (1942). Preliminary standardization of a social insight scale. *American Sociological Review, 7*, 214–225.
Cialdini, R. B., Brown, S. L., Lewis, B. P., Luce, C., & Neuberg, S. L. (1997). Reinterpreting the empathy-altruism relationship: When one into one equals oneness. *Journal of Personality and Social Psychology, 73*, 481–494.
Cronbach, L. J. (1955). Processes affecting scores on understanding of others and assuming "similarity." *Psychological Bulletin, 52*, 177–193.
Davis, M. (1980). A multidimensional approach to individual differences in empathy. *Catalog of Selected Documents in Psychology, 10*, 85.
Davis, M. H., Conklin, L., Smith, A., & Luce, C. (1996). Effect of perspective taking on the cognitive representations of self and other. *Journal of Personality and Social Psychology, 70*, 713–726.
Davis, M. H., & Kraus, L. A. (1997). Personality and empathic accuracy. In W. J. Ickes (Ed.), *Empathic accuracy* (pp. 144–168). New York: Guilford Press.
Dunning, D., Johnson, K., Ehrlinger, J., & Kruger, J. (2003). Why people fail to recognize their own incompetence. *Current Directions in Psychological Science, 12*, 83–87.

Dymond, R. F. (1948). A preliminary investigation of the relation of insight and empathy. *Journal of Consulting Psychology, 12,* 228–233.

Dymond, R. F. (1949). A scale for the measurement of empathic ability. *Journal of Consulting Psychology, 13,* 127–133.

Eisenberg, N. (1986). *Altruistic emotion, cognition, and behavior.* Hillsdale, NJ: Erlbaum.

Epley, N., Keysar, B., Van Boven, L., & Gilovich, T. (2004). Perspective taking and egocentric anchoring and adjusting. *Journal of Personality and Social Psychology, 87,* 327–339.

Gage, N. L., & Cronbach, J. L. (1955). Conceptual and methodological problems in interpersonal perception. *Psychological Review, 62,* 411–422.

Gesn, P. R., & Ickes, W. (1999). The development of meaning contexts for empathic accuracy: Channel and sequence effects. *Journal of Personality and Social Psychology, 77,* 746–761.

Gottman, J. M., & Levenson, R. W. (1992). Marital processes predictive of later dissolution: Behavior, physiology, and health. *Journal of Personality and Social Psychology, 63,* 221–233.

Hodges, S. D. (2005). Is how much you understand me in your head or mine? In B. F. Malle & S. D. Hodges (Eds.), *Other minds: How humans bridge the divide between self and others* (pp. 298–309). New York: Guilford Press.

Hodges, S. D., & Klein, K. J. K. (2000, February). *Getting what you pay for: Empathic accuracy and empathic concern.* Poster presented at the first annual Society of Personality and Social Psychology Conference, Nashville, TN.

Hodges, S. D., & Myers, M. W. (2007). Empathy. In R. Baumeister and K. Vohs (Eds.), *Encyclopedia of social psychology* (pp. 296–298). Thousand Oaks, CA: Sage.

Ickes, W. (1993). Empathic accuracy. *Journal of Personality, 61,* 587–610.

Ickes, W. (2001). Measuring empathic accuracy. In J. A. Hall & F. J. Bernieri (Eds.), *Interpersonal sensitivity: Theory and measurement* (pp. 219–241). Mahwah, NJ: Erlbaum.

Ickes, W. (2003). *Everyday mind reading: Understanding what other people think and feel.* Amherst, NY: Prometheus Books.

Ickes, W., Buysse, A., Pham, H., Rivers, K., Erickson, J. R., Hancock, M., et al. (2000). On the difficulty of distinguishing "good" and "poor" perceivers: A social relations analysis of empathic accuracy data. *Personal Relationships, 7,* 219–234.

Ickes, W., Stinson, L., Bissonnette, V., & Garcia, S. (1990). Naturalistic social cognition: Empathic accuracy in mixed-sex dyads. *Journal of Personality and Social Psychology, 59,* 730–742.

Kilpatrick, S. D., Bissonnette, V. L., & Rusbult, C. E. (2002). Empathic accuracy and accommodative behavior among newly married couples. *Personal Relationships, 9,* 369–393.

Klein, K. J. K., & Hodges, S. D. (2001). Gender differences, motivation, and empathic accuracy: When it pays to understand. *Personality and Social Psychology Bulletin, 27,* 720–730.

Kohler, W. (1929). *Gestalt Psychology.* New York: Liveright.

Kruger, J., & Dunning, D. (1999). Unskilled and unaware of it: How difficulties in recognizing one's own incompetence lead to inflated self-assessments. *Journal of Personality and Social Psychology, 77,* 1121–1134.

Laurent, S. M., & Hodges, S. D. (2008). Gender roles and empathic accuracy: The role of communion in reading minds. Manuscript submitted for publication.

Malatesta, C. Z., Izard, C. E., Culver, C., & Nicolich, M. (1987). Emotion communication skills in young, middle-aged, and older women. *Psychology and Aging, 2,* 193–203.

Marangoni, C., Garcia, S., Ickes, W., & Teng, G. (1995). Empathic accuracy in a clinically relevant setting. *Journal of Personality and Social Psychology, 68,* 854–869.

Mead, G. H. (1934). *Mind, self, and society.* Chicago: University of Chicago Press.

Mitchell, J. P., Macrae, C. N., & Banaji, M. R. (2006). Dissociable medial prefrontal contributions to judgments of similar and dissimilar others. *Neuron, 50,* 655–663.

Rowling, J. K. (1999, October). Radio interview, *The Diane Rehm Show,* NPR.

Simpson, J. A., Ickes, W., & Blackstone, T. (1995). When the head protects the heart: Empathic accuracy in dating relationships. *Journal of Personality and Social Psychology, 69,* 629–641.

Simpson, J. A., Oriña, M. M., & Ickes, W. (2003). When accuracy hurts, and when it helps: A test of the empathic accuracy model in marital interactions. *Journal of Personality and Social Psychology, 85,* 881–893.

Stinson, L., & Ickes, W. (1992). Empathic accuracy in the interactions of male friends versus male strangers. *Journal of Personality and Social Psychology, 62,* 787–797.

Taylor, M., Hodges, S. D., & Kohanyi, A. (2003). The illusion of independent agency: Do adult fiction writers experience their characters as having minds of their own? *Imagination, Cognition and Personality, 22,* 361–380.

Thomas, G., Fletcher, G. J. O., & Lange, C. (1997). On-line empathic accuracy in marital interaction. *Journal of Personality and Social Psychology, 72,* 839–850.

Zebrowitz, L. A. (1990). *Social perception.* Pacific Grove, CA: Brooks/Cole.

20 Perspective Taking: Misstepping Into Others' Shoes

Nicholas Epley and Eugene M. Caruso

INTRODUCTION

The ability to intuit another person's thoughts, feelings, and inner mental states is surely among the most impressive of human mental faculties. Adopting another's perspective requires the ability to represent the self as distinct from others, the development of a theory of mind to realize that others have mental states in the first place (see also Saxe, Chapter 17, this volume), and the explicit recognition that others' mental states and perceptions could differ from one's own. Humans appear to be born with absolutely none of these capacities but instead develop them during the first few years of life (Callaghan et al., 2005; Flavell, 1999; Gopnik & Meltzoff, 1994). Developing these perspective-taking abilities appears critical for many of the good things in social life, from empathy, to cooperation, to possible acts of altruism. Not all humans develop these skills to equivalent degrees, and those who do not develop these skills to any degree are among the most puzzling members of society as they look perfectly human but act completely *un*human. Of course, humans are not alone in their capacity for self-awareness, their considerations of others' mental states, or perhaps even their awareness of differing perspectives and resulting mental states, but comparing the abilities of even the closest nonhuman relative is a bit like comparing sandcastles to skyscrapers (Hare, 2007).

But, as anyone who has recently purchased a cell phone, computer, or almost any other technological gadget knows all too well, owning impressive technology and using it correctly are two entirely different things. One of us, for instance, owns a cellular telephone that is also able to take pictures, play music, and do something called "texting," but so far is only able to use it to call other telephones. The same gap also holds for mental technologies, for which the possibility of performing some impressive mental operation need not equate with one's actual ability to perform this operation. From memory, to altruism, to self-control, the gap between what is possible with one's psychological abilities and what is probable can appear somewhat "canyonesque." The same, we argue, is also true of perspective taking. Humans possess the mental capability necessary to adopt another's perspective and consider another's thoughts, feelings, and internal mental states. This may happen when trying to consider another person's perspective in the present, such as when we wonder how our children could possibly have believed *that* was a good idea, or when people are trying to consider their own perspective at some other point in time, such as when a person anticipates how happy she would be in a new job or 1 year following her own wedding ceremony (see also Dunn, Forrin, & Ashton-James, Chapter 22, this volume). Possessing this capability does not, however, mean that people will necessarily use their perspective-taking skills when they should, or that their skills will actually lead them to accurately identify another person's mental states. Recent advancements in research on the processes underlying perspective taking, in fact, suggest several important challenges to using one's perspective-taking capabilities to their fullest potential and demonstrate a series of reliable missteps that perspective takers are likely to take when stepping (or failing to step) into others' shoes.

Making any kind of general statement about the accuracy of perspective taking is about as hopeless as making a general statement on the value of the U.S. dollar—it depends where you look, when you look, and how you measure it. People are quite capable, for instance, of recognizing the emotion a person is experiencing by looking at his or her facial expressions (Ekman, 1982) and can even detect certain false displays of emotion from truly felt displays (Frank, Ekman, & Friesen, 1993). Empathy for others in distress can be evoked automatically when one is explicitly directed to attend to another's pain and suffering (Batson, 1998), yet in the absence of such explicit direction, empathy is likely to be considerably less automatic (Batson, Chapter 18, this volume; Batson & Shaw, 1991; Hodges & Wegner, 1997; Myers & Hodges, Chapter 19, this volume). People are also reasonably good at recognizing what future versions of themselves will like and dislike but have considerably less ability to predict how much or for how long they will like or dislike those things (Wilson & Gilbert, 2003). Young children before age 4 have difficulty recognizing that others may have beliefs that differ very considerably from their own (Flavell, 1986; Perner, 1991; Wimmer & Perner, 1983) but come to appreciate this as a relatively common occurrence in everyday life as they get older (Wellman, Cross, & Watson, 2001). And people are reasonably good at intuiting the impressions they convey to others in general but are considerably less good at intuiting any specific individual's impression of them (Kenny & DePaulo, 1993). It is not clear that people's beliefs about their ability to accurately adopt another person's perspective reflect their actual ability to do so in any meaningful way (Realo et al., 2003), and confidence in one's ability to intuit another's thoughts consistently appears to outstrip accuracy—even among married couples (Swann & Gill, 1997). About the only general conclusion one can render is that the ability to accurately adopt someone's perspective is better than chance but less than perfect. Thankfully for psychologists, that conclusion leaves plenty of explaining to do.

Understanding how perspective taking operates in everyday social life requires both a consideration of the impressive strengths of this mental ability as well as a recognition of its weaknesses. There is no question that humans are capable of adopting others' perspectives and that doing so can increase social coordination, cooperation, and even psychological altruism. Discussions of such desirable consequences of perspective taking in social interaction are numerous (e.g., Batson, 1994; Galinsky, Ku, & Wang, 2005; Galinsky & Moskowitz, 2000; Lozano, Hard, & Tversky, 2006; Paese & Yonker, 2001; Wade-Benzoni, Tenbrunsel, & Bazerman, 1996).

Our treatment is decidedly less flattering, however, and considers in more detail the barriers that keep people from using their perspective-taking ability to its full potential. That considering another's perspective is difficult and less than perfect will be a surprise to none, but to understand why it is less than perfect and what one might do to improve the accuracy of this ability in everyday life requires an appreciation of the major barriers that keep people from using their potential abilities more completely. We believe there are three critical barriers—activating the ability, adjusting an egocentric default, and accessing accurate information about others. Perspective taking inherently involves simulating another person's thoughts and feelings, and our goal in this chapter is to outline in turn how each of these barriers can influence use of this particular aspect of mental simulation. This treatment is not meant as an implicit or explicit endorsement of the flawed nature of this particular aspect of human judgment, as a pejorative statement about the quality of human mental faculties more generally, or as an implication that accuracy in judgment is always desirable. Indeed, we suggest that many of the factors that reduce accuracy in perspective taking can, at times, also be responsible for many of the desirable outcomes of perspective taking in daily life. Instead, we believe that identifying the barriers that keep people from using their perspective-taking abilities to their full potential provides insights into how this ability is likely to operate in the barrier-heavy nature of social life and how people might go about improving on this already-impressive human faculty.

GAINING PERSPECTIVE ON PERSPECTIVE TAKING

Psychologists communicate their ideas in words rather than numbers, which means that ambiguity is an inherent feature of psychological discourse. Different words can be used to describe the same phenomena, and the same word can be used to describe very different phenomena. This latter problem characterizes discussions of perspective taking, for which the term has been used to describe everything from experiencing another person's emotion, to sympathizing with someone's experience, to anticipating another person's thoughts, to adopting another's visual perspective.

Although the underlying psychological mechanisms may vary (see Batson, Chapter 18, this volume), the feature shared by all instantiations of perspective taking is the need to get beyond one's own point of view to consider the world from another's perspective. Sometimes, psychologists mean this quite literally and measure people's ability to recognize what another person is able to see (Piaget, 1932/1965) or to consider a situation from a completely different visual perspective (Keysar, Barr, Balin, & Brauner, 2000; Libby & Eibach, Chapter 24, this volume, and 2002). But more often point of view is used figuratively to describe assessments based on one's own ideology, emotion, direct experience, or preexisting attitudes and knowledge. Perspective taking then requires getting beyond one's own literal or psychological point of view to consider the perspective of another person who is likely to have a very different psychological point of view. Overcoming egocentrism and one's own current state is therefore the litmus test for attempted perspective taking. People can certainly consider the mental states of someone who happens to share their own perspective, but doing so cannot meaningfully be distinguished from not doing so at all and remaining completely egocentric.

BARRIERS TO ACCURATE PERSPECTIVE TAKING

Successfully performing this particular feat of mental gymnastics requires at least three mental operations. The absence or erroneous operation of any of these can be a source of inaccuracy or miscalibration in perspective taking. First, the mental process of perspective taking must be activated. This requires people to actively think about another person's mental state when it is appropriate to do. Some situations automatically elicit empathic attempts to perceive the world from another person's perspective, such as seeing one's child in pain (Decety & Sommerville, 2003; Decety & Stevens, Chapter 1, this volume), but many do not and require explicit attempts to understand the world from another's perspective. Abilities are of practical importance only when people try to use them, and there is no more immediate barrier to accurate perspective taking than failing to use it in the first place.

Second, people who are actively attempting to adopt another's perspective must first get over their own to try to experience, simulate, or infer the perceptions of another person. One's own perspective is typically immediate, automatic, and easy, whereas reasoning about another's perspective is typically slow, deliberate, and difficult. Because people tend to perform easy tasks more readily than hard ones, the second major barrier to perspective taking is failing to get beyond the easy default of one's egocentric experiences to consider the perceptions of another in a different psychological state.

Finally, overcoming one's egocentric perspective may require using some other information in its place to intuit another's perspective. Such substitutes include stereotypes or other idiosyncratic information known about the target being evaluated. Everyday life provides people with a wealth of nonegocentric information about others that can be used to make inferences about their beliefs, attitudes, and motivations. Some of this information is likely to be quite accurate and revealing, such as a facial expression of disgust or happiness, whereas other information is likely to be fairly inaccurate and misleading, such as gossip or erroneous stereotypes. Accurate perspective taking requires using diagnostic and useful information about another's mental state and avoiding nondiagnostic or useless information, and this differentiation serves as what we believe to be the third major barrier to accurate perspective taking.

Barrier 1: Failing to Activate

One of our favorite urban legends is that people only use 10% of their brains. The statement for any psychologist is instantly hilarious, as if an fMRI scan might show that 90% of the brain is doing absolutely nothing at any given time, but the legend does capture some element of truth. People's brains are capable of a great deal of effortful thinking, but effortful thinking is hard, and people may therefore avoid doing it. People rely, for instance, on defaults in judgment, rapid first impressions when evaluating others, and simple heuristics for important decisions (Gigerenzer, Todd, & the ABC Research Group, 1999; Kahneman & Frederick, 2002). Adopting another's perspective is exactly the kind of mental effort and hard thinking that people may do considerably less often than they could (or than they should).

As barriers to almost anything go, this particular barrier to accurate perspective taking would seem relatively minor. People, after all, have been described as chronic mind readers (Baron-Cohen, 1995) who, after a certain point in development, seem to rapidly and automatically think about others' perspectives (Ickes, 2003). Being unable to consider others' thoughts is grounds for suffering from a psychological disorder (i.e., autism), and these extreme forms of mind-blindness would seem to leave the rest of us comfortable in our fairly automatic tendencies to at least think about others' perspectives when situations explicitly require us to do so. Experimental evidence, however, suggests that this hurdle may be higher than intuition would suggest.

When people are faced with one task that is easy and one that is hard, they can be counted on first to do the easy thing and only subsequently and unreliably do the hard thing (Fiske & Taylor, 1991; Gilbert, 2002). Because one's own perspective tends to come to mind more rapidly, readily, and reliably than information about others' perspectives, one's own point of view may tend to serve as the default perspective for interpreting the world even among full-grown adults (Krueger, 1998). Reducing the automaticity of this default to see things from another's perspective then requires either repeated and frequent practice, as in collectivistic cultures in which greater value is placed on others' perspectives compared to individualistic cultures (Cohen & Gunz, 2002; Wu & Keysar, 2007), or the strong motivation to exert the mental effort necessary to adopt another's perspective (Epley, Keysar, Van Boven, & Gilovich, 2004; Galinsky, Magee, Inesi, & Gruenfeld, 2006). In the absence of sufficient training or sufficient effort, people in social contexts can fail to consider another's perspective even when it is transparently obvious, on reflection, that they need to do so.

Consider, for instance, the ubiquity of social comparisons that require people to directly compare themselves to others. Stating that one is a good leader, a mediocre guitarist, and a bad hockey player, for instance, all require comparisons between one's own abilities and others' abilities. And yet, research suggests that people in these cases think less about others (if at all) than they should. In one study, for instance, people asked to report "how happy you are compared to the average student" instead appeared to answer the much simpler question, "How happy are you?" (Klar & Giladi, 1997). Being happy, of course, does not necessarily make you *happier* than others. This same tendency leads people to evaluate themselves as consistently above average on tasks that are objectively easy (such as using a computer mouse) but as consistently below average on tasks that are objectively difficult (such as computer programming; Kruger, 1999), and to believe that they are going to gain a unique advantage from benefits that are in fact shared by all in a competition (Windschitl & Chambers, 2004; Windschitl, Kruger, & Simms, 2003). In essence, people substitute the relatively easy assessment of their own absolute performance in the place of a more complicated assessment of their own performance compared to others.

These examples are not strictly about perspective taking, but they do make it clear that the self is likely to be a strong focus of attention that will exert inordinate influence on judgment in social contexts that explicitly require consideration of others. More compelling are demonstrations involving social interaction in which perspective taking is clearly required but not necessarily activated. The most blatant example of this is self-presentation, in which people strategically attempt to convey a desired impression to another person. Such self-presentation inherently requires considering how one will look through the eyes of another, and conveying a desired impression necessitates thinking about what one's target will find desirable. This does not, however, appear to be what people actually do.

In one recent experiment, for instance (Myrseth & Epley, 2008), participants were asked to indicate the likelihood that they would tell each of a series of jokes to a new acquaintance to make that person laugh and thereby make a good impression. In addition to these likelihood ratings, participants also rated the extent to which they personally found each of the jokes to be funny and the extent to which they thought their intended target would find the jokes funny. Results demonstrated a strong partial correlation between how funny participants themselves found the jokes and their reported likelihood of telling the joke to their acquaintance ($r = .42$, controlling for how funny they believed their acquaintance would find the joke) but no relationship between the reported likelihood of telling the joke and how funny they thought their acquaintance would find the joke ($r = .00$, controlling for how funny they personally found the joke). Similar strong and significant effects of one's egocentric evaluations were found in contexts ranging from using pickup lines, to constructing a résumé for a job, to providing excuses to a professor for turning in a paper late. Self-presentation involves presenting oneself to others, but these data suggest that people may be presenting primarily to themselves (see also Leary, 1995, p. 161).

Perhaps the clearest evidence, however, of this failure to consider others' perspectives comes from experiments that explicitly manipulate the instruction to consider another's perspective or not. If people in social contexts are already getting beyond themselves and engaging their perspective-taking abilities, then such an instruction should strike participants as redundant and have no measurable effect on thought or action. This does not seem to be the case. Participants in one condition of a prisoner's dilemma game, for instance, were shown the standard payoff matrix and asked to indicate whether they would cooperate or defect (Caruso, Epley, & Bazerman, 2007). In another condition, participants first were asked to consider what their partner would be thinking about this game before indicating whether they personally would cooperate or defect. Because one's payoff depends on his or her own behavior as well as the partner's behavior, it is obvious that participants should already be considering what their partner is likely to be thinking even if not explicitly instructed to do so. They were not. A full 60% of participants in the control condition chose to cooperate, but less than half of this figure (27.5%) chose to do so when first asked to think about others' thoughts (see also Croson, 2000; Idson et al., 2004; Samuelson & Bazerman, 1985). That being explicitly asked to consider the other player's thoughts has such a noticeable effect on behavior, for whatever reason, suggests that participants in the control condition were not already doing so.

In another set of experiments that manipulated the focus on relevant others (Savitsky, Van Boven, Epley, & Wight, 2005), participants were asked to indicate the percentage they personally contributed to a variety of different group tasks, from fourth graders working in a statewide debate team competition to college students recalling group tasks. Of course, the percentage of work one has contributed depends on how much he or she personally contributed compared to how much others in the group contributed. But, people seem to think far more about their own contributions than about others' (Ross & Sicoly, 1979; Thompson & Kelly, 1981), which leads them to reliably claim that they personally contributed far more than is logically possible (for a review, see Leary & Forsyth, 1987). This "overclaiming" result consistently emerged in the control conditions of these experiments, such that self-reported responsibility summed to more than 100%. More important, however, participants in other conditions were explicitly asked to think about others' contributions by first reporting the percentage that others contributed to the group task or were implicitly asked to think about others' contributions by simply listing the initials of each of their other group members. Both of these manipulations that led people to think beyond their own egocentric perspective significantly reduced the amount participants claimed they personally contributed (from 155% to 106% in the experiment with the student debate teams, for instance). In addition, explicitly being led to consider other group members tended to systematically decrease reported enjoyment and interest in working with this group again in the future among those who believed they contributed much to the group itself (Caruso, Epley, & Bazerman, 2006).

Every parent at one point or another has told his or her child to try to see things from another's point of view, and these experiments in some ways can make people look fairly childish. Piaget (1932/1965) recognized some time ago that childhood was characterized by an inability to see things from any perspective other than one's own, but people seem to outgrow this soon enough and move on to higher levels of cognitive development. These results serve as a reminder, however, that perspective taking is not a skill that turns on somewhere around the age of 5 and remains active thereafter. It is instead more like a light switch that must be switched on when needed. Failing to switch on one's perspective-taking ability when needed—perhaps because one lacks the attentional resources, time, or motivation to do so—can easily leave people reasoning in the dark.

Barrier 2: Miscalibrated Adjustment

If activating one's perspective-taking abilities were the only requirement for accurately adopting another's perspective, then this section could serve as our chapter's last. Adopting another person's perspective requires getting over one's own, and simply because people are trying to leave their own perspective behind does not ensure that they will do so completely. Many human judgments, from social comparisons (Mussweiler, 2003), to probability estimates (Griffin & Tversky, 1992), to dispositional inference (Gilbert, 2002), seem to be inordinately influenced by the first information that comes to mind. Perspective taking is no exception, and the first perspective that comes to one's mind often tends to be one's own.

This primacy may have such a profound effect on people's perceptions of an event that it may not even occur to them that others' perceptions may differ from their own and may therefore be in need of adjustment. Consider, for instance, an experiment in which participants were asked to send either sincere or sarcastic messages to another participant, either over the telephone or via e-mail (Kruger, Epley, Parker, & Ng, 2005, Study 1). Participants were asked to predict, for each of 10 sincere and 10 sarcastic messages, whether the recipient would interpret the message correctly or incorrectly. Sarcasm involves interpreting a message in precisely the opposite tone of its literal content and is therefore communicated by the tone in one's voice or other paralinguistic cues rather than by the literal content of the message—cues that are decidedly absent over e-mail.

It is perhaps not surprising, then, that recipients were not significantly better than chance (50.0%) at distinguishing between sarcasm and sincerity over e-mail ($M = 56.0\%$) but were significantly more accurate over the telephone ($M = 73.1\%$). More interesting, however, was that senders of these messages anticipated no difference in the recipients' accuracy when communicating over e-mail or the telephone ($M = 78.0\%$ vs. 77.9%, respectively). The senders' intentions to communicate sarcasm or sincerity were so clear that it rendered them unable to appreciate, it appears, that the perception of the person on the other end of the computer monitor would be very different from the person on the other end of the telephone. Similar difficulties plague teasers, for whom it is so clear that they are "just kidding" that they may completely fail to recognize that their target may take the "obvious" joke quite literally (Kruger, Gordan, & Kuban, 2006).

Even when people are fully aware that another's perspective is likely to differ from theirs, this initial egocentric assessment is likely to serve as a starting point in judgment that is subsequently corrected or adjusted. For instance, teachers know what they are trying to communicate to their students and need to overcome this knowledge to accurately assess the clarity of their lecture. Attempts to adopt others' perspectives can retain some traces of this initial egocentric assessment because attempts to adjust or correct such starting points in judgment tend to be insufficient (for reviews, see Epley, 2004; Keysar & Barr, 2002; Nickerson, 1999; Royzman, Cassidy, & Baron, 2003), leaving final judgments biased in the direction of the initial egocentric default.

Several empirical findings are consistent with this egocentric adjustment account of at least some instances of perspective taking. First, explicit instructions to adopt another person's perspective tend to increase the accessibility of self-related thoughts (Davis et al., 2004) and decrease the accessibility of stereotypes applicable to the target (Galinsky & Moskowitz, 2000). When given no explicit instructions about how to adopt another's perspective, people appear to start by using themselves as a default or a guide. This helps to explain why adopting the perspective of another person tends to increase the perceived similarity with the target and a merging of the self and the other (Davis, Conklin, Smith, & Luce, 1996).

In fact, when asked explicitly to predict how other people feel, people's own current feelings heavily influence their evaluations. When participants were asked to predict the level of unpleasantness experienced by a group of hungry and thirsty hikers who had gotten lost in the woods, those participants who were themselves thirsty thought that the hikers would be more bothered by thirst than hunger relative to participants who were not thirsty (Van Boven & Loewenstein, 2003). Such egocentric projection of drive states suggests again that people make predictions about how others will feel by first imagining what they themselves would feel in the others' situation and do not adjust sufficiently to overcome their own egocentric perspective.

Second, people tend to make egocentric inferences more quickly than nonegocentric inferences. In one experiment, participants were told that a telephone message left for another person was intended to be either sincere or sarcastic (Epley, Keysar et al., 2004). Participants were faster to indicate that the recipient of the message would interpret the message in a manner consistent with their own interpretation than in a manner inconsistent with their own interpretation. In another experiment, participants who saw pictures of a person holding an object in one of their hands were faster to indicate which side of the computer screen the object was on (consistent with their own perspective) than to indicate which hand the person was holding the object with (consistent with the target's perspective; Amorim, 2003; Michelon & Zacks, 2006; Presson, 1982).

Researchers armed with more sophisticated video equipment are even able to catch people in the very act of adjusting an initial egocentric assessment. In the most telling research paradigm, participants are asked to play a referential communication game in which they are told to move objects around a grid of boxes. On critical trials, participants are given an ambiguous instruction that will lead them to look at one object if they interpret the instruction from their own egocentric perspective but to look at another object if they interpret the instruction correctly from the director's perspective. Eye-tracking measures reveal that participants consistently look first at the object suggested by an egocentric interpretation and only subsequently (and not universally) look at the object suggested by adopting the other person's perspective (Keysar et al., 2000). This tendency is even increased when people are in states, such as a happy mood, that increase reliance on immediate defaults in judgment (Converse, Lin, Keysar, & Epley, 2008).

This ability to overcome or adjust an egocentric default may even help to explain the well-known perspective-taking differences between children and adults. In a replication of the eye-tracking procedure just described, children and adults were both equally quick (after controlling for baseline differences in reaction times) and equally likely to look at an object suggested by an egocentric interpretation and differed only in the speed and likelihood with which they corrected that egocentric interpretation to look at the correct object from the other person's perspective (Epley, Morewedge, & Keysar, 2004). Development brings with it the recognition that others' perspectives may differ very considerably from one's own, but that does not mean that people outgrow their initial egocentric tendencies.

Third, overcoming any default in judgment requires deliberate reasoning that takes time, attention, and motivation to expend mental effort. Anything that hinders people's ability to engage in such deliberate reasoning should therefore increase reliance on an egocentric default among perspective takers. Consistent with this account, such egocentric biases tend to increase when people are asked to respond quickly and decrease when people are given financial incentives to be accurate in their judgments (Epley, Keysar et al., 2004).

Fourth, adjusting an egocentric default requires some assessment of when to stop. Homeowners may recognize that they have overvalued their house and need to adjust their asking price downward, but how far? Research demonstrates that altering the likelihood of accepting a value encountered early in the adjustment process tends to increase egocentric biases, such that the extent of adjustment can be influenced by manipulating people's tendency to accept an intermediate estimate (Epley, Keysar et al., 2004). A downward-adjusting home owner may ask a higher price if he or she is rushed for time, for instance, or unable to think very carefully at the time of judgment.

These findings demonstrate that self-knowledge can produce assimilation effects in judgment, and a wide variety of egocentric biases attest to the generality of this process. This insufficient adjustment account can help to explain why people tend to overestimate the extent to which others share their attitudes, beliefs, and knowledge (Birch & Bloom, 2007; Keysar & Barr, 2002; Krueger & Clement, 1994), the extent to which their internal states and intentions are transparent to others (Gilovich, Medvec, & Savitsky, 2000), and their personal contribution in collective endeavors (Ross & Sicoly, 1979), among many others (Nickerson, 1999; Royzman et al., 2003). But, general rules are not without their exceptions, and the self can also serve as a source of contrast when adopting the perspective of others (Beauregard & Dunning, 1998; Dunning & Hayes, 1996).

In particular, others who are centrally defined by their dissimilarity to the self lead to judgments that highlight these differences and can induce contrast with the self. Labor versus management, Republican versus Democrat, Yankees fan versus Red Sox fan—all of these groups are defined by their dissimilarity to each other on specific dimensions that can lead perspective takers to use their own beliefs as a point of contrast when stepping into the shoes of the opposing side. In these cases, it is possible for perspective takers to overestimate the extent to which the beliefs of opposing groups differ from their own (Robinson, Keltner, Ward, & Ross, 1995), often on the very beliefs that people themselves hold with the greatest conviction (Chambers, Baron, & Inman, 2006; Chambers & Melnyk, 2006).

All of these findings converge on the conclusion that people's attempts to adopt another's perspective are likely to retain some residue of their own. When there are few cues that others are likely to see the world very differently, people may not adjust or correct an egocentric default at all. When the cues are ambiguous and there is some uncertainty about others' perspectives, attempts to adjust one's own perspective will tend to be insufficient, and resulting judgments are likely to be egocentrically biased. And, when the target of perspective taking is defined by its polar opposition to the self, people are likely to assume that the other person's perspective is also the polar opposite of their own—a belief that can exaggerate the differences between opposing sides that actually exist (see Markman & McMullen, 2003, and Mussweiler, 2003, for theoretical accounts related to egocentric assimilation and contrast effects). Perspective takers may get beyond the first hurdle mentioned in this chapter and be fully motivated to see things from another person's shoes, but such motivation does not ensure that they will leave their own perspective behind entirely.

Barrier 3: Inaccurate Adjustment

The research described thus far makes it clear that people often use themselves as a guide when perspective taking, using their own knowledge or perceptions as an anchor that can be subsequently adjusted as people attempt to get over themselves. Getting over the self to achieve an accurate sense of another's perspective, however, requires that the information used in place of an egocentric simulation or judgment itself be accurate. Considering the perspective of a child, a pet, or an elderly neighbor may call to mind a host of information about how these targets are likely to perceive the world, and using that information in place of an egocentric perspective will yield accurate judgments only to the extent that this alternate information itself is accurate. Using accurate information in place of one's own perspective is therefore the third and last major barrier to accurate perspective taking that we discuss.

To illustrate this point, consider the (often-painful) task of purchasing a birthday gift for a loved one. Identifying one's own favorite gift is simple, but few buy others exactly what they would like to be given themselves and instead try to infer what their loved one would like best. Similarity attracts in relationships, and loved ones become loved precisely because their preferences tend to match one's own. It is a good idea to use one's preferences when anticipating the preferences of a highly similar other and a bad idea to use them when picking for dissimilar others, yet people's sense of when exactly they should use themselves as a guide and when they should use other information does not seem completely calibrated with reality. People may differentiate too much between their own preferences and others' when thinking about others who are highly similar—such as a spouse (Hoch, 1987)—but differentiate too little when thinking about others whose preferences and perspectives are actually considerably different from their own (Lerouge & Warlop, 2006). Given these difficulties, it is understandable how gift-givers can reliably pay more money for their gifts than their recipients would be willing to pay for them (Waldfogel, 1993).

When people fail to use themselves as a guide for others' perspectives, they tend to rely on stored knowledge about the target under consideration. This may include stereotypes about what humans are like in general, attributes presumably shared by group members, or idiosyncratic knowledge about specific individuals derived from direct or indirect experience (Ames, 2004a, 2004b; Gopnik & Wellman, 1994). The use of such stored knowledge and stereotypes appears to be triggered, quite rationally, from the perception of dissimilarity between the self and a target. When another person seems similar to the self, egocentrism dominates perspective taking, but when another person seems very dissimilar to the self, stored knowledge may be used when trying to adopt another's perspective. In one experiment, for instance, Columbia University students used their own preferences when predicting the preferences of another Columbia student but used their stereotypes about University of California at Berkeley students when predicting the preferences of another Berkeley student (Ames, 2004b). In a more recent neuroimaging experiment, neural regions associated with self-referential thoughts were activated when participants reasoned about the mental states of a person perceived to be similar to themselves but not when they reasoned about a person perceived to be very different (Mitchell, Macrae, & Banaji, 2006).

More interesting, however, are systematic biases in the stored knowledge that people possess about others that may lead to systematically mistaken inferences about another person's thoughts, feelings, or likely behavior. The list of these systematic biases may be long, but we believe the most problematic for perspective takers is the tendency to be overly cynical about others' intentions and motivations. People do not need training in economics to believe that others are powerfully (if not exclusively) motivated by their own self-interest (although such training tends to help; Frank, Gilovich, & Regan, 1993). In one set of experiments, for instance, children as young as those in the second grade actively used a target's self-interest to evaluate the credibility of his or her statements, whereas kindergarteners did not (Mills & Keil, 2005). Such learning obviously did not come from first-grade classes on the power of self-interest but rather from informal instruction in the classroom of everyday life.

Like many other basic bits of learning at this time in life, cynicism provides a set of beliefs that can forever after serve as the basis of folk psychology and people's intuitive understanding of how the mind works (Miller, 1999). By adulthood, however, beliefs about the power of self-interest appear to have become so strong that they can sometimes exaggerate the actual power of self-interest. In one experiment (Miller & Ratner, 1998), participants predicted that nearly 30% more people would donate blood if they were paid $15 to do so than if they were paid nothing (62% vs. 33%, respectively). The actual difference in the percentage who indicated that they would be willing to donate among the same sample was only 11% between those who would be paid $15 versus nothing (73% vs. 63%, respectively). In another study (Kruger & Gilovich, 1999), spouses were asked to indicate how much credit they deserved for a variety of household tasks (e.g., walking the dog, doing the dishes, etc.). Spouses believed that their loved ones would claim responsibility self-servingly, so that they would happily accept more responsibility than they were due for desirable activities but deny more responsibility than they were due for undesirable activities. In reality, spouses tended to claim more responsibility than they were due for both desirable and undesirable activities. As Miller and Ratner (1998, p. 60) suggested, people may not always be ardent self-interested agents, but they are certainly ardent self-interested theorists.

These cynical beliefs about the power of self-interest are especially relevant for perspective taking because people tend to use them primarily when thinking about others. What people learn about self-interest as they age, in other words, is that other people are the ones primarily motivated by self-interest. In one series of experiments, participants consistently predicted that other people would behave more selfishly than they would themselves in contexts ranging from giving donations to support the American Cancer Society, to voting in a U.S. presidential election, to cooperating in a prisoner's dilemma game (Epley & Dunning, 2000, 2006). In another, customer service managers reported being equally motivated by extrinsic incentives (e.g., salary, fringe benefits) and intrinsic incentives (e.g., developing skills, accomplishing something worthwhile) but believed that other managers in the firm were considerably more motivated by extrinsic incentives than by intrinsic ones (Heath, 1999). Cynicism may be the foundation on which folk psychology is built, but that foundation is particularly strong when people are thinking about others.

The tendency toward egocentrism means that leading people to adopt another's view of the world and consider another's thoughts and feelings may have problematic effects in the very contexts in which it could be most beneficial. In particular, conflict between individuals and groups is typically marked by a divergence in perspective, a divergence that nearly every thinker on the human condition, including one's mother, has believed could be overcome by a concerted effort to see things from the other side's perspective. If people are inclined to overcome egocentrism and rely on stored knowledge when they are adopting the perspective of someone who appears different from them, and if self-interest is a basic piece of stored knowledge that people use when thinking about others, then adopting the perspective of another person in the midst of conflict can actually make matters worse rather than better (but see Myers & Hodges, Chapter 19, this volume, for a somewhat different view). Perspective takers who look across ideological divides and try to see things from the opposite side's perspective may not, after all, like what they see.

Consider the paradigmatic conflict scenario of separate parties (industrialists vs. environmentalists, for instance) vying over a portion of the same (presumably) fixed resources. Far from reducing conflict, trying to adopt the other side's perspective in these cases may activate a variety of cynical thoughts about the other side's motivations, intentions, and likely behavior. Such perspective taking may activate cynically biased knowledge and therefore undermine trust, diminish the apparent credibility of the other side, and perhaps more problematically increase how selfishly people behave themselves. Those who adopt the perspective of others in conflict may therefore come to behave more selfishly themselves out of the (often overly extreme) belief that others will behave selfishly, a phenomenon we have called *reactive egoism* (Epley, Caruso, & Bazerman, 2006).

To test for this possibility, participants in one experiment were asked to take part in a simulated social dilemma about the problem of overfishing in one portion of the world's oceans. Each member of a four-party group was asked to imagine being the representative for one particular fishing association who was meeting with members from three other associations to determine how to reduce harvest levels to preserve the species and retain long-term profitability. In the original demonstration, participants tended to claim that it was fair for them to receive more of the overall harvest than other group members believed was fair for them to receive (Wade-Benzoni et al., 1996). In a revised version of this paradigm, participants who were first asked to adopt the perspective of each of the other group members and consider what each of them would think was a fair amount to harvest actually chose to take more of the fixed resources than those who were not induced to adopt the other group members' perspectives. This occurred because considering the perspective of the other group members highlighted cynical thoughts about their likely behavior and led participants to think that others would behave more selfishly and that they should therefore behave more selfishly in return (Epley et al., 2006).

We suggest that using such cynical theories as a perspective-taking guide is a barrier to accuracy because participants in these experiments who were not led to adopt another's perspective did not behave as selfishly as perspective takers would have predicted. Notice, however, that this inaccuracy is hard to identify within any of these groups because people's cynical beliefs about others can become self-fulfilling. Members of groups who consider each others' thoughts using the same cynical theories will come to act in ways that are consistent with others' beliefs about them, but not because the beliefs themselves are necessarily accurate but rather because all members of the group are operating with the same biased pieces of stored knowledge. In this way, cynical beliefs about others' motivations and interests may come to be a self-fulfilling prophecy that can mask the inaccuracy of perspective taking (Miller & Ratner, 1998).

Given the current state of research, it is impossible to calculate how widespread such inaccurate perspective taking is outside the laboratory. Certainly, some perspective-taking tasks are dramatically easier than others. Recognizing that a grimacing person is in pain can be accurately accomplished by a 3-year-old, but reliably recognizing that a person is being dishonest can be remarkably difficult at any age. Given the difficulty people appear to have evaluating the validity and accuracy of even their own knowledge (Burson, Larrick, & Klayman, 2006; Kruger & Dunning, 1999), it is perhaps no wonder that people have such difficulty recognizing when the information they are using to adopt another's perspective is likely to be accurate and when it is not.

CONCLUDING THOUGHTS

Humans are endowed with a remarkable array of abilities, not the least of which is their ability to think about the mental states of others. Although the capacity to appreciate another's mind may be universal (Avis & Harris, 1991), the success and accuracy of this skill are anything but. At times, people will not recognize the need to activate their perspective-taking abilities and will therefore fail to take the first step toward understanding another's point of view. When they are able and motivated to take that first step, however, they may fall short of another's perspective because they are too heavily influenced by their own egocentric viewpoint. And, even when they manage to step beyond their own perspective, they may trip over the inaccurate or incomplete information of stored knowledge on which they rely when intuiting another's mind.

A better understanding of these barriers can help not only to determine ways to overcome them but also to determine when we should and should not try to overcome them. Although we have identified a number of biases that tend to reduce the accuracy of perspective taking, it is not clear whether such a reduction in accuracy is always desirable. Egocentrism may be a necessary ingredient for psychological altruism, may aid in the reduction of stereotype activation, and may help to avoid the cynical theories that are activated when people attempt to infer the motives and minds of others. As such, the functional consequences of perspective taking may be independent of accuracy. For instance, the extent to which members of a couple idealize each other predicts relationship satisfaction, even though these inflated perceptions are based on objectively inaccurate beliefs (Murray, Holmes, & Griffin, 1996).

Because the reduction of bias is not necessarily desirable or undesirable, perhaps the biggest benefit to a balanced assessment of perspective taking is the ability to specify the situations in which adopting another's perspective will produce beneficial outcomes and when it will not. For instance, in the simulated fishing conference study mentioned, the competitive environment led perspective takers to adopt cynical theories about how others would behave, ultimately making all parties pay for their selfish beliefs and subsequent selfish behavior. However, in a structurally similar dilemma that was framed as a cooperative, rather than competitive, interaction, perspective taking actually decreased selfish behavior and led groups to achieve more optimal outcomes (Epley et al., 2006). Such examples illustrate how a better understanding of the barriers to perspective taking may allow us to specify when, how far, and in what direction people should step when attempting to place themselves in the shoes of others.

REFERENCES

Ames, D. R. (2004a). Inside the mind-reader's toolkit: Projection and stereotyping in mental state inference. *Journal of Personality and Social Psychology, 87*, 340–353.

Ames, D. (2004b). Strategies for social inference: A similarity contingency model of projection and stereotyping in attribute prevalence estimates. *Journal of Personality and Social Psychology, 87*, 340–353.

Amorim, M. A. (2003). "What is my avatar seeing?": The coordination of "out-of-body" and "embodied" perspectives for scene recognition across views. *Visual Cognition, 10*, 157–199.

Avis, J., & Harris, P. (1991). Belief-desire reasoning among Baka children: Evidence for a universal conception of mind. *Child Development, 62*, 460–467.

Baron-Cohen, S. (1995). *Mindblindness: An essay on autism and theory of mind.* Boston: MIT Press.

Batson, C. D. (1994). Prosocial motivation: Why do we help others? In A. Tesser (Ed.), *Advanced social psychology* (pp. 333–381). Boston: McGraw-Hill.

Batson, C. D. (1998). Altruism and prosocial behavior. In D. Gilbert, S. Fiske, & G. Lindsay (Eds.), *Handbook of social psychology* (pp. 282–316). New York: McGraw-Hill.

Batson, C. D., & Shaw, L. (1991). Evidence for altruism: Toward a pluralism of prosocial motives. *Psychological Inquiry, 2*, 107–122.

Beauregard, K. S., & Dunning, D. (1998). Turning up the contrast: Self-enhancement motives prompt egocentric contrast effects in social judgments. *Journal of Personality and Social Psychology, 74*, 606–621.

Birch, S., & Bloom, P. (2007). The curse of knowledge in reasoning about false beliefs. *Psychological Science, 18*, 382–386.

Burson, K. A., Larrick, R. P., & Klayman, J. (2006). Skilled or unskilled, but still unaware of it: How perceptions of difficulty drive miscalibration in relative comparisons. *Journal of Personality and Social Psychology, 90*, 60–77.

Callaghan, T., Tochat, P., Lillard, A., Claux, M. L., Odden, H., Itakura, S., et al. (2005). Synchrony in the onset of mental-state reasoning: Evidence from five cultures. *Psychological Science, 16*, 378–384.

Caruso, E. M., Epley, N., & Bazerman, M. H. (2006). The costs and benefits of undoing egocentric responsibility assessments in groups. *Journal of Personality and Social Psychology, 91*, 857–871.

Caruso, E. M., Epley, N., & Bazerman, M. H. (2007). *Reactive egoism and unwarranted distrust.* Unpublished manuscript, Harvard University, Cambridge, MA.

Chambers, J. R., Baron, R. S., & Inman, M. L. (2006). Misperceptions in intergroup conflict: Disagreeing about what we disagree about. *Psychological Science, 17*, 38–45.

Chambers, J. R., & Melnyk, D. (2006). Why do I hate thee? Conflict misperceptions and intergroup mistrust. *Personality and Social Psychology Bulletin, 32*, 1295–1311.

Cohen, D., & Gunz, A. (2002). As seen by the other … : Perspectives on the self in the memories and emotional perceptions of Easterners and Westerners. *Psychological Science, 13*, 55–59.

Converse, B. A., Lin, S., Keysar, B., & Epley, N. (2008). *In the mood to get over yourself: Mood affects theory-of-mind use.* Manuscript submitted for publication.

Croson, R. T. A. (2000). Thinking like a game theorist: Factors affecting the frequency of equilibrium play. *Journal of Economic Behavior and Organization, 41*, 299–314.

Davis, M. H., Conklin, L., Smith, A., & Luce, C. (1996). Effect of perspective taking on the cognitive representation of persons: A merging of self and other. *Journal of Personality and Social Psychology, 70*, 713–726.

Davis, M. H., Soderlund, T., Cole, J., Gadol, E., Kute, M., Myers, M., et al. (2004). Cognitions associated with attempts to empathize: How do we imagine the perspective of another? *Personality and Social Psychology Bulletin, 30*, 1625–1635.

Decety, J., & Sommerville, J. A. (2003). Shared representations between self and others: A social cognitive neuroscience view. *Trends in Cognitive Science, 7*, 527–533.

Dunning, D., & Hayes, A. F. (1996). Evidence for egocentric comparison in social judgment. *Journal of Personality and Social Psychology, 71*, 213–229.

Ekman, P. (1982) *Emotion in the human face.* New York: Cambridge University Press.

Epley, N. (2004). A tale of tuned decks? Anchoring as adjustment and anchoring as activation. In D. J. Koehler & N. Harvey (Eds.), *Blackwell handbook of judgment and decision making* (pp. 240–256). London: Blackwell.

Epley, N., Caruso, E. M., & Bazerman, M. H. (2006). When perspective taking increases taking: Reactive egoism in social interaction. *Journal of Personality and Social Psychology, 91*, 872–889.

Epley, N., & Dunning, D. (2000). Feeling "Holier than thou": Are self-serving assessments produced by errors in self or social prediction? *Journal of Personality and Social Psychology, 79*, 861–875.

Epley, N., & Dunning, D. (2006). The mixed blessings of self-knowledge in behavioral prediction: Enhanced discrimination but exacerbated bias. *Personality and Social Psychology Bulletin, 32,* 641–655.

Epley, N., Keysar, B., Van Boven, L., & Gilovich, T. (2004). Perspective taking as egocentric anchoring and adjustment. *Journal of Personality and Social Psychology, 87,* 327–339.

Epley, N., Morewedge, C., & Keysar, B. (2004). Perspective taking in children and adults: Equivalent egocentrism but differential correction. *Journal of Experimental Social Psychology, 40,* 760–768.

Fiske, S. T, & Taylor, S. E. (1991). *Social cognition.* New York: McGraw-Hill.

Flavell, J. H. (1986). The development of children's knowledge about the appearance-reality distinction. *American Psychologist, 41,* 418–425.

Flavell, J. H. (1999). Cognitive development: Children's knowledge about the mind. *Annual Review of Psychology, 50,* 21–45.

Frank, M. G., Ekman, P., & Friesen, W. V. (1993). Behavioral markers and recognizability of the smile of enjoyment. *Journal of Personality and Social Psychology, 72,* 1429–1439.

Frank, R. H., Gilovich, T., & Regan, D. T. (1993). Does studying economics inhibit cooperation? *Journal of Economic Perspectives 7,* 159–171.

Galinsky, A. D., Ku, G., & Wang, C. S. (2005). Perspective-taking: Fostering social bonds and facilitating social coordination. *Group Processes and Intergroup Relations, 8,* 109–125.

Galinsky, A. D., Magee, J. C., Inesi, M. E., & Gruenfeld, D. H. (2006). Power and perspectives not taken. *Psychological Science, 17,* 1068–1074.

Galinsky, A. D., & Moskowitz, G. B. (2000). Perspective-taking: Decreased stereotype expression, stereotype accessibility, and in-group favoritism. *Journal of Personality and Social Psychology, 78,* 708–724.

Gigerenzer, G., Todd, P. M., & the ABC Research Group. (1999). *Simple heuristics that make us smart.* New York: Oxford University Press.

Gilbert, D. T. (2002). Inferential correction. In T. Gilovich, D. Griffin, & D. Kahneman (Eds.), *Heuristics and biases: The psychology of intuitive judgment* (pp. 167–184). Cambridge, England: Cambridge University Press.

Gilovich, T., Medvec, V. H., & Savitsky, K. (2000). The spotlight effect in social judgment: An egocentric bias in estimates of the salience of one's own actions and appearance. *Journal of Personality and Social Psychology, 78,* 211–222.

Gopnik, A., & Meltzoff, A. N. (1994). Minds, bodies, and persons: Young children's understanding of the self and others as reflected in imitation and "theory of mind" research. *Behavioral and Brain Sciences, 16,* 1–14.

Gopnik, A., & Wellman, H. M. (1994). The theory theory. In L. A. Hirschfeld & S. A. Gelman (Eds.), *Mapping the mind: Domain specificity in cognition and culture* (pp. 257–293). New York: Cambridge University Press.

Griffin, D. W., & Tversky, A. (1992). The weighing of evidence and the determinants of confidence. *Cognitive Psychology, 24,* 411–435.

Hare, B. (2007). From nonhuman to human mind: What changed and why? *Current Directions in Psychological Science, 16,* 60–64.

Heath, C. (1999). On the social psychology of agency relationships: Lay theories of motivation overemphasize extrinsic rewards. *Organizational Behavior and Human Decision Processes, 78,* 25–62.

Hoch, S. J. (1987). Perceived consensus and predictive accuracy: The pros and cons of projection. *Journal of Personality and Social Psychology, 53,* 221–234.

Hodges, S., & Wegner, D. M. (1997). Automatic and controlled empathy. In W. J. Ickes (Ed.), *Empathic accuracy* (pp. 311–339). New York: Guilford.

Ickes, W. (2003). *Everyday mind reading: Understanding what other people think and feel.* Amherst, NY: Prometheus Books.

Idson, L. C., Chugh, D., Bereby-Meyer, Y., Moran, S., Grosskopf, B., & Bazerman, M. H. (2004). Overcoming focusing failures in competitive environments. *Journal of Behavioral Decision Making. 17,* 159–172.

Kahneman, D., & Frederick, S. (2002). Representativeness revisited: Attribute substitution in intuitive judgment. In T. Gilovich, D. Griffin, & D. Kahneman (Eds.), *Heuristics and biases: The psychology of intuitive judgment* (pp. 49–81). New York: Cambridge University Press.

Keysar, B., & Barr, D. J. (2002). Self-anchoring in conversation: Why language users do not do what they "should." In T. Gilovich, D. Griffin, & D. Kahneman (Eds.), *Heuristics and biases: The psychology of intuitive judgment* (pp. 150–166). New York: Cambridge University Press.

Keysar, B., Barr, D. J., Balin, J. A., & Brauner, J. S. (2000). Taking perspective in conversation: The role of mutual knowledge in comprehension. *Psychological Science, 11,* 32–39.

Kenny, D. A., & DePaulo, B. M. (1993). Do people know how others view them? An empirical and theoretical account. *Psychological Bulletin, 114,* 145–161.

Klar, Y., & Giladi, E. E. (1997). No one in my group can be below the group's average: A robust positivity bias in favor of anonymous peers. *Journal of Personality and Social Psychology, 73,* 885–901.

Krueger, J. (1998). On the perception of social consensus. In M. P. Zanna (Ed.), *Advances in experimental social psychology* (Vol. 30, pp. 163–240). San Diego, CA: Academic Press.

Krueger, J., & Clement, R. (1994). The truly false consensus effect: An ineradicable and egocentric bias in social perception. *Journal of Personality and Social Psychology, 65,* 596–610.

Kruger, J. (1999). Lake Wobegon be gone! The "below-average effect" and the egocentric nature of comparative ability judgments. *Journal of Personality and Social Psychology, 77,* 221–232.

Kruger, J., & Dunning, D. (1999). Unskilled and unaware of it: How difficulties in recognizing one's own incompetence lead to inflated self-assessments. *Journal of Personality and Social Psychology, 77,* 1121–1134.

Kruger, J., Epley, N., Parker, J., & Ng, Z. (2005). Egocentrism over email: Can we communicate as well as we think? *Journal of Personality and Social Psychology, 89,* 925–936.

Kruger, J., & Gilovich, T. (1999). "Naive cynicism" in everyday theories of responsibility assessment: On biased assumptions of bias. *Journal of Personality and Social Psychology, 76,* 743–753.

Kruger, J., Gordan, C., & Kuban, J. (2006). Intentions in teasing: When "just kidding" just isn't good enough. *Journal of Personality and Social Psychology, 90,* 412–425.

Leary, M. R. (1995). *Self-presentation: Impression management and interpersonal behavior.* Boulder, CO: Westview Press.

Leary, M. R., & Forsyth, D. R. (1987). Attributions of responsibility for collective endeavors. In C. Hendrick (Ed.), *Review of personality and social psychology* (Vol. 8, pp. 167–188). Newbury Park, CA: Sage.

Lerouge, D., & Warlop, L. (2006). Why it is so hard to predict our partner's product preferences: The effect of target familiarity on prediction accuracy. *Journal of Consumer Research, 33,* 393–402.

Libby, L. K., & Eibach, R. P. (2002). Looking back in time: Self-concept change affects visual perspective in autobiographical memory. *Journal of Personality and Social Psychology, 82,* 167–179.

Lozano, S. C., Hard, B. M., & Tversky, B. (2006). Perspective taking promotes action understanding and learning. *Journal of Experimental Psychology: Human Perception and Performance, 32,* 1405–1421.

Markman, K. D., & McMullen, M. N. (2003). A reflection and evaluation model of comparative thinking. *Personality and Social Psychology Review, 7,* 244–267.

Michelon, P., & Zacks, J. M. (2006). Two kinds of visual perspective taking. *Perception and Psychophysics, 68,* 327–337.

Miller, D. T. (1999). The norm of self-interest. *American Psychologist, 54,* 1053–1060.

Miller, D. T., & Ratner, R. K. (1998). The disparity between the actual and assumed power of self-interest. *Journal of Personality and Social Psychology, 74,* 53–62.

Mills, C., & Keil, F. C. (2005). The development of cynicism. *Psychological Science, 16,* 385–390.

Mitchell, J. P., Macrae, C. N., & Banaji, M. R. (2006). Dissociable medial prefrontal contributions to judgments of similar and dissimilar others. *Neuron, 50,* 655–663.

Murray, S. L., Holmes, J. G., & Griffin, D. W. (1996). The benefits of positive illusions: Idealization and the construction of satisfaction in close relationships. *Journal of Personality and Social Psychology, 70,* 79–98.

Mussweiler, T. (2003). Comparison processes in social judgment: Mechanisms and consequences. *Psychological Review, 110,* 472–489.

Myrseth, K., & Epley, N., (2008). *Putting the self in self-presentation: Egocentric biases in the strategic presentation of oneself to others.* Unpublished manuscript, University of Chicago.

Nickerson, R. S. (1999). How we know—and sometimes misjudge—what others know: Imputing one's own knowledge to others. *Psychological Bulletin, 125,* 737–759.

Paese, P. W., & Yonker, R. D. (2001). Toward a better understanding of egocentric fairness judgments in negotiation. *The International Journal of Conflict Management, 12,* 114–131.

Perner, J. (1991). *Understanding the representational mind.* Cambridge, MA: MIT Press.

Piaget, J. (1965). *The moral judgment of the child* (M. Gabain, Trans.). New York: Free Press. (Original work published 1932)

Presson, C. C. (1982). Strategies in spatial reasoning. *Journal of Experimental Psychology: Learning, Memory, and Cognition, 8,* 243–251.

Realo, A., Allik, J., Nolvak, A., Valk, R., Ruus, T., Schmidt, M., et al. (2003). Mind-reading ability: Beliefs and performance. *Journal of Research in Personality, 37,* 420–445.

Robinson, R., Keltner, D., Ward, A., & Ross, L. (1995). Actual versus assumed differences in construal: "Naive realism" in intergroup perceptions and conflict. *Journal of Personality and Social Psychology, 68,* 404–417.

Ross, M., & Sicoly, F. (1979). Egocentric biases in availability and attribution. *Journal of Personality and Social Psychology, 37,* 322–336.

Royzman, E. B., Cassidy, K. W., Baron, J. (2003). "I know, you know": Epistemic egocentrism in children and adults. *Review of General Psychology, 7,* 38–65.

Samuelson, W. F., & Bazerman, M. H. (1985). The winner's curse in bilateral negotiations. In V. Smith (Ed.), *Research in experimental economics* (Vol. 3, pp. 103–137). Greenwich, CT: JAI Press.

Savitsky, K., Van Boven, L., Epley, N., & Wight, W. (2005). The unpacking effect in responsibility allocations for group tasks. *Journal of Experimental Social Psychology, 41,* 447–457.

Swann, W. B., Jr., & Gill, M. J. (1997). Confidence and accuracy in person perception: Do we know what we think we know about our relationship partners? *Journal of Personality and Social Psychology, 73,* 747–757.

Thompson, S. C., & Kelly, H. H. (1981). Judgments of responsibility for activities in close relationships. *Journal of Personality and Social Psychology, 41,* 469–477.

Van Boven, L., & Loewenstein, G. (2003). Social projection of transient drive states. *Personality and Social Psychology Bulletin, 29,* 1159–1168.

Wade-Benzoni, K. A., Tenbrunsel, A. E., & Bazerman, M. H. (1996). Egocentric interpretations of fairness in asymmetric, environmental social dilemmas: Explaining harvesting behavior and the role of communication. *Organizational Behavior and Human Decision Processes, 67,* 111–126.

Waldfogel, J. (1993). The deadweight loss of Christmas. *American Economic Review, 83,* 1328–1336.

Wellman, H. M., Cross, D., & Watson, J. (2001). Meta-analysis of theory-of-mind development: The truth about false belief. *Child Development, 72,* 655–684.

Wilson, T. D., & Gilbert, D. T. (2003). Affective forecasting. In M. Zanna (Ed.), *Advances in experimental social psychology* (Vol. 35, pp. 345–411). New York: Elsevier.

Wimmer, H., & Perner, J. (1983). Beliefs about beliefs: Representation and constraining function of wrong beliefs in young children's understanding of deception. *Cognition, 13,* 103–128.

Windschitl, P. D., & Chambers, J. R. (2004). The dud-alternative effect in likelihood judgment. *Journal of Experimental Psychology: Learning, Memory, and Cognition, 30,* 198–215.

Windschitl, P. D., Kruger, J., & Simms, E. N. (2003). The influence of egocentrism and focalism on people's optimism in competitions: When what affects us equally affects me more. *Journal of Personality and Social Psychology, 85,* 389–408.

Wu, S., & Keysar, B. (2007). The effect of culture on perspective taking. *Psychological Science, 18,* 600–606.

Section VI

Simulating and Preparing for the Future

21 Imagining a Rosy Future: The Psychology of Optimism

William M. P. Klein and Laura E. Zajac

INTRODUCTION

One of the prevailing themes in this volume is that people's mental simulations regarding future events are associated with a fascinating and complex array of biological, neurological, psychological, and social processes. How people think about the future holds important consequences for decision making, productivity, and mental and physical health. To what extent does it matter whether these views of the future are tinged with optimism? If optimism is an important facet of how people think about the future, it is essential to determine how we should best define optimism, as different definitions may lead to strikingly different conclusions. It also seems essential to understand the mechanisms that underlie optimism (however optimism is defined), as well as to understand the extent to which optimism about the future influences the chances of obtaining the very outcomes about which people are optimistic.

Our goal in this chapter is to explore some of the ways in which the construct of optimism is defined and the extent to which these various conceptualizations are related. In so doing, we hope to illustrate the variability with which this seemingly simplistic concept can be defined, with attendant differences in the conclusions we might draw about its role in various life outcomes and about the processes involved. We begin by briefly considering some standard conceptualizations of optimism.

DIMENSIONS OF OPTIMISM

There are several key dimensions that help to differentiate the many ways in which optimism can be conceptualized. One can think of optimism as a generic personality trait—a predisposition to "expect the best." This conceptualization of optimism is captured well by Scheier and Carver's (1993) Life Orientation Test (LOT), which includes such items as "I'm always optimistic about my future" and "If something can go wrong for me, it will." On the other hand, optimism can be defined in terms of whether predictions about future events are positively valenced. Such a perspective moves away from characterizing optimism as an enduring individual difference variable and rather considers optimism to be a function of context. For example, people are generally less optimistic about a wide variety of personal life events following a natural disaster or terrorist attack or after a negative mood induction (Helweg-Larsen, 1999; Johnson & Tversky, 1983; Lerner & Keltner, 2000). This distinction may be important given that it would be easier to design interventions to increase optimism (assuming doing so was considered beneficial) if optimism was a product of the situation than if it was a relatively stable personality trait.

It is also important to consider whether optimism is defined in part by contrasting it with pessimism. Is it necessary to have a positive outlook to be optimistic or simply not to have a negative outlook? Recent work using the Scheier and Carver (1993) LOT scale has demonstrated that positively valenced and negatively valenced items form independent factors (Herzberg, Glaesmer, & Hoyer, 2006). This suggests that optimism is by no means the opposite of pessimism. High levels of optimism and pessimism may simply reflect high levels of engagement or emotional lability, a notion that deserves greater attention in the literature.

The most common way of measuring optimism in the literature is to ask participants to rate their personal chances of experiencing one or more events and then assess whether their responses reflect an expectation of favorable outcomes in the future. For purposes of this chapter, we call this *single-event optimism*. However, there are many ways to measure single-event optimism, and the possibilities vary across several important psychological dimensions. Next, we consider four.

COGNITIVE VERSUS AFFECTIVE JUDGMENTS

In the conventional risk perception literature, people are asked to make largely cognitive judgments about their risk. Standard scales include a 0–100% scale, a likelihood scale with verbal labels (e.g., "not at all likely" through "extremely likely") and a "magnifier" scale in which the 0–1% portion of a standard percentage scale is magnified to encourage greater awareness that many risks fall in that range (Gurmankin, Helweg-Larsen, Armstrong, Kimmel, & Volpp, 2005). Because lower ratings on these scales signify lower risk, these ratings might be labeled as optimistic.

There are several problems with these types of judgments. First, the more numerical judgments assume a certain facility with numerical content, and many people have trouble generating and interpreting meaningful numerical risk information (Lipkus, Samsa, & Rimer, 2001). A substantial literature has identified a variety of biases in the way people use numbers, such as focusing more on the numerator than the denominator of a fraction (Gigerenzer & Hoffrage, 1995; Schwartz, Woloshin, Black, & Welch, 1997) and overestimating statistical associations between two events (e.g., antibiotic use and breast cancer occurrence) because of a disproportionate focus on when the two events co-occur (Chapman & Chapman, 1967). The second problem is these judgments are often only moderately correlated with a variety of cognitive and behavioral measures (Reyna, 2004), suggesting the possibility that they do not truly represent the way people mentally represent their personal risk.

Research in the decision sciences has begun to pay more attention to the significant role that affect plays in risk judgments and decision making under uncertainty (Loewenstein, Weber, Hsee, & Welch, 2001; Slovic, Peters, Finucane, & MacGregor, 2005). There is now much accumulated evidence that "feelings" about risk may be highly predictive of behavior and decisions under uncertainty. For example, one study showed that a measure in which participants indicated whether they "felt at risk" for getting the flu was more predictive of whether they got a flu shot than any of the more conventional measures discussed above (Weinstein et al., 2007). Epstein (1994) argued in his cognitive-experiential self theory (CEST) that information processing occurred in two parallel modes—a rational cognitive system accompanied by an experience-based emotional system—and often the two systems lead to conflicting judgments and decisions (see also Dunn, Forrin, & Ashton-James, Chapter 22, this volume). In a classic example, Denes-Raj and Epstein (1994) presented undergraduates with two bowls of jelly beans and informed them that they would win a prize if they randomly selected a red jelly bean. They then chose a bowl from which to draw a bean. One bowl had 1 red jelly bean out of 10 (10% chance of winning) and the other 7 reds out of 100 (7% chance of winning). Despite the lower chance of winning with the second bowl, participants tended to prefer it over the first bowl. The authors argued this was so because the experience of seeing 7 jelly beans (and therefore 7 ways of winning) was more affectively appealing.

Other work shows that worry (which could be viewed to some degree as antithetical to optimism) is predictive of behavior and other outcomes (McCaul, Branstetter, Schroeder, & Glasgow, 1996; McCaul & Mullens, 2003). In a recent study, we found that worry predicted behavior change even when controlling for more conventional measures of perceived risk as well as constructs in the theory of planned behavior (e.g., Schmiege, Bryan, & Klein, in press). In short, it may be appropriate to define optimism not as a belief that one's risk is low but rather as a feeling that this is the case. More research using affective measures of perceived vulnerability are clearly necessary.

ABSOLUTE VERSUS COMPARATIVE JUDGMENTS

Instead of asking people to estimate their chances of experiencing a future life event on an absolute scale such as those noted (e.g., a percentage scale or a likelihood scale), people might also be asked to estimate these chances relative to the chances of another person or persons. Typically, the scale accompanying such an item includes a midpoint signifying "same" risk, with responses below this midpoint signifying a perception that one's chances are lower than those of the referent and those above the midpoint that one's chances are higher. In most studies, the referent is the "average" person in one's peer group; for example, a woman might be asked to estimate her chances of getting breast cancer relative to other women of the same age.

This comparative measure of personal risk is the most common one used to measure unrealistic optimism (Weinstein & Klein, 1996), largely because it is fairly easy to identify bias in a large group by showing that the mean response deviates from the midpoint of the scale. Such a bias has generally been called "optimistic bias" or "unrealistic optimism." Dozens of studies have demonstrated unrealistic optimism using this scale in many different domains (Helweg-Larsen & Shepperd, 2001). It is interesting to note, however, that bias on one type of scale (absolute or comparative) does not suggest that one will observe bias on the other type of scale. For example, women tend to overestimate their absolute breast cancer risk and yet often believe their risk is lower than that of other women—representing pessimism about absolute risk and optimism about comparative risk (Lipkus, Biradavolu, Fenn, Keller, & Rimer, 2001). Moreover, absolute and comparative risk perceptions are often only moderately correlated (Lipkus, Klein, Skinner, & Rimer, 2005; Zajac, Klein, & McCaul, 2006), suggesting they capture somewhat independent psychological constructs.

RAW VERSUS CALIBRATED JUDGMENTS

As noted, optimistic judgments are not necessarily optimistically biased judgments. If a man who does not smoke or come into contact with radon or polluted air rates his risk of getting lung cancer to be low, then he would be right to do so. In fact, his risk might be even lower than he thinks it is, in which case he should be regarded as *pessimistically* biased. The only way to label a person's prediction as biased (optimistically or pessimistically) is to obtain information that might be used to calibrate this prediction, such as standing on relevant risk factors. Most studies do not go to these lengths. Instead, they measure people's predictions and then correlate the predictions with other variables such as anxiety and behavior (see review by Klein & Cooper, 2008). Such relationships are informative—they tell us whether optimism (independent of accuracy) is related to other important psychological variables such as anxiety (Dewberry & Richardson, 1990). Indeed, being optimistic about future outcomes seems to have a multitude of positive consequences, ranging from behavioral to psychophysiological (see review by Nes & Segerstrom, 2006). On the other hand, there are far fewer studies that assess how optimistic biases are related to psychological processes (Klein & Cooper, 2008). We return to this issue in the section entitled "Causes and Consequences of Optimism" on page 319.

CONDITIONAL VERSUS UNCONDITIONAL JUDGMENTS

Optimism about the chances of an event happening is not equivalent to optimism about the chances of an event happening given the presence of some other factor. For example, a smoker may be optimistic about not getting cancer (unconditional risk judgment), yet pessimistic about the prospects of reducing his or her risk by quitting (conditional risk judgment). Conditional risk judgments are often used to assess people's optimism about avoiding future events if they take or fail to take precautions to prevent those outcomes (e.g., What are your chances of getting heart disease if you maintain your current sedentary lifestyle?). Although conditional risk judgments more clearly demonstrate the temporal relationship between risk perceptions and behavior (Weinstein, Rothman, & Nicolich, 1998) because the nature of the question effectively controls for past behavior, they are not used frequently in the risk perception literature. Thus, it is difficult to know whether optimism is more or less likely to emerge with these types of judgments.

SHORT-TERM VERSUS LONG-TERM JUDGMENTS

Optimism is by definition a temporal phenomenon—it reflects beliefs about the future. But, some events are more temporally proximal than others. Most research in the area of unrealistic optimism asks participants about long-term events, such as the chances of experiencing serious health problems later in life. However, one could also ask about events that will occur in the short term, such as whether one will be able to complete a task on time (Buehler, Griffin, & Ross, 1994). The temporal proximity of an event turns out to be important when attempting to establish the presence of optimism, such that people are considerably more optimistic about long-term than short-term outcomes (Gilovich, Griffin, & Kahneman, 2002; Shepperd, Helweg-Larsen, & Ortega, 2003). Outcomes that are imminent often evoke a substantial diminution of optimism, perhaps because people are "bracing" for potentially bad news (Shepperd, Findley-Klein, Kwavnick, Walker, & Perez, 2000; Carroll & Shepperd, Chapter 28, this volume; but see also Perunovic & Wilson, Chapter 23, this volume).

OPTIMISM FOR SINGLE EVENTS VERSUS MULTIPLE EVENTS

A final distinction can be made between optimism defined at the level of the single event (e.g., whether one will die of heart disease) or at the level of multiple events. Most risk perception studies include measures of perceived risk for single events, which may be defined as optimistic (if the ratings are on the low-risk end of the scale), or unrealistically optimistic (if the ratings are lower than what they should be based on an objective criterion). A notable exception would be studies that explicitly examine correlates of unrealistically optimistic judgments. As noted, it is easier to demonstrate unrealistic optimism at the level of the group than it is to do so at the level of the individual. Consequently, many studies (particularly early demonstrations of unrealistic optimism; see Weinstein, 1980, 1982, 1984, 1987) presented individuals with an extensive list of life events and had them rate their personal risk of each event. Mean responses across the multiple events were then correlated with mean responses on other variables, such as the extent to which participants believed each event was controllable. Because these analyses used the event as the unit of analysis, it was possible to discuss the findings in the context of *unrealistic* optimism rather than optimism more generally.

Several other studies have asked participants to rate their chances of experiencing multiple events, and these ratings are then summed into a scale purportedly measuring unrealistic optimism (e.g., Davidson & Prkachin, 1997; Tusaie & Patterson, 2006). As noted, it is probably more appropriate to call this summed score a measure of optimism rather than unrealistic optimism, given that objective criteria are not available to examine the accuracy of each and every rating. Moreover, the reliability of such a score is likely to be quite low in many circumstances, given that risk ratings for some types of life events (e.g., being burglarized) do not necessarily have anything to do with risk ratings for others (e.g., having a child with a congenital defect).

HOW ARE DIFFERENT CONCEPTUALIZATIONS OF OPTIMISM RELATED?

Given the many possible different conceptualizations of optimism, how might they be related to each other? Surprisingly few studies have included multiple measures of optimism. One study assessed how dispositional, unrealistic, and comparative optimism were related to each other and to personal risk beliefs (Radcliffe & Klein, 2002). Participants completed the LOT dispositional optimism scale (Scheier & Carver, 1993) and estimated their comparative risk of having a fatal heart attack relative to that of the average same-age, same-sex person. Participants also completed a Health Risk Appraisal (HRA), making it possible to calculate their actual comparative risk of having a heart attack. Participants were defined as unrealistically optimistic if they underestimated their comparative risk (as computed by the HRA). The authors found that dispositional optimism and unrealistic optimism were not correlated, but that individuals who gave optimistic comparative risk ratings (irrespective of accuracy) reported higher levels of dispositional optimism ($r = -.31$).

In another study, Tusaie and Patterson (2006) surveyed rural adolescents and measured dispositional optimism as well as "situational" and comparative optimism with what they called the Optimistic Bias Scale (OBS). The OBS was a 19-item measure in which respondents rated the likelihood of negative events happening to themselves and to other people. Items included health, lifestyle, and environmental events such as contracting HIV, developing cancer, being a victim of gang violence, and getting too little exercise. The authors defined *situational optimism* as the total score of the likelihood of events happening to the respondents themselves and *comparative optimism* as the difference between ratings of self-risk and others' risk. The authors found that only 37% of the situational optimism items were significantly associated with dispositional optimism; correlations ranged from $r = -.16$ (having a heart attack) to $r = -.33$ (being a victim of violence). Only 11% of comparative optimism scores were significantly correlated with dispositional optimism. These findings suggest that although dispositional, situational, and comparative optimism are correlated, the relationships are modest.

Similarly, Davidson and Prkachin (1997) asked participants to make comparative risk ratings for 11 negative health-related items (e.g., mugging, tooth decay, high blood pressure) relative to other individuals of the same age and sex. As in the previous study, although the authors defined a composite index of these ratings as a measure of unrealistic optimism, no objective information was obtained to assess the accuracy of these ratings. Thus, we refer to them solely as comparative risk ratings. Dispositional and comparative optimism across the 11 events were positively correlated ($r = .27$).

A study of Anglo Americans and Mexican Americans examined the correlation between dispositional optimism and the Revised Generalized Expectancy for Success Scale (GESS-R), a 25-item Likert scale that lists statements about future situations and asks participants to rate the likelihood of being in that specific situation (Schutte & Hosch, 1996). The measures were significantly correlated for both Anglo Americans ($r = .58$) and for Mexican Americans ($r = .49$).

Two studies of people at risk for HIV included measures of dispositional optimism and situational optimism about risk of HIV infection. In the first, gay men reported their dispositional optimism and their perceived risk of developing AIDS (Taylor et al., 1992). The two measures were significantly, although only moderately, correlated ($r = -.14$). The other study found no significant correlation between dispositional optimism and perceived risk of contracting HIV in a sample of high-risk adolescents (Goodman, Chesney, & Tipton, 1995).

To illustrate how various types of optimism are related to each other and to relevant constructs such as behavior, we report here preliminary data from our ongoing study of beliefs about cardiovascular risk among individuals diagnosed with Type 2 diabetes (Klein, Zajac, & de Groot, unpublished data, 2008). There is substantial evidence that diabetes greatly increases the risk of various cardiac problems such as atherosclerosis and macrovascular complications (Grundy et al., 1999). However, it is unclear whether people with Type 2 diabetes understand that they are at increased risk. Moreover, to date there are no studies that assess different types of optimism in a sample of individuals already coping with a major health problem.

In this study, Pittsburgh residents with Type 2 diabetes are being recruited into a study in which we collect blood samples, blood pressure, body mass index (BMI), demographic variables, and beliefs about cardiovascular risk in a variety of formats. All data are collected at the University of Pittsburgh Medical Center's General Clinical Research Center (GCRC). Much of the physiological information can then be used to compute the patient's 10-year risk of getting (or dying from) cardiovascular disease using a risk algorithm developed by the United Kingdom Prospective Diabetes Study (UKPDS; Stevens, Kothavi, Adler, Stratten, & Holman, 2001). Participants are asked to report their perceived risk of cardiovascular disease using many of the formats discussed: absolute risk on a graduated percentage scale, comparative risk (relative to the typical person with diabetes and to the typical person without diabetes), conditional risk (risk if your level of physical activity does not change), and feelings of risk (worry, concern, and anxiety about getting cardiovascular disease). We also measure dispositional optimism using Scheier and Carver's LOT (1993).

Our analyses are based only on a preliminary sample of 28, but the pattern of relationships nevertheless illustrates a number of important points. First, the various measures of risk perception for cardiovascular disease (10-year risk of disease occurrence and well as 10-year fatality risk) were largely uncorrelated with actual UKPDS risk, all $rs < .21$. Thus, individuals having elevated risk based on high levels of glycosolated hemoglobin (HbA1c), high blood pressure, and other risk factors did not necessarily see themselves as higher in cardiovascular risk. Participants rate their risk of coronary heart disease (CHD) as higher than that of people without diabetes and about the same as other people with diabetes, and these ratings are unrelated to actual risk. Likelihood judgments (i.e., absolute risk perceptions) are highly correlated with comparative risk perceptions relative to the "average person with diabetes," $r = .76$, demonstrating an unusually high degree of association between how participants think about their absolute and comparative risk. Affective judgments regarding CHD risk were highly correlated with the various types of cognitive risk perceptions (absolute, comparative, and conditional), unlike other studies in which the correlations are more moderate (Lipkus et al., 2005). These findings suggest that among people with diabetes, there is greater coherence among their cognitive and affective risk perceptions than is typically observed, offering the possible hypothesis that risk perceptions become more consistent among individuals already facing a threatening health problem.

Our preliminary analyses also show that people who are high in dispositional optimism believe they are less at risk on nearly all the conventional risk perception measures and are less concerned about their risk. However, there is no correlation between dispositional optimism and actual UKPDS risk, so dispositional optimists are not necessarily lower in risk. This pattern of findings suggests that dispositional optimists in this population may be more likely to be optimistically biased. Indeed, the relationship between dispositional optimism and risk perceptions holds when controlling for actual risk (not surprisingly given the lack of association between actual risk and the other variables), meaning that dispositional optimists are indeed more biased.

Finally, we correlated each of our measures (risk perceptions, affect, dispositional optimism) with intentions to increase level of physical activity and reduce salt, saturated fat, and cholesterol (in separate questions for each change). Conditional risk perceptions—that is, risk perceptions conditioned on changes in future behavior—were the only type of risk perception significantly associated with intentions to change behavior. In other words, people who thought they would be less at risk if they changed their behavior were in fact more likely to intend to change their behavior. These findings indicate that feeling at risk is not enough; it is also important to feel that one's actions will reduce personal risk or what some call *response efficacy* (Ruiter, Abraham, & Kok, 2001).

Further research needs to be done to clarify the relationships among different types of optimism. Correlations in the various studies discussed here varied by health event and by population. Among adolescents and young adults in particular there seems to be little or no correlation between dispositional optimism and situational optimism. Overall, correlations among the different types of optimism suggest that they represent different psychological processes.

SIMILAR PSYCHOLOGICAL CONSTRUCTS

There are several other psychological constructs that share similarities with the way optimism is conceptualized. One is the "optimistic attributional style" introduced by Seligman, Peterson, and colleagues (e.g., Peterson, 2000). People are considered to have such a style if they attribute negative life events to unstable, external, and specific factors and positive life events to stable, internal, and global factors. One's explanatory style is likely to influence predictions about the future but is not necessarily a measure of optimism in the way we have discussed it here because explanatory style primarily captures the way in which people explain events that have already occurred.

Other work identifies a series of self-serving biases in people's judgments, such as overestimations of their abilities relative to that of other people (Dunning, Heath, & Suls, 2004). The processes underlying such biases are concurrently cognitive (Windschitl, Kruger, & Simms, 2003) and motivational (Dunning et al., 2004). It is likely that the processes underlying optimism are similar, although there are likely important differences given that optimism inherently involves uncertainty about the future. More work is necessary to distinguish the psychology of optimistic predictions from the psychology of self-favoring judgments.

The dispositional form of optimism is clearly related to other personality dimensions, such as self-esteem, depression, and faith (Ai, Peterson, Tice, Bolling, & Koenig, 2004; Giltay, Zitman, & Kromhout, 2006; Heinonen, Raikkonen, & Keltikangas-Jarvinen, 2005). Although dispositional optimism is distinguishable from these constructs both conceptually and statistically (Ai et al., 2004; Giltay et al., 2006; Heinonen et al., 2005), all of these constructs are likely to have common antecedents ranging from genetic to contextual. As noted, there is a dearth of work on the development of optimistic beliefs, yet a more substantial literature on the development of depression, which may be informative.

CAUSES AND CONSEQUENCES OF OPTIMISM

What causes a person to make an optimistic estimate of the chances of experiencing a future life event? And, what are the consequences of holding such an optimistic belief about these chances? Not surprisingly, effective answers to these questions depend to some extent on the type of optimism addressed.

SINGLE-EVENT OPTIMISM

The causes of single-event optimism can be divided loosely into the categories of cognitive, motivational, and affective. Much of the literature focuses on *unrealistic optimism*, the mistaken belief that one's chances of experiencing a future event are higher for positive events (and lower for negative events) than the chances are for other people. One cognitive cause of this bias is *egocentrism*, focusing more on one's own risk factors than on those of the reference group to which one is comparing (Kruger, 1999; Weinstein, 1982). People may also use differential standards when rating single targets like the self than when rating aggregated targets like "the average person" (Klar, Medding, & Sarel, 1996), and they may be more regressive when rating known targets (the self) than when rating less-known targets (Moore & Small, 2007). They may apply a "better-than-average" heuristic (Alicke, LoSchiavo, Zerbst, & Zhang, 1997) or any of the conventional heuristics that have been shown to influence judgment, such as availability and representativeness (Kahneman & Tversky, 1990). In a review of the literature on comparative judgments (such as those used to demonstrate unrealistic optimism), Chambers and Windschitl (2004) argued persuasively that cognitive processes may underlie many of the comparative biases observed in the literature.

Nevertheless, there is no doubt that motives also play a role in the emergence and maintenance of optimism. People want to think that their future is more positive than that of other people, and when given information challenging this belief, they do not simply accept it. For example, in one study (Rothman, Klein, & Weinstein, 1996), young adults were given risk information for a variety of negative life events (e.g., divorce, human papilloma virus [HPV], diabetes) tailored to their peer group. The information challenged participants' belief that they were less at risk than other people to experience these events. In response, they lowered their personal risk perceptions, presumably to sustain the self-favoring difference between their own risk and that of their peers.

These findings point to the role that a self-protection motive may play in predictions about the future. However, people hold several other motives that may influence their predictions, and these motives may at times have conflicting effects. For example, much evidence suggests that people desire to appear as rational judges to themselves and to others (Kunda, 1990). Consequently, in contexts in which people's predictions are verifiable, they are less likely to be optimistic and may even be pessimistic (Gilovich et al., 2002; Gilovich & Medvec, 1995)—contrary to the self-enhancement motive.

A related motive is to be adequately prepared for threatening feedback. People may generally believe that they are not at risk for a negative life event, but when they are about to find out whether their belief is accurate (such as when getting diagnostic or genetic test results), they "brace" for potential bad news and become pessimistic (K. Taylor & Shepperd, 1998). Moreover, when people are in a deliberative state—one in which making the right decision is highly salient—they are less optimistic than when they are in an implemental mindset (that is, one in which they are now carrying out a chosen course of action) (Gollwitzer, Heckhausen, & Steller, 1990). That they are more optimistic when carrying out a course of action is sensible because optimism is likely to promote motivation to achieve the desired goal (Armor & Taylor, 1998). Interestingly, mindset regarding a personal decision can influence risk perceptions for unrelated events in exactly the same way—greater optimism about future life events when in an implemental than in a deliberative mindset (S. E. Taylor & Gollwitzer, 1995).

Pessimism also appears when people are faced with ambiguous risk information. One study showed that people who think there are too many conflicting recommendations about how to prevent cancer were more pessimistic about their chances of getting cancer themselves (Han, Moser, & Klein, 2006). Ambiguity aversion as a motive has been shown to cause people to make counterproductive decisions (Fox & Tversky, 2004). People are also averse to losses—causing them to take more risks when faced with loss than when faced with gain (Kahneman & Tversky, 1990). Loss may therefore make people even more likely to be optimistic about future outcomes. Finally, people are averse to regret, often making decisions designed primarily to reduce regret (Miller & Taylor, 1995). When people are highly concerned about regretting their decisions, they feel less optimistic and choose more conservative courses of action (e.g., Ritov & Baron, 1995; Zeelenberg & Pieters, Chapter 27, this volume).

The fact that regret influences optimism about future life events highlights an emerging area in decision science that explores the role of affect in risk perception and decision making. When people evaluate the chances of experiencing future events, they often rely on their affective reaction as much as anything else, depending on what Slovic has called the "affect heuristic" (e.g., Slovic et al., 2005). For example, people are pessimistic about high-risk/high-benefit technology such as nuclear reactors because of the dread they feel about worst-case scenarios involving this technology (Slovic et al., 2005). Indeed, people erroneously regard the correlation between risk and benefit to be negative (the higher the risk, the less the benefit) and are even more likely to do so when negative affect is high (Finucane, Alhakami, Slovic, & Johnson, 2000). Another line of work shows that sadness and other forms of negative affectivity dampen optimism regarding personal risk, whereas anger and happiness increase it (Helweg-Larsen & Shepperd, 2001; Lerner & Keltner, 2000). As noted, affect and cognition often conflict in the context of decision making (Epstein, 1994).

The preceding work demonstrates that single-event optimism may result from a constellation of cognitive, motivational, and affective processes. What are the subsequent consequences of this single-event optimism? The answer, of course, depends on the type of optimism. If we use raw risk perceptions (that is, uncorrected for actual risk) as a measure of optimism, it would appear that optimism is related to lower adoption of risk-reducing behaviors. This conclusion is based on a large literature linking risk perceptions with protective behavior, which shows that higher risk perceptions are associated (although moderately) with such behaviors (e.g., Brewer et al., 2007; McCaul et al., 1996; van der Pligt, 1998; Vernon, 1999). It would be nonsensical to argue that optimism of this sort has negative consequences because it should be the people who are more at risk who take the precautions. Such a conclusion assumes, of course, that people's risk perceptions are positively correlated with their actual risk, which is generally true (e.g., Radcliffe & Klein, 2002).

The more interesting question, in our view, is whether unrealistically optimistic beliefs about the future are consequential. Testing this question is methodologically difficult, which may explain the relative lack of research (Klein & Cooper, 2008). As noted, it requires collecting information about each person's actual risk to determine which members of the sample are biased and which are not. Most studies that have taken this approach point to negative consequences of optimistic biases. For example, Dillard, McCaul, and Klein (2006) asked smokers to estimate their lung cancer risk and collected risk factor information that could be used to compute each smoker's risk with a risk algorithm (based on epidemiological data). When controlling for actual risk, Dillard et al. found that smokers who were more optimistic about their chances of avoiding lung cancer (and therefore were more optimistically biased because actual risk was already partialed out) revealed lower intentions to quit. On the other hand, S. E. Taylor et al. (1992) observed that HIV-seropositive individuals who were optimistically biased about their chances of getting AIDS engaged in relatively more health-promoting behaviors. Klein and Cooper (2008) postulated that optimistic biases may be more adaptive among individuals who are already coping with a health problem than among those far removed from a health problem, an idea that has not yet been put to an empirical test.

Behavior, of course, is only one possible consequence of optimistic biases. Radcliffe and Klein (2002) found that people who were optimistically biased about their risk of having a heart attack knew relatively less about the risk factors for a heart attack and retained less information from an essay they read in the laboratory about these risk factors. These individuals were also more likely to choose to read information about risk factors that would paint their own risk status in a positive light. Biased beliefs about the future may therefore be associated with important precursors to behavior such as the processing of important health information (see also Wiebe & Black, 1997). However, studies testing this hypothesis are largely correlational, pointing to a need for research in which optimistic beliefs are manipulated in an experimental context.

Are some types of single-event optimism more predictive of behavior and other consequences than others? As noted, affective perceptions of vulnerability such as "I feel at risk" are sometimes more predictive of behavior than are more conventional measures of risk perception, such as responses on a 7-point likelihood scale or a 0–100% percentage scale (Weinstein et al., 2007). Worry is significantly associated with protective action (McCaul et al., 1996), although not necessarily more so than conventional risk perceptions. These findings suggest that, at times, "hot" optimism may be more consequential than "cold" optimism, but the boundary conditions have yet to be examined.

Several studies have sought to determine whether absolute and comparative optimism vary in their ability to predict important outcomes such as behavior. We might expect that absolute judgments would be the best predictors because people should recognize that being at high risk necessitates behavioral change irrespective of how one's risk compares with that of others. Yet, some work suggests that people's beliefs about their comparative risk are very important to them. In fact, several studies have shown greater responsiveness to comparative risk feedback than to absolute risk feedback (Klein, 1997, 2003; although see Sparks, Harris, & Raats, 2003). In correlational studies, comparative risk perceptions are sometimes more predictive than absolute risk perceptions of behavior (Blalock, DeVellis, Afifi, & Sandler, 1990), but other studies show the opposite (e.g., Weinstein, Sandman, & Roberts, 1990). Perhaps of most importance, comparative risk perceptions clearly do explain a significant portion of the variance in several different types of outcomes when controlling for absolute risk perceptions (Klein, 2002).

Other theorists have attempted to make distinctions between types of optimism with regard to their consequences. For example, Baumeister (1989) suggests that there is an "optimal margin of illusion" within which optimism is adaptive and outside of which it is not. Wallston (1994) distinguishes between "cautious" and "cockeyed" optimism, suggesting of course that the latter holds more negative consequences. Some of the cognitive, motivational, and affective processes underlying the various types of optimism discussed may help determine when people are inside Baumeister's optimal margin and when their optimism becomes cockeyed in the Wallston sense.

DISPOSITIONAL OPTIMISM

We know very little about the causes of dispositional optimism. It likely has some genetic basis given its stature as a relatively stable personality trait throughout the life span (Plomin et al., 1992), which should also make it more resistant to change following the experience of negative life events (Peterson, 2000). Indeed, dispositional optimism helps people to cope with negative life events, making it less likely that such events would reduce optimism. On the other hand, we know a great deal about the consequences of dispositional optimism, at least in the context of personal health. Such work shows that people who are high in dispositional optimism have better overall physical health, report fewer symptoms of illness, cope better with stress, use more problem-focused coping strategies, handle illness more effectively, and are lower in all-cause mortality (e.g., Aspinwall & Taylor, 1992; Giltay, Geleijnse, Zitman, Hoekstra, & Schouten, 2004; Scheier & Carver, 1993). Suggesting they are resilient, such individuals are also more likely to engage in anxiety-provoking activities such as genetic testing (Peters & Biesecker, 2000). On the other hand, one study suggests that dispositional optimism, in combination with comparative optimism, can produce less interest in health-protective behaviors (Davidson & Prkachin, 1997). All in all, though, dispositional optimism seems to have mostly beneficial consequences.

CAN OPTIMISM BE CHANGED?

Is it possible to increase optimism? Dispositional optimism is generally considered to be a stable trait, a dimension of personality, and does show significant heritability (Plomin et al., 1992; Schulman, Keith, & Seligman, 1993). The most common measure of dispositional optimism, the LOT, shows a high level of test-retest reliability (Scheier & Carver, 1993) suggesting that dispositional optimism is stable over time. However, when people may be artificially pessimistic, as in the case of depressed individuals, what might appear to be "dispositional" optimism could be more malleable.

Research suggests that a pessimistic explanatory style can be a risk factor for depression, and several interventions have been aimed at preventing depression through optimism training (e.g., Riskind, Sarampote, & Mercier, 1996). These interventions have attempted to prevent depression by identifying individuals with a pessimistic explanatory style (who are thus at risk for depression) and treating them with an optimism training intervention. The interventions do seem to raise patients' self-reported level of optimism (measured through face-valid explanatory style measures) (Gillham, Hamilton, Freres, Patton, & Gallop, 2006; Riskind et al., 1996). They tend to use cognitive therapy techniques to target and change the dysfunctional thoughts that are characteristic of depressed individuals. Of course, changing thoughts about the past does not necessarily elicit more optimistic views of the future.

Several studies using cognitive therapy to treat major depression did find that patients reported increased levels of optimism following treatment (Antoni et al., 2001; Muran, Gorman, Safran, & Twining, 1995). The clinical measures of optimism are somewhat different from the LOT, and most clinical research uses single-item face-valid measures of optimism (e.g., "How optimistic are you feeling right now?"). Evidence suggests that cognitive therapy can change reported levels of optimism among individuals at risk for depression as well as those suffering from major depression. However, pessimistic, unrealistic thinking does seem to be a temporary characteristic of depression, and it is not known whether treating depression actually makes people more optimistic (which leads to the remission of depression) or whether the lifting of depression leads patients to revert to a more normal state of optimism. There has been no research aimed at changing dispositional optimism in a healthy population.

Other work suggests that it is very difficult to change people's optimistic biases. For example, Weinstein and Klein (1995) varied the presentation of risk factor information in a series of four studies. The interventions included educating participants about risk factors for several hazards (including having a heart attack, finding high home radon levels, and being injured in a car accident), focusing on either an ideal or worst-case list of risk factors, asking participants to form a mental image of someone at high or low risk for having a weight problem, and asking participants to generate their own list of risk factors relating to a weight or drinking problem. Each of the interventions was unsuccessful at reducing optimistic bias, and some actually increased the bias. Affective manipulations such as mood inductions do influence situational optimism (e.g., Helweg-Larsen & Shepperd, 2001; Johnson & Tversky, 1983), although the temporal durability of these effects is likely to be low.

Overall, then, dispositional optimism might be changed in people at risk or suffering from depression, but more work is necessary to determine the feasibility of changing dispositional optimism in a healthy population. Situational optimism—and the optimistic bias in particular—seem very difficult to change. Interventions that give participants comparative feedback on their risk factors relative to other individuals show some promise for changing optimistic bias (Lipkus & Klein, 2006), but more work needs to be done in this area.

FUTURE DIRECTIONS

A review of the collective literature on optimism reveals a glaring weakness: Most research has taken a fairly descriptive or "main effects" approach. In other words, investigators (including ourselves) tend to investigate direct and unmoderated relationships between measures of optimism and measures of other critical variables like behavior and mental health. Much less work has addressed mediational questions (i.e., the psychological processes that explain why optimism is related to other constructs). Research in other areas has demonstrated a similar problem. For example, much early work examined the relationship between attitudes and behavior, followed later by interest in variables that moderated this relationship (Zanna & Fazio, 1982).

Growing interest in mediators is now apparent in the area of dispositional optimism, which shows, for example, that optimism instigates beneficial physiological effects such as immune system buffering and dampened cardiovascular reactivity (Cohen et al., 1999; Segerstrom & Miller, 2004). Much less work identifies mediators when defining optimism in terms of risk perceptions or optimistic bias. Armor and Taylor (1998) offered the intriguing idea that optimistic biases may enhance motivation by promoting reinterpretations of negative outcomes and self-fulfilling prophecies. These and other ideas need to be tested. For example, optimism may increase self-regulatory resources or reduce resistance and other defensive responses to threat. Unfortunately, testing mediation is much easier when it is possible to manipulate the posited causal variable. As noted, however, risk perceptions—especially inaccurate risk perceptions—can be very resistant to change (Weinstein & Klein, 1995).

The main effects approach in the optimism literature also obfuscates potentially meaningful interactions between different types of optimism and between optimism and other variables. In a key exception, Davidson and Prkachin (1997) measured both risk perceptions and dispositional optimism and observed an interaction such that a combination of low-risk perceptions and high dispositional optimism produced the weakest comprehension of a risk message. Few other studies derived hypotheses involving interactions. We find this surprising given the low-to-moderate relationship between risk perceptions and behavior (e.g., Gerrard, Gibbons, & Bushman, 1996). It seems quite likely that the magnitude of this relationship is dampened because of insufficient attention to other variables that moderate it. As an example, we found in a sample of smokers that level of worry about lung cancer moderated the relationship between lung cancer risk perceptions and intentions to quit (Klein, Zajac, & Monin, unpublished data, 2008). In particular, there was a relatively strong (and positive) linear relationship between risk perceptions and quit intentions among smokers who were low in worry but a minimal relationship among those high in worry. We urge future researchers of the optimism-behavior relationship to pay greater attention to possible interactions.

Our examples so far have concerned the way in which one type of optimism moderates another. However, one must also consider a litany of other variables that could moderate the effects of optimism. Consider the following novel, yet untested, hypotheses:

1. *The effects of optimistic biases on behavior depend on whether one is promotion focused or prevention focused.* People are promotion focused when concerned primarily with achievement and prevention focused when concerned instead with security (Higgins, 1998). Recent work suggests that people are more satisfied with their pursuits to the extent that their regulatory focus (promotion or prevention) matches the means by which they attempt to accomplish these pursuits (e.g., Spiegel, Grant-Pillow, & Higgins, 2004). Optimistic biases are stronger for negative events (which one hopes to avoid) than for positive events (which one hopes to attain) (Hoorens, 1996), suggesting the possibility that optimistic biases are enhanced and may be more likely to hinder precautionary behavior in a prevention focus. No research has considered the effects of regulatory focus on optimistic biases or on the effects of these biases.

2. *Affective risk perceptions may be more predictive of behavior than cognitive risk perceptions if risk information is ambiguous.* Very few studies have compared the percentage of variance explained in behavior by competing sources of optimism (e.g., Weinstein et al., 2007), and future studies would do well not only to assess how the variance in behavior is partitioned but also to identify variables that may influence such partitioning. For example, affective risk perceptions such as "feeling at risk" may be more predictive of behavior if it is difficult to compute one's statistical risk or perhaps if one's perception of risk is cognitively inaccessible (such as when one is under the influence of alcohol or other drugs).

3. *Optimistic biases are more adaptive among individuals having faced or currently facing a significant health threat than among those yet to face such a threat.* As observed by Klein and Cooper (2008), studies demonstrating beneficial effects of optimistic biases are generally conducted in affected populations such as HIV-seropositive individuals (e.g., S. E. Taylor et al., 1992), whereas those demonstrating harmful effects are conducted in young samples or community samples who are asymptomatic (e.g., Radcliffe & Klein, 2002). To our knowledge, no study has manipulated prior experience with an event to assess whether such experience moderates the effects of optimism. Doing so would require a laboratory setting involving a fairly unremarkable event (for obvious ethical reasons) but may shed light on conflicting findings in the literature. It would also be interesting to determine whether optimistic biases foster promotion goals among those unaffected by a negative life event yet prevention goals among those already affected.

These are a few of the many possible hypotheses that could be tested in a framework that deviates from the "main effects" approach so far adopted in this literature. Testing these hypotheses properly does require larger sample sizes and greater theoretical development but would go a long way toward bettering our understanding of the psychology of optimism.

CONCLUSION

On the surface, it would appear that defining optimism about the future is an uncomplicated task: If someone has positive expectations about a future event, then we call that optimism. One of our principal goals in this chapter was to demonstrate that this task may in fact be more complicated than it seems (see also Peterson, 2000). People can be optimistic about their comparative risk of experiencing an event yet pessimistic about their absolute risk of experiencing this event. They can be realistically or unrealistically optimistic, with potentially serious consequences. Conditional risk perceptions may be more or less optimistic than nonconditional risk perceptions. Having generically positive beliefs about the future does not necessarily have much to do with predictions about future outcomes, as shown by the relatively small correlation between dispositional optimism and event-specific optimism. Our new data collected from people struggling with diabetes suggests the possibility that associations among different types of optimism may be stronger among individuals already coping with a negative life event, an idea necessitating empirical testing.

We hope that our review of this literature also draws greater attention to the conventional assumption that optimistic expectations promote adaptive behavior and, ultimately, positive outcomes. The relationship between perceptions of vulnerability and behavior may vary considerably based on how perceptions of vulnerability are conceptualized, for example, as affective or cognitive perceptions. The notion that optimism is adaptive seems reasonable for dispositional optimism but less so for unrealistic optimism at the event-specific level. The latter observation brings into question whether it is appropriate to try to increase optimism, and even if one tried to do so, the evidence suggests that doing so is difficult. Dispositional optimism is considered to be a fairly stable personality trait (Plomin et al., 1992; Schulman et al., 1993), and unrealistic optimism is not easily altered (Weinstein & Klein, 1995).

In contrast to well-entrenched cultural beliefs about what optimism is and whether it is adaptive in a variety of life domains, it seems to us that there are fewer cultural beliefs about what mediates and moderates the effects of optimism. Perhaps this lack of a priori beliefs will facilitate more cultural acceptance of what we hope will be the next generation of research on optimism—research that addresses the "how" and "when" of optimism effects. A more incisive understanding of optimism as a psychological construct is certain to enhance our knowledge of personality development and our theoretical approaches to risk perception. Just as important, it should also assist in the development of strategies to help people make more effective decisions in the many domains of their lives in which optimism may exert an influence.

ACKNOWLEDGMENTS

The writing of this chapter was supported by grants from the National Science Foundation (SES-0648044) and the Pittsburgh Mind-Body Center (PMBC; National Institute of Health grants HL076852/076858). We thank Katy Griffith for her assistance in the preparation of the chapter and Keith Markman for helpful comments on an earlier version.

REFERENCES

Ai, A. L., Peterson, Tice, C. N. T., Bolling, S. F., & Koenig, H. G. (2004). Faith-based and secular pathways to hope and optimism subconstructs in middle-aged and older cardiac patients. *Journal of Health Psychology, 9*, 435–450.

Alicke, M. D., LoSchiavo, F. M., Zerbst, J., & Zhang, S. T. (1997). The person who outperforms me is a genius: Maintaining perceived competence in upward social comparison. *Journal of Personality and Social Psychology, 73*, 781–789.

Antoni, M. H., Lehman, J. M., Klibourn, K. M., Boyers, A. E., Culver, J. L., Alferi, S. M., et al. (2001). Cognitive-behavioral stress management intervention decreases the prevalence of depression and enhances benefit finding among women under treatment for early-stage breast cancer. *Health Psychology, 21*, 20–32.

Armor, D. A., & Taylor, S. E. (1998). Situated optimism: Specific outcome expectancies and self-regulation. In M. P. Zanna (Ed.), *Advances in experimental social psychology* (Vol. 30, pp. 309–379). New York: Academic Press.

Aspinwall, L. G., & Taylor, S. E. (1992). Modeling cognitive adaptation: A longitudinal investigation of the impact of individual differences and coping on college adjustment and performance. *Journal of Personality and Social Psychology, 62*, 989–1003.

Baumeister, R. F. (1989). The optimal margin of illusion. *Journal of Social and Clinical Psychology, 8*, 176–189.

Blalock, S. J., DeVellis, B. M., Afifi, & Sandler, R. A. (1990). Risk perceptions and participation in colorectal cancer screening. *Health Psychology, 9*, 792–806.

Brewer, N. T., Chapman, G. B., Gibbons, F. X., Gerrard, M., McCaul, K. D., & Weinstein, N. D. (2007). Meta-analysis of the relationship between risk perception and health behavior: The example of vaccination. *Health Psychology, 26*, 136–145.

Buehler, R., Griffin, D., & Ross, M. (1994). Why people underestimate their task completion times. *Journal of Personality and Social Psychology, 67*, 366–381.

Chambers, J. R., & Windschitl, P. D. (2004). Biases in social comparative judgments: The role of nonmotivated factors in above-average and comparative-optimism effects. *Psychological Bulletin, 130,* 813–838.

Chapman L. J., & Chapman J. P. (1967). Genesis of popular but erroneous diagnostic observations. *Journal of Abnormal Psychology, 72,* 193–204.

Cohen, F., Kearney, K. A., Zegans, L. S., Kemeny, M. E., Neuhaus, J. M., & Stites, D. P. (1999). Differential immune system changes with acute and persistent stress for optimists versus pessimists. *Brain, Behavior, and Immunity, 13,* 155–174.

Davidson, K., & Prkachin, K. (1997). Optimism and unrealistic optimism have an interacting impact on health-promoting behavior and knowledge changes. *Personality and Social Psychology Bulletin, 23,* 617–624.

Denes-Raj, V., & Epstein, S. (1994). Conflict between intuitive and rational processing: When people behave against their better judgment. *Journal of Personality and Social Psychology, 66,* 819–829.

Dewberry, C., & Richardson, S. (1990). Effect of anxiety on optimism. *Journal of Social Psychology, 130,* 731–738.

Dillard, A. J, McCaul, K. D., & Klein, W. M. P. (2006). Unrealistic optimism in smokers: Implications for smoking myth endorsement and self-protective motivation. *Journal of Health Communication, 11,* 93–102.

Dunning, D., Heath, C., & Suls, J. M. (2004). Flawed self-assessment: Implications for health, education, and the workplace. *Psychological Science in the Public Interest, 5,* 69–106.

Epstein, S. (1994). Integration of the cognitive and the psychodynamic unconscious. *American Psychologist, 49,* 709–724.

Finucane, M. L., Alhakami, A., Slovic, P., & Johnson, S. M. (2000). The affect heuristic in judgments of risks and benefits. *Journal of Behavioral Decision Making, 13,* 1–17.

Fox, C. R., & Tversky, A. (2004). Ambiguity aversion and comparative ignorance. In E. Shafir (Ed.), *Preference, belief, and similarity: Selected writings by Amos Tversky* (pp. 777–793). Cambridge, MA: MIT Press.

Gerrard, M., Gibbons, F. X., & Bushman, B. J. (1996). Relation between perceived vulnerability to HIV and precautionary social behavior. *Psychological Bulletin, 119,* 390–409.

Gigerenzer, G., & Hoffrage, U. (1995). How to improve Bayesian reasoning without instruction: Frequency formats. *Psychological Review, 102,* 684–704.

Gillham, J. E., Hamilton, J., Freres, D. R, Patton, K., & Gallop, R. (2006). Preventing depression among early adolescents in the primary care setting: A randomized controlled study of the Penn Resiliency Program. *Journal of Abnormal Child Psychology, 34,* 203–219.

Gilovich, T., Griffin, D., & Kahneman, D. (Eds.). (2002). *Heuristics and biases: The psychology of intuitive judgment.* New York: Cambridge University Press.

Gilovich, T., & Medvec, V. H. (1995). Some counterfactual determinants of satisfaction and regret. In N. J. Roese & J. M. Olson (Eds.), *What might have been: The social psychology of counterfactual thinking.* Hillsdale, NJ: Erlbaum.

Giltay, E. J., Geleijnse, J. M., Zitman, F. G., Hoekstra, T., & Schouten, E. G. (2004). Dispositional optimism and all-cause and cardiovascular mortality in a prospective cohort of elderly Dutch men and women. *Archives of General Psychiatry, 61,* 1126–1135.

Giltay, E. J., Zitman, F. G., & Kromhout, D. (2006). Dispositional optimism and the risk of depressive symptoms during 15 years of follow-up: The Zutphen Elderly Study. *Journal of Affective Disorders, 91,* 45–52.

Gollwitzer, P. M., Heckhausen, H., & Steller, B. (1990). Deliberative and implemental mind-sets: Cognitive tuning toward congruous thoughts and information. *Journal of Personality and Social Psychology, 59,* 1119–1127.

Goodman, E., Chesney, M. A., & Tipton, A. C. (1995). Relationship of optimism, knowledge, attitudes, and beliefs to use of HIV antibody testing by at-risk female adolescents. *Psychosomatic Medicine, 57,* 541–546.

Grundy, S., Benjamin, I., Burke, G., Chait, A., Eckel, R., & Howard, B. (1999). Diabetes and cardiovascular disease: A statement for healthcare professionals from the American Heart Association. *Circulation, 100,* 1134–1146.

Gurmankin, A. D., Helweg-Larsen, M., Armstrong, K., Kimmel, S. E., & Volpp, K. G. (2005). Comparing the standard rating scale and the magnifier scale for assessing risk perceptions. *Medical Decision Making, 25,* 560–70.

Han, P. K. J., Moser, R. P., & Klein, W. M. P. (2006). Perceived ambiguity about cancer prevention recommendations: Relationship to perceptions of cancer preventability, risk, and worry. *Journal of Health Communication, 11*(Suppl. 1), 51–69.

Heinonen, K., Raikkonen, K., & Keltikangas-Jarvinen, L. (2005). Self-esteem in early and late adolescence predicts dispositional optimism-pessimism in adulthood: A 21-year longitudinal study. *Personality and Individual Differences, 39*, 511–521.

Helweg-Larsen, M. (1999). (The lack of) optimistic biases in response to the 1994 Northridge earthquake: The role of personal experience. *Basic and Applied Social Psychology, 21*, 119–129.

Helweg-Larsen, M., & Shepperd, J. A. (2001). Do moderators of the optimistic bias affect personal or target risk estimates? A review of the literature. *Personality and Social Psychology Review, 5*, 74–95.

Herzberg, P. Y., Glaesmer, H., & Hoyer, J. (2006). Separating optimism and pessimism: A robust psychometric analysis of the Revised Life Orientation Test (LOT-R). *Psychological Assessment, 18*, 433–438.

Higgins, E. T. (1998). From expectancies to worldviews: Regulatory focus in socialization and cognition. In J. M. Darley & J. Cooper (Eds.), *Attribution and social interaction: The legacy of Edward E. Jones* (pp. 243–309). Washington, DC: American Psychological Association.

Hoorens, V. (1996). Self-favoring biases for positive and negative characteristics: Independent phenomena? *Journal of Social and Clinical Psychology, 15*, 53–67.

Johnson, E. J., & Tversky, A. (1983). Affect, generalization, and the perception of risk. *Journal of Personality and Social Psychology, 45*, 20–31.

Kahneman, D., & Tversky, A. (1990). Prospect theory: An analysis of decision under risk. In P. K. Moser (Ed.), *Rationality in action: Contemporary approaches* (pp. 140–170). New York: Cambridge University Press.

Klar, Y., Medding, A., & Sarel, D. (1996). Nonunique invulnerability: Singular versus distributional probabilities and unrealistic optimism in comparative risk judgments. *Organizational Behavior and Human Decision Processes, 67*, 229–245.

Klein, W. M. (1997). Objective standards are not enough: Affective, self-evaluative, and behavioral responses to social comparison information. *Journal of Personality and Social Psychology, 72*(4), 763–774.

Klein, W. M. P. (2002). Comparative risk estimates relative to the average peer predict behavioral intentions and concern about absolute risk. *Risk Decision and Policy, 7*, 193–202.

Klein, W. M. P. (2003). Effects of objective feedback and "single other" or "average other" social comparison feedback on performance judgments and helping behavior. *Personality and Social Psychology Bulletin, 29*, 418–429.

Klein, W. M. P., & Cooper, K. L. (2008). On the physical health costs of self-enhancement. In E. Chang (Ed.), *Self-criticism and self-enhancement: Theory, research, and clinical implications* (pp. 141–158). Washington, DC: American Psychological Association.

Klein, W. M. P., Zajac, L. E., & de Groot, M. (2007). [Cardiovascular risk perceptions among people with Type 2 diabetes]. Unpublished data.

Kruger, J. (1999). Lake Wobegon be gone! The "below-average effect" and the egocentric nature of comparative ability judgments. *Journal of Personality and Social Psychology, 77*, 221–232.

Kunda, Z. (1990). The case for motivated reasoning. *Psychological Bulletin, 108*, 480–498.

Lerner, J. S., & Keltner, D. (2000). Beyond valence: Toward a model of emotion-specific influences on judgment and choice. *Cognition and Emotion, 14*, 473–493.

Lipkus, I. M., Biradavolu, M., Fenn, K., Keller, P., & Rimer, B. K. (2001). Informing women about their breast cancer risks: Truth and consequences. *Health Communication, 13*, 205–266.

Lipkus, I. M., & Klein, W. M. P. (2006). Effects of communicating social comparison information on risk perceptions for colorectal cancer. *Journal of Health Communication, 11*, 391–407.

Lipkus, I. M., Klein, W. M. P., Skinner, C. S., & Rimer, B. K. (2005). Breast cancer risk perceptions and breast cancer worry: What predicts what? *Journal of Risk Research, 8*, 439–452.

Lipkus, I. M., Samsa, G., & Rimer, B. (2001). General performance on a numeracy scale among highly educated samples. *Medical Decision Making, 21*, 37–44.

Loewenstein, G. F., Weber, E. U., Hsee, C. K., & Welch, N. (2001). Risk as feelings. *Psychological Bulletin, 127*, 267–286.

McCaul, K. D., Branstetter, A. D., Schroeder, D. M., & Glasgow, R. E. (1996). What is the relationship between breast cancer risk and mammography screening? A meta-analytic review. *Health Psychology, 15*, 423–429.

McCaul, K. D., & Mullens, A. B. (2003). Affect, thought, and self-protective health behavior: The case of worry and cancer screening. In J. Suls & K. A. Wallston (Eds.), *Social psychological foundations of health and illness* (pp. 137–168). Malden, MA: Blackwell.

Miller, D. T., & Taylor, B. R. (1995). Counterfactual thought, regret and superstition: How to avoid kicking yourself. In N. J. Roese & J. M. Olson (Eds.), *What might have been: The social psychology of counterfactual thinking* (pp. 305–331). Mahwah, NJ: Erlbaum.

Moore, D. A., & Small, D. A. (2007). Error and bias in comparative social judgment: On being both better and worse than we think we are. *Journal of Personality and Social Psychology, 92,* 972–989.

Muran, J. C., Gorman, B. S., Safran, J. D., & Twining, L. (1995). Linking in-session change to overall outcome in short-term cognitive therapy. *Journal of Consulting and Clinical Psychology, 63,* 651–657.

Nes, L. S., & Segerstrom, S. C. (2006). Dispositional optimism and coping: A meta-analytic review. *Personality and Social Psychology Review, 10,* 235–251.

Peters, K. F., & Biesecker, L. G. (2000). An opportunity for genetic counseling intervention: Depression in parents of individuals with Proteus syndrome. *Journal of Genetic Counseling, 9,* 161–171.

Peterson, C. T. (2000). The future of optimism. *American Psychologist, 55,* 44–55.

Plomin, R., Scheier, M. F., Bergeman, C. S., Pedersen, N. L., Nesselroade, J. R., & McClearn, G. E. (1992). Optimism, pessimism, and mental health: A twin/adoption analysis. *Personality and Individual Differences, 13,* 921–930.

Radcliffe, N. M., & Klein, W. M. P. (2002). Dispositional, unrealistic and comparative optimism: Differential relations with the knowledge and processing of risk information and beliefs about personal risk. *Personality and Social Psychology Bulletin, 28,* 836–846.

Reyna, V. F. (2004). How people make decisions that involve risk: A dual-processes approach. *Current Directions in Psychological Science, 13,* 60–66.

Riskind, J. H., Sarampote, C. S., & Mercier, M. A. (1996). For every malady a sovereign cure: Optimism training. *Journal of Cognitive Psychotherapy, 10,* 105–117.

Ritov, I., & Baron, J. (1995). Outcome knowledge, regret, and omission bias. *Organizational Behavior and Human Decision Processes, 64,* 199–127.

Rothman, A. J., Klein, W. M., & Weinstein, N. D. (1996). Absolute and relative biases in estimations of personal risk. *Journal of Applied Social Psychology, 26,* 1213–1236.

Ruiter, R. A. C., Abraham, C., & Kok, G. (2001). Scary warning and rational precautions: A review of the psychology of fear appeals. *Psychology and Health, 16,* 613–630.

Scheier, M. F., & Carver, C. S. (1993). On the power of positive thinking: The benefits of being optimistic. *Current Directions in Psychological Science, 2,* 26–30.

Schmiege, S. J., Bryan, A. B., & Klein, W. M. P. (in press). Distinctions between worry and perceived risk in the context of the Theory of Planned Behavior. *Journal of Applied Social Psychology.*

Schulman, P., Keith, D., & Seligman, M. E. P. (1993). Is optimism heritable? A study of twins. *Behavior Research and Therapy, 31,* 569–574.

Schutte, J. W., & Hosch, H. M. (1996). Optimism, religiosity, and neuroticism: A cross-cultural study. *Personality and Individual Differences, 20,* 239–244.

Schwartz, L. M., Woloshin, S., Black, W. C., & Welch, G. H. (1997). The role of numeracy in understanding the benefit of screening mammography. *Annals of Internal Medicine, 127,* 966–971.

Segerstrom, S. C., & Miller, G. E. (2004). Psychological stress and the human immune system: A meta-analytic study of 30 years of inquiry. *Psychological Bulletin, 130,* 601–630.

Shepperd, J. A., Findley-Klein, C., Kwavnick, K. D., Walker, D., & Perez, S. (2000). Bracing for loss. *Journal of Personality and Social Psychology, 78,* 620–634.

Shepperd, J. A., Helweg-Larsen, M., & Ortega, L. (2003). Are comparative risk judgments consistent across time and events? *Personality and Social Psychology Bulletin, 29,* 1169–1180.

Slovic, P., Peters, E., Finucane, M. L., & MacGregor, D. G. (2005). Affect, risk, and decision-making. *Health Psychology, 24,* S35–S40.

Sparks, P., Harris, P. R., & Raats, M. (2003). Imagining and explaining hypothetical scenarios: Mediational effects on the subjective likelihood of health-related outcomes. *Journal of Applied Social Psychology, 33,* 869–887.

Spiegel, S., Grant-Pillow, H., & Higgins, E. T. (2004). How regulatory fit enhances motivational strength during goal pursuit. *European Journal of Social Psychology, 34,* 39–54.

Stevens, R., Kothari, V., Adler, A. I., Stratten, I. M., & Holman, R. R. (2001). UKPDS 56: The UKPDS Risk Engine: A model for the risk of coronary heart disease in type 2 diabetes. *Clinical Science, 101,* 671–679.

Taylor, K., & Shepperd, J. A. (1998). Bracing for the worst: Severity, testing, and feedback timing as moderators of the optimistic bias. *Personality and Social Psychology Bulletin, 24,* 915–926.

Taylor, S. E., & Gollwitzer, P. M. (1995). The effects of mindset on positive illusions. *Journal of Personality and Social Psychology, 69,* 213–226.

Taylor, S. E., Kemeny, M. E., Aspinwall, L. G., Schneider, S. G., Rodriguez, R., & Herbert, M. (1992). Optimism, coping, psychological distress, and high-risk sexual behavior among men at risk for acquired immunodeficiency syndrome (AIDS). *Journal of Personality and Social Psychology, 62*, 460–473.

Tusaie, K. R., & Patterson, K. (2006). Relationships among trait, situational, and comparative optimism: Clarifying concepts for a theoretically consistent and evidence-based intervention to maximize resilience. *Archives of Psychiatric Nursing, 20*, 144–150.

van der Pligt, J. (1998). Perceived risk and vulnerability as predictors of precautionary behaviour. *British Journal of Health Psychology, 3*, 1–14.

Vernon, S. W. (1999). Risk perception and risk communication for cancer screening behaviors: A review. *Monographs: Journal of the National Cancer Institute, 25*, 101–119.

Wallston, K. A. (1994). Cautious optimism versus cockeyed optimism. *Psychology and Health, 9*, 201–203.

Weinstein, N. D. (1980). Unrealistic optimism about future life events. *Journal of Personality and Social Psychology, 5*, 441–460.

Weinstein, N. D. (1982). Unrealistic optimism about susceptibility to health problems. *Journal of Behavioral Medicine, 5*, 441–460.

Weinstein, N. D. (1984). Why it won't happen to me: Perceptions of risk factors and susceptibility. *Health Psychology, 3*, 431–457.

Weinstein, N. D. (1987). Unrealistic optimism about susceptibility to health problems: Conclusions from a community-wide sample. *Journal of Behavioral Medicine, 10*, 481–500.

Weinstein, N. D., & Klein, W. M. (1995). Resistance of personal risk perceptions to debiasing interventions. *Health Psychology, 14*, 132–140.

Weinstein, N. D., & Klein, W. M. (1996). Unrealistic optimism: Present and future. *Journal of Social and Clinical Psychology, 15*, 1–8.

Weinstein, N. D., Kwitel, A., McCaul, K. D., Magnan, R. E., Gerrard, M., & Gibbons, F. X. (2007). Risk perceptions: Assessment and relationship to influenza vaccination. *Health Psychology, 26*, 146–151.

Weinstein, N. D., Rothman, A. J., & Nicolich, M. (1998). Use of correlational data to examine the effects of risk perceptions on precautionary behavior. *Psychology and Health, 13*, 479–501.

Weinstein, N. D., Sandman, P. M., & Roberts, N. E. (1990). Determinants of self-protective behavior: Home radon testing. *Journal of Applied Social Psychology, 20*, 783–801.

Wiebe, D. J., & Black, D. (1997). Illusional beliefs in the context of risky sexual behaviors. *Journal of Applied Social Psychology, 27*, 1727–1749.

Windschitl, P. D., Kruger, J., & Simms, E. N. (2003). The influence of egocentrism and focalism on people's optimism in competitions: When what affects us equally affects me more. *Journal of Personality and Social Psychology, 85*, 389–408.

Zajac, L. E., Klein, W. M. P., & McCaul, K. D. (2006). Absolute and comparative risk perceptions as predictors of cancer worry: Moderating effects of gender and psychological distress. *Journal of Health Communication, 11*, 37–49.

Zanna, M. P., & Fazio, R. H. (1982). The attitude-behavior relation: Moving toward a third generation of research. In M. P. Zanna, E. T. Higgins, & C. P. Herman (Eds.), *Consistency in social behavior: The Ontario symposium* (Vol. 2, pp. 283–301). Hillsdale, NJ: Erlbaum.

22 On the Excessive Rationality of the Emotional Imagination: A Two-Systems Account of Affective Forecasts and Experiences

Elizabeth W. Dunn, Noah D. Forrin,
and Claire E. Ashton-James

INTRODUCTION

If imagination is an airplane, then we humans are frequent fliers; emerging research in neuroscience suggests that we devote a large portion of our mental lives to traveling into the future, as well as the past, to envision what other times and places would be like and how we would feel when we got there (Buckner & Carroll, 2007; Buckner & Vincent, 2007; Gilbert & Buckner, 2007; Szpunar & McDermott, Chapter 8, this volume). Indeed, while the average Labrador seems to display some drooling recognition of how much he will enjoy the leftover steak that has just been placed in front of him, humans possess a qualitatively different ability: We can imagine a situation (or steak) that is faraway in time or place and that we have never before experienced, calculating with some degree of accuracy how we would feel if we were plunged into that situation.

While marveling at this "affective forecasting" ability, psychologists have also been quick to identify its shortcomings. An explosion of recent research has shown that people often overestimate (e.g., Buehler & McFarland, 2001; Gilbert, Morewedge, Risen, & Wilson, 2004), sometimes underestimate (e.g., Dunn, Biesanz, Human, & Finn, 2007; Gilbert, Gill, & Wilson, 2002), and occasionally misunderstand entirely (e.g., Woodzicka & LaFrance, 2001) the emotional responses they will experience in the future. In explaining the sources of these errors, researchers have diagnosed a number of specific flaws in the emotional imagination, including immune neglect (Gilbert, Pinel, Wilson, Blumberg, & Wheatley, 1998), focusing illusions (e.g., Dunn, Wilson, & Gilbert, 2003; Schkade & Kahneman, 1998), and empathy gaps (e.g., Loewenstein & Schkade, 1999; Van Boven & Loewenstein, 2005). Although these phenomena have been documented independently—creating the possible appearance of a grab bag of forecasting flaws—we believe that most sources of systematic forecasting errors can be integrated through the unifying theoretical perspective provided by Seymour Epstein's (1994, 1998a) cognitive-experiential self theory (CEST).

COGNITIVE-EXPERIENTIAL SELF THEORY

Similar to other dual-process theories, CEST posits that humans make sense of themselves and the world around them via two distinct information-processing systems that operate in parallel: the rational system and the experiential system (see Table 22.1).[1] As the new kid on the evolu-

TABLE 22.1

Comparison of the Experiential and Rational Systems

Experiential	Rational
1. Holistic	1. Analytic
2. Automatic, effortless	2. Intentional, effortful
3. Affective: pleasure-pain oriented (what feels good)	3. Logical: reason oriented (what is sensible)
4. Associationistic connections	4. Logical connections
5. Behavior mediated by "vibes" from past events	5. Behavior mediated by conscious appraisal of events
6. Encodes reality in concrete images, metaphors, and narratives	6. Encodes reality in abstract symbols, words, and numbers
7. More rapid processing: oriented toward immediate action	7. Slower processing: capacity for long-delayed action
8. Slower and more resistant to change: changes with repetitive or intense experience	8. Changes more rapidly and easily: changes with strength of argument and new evidence
9. More crudely differentiated: broad generalization gradient, stereotypical thinking	9. More highly differentiated
10. More crudely integrated—dissociative, emotional complexes; context-specific processing	10. More highly integrated: context-general principles
11. Experienced passively and preconsciously: We believe we are seized by our emotions	11. Experienced actively and consciously: We believe we are in control of our conscious thoughts
12. Self-evidently valid: "Experiencing is believing"	12. Require justification via logic and evidence

Note: From *The Relational Self: Theoretical Convergences in Psychoanalysis and Social Psychology*, R. C. Curtis (Ed.), 1992, Guilford Press, New York, p. 123. Copyright 1992 by Guilford Press. Adapted with permission.

tionary block, the rational system is probably unique to us big-brained humans and allows us to engage in logical reasoning. Relying largely on conscious appraisals of events, the rational system is highly analytic and readily makes sense of abstract numbers and ideas, changing rapidly as these sources of information change. In contrast, the evolutionarily ancient experiential system is affectively oriented and integrates information holistically, responding primarily to concrete information (e.g., images). The experiential system relies on associations between new information and past experiences, such that change in the operation of this system may occur relatively slowly (Epstein, 1994, 1998a).

According to Epstein (1998a), emotions are a signature product of the experiential system. Affective forecasting, however, is a uniquely human ability that most likely depends to a large extent on the advanced cognitive capacity of the rational system. Thus, in making affective forecasts, humans may rely heavily on the rational system in trying to understand the experiential system. Like an engineer trying to understand a poet or a robot trying to understand a puppy, this cross talk may provide the basis for a host of misunderstandings. Indeed, we suggest that the core differences between the rational and the experiential systems can account for the seemingly disparate sources of recently documented errors in affective forecasting. In the sections that follow, we address each of these core differences in turn, using CEST to integrate separate strands of research on affective forecasting. Finally, we consider implications of this theoretical perspective for improving affective forecasts and for guiding future research.

Analytic Versus Holistic

One of the most important differences between the rational and the experiential systems is that the former processes information more analytically while the latter processes information more holistically. This core difference in processing styles may underlie the most ubiquitous discrepancies between affective forecasts and emotional experiences. To the extent that people adopt an analytic mindset when making affective forecasts about an upcoming event, they are likely to take the approach of an entomologist, separating the specimen under study from its contextual jungle, placing it under the microscope, and then dissecting it into individual parts.

This analytic approach may underlie the common tendency for affective forecasters to exhibit *focalism*, mentally zeroing in on the "signal" of the focal event while isolating it from the "noise" provided by background distractions and other events (Wilson, Wheatley, Meyers, Gilbert, & Axsom, 2000). For example, when asked to imagine how they would feel in the days after their college football team won a big game, football fans focused heavily on the game's outcome and therefore anticipated more lasting, victory-induced delight than they actually experienced. These collegiate fans generated more moderate forecasts only when the researchers prompted them to consider that there might be more to student life than football. Research in our lab suggested that forecasters may not only ignore relevant situational factors but may also succumb to *dispositional neglect*, ignoring their own stable, dispositional level of happiness (Forrin, Dunn, Biesanz, & Aknin, 2007). Thus, forecasters may go astray by isolating a focal event from the larger background provided by other situational events and their own baseline happiness.

As well as separating a particular event or outcome from its broader context, the analytic forecaster would be expected to dissect an outcome into its component parts and focus on those parts or aspects that most clearly differentiate it from other outcomes. This is exactly what forecasters appear to do. For example, just before college freshmen received their dormitory assignments—which would determine where they lived for the subsequent 3 years of school—they were asked to predict how happy they would be living in each of 12 dorms (Dunn et al., 2003). At the time that they made these predictions, the students knew a great deal about the dormitories. But, in making their affective forecasts, the students focused heavily on physical features of the dorms (e.g., location) that strongly differentiated the dorms from each other, while largely neglecting the important features that the dorms had in common; thus, students exhibited an *isolation effect* (Kahneman & Tversky, 1979), mentally zooming in on the features that differed between options while ignoring the options' shared features. Because of this highly analytic approach, students made erroneously extreme forecasts, overestimating how happy they would be in the desirable dorms and how miserable they would be in the less-desirable dorms.

A similar, analytic forecasting style emerged when students in another study were asked to imagine living in California versus the Midwest (Schkade & Kahneman, 1998). Perhaps unsurprisingly, students residing in both states anticipated that living in California would lead to greater life satisfaction than living in the Midwest. This prediction stemmed from the fact that students focused heavily on the differences between the two regions—particularly California's superior weather—when imagining what it would be like to live in the other region. Yet, actual satisfaction may depend on a much broader set of life conditions, including social relationships, job opportunities, daily hassles, and other factors that on balance are fairly similar across regions, such that regional differences in life satisfaction may be quite minimal. Indeed, while acknowledging the objectionable nature of their region's weather, the students actually living in the Midwest reported life satisfaction levels that were equivalent to those of their Californian counterparts. A parallel phenomenon emerged in a study of a 3-week bicycle trip through California (Mitchell, Thompson, Peterson, & Cronk, 1997). Before the trip, the cyclists focused on core aspects of the trip, including the opportunities to bike and make friends, while giving little thought to potential distractions (e.g., bee stings and flat tires) that might diminish their enjoyment of the vacation. These distractions, however, did influence their actual enjoyment during the trip, contributing to the discrepancy that emerged between the cyclists' highly positive forecasts and their more equanimous experiences.

In separating the signal of a focal event from the noise of its background, forecasters may also readily neglect the event's temporal context. Exploring this idea, Gilbert et al. (2002) asked participants to predict how much they would enjoy eating spaghetti with meat sauce either the next morning or the next evening. Their findings suggested that participants first called to mind an image of the saucy spaghetti, isolated from its temporal context, leaving individuals with the initial conclusion that they would enjoy the pasta as much for breakfast as they would for dinner. Only later—and with some effort—were participants able to correct for the influence of mealtime, subtracting out the potentially unpalatable effects of eating spaghetti with meat sauce first thing in the morning.

As well as struggling to take the holistic future context of an upcoming event into account, forecasters may often fail to fully contextualize such an event within the broader framework of other similar past events[2] (Buehler & McFarland, 2001; Morewedge, Gilbert, & Wilson, 2005). For example, left to their own devices, individuals may imagine that an upcoming New Year's Eve party will be the best party ever, overlooking the patchwork of past celebrations that have turned out to be disappointing. Indeed, the more forecasters focus on a future event in isolation from the broad context of similar past events, the more likely they are to overestimate the upcoming event's emotional impact (Buehler & McFarland, 2001).

Taken together, the research described in the preceding paragraphs seems to paint a rather dull view of the emotional experiences contained in daily life; in contrast to the exciting roller coaster of dizzying highs and devastating lows imagined by forecasters, actual emotional experiences may appear relatively pallid. While giving up the devastating lows might not be so bad, can we ever attain and—more importantly—maintain the dizzying highs envisioned by forecasters? Given that forecasters' extreme expectations stem from their tendency to view a focal event in sharp relief from the contextual background, perhaps individuals might be able to experience more potent emotions if a focal event were prevented from being assimilated into the broader fabric of everyday life. Developing this idea, Wilson and his colleagues reasoned that people might have trouble engaging in such assimilation, or "sense-making" if the meaning or cause of the focal event were uncertain (Wilson, Centerbar, Kermer, & Gilbert, 2005). Consistent with this hypothesis, participants in their studies who could not easily make sense of a positive event experienced more prolonged happiness. In one such study, students at the University of Virginia were led to believe that they had received positive feedback from three opposite-sex students after having exchanged information with them over the Internet (the feedback was in fact controlled by the experimenter). Participants who were not given the source of each flattering comment—and thus had trouble making sense of this positive event—experienced elevated mood for longer than those who were given this information.

Summary

A broad array of recent research supports the notion that forecasters tend to adopt a relatively analytic approach in imagining their emotional responses to future events. Like good analysts, forecasters extract the focal event from the noise of its background and break up the event into its most important parts, devoting careful attention to those parts that distinguish it from similar events. Problems arise, however, because the emotional experiences that forecasters are trying to predict may stem from a more holistic response to events. Only when forecasters are reminded to take a more contextualized approach—or experiencers are prevented from letting an event fade into the background—are forecasters and experiencers likely to converge on this important dimension of information processing. Given this fundamental discrepancy, then, it is perhaps no surprise that forecasters so commonly exhibit an *impact bias*, overestimating the intensity and duration of their own emotional responses to events (Gilbert, Driver-Linn, & Wilson, 2002).

COLD VERSUS HOT

In keeping with its analytic nature, a second major feature of the rational system is that it is driven by reason rather than emotion. That is, the rational system is better able to process nonaffective, conceptual information such as facts and figures than affective information such as feelings and emotional reactions, which are more readily processed by the experiential system. The rational system can thus be thought of as a "cold" system in that it generates "logical" responses to events, while the experiential system can be considered a "hot" system because it is associated with more "emotional" responses to events. In short, the rational system is oriented to what is sensible, whereas the experiential system is oriented to what feels good (Epstein, 1998a). As a result, the rational system is likely to promote a dispassionate, balanced view of an event, while the experiential system is likely to promote a more motivated view of the same event—allowing one to view the event in a desired light.

To the extent that the experiential system plays a weaker role in generating affective forecasts than in generating actual emotions, forecasters may readily overlook the experiential system's ability to take the sting out of negative events. For example, Democrats made the (perfectly reasonable) prediction that they would be unhappy a month after George W. Bush was elected governor of Texas (Gilbert et al., 1998). As it turned out though, their happiness had returned to normal by this time. More important, they had developed rosier views of Bush, suggesting that they were making the best of a bad situation. According to Gilbert et al. (1998), forecasters succumb to the impact bias, as in the experiment discussed in the preceding section, because they neglect the power of the *psychological immune system*, which quickly and quietly transforms life's lemons into lemonade. From the perspective of CEST, such *immune neglect* may occur because forecasters envision future outcomes dispassionately, in keeping with the rational system; they fail to take into account the motivated, pleasure-oriented processing that the experiential system will contribute.

This idea is illustrated by an experiment in which students were led to believe that an attractive member of the opposite sex was moderately likely or moderately unlikely to pick them over another student as a preferred dating partner (Wilson, Wheatley, Kurtz, Dunn, & Gilbert, 2004). Before learning the potential date's final decision, participants took a relatively cool, even-handed view, reporting a moderate degree of interest in dating this person, regardless of whether they expected to be chosen. This balanced perspective was quickly replaced by a more motivated one, however, after participants learned the attractive person's final decision; individuals who were randomly assigned to learn that they had been selected viewed the potential date as a more appealing prospect than did those individuals who were assigned to the rejection condition. Because rejected participants were able to devalue the potential date in ways they failed to foresee, the rejectees' actual emotional experiences were less negative than they anticipated. In this dating game study, participants apparently required little time or effort to reconstrue the potential date according to their own best interests; participants reported feeling equally good regardless of whether they were given time to engage in reconstrual after learning if they had been chosen.

Of course, the successful functioning of the psychological immune system is likely to require time and effort when individuals are faced with more troubling forms of feedback (e.g., denial of tenure); under such conditions, we would argue that the experiential system may harness the power of the rational system to marshal the full repertoire of sophisticated human defense mechanisms. In any case, the key point is that the critical role of the experiential system may be missed by forecasters relying on the rational system, contributing to the impact bias. This suggests that the impact bias should not be seen as resulting from the "distorted" nature of forecasts. After all, affective forecasts—guided largely by the rational system—tend to be logical and objective. Rather, immune neglect (a major source of the impact bias) emerges due to the failure of the rational system to appreciate the important role that the experiential system will play in shaping actual emotions.

As well as neglecting the influence of psychological defenses on future emotions, affective forecasters also tend to ignore the influence of visceral factors. As mentioned in the opening of this section, the rational system is a cold system, driven by reason, and the experiential system is a hot system, driven by emotions. Thus, when making affective forecasts, individuals typically imagine how they will feel in a hot state while they are in a cold state. This creates what Loewenstein and Schkade (1999) refer to as a *hot/cold empathy gap* (see also Loewenstein, O'Donoghue, & Rabin, 2003; Van Boven & Loewenstein, 2003). The hot/cold empathy gap reflects the struggle of the cold rational system to understand the hot experiential system, especially when visceral factors come into play. According to Loewenstein and Schkade (1999), it is difficult to predict the intensity of visceral factors, let alone their influence on future emotions and behavior. For example, Christensen-Szalanski (1984) found that pregnant women underestimated the pain of childbirth; consequently, most made a nonbinding decision to forgo anesthesia—a decision that many reversed after the onset of labor.

Several other studies provide additional evidence that an empathy gap exists between the cold, rational system (the primary source of predicted emotions) and the hot, experiential system (the primary source of actual emotions). Individuals who completed a quiz were offered, as reimbursement, either a candy bar or the answers to the quiz questions (Loewenstein, Prelec, & Shatto, 1998). Among those who made their choice before taking the quiz, only 21% chose the answers; however, a substantially higher percentage of individuals (60%) opted for the answers after having taken the quiz. In their cold state, prior to taking the quiz, individuals apparently underestimated their subsequent curiosity and its effect on their behavior. Similarly, students in another study overestimated their willingness to engage in a public performance for money because they failed to predict the embarrassment and fear they would experience as their performance drew near (Van Boven, Loewenstein, Dunning, & Welch, 2004). Again, the cold rational system appears to be ill-suited to make forecasts regarding the hot experiential system. Because of this fundamental mismatch, empathy gaps may be difficult to correct unless forecasters are given an experiential taste of the situation or outcome they will later encounter (Loewenstein, Nagin, & Paternoster, 1997; Van Boven, Dunning, & Loewenstein, 2000; Van Boven & Loewenstein, 2005). Thus, empathy gaps are likely to arise when the response of the experiential system is merely contemplated by the rational system.

Summary

In this section, we outlined two shortcomings of people's overreliance on the rational system in making forecasts regarding the experiential system. The first shortcoming is that the rational system—logical and objective—does not take into account the psychological defenses initiated by the experiential system; this leads to the impact bias for negative events (i.e., forecasts are more negative than experiences). The second shortcoming is that the cold rational system leads individuals to underestimate the influence of hot emotions and drives on their subsequent behavior. This hot/cold empathy gap can lead to severe forecasting errors, which are unlikely to be mitigated unless forecasters are allowed to "step into the phenomenological shoes" (Van Boven et al., 2000, p. 73) of their future selves.

ABSTRACT VERSUS CONCRETE

As well as processing information in different ways, the rational and experiential systems respond to different types of input. In particular, while the rational system is adept at drawing meaning from abstract numbers, words, and symbols, the experiential system is relatively insensitive to such information, instead responding more readily to concrete images, metaphors, and narratives. If the rational system plays a dominant role in affective forecasts and the experiential system plays a dominant role in actual emotions, then affective forecasts and experiences are likely to diverge in part because of their differential sensitivity to abstract information.

According to research by Hsee and Zhang (2004), forecasters may exhibit greater sensitivity to abstract quantitative information in part because people often make affective forecasts in *joint evaluation* (JE) mode—that is, when they are comparing multiple options. For example, in planning a future ski trip, people are likely to engage in affective forecasting as they weigh the tough choice between Whistler and Aspen. Comparing these options side by side, forecasters' attention might be drawn to the fact that Whistler has 200 trails and a vertical rise of 5,280 feet, while Aspen has a relatively paltry 76 trails and a vertical rise of just 3,276 feet. Because such statistics are easy to evaluate when making this direct comparison, avid skiers might predict enjoying a Whistler vacation far more than an Aspen vacation. Once immersed in their vacation, however, skiers inevitably find themselves in *single-evaluation* (SE) mode, in which they are faced with only the mountain they selected. In this mode, Whistler's purely quantitative advantages may no longer be salient, such that Whistler's extra 2,000 feet may fail to lift skiers' enjoyment above that of their counterparts at Aspen. Therefore, predictions made by forecasters in JE may exaggerate the difference between the pleasure of skiing at Whistler versus Aspen, exhibiting what Hsee and Zhang (2004) term the *distinction bias.*

From this perspective, abstract quantitative information has a greater influence on affective forecasts than on emotional experiences because of the common tendency for people to consider multiple options when making affective forecasts. Pushing this further, we would argue that if affective forecasts are primarily processed by the rational system, they should be inherently more sensitive to quantitative information than emotional experiences, even when forecasts are made in SE mode. To test this hypothesis, which was derived from CEST, we exposed participants to information about a deadly forest fire in Spain and manipulated the fire's perceived death toll between subjects by leading participants to believe that either 5 or 10,000 people had been killed (Dunn & Ashton-James, 2008). Participants serving as "experiencers" were asked to read a short newspaper article about the event and to report their feelings afterward. Other participants serving as forecasters were asked to read a brief summary of the article and predict how they would feel after reading the full article. Consistent with the idea that affective forecasts are processed by the rational system, which is sensitive to facts and figures, forecasters in the 10,000-dead condition predicted feeling much more upset than did forecasters in the 5-dead condition. Experiencers, however, exhibited what we term *emotional innumeracy*; they felt no more upset after reading that 10,000 people had been killed in the fire than that 5 people had been killed, reflecting the insensitivity of the experiential system to numerical information.

Of course, experiencers' insensitivity to death tolls might have stemmed from the fact that the target event (a Spanish forest fire) occurred far away from our American participants, and that it was described in dry, journalistic terms. Experiencers also displayed emotional innumeracy, however, when we examined responses to a nearby, high-impact event. In the immediate aftermath of Hurricane Katrina, when the storm's true death toll was unknown, we led students at Duke University to believe that 50 people, 500 people, 1,000 people, or 5,000 people had been killed (thereby manipulating perceived death toll between subjects). Consistent with the hypothesis that emotional experiences are largely insensitive to numerical information—even when those numbers refer to the loss of nearby human lives—we found that students' sadness about the hurricane was unrelated to the storm's perceived death toll. Several weeks later, when another major hurricane was approaching the Southeast, we asked one group of Duke students to predict how sad they would feel if 5 people were killed and another group to predict how sad they would feel if 5,000 people were killed in the hurricane. In contrast to the emotional innumeracy exhibited by experiencers, our forecasters displayed substantial sensitivity to numbers, with those in the 5,000-dead condition predicting that they would feel much greater sadness than those in the 5-dead condition. Thus, death tolls had a more powerful impact on affective forecasts than on actual emotions, consistent with our argument that the former stem primarily from the rational system and the latter primarily from the experiential system.

From this perspective, the number of people killed in a disaster should influence actual emotions if abstract death toll statistics are translated into a form of information that is meaningful to the experiential system, such as concrete images. To test this idea, we asked students to examine a Web site, which (a) informed them that either 15 or 500 college students had been killed in the Iraq war effort and (b) either did or did not contain head shots of each individual killed (Dunn & Ashton-James, 2008). In the absence of pictures, participants reported feeling about equally sad regardless of whether they were led to believe that 15 or 500 students had died, consistent with our previous studies. But, participants did report feeling greater sadness as a function of death toll when these casualties were represented by head shots of each deceased individual, supporting the notion that actual emotions—as a product of the experiential system—are more sensitive to concrete images than to abstract numbers (see also Amit, Algom, Trope, & Liberman, Chapter 4, this volume). Yet, because affective forecasting engages the rational system, forecasts are broadly sensitive to quantitative information, leading people to overestimate how upset they would be in response to grand-scale tragedies.

Indeed, previous research suggests that people may sometimes be more upset by a tragedy that affects only a handful of individuals than by a broader tragedy. For example, when several miners become trapped deep underground, their individual stories are likely to capture media attention, and the details of their lives and pictures of their families may tear at heartstrings around the world—even while statistics about annual mining deaths fail to provoke public concern. Sherman, Beike, and Ryalls (1999) argued that people may be more emotionally responsive to specific, concrete cases (e.g., three men trapped in a mine) than to generalized abstractions (e.g., statistics about mining deaths) because the experiential system is engaged more by the former than the latter. Therefore, to the extent that small-scale tragedies are more likely to provoke a focus on the specific individuals affected, people may actually feel worse in response to a disaster that affects few rather than many. Forecasters may overlook this, however, focusing instead on more abstract information about a disaster.

Interestingly, a separate line of research provides evidence that forecasters may be particularly responsive to abstract information when contemplating temporally distant events. Using a variety of measures, Trope, Liberman, and colleagues (e.g., Amit et al., Chapter 4, this volume; Liberman, Sagristano, & Trope, 2002) have demonstrated that people think more abstractly when imagining an event in the distant future versus the near future. Integrating this work with our own recent findings, we would speculate that affective forecasters may be especially sensitive to abstract quantitative information when considering a temporally distant versus imminent event—potentially magnifying forecasting biases for events in the far-off future.

Summary

The research described suggests that abstract, quantitative information has little influence on actual emotions but substantial influence on affective forecasts—not only because of the circumstances in which forecasts are typically made but also because of the rational system's heavy involvement in affective forecasting. As discussed, affective forecasts are typically made in JE mode, which facilitates attentiveness to quantitative differences between available options. Even when forecasts are made in SE mode, our experiments (which all used between-subjects designs) demonstrated that affective forecasts are more sensitive to abstract numerical information than are actual emotions. More tentatively, we would suggest that people may be particularly sensitive to such abstract information when making forecasts for temporally distant versus more imminent events.

DOES FORECASTING PRIME THE RATIONAL SYSTEM?

The diverse lines of research described thus far are remarkably consistent with our theoretical position that the rational system drives affective forecasts, while the experiential system drives actual emotions. Still, with the exception of our recent work on responses to tragedies, the research we have described was developed primarily on the basis of theories other than CEST. It is therefore critical to obtain more direct evidence for our dual-systems account of predicted and actual emotions.

With this goal in mind, we examined whether making affective forecasts triggers the operation of the rational system; specifically, we assigned participants to report either affective forecasts or actual emotions and then asked them to complete a seemingly unrelated temporal discounting task (Dunn & Ashton-James, 2008). Previous research suggests that activating the experiential system promotes high levels of temporal discounting—such that people are willing to pay much more to receive an item immediately versus at a delay—whereas activating the rational system reduces temporal discounting (e.g., Frederick, 2005). Therefore, if the act of affective forecasting serves to prime the rational system, then people should exhibit lower levels of temporal discounting after reporting affective forecasts versus actual feelings. This is exactly what we found; compared to participants who were asked to report their actual feelings, participants who were asked to report affective forecasts later reported little difference in their willingness to pay for products (e.g., movie vouchers) immediately versus at a delay.[3]

Summary

To the extent that making affective forecasts effectively triggers the rational system, there should be downstream cognitive consequences of affective forecasting, even on seemingly unrelated tasks. Providing one piece of initial support for this proposition, we found that after making affective forecasts, people exhibited reduced temporal discounting, a pattern that implicates the activation of the rational system.

Bridging the Rational-Experiential Divide

If predicted and actual emotions are generated in large part by different systems, as we argue, then there may be little hope for more than occasional, accidental convergence between affective forecasts and emotional experiences. Consistent with this, people seem hard-pressed to learn from their past experiences in making affective forecasts (Wilson, Meyers, & Gilbert, 2001). For example, participants who had just received positive feedback on a social aptitude test failed to use their own emotional response to this event as a guide in predicting how they would feel in the future after receiving very similar forms of positive feedback (Wilson et al., 2001). More broadly, Wilson, Laser, and Stone (1982) found that people possess little insight into the predictors of their own moods. Participants in this study were asked to rate their mood on a daily basis, as well as rating the day's weather, how much exercise they had gotten that day, how much sleep they had gotten the night before, and other predictor variables that could affect mood. At the end of the study, participants were asked to estimate the extent to which each of the predictor variables had been associated with their mood during the study period. In addition, "observers" (students at the same university who did not complete daily ratings) were asked to estimate the relationships that would emerge between the predictor variables and the daily moods of participants in the study. Amazingly, participants were no more accurate at estimating these relationships—between the predictor variables and their own personal daily moods—than were observers, who had no direct access to participants' emotional experiences. This suggests that in attempting to decipher the determinants of their own moods, individuals must rely heavily on the rational system, which lacks direct access into the workings of the experiential system.

Given this potential for misunderstandings between the rational and experiential systems, how can affective forecasts be improved? One productive strategy may lie in tuning out the rational system. Because the rational system requires mental effort to operate, this system can be distracted from pursuing one task by the demands of another task. Under such conditions, the experiential system may be left to its own devices, producing potential benefits for decision making (Dijksterhuis, 2004; Dijksterhuis, Bos, Nordgren, & van Baaren, 2006; Dijksterhuis & Meurs, 2006; Dijksterhuis & Nordgren, 2006; Dijksterhuis & van Olden, 2006). For example, when students were asked to choose an art poster to take home, they were more satisfied with their poster weeks later if they were distracted before making their choice than if they engaged in conscious deliberation (Dijksterhuis & van Olden, 2006). By tuning out the rational system through distraction, then, the intuitive outputs of the experiential system may receive greater weight in the generation of predicted (as well as actual) emotions, thereby increasing the correspondence between affective forecasts and experiences regarding complex events or outcomes.

The rational system, however, may be effective when it comes to making decisions between relatively simple options. For example, Dijksterhuis et al. (2006) argued that when consumers choose between simple products (e.g., oven mitts), they should rely on conscious thought (engaging the rational system). Conversely, when consumers choose between complex products (e.g., cars), they should tune out the rational system and rely on unconscious thought (engaging the experiential system). As discussed in the Analytic Versus Holistic section, the rational system tends to break the available options down into a few key components, an approach that may work better for simple than complex decisions.

Forecasts might be improved not only by tuning out the rational system but also by tuning in the experiential system. Consistent with the idea that these two systems can operate in parallel, an individual who imagines tomorrow's root canal may generate a mental prediction about the level of pain that will be felt tomorrow, while also experiencing a visceral feeling of dread in the present (Clore, 1992; Damasio, 1994; Loewenstein, 2000; Loewenstein & Lerner, 2003; Loewenstein, Weber, Hsee, & Welch, 2001; Schwarz, 1990; Slovic, Finucane, Peters, & MacGregor, 2002). Whereas the rational system may be largely responsible for generating the prediction about expected pain tomorrow, the experiential system may be largely responsible for generating the anticipatory emotion of dread the patient feels today. Often, the output provided by these two systems will closely converge; the patient who predicts greater pain tomorrow will typically feel greater dread today. Yet, there are common circumstances in which the outputs of these two systems may diverge (for a review, see Loewenstein & Lerner, 2003), and under such circumstances, the information provided by the two systems will be nonredundant, such that taking both sources into account may allow for a more diagnostic prediction of future feelings.

Drawing on CEST, Rawn and Dunn (2007) examined one such circumstance. Dieters and nondieters were presented with a gooey chocolate chip cookie. As soon as the cookie was unveiled, two research assistants unobtrusively rated each participant's facial expression, providing a measure of anticipatory emotions (i.e., the emotions experienced in anticipation of devouring the cookie). Participants then predicted how much they would enjoy eating the cookie, providing a measure of expected emotions (i.e., affective forecasts). Finally, participants ate the cookie and reported how much they had actually enjoyed it. For dieters, being presented with a cookie in this way may create a potential conflict between the rational and experiential systems. According to CEST, the rational system is capable of switching quickly to a new set of rules, allowing it to readily adopt a new set of diet-friendly guidelines specifying that cookies and other high-fat foods might not be so delectable after all. The experiential system, by contrast, is more resistant to change, potentially leaving it clinging to the long-held notion that eating a chocolate chip cookie is one of life's finest pleasures. Consistent with this perspective, Rawn and Dunn (2007) found that participants' anticipatory emotions predicted unique variance in actual enjoyment (above expected emotions) but only among dieters—for whom a divergence in the output of the two systems would be expected. Tentatively, then, we would suggest that people may sometimes be able to more accurately foresee their own future feelings if they pay attention to the flash of affect that the experiential system generates when the future outcome is imagined (although whether such accuracy is always desirable is another question).

Tuning in the experiential system in this way may be easier for events that lie in the near versus distant future; a variety of research suggests that people experience stronger flashes of affect as an event draws closer in time (Loewenstein & Lerner, 2003). Engaging the experiential system may also be easier when the occurrence of an outcome is relatively certain. As discussed, when participants in Wilson et al.'s (2004) "dating game" study were led to believe that there was a strong, but still uncertain, chance that an attractive person would end up selecting them for a date, forecasters exhibited the balanced, objective style characteristic of the rational system. But, when participants in a follow-up study were led to believe that the attractive person was virtually certain to select them, forecasters took a more motivated approach, seeing the person in a rosier light, suggesting that the experiential system had begun to kick in. Thus, particularly for imminent, highly certain future events, the experiential system may offer a readout on the value of the event—which may provide a useful source of information in predicting how the event will actually feel when it happens.

Arguably, the predictions people make about imminent, highly certain events may be less important for shaping appropriate planning behavior than the predictions they make about more distant, uncertain events. For example, recognizing that one would feel embarrassed about flubbing a conference talk is more likely to promote successful preparatory behavior if this affective forecast is made several days before the talk, as opposed to moments beforehand. Is it ever possible to engage the experiential system in making affective forecasts about relatively remote events? Research suggested that the answer may be yes, at least for people who have grown up in cultures in which experiential thinking is valued and cultivated. In an elegant series of studies, Lam and his colleagues demonstrated that East Asians are less prone to exhibit focalism than are Westerners because East Asians engage in more holistic thinking, situating a focal event within its broader context (Lam, Buehler, McFarland, Ross, & Cheung, 2005). For example, when forecasting how they would feel on the first warm day of spring, Euro-Canadian students focused more heavily on the warm weather (the focal event) than Asian students; consequently, only the Euro-Canadian students exhibited the impact bias (Lam et al., 2005, Study 1). Although this research specifically examined cultural differences in holistic versus analytic thinking, East Asians may also be relatively adept at tuning in the experiential system more broadly when making affective forecasts.

For those of us who rely largely on the rational system in making affective forecasts, the best bet may lie in training the rational system to better understand the workings of the experiential system; with a more fine-tuned understanding of the inner workings of the experiential system, the rational system would have a stronger information base on which to predict future emotional experiences. This form of knowledge is captured by Salovey and Mayer's (1990) conceptualization of emotional intelligence (EI), which they defined as knowledge about the causes and consequences of one's own and others' experience of emotions, including the automatic processes that underlie the sensory perception, interpretation, experience, and management of emotions. As noted by Epstein (1998b), this approach to EI essentially reflects how well the rational system understands the workings of the experiential system. Hence, we would argue that individuals who are high in EI should be able to generate more accurate affective forecasts.

To test the hypothesis that individuals with more emotionally intelligent rational systems make more accurate affective forecasts, we asked participants who had previously completed a performance measure of EI (the Mayer-Salovey-Caruso Emotional Intelligence Test; Salovey, Mayer, & Caruso, 2003) to predict how they would feel 2 days after a political event (Study 1, U.S. presidential election), 3 weeks after a personal event (Study 1, academic exam), or the morning following a sporting event (Study 2, college basketball game). At the specified time following each event, participants were asked to report how they were actually feeling (Dunn, Brackett, Ashton-James, Schneiderman, & Salovey, 2007). In support of the idea that EI should facilitate accurate affective forecasts, we found that there was less discrepancy across these diverse events between the affective forecasts and experiences of individuals high in EI compared to individuals low in EI.

From our theoretical perspective, affective forecasting accuracy depends in part on the extent to which the rational system has access to complete and correct information about the reality of emotional experiences in everyday life. Consistent with this, we found that forecasting accuracy was most strongly related to the "emotional management" component of EI (Dunn, Brackett, et al., 2007), which measures knowledge of social, environmental, and cognitive factors that influence the intensity and duration of emotional experiences (Mayer & Salovey, 1997). Hence, a viable route to reducing errors in affective forecasting may be to develop one's EI so that the rational system has sufficient information on which to base predictions about emotional experiences.

Summary

The gulf between affective forecasts and experiences may be bridged either by increasing the role of the experiential system in the formulation of affective forecasts or by improving the rational system's understanding of the experiential system. Tuning in the experiential system may entail quieting the rational system through distraction (e.g., Dijksterhuis et al., 2006) or directing people's attention to their current affective states as a source of information about their future affective state (Rawn & Dunn, 2007). Alternatively, affective forecasting accuracy may be improved by increasing the "emotional intelligence" of the rational system—that is, improving one's knowledge about the causes and consequences of emotions. Thus, separate strands of research conducted by Dijksterhuis and colleagues and Dunn and colleagues provide support for the viability of a two-systems approach to understanding when forecasts and experiences will converge.

CONCLUSION AND IMPLICATIONS

In view of the recent proliferation of research demonstrating systematic errors in affective forecasting, it is clear that our frequent flights to the emotional future rarely arrive at the correct destination. Previous research has identified a number of seemingly unrelated factors that steer us off course, leading to affective forecasts that either overshoot or undershoot the emotional mark, including immune neglect (Gilbert et al., 1998), focusing illusions (e.g., Dunn et al., 2003; Schkade & Kahneman, 1998), and empathy gaps (e.g., Loewenstein & Schkade, 1999; Van Boven & Loewenstein, 2005).

Throughout this chapter, we have argued that CEST provides a coherent theoretical framework for understanding the relationship between these seemingly disparate sources of affective forecasting errors. Specifically, we have suggested that discrepancies between affective forecasts and experiences stem in large part from a tendency for humans to rely heavily on the rational system in making predictions about affective responses that are generated predominantly by the experiential system. Because the rational and experiential systems process information about the world in fundamentally different ways—the rational system is relatively analytic, cold, and conceptual, while the experiential system is relatively holistic, hot, and sensual—errors in affective forecasting should occur to the extent that individuals rely on the rational system in making forecasts about their emotional experiences.

Supporting this idea, we have reviewed several factors that create biases in affective forecasting and have argued that, in different ways, each of these variables is associated with reliance on the rational system. In line with the rational system's analytic style, forecasters tend to pluck a target outcome from its broader contextual framework, focusing on a few key features that distinguish it from other similar outcomes, while largely neglecting background events and distractions, similar past events, and the temporal context—all of which are relevant to actual emotional experiences. Furthermore, exhibiting the cold, logical approach typical of the rational system, forecasters commonly overlook the motivated processes that will take the sting out of negative events, as well as the hot, visceral factors that will shape their future feelings and behaviors. Forecasters are also highly responsive to abstract quantitative information, consistent with the rational system's sensitivity to abstract numbers, words, and symbols. Of course, our argument is not meant to imply that forecasts are fully rational; the rational system surely plays a less-dominant role in driving affective forecasts than in driving some other types of judgments. Our key point is that the rational system appears to play a larger role in shaping affective forecasts than in shaping the emotional experiences that those forecasts are meant to predict—producing diverse, yet systematic discrepancies between forecasts and experiences.

Such discrepancies may be reduced when this imbalance is corrected. Emerging research suggests that this may be accomplished by usurping the rational system's resources, leaving the experiential system free to take the lead in information processing. As well as tuning out the rational system, forecasters may be able to tune in the experiential system. New research in our lab implies that when people contemplate an impending event, the experiential system produces a flash of affect—detectable in individuals' facial expressions—that in some cases predicts actual emotional experiences above and beyond more rational, thoughtful affective forecasts. Although anyone may be able to learn to tune in to such information, individuals who have been raised in cultures that value experiential thinking may have a leg up in this domain. Finally, individuals who possess strong, verbalizable knowledge about the inner workings of the experiential system also appear to be particularly adept at affective forecasting.

The two-systems account of affective forecasts and experiences that we have proposed in this chapter allows us to go beyond existing research and make novel predictions about potential sources of affective forecasting errors, as well as identify conditions under which affective forecasting accuracy should be improved. For example, our two-systems perspective suggests that forecasters may often go astray by neglecting emergent properties of future experiences; that is, given the analytic nature of the rational system, forecasters might take a piecemeal approach, selecting a favorite wine and favorite entrée at a restaurant while giving insufficient weight to the holistic quality of the food-wine pairing.

Our perspective also implies that affective forecasting accuracy may be improved by a number of variables that promote experiential processing or direct attention to the outputs of the experiential system. For example, attention may be subtly directed to experiential cues by the presence of a mirror, which enables visual processing of one's own facial expression. Given that facial expressions of emotion are perceived automatically and often guide judgments without conscious awareness (Murphy & Zajonc, 1993; Winkielman, Berridge, & Wilbarger, 2005), the information provided by one's facial expressions while imagining future events should be automatically integrated into the construction of an affective forecast, potentially improving accuracy.

Our theoretical perspective also leads to the novel prediction that individual difference variables associated with rational versus experiential thinking styles may be correlated with forecasting accuracy. If the discrepancy between affective forecasts and experiences stems from an overreliance on the rational system to make predictions about phenomena that are processed and generated largely by the experiential system, then seemingly desirable dispositional qualities such as need for cognition may be negatively correlated with affective forecasting accuracy. Need for cognition is a trait associated with a preference for analytic, thorough, logic-based thought and systematic information processing over the use of cognitive shortcuts, intuition, experiential cues, and heuristic processing (Cacioppo & Petty, 1982). Thus, someone who is high in need for cognition would tend to process information using the rational system, while a person with a low need for cognition may rely more heavily on the experiential system (Epstein et al., 1996). Individuals who are high in need for cognition should therefore be more susceptible to affective forecasting errors due to their dispositional tendency to utilize the rational system over the experiential system in information processing.

In conclusion, building on CEST, the two-systems model of affective forecasts and experiences that we have proposed not only provides a broad explanation for diverse sources of error in affective forecasting but also provides a clear framework on which to predict and prevent significant errors in affective forecasting. In essence, we posit that predicted emotions are primarily driven by the rational system, while actual emotions are primarily driven by the experiential system. Like an engineer and a poet or a robot and a puppy, the rational and experiential systems process the world in fundamentally different ways, often leading to divergent outputs despite similar inputs. To the extent that we can encourage the engineer to think like a poet or program the robot to utilize the experience of the puppy, our affective forecasts and experiences may be reconciled.

NOTES

1. Akin to the distinction between the rational and experiential systems, related dual-process accounts draw a parallel distinction between rule-based and associative processing (Smith & DeCoster, 2000; see also Sloman, 1996), systematic versus heuristic processing (Chaiken, 1980), information-based versus experience-based processing (Koriat & Levy-Sadot, 1999), and central versus peripheral processing (Petty & Cacioppo, 1986).
2. Individuals may be particularly inclined to overlook past negative events when making affective forecasts. According to Taylor's (1991) mobilization-minimization hypothesis, people are quick to respond

to negative events and minimize their impact, causing such events to fade from memory quickly. This may help to explain why individuals overlook the disappointments associated with past events (e.g., last year's party) when making forecasts for future events (e.g., the upcoming party). Moreover, the memories associated with past events may be colored by implicit theories (Ross, 1989). When these implicit theories are positive (e.g., parties are fun), they may lead to past events being recalled in a more positive light, which may in turn generate more positive affective forecasts.

3. One might argue that the act of forecasting simply led people to place greater value on the distant future. However, participants in this experiment were asked to predict how they would feel in the immediate future, not the distant future; specifically, participants were asked to complete the temporal discounting measure after reporting their predicted or actual feelings in response to a Spanish forest fire as part of the experiment described in this chapter.

REFERENCES

Buckner, R. L., & Carroll, D. C. (2007). Self-projection and the brain. *Trends in Cognitive Science, 2,* 49–57.

Buckner, R. L., & Vincent, J. L. (2007). Unrest at rest: Default activity and spontaneous network correlations. *NeuroImage, 37,* 1073–1082.

Buehler, R., & McFarland, C. (2001). Intensity bias in affective forecasting: The role of temporal focus. *Personality and Social Psychology Bulletin, 27,* 1480–1493.

Cacioppo, J. T., & Petty, R. E. (1982). The need for cognition. *Journal of Personality and Social Psychology, 42,* 116–131.

Chaiken, S. (1980). Heuristic versus systematic information processing and the use of source versus message cues in persuasion. *Journal of Personality and Social Psychology, 39,* 752–766.

Christensen-Szalanski, J. J. J. (1984). Discount functions and the measurement of patients' values: Women's decisions during child-birth, *Medical Decision Making, 4,* 47–58.

Clore, G. L. (1992). Cognitive phenomenology: Feelings and the construction of judgment. In L. L. Martin & A. Tesser (Eds.), *The construction of social judgments* (pp. 133–163). Hillsdale, NJ: Erlbaum.

Damasio, A. R. (1994). *Descartes' error: Emotion, reason, and the human brain.* New York: Putnam.

Dijksterhuis, A. (2004). Think different: The merits of unconscious thought in preference development and decision making. *Journal of Personality and Social Psychology, 87,* 586–598.

Dijksterhuis, A., Bos, M. W., Nordgren, L. F., & van Baaren, R. B. (2006). On making the right choice: The deliberation-without attention effect. *Science, 311,* 1005–1007.

Dijksterhuis, A., & Meurs, T. (2006). Where creativity resides: The generative power of unconscious thought. *Consciousness and Cognition: An International Journal, 15,* 135–146.

Dijksterhuis, A., & Nordgren, L. F. (2006). A theory of unconscious thought. *Perspectives of Psychological Science, 1,* 95–109.

Dijksterhuis, A., & van Olden, Z. (2006). On the benefits of thinking unconsciously: Unconscious thought can increase post-choice satisfaction. *Journal of Experimental Social Psychology, 42,* 627–631.

Dunn, E. W., & Ashton-James, C. (2008). On emotional innumeracy: Predicted and actual affective responses to grand-scale tragedies. *Journal of Experimental Social Psychology, 44,* 692–698.

Dunn, E. W., Biesanz, J.C., Human, L. J., & Finn, S. (2007). Misunderstanding the affective consequences of everyday social interactions: The hidden benefits of putting one's best face forward. *Journal of Personality and Social Psychology, 92,* 990–1005.

Dunn, E. W., Brackett, M. A., Ashton-James, C., Schneiderman, E., & Salovey, P. (2007). On emotionally intelligent time travel: Individual differences in affective forecasting ability. *Personality and Social Psychology Bulletin, 33,* 85–93.

Dunn, E. W., Wilson, T. D., & Gilbert, D. T. (2003). Location, location, location: The misprediction of satisfaction in housing lotteries. *Personality and Social Psychology Bulletin, 29,* 1421–1432.

Epstein, S. (1994). Integration of the cognitive and the psychodynamic unconscious. *American Psychologist, 49,* 709–724.

Epstein, S. (1998a). Cognitive-experiential self-theory. In D. F. Barone, M. Hersen, & V. B. Van Hasselt (Eds.), *Advanced personality* (pp. 211–238). New York: Plenum Press.

Epstein, S. (1998b). *Constructive thinking: The key to emotional intelligence.* Westport, CT: Praeger.

Epstein, S., Pacini, R., Denes-Raj, V., & Heier, H. (1996). Individual differences in intuitive-experiential and analytical-rational thinking styles. *Journal of Personality and Social Psychology, 71,* 390–405.

Forrin, N. D., Dunn, E. W., Biesanz, J. C., & Aknin, L. B. (2007). [Differences in affective forecasts made for the self versus others]. Unpublished raw data.

Frederick, S. (2005). Cognitive reflection and decision making. *Journal of Economic Perspectives, 19,* 25–42.

Gilbert, D. T., & Buckner, R. L. (2007, January 29). Time travel in the brain. *Time, 169,* 91.

Gilbert, D. T., Driver-Linn, E., & Wilson, T. D. (2002). The trouble with Vronsky: Impact bias in the forecasting of future affective states. In L. Feldman-Barrett & P. Salovey (Eds.), *The wisdom of feeling* (pp. 114–143). New York: Guilford Press.

Gilbert, D. T., Gill, M. J., & Wilson, D. T. (2002). The future is now: Temporal correction in affective forecasting. *Organizational Behavior and Human Decision Processes, 88,* 690–700.

Gilbert, D. T., Morewedge, C. K., Risen, J. L., & Wilson, T. D. (2004). Looking forward to looking backward: The misprediction of regret. *Psychological Science, 15,* 346–350.

Gilbert, D. T., Pinel, E. C., Wilson, T. D., Blumberg, S. J., & Wheatley, T. P. (1998). Immune neglect: A source of durability bias in affective forecasting. *Journal of Personality and Social Psychology, 75,* 617–638.

Hsee, C. K., & Zhang, J. (2004). Distinction bias: Misprediction and mischoice due to joint evaluation. *Journal of Personality and Social Psychology, 86,* 680–695.

Kahneman, D., & Tversky, A. (1979). Prospect theory: An analysis of decision under risk. *Econometrica, 47,* 263–291.

Koriat, A., & Levy-Sadot, R. (1999). Processes underlying metacognitive judgments: Information-based and experience-based monitoring of one's own knowledge. In S. Chaiken & Y. Trope (Eds.), *Dual-process theories in social psychology* (pp. 483–502). New York: Guilford Press.

Lam, K. C. H., Buehler, R., McFarland, C., Ross, M., & Cheung, I. (2005). Cultural differences in affective forecasting: The role of focalism. *Personality and Social Psychology Bulletin, 31,* 1296–1300.

Liberman, N., Sagristano, M., & Trope, Y. (2002). The effect of temporal distance on level of mental construal. *Journal of Experimental Social Psychology, 38,* 523–534.

Loewenstein, G. (2000). Emotions in economic theory and economic behaviour. *The American Economic Review, 90,* 426–432.

Loewenstein, G., & Lerner, J. (2003). The role of affect in decision making. In R. J. Davidson, H. H. Goldsmith, & K. R. Scherer (Eds.), *Handbook of affective science* (pp. 619–642). Oxford, England: Oxford University Press.

Loewenstein, G., Nagin, D., & Paternoster, R. (1997). The effect of sexual arousal on sexual forcefulness. *Journal of Research in Crime and Delinquency, 34,* 443–473.

Loewenstein, G., O'Donoghue, T., & Rabin, M. (2003). Projection bias in predicting future utility. *Quarterly Journal of Economics, 118,* 1209–1248.

Loewenstein, G., Prelec, D., & Shatto, C. (1998). *Hot/cold intrapersonal empathy gaps and the underprediction of curiosity.* Unpublished manuscript, Carnegie Mellon University, Pittsburgh, PA.

Loewenstein, G. F., & Schkade, D. (1999). Wouldn't it be nice? Predicting future feelings. In D. Kahneman, E. Diener, & N. Schwartz (Eds.), *Well-being: The foundations of hedonic psychology* (pp. 85–105). New York: Russell Sage Foundation.

Loewenstein, G. F., Weber, E. U., Hsee, C. K., & Welch, E. (2001). Risk as feelings. *Psychological Bulletin, 127,* 267–286.

Mayer, J. D., & Salovey, P. (1997). What is emotional intelligence? In P. Salovey & D. J. Sluyter (Eds.), *Emotional development and emotional intelligence: Educational implications* (pp. 4–30). New York: Basic Books.

Mitchell, T. R., Thompson, L., Peterson, L., & Cronk, R. (1997). Temporal adjustments in the evaluation of events: The "rosy view." *Journal of Experimental Social Psychology, 33,* 421–448.

Morewedge, C. K., Gilbert, D. T., & Wilson, T. D. (2005). The least likely of times: How remembering the past biases forecasts of the future. *Psychological Science.*

Murphy, S. T., & Zajonc, R. B. (1993). Affect, cognition, and awareness: Affective priming with optimal and suboptimal stimulus exposures. *Journal of Personality and Social Psychology, 64,* 723–739.

Petty, R. E., & Cacioppo, J. T. (1986). The elaboration likelihood model of persuasion. In L. Berkowitz (Ed.), *Advances in experimental social psychology* (pp. 123–205). New York: Academic Press.

Rawn, C. D., & Dunn, E. W. (2007). [Thoughtful versus gut forecasts]. Unpublished raw data.

Ross, M. (1989). Relation of implicit theories to the construction of personal histories. *Psychological Review, 96,* 341–357.

Salovey, P., & Mayer, J.D. (1990). Emotional intelligence. *Imagination, Cognition, and Personality, 9,* 185–211.

Salovey, P., Mayer, J. D., & Caruso, D. (2003). Measuring emotional intelligence as a set of abilities with the Mayer-Salovey-Caruso emotional intelligence test. In S. J. Lopez & C. R. Snyder (Eds.), *Positive psychology assessment: A handbook of models and measures* (pp. 251–265). Washington, DC: American Psychological Association.

Schkade, D. A., & Kahneman, D. (1998). Does living in California make people happy? A focusing illusion in judgments of life satisfaction. *Psychological Science, 9,* 340–346.

Schwarz, N. (1990). Feelings as information: Informational and motivational functions of affective states. In E. T. Higgins & R. M. Sorrentino (Eds.), *Handbook of motivation and cognition: Foundations of social behavior* (Vol. 2, pp. 527–561). New York: Guilford Press.

Sherman, S. J., Beike, D. R., & Ryalls, K. R. (1999). Dual-processing accounts of inconsistencies in responses to general versus specific cases. In S. Chaiken & Y. Trope (Eds.), *Dual-process theories in social psychology* (pp. 203–227). New York: Guilford Press.

Sloman, S. A. (1996). The empirical case for two systems of reasoning. *Psychological Bulletin, 119,* 3–22.

Slovic, P., Finucane, M., Peters, E., & MacGregor, D. (2002). The affect heuristic. In T. Gilovich, D. Griffin, & D. Kahneman (Eds.), *Heuristics and biases* (pp. 397–420). New York: Cambridge University Press.

Smith, E. R., & DeCoster, J. (2000). Dual-process models in social and cognitive psychology: Conceptual integration and links to underlying memory systems. *Personality and Social Psychology Review, 4,* 108–131.

Taylor, S. E. (1991). Asymmetrical effects of positive and negative events: The mobilization-minimization hypothesis. *Psychological Bulletin, 110,* 67–85.

Van Boven, L., Dunning, D., & Loewenstein, G. (2000). Egocentric empathy gaps between owners and buyers: Misperceptions of the endowment effect. *Journal of Personality and Social Psychology, 79,* 66–76.

Van Boven, L., & Loewenstein, G. (2003). Social projection of transient drive states. *Personality and Social Psychology Bulletin, 29,* 1159–1168.

Van Boven, L., & Loewenstein, G. (2005). Empathy gaps in emotional perspective taking. In S. Hodges & B. Malle (Eds.), *Other minds: How humans bridge the divide between self and others* (pp. 284–297). New York: Guilford Press.

Van Boven, L., Loewenstein, G., Dunning, D., & Welch, N. (2004). *The illusion of courage: Underestimating the impact of fear of embarrassment on the self.* Unpublished manuscript, University of Colorado, Boulder.

Wilson, T. D., Centerbar, D. B., Kermer, D. A., & Gilbert, D. T. (2005). The pleasures of uncertainty: Prolonging positive moods in ways people do not anticipate. *Journal of Personality and Social Psychology, 88,* 5–21.

Wilson, T. D., Laser, P. S., & Stone, J. I. (1982). Judging the predictors of one's own mood: Accuracy and the use of shared theories. *Journal of Experimental Social Psychology, 18,* 537–556.

Wilson, T. D., Meyers, J., & Gilbert, D. T. (2001). Lessons from the past: Do people learn from experience that emotional reactions are shortlived? *Personality and Social Psychology Bulletin, 27,* 1648–1661.

Wilson, T. D., Wheatley, T., Kurtz, J., Dunn, E., & Gilbert, D. T. (2004). When to fire: Anticipatory versus postevent reconstrual of uncontrollable events. *Personality and Social Psychology Bulletin, 30,* 1–12.

Wilson, T. D., Wheatley, T. P., Meyers, J. M., Gilbert, D. T., & Axsom, D. (2000). Focalism: A source of the durability bias in affective forecasting. *Journal of Personality and Social Psychology, 78,* 821–836.

Winkielman, P., Berridge, K. C., & Wilbarger, J. L. (2005). Unconscious affective reactions to masked happy versus angry faces influence consumption behavior and judgments of value. *Personality and Social Psychology Bulletin, 31,* 121–135.

Woodzicka, J. A., & LaFrance, M. (2001). Real versus imagined gender harassment. *Journal of Social Issues, 57,* 15–30.

23 Subjective Proximity of Future Selves: Implications for Current Identity, Future Appraisal, and Goal Pursuit Motivation

Wei Qi Elaine Perunovic and Anne E. Wilson

INTRODUCTION

People often think to the past or to the future when considering issues pertinent to their current identity. It is difficult, if not impossible, to answer the question "Who am I?" without looking back over a lifetime of experiences and without thinking ahead to one's hopes and plans for the future. In describing the notion of "specious present," William James (1890/1950) noted that "the knowledge of some other part of the stream, past or future, near or remote, is always mixed in with our knowledge of the present thing" (p. 606). A large part of individuals' conceptualization of their present self draws from their memories of the past and imaginations of the future. At the same time, their reconstructions of their past and predictions for their future are influenced by present beliefs, feelings, and self-views.

From the perspective of temporal self-appraisal (TSA) theory (Ross & Wilson, 2000; Wilson & Ross, 2003), past and future selves can be thought of as temporally extended selves that vary in proximity to the current self. Ross and Wilson were primarily concerned with the subjective proximity of past and future selves. They used the term *subjective temporal distance* to refer to how close or far away people feel psychologically from their past or future, and they have demonstrated an intimate connection between the subjective temporal distance of former and future selves and current identity (Ross & Wilson, 2000, 2002, 2003; Wilson, Buehler, Lawford, & Schmidt, 2007; Wilson & Ross, 2001, 2003). They have discovered a number of intriguing parallels between how people remember their past and how they think about their future.

In this chapter, we briefly describe TSA research examining subjective proximity of past selves and then illustrate how this work may be extended to the investigation of future self-appraisal. Our current self-view, motivation, decisions, and behavior can be affected by what we predict or speculate that the future might hold, even though these future selves are always hypothetical or imagined. We describe our ongoing research exploring how the subjective distance of imagined future selves not only has implications for identity but also may play an important role in motivation and goal pursuit.

PSYCHOLOGICAL TEMPORAL DISTANCE AND PAST SELF-APPRAISALS

In general, events that happened a month ago feel closer than events that happened a year ago. The association between subjective and actual time, however, is far from perfect (Block, 1989; Brown,

Rips, & Shevell, 1985; Ross & Wilson, 2002; Vohs & Schmeichel, 2003). Some distant past events may subjectively feel like they occurred just yesterday, whereas other recent events may subjectively feel very remote, regardless of calendar time. For instance, a person may think that her wedding day, which had actually occurred a year ago, feels as though it occurred only yesterday; yet, this same person may feel that a conflict with her spouse (which actually occurred yesterday) feels like ancient history. The psychological experience of time, hence, may diverge markedly from actual calendar time. There are a number of psychological factors that can influence the subjective feeling of time independent of calendar time. For example, events that reflect favorably on the self tend to be experienced as psychologically more recent than unfavorable events (Ross & Wilson, 2002). In addition, events that are thought about more frequently, described more vividly, or ruminated on to a greater extent tend to be experienced as psychologically closer in time (Wilson, McLellan, & Ross, 2006; Wilson, McTeer, & Gunn, 2006).

Why do we care about the subjective experience of temporal distance? For one thing, there may be an intriguing connection between how close or far away the past feels subjectively and one's current identity. According to TSA theory, subjectively recent past selves should reflect directly on present identity, whereas distant past selves do not but may be contrasted instead. In other words, individuals may feel that their past continues to reflect on their current self when the past self feels psychologically close (Wilson & Ross, 2003). In contrast, when a past self is psychologically distant, then it may no longer reflect on the self today. Instead, it may feel like a detached "old me" who is quite different from the self now and whose attributes and experiences have little bearing on the present. Because people are motivated to maintain favorable views of their current selves (Baumeister, 1998; Higgins, 1996), they should be motivated to praise subjectively recent selves and deprecate remote selves, providing them with evidence of their impressive (and improving) current attributes. In research supporting this theory, Wilson and Ross (2001) demonstrated that people evaluated a past self more favorably when it was described as recent than when it was described as distant (holding actual calendar time constant). Ross and Wilson (2002) also observed that perceived time is malleable: People can shift the psychological distance of past events, feeling subjectively closer to past successes than past failures, regardless of calendar time. Presumably, feeling close to past successes allows people to continue to take credit for them, and feeling distant from past failures shields the present self from blame. Furthermore, supporting their motivational interpretation, Ross and Wilson (2002) also found that individuals show this pattern of distancing for their own but not acquaintances' positive and negative events. Finally, Wilson and Ross (2003) reported evidence that this pattern of distancing does benefit current identity: People feel better about their current selves when induced to feel close to (rather than distant from) past glories and far from (rather than close to) former shortcomings.

PSYCHOLOGICAL TEMPORAL DISTANCE AND FUTURE SELF-APPRAISAL

It is one thing to think about one's earlier exploits and another to imagine what one will become in the future. Understanding how people view themselves in the future has long been a topic of interest for social psychologists (e.g., Johnson & Sherman, 1990; Karniol & Ross, 1996). People's expectations about their future can have implications for their present, influencing their current self-view, motivation, and behavior (e.g., in this volume, Carroll & Shepperd, Chapter 28; Dunn, Forrin, & Ashton-James, Chapter 22; Faude, Wuerz, & Gollwitzer, Chapter 5; Klein & Zajac, Chapter 21; Markus & Nurius, 1986; Oettingen & Kappes, Chapter 26; Oyserman & James, Chapter 25). Although the past and future self are not identical constructs, the two share the element of flexibility. Both are temporally extended selves created mentally in the present time (see also Libby & Eibach, Chapter 24, this volume). Neuropsychological evidence indicates that there is an intimate relation between recollection of the past and imagination of the future (Szpunar & McDermott, Chapter 8, this volume; Tulving, 2005). Individuals who lost their ability to recall past episodic memories also experienced the incapability to imagine their future (Klein, Loftus, & Kihlstrom,

2002). However, although people are afforded some poetic license to reconstruct the past according to their desires, they are limited to some extent by reality constraints (see also Van Boven, Kane, & McGraw, Chapter 9, this volume). In contrast, future selves by definition are still hypothetical and hence may be even less constrained by reality and more colored by one's current beliefs and desires (Newby-Clark & Ross, 2003; Robinson & Ryff, 1999).

According to TSA theory, there should be parallels between the ways that people recall their former selves and think about their future selves. In particular, just as subjectively recent past selves reflect directly on current identity, so should subjectively close future selves. In contrast, like distant past selves, remote future selves carry few implications for current selves. Based on this reasoning, one should predict that people will be more motivated to praise psychologically close upcoming selves to a greater extent than future selves that still feel psychologically far-off. However, future expectations differ from recollections of the past in a crucial way. Whether sooner or later, people anticipate becoming the future self that they predict. Therefore, people might not exaggerate the inferiority of distant future selves to allow their present self to appear superior in comparison, as they might with former selves. Indeed, people tend to view themselves as improving over time (Wilson & Ross, 2000, 2001) and tend not to predict future decline (Wilson et al., 2007).

Hence, there is an interesting paradox: Although people tend to anticipate getting better and better through actual calendar time, when they evaluate a future self at any given point in time, they will be more inclined to praise it if it feels psychologically closer rather than farther away. This phenomenon should occur because of people's concern with feeling good about their current state: Glorifying psychologically closer future selves holds greater promise of immediate gratification than applauding psychologically intangible distant future selves. The aforementioned irony may become more apparent when one considers the finding that people tend to feel more optimistic about a distal future than a proximal future because the former is mentally represented more abstractly and the latter more concretely (see Amit, Algom, Trope & Liberman, Chapter 4, this volume) and the finding that people tend to lose confidence as the "moment of truth" draws near in actual time (Gilovich, Kerr, & Medvec 1993). However, TSA theory is based on two important premises—that self-appraisal involves motivational processes and that individuals are concerned with the valence of their present identity when evaluating their temporal self. Therefore, when people are asked to appraise their future selves, the motivation to boost their current self-regard will steer them to engage in evaluative processes that maximize positive implication for their current identity: When a future self feels psychologically closer to, rather than more distant from, the present, this future self is appraised more favorably.

The prediction that people enhance subjectively proximal future selves to a greater degree than their subjectively distant future selves has been supported in a series of studies in which temporal distance was experimentally varied. Wilson et al. (2007) manipulated the subjective temporal distance of a specific point in time in the future using a timeline procedure (also see Pennington & Roese, 2003; Sanna, Chang, Carter, & Small, 2006; Wilson & Ross, 2003) and examined its effect on appraisals of the future self. Participants were asked to mark a specific target point in the future (e.g., yourself 2 months from today) on a timeline. Across several studies, participants evaluated their anticipated future attributes and expected performance on an upcoming test. The findings indicated that participants who were made to feel closer to their future selves viewed their future selves more favorably than participants who were induced to feel more distant from their future selves. This effect of subjective temporal distance on future self-appraisals was unique to participants' evaluations of their own future selves and did not apply to their evaluations of their acquaintances' future selves, suggesting that the effect does not simply reflect a general cognitive tendency. Instead, results are consistent with the TSA suggestion that people's evaluations of temporally extended selves (in the past or future direction) are often constructed in ways that bolster present self-regard (Wilson & Ross, 2001, 2003). Regardless of whether a temporally extended self is in the past or the future, its subjective proximity can have an impact on its subjective valence:

Individuals should be more motivated to evaluate close temporal selves favorably because those selves reflect directly on current identity.

PSYCHOLOGICAL TEMPORAL DISTANCE OF FUTURE SELVES AND CURRENT IDENTITY

People spend a considerable amount of time thinking about their future. We may imagine great success in our careers, increased wealth, a happy family life, good health, and fulfilling retirement years. But, just who is that future person who is reaping all of the benefits of our current hard work and self-discipline? Is that 40-, 50-, or 60 year-old person in the future actually me? In other words, are anticipated future selves assimilated as part of our present identity, or are they viewed as akin to no more than casual acquaintances or even strangers? Research on counterfactual thinking and social comparison suggests that assimilation occurs when aspects of a target are included in one's self-construal (e.g., Markman & McMullen, 2003; McFarland, Buehler, & McKay, 2001; Stapel & Koomen, 2000). We suppose that the future self could become assimilated to the present under certain conditions and suggest that that there is an intimate link between the subjective temporal distance of future selves and current identity. Just as identities of psychologically close others can be treated as one's own through self-expansion (Aron & Aron, 1996), so can a future self that feels psychologically close. When a future self is experienced as psychologically proximal (controlling for actual distance), people should identify more with that self: It should feel to some meaningful extent like "me." In contrast, psychologically distant future selves may be more likely to seem like another person. We propose that identification with future selves has important implications not only for future self-appraisal, but also perhaps for current decision making that will affect future outcomes and future goal pursuit.

Although our research examining the precise nature of the relationship between temporal distance of future self and current identity is in a nascent stage, our existing data suggest that the two are closely connected. We have measured people's current identification with future selves by asking participants to select one of four options that best describes what their future self feels like to them now (Perunovic, Gorman, & Wilson, 2006). Does a specified future self feel like "1 - myself today, 2 - someone who is very close to me, 3 - someone I know but who is not close to me, or 4 - a stranger"? We found that individuals are more likely to identify with a future self (to experience it like "myself today") when it feels subjectively close in time. In contrast, when people view a future self as psychologically remote, they are more likely to view that self as a stranger—an unfamiliar outsider with whom one identifies minimally. Importantly, we find that individuals do not necessarily identify with future selves who are closer in calendar time to a greater degree. That is, they may not identify with themselves in 5 years any more than they identify with themselves in 10 years. Indeed, the association between actual temporal distance and identification tends to be weak or nonexistent and does not alter the relation between subjective temporal distance and identification with future selves when it is held constant (Perunovic & Wilson, 2006).

If subjectively closer future selves are more likely to be viewed as part of the current identity, then people should be more inclined to take credit now for future successes that feel temporally close rather than far away. Supporting this contention, Wilson et al. (2007) found that when participants were induced to feel close to an anticipated future success they enjoyed a current identity boost: Their present self-appraisals were more positive than those of participants who were induced to feel subjectively distant from expected future glories. Wilson et al. argued that participants' current self-regard increased because they identified with the self that experienced a close future success; hence, that future success was assimilated with current identity. How did people feel after thinking about a distant success? On the one hand, conceivably even distant success could make people feel good about themselves if they were simply happier after anticipating something that they would eventually accomplish. On the other hand, if a successful future self was experienced as sufficiently distinct from the present, then its superiority may make the present appear pale in comparison. In this study, however, thinking about a psychologically distant future success did not lead participants to appraise the current self more or less positively than a control group who did not think of a future success at all. Apparently, experiencing a future success as remote was neither flattering nor threatening to the current self; it simply had little bearing on current identity.

We also expected that, like they do for past selves (Ross & Wilson, 2002), individuals might shift the perceived distance of future selves in ways that enhance current identity. Evidence supports this prediction: Peetz, Wilson, and Strahan (in press) observed that people judge expected future successes to be subjectively closer than anticipated failures. For instance, students were asked to predict their scores on an upcoming exam and to report the subjective distance of that future test. Those who expected their future self to perform better on the exam indicated that they felt closer to the time of the exam. Because subjective temporal distance is malleable, people may be able to reap the benefit from anticipated glory by drawing it subjectively nearer to the present while keeping threatening future failures at bay by viewing them as still remote.

PSYCHOLOGICAL TEMPORAL DISTANCE AND GOAL PURSUIT MOTIVATION

So far, we have described the connection between variations in subjective temporal distance from the future and self-appraisals. We also theorize that subjective proximity of the future may play an important role in goal pursuit motivation. Goal pursuit is a pervasive aspect of human behavior and is integral to self-improvement. Thinking about possible future selves has long been thought to influence people's current motivation and actions (e.g., Markus & Nurius, 1986; Oettingen & Kappes, Chapter 26, this volume; Oyserman & James, Chapter 25, this volume; Ruvolo & Markus, 1992). We suggest that the subjective temporal distance of future selves and goals can affect current motivation to approach those goals. In the next section, we describe our research attempting to uncover the role of psychological temporal distance in goal pursuit motivation.

PSYCHOLOGICAL TEMPORAL DISTANCE AND WILLINGNESS TO BEAR SHORT-TERM COSTS FOR LONG-TERM HEALTH BENEFITS

Sometimes, pursuing future successes involves making sacrifices in the present. Many behaviors that promote long-term health have some immediate consequences that diverge from their future benefits. In our research in the domain of health, we have focused on exercising and healthy eating. Physical exercise, for example, has significant long-term future benefits (e.g., better health, longer life), but it is not without immediate costs at the time of action (e.g., inconvenience, effort). Individuals are often aware of the long-term consequences of these behaviors and know that these consequences can be far more substantial than the immediate costs, yet often they still behave in ways that are inconsistent with attaining their long-term goals. This kind of behavioral decision making may be due to the temporal imbalance between the imminent and remote outcomes of these behaviors (Hall & Fong, 2003, 2007). Temporally close outcomes can appear larger than temporally distant outcomes in the same way that spatial perspective leads something within arm's reach to appear larger than something located off on the horizon. Thus, even when people are aware that distant benefits (e.g., enjoying a long, healthy life) are rationally more significant than immediate costs (e.g., forgoing an episode of *Survivor* in favor of a trip to the gym), at the moment of truth (when one must get off the couch), the psychological magnitude of the distant benefit may recede, and the significance of the proximal cost may loom large. Indeed, much of the research on temporal discounting and time preference suggests that people often value more immediate rewards to a greater extent than more distant rewards, even if distant rewards are objectively better (Ainslie & Haslam, 1992; Hall & Fong, 2007; Loewenstein, & Thaler, 1989; Mischel, Shoda, & Rodriguez, 1989). Similarly, in their temporal self-regulation theory, Hall and Fong (2007) incorporated the role of temporal contingencies in understanding the mechanism through which people make irrational health choices. They argued that people's failure to engage in adaptive behavior is in part due to the fact that these "rational" behaviors often come with significant immediate costs and little immediate benefit.

Another reason that people may be disproportionately swayed by proximal consequences is that these outcomes may be clearly experienced as costs or benefits to the current self. Recalling our discussion about the degree to which people identify with future selves, we may suppose that most people would readily agree that watching their favorite television show today would represent a consequence for themselves. However, people report that psychologically distant selves are often experienced as akin to casual acquaintances or strangers. Hence, the long-term future consequence may also be experienced as a benefit bestowed on a stranger. If so, then the psychological decision that individuals may be making is, "Should I give up a clear benefit to myself today to provide a possible benefit to a stranger later?" We do not suggest that anyone actually thinks about the decision explicitly in these terms, but that individuals' experiences of future selves may lead to a psychological weighting of consequences along these lines. This reasoning is reflected in philosopher Parfit's (1984) statement that, "My concern for the future may correspond to the degree of connectedness between me now and myself in the future. ... Since connectedness is nearly always weaker over long periods, I can rationally care less about my farther future" (p. 313). If the distant future self is experienced as a different person, then the benefit enjoyed in the distant future can be conceived as rewarding someone else rather than the self.

The majority of the theory and research pertaining to these issues has contrasted outcomes that are objectively close versus far off in calendar time only. We are, however, also interested in people's subjective experience of the temporal distance of these consequences. It is likely that in almost every case, a consequence occurring today will feel closer than a consequence expected in 20 years. Nonetheless, we do propose that the subjective distance of that future consequence can vary to a meaningful degree. One person may view an outcome expected in 20 years as simply impossibly distant and scarcely worth a second thought, whereas another individual may view this anticipated outcome as almost within reach and quite pertinent to his or her current lifestyle. Indeed, preliminary evidence indicates that individual differences in the degree to which people see the long-term future as subjectively close or remote is related to their propensity for considering long-term consequences of their actions (e.g., "I am willing to sacrifice my immediate happiness or well-being in order to achieve future outcomes," Strathman, Gleicher, Boninger, & Edwards, 1994) and even their generativity (concern for future generations; e.g., "I feel as though my contributions will exist after I die," McAdams & de St. Aubin, 1992).

We propose that the psychological distance of future consequences, then, could influence people's current decisions for at least a couple of reasons. First, a subjectively closer future consequence might seem larger and more significant. Second, people might identify with the future self that is expected to benefit from a long-term consequence of their decision: If the future benefit will belong to "me" rather than to "another person," it should be more compelling and hence should inspire stronger efforts to achieve long-term outcomes. Thus, we propose that feelings of closeness to the future self should play an important role in people's decisions to behave in ways that promote future benefits.

In a study examining individuals' motivation to engage in regular physical activity, Perunovic and Wilson (2006) reminded undergraduate university students about various future health benefits (e.g., reduced chance of developing heart disease and certain cancers; healthier muscles, bones, and joints) that they are likely to obtain in their mid-30s if they engage in regular physical activity now. Students who felt psychologically closer to their 35-year-old future selves reported greater identification with their future selves, indicated higher motivation to engage in regular physical activity, and planned to devote a greater number of hours to exercising in the next 2 months than those who viewed their 35-year-old selves as more remote. In another study, undergraduate university students were provided with information on healthy eating and were explicitly made aware of both short-term costs (e.g., inconvenience, taste compromises) and long-term benefits (e.g., reduced risk of obesity, maintenance of healthy organs) of healthy eating (Perunovic et al., 2006). The students were also told that if they continue to eat healthfully now until their 30s they will reap a number of the long-term benefits in the future when they are 35 years old. We expected that psychological temporal distance would significantly predict identification with the future self, which would in turn predict people's motivation to bear short-term costs for long-term benefits. The study's findings supported our prediction, indicating that students who felt closer to their 35-year-old future selves identified with their 35-year-old selves to a greater degree, which in turn elicited greater motivation to eat healthy at their current age. Although the research is preliminary and correlational at this stage, these findings are consistent with the contention that if the future feels close, then people may identify with their future selves to a greater degree and increase their willingness to bear short-term costs in pursuit of future benefits. Additional studies in which temporal distance is manipulated are clearly needed to directly examine its causal role in motivation to engage in health-related behaviors.

PSYCHOLOGICAL TEMPORAL DISTANCE AND ACADEMIC MOTIVATION

Students' academic goal pursuit can be thought of as another domain in which individuals accept short-term costs for the promise of long-term benefits. Students must give up attractive alternatives (e.g., partying, relaxing, sleeping) to study for tests, complete assignments, and go to class if they wish to attain academic success in the longer term. For most students, of course, the short-term alternatives win out at least some of the time, and individual differences in procrastination and conscientiousness might predict the relative balance between students' short-term and long-term choices. Subjective temporal distance from future potential outcomes can also play a significant role in students' academic motivation and behavior.

Peetz et al. (in press) found evidence that suggested the possible effect of subjective temporal distance on motivation in the study mentioned in which students were asked to predict their expected grade on an upcoming exam and the psychological distance of the exam. Those who expected to do well reported feeling significantly closer to the exam than those who expected to do poorly. In addition, Peetz et al. collected actual grades (from the instructor) following the exam and found that students who had reported feeling closer to the time of the exam 2 weeks earlier obtained better grades on the test than those who felt more distant from the exam, even after controlling for their expected grade on the test. Conceivably, feeling close to the future exam may have served as an impetus to encourage motivational or behavioral processes that helped actually to achieve success on the exam.

Of course, this correlational finding simply shows a link between subjective distance and subsequent test performance and provides no direct evidence for the causal role of temporal distance or the mechanism through which it leads to improved performance. In a subsequent study, Peetz et al. found that students who were experimentally induced to feel close to their future selves at graduation (about 3 years hence) reported greater motivation to work hard now to attain their goal of successful graduation than those who were led to feel that graduation was psychologically very remote. An additional study demonstrated the process by which temporal distance could lead to behavioral effects. Students were told that as part of a study, they would be asked to complete a test in 2 weeks. They were informed that studying was known to increase performance, and they would be given the opportunity to study online over the next 2 weeks. To motivate them to prepare for the test, the researcher informed them that the exam (a test like the Graduate Record Examination [GRE]) was indicative of success at the university, and that top performers would receive an additional cash reward. Participants were then induced to feel close to or distant from the upcoming exam, and they reported their motivation to prepare for and to succeed on the test. Participants could also log on to the study pages online at any time over the next 2 weeks, and their studying activities were recorded. Peetz et al. found that, relative to participants who were induced to feel far from the time of the test, those who were led to feel close to the exam reported greater psychological proximity to the exam, which in turn led to increased motivation to both prepare for and perform well on the test. Increased motivation, in turn, predicted greater time spent preparing for the test using the online tutorial.

Hence, it appears that feeling close to future outcomes may enhance performance by increasing motivation and preparatory behavior.

Taken together, these findings related to subjective temporal distance and motivation in the domain of academics suggest a self-fulfilling prophecy in which students might engage. Students may draw anticipated successes close (to provide a boost to current self-view) but push away expected failures (to protect current self-regard). Increasing the psychological proximity of successes may increase students' motivation to study, whereas distancing expected failures may reduce motivation. These motivational and behavioral processes in turn increase the likelihood that the outcome that students hoped for (or dreaded) actually comes to pass.

PSYCHOLOGICAL TEMPORAL DISTANCE AND THE EFFECTS OF RESOLUTION SETTING

Our investigations of the role of the psychological time of the future has led to some intriguing preliminary evidence concerning identification with future self, motivation, and goal-pursuit behavior, although additional research must be done to flesh out the precise processes. Our interest in these research questions also led us to begin a related line of inquiry pertaining to the psychology of future resolution setting.

Sometimes, people set behavioral goals that are associated with a specific time in the future (they will begin a desired behavior, or end an undesirable one, starting on a specified future date). The New Year, for instance, is a popular time during which people resolve to pursue self-improvement goals. Although considerable research has addressed the outcomes of resolution setting (people's success in following resolutions, etc.), little is known about the consequences of resolution setting on people's behavior prior to the resolution onset (i.e., does making a New Year's resolution affect one's behavior in the relevant domain prior to New Year's Day?) This question would be reasonably trivial if people actually kept most of their resolutions: Why would it matter what people do for a week or two prior to a resolution date if they subsequently shaped up and fulfilled their self-improvement promises? However, people often do not adhere to their resolutions. Research shows that although some resolvers successfully attain their goals, many New Year's resolutions are abandoned not long after the New Year (Norcross, Mrykalo, & Blagys, 2002; Norcross, Ratzin, & Payne, 1989; Norcross & Vangarelli, 1989). As a result, people may make (and then break) new self-improvement resolutions year round, not just at the New Year. Indeed, some people may spend as much time in "preresolution limbo" as they do attempting to follow any given goal before abandoning it. To the extent that this is true, then, it is interesting and nontrivial to examine preresolution psychology.

How do people react to an upcoming resolution onset? Setting New Year's resolutions could have either beneficial or harmful effects prior to the intended commencement date of the resolution. Expecting to follow a resolution may make some people feel that they have the license to "stock up" now on the preresolution behavior before the onset of their self-restraint. This idea is consistent with the "last supper effect" (Eldredge, Agras, & Arnow, 1994), suggesting that anticipating deprivation may give some people justification for overindulgence. In contrast, it is also conceivable that some people might be inspired by their wholesome self-improvement goals and begin emulating their future, improving self prior to the projected resolution onset date. For instance, Mary and Joanna might both set a New Year's resolution to eat healthier. Mary might use this good intention as a green flag to overindulge on turkey, sweets, and wine over the preceding holidays, whereas Joanna might look forward to her healthier, svelter self and already be motivated to forgo a few extra helpings at holiday parties.

Improving health-related behaviors has become a common goal that many people resolve to achieve in our society. Many North Americans do not maintain a well-balanced diet that is optimal for long-term health, instead consuming excess fat and insufficient vegetables, fruits, and calcium-rich products (Statistics Canada, 2006; U.S. Department of Health & Human Services, 2005). Most people, however, do report intentions to eat more healthfully, and the goal to improve their diet represents a common New Year's resolution (Heart and Stroke Foundation of Canada, 2002).

Individuals often set their resolutions days or weeks before New Year's Day. What implications do anticipated resolutions have for resolvers during the holiday season before the New Year?

To examine this question, in mid-December we studied individuals who reported intending to improve their eating habits in the future (Perunovic & Wilson, 2007). We assumed that mid-December may be a time that many individuals contemplate possible resolutions for the upcoming New Year. Therefore, in an attempt to experimentally manipulate resolution setting, we either induced participants to think explicitly about improving their eating behavior as a New Year's resolution (resolvers) or simply asked them to think about improving their eating behavior without linking it to New Year's resolutions (nonresolvers). We assessed participants' subjective temporal distance to the New Year by asking them how close or far away they felt from the coming New Year's Day at that time. Just as subjective closeness to academic goal motivated current goal-pursuit behavior (Peetz et al., in press), we thought that those who felt close to their New Year's "new self" would be more inspired to start emulating that behavior even before the resolution date. We then asked various questions assessing their motivation to eat healthy now and during the holidays. The findings indicated that individual differences in subjective distance from the New Year moderated the effect of resolution setting on intentions to engage in healthy eating now and during the holiday season. Among those who set a New Year's resolution to eat healthy, individuals who felt psychologically closer (1 standard deviation above the mean) to the New Year felt better about themselves when imagining their upcoming self-improvement. According to TSA theory (Wilson & Ross, 2003), these participants may have experienced an affective boost because they incorporated anticipated future improvements into their current identity. In turn, this may have led participants to plan to behave in a manner consistent with this aspect of their identity. Accordingly, these participants also planned to eat healthier prior to the New Year, intended to avoid unhealthy food during the holidays, and felt guiltier when imagining holiday overeating. The motivating effects of resolution setting were absent and sometimes reversed among those who felt relatively distant (1 standard deviation below the mean) from the New Year, perhaps because they felt disconnected with the self they would become starting in the New Year.

Our findings suggest that setting a future resolution can have a powerful effect on people's current motivation even before the resolution onset. This effect, however, is moderated by psychological temporal distance of the New Year. We suggest that psychological distance is closely tied to identification with future self (Perunovic et al., 2006; Strahan & Wilson, 2006): Resolvers may benefit if they already incorporate their "improving self" into current identity but may instead feel unmotivated or even justified to overindulge if they perceive their future improvements to be distinct from their current, less-disciplined, pre-New Year self. We are currently conducting additional New Year's resolutions studies in which temporal distance is experimentally manipulated to examine its causal role. Nevertheless, taken together, findings from the resolution study and the academic motivation studies discussed in this chapter (Peetz et al., in press) support the notion that when people feel closer to a future point in time (keeping calendar time constant), they may be more motivated to pursue future goals right now than if they feel that the future is still remote.

SUMMARY AND CONCLUSIONS

Philosophers and psychologists have long been concerned with understanding the subjective experience of time and have noted that psychological time can be experienced as independent from calendar time (e.g., Block, 1989; Brown et al., 1985; James, 1890/1950; Ross & Wilson, 2002; Vohs & Schmeichel, 2003). Recent work in our program of research suggests that an understanding of subjective time may help researchers to better comprehend the connections among current identity, future selves, motivation, and goal pursuit. The research described in this chapter suggests that people are able to enhance present self-regard by evaluating psychologically proximal and remote future selves differently, and that psychologically close and distant future selves have different implications for current self-identity. Our research also suggests that anticipated future goals have a greater current motivational impact when they feel psychologically imminent rather than remote. Subjective temporal distance may play a pivotal role in the self-regulation necessary for effective goal pursuit.

Our investigation of subjective time is consistent with research on related constructs such as time perspective, temporal orientation, and consideration of future consequences (Hall & Fong, 2003; Strathman et al., 1994; Zimbardo & Boyd, 1999), which also point to the role of temporal focus in people's pursuit of immediate or delayed gratification. For example, whereas future-focused individuals forgo immediate gain and endure short-term costs to reap their long-term benefits, present-oriented people are more likely to give in to short-term temptations. Present-oriented individuals are more likely to smoke, drink, use drugs, and engage in other risky behaviors, whereas people high in future focus tend to exercise more, perform better academically, and make more proenvironmental choices (Hall & Fong, 2003; Rothspan & Read, 1996; Strathman et al., 1994; Teahan, 1958; Zimbardo, Keough, & Boyd, 1997). Experimental evidence also suggests a causal role of time perspective. Researchers have attempted to encourage greater future focus by communicating long-term outcomes and explicitly linking current behaviors and long-term outcomes (e.g., Hall & Fong, 2003, 2007).

Of course, temporal distance of an object, a temporally extended self, or a point in time is only one form of psychological distance that may affect goal pursuit. Research on delay of gratification shows that the form in which objects are mentally represented can affect self-regulation in children. Thinking about a tempting object in an abstract form (e.g., thinking about marshmallows as clouds) serves as a "cooling" strategy that facilitates resistance to the tempting object (Mischel, Shoda, & Rodriguez, 1989). The abstracting strategy may operate to induce psychological distance from the object (Bar-Anan, Liberman, & Trope, 2006). There may also be a close connection between psychological distance factors and subjective temporal distance. For example, seeing a future outcome as close or far might make the outcome seem more probable or more "fantasy-like" (see Oettingen & Mayer, 2002), might alter construals of goals (Trope & Liberman, 2003), and might affect regulatory focus (Pennington & Roese, 2003). Future research should further explore the interconnections between different types of psychological distance (e.g., Trope, Liberman, & Wakslak, 2007) and elucidate the powerful role of subjective proximity in understanding goal-pursuit motivation and behavior.

REFERENCES

Ainslie, G., & Haslam, N. (1992). Self-control. In G. Loewenstein & J. Elster (Eds.), *Choice over time* (pp. 177–209). New York: Russell Sage Foundation.

Aron, A., & Aron, E. N. (1996). Self and self-expansion in relationships. In G. J. O. Garth & J. Fitness (Eds.), *Knowledge structures in close relationships: A social psychological approach* (pp. 325–344). Hillsdale, NJ: Erlbaum.

Bar-Anan, Y., Liberman, N., & Trope, Y. (2006). The association between psychological distance and construal level: Evidence from an implicit association test. *Journal of Experimental Psychology: General, 135*(4), 609–622.

Baumeister, R. F. (1998). The self. In D. T. Gilbert, S. T. Fiske, & G. Lindzey (Eds.), *Handbook of social psychology* (4th ed., pp. 680–740). New York: McGraw-Hill.

Block, R. A. (1989). Experiencing and remembering time: Affordances, context, and cognition. In I. Levin & D. Zakay (Eds.), *Advances in psychology: Vol. 59. Time and human cognition: A life-span perspective* (pp. 333–363). Amsterdam: North-Holland.

Brown, N. R., Rips, L. J., & Shevell, S. K. (1985). The subjective dates of natural events in very long-term memory. *Cognitive Psychology, 17,* 139–177.

Eldredge, K. L., Agras, W. S., & Arnow, B. (1994). The last supper: Emotional determinants of pretreatment weight fluctuation in obese binge eaters. *International Journal of Eating Disorders, 16,* 83–88.

Gilovich, T., Kerr, M., & Medvec, V. H. (1993). Effect of temporal perspective on subjective confidence. *Journal of Personality and Social Psychology, 64,* 552–560.

Hall, P. A., & Fong, G. T. (2003). The effects of a brief time perspective intervention for increasing physical activity among young adults. *Psychology & Health, 18,* 685–706.

Hall, P. A., & Fong, G. T. (2007). Temporal self-regulation theory: A model for individual health behavior. *Health Psychology Review, 1,* 6–52.

Heart and Stroke Foundation of Canada. (2002). *New Heart and Stroke Foundation campaign helps consumers shop heart healthy.* Retrieved July 18, 2006, from http://ww2.heartandstroke.ca/Page.asp?PageID=33&ArticleID=1126&Src=living&From=SubCategory

Higgins, E. T. (1996). The "self digest": Self-knowledge serving self-regulatory functions. *Journal of Personality and Social Psychology, 71,* 1062–1083.

James, W. (1950). *Principles of psychology.* New York: Dover. (Originally published 1890)

Johnson, M. K., & Sherman, S. J. (1990). Constructing and reconstructing the past and the future in the present. In E. T. Higgins & R. M. Sorrentino (Eds.), *Handbook of motivation and cognition: Foundations of social behavior* (Vol. 2, pp. 482–526). New York: Guilford Press.

Karniol, R., & Ross, M. (1996). The motivational impact of temporal focus: Thinking about the future and the past. *Annual Review of Psychology, 47,* 593–620.

Klein, S. B., Loftus, J., & Kihlstrom, J. F. (2002). Memory and temporal experience: The effects of episodic memory loss on an amnesic patient's ability to remember the past and imagine the future. *Social Cognition, 20,* 353–379.

Loewenstein, G., & Thaler, R. (1989). Anomalies: Intertemporal choice. *Journal of Economic Perspectives, 3,* 181–193.

Markman, K. D., & McMullen, M. N. (2003). A reflection and evaluation model of comparative thinking. *Personality and Social Psychology Review, 7,* 244–267.

Markus, H., & Nurius, P. (1986). Possible selves. *American Psychologist, 41,* 954–969.

McAdams, D. P., & de St. Aubin, E. (1992). A theory of generativity and its assessment through self-report, behavioral acts, and narrative themes in autobiography. *Journal of Personality and Social Psychology, 62,* 1003–1015.

McFarland, C., Buehler, R., & McKay, L. (2001). Affective responses to social comparisons with extremely close others. *Social Cognition, 19,* 547–586.

Mischel, W., Shoda, Y., & Rodriguez, M. L. (1989). Delay of gratification in children. *Science, 244,* 933–938.

Newby-Clark, I. R., & Ross, M. (2003). Conceiving the past and future. *Personality and Social Psychology Bulletin, 29,* 807–818.

Norcross, J. C., Mrykalo, M. S., & Blagys, M. D. (2002). Auld lang syne: Success predictors, change processes, and self-reported outcomes of New Year's resolvers and nonresolvers. *Journal of Clinical Psychology, 58,* 397–405.

Norcross, J. C., Ratzin, A. C., & Payne, D. (1989). Ringing in the new year: The change processes and reported outcomes of resolutions. *Addictive Behaviors, 14,* 205–212.

Norcross, J. C., & Vangarelli, D. J. (1989). The resolution solution: Longitudinal examination of New Year's change attempts. *Journal of Substance Abuse, 1,* 127–134.

Oettingen, G., & Mayer, D. (2002). The motivating function of thinking about the future: Expectations versus fantasies. *Journal of Personality and Social Psychology, 83,* 1198–1212.

Parfit, D. (1984). *Reasons and persons.* New York: Oxford University Press.

Peetz, J., Wilson, A. E., & Strahan, E. J. (in press). The role of subjective temporal distance to future goals in motivation and behavior. *Social Cognition.*

Pennington, G. L., & Roese, N. J. (2003). Regulatory focus and temporal distance. *Journal of Experimental Social Psychology, 39,* 563–576.

Perunovic, W. Q. E., Gorman, G., & Wilson, A. E. (2006). *Temporal distance and predicting healthy eating behavior at the moment of truth.* Poster presented at Association for Psychological Science Convention, May 2006, New York.

Perunovic, W. Q. E., & Wilson, A. E. (2006). [Subjective temporal distance, current self-identity, and healthy decisions about future consequences]. Unpublished raw data, Wilfrid Laurier University, Waterloo, Ontario, Canada.

Perunovic, W. Q. E., & Wilson, A. E. (2007). [Resolving to eat healthier in the New Year: The role of psychological temporal distance in pre-New Year motivation]. Unpublished raw data, Wilfrid Laurier University, Waterloo, Ontario, Canada.

Robinson, M. D., & Ryff, C. D. (1999). The role of self-deception in perceptions of past, present, and future happiness. *Personality and Social Psychology Bulletin, 25,* 595–606.

Ross, M., & Wilson, A. E. (2000). Constructing and appraising past selves. In D. L. Schacter & E. Scarry (Eds.), *Memory, brain and belief* (pp. 231–258). Cambridge, MA: Harvard University Press.

Ross, M., & Wilson, A. E. (2002). It feels like yesterday: Self-esteem, valence of personal past experiences, and judgments of subjective distance. *Journal of Personality and Social Psychology, 82,* 792–803.

Ross, M., & Wilson, A. E. (2003). Autobiographical memory and conceptions of self: Getting better all the time. *Current Directions in Psychological Science, 12,* 66–69.

Rothspan, S., & Read, S. J. (1996). Present versus future time perspective and HIV risk among heterosexual college students. *Health Psychology, 15,* 131–134.

Ruvolo, A. P., & Markus, H. (1992). Possible selves and performance: The power of self-relevant imagery. *Social Cognition, 10,* 95–124.

Sanna, L. J., Chang, E. C., Carter, S. E., & Small, E. M. (2006). The future is now: Prospective temporal self-appraisals among defensive pessimists and optimists. *Personality and Social Psychology Bulletin, 32,* 727–739.

Stapel, D. A., & Koomen, W. (2000). Distinctness of others and malleability of selves: Their impact on social comparison effects. *Journal of Personality and Social Psychology, 79,* 1068–1087.

Statistics Canada (2006). *Canadian community health survey: Overview of Canadians' eating habits.* Retrieved July 18, 2006, from http://www.statcan.ca/Daily/English/060706/d060706b.htm

Strathman, A., Gleicher, F., Boninger, D. S., & Edwards, C. S. (1994). The consideration of future consequences: Weighing immediate and distant outcomes of behavior. *Journal of Personality and Social Psychology, 66,* 742–752.

Strahan, E. J., & Wilson, A. E. (2006). Temporal comparisons and motivation: The relation between past, present, and possible future selves. In C. Dunkel & J. Kerpelman (Eds.). *Possible selves: Theory, research, and application.* Nova Science Publishing.

Teahan, J. E. (1958) Future time perspective, optimism, and academic achievement. *The Journal of Abnormal and Social Psychology, 17,* 379–380.

Trope, Y., & Liberman, N. (2003). Construal level theory of intertemporal judgment and decision. In G. Loewenstein, D. Read, & R. Baumeister (Eds.), *Time and decision: Economic and psychological perspectives on intertemporal choice* (pp. 245–276). New York: Russell Sage Foundation.

Trope, Y., Lieberman, N., & Wakslak, C. (2007). Construal levels and psychological distance: Effects on representation, prediction, evaluation, and behavior. *Journal of Consumer Psychology, 17,* 83-95.

Tulving, E. (2005). Episodic memory and autonoesis: Uniquely human? In H. S. Terrace & J. Metcalfe (Eds.), *The missing link in cognition: Origins of self-reflective consciousness: The missing link in cognition* (pp. 3–56). New York: Oxford University Press.

U.S. Department of Health and Human Services (2005). *Dietary guidelines for Americans 2005.* Retrieved July 18, 2006, from http://www.healthierus.gov/dietaryguidelines/

Vohs, K. D., & Schmeichel, B. J. (2003). Self-regulation and extended now: Controlling the self alters the subjective experience of time. *Journal of Personality and Social Psychology, 85,* 217–230.

Wilson, A. E., Buehler, R., Lawford, H., & Schmidt, C. (2007). *Basking in the projected glory: The role of subjective temporal distance in future self-appraisal.* Unpublished manuscript.

Wilson, A. E., McLellan, L., Ross, M., & Anti, S. (2008). *To dwell or distract: The role of rumination in subjective distance.* Manuscript in preparation.

Wilson, A. E., Gunn, G., & McTeer, T. P. (2008). *Objective and subjective date estimates of past news events.* Manuscript in preparation.

Wilson, A. E., & Ross, M. (2000). The frequency of temporal-self and social comparisons in people's personal appraisals. *Journal of Personality and Social Psychology, 78,* 928–942.

Wilson, A. E., & Ross, M. (2001). From chump to champ: People's appraisals of their earlier and present selves. *Journal of Personality and Social Psychology, 80,* 572–584.

Wilson, A. E., & Ross, M. (2003). The identity function of autobiographical memory: Time is on our side. *Memory: Special Issue Exploring the Functions of Autobiographical Memory, 11,* 137–149.

Zimbardo, P. G., & Boyd, J. N. (1999). Putting time in perspective: A valid, reliable individual-differences metric. *Journal of Personality and Social Psychology, 77,* 1271–1288.

Zimbardo, P. G., Keough, K. A., & Boyd, J. N. (1997). Present time perspective as a predictor of risky driving. *Personality and Individual Differences, 23,* 1007–1023.

24 Seeing the Links Among the Personal Past, Present, and Future: How Imagery Perspective in Mental Simulation Functions in Defining the Temporally Extended Self

Lisa K. Libby and Richard P. Eibach

INTRODUCTION

Joan Didion's autobiographical play, *The Year of Magical Thinking,* is based on her memoir of the same title and depicts the events from a period in her life that included both the unexpected death of her husband and the prolonged illness and eventual death of her only child. Describing the process of adapting the story for the Broadway stage, Didion commented:

> I never thought of the character who would appear onstage in this play as me. I thought of her as "the speaker," or "she." I thought of myself as the witness, the watcher, the auditor, the audience. ... It would be logical to assume that I adopted this distance to protect myself. It would also be wrong. The idea that whoever appeared onstage would play not me but a character was central to imagining how to make the narrative: I would need to see myself from outside. (2007, p. B7)

Didion's remarks suggest that reflecting on life experiences from an outside perspective facilitates the process of making sense of those events and constructing a coherent story. Few of us will ever write a formal autobiography, let alone see our life events played out by an actor on the Broadway stage. However, in the process of developing a self-concept, people do tend to integrate their life experiences into a coherent framework that follows a narrative structure (McAdams, 2001; Singer, 2004), and when thinking about life events people do often see those events played out with imagery in their mind's eye (Atance & O'Neill, 2001; Pillemer, 1998). Further, in this mental imagery people sometimes use an observer's visual perspective so that they see themselves from the outside (Nigro & Neisser, 1983). Does the visual perspective people use to picture life events play a role in the process of integrating those events into a broader framework, as Didion's remarks suggest? If so, what are the consequences for the self-concept, self-judgment, and behavior?

IMAGERY PERSPECTIVE[1]

Visual imagery is integral to mental simulations of life events, both past (Pillemer, 1998) and future (Atance & O'Neill, 2001). In this imagery, people often picture life events from the same point of view they would have if the events were actually happening; that is, they use a *first-person perspective* so that they are looking out at the situation through their own eyes. However, other times people picture life events from the point of view an observer would have if the events were actually happening; that is, they use a *third-person perspective*, so that they see themselves in the image. References to this phenomenon appear across a range of sources, from philosophy (Wollheim, 1984), to literature (Oe, 1974), to folk psychology (Schacter, 1996), suggesting that the experience of shifting between one's own and an outsider's perspective in mental imagery is a familiar part of everyday phenomenology. Indeed, empirical investigations verify that although first-person imagery is generally more common than third-person imagery, most people experience images from both perspectives and can dynamically shift perspective at will (Nigro & Neisser, 1983; Robinson & Swanson, 1993).

Research from several traditions converges on the idea that visual perspective in mental imagery of events could be functionally related to the way people process information about those events and make related judgments. For example, the ability to shift between one's own and an outsider's perspective on dimensions other than visual imagery (e.g., emotion, identity, conceptual knowledge) is fundamental to a variety of psychological processes (e.g., cognitive development: Piaget, 1932; perception of agency: Decety & Grezes, 2006; Decety & Stevens, Chapter 1, this volume; self-concept: Baldwin & Holmes, 1987; self-control: Prencipe & Zelazo, 2005; attitude change: Bem, 1972; social understanding: Barresi & Moore, 1996; empathy: Batson, Chapter 18, this volume; Batson, Early, & Salvarani, 1997). In addition, manipulation of camera perspective in video imagery demonstrates that self-other differences in visual perspective per se can affect event-related judgments (Storms, 1973). The idea that shifts of visual perspective in mental imagery could also have important psychological effects is consistent with a tradition of research suggesting that mental imagery functions in the representation and manipulation of information (Kosslyn, 1980, 1994; Kosslyn & Moulton, Chapter 3, this volume; Kosslyn, Thompson, & Ganis, 2006; Shepard & Cooper, 1982).

Despite the many reasons to believe that perspective in mental imagery should have important psychological consequences, empirical research directly investigating the phenomenon has been relatively slow to develop. Psychologists have long been aware of people's ability to shift visual perspectives in mental imagery (e.g., Freud, 1907/1960; Galton, 1883), but it was not until the early 1980s that the first empirical studies were conducted (Nigro & Neisser, 1983). Since then, however, a growing body of work attests to the notion that imagery perspective in mental simulations of life events is a meaningful psychological variable. For example, imagery perspective is related to a broad variety of phenomena, including clinical disorders (Clark & Wells, 1995; Coles, Turk, Heimberg, & Fresco, 2001; McIsaac & Eich, 2004), cultural differences (Cohen, Hoshino-Browne, & Leung, 2007), and aging processes (Piolino et al., 2006).

In the present chapter, we focus on how imagery perspective in mental simulations of past and future events functions in defining the temporally extended self-concept. We begin by reviewing work that explores how imagery perspective is related to social cognition on a very basic level in terms of the mental focus people adopt when thinking about life events. This work sets the stage for a discussion of the role of perspective in connecting past and future events to self-judgments and behaviors in the present. The resulting model suggests that imagery perspective is an integral component of the self-concept.

IMAGERY PERSPECTIVE AND MENTAL FOCUS

Look at yourself.
Step back and look at what you're doing.
Watch what you do.

Any given life event is characterized by a particular experience in and of itself but also has the potential to take on broader meaning when considered in the context of one's life as a whole (McAdams, 2001; Pillemer, 1998). The expressions above suggest that a person's visual perspective on an event is related to whether the person focuses on the immediate experience of an event or reflects on what it means in a broader context. For example, when a student is bogged down in the immediate challenges of writing a dissertation we might encourage her to revel in the broader significance of her efforts, saying, "Look at yourself—you're earning a Ph.D.!" Or, when a friend is enjoying that second piece of cake, we might warn him of the implications for his waistline, saying, "Look at yourself, you're throwing away your diet!" When we use such expressions we do not expect a person to literally step outside themselves and take a look, but research on imagery perspective in mental simulations of past and future events suggests that there is literal truth to the metaphor underlying these figures of speech. Specifically, picturing an event from a first-person visual perspective is related to adopting an experiential mindset in which people attend to the specific actions, sensory information, and thoughts and feelings that characterize their response to the event in and of itself. On the other hand, picturing an event from a third-person visual perspective is related to adopting a reflective mindset in which people integrate the pictured event with other events or self-knowledge, drawing broad conclusions about personal traits, goals, or life themes (Libby & Eibach, 2008).

For example, research investigating the emotional experience that accompanies the mental simulation of events from the personal past shows that there is a bidirectional relationship between imagery perspective and the reliving of past emotion: Focusing on reliving past emotional reactions causes people to picture events from the first-person perspective (Nigro & Neisser, 1983), and deliberately switching from first-person to third-person imagery can reduce reliving of past emotion (Kross, Ayduk, & Mischel, 2005; Robinson & Swanson, 1993). Other research has investigated the causal inferences people make about their own past behavior, depending on the perspective they use to picture it. Using the third-person as opposed to first-person perspective when recalling a social interaction caused individuals to interpret their own past behavior as more a function of their personal dispositions (Frank & Gilovich, 1989). Dispositional inferences suggest a focus on the broader significance of an event: If behavior is caused by an individual's disposition, it implies something about that individual that transcends the specific situation in which the behavior occurred.

In our own research, we have shown that imagery perspective affects not only the perceived cause of actions but the very definition of what those actions are and has an effect not only on inferences regarding traits but on inferences regarding goals as well (Libby, Shaeffer, & Eibach, 2008). Any action (e.g., locking a door) can be defined in many different ways, and these descriptions can be ordered on a continuum from concrete to abstract. Concrete construals (e.g., turning a key) describe a behavior in terms of discrete actions, whereas abstract construals ascribe a broader meaning, often suggesting something about the superordinate goals or traits of the actor (e.g., securing the house, being responsible). In a test of whether imagery perspective affects construal level, participants were assigned to use either the first-person or third-person perspective to picture themselves doing a range of common everyday actions such as locking a door and were asked to choose between concrete and abstract construals of those actions. Results showed that participants were more likely to choose abstract construals when they pictured actions from the third-person than from the first-person perspective. This effect held both for items for which abstract construals referred to traits (e.g., being responsible) and items for which abstract construals referred to superordinate goals (e.g., securing the house) (Libby, Shaeffer, & Eibach, 2008). As do traits, superordinate goals highlight the reasons and consequences for actions rather than the concrete details of the action itself (Vallcher & Wegner, 1985), and thus the results support the idea that third-person imagery leads people to reflect on the broader meaning of actions.

Analogous effects emerge with regard to the way people describe actual events from their lives. For example, in one study participants were assigned to picture an event from either the first-person or third-person perspective and later describe what went through their minds while picturing the event (Kross et al., 2005). Analysis of these responses revealed that participants who were assigned

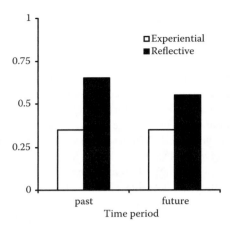

FIGURE 24.1 Proportion of participants who pictured their graduation from the third-person perspective depending on whether the event was in the past or the future and whether they were instructed to adopt an experiential or reflective focus.

to use the first-person perspective were more likely to have thought about the concrete details of the event than were those assigned to use the third-person perspective. On the other hand, third-person participants were more likely than first-person participants to have thought about the event in terms of its abstract meaning, applying theories to explain why things happened as they did and how the event related to other events.

In our own research, we sought to determine whether thinking about the broader meaning of a real event in one's life prompts people to picture it from the third-person perspective. In other words, do people actually "step back and look at the big picture" in their imagery when they are trying to place a specific event in the context of their life as a whole? To address this question, we asked a group of undergraduates to think of an event from their lives, either their high school graduation (a past event) or university graduation (a future event) (Libby & Eibach, 2008). We asked all participants to describe the event, but we varied the instructions they received. Within each time period condition, one group of participants was assigned to focus their description on the concrete details of the event, such as where the event took place, what specific actions they engaged in, and what they saw and heard. The other group of participants in each time period condition was assigned to focus their description on the broader meaning of the event in their lives—how the event related to previous experiences and accomplishments, how it related to the future, and its meaning in the context of their lives as a whole. After participants had written about the event in the specified way, they closed their eyes and pictured it, reporting on the visual perspective they used. Results revealed that, regardless of time period—past or future—participants who were told to reflect on the broader meaning of the event in their life as a whole (reflective focus) were more likely to visualize it from the third-person perspective than were those told to focus on the details of the event in isolation (experiential focus; see Figure 24.1).

Thus, consistent with linguistic metaphors, research suggests that people see events in a broader context, linking them to traits, goals, and theories, if they picture those events from the third-person rather than the first-person perspective. Given that the third-person perspective affords a distanced view of events, this pattern is theoretically consistent with research demonstrating that psychological distance on many dimensions—including spatial, temporal, and interpersonal—is related to abstraction, with greater distance corresponding to more abstract representations (Amit, Algom, Trope, & Liberman, Chapter 4, this volume; Liberman, Trope, & Stephan, 2007). The research reviewed here, however, makes a unique contribution by highlighting the role of visual imagery in the mental representation of events.

One challenge in making the case for mental imagery effects is that it is impossible to directly observe the images people report to have when thinking about events. However, converging evidence for the idea that it is the visual perspective of mental images that is responsible for the effects described thus far comes from research that replicates the effects using manipulations of camera angle in photographic and video imagery. In such studies, researchers can directly control the visual perspective of images, and results are consistent with those from experiments that measure and manipulate visual perspective in mental imagery. For example, the same relationships between perspective and causal inferences that emerge when perspective is measured and manipulated via mental imagery (Frank & Gilovich, 1989) also emerge when perspective is manipulated via camera angle in video imagery (Storms, 1973). In addition, we have replicated the pattern we described, linking third-person mental imagery and abstract construal, using photographs rather than mental imagery to manipulate visual perspective (Libby, Shaeffer, & Eibach, 2008). Such findings provide added support for the notion that visual perspective in mental imagery is functionally related to the mindset people adopt when thinking about life events. What are the implications of these perspective effects for the definition of the self-concept?

IMAGERY PERSPECTIVE AND THE SELF

Moment to moment, lives are made up of a series of concrete experiences. Out of these experiences people construct a notion of a continuous self that spans across time (James, 1890/1950; McAdams, 2001). We began this chapter with Didion's (2007) remarks that observing life events from an outside perspective was essential to integrating those events into a coherent whole. We suggested that, for this reason, visual perspective in mental imagery could be an important component of the temporally extended self-concept. The relationship between imagery perspective and the tendency to focus on the experiential details of a life event versus reflect on what it means in a broader context provides a rationale for how imagery perspective may function in self-construction.

In the course of daily life, people are generally focused on their immediate experience of events and spend relatively little time reflecting on themselves (Csikszentmihalyi & Figurski, 1982). The fact that first-person imagery is generally more common than third-person imagery (e.g., Nigro & Neisser, 1983) suggests that an experiential focus is likely to be the default in mental simulations of events as well. Nevertheless, the process of reflection does appear to play an important role in self-construction. The more people tend to reflect on actions and life events in terms of their broader significance as opposed to their concrete details, the more well defined their self-concepts are: They are more certain about their traits, have a stronger internal locus of control, show more consistent behavior over time, and are less distracted by impulse (Vallacher & Wegner, 1989). Thus, even if third-person imagery is not the predominant mode of mental simulation, the fact that this perspective involves a reflective focus on events suggests that third-person imagery could play a crucial role in defining the temporally extended self. In particular, we propose that third-person imagery functions in self-construction by linking specific events to more general beliefs and theories about the self and one's life as a whole.

In the remainder of this chapter, we describe research that demonstrates this role of imagery perspective in defining the self-concept. We first focus on a series of studies that investigated imagery perspective in mental simulations of past events and then describe research extending these findings to the process of mentally simulating future life events. Both lines of research show how imagery perspective connects with self-judgment and behavior, supporting the role of imagery perspective in defining the temporally extended self.

LOOKING INTO THE PAST: IMAGERY PERSPECTIVE AND PERCEPTIONS OF CHANGE IN THE SELF

I still remember the first time I saw the birth of a baby and my overwhelming awe at the experience. Through my 17-year-old eyes, as a nursing student, I was moved to tears watching the excitement and the emotions of the parents. I immediately knew I wanted to work in that environment.

Kim Richards, RN (Cato, 2007, p. 12)

I am completely different. I've been through a metamorphosis.... I feel as if I woke up one morning to find myself completely different. ... I am just not the same person I was three months ago. I look back and cannot believe that I was her.

Woman changed by feminist movement (Goodman, 1979, p. 69)

These examples highlight the phenomenological differences associated with recalling events, depending on whether one still identifies with a past self. When the nurse recalls her first time in the delivery room—an event central to her present identity—she focuses on the experience of the event in and of itself, reliving it in the present as if she were her past self again. On the other hand, the woman changed by the feminist movement adopts a reflective stance on her past, noting the inconsistencies that emerge when that past is placed in relation to the present. This woman's remark that her past self seems like a different person is not uncommon among people who have experienced a major life change (e.g., Biernacki, 1986; Mathieson & Stam, 1995). In light of the research we have just reviewed, these anecdotal observations raise the question of whether self-change prompts people to picture past selves from a third-person perspective and whether a shift in focus from the experience of an event to its broader meaning might contribute to such an effect. Further, given that people often seek to change themselves in desirable ways by overcoming negative past selves, would deliberately adopting one perspective or the other when recalling a past self have any impact on perceived or actual self-improvement?

How Self-Change Affects Imagery Perspective

We have found that self-change is indeed associated with a tendency to picture past selves from the third-person perspective. For example, in one study undergraduates recalled five memories from high school related to an aspect of themselves that had since changed and five memories from the same time period but related to an aspect that had remained stable up to the present. Participants' reports of memory perspective showed that they used the third-person perspective for 60% of their memories related to changed aspects of themselves but for only 33% of their memories related to stable aspects (Libby & Eibach, 2002). Why does self-change produce this tendency to view one's past self from an outside perspective?

When people think about changes in themselves, they tend to focus on changes for the better because improvement reflects positively on the present self (Perunovic & Wilson, Chapter 23, this volume; Ross & Wilson, 2000; Wilson & Ross, 2000). Thus, it is possible that one reason people tend to picture prechange selves from the third-person perspective is to separate their present self from an undesirable past. Such an effect would be consistent with research showing that people manage subjective perceptions of temporal distance in the service of protecting the present self from undesirable past selves: People report feeling as if their past faults and foibles occurred longer ago in time than did their past successes, even when the objective distance is the same (Ross & Wilson, 2002). On the other hand, the anecdotal examples we have cited so far in this chapter suggest that imagery perspective could function differently with regard to the self-concept than subjective temporal distance does. In the opening quotation of the chapter, Didion (2007) claimed that she adopted a distanced observer perspective on her past experiences not to protect herself but rather to facilitate the process of fitting her experiences into a coherent narrative. The quotations at the beginning of this section suggest that self-change may affect whether a person focuses on the experience of a past event when recalling it or on how that event relates to broader patterns in their life. Perhaps it is this shift in mental focus, rather than a motivation to protect the present self, that explains the shift in imagery perspective that occurs when people change.

To test the viability of these two accounts, we again conducted a study in which undergraduates recalled high school memories (Libby & Eibach, 2008, Study 1). This time, however, we not only specified that those memories either be related to changed or stable aspects of the self but also whether the changed aspects should represent improvements or decline and whether the stable

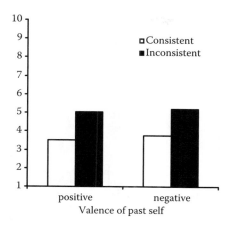

FIGURE 24.2 Mean memory perspective ratings, depending on past-self consistency and past-self valence. Ratings were made on a scale ranging from 1 (entirely first person) to 10 (entirely third person).

aspects should be positive or negative. Thus, across four conditions in the experiment participants recalled memories of positive or negative past selves that were either consistent or inconsistent with the present self. To the extent that the tendency to use third-person imagery when recalling prechange events is driven by a motivation to separate the present self from undesirable past selves, the relationship between self-change and third-person imagery should depend on the valence of the past self. Specifically, people should experience less third-person imagery when they recall events related to ways their past selves were superior to the present and more third-person imagery when they recall events related to enduring negative qualities of the self. Participants' reports of memory perspective provided no support for such a conclusion, however. Participants experienced more third-person imagery when their past selves were inconsistent with their present selves than when they were consistent, regardless of whether those past selves were perceived to be negative or positive (see Figure 24.2). Thus, the tendency to recall prechange selves from the third-person perspective does not appear to be motivated by a desire to separate the present self from negative past selves.

Further research suggests that, instead, the effect of self-change on imagery perspective is a function of how self-change influences people's focus on the experience of past events versus their meaning in a broader context. People are motivated to maintain a coherent sense of self over time (McAdams, 1997; Vinitzky-Seroussi, 1998). When people change, their past selves are no longer consistent with their present self. Such inconsistency creates a threat to coherence, but people can successfully resolve the threat by generating an explanation for the past self's behavior that links it to their current personality (Ross & McFarland, 1988). For example, they may frame a discrepant past event as a turning point or as a stage in the evolution of their present self (McAdams, Josselson, & Lieblich, 2001). Doing so involves thinking about the event in terms of its relation to broader themes in one's life rather than focusing on the concrete experience, and it is this shift in mental focus that appears to be responsible for the effect of self-change on imagery perspective.

Supporting this account, when consistency between past and present selves is experimentally manipulated, inconsistency causes people to picture past selves from a third-person perspective (Libby & Eibach, 2002, Studies 2 and 3). Furthermore, inconsistency between past and present selves encourages a focus on the meaning of an event in relation to one's life as a whole (Libby & Eibach, 2007, Study 2). To test whether these effects explain the relationship between self-change and imagery perspective, we asked participants to recall an event related either to a dimension of themselves that had since changed or a dimension that had remained the same up to the present. In addition to reporting the visual perspective of the images they experienced when picturing the event, participants also described the event in writing and completed a checklist measuring the

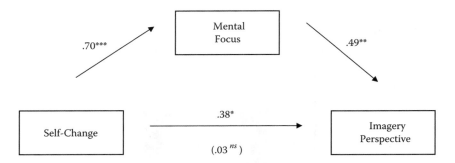

FIGURE 24.3 Path diagram relating self-change and mental focus to imagery perspective. Numbers on paths represent standardized regression coefficients. Self-change was coded –1 for participants who had not changed and +1 for participants who had changed. Higher numbers on the mental focus index correspond to greater reflective focus and less experiential focus; higher numbers on the imagery perspective measure indicate more third-person imagery. The number in parentheses is the standardized regression coefficient for self-change when mental focus was included in the equation. $*p < .05$, $**p < .01$, $***p < .001$; Sobel $z = 2.55$, $p < .05$.

extent to which they were focusing on the concrete experience of the event as they recalled it (e.g., feeling the same feelings and thinking the same thoughts as when the event happened originally) or reflecting on how to integrate it into their life as a whole (e.g., thinking about why they behaved the way they did).

Participants' imagery perspective reports replicated previous results showing that people are more likely to recall an event from the third-person perspective when they have since changed. Participants' event descriptions and their responses on the checklist replicated previous results showing that people are less likely to focus on the experience of a past event and more likely to reflect on its relationship to broader themes in their lives when the past self is inconsistent with the present self than when the two are consistent. Finally, mediational analyses demonstrated that the relationship between self-change and mental focus statistically accounted for the relationship between self-change and imagery perspective (see Figure 24.3). Thus, it appears that the reason changed people look back on their past selves from a third-person perspective is that self-change leads people to think about past events on a broader level in order to maintain a coherent sense of self over time.

The fact that third-person recall is not a direct result of change in the self, but a function of how self-change affects the mindset people adopt when thinking about the past suggests that any factor that causes people to adopt a reflective orientation toward the past should promote third-person imagery. All else being equal, people are more likely to reflect on the meaning of a past event, and thus picture it from the third-person perspective, if it is inconsistent with the present self than if it is consistent, but there are likely to be circumstances under which people would be prompted to reflect on the meaning of a past event that is consistent with the present. Under such circumstances, we would expect people to picture the event from the third-person perspective. For example, if a person encounters a present challenge or dilemma that leads them to ponder who they "really are" as a person, they might reflect on self-consistent past events in an effort to answer the question (Singer & Salovey, 1993) and, as a result, use third-person imagery to represent their past self. The important point is that it is not consistency or inconsistency of the past self per se, but rather a person's mindset—experiential versus reflective—that determines imagery perspective.

How Imagery Perspective Affects Self-Change

The research we reviewed shows that reflection on the broad meaning of an event is not only an inducement to picture it from the third-person perspective, but also a consequence of using this perspective; further, people can shift perspective at will. Given that people's beliefs about change in the self can have important consequences for well-being (Brickman & Campbell, 1971; Carver & Scheier, 1990; Hsee & Abelson, 1991) and success at self-improvement (Rothman, 2000), we wondered whether imagery perspective could be deliberately controlled to influence perceptions of change in the self since an event occurred. If the third-person perspective leads people to think about the meaning of an event as it relates to broader patterns in their life, the third-person perspective should accentuate perceived change when people consider an event to be part of a trajectory of change but should accentuate perceived continuity when people consider an event to be related to an enduring aspect of the self, and this could have important consequences for self-judgments and behavior in the present.

No doubt, one determinant of people's beliefs about change in the self over time is how much they have actually changed. However, perceptions of change and stability are also influenced by subjective and contextual factors. One such factor is whether the past self is positive or negative. People are generally motivated to see themselves developing over time in a way that maintains a positive view of the present self (Perunovic & Wilson, Chapter 23, this volume; Ross & Wilson, 2000). This is not to say that people will not acknowledge enduring negative aspects of themselves or ways they may have declined over time (in fact, a study we described earlier provides an example of just such awareness, Libby & Eibach, 2008); however, to the extent there is any ambiguity about change or stability in the self, people appear to give themselves the benefit of the doubt. Third-person imagery causes people to try to integrate an event into their life as a whole. If people tend to give themselves the benefit of the doubt, then all else being equal, the process of integrating an event into one's life should highlight themes of continuity when a past self is positive but themes of change when the past self is negative. Thus, the third-person perspective should tend to accentuate perceived stability in the self when people recall positive past selves but perceived change when they recall negative past selves.

For example, returning to one's alma mater for a college reunion might trigger memories of events—good and bad—that occurred during one's college years. All else being equal, when one reflects from the third-person perspective on how a positive past moment, such as winning an award, fits into one's life as a whole one is likely to think about a chain of similar achievements in the course of one's life, thus accentuating continuity in the self over time. However, when one reflects from the third-person perspective on a less-flattering college moment, such as a night spent partying when one should have been hitting the books, one is likely to think about the ways one has matured and grown over time, thus accentuating change in the self. Consistent with this line of reasoning, we have found that picturing a proud past moment from the third-person perspective causes people to believe they have changed less since the event occurred than when they picture it from the first-person perspective, but that picturing a past social blunder from the third-person perspective causes them to believe they have changed more since the event occurred than when they picture it from the first-person perspective (Libby, Eibach, & Gilovich, 2005).[2]

Such subjective perceptions of change can even have effects on observable behavior. In the study in which people recalled a social blunder they not only said they changed more after picturing the event from the third-person perspective, they also acted as if they had changed more by demonstrating greater social skill in a social interaction following the memory task. Additional data support the idea that the pattern of results observed when people recalled positive and negative past selves is a function of the differential theories of change that are invoked when people consider positive versus negative events in the broader context of their life as a whole and not a function of the positivity or negativity of the events per se. A similar pattern of results emerges—with third-person imagery accentuating the influence of default assumptions about continuity or change in the self over time—regardless of whether these default assumptions are a function of goals, experimental instructions, or individual differences (Libby et al., 2005).

The fact that third-person imagery appears to accentuate the subjective meaning of life events, influencing beliefs about the self, and even behavior, suggests that third-person imagery should lead people to draw more extreme conclusions in line with their broad theories not just regarding continuity and change but other dimensions as well. Preliminary results from our lab, investigating the role of individual difference variables such as self-esteem and attachment style in moderating the effect of perspective on related judgments and emotion, provide support for this idea. Overall, our research suggests that when people step outside of themselves and picture past events from an external perspective, they do not adopt a dispassionate, objective view but rather tend to see an exaggerated image of who they think they are. Given that the temporally extended self includes both past and potential future events, the findings we have described involving imagery perspective in memory raise the question of whether imagery perspective also plays a role in integrating potential future actions with the temporally extended self. Before concluding, we describe the beginnings of a new line of research that investigates this question.

LOOKING INTO THE FUTURE: IMAGERY PERSPECTIVE AND FOLLOWING THROUGH ON GOOD INTENTIONS

Relative to first-person imagery, third-person imagery makes people more likely to integrate a specific event with broader knowledge and beliefs about the self. Specifically, our own research demonstrates that people are more likely to construe imagined actions in relation to goals and identities when picturing those actions from the third-person perspective. For these reasons, the perspective people use to picture the future has the potential to affect the self-concept—including goals and personal strivings—with important implications for present behavior. In an initial investigation of these possibilities, we focused on the question of how imagery perspective might influence people's abilities to follow through with good intentions.

George Bernard Shaw (1921, p. 9) suggested the power of imagination in helping people follow through with their goals: "Imagination is the beginning of creation. You imagine what you desire, you will what you imagine and at last you create what you will." Indeed, there is evidence that imagining one's self engaging in actions makes one more likely to actually engage in those actions (Gregory, Cialdini, & Carpenter, 1982). However, despite intuitive notions about the role of imagery in goal pursuit—when people have an important goal they are often given the advice to "picture" themselves achieving it—there is relatively little work that directly investigates the process (cf. Conway, Meares, & Standart, 2004; Kosslyn & Moulton, Chapter 3, this volume; Miller, Galanter, & Pribram, 1960; Schultheiss & Brunstein, 1999). We were interested in whether the visual perspective that people adopt when picturing desired future actions would affect the inferences they drew about themselves and thus their likelihood of following through with the imagined actions. We chose to address this question in the context of the 2004 U.S. presidential election.

There are many Americans who register to vote, presumably with the goal of being a voting citizen, but then never make it to the polls on election day. We were interested in whether the visual perspective that registered voters used to picture themselves voting in an upcoming election would influence their likelihood of following through with their goal to vote. Given that people tend to think about specific actions in terms of broader life themes, including goals and identities, when they picture those actions from the third-person than from the first-person perspective, we predicted that picturing voting from the third-person as opposed to the first-person perspective would highlight registered voters' identities as voters and make them more likely to behave in line with this goal come election day.

To test this hypothesis, we recruited registered voters in Ohio to take part in an online study the night before the 2004 U.S. presidential election (Libby, Shaeffer, Eibach, & Slemmer, 2007). Participants were randomly assigned to use the first-person or third-person perspective to picture themselves voting the next day and then completed measures designed to tap into their self-perceptions as voters (e.g., importance of voting, how much their vote made a difference). After the election, we followed up with participants to find out whether they voted. Results revealed that not only did third-person imagery cause registered voters to express stronger identities as voters the night before the election, but as a result, it also caused them to be more likely to turn out to the polls on election day: 90% of participants in the third-person condition voted compared with 72% in the first-person condition. Another pair of studies provided converging evidence that third-person imagery of desired future actions can facilitate goal pursuit by enhancing motivation relative to first-person imagery (Vasquez & Buehler, 2007).

These findings suggest that because third-person imagery leads people to think about specific actions in relation to broader themes in their lives such as goals and identities, the visual perspective people use to imagine desirable future behavior can have important consequences for their ability to follow through on good intentions. Other research demonstrates that framing specific actions in relation to broader goals and identities has a range of implications for the process of goal pursuit (Fishbach & Dhar, 2005; Fishbach, Dhar, & Zhang, 2006). Thus, we expect that our ongoing investigations will reveal further ways in which imagery perspective is a useful tool for successful goal completion. More generally, the present results provide reason to believe that third-person imagery functions to integrate the self across time, not only looking into the past, but also looking into the future.

CONCLUSION

The visual perspective people use to picture life events is related to the mental focus people adopt when simulating those events. Reflecting on how a specific event relates to broader themes in one's life prompts people to picture that event from the third-person perspective. Moreover, adopting this perspective facilitates the process, causing people's reactions to be driven more by the broad meaning of those events in their lives when they picture those events from the third-person than from the first-person perspective. Consistent with the intuitions Didion (2007) expressed in the opening quotation of this chapter, the research we have reviewed here suggests that third-person imagery serves as a phenomenological equivalent of narrative, linking specific events with life themes and general beliefs about the self. Through this mechanism, imagery perspective functions in defining the temporally extended self-concept, influencing self-judgment and shaping behavior. Thus, when people look into the past and the future from a third-person perspective they see the self across time, and this has important implications for who they are in the present moment.

NOTES

1. People experience mental imagery in both visual and nonvisual sensory domains (Neisser, 1967), and perspective can be defined on various dimensions, including visual point of view, conceptual knowledge, and emotion. In the present chapter, we focus specifically on visual point of view in mental images. Thus, for ease of presentation, unless otherwise indicated we use the term *imagery perspective* to refer specifically to the visual point of view in internally generated mental images.
2. Previous work suggests that temporal self-comparisons result in assimilation when a past self is included in the present self but contrast when the past self is excluded from the present self (Markman & McMullen, 2003; Schwarz & Bless, 1992). Although it could be hypothesized that imagery perspective would serve as a direct cue to include (first person) or exclude (third person) the past self in the present, the pattern of results described here, which is representative of the pattern observed across multiple experiments (Libby et al., 2005; Libby, Pfent, Valenti, & Eibach, 2008; Marigold, Libby, Ross, & Holmes, 2008), contradicts this hypothesis. Rather than functioning as a direct cue for inclusion/exclusion, imagery perspective affects mindset (experiential or reflective), and a reflective mindset can accentuate the impact of inclusion and exclusion on self-judgment. That imagery perspective is related to mindset and not inclusion/exclusion is also supported by results we described showing that third-person imagery is not a direct result of self-change but rather a result of the fact that self-change shifts people from an experiential to reflective mindset.

REFERENCES

Atance, C. M., & O'Neill, D. K. (2001). Episodic future thinking. *Trends in Cognitive Science, 5,* 533–539.
Baldwin, M. W., & Holmes, J. G. (1987). Salient private audiences and awareness of the self. *Journal of Personality and Social Psychology, 52,* 1087–1098.

Barresi, J., & Moore, C. (1996). Intentional relations and social understanding. *Behavioral and Brain Sciences, 19,* 107–154.

Batson, C. D., Early, S., & Salvarani, G. (1997). Perspective taking: Imagining how another feels versus imagining how you would feel. *Personality and Social Psychology Bulletin, 23,* 751–758.

Bem, D. J. (1972). Self-perception theory. In L. Berkowitz (Ed.), *Advances in experimental social psychology* (Vol. 6, pp. 1–62). New York: Academic Press.

Biernacki, P. (1986). *Pathways from heroin addiction: Recovery without treatment.* Philadelphia: Temple University Press.

Brickman, P., & Campbell, D. T. (1971). Hedonic relativism and planning the good society. In M. H. Appley (Ed.), *Adaptation level theory: A symposium* (pp. 287–304). San Diego, CA: Academic Press.

Carver, C. S., & Scheier, M. F. (1990). Origins and functions of positive and negative affect: A control-process view. *Psychological Review, 97,* 19 –35.

Cato, J. (2007). Leader to watch: Kim Richards, R.N. *Nurse Leader, 2,* 12 – 16.

Clark, D. M., & Wells, A. (1995). A cognitive model of social phobia. In R. G. Heimberg, M. R. Liebowitz, D. A. Hope, & F. R. Schneier (Eds.), *Social phobia: Diagnosis, assessment and treatment* (pp. 69–93). New York: Guilford Press.

Cohen, D., Hoshino-Browne, E., & Leung, A.K. (2007). Culture and the structure of personal experience. In M. P. Zanna (Ed.), *Advances in experimental social psychology* (Volume 39, pp. 1–67). San Diego: Academic Press.

Coles, M. E., Turk, G. L., Heimberg, R. G., & Fresco, D. M. (2001). Effects of varying levels of anxiety within social situations: Relationship to memory perspective and attributions in social phobia. *Behaviour Research and Therapy, 39,* 651–665.

Conway, M. A., Meares, K., & Standart, S. (2004). Images and goals. *Memory, 12,* 525–531.

Csikszentmihalyi, M., & Figurski, J. (1982). Self-awareness and aversive experience in everyday life. *Journal of Personality, 50,* 15–28.

Decety, J., & Grezes, J. (2006). The power of simulation: Imagining one's own and other's behavior. *Brain Research, 1079,* 4–14.

Didion, J. (2007, March 4). The year of hoping for stage magic. *New York Times,* p. B1, B7.

Fishbach, A., & Dhar, R. (2005). Goals as excuses or guides: The liberating effect of perceived goal progress on choice. *Journal of Consumer Research, 32,* 370–377.

Fishbach, A., Dhar, R., & Zhang, Y. (2006). Subgoals as substitutes or complements: The role of goal accessibility. *Journal of Personality and Social Psychology, 91,* 232–242.

Frank, M. G., & Gilovich, T. (1989). Effect of memory perspective on retrospective causal attributions. *Journal of Personality and Social Psychology, 57,* 399–403.

Freud, S. (1960). Childhood memories and screen memories. In J. Strachey (Ed.), *The standard edition of the complete psychological works of Sigmund Freud* (Vol. 6, pp. 43–52). London: Hogarth Press. (Original work published 1907)

Galton, F. (1883). *Inquiries into human faculty.* London: Macmillan.

Goodman, E. (1979). *Turning points: How people change, through crisis and commitment.* New York: Doubleday.

Gregory, W. L., Cialdini, R. B., & Carpenter, K. M. (1982). Self-relevant scenarios as mediators of likelihood estimates and compliance: Does imagining make it so? *Journal of Personality and Social Psychology, 43,* 89–99.

Hsee, C. K., & Abelson, R. P. (1991). Velocity relation: Satisfaction as a function of the first derivative of outcome over time. *Journal of Personality and Social Psychology, 60,* 341–347.

James, W. (1950). *The principles of psychology* (Vol. 1). New York: Dover. (Original work published 1890)

Kosslyn, S. M. (1980). *Image and mind.* Cambridge, MA: Harvard University Press.

Kosslyn, S. M. (1994). *Image and brain.* Cambridge, MA: MIT Press.

Kosslyn, S. M., Thompson, W. L., & Ganis, G. (2006). *The case for mental imagery.* New York: Oxford University Press.

Kross, E., Ayduk, O., and Mischel, W. (2005) When asking "why" does not hurt. Distinguishing rumination from reflective processing of negative emotions. *Psychological Science, 16,* 709–715.

Libby, L. K., & Eibach, R. P. (2002). Looking back in time: Self-concept change affects visual perspective in autobiographical memory. *Journal of Personality and Social Psychology, 82,* 167–179.

Libby, L. K., & Eibach, R. P. (2008). *Reflecting on personal change: Why past-self consistency affects visual perspective in autobiographical memory images.* Manuscript submitted for publication.

Libby, L. K., Eibach, R. P., & Gilovich, T. (2005). Here's looking at me: The effect of memory perspective on assessments of personal change. *Journal of Personality and Social Psychology, 88,* 50–62.

Libby, L. K., Shaeffer, E. M., & Eibach, R. P. (2008). *Seeing meaning in action: The relationship between imagery perspective and action identification.* Manuscript submitted for publication.

Libby, L. K., Shaeffer, E. M., Eibach, R. P., & Slemmer, J. A. (2007). Picture yourself at the polls: Visual perspective in mental imagery affects self-perception and behavior. *Psychological Science, 18,* 199–203.

Libby, L. K., Pfent, A., Valenti, G., & Eibach, R. P. (2008). *Imagery perspective, self-esteem, and the experience of shame.* Manuscript in preparation.

Liberman, N., Trope, Y., & Stephan, E. (2007). Psychological distance. In E. T. Higgins & A. W. Kruglanski (Eds.), *Social psychology: Handbook of basic principles* (Vol. 2). New York: Guilford Press.

Marigold, D., Libby, L. K., Ross, M., & Holmes, J. G. (2008). *Framing memories of relationship transgressions: The influence of attachment anxiety and visual imagery perspective.* Manuscript submitted for publication.

Markman, K. D., & McMullen, N. (2003). A reflection and evaluation model of comparative thinking. *Personality and Social Psychology Review, 7*(3), 244–267.

Mathieson, C. M., & Stam, H. J. (1995). Renegotiating identity: Cancer narratives. *Sociology of Health and Illness, 17,* 283–306.

McAdams, D. P. (1997). The case for unity in the (post)modern self: A modest proposal. In R. D. Ashmore & L. J. Jussim (Eds.), *Self and identity: Fundamental issues* (pp. 46–78.). New York: Oxford University Press.

McAdams, D. P. (2001). The psychology of life stories. *Review of General Psychology, 5,* 100–122.

McAdams, D. P., Josselson, R., & Lieblich, A. (Eds.) (2001). *Turns in the road: Narrative studies of lives in transition.* Washington, DC: American Psychological Association.

McIsaac, H. K., & Eich, E. (2004). Vantage point in traumatic memory. *Psychological Science, 15,* 248–253.

Miller, G. A., Galanter, E., and Pribram, K. H. (1960). *Plans and the structure of behavior.* New York: Holt, Rinehart, and Winston.

Neisser, U. (1967). *Cognitive psychology.* Norwalk, CT: Appleton-Century-Crofts.

Nigro, G., & Neisser, U. (1983). Point of view in personal memories. *Cognitive Psychology, 15,* 467–482.

Oe, K. (1974). *The silent cry.* New York: Kodansha International.

Piaget, J. (1932). *The moral judgment of the child.* London: Kegan Paul, Trench, and Trubner.

Pillemer, D. B. (1998). *Momentous events, vivid memories: How unforgettable moments help us understand the meaning of our lives.* Cambridge, MA: Harvard University Press.

Piolino, P., Desgranges, B., Clarys, D., Guillery-Girard, B., Taconnat, L., Isingrini, M., et al. (2006). Autobiographical memory, autonoetic consciousness, and self perspective in aging. *Psychology and Aging, 21,* 510–525.

Prencipe, A., & Zelazo, P. D. (2005). Development of affective decision making for self and other. *Psychological Science, 16,* 501–505.

Robinson, J. A., & Swanson, K. L. (1993). Field and observer modes of remembering. *Memory, 1,* 169–184.

Ross, M., & McFarland, C. (1988). Constructing the past: Biases in personal memories. In D. Bar-Tal & A. W. Kruglanski (Eds.), *The social psychology of knowledge* (pp. 299–314). New York: Cambridge University Press.

Ross, M., & Wilson, A. E. (2000). Constructing and appraising past selves. In D. L. Schacter & E. Scarry (Eds.), *Memory, brain, and belief* (pp. 231–258). Cambridge, MA: Harvard University Press.

Ross, M., & Wilson, A. E. (2002). It feels like yesterday: Self-esteem, valence of personal past experiences, and judgments of subjective distance. *Journal of Personality and Social Psychology, 82,* 792–803.

Rothman, A. J. (2000). Toward a theory-based analysis of behavioral maintenance. *Health Psychology, 19,* 64–69.

Schacter, D. L. (1996). *Searching for memory: The brain, the mind, and the past.* New York: Basic Books.

Schultheiss, O. C., & Brunstein, C. (1999). Goal imagery: Bridging the gap between implicit motives and explicit goals. *Journal of Personality, 67*(1), 1–38.

Schwarz, N., & Bless, H. (1992). Constructing reality and its alternatives: An inclusion/exclusion model of assimilation and contrast effects in social judgment. In L. Leonard & A. Tesser (Eds.) *The construction of social judgments* (pp. 217–245). Hillsdale, NJ: Lawrence Erlbaum Associates.

Shaw, G. B. (1921). *Back to Methuselah: A metabiological pentateuch.* New York: Brentano's.

Shepard, R. N., & Cooper, L. (1982). *Mental images and their transformations.* Cambridge, MA: MIT Press.

Singer, J. A. (2004). Narrative identity and meaning making across the adult lifespan: An introduction. *Journal of Personality, 72,* 437–459.

Singer, J. A., & Salovey, P. (1993). *The remembered self: Emotion and memory in personality.* New York: Free Press.

Storms, M. D. (1973). Videotape and the attribution process: Reversing actors' and observers' points of view. *Journal of Personality and Social Psychology, 27*, 65–175.

Vallacher, R. R., & Wegner, M. (1989). Levels of personal agency: Individual variation in action identification. *Journal of Personality and Social Psychology, 57*, 660–671.

Vallacher, R. R., & Wegner, D. M. (1985). *A theory of action identification*. Hillsdale, NJ: Lawrence Erlbaum Associates.

Vasquez, N. A., & Buehler, R. (2007). Seeing future success: Does imagery perspective influence achievement motivation? *Personality and Social Psychology Bulletin*.

Vinitzky-Seroussi, V. (1998). *After pomp and circumstance: High school reunion as an autobiographical occasion*. Chicago: University of Chicago Press.

Wilson, A. E., & Ross, M. (2000). The frequency of temporal-self and social comparisons in people's personal appraisals. *Journal of Personality and Social Psychology, 78*, 928–942.

Wollheim, R. (1984). *The thread of life*. New Haven, CT: Yale University Press.

25 Possible Selves: From Content to Process

Daphna Oyserman and Leah James

INTRODUCTION

Possible selves are visions of the self in a future state; like guideposts, possible selves can orient current choices and behavior. Envisioning ones' future "healthy self," the self who can take the stairs without becoming breathless, or ones' future "unhealthy, smoking self," the self who can no longer do so, can make current choices—refraining from buying a new package of cigarettes, or going to the gym—feel meaningful rather than simply painful. Yet, people do not always act in ways that enhance their chances of attaining their positive and avoiding their negative possible selves. They push the button and wait for the elevator instead of taking the stairs and do not pass on the second dessert or third roll. Why not?

We suggest three factors that may increase the likelihood of discrepancies between possible selves and self-regulatory behaviors: (mis)match, (no) gap, and (mis)interpretation of subjective experience. Discrepancies may arise when there is a mismatch between possible selves and what is cued or made accessible and salient in social context, when no gap is perceived between current effort and what is needed to attain the possible self, and when subjective affective experience (e.g., difficulty) is interpreted as meaning that the possible self is too hard to attain or that enough effort has already been expended. Conversely, self-regulatory behaviors are cued when possible selves match or feel congruent with other aspects of self-concept, when relevant gaps—between one's current situation and future goal and between one's current level of effort and the effort required to attain this goal—are salient and when subjective experience is interpreted to mean that effort is needed (e.g., "This is hard work. … This goal must be really important to me"). To make the case for this model, we synthesize a possible self-approach with other self-regulation and motivation perspectives to suggest how and when possible selves are likely to be effective self-regulators.

POSSIBLE SELVES: A WORKING DEFINITION

Possible selves are the future-oriented aspects of self-concept, the positive and negative selves that one expects to become or hopes to avoid becoming (Markus & Nurius, 1986). They are the desired and feared images of the self already in a future state—the "clever" self who passed the algebra test, the "unhealthy" self who failed to lose weight or quit smoking, and the "off-track" self who became pregnant (Oyserman & Markus, 1990a, 1990b; see also Perunovic & Wilson, Chapter 23, this volume). Individuals possess multiple positive and negative possible selves. These possible selves are often linked with differing social roles and identities, so that possible selves are likely to develop in domains relevant to current life tasks such as being a student, a parent, or a life partner (Cross & Markus, 1994). Possible selves also differ along a continuum of detail; some possible selves are filled with vivid detail of how, when, and in what way the possible self will be attained and what it will feel like to be that self in the future. Other possible selves are much simpler. Possible self content and likage with current action strategies have implications for behavior in the present. A "college student" possible self may cue current effort to the extent that current schoolwork is perceived to be connected with attaining a positive college student possible self and avoiding a feared "failed college student" possible self of not going to college or not getting into one's first-pick college. The possible self can work effectively to regulate current behavior focused on school or other college preparatory activities, even if which college or what major or how it would feel to be a college student are not articulated.

CONTENT OF POSSIBLE SELVES

Much of the research on possible selves has focused on the content of possible selves rather than on testing the motivational consequences of possible selves (for reviews, see Hoyle & Sherrill, 2006; Oyserman & Fryberg, 2006). Differences in measurement techniques reduce our ability to generalize about likely content or detail of possible selves (Hoyle & Sherrill, 2006; for a summary of existing measures with adolescents, see Oyserman & Fryberg, 2006). However, some outlines of content of possible selves emerge across studies. Importantly, it seems that possible self content typically reflects developmentally and contextually salient projects and challenges (Oyserman & Fryberg, 2006; Oyserman & Markus, 1990a, 1990b; Oyserman, Terry, & Bybee, 2002; see also Klinger, Chapter 15, this volume).

For example, a number of studies with middle-class young adults suggested that their possible selves are focused on occupational and interpersonal issues such as getting married, and that family and parenting possible selves become more important in middle adult years (Cross & Markus, 1991; Hooker, Fiese, Jenkins, Morfei, & Schwagler, 1996; Strauss & Goldberg, 1999). Although little research has focused on low-income adults, one study suggested that securing employment and caring for and providing for children were pervasive themes of the possible selves of mothers receiving welfare or transitioning to work (Lee & Oyserman, in press), and a study with imprisoned fathers suggested that becoming like their own fathers is a common feared possible self for these men (Meek, 2007). As adults age, the centrality of job-focused possible selves recedes (Cross & Markus, 1991), and physical health-related possible selves become more prominent (Frazier, Hooker, Johnson, & Kaus, 2000; Hooker & Kaus, 1994). During adolescence, education and future occupations are among the most common foci of young teens' possible selves (Knox, Funk, Elliott, & Bush, 2000; Shepard & Marshall, 1999). These possible selves are equally common among low-income and minority early teens (Oyserman, Bybee, Terry, & Hart-Johnson, 2004), as are, to a lesser degree, fears about becoming off-track and possible selves focused on peer relations (Oyserman, Johnson, & Bybee, 2007).

IMAGINING POSSIBLE SELVES

As future states, all possible selves involve some change from the present, but how possible selves are imagined differs among individuals and contexts in critical ways. Of particular importance are differences in detail and link to strategies, perceived likelihood or certainty of attainment, valence, and temporal distance (how far in the future the imagined self is located). The implications of these differences are summarized in this section.

Detail and Link to Strategies

Some possible selves include concrete strategies for how to achieve them, whereas others do not. When possible selves do not feel connected to other aspects of self-concept, and are not linked with strategies, they are less likely to trigger self-regulatory action. Failing to work toward a future that one does not see as linked to important self-concept features, a future that one can hardly imagine anyway, is unlikely to feel devastating. Similarly, even a vividly detailed possible self is unlikely to produce self-regulation if the action to be taken to attain it is not clear.

Perceived Likelihood or Certainty of Attainment

Some possible selves feel comfortably certain, the selves one will become if nothing much changes from the way things are now. Other possible selves are "within one's grasp," yet uncertain enough to instill a sense of urgency in action. These less-certain possible selves are the selves one can expect to attain or to avoid becoming if one invests reasonable effort and energy. Still other possible selves are quite remote in their likelihood; these are the "long-shot" possible selves, ones so unlikely that action feels pointless. Having these possible selves may make for pleasant dreams or sleepless nights, but these possible selves are unlikely to change behavior unless, for whatever reason, the perceived likelihood of their potential reality increases beyond some minimal threshold. Thus, the motivational value of possible selves may have an inverted U-shaped function, low when expectancy of attainment is either too high or too low to warrant additional effort.

Valence

Possible selves may be positive (selves one expects, believes one can, or hopes to become) or negative (selves one expects or wants to avoid becoming or fears becoming). Whether a possible self-image is positive or negative has consequences for the likely impact of the possible self on mood and motivation. Feared possible selves focus attention on what one would be like if things went wrong. Feared possible selves could be focused on small bumps in life's pathway or on larger roadblocks resulting in failure to attain significant milestones. Some of these feared possible selves are likely to be experienced, even repeatedly, but over time efforts to avoid the bumps in the road may reduce one's likelihood of experiencing blocked milestones. For example, a graduate student may have a feared possible self in which all her manuscripts have been rejected from the journal of her choice, as well as a feared possible self in which she fails to get tenure. Working with added vigilance to make sure that her studies are well done, her write-ups clear, and her choice of target journals reasonable should minimize the chance that everything she writes is rejected (although some papers may very well require multiple submissions). Moreover, the more effort she expends on ensuring that the always-rejected possible self does not materialize, the less likely it is that the "denied tenure" possible self will come to be.

Temporal Distance

As is clear in the example, possible selves also differ with regard to temporal distance from the present. While all possible selves focus on the future, the distance between the present and the future can be near or far. Time units can be marked vaguely (e.g., "when I am an adult and on my own") or clearly (e.g., "next September" or "next semester"). Time can be marked by meaning unit ("by the time I have to buy another swimsuit," "by the time I retire") or by date ("by Valentine's Day"). How time is marked is likely to influence how vividly this future is imagined or whether the future is imagined at all. For example, soldiers, prisoners, and high school students may mark time until the future begins (after discharge, once parole begins, after graduation) such that the present is experienced as separate from the future, and the future feels distal, vague, and open. Conversely, the present can be seen as setting the groundwork for what will become possible in the future, such as getting training that can be used after military service to enhance one's appeal to employers or taking advanced placement classes to increase the likelihood of college acceptance. We examine the implications of each of these variables for the self-regulatory effectiveness of possible selves.

FUNCTIONS OF POSSIBLE SELVES

The notion that future images could have motivational force is not new; for example, almost half a century ago, Miller, Galanter, and Pribram (1960) made reference to images of the future and plans for their attainment. They proposed that behavior is cued by experience of discrepancy between one's current and planned outcomes, and that plans for attainment can be automatically enacted when discrepancy is cued. Indeed, the importance of temporal focus on motivation, the idea that self-concept contains temporal components, and the hypothesis that current self-regulation is linked with future goals is deeply rooted in psychological formulations of self-concept since William James (1890). Currently, these future images have become known as possible selves, personal projects, and personal strivings (for reviews, see Markus & Wurf, 1987; Oyserman, 2001).

WELL-BEING

A number of authors have argued that making salient one's most successful future or possible selves improves well-being (e.g., King, 2001). Simply by serving as a reminder of the malleability of the self (e.g., "I may not be doing well in school this year, but I will next year"), positive possible selves can promote current well-being and optimism about the future (Cross & Markus, 1994; Markus & Wurf, 1987). Possible selves can facilitate optimism and belief that change is possible because they provide a sense that the current self is mutable (Markus & Nurius, 1986; see also Klein & Zajac, Chapter 21, this volume). Thus, goals or possible selves may simply make us feel good about ourselves, particularly if the goal or future self is vague and carries no specified action plan (Gonzales, Burgess, & Mobilio, 2001). Indeed, at least in Western culture, a dominant self-goal is simply to feel good about the self—to self-enhance (Brown, 1998). By allowing one to feel good about the self and providing hope for a better future, possible selves may fulfill self-enhancement goals. For example, a student may say to herself, "I may not be doing well in school now, but I'm sure I'll do better next year," in this way buffering self-esteem from current bad grades, although not engaging in any behavioral strategies to actually increase the chance of earning better grades in the coming year.

Supporting this notion, Gonzales and colleagues (2001) found that articulating a goal elevated mood, improved well-being, and created a sense of optimism about the likelihood of attaining the goal for participants, compared with participants who did not articulate a goal (see also Faude, Wuerz, & Gollwitzer, Chapter 5, this volume). Self-enhancing possible selves promote positive feelings and maintain a sense of optimism and hope for the future without evoking behavioral strategies. For example, simply having a New Year's resolution that one will turn over a new leaf, live healthfully, and lose weight may be so satisfying that it can serve as sufficient reason to have an extra slice of cake on New Year's Eve (see also Fishbach, Dhar, & Zhang 2006; Perunovic & Wilson, Chapter 23, this volume). But, setting goals can also improve performance under certain circumstances (e.g., Brickman & Bulman, 1977; Taylor, Neter, & Wayment, 1995). For example, the more self-directed goals are linked to specific strategies, the more likely they are to be carried out (Faude et al., Chapter 5, this volume; Gollwitzer, 1996; Oettingen & Kappes, Chapter 26, this volume).

SELF-REGULATION

Possible selves are not just about feeling good; they can also serve to promote self-regulation. That is, they can produce current behavior in pursuit of becoming like one's positive future selves and avoiding becoming like one's negative future selves. As noted, possible selves are more likely to be effective in this self-regulatory function when they provide concrete and detailed future images linked with strategies that connect current behaviors to future states and when they do not feel contradictory to important social identities (e.g., "I may not be doing well in school this year, but to make sure I do better next year, I have signed up for summer tutoring. Doing well in school is important for me as an African American").

Thus, possible selves can serve two important self-functions, promoting well-being (Gonzales et al., 2001) and invigorating self-improvement efforts (Brickman & Bulman, 1977; Taylor et al., 1995). The self-enhancement and self-improvement functions of possible selves are separate but not necessarily orthogonal. Depending on how self-enhancement and self-improvement successes and failures are interpreted, focus on self-improvement can complement or compete with focus on self-enhancement. Thus, for example, taking action to attain a possible self can serve both self-improvement and self-enhancement functions if that effort results in increased optimism about one's future and increased optimism bolsters effort (Oettingen & Kappes, Chapter 26, this volume).

However, the reverse can also happen when action taken to attain a goal increases optimism and thereby serves to distract attention from ongoing effort. In this chapter, we focus particularly on the self-improvement function of possible selves by asking when possible selves will be effective self-regulators.

WHAT MAKES POSSIBLE SELVES EFFECTIVE SELF-REGULATORS?

Possible selves are not always effective self-regulators. A number of factors are likely to increase the effectiveness of possible selves in regulating behavior. These can be organized loosely as pertaining to context, features of possible selves, and interpretation of subjective experience such as mood or feelings of ease or difficulty. Thus, possible selves are unlikely to regulate behavior if the future does not feel salient, the present does not feel linked to the future, or one does not believe one's actions have any impact on the future and if discrepancies between one's current and future selves are not salient and accessible. Moreover, action to work on possible selves is less likely when possible selves are perceived as irrelevant to or conflicting with other important components of self-concept, including gendered racial-ethnic or national identities and when the subjective experience of working on a possible self is interpreted to mean either that the possible self is not attainable or that sufficient effort has already been put forth. In this section, we discuss each of these components in detail.

LINKING THE PRESENT TO THE FUTURE

> When engaged in safe occupations, and living in healthy countries, men are much more apt to be frugal, than in unhealthy, or hazardous occupations, and in climates pernicious to human life. Sailors and soldiers are prodigals. In the West Indies, New Orleans, the East Indies, the expenditure of the inhabitants is profuse. The same people, coming to reside in the healthy parts of Europe, and not getting into the vortex of extravagant fashion, live economically. War and pestilence have always waste and luxury, among the other evils that follow in their train. (Rae 1834/1905, p. 57, taken from Shane, Loewenstein, & O'Donoghue, 2002, p. 353)

As can be seen in this quotation, in hazardous contexts in which present risk is salient and the future is uncertain and distant, people live their lives quite differently than they do when the future feels more predictable and controllable. According to Shane et al. (2002), the idea that choices made about the future may differ from those that are made about the present has been established as a topic within the social sciences, especially sociology and economics, since 1834, with John Rae's publication of *The Sociological Theory of Capital*. Rae (1834/1905) suggested that accumulating (rather than spending now) is limited by uncertainty about the future and by the immediate pleasures of spending and is therefore a function of self-restraint and of the desire to provide the benefits of one's savings to others (e.g., close others, family and kin). In this sense, life is lived in the moment, with one eye on the past and the other on the future. That is, present action can be thought of in terms of current hedonic potential, continuity or discontinuity with the past, or likely consequences of current action for the future (Simons, Vansteenkiste, Lens, & Lacante, 2004). Current and future consequences may be congruent but often are not. Eating ice cream is tasty now and may be a nostalgic reminder of other happy ice cream events from one's past, but eating ice cream now may also result in undesirable weight gain later. As temporal orientation shifts, so does the felt salience of the future. When the present is salient, focus is likely to be on current consequences of action, including both hedonic potential (pleasant taste, satisfaction) and meaning imbued by links with the past ("Eating a banana split reminds me of the summers I spent with my grandmother!"; e.g., Boyd & Zimbardo 2005; Zimbardo & Boyd, 1999).

Conversely, when the future is salient, discrepancies between one's current state or current pathway and one's intended goals are likely to be cued. The ice cream may no longer look so good when conceptualized as a step away from one's positive "ideal weight" possible self or as a step toward one's negative "heavy weight" possible self. When the future feels real, it looms large in the sense that it grabs attention and resources. When the future is salient, current hedonic potential and links to the past should be less consequential for behavior choice than making progress toward one's future goals.

Belief in the self-relevant impact of present behavior on attainment of future goals has been studied from a variety of perspectives within psychology and education. For example, a number of independent research programs documented a positive association between salience of the future and increased positive outcomes, including higher belief in the importance of education (Brown & Jones, 2004; Cretin, Lens, & Simons, 2001) and better grades (Boyd & Zimbardo, 2005). Some research also showed an association between future orientation and decreased risky behavior, including driving after drinking alcohol (Boyd & Zimbardo, 2005).

Within the possible self framework, it is clear that the belief that present action matters for one's future can itself be positively motivating. The routines of daily life are predicated on this belief. Consider the routines of doing well in school and the repetitious, not particularly hedonically pleasing steps required. The aspiring good student must repeatedly go to bed before he or she would prefer, get out of bed and go to school at an early hour, and sit still and face the teacher when chatting with one's friends is far more tempting. After school, the aspiring good student must do homework, study and get help as needed, even when the homework is hard, long and tedious, the teacher is boring, and the subject matter is dry. School and homework are to be attended to even when the alternatives are more hedonically pleasing in the moment.

Such self-denial, self-sacrifice, and continued effort on difficult or boring tasks in the present make intuitive sense when linked to belief in future attainment of self-relevant goals but not otherwise. By connecting current study with good grades and, farther down the road, with a career or the kind of job that allows for pleasure and self-fulfillment, today's sacrifices make sense. In other words, future relevance can add utility to present-day activities (Simons et al., 2004).

SALIENCE OF FUTURE GOALS

The question follows of how best to make the future feel relevant. The salience of future goals clearly varies between persons, but also between contexts and settings. Such differences may be grounded in cultural syndromes, particularly variation in the belief that one's actions in the present influence the course of one's future, and that luck and contextual factors outside of one's control play important roles in attaining successes and avoiding failures (Chandler, Shama, Wolf, & Planchard, 1981).

For some, in some settings, the future feels tangible—proximal, certain, and in one's control, at least to some extent. For others, at least in some settings, the future is more likely to feel distal, uncertain and unpredictable. In other cases, the future can feel unknowable, in the hands of others, or based on chance. In the extreme, these beliefs make behavior focused on long-term consequences seem irrational.

OBSERVING A GAP BETWEEN CURRENT AND FUTURE SELVES

Even when the future is salient, attempts to shift motivation by cuing possible selves will only work when there is an observable gap between current and future selves. Sometimes possible selves do not differ much from current selves, making increased effort feel unnecessary—in this case, cuing these selves has little effect on self-regulation. For example, Hoyle and Sherrill (2006) primed hoped-for and feared possible selves by asking healthy college students to write about their positive healthy possible selves as well as their negative unhealthy possible selves. Afterward, all students were given a chance to work with a personal trainer and to choose from various health brochures. Compared to control group students who did not write about possible selves, students in the feared possible self condition were more likely to choose the trainer and to choose more brochures. No effect was found among the students in the hoped-for possible selves condition. The authors proposed that the students were healthy already, so that priming a healthy possible self did not prime a discrepancy with one's current self.

To the extent that the future feels like a seamless flow from the present, the gap between present and future may not be salient, reducing goal-focused effort. Only when bringing to mind positive or negative future selves makes salient the comparison (and discrepancy) between current and potential future selves is it likely that motivation to work toward the goal will increase (Carver, 2001). Building on earlier feedback models (e.g., Miller et al., 1960) and earlier Expectancy × Value models (such as early work by Lewin, Dembo, Festinger, & Sears, 1944), Carver and Scheier (1982) outlined how discrepancy reduction processes may work in their control theory. They postulated the existence of a negative-feedback loop that acts to reduce deviations from a desired state and so regulates behavior. If the system senses a discrepancy between the current state and a desired reference point, it dictates that a behavior be performed to reduce this discrepancy. The resulting state is then recompared to the reference point to determine if the dictated behavior has succeeded in reducing the discrepancy—if not, the system incites a new behavior. Of course, if there is no detectable discrepancy, the system fails to produce a behavioral output.

Thus, for healthy, middle-class individuals, thinking about feared possible selves of being unhealthy might be more likely to cue discrepancies than thinking about healthy possible selves. However, Hoyle and Sherrill's (2006) study should not be interpreted to mean that feared possible selves always have greater motivational force than positive, expected, or hoped-for possible selves. Rather, that cuing a possible self that feels discrepant with one's present self may generally be beneficial for motivational focus. Because self-concept content tends to be predominantly positive, for positive possible selves to result in self-regulatory action, care must be taken to cue discrepancy between current and future selves. As described in the section on "balance," one way to do that is for positive possible selves to be coupled with "balanced" feared possible selves in the same domain (e.g., Oyserman & Markus, 1990a, 1990b). A balanced perspective implies that positive goals alone are not enough to sustain motivation, and that to provide reminders of what one has to lose, one's feared possible selves are also needed. This perspective is congruent with Kahneman and Tversky's (1979) prospect theory. Kahneman and Tversky noted that losses loom psychologically larger than gains so that, all things being equal, individuals should be more motivated to avoid losses than to attain gains of similar sizes, and situations in which losses are possible should be more eye-catching than situations in which gains are possible.

ATTAINABILITY, CONTROL BELIEFS, AND EFFORT

We have proposed that the motivational value of possible selves may have an inverted U-shaped function. That is, individuals are unlikely to engage in self-regulatory behavior when certainty of attaining possible self goals or of controlling future outcomes is either too low—prompting the feeling that future goals cannot be attained no matter how high the effort, or when certainty is too high—prompting the feeling that future goals will certainly be attained no matter how low the effort. When the future feels completely certain, simply a continuation of the present, current and possible selves are unlikely to feel discrepant. Lacking discrepancy, cuing possible selves should not influence motivation. Certainty, in other words, can become so high that it undermines effort. At the other end of the continuum, there is no reason to engage in efforts to attain future possible selves if the goals are not attainable or if life is beyond one's control. Thus, when a desired future is completely unachievable or out of one's hands completely, cuing possible selves should not influence motivation. While related, certainty about attainability of goals and certainty about controllability of the future involve somewhat different processes. In the following sections, we distinguish effects of certainty about goal attainment from effects of certainty about controllability of the future. In addition, moving beyond the goal engagement and disengagement effects of certainty, we also propose that optimal levels of certainty should produce positive spillover effects whereas lower or higher than optimal levels of certainty should produce negative spillover effects. Positive spillover effects involve a self-constructive approach beyond pursuit of a particular goal, a willingness to engage in positive future-oriented behaviors such as wearing safety belts or helmets. Negative spillover effects involve a self-destructive approach beyond pursuit of a particular goal, a willingness to engage in behaviors likely to be risk increasing in the future such as smoking, drug, or alcohol use.

Certainty about Attainability

Up to a point, increasing certainty about goal attainment should have positive effects on effort—one has to believe that there is some chance of success to sustain effort over time. Indeed, strategies to increase effort often focus on ways to increase belief that a goal is attainable, either by providing feedback that progress has been made or by highlighting that current failure does not close off options. Thus, weight watchers can use their weekly weigh-in to see that progress is being made toward their weight loss goal and on weeks in which too many cakes were consumed to produce weight loss; one can be consoled by the fact that each new week brings new weight loss chances.

However, beyond a certain point, these very cues can also increase the likelihood of motivation-undermining feelings of certainty about goal attainment. As outlined below, one way to undermine motivation is to provide too many concrete markers of goal progress. Another way to undermine motivation is to provide very clear information that second chances are possible. While quite different on the surface, both kinds of cues have in common that individuals do not need to maximize effort in the moment and may be able to "coast" a bit, reducing effort on a particular goal and turning attention either to other goals or to more immediate pleasures. Things that can be done again do not feel as consequential, even though, of course, most goals are attained only through repeated as opposed to single choices.

A set of studies illustrates this point. The undermining effect of specific feedback was demonstrated in a computer game setting. Effort (operationalized as speed of button press) was impaired among computer gamers who concluded that success was certain after receiving both clear feedback about goal progress and specific information about distance from a goal (Amir & Ariely, 2006). The undermining effect of second chances was demonstrated in a tempting choices setting. Succumbing to temptation (operationalized as unhealthy snack and entertaining as compared to edifying magazines and movies) was increased among participants told that they would be able to choose multiple times. "Single shot" participants who were told that they were to make a single choice were likely to eat healthy snacks and choose highbrow magazines and movies than multiple chance participants who were told that they would be making the choice again later (Khan & Dhar, 2007). Knowing for sure that one will have the chance to do the right thing again later reduces the chance that one will do it now (or later). Thus, when told that they would be able to make the choice again later, participants opted for the short-term pleasure more often than when they perceived the choice as non-repeating.

Moreover, when asked to make a choice again, a week later, they were not more likely to pick the goal-focused choice.

Just as high levels of certainty that a goal can be attained undermine effort by suggesting that attention *can* be shifted to other goals, high levels of uncertainty can undermine effort by suggesting that attention *should* be shifted to other goals. This line of reasoning is articulated in control theory in terms of assessed likelihood of reducing discrepancy between current and desired states (or of increasing discrepancy between current and undesired states). If likelihood is assessed as below a certain criteria, goal disengagement is postulated (Carver & Scheier, 1982; Wrosch, Scheier, Carver, & Schulz, 2003). Going beyond a control theory prediction of simple engagement vs. disengagement, we propose that high levels of uncertainty about attainability, the feeling that attaining positive and avoiding negative possible selves are hopelessly beyond one's reach, can have negative spillover effects. That is, feeling that one cannot attain important life goals can increase risk of engaging in present-focused and future self-destructive behaviors. The reverse may also be true, that is, optimal levels of felt attainability may result in positive spillover effects, that is, willingness to work maximally to attain possible self goals as well as a more generally willingness to engage in self-constructive behaviors.

Two studies, the first using a large sample of New York City, primarily minority, middle school students and the second using a nationally representative sample of eighth graders, illustrate the negative spillover effects. Certainty of attaining positive goals and binge drinking were assessed across a three-year interval from seventh to ninth grade. Students who believed that their chances of graduating from high school, finding an enjoyable job and having a happy family life were low were later more likely to report binge drinking (Griffin, Botvin, Nichols, and Scheier (2003). Academic goals, efficacy about their attainment, and in-school violent behavior were assessed in the second study. Students with high goals but low efficacy about their attainment were more likely to engage in in-school violence (Honora & Rolle, 2002). Taken together both studies provide ecological validity to our argument that perceived insurmountable gaps between goals and ability to attain them will be associated not simply with goal disengagement but with negative spillover—increased engagement in problem behavior. Future experimental research is needed to clarify that the causal process implied by our model is indeed operating.

In the next section, we shift focus from the effects of beliefs about goal attainability on effort to attain possible selves to the effects of beliefs about controllability of the future on effort. Although effort is likely to be influenced by both, the process involved differs somewhat. Controllability refers to the perception that effort matters either because one's qualities—athletic, intellectual, and other abilities—are malleable and likely to change with effort or more generally because the world is rule-governed so that following the rules will help. Just as with beliefs about goal attainability, beliefs about controllability should have an inverted U-shaped function. Felt lack of control, either because one's qualities are not malleable or because the world is not rule-governed for people like oneself, should result in reduced effort, as should overly high sense of control.

Perceived Controllability

Fatalistic beliefs focusing on lack of control (e.g., "everyone has a bullet with his or her name on it", "when your number is up, you gotta go") make pursuit of future goals unlikely. Wearing safety belts, refraining from tobacco, alcohol or other drugs, and even turning off the television to focus on studying all involve beliefs about the controllability and malleability of one's destiny. If life itself feels outside one's control, then the future is outside one's control and possible selves should feel unattainable by stint of personal effort.

Thus, while attainability matters—instigating maximal effort when certainty of attaining a possible self goal is neither too high nor too low, so does controllability. Controllability refers to the belief that one's own actions can change the course of future events. The association between control beliefs and willingness to take action to improve one's situation has been demonstrated across a range of outcomes including well-being and physical health (Taylor, Kemeny, Reed, Bower, & Gruenewald, 2000) and academic outcomes (Dweck, 1996, 2000). Although the models differ, they have in common the idea that willingness to take action to improve one's future is more likely if one believes that outcomes are within one's control.

In the domain of school and academic attainments, belief that intelligence is subject to one's own control should result in increased effort. Students who believe that intelligence is malleable, open to their own control, should be more willing to engage in effort to improve than students who don't believe this and instead believe that their intelligence is a fixed entity beyond their control. In a recent demonstration of just this effect, white and African American Stanford undergraduate participants were randomly assigned to one of two treatment conditions or a no-treatment control group (Aronson, Fried, & Good, 2002). Positive effects on end of semester grades were found for African American students in the treatment condition involving both writing letters to pen-pals and being primed with the malleability of intelligence. To produce this effect, participants needed to convince themselves that one can control one's own academic outcomes. The intervention involved participants who had agreed to be pen pals with low income students at risk of school failure. Participants were shown a movie in which an animated brain actually grew and changed with effort and then were asked to write a response to their pen pal describing intelligence as malleable, giving examples from their own life when hard work had paid off in better performance. Next, 10 days later, participants were given thank you notes from the student and his or her teacher and another handwritten letter and again asked to respond with a letter focusing on the malleability of intelligence with examples from their own life. Finally, 10 days later, participants were asked to write, revise, and practice persuasive speeches on the malleability of intelligence. Speeches were videotaped and shown to participants, who were told that the videotapes would be used in interventions with at-risk middle school students.

Results suggest that even college students can benefit from viewing intelligence as malleable. The controllability implied by viewing the future as malleable contrasts with perceptions of the future as pre-set and therefore uncontrollable. Students who view their academic future as predetermined by their unalterable level of intelligence are unlikely to put forth effort to improve performance. Similarly, the individual who believes that "when your number is up, you gotta go" or that "everyone has a bullet with their name on it" will not be particularly worried about eating sweet or salty foods, drinking, or smoking. Belief in the future as pre-determined by external forces such as fate or luck may, in such cases, undermine personal effort.

Cultural Influences on Control Beliefs

Feelings of control can be experienced relationally, at the group level (e.g., "I have to overcome these obstacles, or I'll disappoint my group," "We can do this") or at the individual level (e.g., "I have to do this to be who I want to be, I can do this for myself"). Focus on relational or individual control is likely to vary by gender and cross culturally (see Yamaguchi, Gelfand, Ohashi, & Zemba, 2005). In both cases, to the extent that a primary way of controlling one's outcomes is by sustained effort, taking action in the present to attempt to change the course of one's future life makes sense.

Other's successes can increase perceived efficacy in a number of ways: either directly through assimilation of like-others' results ("If others like me can do it, so can I") or use of like-others as role models ("If I work hard, I can become like that"). The perspective taken will depend on cultural dominance of an interdependent or an independent perspective. Upward social comparison makes positive possible selves salient among women and those higher in interdependence, perhaps because they include the other's success into what may be possible for the self with effort (Kemmelmeier & Oyserman, 2001a, 2001b). Similarly, a salient superachieving standard is motivating for younger students who can view the achiever as a future model, but not for students who should be at the same level as the superachiever (Lockwood & Kunda, 1997). A related literature on performance versus mastery goals suggests that seeking to outperform one's peers has positive effects on effort (for a review and relevant studies, see Senko & Harackiewicz, 2005).

Although cultures vary in their belief in the power of fate and luck, a cross-cultural comparison of students from diverse countries such as China, India, and the United States suggests that students most commonly evoke effort in explaining their academic successes and failures (Tuss, Zimmer, & Ho, 1995). Whether framed as personal effort or effort for the good of one's in-group, willingness to try more, try again, and keep going matters; belief in the malleability of one's results based on effort is associated with better academic outcomes (e.g., Dweck, 2000). Across various age groups, interventions that change beliefs about effort also change willingness to persist in goal pursuit (Dweck, 2000).

Spirituality, while not always assessed, can clearly be part of a cultural perspective and can be powerfully implicated in self-regulatory effort. Faith-based initiatives seek to harness the motivational resource of connecting one's own self-regulatory efforts to higher beliefs about the goals, strategies, and selves that are acceptable and worth attaining within one's meaning-making framework. Self-help groups, especially Alcoholics Anonymous, are often loosely or more explicitly linked to faith and spirituality as mechanisms of self-regulation.

Detail, Strategies, and Sequential Steps

As we outline in this section, results across a number of research programs converge in suggesting that possible selves matter not only because they focus attention on the future, but also because they link vivid images of oneself in a future state to current action that can be taken to move toward positive and away from negative future selves. For proximal possible selves to matter, they need to cue action in the present. For distal possible selves to matter, action in the present needs to be linked to outcomes in the future via more proximal possible selves that can serve as evidence that progress is being made and as markers for whether current effort is sufficient, needs to be increased, or plans of action need to be revised for the distal possible self to be attained.

Thinking only of one's best future (Oettingen & Kappes, Chapter 26, this volume; Oettingen, Pak, & Schnetter, 2001) or vaguely reminding people of future utility is no more helpful in inducing behavior change than failing to mention the future entirely (Vansteenkiste, Simons, Soenens, & Lens, 2003). Oettingen and colleagues (2001) found that simply dreaming about a wonderful future without explicitly also thinking about the gap between the present and this future had no motivational effect. Vansteenkiste et al. (2003) found that reminding participants that a particular task had future utility without any specific content about this future or any concrete rationale regarding why this task was relevant displayed no additional motivational effects when compared to a no-future control group.[1]

Further, imagining becoming a doctor can only improve the chances of actually becoming one (or at least the likelihood of completing some sort of college degree) if this distal possible self is linked to current steps and more proximal possible selves. Persistent goal pursuit involves a series of steps, and the more distal the goal, the less clearly linked current steps may be to distal future goals and the greater the need for linkage to detailed proximal possible selves. Vague, general possible selves lacking behavioral strategies cannot function to guide self-regulation because they provide neither a specific picture of one's goals nor a road map of how to reduce discrepancies between the present and one's future possible selves (e.g., Carver, 2001).

Strategies should take into account the need for persistence over time. Most possible self goals involve persistence over time because the goal involves ongoing work rather than single criteria. For example, maintaining a healthy weight through exercise and diet does not involve one trip to the gym or one forgone cookie. Even what would appear to be a discrete attainment-focused possible self—the "accepted-to-college" possible self or the "published" possible self—typically involves repeated effort over time. Effective strategies include both one's own actions over time and how to engage in these actions in context. Thus, doing homework and getting to bed by 10 every night can be effective strategies for attaining a next-year school-focused possible self, but these strategies alone will not be enough in social contexts with friends who want to hang out during homework time or stay out late on school nights. Strategies need to include ways of dealing with relevant others, including friends, classmates, and teachers who may reduce or increase chances of goal attainment (Oyserman et al., 2004).

In addition to cuing the repetition of actions needed to attain more proximal possible selves, strategies may also serve as pathways from more proximal to more distal possible selves. Thus, next-year possible selves may be associated with more distal possible selves via a common set of strategies. For example, doing homework is a strategy to attain proximal school-focused possible selves, but doing homework can also improve chances of attaining more distal possible selves. In this way, doing homework as a way of working toward school-focused possible selves can link present action to attainment of distal possible selves focused on successful engagement with valued social identities, such as reflecting well on one's parents or becoming a valued member of one's racial/ethnic, national, or religious group (e.g., Oyserman, 2007). Strategies create steppingstones from possible self to possible self at different temporal distances from the present, linking current action to both proximal and more distal possible selves.

RELEVANCE TO SELF-CONCEPT

Strategies to attain a possible self are likely to be cued frequently when the possible self converges or meshes well with other aspects of self-concept, important social identities, or contextually relevant stereotypes about one's in-group. Consider, for example, Asian American students for whom the model minority stereotype, the link between filial piety and academic attainment, and personal goals may all converge to make gaps between one's current academic situation and one's possible selves chronically salient. Conversely, consider Mexican American and African American students, for whom in-groups are stereotyped as not wanting to do well in school. Because they are not likely to be reminded of their school-focused possible selves and may find that others do not see school-focused possible selves as congruent with their racial/ethnic identities, these students are likely to find it more difficult to remain focused on working toward their school-focused possible selves. A number of interventions have been developed to create positive conditions for these students to focus on their possible self goals in school.

For example, in two studies, Cohen, Garcia, Apfel, and Master (2006) focused on making positive self-views salient to African American students as a way to increase their likelihood of attaining academic possible selves by combating negative stereotypes about African Americans (Steele & Aronson, 1995). Specifically, they asked teachers to hand out name-labeled envelopes containing instructions to students to write about either their most central values or least central values and explain why these are important to them (or in the case of least central values, why they might be important to others), then return the envelope to the teacher. Students were told that this was a regular class assignment (rather than an experiment), and each returned envelope was labeled with the student's name. Relative to those who wrote about their least central values, African American students who wrote about their most central values attained improved end-of-term grade point average.

Effects were most pronounced for previously low-performing students, and no effects were found for European American students. Although salience of racial stereotypes did not mediate the process, these stereotypes were less accessible among the students who wrote about their salient values. The authors inferred that the students who wrote about their values were reminded of why school mattered to them, and that this had helped buffer them from stereotype threat, that is, worse performance in a stereotyped domain. From an identity-based motivation perspective, these results imply that the intervention had an effect on low-performing African American students because it helped them link their valued possible selves to school when they might otherwise have felt conflict between focusing on school goals and the stereotypic content of racial identity (e.g., Oyserman, 2007).

Lack of convergence between racial/ethnic identities and possible selves has also been implicated in health-focused self-regulation (Oyserman, Fryberg, & Yoder, 2007). In these studies, when primed to think about their racial/ethnic group membership, low-income Latino and African American students were more pessimistic about their chances of maintaining good health. This undermining effect occurred for participants who associated risky health behavior with racial/ethnic group membership.

LINKING POSSIBLE SELVES TO OTHER SELF-REGULATION AND MOTIVATION PERSPECTIVES

TEMPORAL PROXIMITY MODELS

Action occurs in the present yet has consequences for the future. Indeed, the meaning of current action can be construed in terms of both the present and the future. A number of theoretical frameworks have attempted to articulate how and when the future is perceived to be temporally proximal enough to matter for current action. One version of temporal proximity model comes from economics. Here the assumption is that the future is less real than the present—future benefits provide less pleasure and future costs produce less pain than parallel events in the present. Another version of temporal proximity model comes from psychology. Here the assumption is not that the future is discounted compared to the present but rather that when the future is taken into account, long term outcomes are more likely to be pursued.

Within the self-concept literature, this discussion has been less salient. However, possible selves are commonly defined as future-oriented components of the self-concept. That is, possible selves create a link between the present and future and make the future feel more tangible and in that sense, more proximal.

When the future appears to start in the present, current effort should be engaged. Of course futures can be temporally near (tomorrow) or far (in twenty years). The question follows of how far in the future possible selves should reside in order to be optimally motivating. In the following section, we articulate relevant temporal proximity models.

Estimating the Future via Willingness to Delay Consumption

In this way, an economic perspective would provide an estimate of how far into the future is too far to be motivating by examining the extent to which the future is discounted, how much more people would need in the future in order to delay consumption in the present. For instance, from an economic perspective, individuals should be willing to delay current consumption when they feel psychologically connected with a future self (Frederick, 2002; Frederick, Loewenstein, & O'Donoghue, 2002). When the future is too far away, the connection is no longer psychologically meaningful, one may be dead or be so different from now that a meaningful connection with one's present self is hard to imagine. Taking an economic perspective, there is no point saving for a retirement that one does not expect to live long enough to enjoy and no point in saving for an elderly and frail future self that one cannot imagine becoming or with whom one does not feel close.

Estimating Psychological Distance

Psychologists examining this issue have used various time points into the future. Unfortunately, measures differ in other ways as well, making integrative synthesis about potential differential effects of cuing possible selves focused on the near or more distal future premature (e.g., Hoyle & Sherrill, 2006; Oyserman & Fryberg, 2006). Therefore, in this section, we link possible self research to two other models or classes of models: temporal construal (Trope & Liberman, 2003) and future time perspective models (e.g., Simons et al., 2004). While distinct in their development and focus, both models would suggest that it is not how far chronologically into the future a possible self is, but rather how psychologically proximate or distal it feels that should influence the self-regulatory impact of a possible self (see also Perunovic & Wilson, Chapter 23, this volume). To the extent that close chronology is likely to cue close psychological proximity, then more distal possible selves are unlikely to influence behavior over time unless they are linked to a sequence of more proximal possible selves—possible selves that will occur in the nearer future and feel psychologically closer.

This means that the way that questions about time are framed in one's mind should have an impact on the extent that a possible self becomes salient as well as the extent that it continues to be the focus of self-regulatory effort. Thus, if the question is "Is the planned-for future near?" then vivid images of the possible self linked to detailed strategies should result in feeling that the future is proximal, so that one should focus on how to get needed tasks accomplished (see Libby & Eibach, Chapter 24, this volume; Trope & Liberman, 2003). More abstract images of the possible self that are not linked to detailed strategies should result in feeling that the future is distal, so that one does not really need to engage in any action in the present even though the future goals are valued.

Indeed, experimental evidence documents the impact of temporal construal on both psychologically experienced closeness and subsequent response (Amit, Algom, Trope, & Liberman, chapter 4, this volume; Smith & Trope, 2006; Trope & Liberman, 2003). Once a feeling of psychological closeness is cued, then participants focus on how to carry out a task rather than focusing on whether they should carry it out (see also Faude et al., Chapter 5, this volume). Conversely, psychological distance, once cued, focuses participants on whether the task is of value rather than on how the task would fit into one's daily schedule. In some ways, being able to see a goal as both temporally close (the future starts "now") and also distal (the future has meaning) should produce optimal striving in terms of both how and why a goal should be attained.

The temporal construal model fits well with correlational evidence stemming from future time orientation or perspective models (e.g., Eccles & Wigfield, 2002; Feather, 1990, 1992). This work shows that there are individual differences in future time perspective, such that specific points in the future (e.g., "when I graduate from high school," "4 years from now") feel closer for individuals able to imagine farther into the future. Thus, having a long future time perspective creates a greater sense of psychological closeness with future events than having a short future time perspective. If one cannot imagine one's future past the age of 20, then 20 seems farther away than if one can imagine one's future through grandparenthood. From the perspective of the temporal construal model, one would expect youth with a long future time perspective to engage in more current action to attain their possible selves for these psychologically "close" futures.

MULTIPLE GOALS, MULTIPLE STRATEGIES, AND CONTEXTUAL CUING

The self is multidimensional and includes multiple potentially competing goals (e.g., Abrams, 1994; Burke, 2003; King & Smith, 2004; Oyserman, 2001; Settles, 2004). Therefore, possible selves may compete not only with other aspects of identity but also with other possible selves. The problem of goal competition was noted by William James (1890); he described the competition within one's person between the aspiring bon vivant who argues for going out and the aspiring scholar who argues for focusing on studies. Since James's initial conceptualization, a number of self-regulation models have focused explicitly on juggling multiple, conflicting self-goals. Each of these models suggests that handling multiple goals is likely to involve tradeoffs between working on one goal and working on other goals. Because goals compete for time and resources, success in making progress toward a goal may result in shift of effort to another self-goal that seems more in need of one's time and energy (e.g., Carver & Scheier, 1982; Fishbach et al., 2006). Conversely, when progress toward goal attainment is slower than expected, increased time and resources should be diverted from other goal pursuits to improve goal attainment pace and likely success. As a result, the way that one interprets and frames progress has important implications for goal pursuit. For example, Fishbach and colleagues (2006) showed students information about how much they had left to study by pointing out that they still had halfway to go. These students were more likely to predict that they would continue studying than were students shown that they had already completed half of their study time.

FLUENCY MODELS

Because possible selves focus on an ultimately uncertain future, maintaining self-regulatory focus requires sustained effort in the face of difficulty. Experienced difficulty or ease of goal attainment can have unexpected effects on goal persistence, depending on how these subjective experiences are interpreted (for a review of the fluency literature as it relates to attitudes, judgment, and behavior, see Sanna, Schwarz, & Kennedy, Chapter 13, this volume; Schwarz & Clore, 2007; for related research on the informational value of good mood, see Martin et al., 1990). Because sustaining self-regulatory effort over time is difficult, difficulty may be misinterpreted as evidence that the possible self is not a reasonable goal and should be abandoned (Oyserman, Bybee, & Terry, 2006). This may happen if experienced difficulty is used to answer the implied question, "Is this possible self really part of the true me?" or "Have I worked enough?" In these cases, difficulty implies that the answer to these questions is "Yes, you have tried enough, and no, this isn't really possible for you."

Conversely, difficulty and expended effort can also serve as reminders that the goal is important, and therefore effort should be continued without reduction in effort (Fishbach et al., 2006). This is likely if effort in the face of difficulty is understood as an answer to the implied question, "Is this important to me?" or "Do I care about this goal?" In these cases, feelings of fatigue and difficulty should suggest that one really cares and is willing to put in the needed effort.

Experiences of ease or difficulty can be evoked by ease or difficulty either in pursuing strategies or in imagining the relevant possible self in the first place. Thus, finding homework difficult may lead a student to infer that "Math is not for me," resulting in disengagement from proximal school-focused possible selves and even from more distal possible selves seen as linked to school-focused possible selves. The student may conclude, for example, that becoming a doctor is unlikely as well. Difficulty in imagining a pathway from the present to more distal possible selves can also produce disengagement from the goal. For example, when primed to think of college as expensive, low-income middle school students reduced planned homework time for that very evening compared with students primed to think of college as affordable via financial aid (Destin & Oyserman, 2008a). Further if a student finds it hard to picture himself or herself in college or as a doctor in the first place, this may signal that these possible selves are unachievable.

Yet, difficulty need not always be interpreted as a sign that the possible self is unlikely or that sufficient effort has already been supplied. Following from the fluency perspective, difficulty takes on different meanings depending on the implications drawn from it. For example, in sports, the saying "no pain, no gain" implies that painful effort is rewarded with movement toward important goals; indeed, it also seems to imply that more effort shows more commitment. To the extent that difficulty appears to answer such an alternative implied question, then difficulty should cue increased goal focus and a decreased tendency to refocus effort to alternative goals. Schwarz and Clore (2007) reviewed the literature on the meaning implied by subjective experiences, such as the experience of difficulty. They demonstrated, for example, that having difficulty listing eight fine Italian restaurants in one's hometown either leads to the conclusion that there are not many or that one is not an expert on fine Italian restaurants, depending on which question was posed immediately after the listing task. Their work strongly suggests that experiences of difficulty can mean very different things depending on what one asks oneself about the experience.

In their work on performance-based stop rules, Martin, Ward, Achee, and Wyer (1993) similarly focused on feelings as information. Specifically, Martin and his colleagues also found that an interaction exists between subjective experience and the question one poses about how the experience influences persistence. Focusing on the interaction between question posed and good mood, they found that when one asks oneself if a task is enjoyable, positive mood implies that it is indeed enjoyable, encouraging further effort. Conversely, when one asks oneself whether a task has been adequately completed, positive mood implies satisfaction with one's performance, encouraging disengagement from the task.

Self-Regulatory Focus

While fluency models speak to whether individuals will persist in goal pursuit, Higgins's (1996) self-regulatory focus model focuses not on whether goals will be pursued, but how they will be pursued. Goals can be pursued by avoiding failures and mistakes or by focusing on chances for successes and opportunities to make progress. Higgins termed these foci *prevention* and *promotion focus*, respectively. When success is defined as lack of failure, Higgins described the self-regulatory focus as prevention oriented. When failure is defined as lack of success, Higgins described the self-regulatory focus as promotion oriented. Promotion focus entails eagerly working toward positive outcomes, whereas prevention focus entails vigilantly working to avoid negative outcomes. Considerable research showed that primed or chronic promotion focus is associated with eagerness, risk taking, and sensitivity to the presence or absence of gains. Conversely, primed or chronic prevention focus is associated with minimizing risk and sensitivity to the presence or absence of losses (Camacho, Higgins, & Luger, 2003; Higgins, 1997; Liberman, Idson, Camacho, & Higgins, 1999; Liberman, Molden, Idson, & Higgins, 2001; O'Brien & Oyserman, in press; see also Markman et al., Chapter 12, this volume).

Much as the possible self literature has assumed that all individuals have both positive and negative possible selves, the self-regulatory focus literature has assumed that all individuals can be promotion or prevention focused, depending on the context (Camacho et al., 2003; Higgins, 1997; Liberman et al., 1999, 2001). Promotion focus makes salient the possibility of success, encouraging action and chance taking. Conversely, prevention focus makes salient the possibility of failure, encouraging caution and deliberation. Importantly, pursuing goals in ways that match the regulatory orientation of the goal feels good and increases motivational strength (Spiegel, Grant-Pillow, & Higgins, 2004). Thus, eagerly pursuing success and vigilantly avoiding failures may feel right in a way that vigilantly seeking success and eagerly avoiding failure does not. Moreover, motivation increases when chronic or momentarily primed prevention or promotion focus is matched with prevention- or promotion-focused strategies.

Following this logic, it may be that self-regulation will improve when possible selves and strategies fit. Thus, expected possible selves are more likely to be pursued when strategies are promotion focused, involving pursuit of success, whereas feared possible selves may be more likely to be pursued when strategies are prevention focused, involving vigilant care to avoid failures. Moreover, in risky contexts, individuals may be likely to focus attention on the possibility of failures, whereas in lower-risk contexts, individuals are freer to focus on successes. This implies that in risky contexts, discrepancy between current and feared possible selves should be accessible and salient. Conversely, in low-risk contexts, discrepancies between current and positive desired selves should be accessible and salient. One recent study began to examine this possibility. In a 2 × 2 between-subjects design, Destin and Oyserman (2008b) primed participants to think about the college years as risky and failure prone or as safe and success prone. Participants were then asked about either their feared possible selves or their expected possible selves. Motivation to study and hours set aside for academics increased when context and possible self-focus matched; thinking of school as risky and of one's feared possible selves improved effort as did thinking of school as safe and of one's expected possible selves.

BALANCE

A related line of research suggests improved self-regulation among individuals whose salient or on-line possible selves include both positive (expected) and negative (feared) possible selves in the same domain, termed *balance* (Oyserman & Markus, 1990a, 1990b). When possible selves are balanced, individuals select strategies that both increase the likelihood of becoming like the positive possible self and decrease the likelihood of becoming like the negative possible self, thereby focusing self-regulation and broadening effort (Oyserman & Markus, 1990a, 1990b). When possible selves are balanced, individuals select strategies that both increase the likelihood of attaining the positive possible self and decrease the likelihood of becoming more like the negative possible self. In this way, balance narrows focus to those strategies that can serve both goals or at least are not likely to undermine one of the goals. By focusing on both the positive and the potential negative consequences of goal pursuit, self-regulatory effort is bolstered. Not only are youth with balanced possible selves likely to target narrower and more effective strategies, they are also more likely to work on their possible selves because discrepancy between current and possible selves can be cued either by focus on feared possible selves or by focus on positive expected or desired possible selves. Possible selves and strategies are thus likely to be cued whether the context is perceived as high risk (relevant to feared possible selves) or low risk (relevant to expected possible selves).

In a number of studies, European American and African American high school students with balanced pairs of positive and negative school-focused possible selves were less likely to report involvement with delinquency (Oyserman & Markus, 1990a, 1990b), particularly if they also reported doing something currently to work on these possible selves (Oyserman & Saltz, 1993). When strategies are detailed and concrete, youth are particularly able to engage in sustained effort in pursuit of their possible selves. Thus, low-income African American and Latino youths whose possible selves included both positive and negative elements and strategies were less at risk for loss of academic efficacy and drop in grade point average than youth whose possible selves did not contain all of these elements (Oyserman et al., 2004).

Oyserman et al. (2006) designed an intervention to test a socially contextualized model of possible selves such as we have described here. They hypothesized that academic outcomes would improve if the conditions specified in the model were met. Specifically, academic improvement should occur if school-focused possible selves were balanced, linked to detailed strategies, contextually cued and perceived congruent with important social identities (especially gendered racial/ethnic identities), and if difficulty in pursuing these possible selves was interpreted to mean that doing well in school was an important self-goal. They worked with the eighth-grade cohort in three middle schools that enrolled low-income, predominantly African American and Latino students. A staff member randomly assigned students to attend their elective as usual or to attend the intervention. The intervention lasted for a single class period, twice a week, for a total of 11 sessions. In each session, students participated in activities designed to make possible selves and strategies salient, create a positive link between possible selves and social identities, and affirm the belief that difficulty is normal when working on an important goal. For example, youth picked pictures of their adult images, drew timelines into the future, and drew posters connecting current strategies with proximal and distal possible selves. Compared to a control group, students in the possible selves-focused intervention condition had improved academic outcomes as assessed by grade point average, attendance, in-class behavior, and time spent doing homework. Effects were assessed both at the end of the school year and at the end of a second school year and showed steady or increasing effect size over time.

Importantly, these academic effects were mediated by change in the possible selves students reported as expected and feared in the coming year. Specifically, the intervention resulted in an increase in both possible selves focused on becoming off track (delinquent, on drugs, pregnant) or doing poorly in school and an increased focus on school-based strategies such as going to class rather than skipping school to avoid these outcomes. It also resulted in an increase in the number of balanced school-focused possible selves that included both positive expectations and selves to avoid. Moreover, while these results were interpreted in terms of the risk-reducing effects of possible selves, mediation of the effect of parent-school involvement via its effect on possible selves could not be tested because parent-school involvement was only assessed at one point in time. However, it seems reasonable to assume that high parent-school involvement has a positive impact on children's in-school behavior and grades in part by reinforcing and sustaining children's school-focused possible selves. By attending school functions, parents let their children know that they see school as an important context for investment of time, implying that effort in school is worthwhile for the child and congruent with in-group identity. Moreover, by spending time at school, parents make school-focused goals more salient and accessible for their children, reducing the likelihood that competing goals will take precedence over school.

A PROCESS MODEL

In this chapter, we have linked possible selves theory with other relevant self-regulation models and outlined a process model of when and how possible selves are likely to influence self-regulation and outcomes. To provide a visualization of this process model and how it is likely to unfold over time, we developed the schematic drawing presented in Figure 25.1. Of necessity, the model is simplified to focus on a particular possible self. It does not depict movement between possible selves

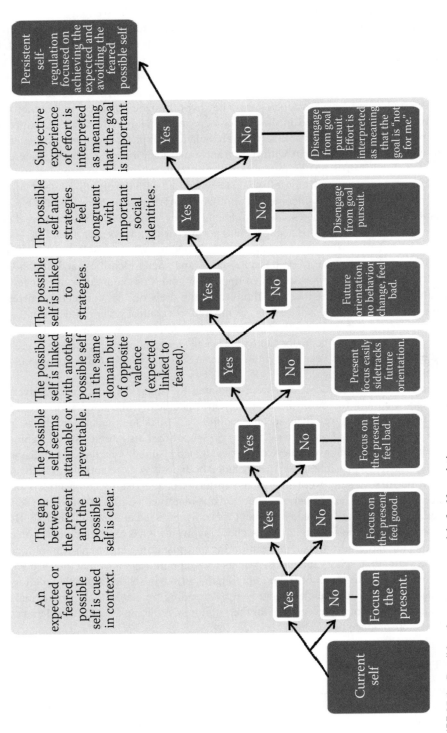

FIGURE 25.1 Possible selves: a process model of self-regulation.

and focuses on optimal certainty that a goal can be attained rather than detailing the full inverted U-shaped function we described earlier.

As depicted graphically in this figure, we propose that self-regulation involves a series of elements that must be present for sustained action toward future goals. If these requirements are not met, individuals are likely to be oriented toward the present rather than the future and so will not engage in persistent self-regulation. While the model presents a specific linear progression, we are not suggesting that the series must occur in this order, but rather that all the elements must be turned on. As laid out in Figure 25.1, the sequence can be outlined in seven parts (Oyserman, 2007; Oyserman et al., 2004, 2006):

1. A possible self is cued in context.
2. The gap between present and the possible self is clear.
3. The possible self seems attainable or preventable.
4. The possible self is linked to another possible self in the same domain but of opposite valence (e.g., a carrot-stick or balanced vision of where to go and what may happen if one does not stay focused).
5. The possible self is linked to strategies.
6. The possible self and strategies feel congruent with important social identities.
7. Subjective experience of effort is interpreted as meaning that the goal is important.

The process model suggests a testable sequence and allows for integration of possible selves research with other self-regulatory models. By outlining a specific process model, we hope to increase the usefulness of this integrative model for future basic and applied research efforts.

ACKNOWLEDGMENTS

Some of the research reported in this chapter was funded by National Institute of Mental Health grant R01 MH 58299 (D. Oyserman, principal investigator). While writing this chapter, Leah James was a Prevention Research Training Fellow supported by the Michigan Prevention Research Training Grant (National Institutes of Health grant T32 MH63057-03, D. Oyserman, principal investigator).

NOTE

1. Discrepancy effects can also be motivating when the past is compared with the present, as demonstrated by Markman and colleagues (Markman & McMullen, 2003; Markman, Karadogan, Lindberg, & Zell, Chapter 12, this volume). In these studies, explicitly comparing the present to a better alternative past is more motivating than simply reflecting on how a better past alternative outcome could have been possible in the present.

REFERENCES

Abrams, D. (1994). Social self-regulation. *Personality and Social Psychology Bulletin, 20,* 473–483.
Amir, O., & Ariely, D. (2006, December 1). Resting on laurels: The effects of discrete progress markers on task performance and preferences. Retrieved August 8, 2007, from http://ssrn.com/abstract=951144
Aronson, J., Fried, C., & Good, C. (2002). Reducing the effects of stereotype threat on African American college students by shaping theories of intelligence. *Journal of Experimental Social Psychology, 38,* 113–125.
Boyd, J., & Zimbardo, P. (2005). Time perspective, health, and risk-taking. In A. Strathman and J. Joireman (Eds.), *Understanding behavior in the context of time: Theory, research, and application* (pp. 85–107). Mahwah, NJ: Erlbaum.
Brickman, P., & Bulman, R. (1977). Pleasure and pain in social comparison. In J. Suls and R. Miller (Eds.), *Social comparison processes: Theoretical and empirical perspectives* (pp. 149–186). Washington, DC: Hemisphere.

Brown, J. (1998). *The self*. New York: McGraw-Hill.

Brown, W., & Jones, J. (2004). The substance of things hoped for: A study of the future orientation, minority status perceptions, academic engagement, and academic performance of Black high school students. *Journal of Black Psychology, 30*, 248–273.

Burke, P. J. (2003). Relationships among multiple identities. In P. J. Burke, T. J. Owens, R. T. Serpe, & P. A. Thoits (Eds.), *Advances in identity theory and research* (pp. 195–214). New York: Kluwer Academic/Plenum.

Camacho, C., Higgins, E. T., & Luger, L. (2003). Moral value transfer across regulatory fit: What feels right *is* right, what feels wrong *is* wrong. *Journal of Personality and Social Psychology, 84*, 498–510.

Carver, C. (2001). Self-regulation. In A. Tesser & N. Schwarz (Eds.), *Blackwell handbook of social psychology* (pp. 307–328). Malden, MA: Blackwell Press.

Carver, C., & Scheier, M. (1982). Control theory: A useful conceptual framework for personality-social, clinical and health psychology. *Psychological Bulletin, 92*, 111–135.

Chandler, T., Shama, D., Wolf, F., & Planchard, S. (1981). Multiattributional causality: A five cross-national samples study. *Journal of Cross-Cultural Psychology, 12*, 207–221.

Cohen, G., Garcia, J., Apfel, N., & Master, A. (2006). Reducing the racial achievement gap: A social-psychological intervention. *Science, 313*, 1307–1310.

Cretin, H., Lens, W., & Simons, J. (2001). The role of perceived instrumentality in student motivation. In A. Efklides, J. Kuhl, and R. M. Sorrentino (Eds.), *Trends and prospects in motivation research* (pp. 37–45). Dordrecht, The Netherlands: Kluwer Academic.

Cross, S., & Markus, H. (1991). Possible selves across the life span. *Human Development, 34*, 230–255.

Cross, S., & Markus, H. (1994). Self-schemas, possible selves, and competent performance. *Journal of Educational Psychology, 86*, 423–438.

Dweck, C. (1996). Motivational processes affecting learning. *American Psychologist, 41*, 1040–1048.

Dweck, C. (2000). *Self-Theories: Their role in motivation, personality, and development*. Philadelphia: Psychology Press.

Eccles, J. S., & Wigfield, A. (2002). Motivation beliefs, values, and goals. *Annual Review of Psychology, 53*, 109–132.

Feather, N. T. (1990). Bridging the gap between values and actions: Recent applications of the expectancy-value model. In E. T. Higgins & R. Sorrentino (Eds.), *Handbook of motivation and cognition* (Vol. 2, pp. 151–192). New York: Guilford Press.

Feather, N. T. (1992). Values, valences, expectations, and actions. *Journal of Social Issues, 48*, 109–124.

Fishbach, A., Dhar, R., & Zhang, Y. (2006). Subgoals as substitutes or complements: The role of goal accessibility. *Journal of Personality and Social Psychology, 91*, 232–242.

Frazier, L. D., Hooker, K., Johnson, P. M., & Kaus, C. R. (2000). Continuity and change in possible selves in later life: A 5-year longitudinal study. *Basic and Applied Social Psychology, 22*, 237–243.

Frederick, S. (2002). Time preference and personal identity. In G. Loewenstein, D. Read, & R. Baumeister (Eds.), *Time and decision: Economic and psychological perspectives on intertemporal choice* (pp. 89–113). New York: Russell Sage.

Frederick, S., Loewenstein, G., & O'Donoghue, T. (2002). Time discounting and time preference: A critical review. *Journal of Economic Literature, 40*, 351–401.

Gollwitzer, P. (1996). The volitional benefits of planning. In P. Gollwitzer & J. A. Bargh (Eds.), *The psychology of action: Linking cognition and motivation to behavior* (pp. 287–312). New York: Guilford Press.

Gonzales, M., Burgess, D., & Mobilio, L. (2001). The allure of bad plans: Implications of plan quality for progress toward possible selves and postplanning energization. *Basic and Applied Social Psychology, 23*, 87–108.

Griffin, K., Botvin, G., Nichols, T., & Scheier, M. (2004). Low perceived chances for success in life and binge drinking among inner-city minority youth. *Journal of Adolescent Health, 34*, 501–507.

Higgins, E. T. (1996). The "self-digest": Self-knowledge serving self-regulatory functions. *Journal of Personality and Social Psychology, 71*, 1062–1083.

Higgins, E. T. (1997). Beyond pleasure and pain. *American Psychologist, 80*, 1280–1300.

Honora, D., & Rolle, A. (2002). A discussion of the incongruence between optimism and academic performance and its influence on school violence. *Journal of School Violence, 1*, 67–81.

Hooker, K., Fiese, B., Jenkins, L., Morfei, M. Z., & Schwagler, J. (1996). Possible selves among parents of infants and preschoolers. *Developmental Psychology, 32*, 542–550.

Hooker, K., & Kaus, C. R. (1994). Health-related possible selves in young and middle adulthood. *Psychology and Aging, 9*, 126–133.

Hoyle, R., & Sherrill, M. (2006). Future orientation in the self-system: Possible selves, self-regulation, and behavior. *Journal of Personality, 74,* 1673–1696.

James, W. (1890). *The principles of psychology* (Vol. 1). New York: Dover.

Kahneman, D., & Tversky, A. (1979). Prospect theory: An analysis of decision under risk. *Econometrica, 47,* 263–292.

Kemmelmeier, M., & Oyserman, D. (2001a). Gendered influence of downward social comparison on current and possible selves. *Journal of Social Issues, 57,* 129–148.

Kemmelmeier, M., & Oyserman, D. (2001b). The ups and downs of thinking about a successful other: Self-construals and the consequences of social comparisons. *European Journal of Social Psychology, 31,* 311–320.

Khan, U., & Dhar, R. (2007). Where there is a way, is there a will? The effect of future choices on self control. *Journal of Experimental Psychology: General, 136,* 277–288.

King, L. (2001). The health benefits of writing about life goals. *Personality and Social Psychology Bulletin, 27,* 798–807.

King, L., & Smith, N. G. (2004). Gay and straight possible selves: Goals, identity, subjective well-being, and personality development. *Journal of Personality, 72,* 967–994.

Knox, M., Funk, J., Elliott, R., & Bush, E. G. (2000). Gender differences in adolescents' possible selves. *Youth & Society, 31,* 287–309.

Lee, S. J., & Oyserman, D. (in press). Expecting to work, fearing homelessness: The possible selves of low-income mothers. *Journal of Applied Social Psychology.*

Lewin, K., Dembo, T., Festinger, L., & Sears, P. (1944). Level of aspiration. In J. M. Hunts (Ed.), *Personality and the behavior disorders* (pp. 333–378). New York: Ronald Press.

Liberman, N., Idson, L., Camacho, C., & Higgins, E. T. (1999). Promotion and prevention choices between stability and change. *Journal of Personality and Social Psychology, 77,* 1135–1145.

Liberman, N., Molden, D., Idson, L., & Higgins, E. T. (2001). Promotion and prevention focus on alternative hypotheses: Implications for attributional functions. *Journal of Personality and Social Psychology, 80,* 5–18.

Lockwood, P., & Kunda, Z. (1997). Superstars and me: Predicting the influence of role models on the self. *Journal of Personality and Social Psychology, 73,* 91–103.

Lockwood, P., & Kunda, Z. (1999). Increasing the salience of one's best selves can undermine inspiration by outstanding role models. *Journal of Personality and Social Psychology, 76,* 214–228.

Markman, K., & McMullen, M. (2003). A reflection and evaluation model of comparative thinking. *Personality and Social Psychology Review, 3,* 244–267.

Markus, H., & Nurius, P. (1986). Possible selves. *American Psychologist, 41,* 954–969.

Markus, H., & Wurf, E. (1987). The dynamic self-concept. *Annual Review of Psychology,* 299–337.

Martin, L. L., Ward, D. W., Achee, J. W., & Wyer, R. S., Jr. (1993). Mood as input: People have to interpret the motivational implications of their moods. *Journal of Personality and Social Psychology, 64,* 317–326.

Martin, L. L., Seta, J. J., & Crelia, R. A. (1990). Assimilation and contrast as a function of people's willingness and ability to expend effort in forming an impression. *Journal of Personality and Social Psychology, 59,* 27–37.

Meek, R. (2007).The parenting possible selves of young fathers in prison. *Psychology Crime and Law, 13,* 371–382.

Miller, G. A., Galanter, E., & Pribram, K. H. (1960). *Plans and the Structure of Behavior.* New York: Holt, Rinehart & Winston.

O'Brien, B., & Oyserman, D. (in press). It's not what you think, but how you think about it: The effect of situationally primed mindsets on legal judgments and decision making. *Marquette Law Review, 92.*

Oettingen, G., Pak, H., & Schnetter, K. (2001). Self-regulation of goal-setting: Turning free fantasies about the future into binding goals. *Journal of Personality and Social Psychology, 80,* 736–753.

Oyserman, D. (2001). Self-concept and identity. In A. Tesser & N. Shwarz (Eds.), *Blackwell handbook of social psychology* (pp. 499–517). Malden, MA: Blackwell Press.

Oyserman, D. (2007). Social identity and self-regulation. In A. Kruglanski & T. Higgins (Eds.), *Handbook of social psychology* (2nd ed., pp. 432–453). New York: Guilford Press.

Oyserman, D., Brickman, D., & Rhodes, M. (2007). School success, possible selves and parent school-involvement. *Family Relations, 56,* 279–289.

Oyserman, D., Bybee, D., & Terry, K. (2006). Possible selves and academic outcomes: How and when possible selves impel action. *Journal of Personality and Social Psychology, 91,* 188–204.

Oyserman, D., Bybee, D., Terry, K., & Hart-Johnson, T. (2004). Possible selves as roadmaps. *Journal of Research in Personality, 38,* 130–149.

Oyserman, D., & Fryberg, S. A. (2006). The possible selves of diverse adolescents: Content and function across gender, race, and national origin. In C. Dunkel & J. Kerpelman (Eds.), *Possible selves: Theory, research, and application* (pp. 17–39). Huntington, NY: Nova.

Oyserman, D., Fryberg, S., & Yoder, N. (2007). Identity-based motivation and health. *Journal of Personality and Social Psychology, 93,* 1011–1027.

Oyserman, D., Johnson, E., & Bybee, D. (2007). *Not doing much about it: Early adolescents' possible selves, imagined but not engaged.* Unpublished manuscript.

Oyserman, D., & Markus, H. (1990a). Possible selves in balance: Implications for delinquency. *Journal of Social Issues, 42,* 141–157.

Oyserman, D., & Markus, H. (1990b). Possible selves and delinquency. *Journal of Personality and Social Psychology, 59,* 112–125.

Oyserman, D., & Saltz, E. (1993). Competence, delinquency, and attempts to attain possible selves. *Journal of Personality and Social Psychology, 65,* 360–374.

Oyserman, D., Terry, K., & Bybee, D. (2002). A possible selves intervention to enhance school involvement. *Journal of Adolescence, 24,* 313–326.

Rae, J. (1905). *The sociological theory of capital.* New York: Macmillan. (Original work published 1834 as *The new principles of political economy*)

Schwarz, N., & Clore, G. L. (2007). Feelings and Emotional Experiences. In A. W. Kruglanski & E. T. Higgins (Eds.), *Social Psychology: Handbook of Basic Principles* (Second ed., pp. 385–407). New York: Guilford Press.

Senko, C., & Harackiewicz, J. (2005). Achievement goals, task performance, and interest: Why perceived goal difficulty matters. *Personality and Social Psychology Bulletin, 31,* 1739–1753.

Settles, I. H. (2004). When multiple identities interfere: The role of identity centrality. *Personality and Social Psychology Bulletin, 30,* 487–500.

Shane, F., Loewenstein, G., & O'Donoghue, T. (2002). Time discounting and time preference: A critical review. *Journal of Economic Literature, 40,* 351–401.

Shepard, B., & Marshall, A. (1999). Possible selves mapping: Life-career exploration with young adolescents. *Canadian Journal of Counselling, 33,* 37–54.

Simons, J., Vansteenkiste, M., Lens, W., & Lacante, M. (2004). Placing motivation and future time perspective theory in a temporal perspective. *Education Psychology Review, 16,* 121–139.

Smith, P. K., & Trope, Y. (2006). You focus on the forest when you're in charge of the trees: Power priming and abstract information processing. *Journal of Personality and Social Psychology, 90,* 578–596.

Spiegel, S., Grant-Pillow, H., & Higgins, E. T. (2004). How regulatory fit enhances motivational strength during goal pursuit. *European Journal of Social Psychology, 34,* 39–54.

Steele, C. M., & Aronson, J. (1995). Stereotype threat and the intellectual test performance of African-Americans. *Journal of Personality and Social Psychology* 69(5), 797–811.

Strauss, R., & Goldberg, W. A. (1999). Self and possible selves during the transition to fatherhood. *Journal of Family Psychology, 13,* 244–259.

Taylor, S., Kemeny, M., Reed, G., Bower, J., & Gruenewald, T. (2000). Psychological resources, positive illusions, and health. *American Psychologist, 55,* 99–109.

Taylor, S., Neter, E., & Wayment, H. (1995). Self-evaluation processes. *Personality and Social Psychology Bulletin, 21,* 1278–1287.

Trope, Y., & Liberman, N. (2003). Temporal construal. *Psychological Review, 110,* 403–421.

Tuss, P., Zimmer, J., & Ho, H. (1995). Causal attributions of underachieving fourth-grade students in China, Japan, and the United States. *Journal of Cross-Cultural Psychology, 26,* 408–425.

Vansteenkiste, M., Simons, J., Soenens, B., & Lens, W. (2003). How to become a lifelong exerciser: The importance on presenting a clear future goal in an autonomy-supportive way. *Journal of Sport Exercise Psychology, 26(2),* 232–250.

Wrosch, C., Scheier, M., Carver, C., & Schulz, R. (2003). The importance of goal disengagement in adaptive self-regulation: When giving up is beneficial. *Self & Identity, 2,* 1–20.

Yamaguchi, S., Gelfand, M., Ohashi, M., & Zemba, Y. (2005). The cultural psychology of control: Illusions of personal versus collective control in the United States and Japan. *Journal of Cross-Cultural Psychology, 36,* 750–761.

Zimbardo, P., & Boyd, J. (1999). Putting time in perspective: A valid, reliable individual-differences metric. *Journal of Personality and Social Psychology, 77,* 1271–1288.

26 Mental Contrasting of the Future and Reality to Master Negative Feedback

Gabriele Oettingen and Andreas Kappes

INTRODUCTION

Negative feedback is an inevitable part of successful goal attainment. For example, one sets out to jog 3 miles but has to stop after 1.5 miles, gasping for breath. This feedback may be acknowledged as important information suggesting that one needs to get into better shape. However, one may also interpret it as an indicator of low athleticism, leading one to give up on the desire to establish a regular exercise routine. Kurt Lewin (1948) described how such dilemmas capture the paradoxical nature of the pursuit of wish fulfillment. For successful wish fulfillment, people need to acknowledge negative feedback without letting it harm their positive beliefs in themselves or their beliefs about what the future holds for them.

Our chapter, in three parts, addresses mental contrasting of the future and reality as a means of effectively responding to negative feedback. First, we provide an overview of research on mental contrasting as a strategy of realizing one's wishes by facilitating goal commitment and goal striving. Second, we show that mental contrasting enables people to extract meaningful information from negative feedback without losing their positive self-view or their optimistic future orientation. Finally, we describe research speaking to the transfer of mental contrasting effects across tasks and life domains and discuss the implications of these findings for using mental contrasting as a self-regulatory tool that yields benefits for performance and achievement beyond attaining the specified goal.

EFFECTS ON GOAL COMMITMENT

A long tradition of research suggests that people commit to and strive for goals that are desirable and feasible (e.g., Atkinson, 1957; Bandura, 1997; Faude, Wuerz, & Gollwitzer, Chapter 5, this volume; Gollwitzer, 1990; Klinger, 1975, Chapter 15, this volume; Locke & Latham, 1990). *Desirability* comprises the summarized expectations of the pleasantness of short-term and long-term consequences of goal attainment (Heckhausen, 1977). *Feasibility* is defined as expectations that future events and actions will occur (Gollwitzer, 1990). Prominent examples include expectations of whether one can execute a behavior necessary for realizing a specific outcome (i.e., self-efficacy expectations; Bandura, 1977), expectations that a behavior will lead to a specified outcome (i.e., outcome expectations, Bandura, 1977; instrumentality beliefs, Vroom, 1964), and judgments about the general probability of a certain outcome (i.e., general expectations; Heckhausen, 1991; Oettingen & Mayer, 2002).

Self-regulatory approaches to goal attainment spell out the processes by which perceived desirability and feasibility are translated into goal commitment and goal striving (e.g., Oettingen, Pak, & Schnetter, 2001) and how goal striving can be made more effective to increase the rate of goal attainment (e.g., Gollwitzer & Sheeran, 2006). Most self-regulation research focuses on how to increase the rate of goal attainment rather than on the question of how desirability and feasibility are translated into goal commitment and goal striving. However, the model of fantasy realization (Oettingen, 1999; Oettingen et al., 2001), addressing the question of how goal commitment emerges as a function of self-regulatory processes, identifies a mode of thinking about the future that translates feasibility into goal commitment with subsequent goal striving: mental contrasting of a desired future (e.g., becoming a medical doctor) with the reality that impedes its realization (e.g., having not taken the necessary exams yet).

In mental contrasting, people first imagine the attainment of a desired future (e.g., becoming a lawyer, writing an article) and thereafter reflect on the present reality that stands in the way of attaining the desired future (e.g., excessive partying, having little time). Thus, contrasting fantasies about the future with reflections on reality is a problem-solving strategy: The person wants to achieve a desired future and needs to engage in actions to realize it. In their theory of problem solving, Newell and Simon (1972) distinguished between an objective and a subjective problem space. The objective problem space is defined by the demands of the task. In the case of realizing a desired future, the objective problem space is composed of the desired future and the impediments to getting there. The subjective problem space is defined by the internal representations of the problem. Mental contrasting matches the subjective problem space with the objective problem space and thereby enables people to recognize that they need to take action to achieve the desired future. Therefore, expectations of attaining the desired future become activated and determine the person's commitment and striving to attain the desired future.

Specifically, conjointly envisioning the future and reality makes both simultaneously accessible and links them in a manner suggesting that reality impedes the realization of the desired future. This linkage thus elicits a necessity to act that in turn activates expectations of success. Subsequently, these expectations set the course for a person's goal commitment and goal striving: When expectations of success are high, people will actively commit to and strive toward reaching the desired future; when expectations of success are low, people will refrain from doing so.

The model of fantasy realization specifies two other modes of thinking about the future, both of which fail to lead to goal commitment and goal striving guided by the perceived likelihood of attaining the desired future. People may either solely envision the attainment of the wished-for future (i.e., indulging) or solely reflect on the negative reality (i.e., dwelling). Considered again from a problem-solving perspective (Newell & Simon, 1972), both modes of thinking create a subjective problem space that does not correspond to the objective problem space. Because the objective problem space is not subjectively accessible, a discrepancy or tension between future and reality is not perceived, and thus there is no signal indicating that actions would be necessary or instrumental to achieve the desired future. Therefore, expectations of success do not become activated, and goal commitment and goal striving do not reflect the perceived likelihood of reaching the desired future. The level of goal striving is determined by the a priori commitment that the person holds with respect to attaining the desired future. Thus, it is mental contrasting, and not indulging and dwelling, that succeeds in strengthening goal commitment with subsequent goal striving when expectations of success are high and in weakening it when expectations of success are low.

EMPIRICAL EVIDENCE

A multitude of studies have tested the effects of mental contrasting, indulging, and dwelling on goal commitment and goal striving (Oettingen, 2000; Oettingen, Hönig, & Gollwitzer, 2000; Oettingen, Mayer, Thorpe, Janetzke, & Lorenz, 2005; Oettingen et al., 2001). For example, in one study, freshmen enrolled in a vocational school for computer programming (Oettingen et al., 2001, Study 4) first indicated their expectations of excelling in mathematics. Thereafter, they named aspects that they associated with excelling in mathematics (e.g., feelings of pride, increasing job prospects) and aspects of reality that might impede its fulfillment (e.g., being distracted by peers, feeling lazy). Subsequently, three experimental conditions were established to correspond with the three modes of thought specified by the model. In the mental contrasting condition, participants elaborated two positive aspects of the future and two aspects of reality, in alternating order, beginning with a positive aspect of the future; in the indulging condition, participants elaborated four positive aspects of the future; and in the dwelling condition, participants elaborated four negative aspects of reality. As a dependent variable, participants indicated how energized they felt with respect to excelling in mathematics (e.g., how active, eventful, energetic). Furthermore, 2 weeks after the experiment, participants' teachers reported how much effort each student had invested for the last 2 weeks and provided each student with a grade for that time period. As predicted, only in the mental contrasting group did the students feel energized, exert effort, and earn grades based on their expectations. Participants in the mental contrasting group with high expectations of success felt the most energized, invested the most effort, and received the highest grades. Conversely, participants in the mental contrasting group with low expectations of success felt the least energized, invested the least effort, and received the lowest course grades. Participants in the indulging and dwelling conditions did not differ in their moderate and expectancy-independent feelings of energization. This was also true for teacher-rated effort and grades.

This pattern of results was replicated in a variety of studies, including ones pertaining to studying abroad (Oettingen et al., 2001, Study 2), acquiring a second language (Oettingen et al., 2000, Study 1), getting to know an attractive stranger (Oettingen, 2000, Study 1), finding a balance between work and family life (Oettingen, 2000, Study 2), improving one's self (Oettingen et al., 2005, Study 1), and idiosyncratic interpersonal wishes of great importance (Oettingen et al., 2001, Study 1 and 3). Furthermore, goal striving was assessed by cognitive (e.g., making plans), affective (e.g., feeling responsible for the wished-for ending), motivational (e.g., feelings of energization), and behavioral indicators (e.g., invested effort and achievements). Such indicators were measured via self-report or observations either immediately after or weeks after the experiment. In all of these studies, the same pattern of results emerged. Given high expectations of success, participants in the mental contrasting group showed the strongest goal commitment and goal striving, whereas given low expectations, people showed the least goal commitment and goal striving. Participants who indulged in positive images about the future or dwelled on negative images of reality moderately committed to and strived toward realizing their wishes without considering their expectations of success.

MECHANISMS

Two mechanisms mediate the translation of expectations into goal attainment: planning and energization (Oettingen & Mayer, 2007; Oettingen, Mayer, Sevincer, Stephens, & Hagenah, 2008). Research on the cognitive mechanism of planning assumes that planning out the route to goal attainment facilitates actual goal attainment (e.g., Armor & Taylor, 2003; Faude et al., Chapter 5, this volume; Gollwitzer, 1999; Gollwitzer, Fujita, & Oettingen, 2004). Research on the motivational mechanism of energization is based on the idea that energization helps to initiate and maintain goal striving, a resource-demanding endeavor (e.g., Locke & Latham, 2002; Muraven, Tice, & Baumeister, 1998).

Cognitive Mechanism of Planning

Planning is vital to successful goal attainment because it helps people to overcome volitional problems such as failing to get started, getting derailed during the course of goal-directed actions, or overextending oneself in ongoing goal striving (Gollwitzer & Sheeran, 2006). Planning—that is, preparing oneself for future actions—also fosters positive self-perceptions needed for successful goal attainment. Specifically, planning in the form of furnishing one's goal striving with implementation intentions (Gollwitzer, 1999) alleviates the volitional problems that occur during goal striving (meta-analysis by Gollwitzer & Sheeran, 2006). Framed in an if-then format, implementation intentions link a critical situation (e.g., an obstacle) to an instrumental goal-directed response (e.g., aimed at overcoming said obstacle). Control of the response is thereby delegated to anticipated cues that in turn elicit the response automatically. As a consequence, planning out one's route to goal attainment in the form of implementation intentions fosters successful goal attainment. Further, when compared to deliberating a personal problem, planning fosters positive self-evaluations (e.g., Armor & Taylor, 2003; Gollwitzer & Kinney, 1989; Taylor & Gollwitzer, 1995). Such positive self-evaluations, even if illusory, enhance the likelihood of goal attainment (Taylor & Brown, 1988).

When the present reality is recognized as an obstacle to attaining the desired future and people expect to attain the desired future, they commit themselves to overcoming the obstacle and are thereby inclined to make plans that spell out what needs to be done to overcome the obstacle (Oettingen, 2000; Oettingen et al., 2001). Indeed, when obstacles and threats are salient, people will include them in their preparatory activities (Armor & Taylor, 1998). The procedure of mental contrasting makes obstacles salient, such that when obstacles are recognized as surmountable people commit themselves to overcoming them. As a result, individuals who have used the strategy of mental contrasting should generate efficient plans. By using if-then plans (implementation intentions), perceived obstacles can be linked to an instrumental goal-directed action to overcome them. For example, a person who has the goal of doing well on an exam might form the following plan: "If the phone rings and a friend asks me to go out, then I will make an appointment with him after the exam." Consequently, mental contrasting should lead to expectancy-dependent planning that in turn fosters goal attainment.

To test the hypothesis that mental contrasting leads to expectancy-dependent planning, which subsequently guides goal attainment, participants first named an important interpersonal wish (e.g., solving a conflict with a friend, being friendlier to parents) and thereafter engaged in mental contrasting, indulging, dwelling, or reverse mental contrasting (Oettingen & Mayer, 2007), a fourth condition in which participants started first with the elaboration of the reality followed by the elaboration of the desired future. By reversing the sequence of mental contrasting, the reality should not be perceived as standing in the way of fantasy realization; therefore, we expected no expectancy-dependent planning or goal attainment (for supportive findings, see Oettingen et al., 2001). Participants then rated the extent to which they successfully achieved their goals. To measure the mediating variable (i.e., planning), two independent raters content analyzed participants' elaborations of the negative aspects of the reality in the mental contrasting, dwelling, and reverse-contrasting conditions to assess the number of elicited implementation intentions. A significant benefit of this method is its ability to capture participants' on-line plan formation during the process of mental contrasting versus noncontrasting modes of thought. Because negative aspects of the present reality did not emerge in the indulging condition, plan formation in response to negative aspects of reality could not be assessed in this group.

As predicted, self-rated success in goal achievement showed expectancy dependence in the mental contrasting condition but not in the nonmental contrasting conditions. Importantly, expectancy-congruent plan formation also emerged in the mental contrasting condition but not in the dwelling and reverse mental contrasting conditions. Specifically, the formation of if-then plans (i.e., implementation intentions; Gollwitzer, 1999) showed the same pattern of results as perceived goal achievement and predicted participants' perceived goal achievement over and above the interaction of expectations and experimental condition. In addition, in the mental contrasting condition, forming implementation intentions fully explained the relation between expectations of success and perceived goal achievement. Apparently, mental contrasting allows people with high expectations of success to become not only committed to realizing their wishes, but also triggers plans directed toward overcoming the anticipated obstacles and thereby helps people to perceive themselves as successfully attaining their goals (Oettingen & Mayer, 2007). Assuming that individuals have reasonably accurate expectancies of success (i.e., perceived probabilities of success), expectancy-independent self-evaluations in noncontrasting participants may pose a problem not only for inadequate exertion of effort but also for expectancy appraisal in the future. Performance evaluations failing to respect expectations of success should pave the way to inaccurate appraisals of further probabilities of success.

Motivational Mechanism of Energization

As a motivational mechanism, mental contrasting should instigate expectancy-dependent energization, which then guides goal commitment and goal striving. Motivational research traditionally emphasized the importance of energization for instigating goal-directed action. In line with this research tradition, recent work underlines the importance of energization for the activation and strength of behavior (Brehm & Self, 1989; Locke & Latham, 2002; Wright, 1996). *Energization* is also referred to as activity incitement (Brunstein & Gollwitzer, 1996). In addition, in his theory of motivation, Brehm specified the conditions of energy mobilization (e.g., Brehm & Self, 1989). The theory assumes that energization as an expression of effort furthers goal-directed action in line with a person's needs, expectations, and perceived importance of success. People will mobilize energy in line with the demands of the task as long as they perceive successful goal striving as possible and worthwhile.

Mentally contrasting a desired future induces a necessity to act and thereby activates expectations of success. People with high expectations of success should mobilize effort toward reaching their goal, while people with low expectations and weak commitment should mobilize only little effort. Indeed, energization as an indicator of effort mobilization has been observed as a mediator of mental contrasting effects in two studies (Oettingen et al., 2008). One study assessed feelings of energization via self-report, and another study measured energization via systolic blood pressure (SBP), a reliable indicator of motivational arousal (Gendolla & Wright, 2005; Wright, 1996). In the first study, using an acute stress paradigm (i.e., videotaped public speaking; al' Absi et al., 1997), persistence and quality of performance were observed in the laboratory. Economics students participating in this study were informed that they were to deliver a speech in front of a video camera to help researchers develop a measure of professional skills for a human resource department. Participants were randomly assigned to either a mental contrasting or an indulging condition. Initial feelings of energization were measured via self-report measure (e.g., how energized they felt when thinking about giving their talk), and participants' evaluations of their own presentations were gauged by asking them to rate their actual performance. Persistence was indicated by the duration of each participant's presentation in minutes, and quality of performance was measured via independent raters' evaluations of the quality of the videotaped content (Oettingen et al., 2008, Study 2).

Again, and consistent with findings of previous mental contrasting studies, individuals in the mental contrasting group, contrary to those in the indulging condition, evidenced a strong link between perceived expectations of success and goal commitment as measured by subjective self-evaluations of performance and objective ratings of the videotaped presentations. Moreover, feelings of energization not only showed the same pattern of results as the goal-commitment variables but also predicted objective and subjective presentation quality over and above the interactive effect of experimental condition (i.e., mental contrasting or indulging) and expectations. Finally, in the mental contrasting condition, feelings of energization fully explained the relationship between expectations of success and both subjective and objective performance quality.

Physiological data substantiate these findings of energization as a mediating mechanism. Building on findings that cardiovascular responses are a valid indicator of effort expenditure and reliably relate to applying instrumental behavior (Obrist, 1981; Wright, 1996), mental contrasting versus indulging effects on SBP were investigated (Oettingen et al., 2008, Study 1). Systolic blood pressure responds to the degree of task demands (Gendolla, 1999; Wright, 1996), while diastolic blood pressure and heart rate do less so, showing that it is particularly a strong sympathetic influence on the heart that relates to energization and effort expenditure. Therefore, Oettingen et al., (2008, Study 1) investigated SBP as a mediator of the effect of mental contrasting versus indulging on goal commitment. In this study, SBP was collected at baseline and during the thought processes of mental contrasting versus indulging. Changes in SBP from baseline showed the familiar pattern of results. Specifically, changes in energization and effort expenditure as measured by SBP from before to during the mental contrasting versus indulging procedures emerged as a motivational mediator of the expectation–goal-commitment effects.

These results also relate to the biopsychosocial model of challenge versus threat by Blascovich and Tomaka (1996). The authors postulated and found that making challenge versus threat salient in the laboratory (situational demands meet vs. exceed resources) produces distinct sets of physiological responses (Tomaka, Blascovich, Kibler, & Ernst, 1997), which in turn predict successful performance (e.g., in the athletic domain; Blascovich, Seery, Mugridge, Norris, & Weisbuch, 2004). Future research may investigate whether inducing challenge versus threat by activating expectations through mental contrasting would also lead to the predicted physiological responses and subsequent performance effects.

SUMMARY

The model of fantasy realization identifies mental contrasting as an effective way of translating one's expectations of success into goal commitment and goal striving, and numerous empirical studies supported this assumption. In addition, the differential effects of mental contrasting versus other strategies on expectation-dependent goal attainment were mediated by planning and energization. In the next section, we explore whether mental contrasting enables people to effectively respond to negative feedback.

EFFECTS ON RESPONDING TO NEGATIVE FEEDBACK

According to Lewin (1948), mastering negative feedback is a paradoxical task. On the one hand, persistent and effective goal striving after negative feedback demands keeping an optimistic future outlook and maintaining confidence in oneself. On the other hand, successful goal striving also demands realistic appraisal of the present situation to ensure progress toward the goal. "One might say that this paradox—to be realistic, and at the same time be guided by high goals—lies at the heart of the problem" (1948, p. 119). Following these considerations, we assume that when people are confronted with negative feedback, they need to acknowledge it to extract important information for subsequent goal striving, but they also need to protect their positive self-view and optimistic future outlook to stay motivated on their way to goal achievement. Consequently, the forthcoming research focuses on the role of mental contrasting with regard to the three critical features of upholding goal striving in the face of negative feedback: (a) processing goal-relevant information embedded in negative feedback; (b) protecting one's positive self-view in the face of negative feedback; and (c) maintaining an optimistic future outlook in one's attributions for negative feedback. We hypothesize that mentally contrasting feasible wishes with potential obstacles of reality will enable people to achieve all three: to effectively process negative feedback on the one hand but also to maintain one's positive self-view as well as optimistic outlook. We argue that mental contrasting may achieve these benefits by fostering commitment, facilitating if-then plans, and increasing energization.

First, research on goal commitment strengthens the hypothesis that mental contrasting feasible wishes will support the mastery of negative feedback. An important feature of mental contrasting is that it translates high expectations about achieving a desired future into strong goal commitments (Oettingen, 2000; Oettingen et al., 2001). When people are strongly committed to a certain goal, they react with increased effort when facing negative feedback on their way to goal achievement (Gollwitzer, 1990; Wright, 1996). For example, Wicklund and Gollwitzer (1982; Brunstein & Gollwitzer, 1996), in their model of symbolic self-completion, postulated and observed that negative feedback on a task relevant to participants' self-defining goals (i.e., goals people are committed to) led to enhanced performance on a subsequent task relevant to the same self-defining goals. Conversely, participants who were confronted with negative feedback on a task not relevant to their self-definitions did not enhance their effort. These findings suggest that negative feedback only leads to enhanced performance if it is relevant to goals to which people have firmly committed. Similarly, Klinger (1975; Chapter 15, this volume) maintained that when people have committed to a certain goal (i.e., when they have a current concern), they increase their effort in the face of negative feedback. Finally, Locke and Latham (1990) included in their definition of commitment the degree to which the individual maintains a certain goal when negative feedback occurs (see also Latham & Locke, 1991).

Second, mental contrasting of feasible wishes facilitates planning one's goal striving in the form of if-then plans (Oettingen & Mayer, 2007). If-then plans or implementation intentions, in turn, equip people to link anticipated obstacles to goal-directed behavior, thus facilitating goal attainment (Gollwitzer, 1999). Therefore, mental contrasting should ready people to process negative feedback as useful cues for specifying when, where, and how they may act in a goal-directed way.

Finally, mentally contrasting feasible wishes facilitates energization as measured by self-report and physiological indicators (Oettingen et al., 2008). Energization, in turn, equips people to perceive negative feedback not as failure, but rather as a challenge (Dweck & Leggett, 1988; Wright, 1996). Therefore, mental contrasting should ready people to confront challenge and to process the information entailed in negative feedback rather than avoiding it as unwelcome news of failing one's goal striving.

However, mental contrasting of feasible wishes, inducing commitment, planning, and energization should not solely lead to the effective processing of negative feedback. As commitment, planning and energization foster a positive self-view and optimistic future outlook (Armor & Taylor, 2003; Gollwitzer & Kinney, 1989; Taylor & Gollwitzer, 1995; Wright, 1996), mental contrasting of feasible wishes should help to effectively uphold people's positive self-view and future outlook in the face of negative feedback.

PROCESSING INFORMATION ENTAILED IN NEGATIVE FEEDBACK

Successfully handling negative feedback requires extracting meaningful knowledge from it. For example, being short of breath may motivate one to exercise more often and eventually improve one's physical fitness and shape. Such information may help one to detect errors and adjust behavior effectively (Audia & Locke, 2003), to reduce uncertainty about the behavior and the outcome (Ashford, 1986), and to help individuals to identify ineffective behaviors (Ilgen, Fisher, & Taylor, 1979). Moreover, negative feedback helps people to decide which skills need to be improved and how these skills can be improved (Dweck & Leggett, 1988).

However, negative feedback may not be readily processed because the information entailed in the negative feedback may diminish one's self-view. Indeed, negative stimuli are less likely to be processed than positive stimuli (Taylor, 1991). For example, in one study (Sedikides & Green, 2000, Experiment 1), participants completed a personality inventory, received negative and positive feedback about their personality, and were then confronted with a surprise cued recall task. The recall of negative feedback was limited compared to the recall of positive feedback, even when it was innocuous (Sedikides & Green, 2000, Experiment 2), and this information neglect seems to have been caused by the expenditure of minimal processing resources to negative feedback (Sedikides & Green, 2000, Experiment 3). In addition, it has been found that people tend to neglect negative information regardless of whether their self-view is positive or negative (Sedikides & Green, 2004, Experiment 2).

Effective processing of negative feedback is crucial for successful goal attainment. We hypothesize that mentally contrasting a feasible wish energizes individuals and helps them to plan out their goal striving, fostering the effective processing of negative feedback. Mentally contrasting an unfeasible wish, on the other hand, should not elicit these beneficial consequences. Finally, indulging and dwelling should elicit negative feedback processing that is not moderated by perceived chances of success. These hypotheses were tested in a simple cued recall experiment (Pak, Kappes, & Oettingen, 2008, Study 1).

Students were invited to participate in two supposedly independent studies. In the first part, they named an important interpersonal concern (e.g., improving relationships with one's parents, getting to know somebody) and reported their expectations of successfully dealing with it. In the second part, students completed an ostensible test of social competence. Specifically, students studied a variety of ambiguous pictures and then filled out semantic differential-type questions about their impressions of the people depicted in the pictures. After completing the test, participants received false feedback statements about their social competence that focused on situations in which participants supposedly show interpersonal weaknesses and failings. For example, some false feedback suggested that participants tend to react impulsively in stressful situations or that they tend to be tense in socially challenging situations. As such, the negative feedback was related to the domain of participants' interpersonal concerns. Finally, the three self-regulatory thought modes were induced by asking students to elaborate their previously named interpersonal concern by either alternating between aspects of future and reality (starting with a positive aspect of the future; mental contrasting), focusing only on aspects of the positive future (indulging) or focusing only on aspects of the negative reality (dwelling). At the end of the experiment, all participants were confronted with a surprise cued recall test for the feedback received, with the number of recalled adjectives describing participants' social weaknesses serving as the dependent variable.

Results showed that participants in the mental contrasting condition with high expectations for reaching the desired future were most successful in extracting meaningful information from the negative feedback: They recalled the highest number of adjectives describing their weaknesses and shortcomings. Participants in the mental contrasting condition with low expectations of success were least successful in extracting meaningful information: They recalled the lowest number of adjectives describing their weaknesses and shortcomings. Finally, participants in the indulging and dwelling groups recalled a moderate number of negative adjectives, and recall was independent of expectation level.

These results support the hypotheses that mental contrasting—by energizing people to realize their wishes, form plans, and commiting them in line with their subjective probabilities of success—will lead people to process negative feedback in an expectancy-dependent way. Indulging and dwelling, on the other hand, induce people to process negative feedback irrespective of whether they judge their probabilities of success as high or low.

PROTECTING ONE'S SELF-VIEW AFTER NEGATIVE FEEDBACK

Pak et al. (2008, Experiment 1) found that mental contrasting in light of high expectations led to better processing of negative goal-relevant information. Accessibility of negative goal-relevant information is important for successful goal attainment because it provides useful clues for how to pursue one's goal attainment. Another determinant of successful goal striving is a person's positive self-view, that is, evaluating oneself as being able and as possessing desired attributes. Taylor and Brown (1988) reviewed a large amount of research suggesting that people holding a positive self-view work harder and longer on task goals, perform more effectively, and reach their goals more successfully than do people holding a more negative self-view (see also Taylor, Kemeny, Reed, Bower, & Gruenewald, 2000).

Although mental contrasting feasible wishes benefits goal attainment by promoting effective processing of negative feedback, it may incur the cost of damaging the individual's self-view. Indeed, trainees at the master's level experienced reduced positivity of their domain-specific self-views after they received false negative feedback about their abilities (Daniels & Larson, 2001). Dweck and Leggett (1988) also observed that negative feedback may lead to comparatively negative views about one's abilities. They found this to be particularly true for those who hold entity theories of intelligence (believing that ability is stable over time) as these individuals tend to set performance goals for themselves (wanting to prove their abilities) and consequently interpret negative feedback as an indicator of failure or lack of ability. As a result, entity theorists tend to prematurely abandon their goal striving. On the other hand, when people hold incremental theories (believing that ability is malleable), and thus set learning goals for themselves (wanting to increase their abilities), they interpret negative feedback as a mere setback that provides useful information for increasing ability. As a result, incremental theorists tend to maintain their goal striving. These findings show not only that negative feedback may hurt one's positive self-view and subsequent goal striving, but also that mindsets may influence the way negative feedback has an impact on individuals' self-views (Dweck, 2006; see also Gollwitzer, 1990).

If the processing of negative feedback can damage one's positive self-view (Daniels & Larson, 2001; Dweck & Elliot, 1988), one might argue that mental contrasting of a feasible wish, although beneficial in terms of providing clues for successful goal striving, might nevertheless hurt goal striving. However, because mental contrasting of feasible wishes strengthens goal commitment, leads people to form plans, and energizes them, we hypothesize that mental contrasting of a feasible wish will lead to the maintenance of a person's self-view even when faced with strong negative feedback. This hypothesis was tested in the experiment described next (Pak et al., 2008, Experiment 2).

Again, students were invited to participate in two supposedly independent studies. In the first study, participants named an important interpersonal concern and rated their expectations of success. In the second study, they completed the same aforementioned social competence test. This time, however, normative rather than noncomparative negative feedback was provided. Negative feedback that includes a comparison to a norm has been shown to exert a more detrimental influence on self-views than noncomparative feedback, including task-oriented information (Butler, 1987; Kluger & DeNisi, 1997). Specifically, participants were told that they had achieved only a low number of points on the test, and that their performance, compared to other people in their peer group, was rather poor. After receiving the feedback, the three self-regulatory modes of thought were induced (i.e., mental contrasting, indulging, and dwelling). Participants then rated their social ability and interpersonal intelligence. As there was a baseline rating of these variables, the change in pre- to postmanipulation self-views served as the dependent variable.

Participants in the mental contrasting condition showed expectancy dependence in their self-view change scores: Those with high expectations of success sustained their view of their social abilities (they even showed a small increase), while those with low expectations showed a comparatively diminished self-view. In the other two conditions (i.e., indulging and dwelling), no expectancy-dependent change was observed.

Apparently, mentally contrasting future and reality enables people with high expectations of success to protect their positive self-view when facing negative feedback. Further, the findings suggest that mental contrasting effects extend beyond the particular wish about which people mentally contrasted. For example, participants named as an important interpersonal concern "to get along with my mother" or "to get to know someone I like." Mentally contrasting these specific concerns brought the general view of the self—a more global appraisal of one's abilities—in line with the perceived probabilities that the specific concern would have a happy ending. This finding implies that mentally contrasting concerns of high subjective probability of success may be used to bolster individuals' more general view of ability.

OPTIMISTIC ATTRIBUTIONS AFTER NEGATIVE FEEDBACK

Another facilitator of successful goal striving is an optimistic attribution pattern in response to negative feedback because such attributions influence a person's outlook for future goal striving (Seligman, 1991). Research on attributions assumes that explaining negative feedback in global and stable terms is associated with maladaptive responses (e.g., Abramson, Seligman, & Teasdale, 1978; Peterson, Maier, & Seligman, 1993; Weiner, 1986). For example, attributions to global and stable causes hamper persistence after failure (Weiner, 1986) and impair mastery-oriented behavioral patterns (Diener & Dweck, 1978).

The reformulation of the learned helplessness theory specified in detail the effects of attributions of negative feedback on subsequent goal striving (Abramson et al., 1978; Peterson et al., 1993; Seligman, 1991; see Mikulincer, 1994, for a review). For instance, one way to explain the negative feedback of getting out of breath could be to assume that one lacks the ability to become fit. Attributing negative events to such internal, stable, and global causes (i.e., pessimistic explanatory style; Abramson et al., 1978) has detrimental effects on future goal striving because it fosters the expectation that these negative events will reoccur in the future (stable), be pervasive across situations (global), and relate to personal deficits (internal). Thus, this attribution pattern harms the person's positive outlook for future goal striving and his or her self-esteem. Another way to explain the negative feedback of getting out of breath would be to assume that one felt a bit under the weather (e.g., after a night of not sleeping so well). Explaining negative events with such external, unstable, and specific attributions (i.e., optimistic explanatory style; Seligman, 1991) shelters an individual against a dreary outlook for the future and subsequent performance deficits because he or she forms the expectation that the negative event is modifiable (unstable), stays restricted to the particular situation (specific), and is caused by outside circumstances (external). This optimistic attribution pattern protects the individual's positive outlook and his or her self-esteem. As a consequence, optimistic explanatory style is related to persistence in the face of negative feedback (see Gillham, Shatté, Reivich, & Seligman, 2001, for a review). For example, in one study participants performed a basketball dribbling trial and then received false negative feedback about their performance (Martin-Krumm, Sarrazin, Peterson, & Famose, 2003). In the subsequent trial, participants with an optimistic explanatory style were less anxious, more confident, and performed better than participants with a pessimistic explanatory style. In sum, explaining negative feedback in an optimistic way enhances mastery, and by protecting one's confidence, it also facilitates the realization of the desired future.

Mentally contrasting feasible wishes fosters energization, commitment, and planning. All three factors should help people to maintain a positive future outlook in the form of optimistic attributions when facing negative feedback (Gollwitzer & Kinney, 1989; Latham & Locke, 1991). To test whether mentally contrasting a feasible wish promotes optimistic explanations of negative feedback, students were invited to participate in a study about social competence (Pak et al., 2008, Study 3). In the first part, students were asked about their expectations to perform well on an upcoming social competence test. Next, a mental contrasting condition and an indulging condition were established. Specifically, in the mental contrasting condition participants elaborated fantasies about excelling on the social competence test (e.g., pride, relief, and good feelings) as well as the negative reality (e.g., anxiety, tiredness, and clumsiness), whereas in the indulging condition they only fantasized about excelling on the social competence test. In the second part, students completed the social competence test and then received normative negative feedback on their performance. Finally, based on the explanatory style questionnaire (Peterson et al., 1982), participants indicated what they thought caused their negative performance (e.g., the unusual context) and then rated this cause on the three explanatory dimensions: stable versus unstable, global versus specific, and internal versus external. These three dimensions encompassed an overall index of optimistic attributions (Seligman, 1991). Participants in the mental contrasting condition with high expectations of success used optimistic attributions to explain the negative feedback, whereas those with low expectations of success used pessimistic attributions. Participants in the indulging condition used moderately optimistic attributions to explain their negative feedback, independent of their expectations of success.

SUMMARY

Three studies indicated that mentally contrasting an achievable, desired future with the hindering reality enables the successful mastery of negative feedback. Participants in the mental contrasting condition with high expectations effectively processed negative feedback, protected their self-view from threatening negative feedback, and explained negative feedback in an optimistic way. Apparently, mentally contrasting feasible futures enables people to successfully tackle negative feedback on the way to wish fulfillment.

In all three experiments (Pak et al., 2008), participants were confronted with explicit negative feedback. However, successful goal striving, particularly when solving very difficult tasks, may also present demands to overcome implicit negative feedback. For instance, when trying to make sense of a difficult mathematical problem, one may repeatedly be confronted with approaches that lead to inconclusive or negative implicit feedback (e.g., when arriving at a false intermediate solution or an unbalanced equation). Such feedback posed by facing factual obstacles and difficulties on the way to solving the problem may threaten people in their readiness to process useful information, in terms of both their self-view of competence and their optimistic future outlook. Maintaining readiness for new goal-relevant information and confidence in one's competence and future perspective furthers successful performance. We assume that mental contrasting in light of high expectations of success fosters successful performance in difficult tasks because it fosters information processing as well as the maintenance of one's self-view and optimistic outlook.

Finally, studying the effects of mental contrasting on performance addresses the question of whether the effects of mental contrasting transfer across tasks and life domains (see also Wong, Galinsky, & Kray, Chapter 11, this volume). We assume they do for the following reasons: First, as described, mental contrasting of a specific interpersonal concern created expectancy dependence in participants' self-views of general social competence and in their reported success of general goal attainment, while indulging and dwelling did not. Apparently, high versus low expectancies of successfully solving a very specific concern (e.g., to improve a relationship with a roommate, to accept teachers for who they are) were beneficial for self-evaluations of general social intelligence and goal-striving capacity. In other words, mental contrasting makes high expectations of successfully solving a specific concern benefit self-evaluations of one's general interpersonal ability. Although these transfer effects were so far observed only within one life domain, one might speculate that they would even cross domain boundaries and go beyond self-evaluations to also affect effort and performance. For example, mental contrasting might allow high expectations of successfully solving a specific interpersonal concern (e.g., getting to better know a liked person) to transfer to the attainment of success in an academic task (e.g., solving math problems).

Second, mental contrasting of a specific interpersonal concern led to expectancy-dependent planning as measured by the number of if-then statements generated during elaboration, while indulging and dwelling did not (Oettingen & Mayer, 2007). A planning mindset has also been found to transfer to other task and life domains (Gollwitzer, 1990). Third, mental contrasting of a specific interpersonal concern led to energization as measured by self-report and physiological indicators (Oettingen et al., 2007; see also Wright, 1996). We assume that energy mobilization will transfer beyond the immediate concern to affect behavior in other tasks and different life domains. For these three reasons, we hypothesize that mentally contrasting future and reality in one life domain will facilitate the effects of mental contrasting in a different life domain, a hypothesis that is tested in the study described next.

EFFECTS ON PERFORMANCE

To examine whether mental contrasting of feasible wishes leads to successful performance in tasks that entail implicit negative feedback, participants had to mentally contrast, indulge, or dwell with respect to an important interpersonal wish. They then were asked to solve a very difficult reasoning task (Pak et al., 2008, Experiment 4). Specifically, participants were given the most difficult form of Raven's Progressive Matrices (Raven, Raven, & Court, 1992), a frequently used test for measuring reasoning ability (Mackintosh, 1996). Further, it is considered to be a test well suited for measuring Spearman's g, the general factor assumed to underlie various cognitive abilities (Jensen, 1998). Even though the matrices assess individual differences in intelligence and such differences are assumed to be relatively stable (e.g., Jensen, 1989), they have been found to be amenable to motivational influences (Chaiken, Giner-Sorolla, & Chen, 1996). Thus, mental contrasting should lead to performance in line with expectations of success, whereas this effect should not be observed in the noncontrasting groups.

Students were invited to participate in two supposedly independent studies, one about interpersonal wishes and the other about cognitive skills. First, participants indicated their most important interpersonal wish and their expectations of successfully realizing the wish and listed both positive aspects of realizing the wish and negative aspects of reality standing in the way of realizing it. Thereafter, as in the previous studies, participants either had to mentally contrast aspects of the future and reality (starting with a future aspect), indulge in positive aspects of the future, or dwell on negative aspects of the reality. Next, participants completed the most difficult form of the matrices. Participants in the mental contrasting condition with high expectations of success achieved the best scores on the intelligence test, while those in the mental contrasting condition with low expectations scored the lowest. Participants in the indulging and dwelling conditions evidenced moderate levels of performance independent of their expectations of success.

Apparently, by inducing cognitive processes that benefit solving difficult tasks, mental contrasting was strong enough to make a difference in performance on the Raven intelligence test. As a limitation, the study does not explicitly test which cognitive processes boosted performance on the Progressive Matrices. However, findings from the studies described earlier suggest that by processing information entailed in negative feedback (Pak et al., 2008, Study 1) as well as by sustaining their positive self-view (Pak et al., 2008, Study 2) and optimistic attributions (Pak et al., 2008, Study 3), participants managed to show superior test performance. This interpretation of the results was supported by Jensen (1987), who found substantial correlations between degree of information processing as measured with a memory task and two visual search tasks and performance on the Progressive Matrices. Further, Stankov and Crawford (1997) observed that a positive self-view was linked to heightened performance on the Progressive Matrices. Finally, optimistic attributions that reduce test anxiety (Martin-Krumm et al., 2003) facilitate performance on intelligence tests (see Zeidner, 1995, for a review). Although we do not know which variables are responsible for the results and to what degree, the observed effects are remarkable as performance on intelligence tests are generally viewed as relatively stable (Jensen, 1989).

SUMMARY

Mental contrasting effects transferred from the interpersonal domain to the achievement domain; that is, mental contrasting of a feasible wish in one life domain enabled participants to succeed in solving a very difficult, different task in another life domain (see also Hirt, Kardes, & Markman, 2004; Markman, Lindberg, Kray, & Galinsky, 2007). The transfer of effects from one task to another and across domains suggests that acquiring mental contrasting as a self-regulatory strategy can help people not only to translate their expectations of success into goal commitment and goal striving and to master negative feedback but also to foster achievement on a more general level. Almost everybody has high feasibility desires and could thereby potentially profit from the beneficial effects of mental contrasting. By taking advantage of the transfer effects of mental contrasting, people may be able to use the procedure strategically to influence achievement in other domains, even in those in which the perceived chances of attaining the desired future are not yet high. In sum, mental contrasting seems to be a highly useful self-regulatory tool, and practicing it should promote the fulfillment of one's wishes as well as successful performance in a variety of tasks and life domains.

RELATED APPROACHES

The model of fantasy realization relates to several other approaches to goal pursuit in meaningful ways that may be grouped into those involving set goals, formed intentions, and aspired standards regarding future outcomes on the one hand and mental simulations and free images about future outcomes on the other hand. Therefore, in the final part of the chapter, we consider how mental contrasting relates to goal-setting theory as it specifies goals that are particularly fruitful for enhancing effort and motivation (Locke & Latham, 1990), to the theory of planned behavior as it describes the determinants of intentions (Ajzen, 1991; see also Fishbein & Ajzen, 1975), and to the self-regulatory control-process model of Carver and Scheier (1990) as it involves a discrepancy notion involving standards and feedback. In addition, we relate the model of fantasy realization to models of mental simulation and goal pursuit such as the reflection and evaluation model (REM; Markman, Karadogan, Lindberg, & Zell, Chapter 12, this volume; Markman & McMullen, 2003, 2005) and the model of imagination, goals, and affect (IGoA; Sanna, 2000; Sanna, Carter, & Burkley, 2005) and to the notion of process versus outcome simulations (Taylor, Pham, Rivkin, & Armor, 1998) as all three models specify mental simulations that differentially affect motivation and effort in goal pursuit.

GOALS, INTENTIONS, AND STANDARDS

The ideas as specified by the model of fantasy realization differ from those spelled out in goal-setting theory (Locke & Latham, 1990, 2002) as well as from those put forward in the theory of planned behavior (Ajzen, 1991; see also Fishbein & Ajzen, 1975). Goal-setting theory defines conscious goals as chosen or assigned and analyzes the impact of the quality and content of such goals for action. For example, setting specific, difficult goals leads to higher performance than setting "do-your-best" goals (Locke & Latham, 1990, 2002). The theory of planned behavior specifies the variables that determine behavioral intentions, such as attitudes toward the behavior, subjective norms, and importantly, perceived control over the behavior.

In contrast to goal-setting theory, the model of fantasy realization focuses on forming commitments to attaining one's fantasies rather than setting goals or standards of a certain proficiency (i.e., wanting to achieve an A versus a B on a midterm exam). In contrast to the theory of planned behavior, the model of fantasy realization explores which modes of thought (mental contrasting vs. indulging, dwelling, and reverse contrasting) translate feasibility (control beliefs) into actual behavior. The model of fantasy realization relates in parallel ways to other theories of goal pursuit (summary by Oettingen & Gollwitzer, 2001) that also specify feasibility as a critical determinant of goal striving.

Finally, the model of fantasy realization differs from the self-regulatory control-process model (Carver & Scheier, 1990). The latter tries to adapt Powers's (1973) theory of the control of perception to predict behavior, although "The heart of control theory is that organisms control, and that what they control is not behavior at all, but perception" (Powers, 1994/2005, p. 1). Carver and Scheier (1990) assumed that behavior is regulated by feedback loops. Specifically, in a discrepancy-reducing loop a perceived value (input) is compared by a comparator to a set standard, and if discrepant, the discrepancy will be reduced (output) to bring the input value closer to the standard, thereby taking into account a priori deviations as well as deviations that were caused by external influences.

In contrast, the model of fantasy realization does not assume a set standard; rather, it explicates the processes that build commitments to realizing one's future fantasies and thus are an essential part of goal setting (Locke & Latham, 1990). Second, positive fantasies differ from standards as the former are vague images about a desired future. Only by being subjected to mental contrasting do individuals acquiesce to realize these vague images in reality. Third, the model of fantasy realization does not consider behavior or behavioral effects (neither in their objective nor in their subjective form) as predictors of discrepancy reduction. It only considers perceptions of obstacles to the realization of a fantasized future (either as part of mental contrasting, dwelling, or reverse contrasting). Fourth, it does not postulate a comparator as no perceived effects of behavior are compared with a standard (or a fantasy). The model of fantasy realization simply postulates that the conjoint elaboration of the desired future and impeding reality makes people respect their expectations of success in their goal commitments and goal striving. In sum, the model of fantasy realization, unlike the self-regulatory control-process model (Carver & Scheier, 1990), is not a feedback-loop model that entails feedback, standard, and comparator as central concepts. Rather, it specifies distinct modes of thinking about future and present reality that guide people to form more or less wise goal commitments (i.e., to engage if feasibility is high and to let go if feasibility is low after mental contrasting or to engage independent of feasibility after indulging, dwelling, or reverse contrasting).

MENTAL SIMULATION: REFLECTION VERSUS EVALUATION, OUTCOME VERSUS PROCESS

The model of fantasy realization shares its focus on modes of thought with research on mental simulation and counterfactual thinking. A model that explicitly links mental simulation and counterfactual thinking to motivation and action is the REM (Markman & McMullen, 2003, 2005). This model distinguishes between assimilative and contrastive thoughts in response to upward and downward counterfactual, social, and temporal comparisons. Assimilative thoughts arise via a reflection mode, in which one vividly experiences alternative worlds, whereas contrastive thoughts arise via an evaluation mode, in which alternative worlds function as a reference point in evaluating one's present standing. With regard to emotional and motivational consequences, upward reflection leads to positive affect but diminished effort, whereas downward reflection leads to negative affect and enhanced effort. Conversely, upward evaluation (e.g., "I could have done better than I actually did") leads to negative affect but enhanced effort, whereas downward evaluation (e.g., "I could have done worse than I actually did") leads to positive affect but diminished effort. Interestingly, recent research has shown that generating upward counterfactuals in an evaluative mode elicited strategic thinking (assessed by content analysis) that benefited persistence and successful performance (Markman, McMullen, & Elizaga, 2008).

Similar to the model of fantasy realization that distinguishes between one-sided thinking (indulging and dwelling) and two-sided thinking (mental contrasting), the REM model also posits a one-sided mode of thought (reflection) and a two-sided mode of thought (evaluation). Moreover, both models postulate different emotional and motivational consequences of one-sided versus two-sided thinking. The model of fantasy realization differs, however, from the REM (among others) in three important ways. First, the model of fantasy realization deals with thoughts about the future versus present reality. Second, it postulates a mental link between future and reality by simultaneous activation of both the future and the reality in terms of the relational construct of reality "standing in the way" of realizing the future. Third, it postulates that the two-sided mode of thought of mental contrasting produces expectancy-based goal striving, while the one-sided modes of thought of indulging and dwelling fail to do so.

The REM shares commonalities with the IGoA model (Sanna, 2000; Sanna et al., 2005). Using the terminology of mental contrasting, indulging, and dwelling (Oettingen et al., 2001), the IGoA model, similar to the REM, distinguishes between reflection and evaluation modes of comparisons. The last two models agree that two-sided modes of thoughts lead to self-improvement or mood repair (depending on whether the comparison is directed upward or downward), whereas one-sided modes of thought directed upward may be described as indulging. Interestingly, the models diverge when it comes to downward reflection. The REM postulates that such thoughts serve as "wake-up calls," whereas the IGoA model postulates that they are unprofitable dwellings or ruminations (Markman et al., 2008). The model of fantasy realization might offer an integrative solution: When juxtaposed against fantasies regarding a desired future, downward reflections might trigger thoughts about obstacles standing in the way of attaining a desired future, thus leading to fantasy realization. When considered alone, however, downward reflections may typify sheer ruminative thought (Nolen-Hoeksema, 2000).

A model testing the effects of mental simulations about the future on goal striving has been postulated by Taylor and colleagues (1998). More specifically, mental simulations that focus on having attained a set standard or goal (e.g., imagining approaching the board where the aspired A is posted; outcome simulations) are less effective than mental simulations of the path toward goal attainment (i.e., imagining going home and taking the various steps of studying for an A; process simulations). The model of fantasy realization, to the contrary, holds that mentally contrasting fantasies about a desired future (e.g., doing well in the course) with present reality (e.g., being distracted by partying) leads to goal commitment in line with one's expectations of success (i.e., perceived likelihood of doing well in the course). From this perspective, planning in the form of process simulations is conceptualized as a dependent variable that facilitates goal striving. Indeed, Oettingen (2000, Study 2) observed that female doctoral students whose expectations to combine work and family life were high generated more process simulations geared at integrating the two life tasks in the mental contrasting conditions as compared to the indulging and dwelling conditions.

Mental simulations may also refer to the past, and thereby help or hurt coping with a stressor. Rivkin and Taylor (1999; Taylor et al., 1998) distinguished process versus event simulations. These simulations refer to events and emotional experiences as they happened when the stressor arose and unfolded (event simulations) versus thoughts about having successfully coped with the stressor (outcome simulations). Event simulations lead to more positive affect and active coping strategies than outcome simulations as they are assumed to be based on processing the details of the stressor and its subsequent facilitated emotion- and problem-solving regulation. The effects of mental contrasting future and present reality, to the contrary, are assumed to be based on simultaneous accessibility of future and impeding reality, which then leads to active coping when chances look promising.

CONCLUSION

The described research shows that mentally contrasting a desirable and feasible future with negative reality makes people remain resolute in their goal striving, even when people are confronted with strong negative feedback. Mental contrasting made people derive meaningful information from negative feedback and even preserved their positive self-view, as well as optimistic outlook, despite explicit negative feedback. In addition, the beneficial effects of mental contrasting surpass the striving for any one particular desired future as mental contrasting improved performance even in unrelated tasks and different life domains. The model of fantasy realization adds to the research on goal pursuit by tackling the long-neglected quest for the processes of forming goal commitments. In addition, it specifies the procedures that people can use to make their sense of efficacy fruitful for their goal striving and goal attainment.

REFERENCES

Abramson, L. Y., Seligman, M. E. P., & Teasdale, J. D. (1978). Learned helplessness in humans: Critique and reformulation. *Journal of Abnormal Psychology, 87*, 49–74.

Ajzen, I. (1991). The theory of planned behavior. *Organizational Behavior and Human Decision Processes, 50*(2), 179–211.

al' Absi, M., Bongard, S., Buchanan, T., Pincomb, G., Licinio, J., & Lovallo, W. R. (1997). Cardiovascular and neuroendocrine adjustment to public speaking and mental arithmetic stressors. *Psychophysiology, 34*, 266–275.

Armor, D. A., & Taylor, S. E. (1998). Situated optimism: Specific outcome expectancies and self-regulation. *Advances in Experimental Social Psychology, 30*, 309–379.

Armor, D. A., & Taylor, S. E. (2003). The effects of mindset on behavior: Self-regulation in deliberative and implemental frames of mind. *Personality and Social Psychology Bulletin, 29*, 89–95.

Ashford, S. J. (1986). Feedback-seeking in individual adaptation: A resource perspective. *Academy of Management Journal, 29*, 465–487.

Atkinson, J. W. (1957). Motivational determinants of risk-taking behavior. *Psychological Review, 64*, 359–372.

Audia, P. G., & Locke, E. A. (2003). Benefiting from negative feedback. *Human Resource Management Review, 13*, 631–646.

Bandura, A. (1977). Self-efficacy: Toward a unifying theory of behavioral change. *Psychological Review, 84*, 191–215.

Bandura, A. (1997). *Self-efficacy: The exercise of control*. New York: Freeman.

Blascovich, J., Seery, M. D., Mugridge, C. A., Norris, R. K., & Weisbuch, M. (2004). Predicting athletic performance from cardiovascular indexes of challenge and threat. *Journal of Experimental Social Psychology, 40*, 683–688.

Blascovich, J., & Tomaka, J. (1996). The biopsychosocial model of arousal regulation. *Advances in Experimental Social Psychology, 28*, 1–51.

Brehm, J. W., & Self, E. A. (1989). The intensity of motivation. *Annual Review of Psychology, 40*, 109–131.

Brunstein, J., & Gollwitzer, P. M. (1996). Effects of failure on subsequent performance: The importance of self-defining goals. *Journal of Personality and Social Psychology, 70*, 395–407.

Butler, R. (1987). Task-involving and ego-involving properties of evaluation: Effects of different feedback conditions on motivational, perceptions, interest, and performance. *Journal of Educational Psychology, 79*, 474–482.

Carver, C. S., & Scheier, M. F. (1990). Origins and functions of positive and negative affect: A control-process view. *Psychological Review, 97*, 19–35.

Chaiken, S., Giner-Sorolla, R., & Chen, S. (1996). Beyond accuracy: Defense and impression motives in heuristic and systematic information processing. In P. M. Gollwitzer & J. A. Bargh (Eds.), *The psychology of action: Linking cognition and motivation to behavior* (pp. 553–578). New York: Guilford Press.

Daniels, J. A., & Larson, L. M. (2001). The impact of performance feedback on counseling self-efficacy and counselor anxiety. *Counselor Education and Supervision, 41*, 120–130.

Diener, C. I., & Dweck, C. S. (1978). An analysis of learned helplessness: Continuous changes in performance, strategy, and achievement cognitions following failure. *Journal of Personality and Social Psychology, 36*, 451–462.

Dweck, C. S. (2006). *Mindset: The new psychology of success*. New York: Random House.

Dweck, C. S., & Elliot, E. S. (1988). Goals: An approach to motivation and achievement. *Journal of Personality and Social Psychology, 54*, 5–12.

Dweck, C. S., & Leggett, E. L. (1988). A social cognitive approach to motivation and personality. *Psychological Review, 95*, 256–273.

Fishbein, M., & Ajzen, I. (1975). *Belief, attitude, intention, and behavior: An introduction to theory and research*. Reading, MA: Addison-Wesley.

Gendolla, G. H. E. (1999). Self-relevance of performance, task difficulty, and task engagement assessed as cardiovascular response. *Motivation and Emotion, 23*, 45–66.

Gendolla, G. H. E., & Wright, R. A. (2005). Motivation in social settings studies of effort-related cardiovascular arousal. In J. P. Forgas, K. D. Williams, & S. M. Laham (Eds.), *Social motivation: Conscious and unconscious processes* (pp. 71–90). New York: Cambridge University Press.

Gillham, J. E., Shatté, A. J., Reivich, K. J., & Seligman, M. E. P. (2001). Optimism, pessimism, and explanatory style. In E. C. Chang (Ed.), *Optimism and pessimism: Implications for theory, research, and practice* (pp. 53–75). Washington, DC: American Psychological Association.

Gollwitzer, P. M. (1990). Action phases and mind-sets. In E. T. Higgins & R. M. Sorrentino (Eds.), *Handbook of motivation and cognition: Foundations of social behavior* (pp. 53–92). New York: Guilford Press.

Gollwitzer, P. M. (1999). Implementation intentions. Strong effects of simple plans. *American Psychologist, 54*, 493–503.

Gollwitzer, P. M., Fujita, K., & Oettingen, G. (2004). Planning and the implementation of goals. In R. F. Baumeister & K. D. Vohs (Eds.), *Handbook of self-regulation: Research, theory, and applications* (pp. 211–228). New York: Guilford Press.

Gollwitzer, P. M., & Kinney, R. F. (1989). Effects of deliberative and implemental mind-sets on illusion of control. *Journal of Personality and Social Psychology, 56*, 531–542.

Gollwitzer, P. M., & Sheeran, P. (2006). Implementation intentions and goal achievement: A meta-analysis of effects and processes. *Advances in experimental social psychology, 38*, 69–119.

Heckhausen, H. (1977). Achievement motivation and its constructs: A cognitive model. *Motivation and Emotion, 1*, 283–329.

Heckhausen, H. (1991). *Motivation and action*. New York: Springer.

Hirt, E. R., Kardes, F. R., & Markman, K. D. (2004). Activating a mental simulation mind-set through generation of alternatives: Implications for debiasing in related and unrelated domains. *Journal of Experimental Social Psychology, 40*, 374–383.

Ilgen, D. R., Fisher, C. D., & Taylor, M. S. (1979). Consequences of individual feedback on behavior in organizations. *Journal of Applied Psychology, 64*, 349–371.

Jensen, A. R. (1987). Process differences and individual differences in some cognitive tasks. *Intelligence, 11*, 107–136.

Jensen, A. R. (1989). The relationship between learning and intelligence. *Learning and Individual Differences, 1*, 37–62.

Jensen, A. R. (1998). *The g factor: The science of mental ability.* Westport, CT: Praeger.

Klinger, E. (1975). Consequences of commitment to and disengagement from incentives. *Psychological Review, 82*, 1–25.

Kluger, A. N., & DeNisi, A. (1997). Feedback interventions: Toward the understanding of a double-edged sword. *Current Directions in Psychological Science, 7*, 67–72.

Latham, G. P., & Locke, E. A. (1991). Self-regulation through goal setting. *Organizational Behavior and Human Decision Processes, 50*, 212–247.

Lewin, K. (1948). Time perspective and morale. In G. W. Lewin (Ed.), *Resolving social conflicts: Selected papers on group dynamics* (pp. 103–124). New York: Harper.

Locke, E. A., & Latham, G. P. (1990). *A theory of goal setting and task performance.* Englewood Cliffs, NJ: Prentice-Hall.

Locke, E. A., & Latham, G. P. (2002). Building a practically useful theory of goal setting and task motivation: A 35-year odyssey. *American Psychologist, 57*, 705–717.

Mackintosh, N. J. (1996). Sex differences and IQ. *Journal of Biosocial Science, 28*, 559–571.

Markman, K. D., Lindberg, M. J., Kray, L. J., & Galinsky, A. D. (2007). Implications of counterfactual structure for creative generation and analytical problem solving. *Personality and Social Psychology Bulletin, 33*, 312–324.

Markman, K. D., & McMullen, M. N. (2003). A reflection and evaluation model of comparative thinking. *Personality and Social Psychology Review, 7*, 244–267.

Markman, K. D., & McMullen, M. N. (2005). Reflective and evaluative modes of mental simulation. In D. R. Mandel, D. J. Hilton, & P. Catellani (Eds.), *The psychology of counterfactual thinking* (pp. 77–93). New York: Routledge.

Markman, K. D., McMullen, M. N., & Elizaga, R. A. (2008). Counterfactual thinking, persistence, and performance: A test of the reflection and evaluation model. *Journal of Experimental Social Psychology, 44*, 421–428.

Martin-Krumm, C. P., Sarrazin, P. G., Peterson, C., & Famose, J.-P. (2003). Explanatory style and resilience after sports failure. *Personality and Individual Differences, 35*, 1685–1695.

Mikulincer, M. (1994). *Human learned helplessness: A coping perspective.* New York: Plenum Press.

Muraven, M., Tice, D. M., & Baumeister, R. F. (1998). Self-control as a limited resource: Regulatory depletion patterns. *Journal of Personality and Social Psychology, 74*, 774–789.

Newell, A., & Simon, H. A. (1972). *Human problem solving.* Oxford, England: Prentice-Hall.

Nolen-Hoeksema, S. (2000). The role of rumination in depressive disorders and mixed anxiety/depressive symptoms. *Journal of Abnormal Psychology, 109*, 504–511.

Obrist, P. A. (1981). *Cardiovascular psychophysiology: A perspective.* New York: Plenum.

Oettingen, G. (1999). Free fantasies about the future and the emergence of developmental goals. In J. Brandstädter & R. M. Lerner (Eds.), *Action and self-development: Theory and research through the life span* (pp. 315–342). Thousand Oaks, CA: Sage.

Oettingen, G. (2000). Expectancy effects on behavior depend on self-regulatory thought. *Social Cognition, 18*, 101–129.

Oettingen, G., & Gollwitzer, P. M. (2001). Goal setting and goal striving. In A. Tesser & N. Schwarz (Eds.), *Intraindividual processes. Volume 1, Blackwell Handbook in Social Psychology* (pp. 329–347). Oxford, England: Blackwell.

Oettingen, G., Hönig, G., & Gollwitzer, P. M. (2000). Effective self-regulation of goal attainment. *International Journal of Educational Research, 33*, 705–732.

Oettingen, G., & Mayer, D. (2002). The motivating function of thinking about the future: Expectations versus fantasies. *Journal of Personality and Social Psychology, 83*, 1198–1212.

Oettingen, G., & Mayer, D. (2007). *Mental contrasting and the readiness to form implementation intentions.* Unpublished manuscript.

Oettingen, G., Mayer, D., Sevincer, A. T., Stephens, E. J., & Hagenah, M. (2008). *Making fantasies about the future come true: The role of energization.* Manuscript submitted for publication.

Oettingen, G., Mayer, D., Thorpe, J. S., Janetzke, H., & Lorenz, S. (2005). Turning fantasies about positive and negative futures into self-improvement goals. *Motivation and Emotion, 29*, 237–267.

Oettingen, G., Pak, H., & Schnetter, K. (2001). Self-regulation of goal-setting: Turning free fantasies about the future into binding goals. *Journal of Personality and Social Psychology, 80,* 736–753.

Pak, H., Kappes, A., & Oettingen, G. (2008). *Responding to negative feedback: The role of mental contrasting.* Submitted for publication.

Peterson, C., Maier, S. F., & Seligman, M. E. P. (1993). *Learned helplessness: A theory for the age of personal control.* New York: Oxford University Press.

Peterson, C., Semmel, A., Baeyer, C., Abramson, L. Y., Metalsky, G., & Seligman, M. E. P. (1982). The attributional style questionnaire. *Cognitive Therapy and Research, 6,* 287–299.

Powers, M. A. (1994/2005). Direction_for_psychology.pdf. Retrieved June 18, 2008 from www.livincontrol-systems.com/intro_papers/direction_for_psych.pdf

Powers, W. T. (1973). *Behavior: The control of perception.* New York: Aldine/DeGruyter.

Raven, J., Raven, J. C., & Court, J. H. (1992). *Manual for Raven's Progressive Matrices and Mill Hill Vocabulary Scales.* Oxford, England: Oxford Psychologists Press.

Rivkin, I., & Taylor, S. E. (1999). The effects of mental simulation on coping with controllable stressful events. *Personality and Social Psychology Bulletin, 25,* 1451–1462.

Ryan, R. M., & Frederick, C. (1997). On energy, personality, and health: Subjective vitality as a dynamic reflection of well-being. *Journal of Personality, 65,* 529–565.

Sanna, L. J. (2000). Mental simulation, affect, and personality: A conceptual framework. *Current Directions in Psychological Science, 9,* 168–173.

Sanna, L. J., Carter, S. E., & Burkley, E. (2005). Yesterday, today, and tomorrow: Counterfactual thinking and beyond. In A. Strathman & J. Joireman (Eds.), *Understanding behavior in the context of time: Theory, research, and application* (pp. 165–185). Mahwah, NJ: Erlbaum.

Sedikides, C., & Green, J. D. (2000). On the self-protective nature of inconsistency-negativity management: Using the person memory paradigm to examine self-referent memory. *Journal of Personality and Social Psychology, 79,* 906–922.

Sedikides, C., & Green, J. D. (2004). What I don't recall can't hurt me: Information negativity versus information inconsistency as determinants of memorial self-defense. *Social Cognition, 22,* 4–29.

Seligman, M. E. P. (1991). *Learned optimism.* New York: Knopf.

Stankov, L., & Crawford, J. D. (1997). Self-confidence and performance on tests of cognitive abilities. *Intelligence, 25,* 93–109.

Taylor, S. E. (1991). Asymmetrical effects of positive and negative events: The mobilization-minimization hypothesis. *Psychological Bulletin, 103,* 67–85.

Taylor, S. E., & Brown, J. D. (1988). Illusion and well-being: A social psychological perspective on mental health. *Psychological Bulletin, 103,* 193–210.

Taylor, S. E., & Gollwitzer, P. M. (1995). Effects of mindset on positive illusions. *Journal of Personality and Social Psychology, 69,* 213–226.

Taylor, S. E., Kemeny, M. E., Reed, G. M., Bower, J. E., & Gruenewald, T. L. (2000). Psychological resources, positive illusions, and health. *American Psychologist, 55,* 99–109.

Taylor, S. E., Pham, L. B., Rivkin, I., & Armor, D. A. (1998). Harnessing the imagination: Mental simulation, self-regualtion, and coping. *American Psychologist, 53,* 429–439.

Tomaka, J., Blascovich, J., Kibler, J., & Ernst, J. M. (1997). Cognitive and physiological antecedents of threat and challenge appraisal. *Journal of Personality and Social Psychology, 73,* 63–72.

Vroom, V. H. (1964). *Work and motivation.* Oxford, England: Wiley.

Weiner, B. (1986). Attribution, emotion, and action. In R. M. Sorrentino & E. T. Higgins (Eds.), *Handbook of motivation and cognition: Foundations of social behavior* (pp. 281–312). New York: Guilford Press.

Wicklund, R. A., & Gollwitzer, P. M. (1982). *Symbolic self-completion.* Hillsdale, NJ: Erlbaum.

Wright, R. A. (1996). Brehm's theory of motivation as a model of effort and cardiovascular response. In P. M. Gollwitzer & J. A. Bargh (Eds.), *The psychology of action: Linking cognition and motivation to behavior* (pp. 424–453). New York: Guilford Press.

Zeidner, M. (1995). Adaptive coping with test situations: A review of the literature. *Educational Psychologist, 30,* 123–133.

27 On the Consequences of Mentally Simulating Future Foregone Outcomes: A Regret Regulation Perspective

Marcel Zeelenberg and Rik Pieters

INTRODUCTION

When deciding what to do, we often think about the consequences of our actions and evaluate their attractiveness and likelihood of occurrence. Our choices are then at least partly based on these appraisals. However, when decisions are important enough, we also tend to think about how we would evaluate our outcomes in light of the outcomes forgone. This has sometimes been referred to as *prefactual thinking* (e.g., Sanna, 1996). For example, when choosing to invest all our savings in risky stocks, we may envision the situation that the stock market crashes and compare that outcome to the alternative in which our money would have been securely placed in a savings account. In turn, entertaining such prefactual thoughts arouses emotions. In this particular example, one could already feel the regret on learning that the savings account would have dramatically outperformed the stock market investment. This feeling of potential regret concerning future worlds is often called *anticipated regret* or *anticipatory regret*. More than two decades of research have shown that when this type of regret is elicited, it can exert a strong influence on our behavior (for a review, see Zeelenberg, 1999a). More specifically, decision makers tend to regulate their regrets, such that they behave in a way that allows them to avoid experiencing this emotion in the future. In this chapter, we review what we have learned over these years and what remains to be learned, and we do so by presenting our attempt to formulate a theory of regret that integrates these observations and delineates opportunities for future research. We first address what regret is before turning to the effects of its anticipation.

Regret is the emotion that we experience when realizing or imagining that our current situation would have been better if only we had decided differently. It is a backward-looking emotion signaling an unfavorable evaluation of a decision. It is also an unpleasant feeling, coupled with a clear sense of self-blame concerning its causes and strong wishes to undo the current situation. This retrospective type of regret that is felt when decisions go awry has attracted much research attention from psychologists. As with many topics in decision research, the work of Kahneman and Tversky was influential here (e.g., Kahneman & Tversky, 1982a, 1982b). Their work on the simulation heuristic was the basis for further studies on counterfactual thinking and emotion, and it paved the way for numerous articles addressing the question of whether we regret actions more than inactions. Currently, a good number of things is known about the things that people regret (Gilovich & Medvec, 1995; Roese & Summerville, 2005), how regret feels, and how it relates to other constructs such as disappointment and cognitive dissonance (Landman, 1993; Zeelenberg, Van Dijk, Manstead, & van der Pligt, 1998), how regret may be experienced as a hot emotion or a wistful emotion (Gilovich,

Medvec, & Kahneman, 1998), and how regret may have an impact on subsequent behaviors and choices (Zeelenberg, Inman, & Pieters, 2001).

Less is known about the phenomenology of anticipated regret. This prospective emotion that is forward looking, potentially exerting an influence on the choices we are still to make, has received the most attention from decision researchers. Its effects, however, are reasonably well documented. The notion of anticipated decision regret has been put forward as a possible explanation for why decision makers do not behave in line with theories of rational choice. Perhaps the origin of modern regret research can be found in the proposal of the "minimax regret" principle (Lee, 1971; Luce & Raiffa, 1957; Savage, 1951). According to this principle, decision makers, before making a choice, first compute the maximum of possible regret for each option. Regret is operationally defined as the value difference between an obtained outcome and the best possible outcome that could have resulted from the rejected options. The minimax regret principle prescribes decision makers to choose that option for which the potential maximum regret is minimal. However, the minimax regret principle does not take into account the likelihood of the regret occurring. That is, a particular option may be associated with the highest possible regret, but the chance of ending up with this regret is very low. In this case, the principle still tells one to avoid that option. As such, the minimax regret principle is very conservative or pessimistic.

Later, in the early 1980s, different theorists (Bell, 1982; Loomes & Sugden, 1982; Sage & White, 1983; see also Humphrey, 2004) proposed regret theories that take the probability of regret into account and so provided more plausible accounts for the influence of anticipated regret on decision making. Direct tests of predictions derived from regret theory did not provide unequivocal support (Harless, 1992; Leland, 1998; Starmer & Sugden, 1993), but the main psychological assumptions have been supported (for a review, see Zeelenberg, 1999a). The first assumption is that we may experience emotions as a consequence of our decisions. Decision makers experience regret when the outcome of the rejected option would have been better and rejoice when the outcome of the rejected option would have been worse (Zeelenberg et al., 1998). A subsequent assumption is that these emotions have an impact on how we evaluate decision outcomes (Inman, Dyer, & Jia, 1997; Mellers, Schwartz, & Ritov, 1999; Taylor, 1997).

The most important assumption in these economic regret theories is that the impact of regret is taken into account before we decide and thus may play an important role in determining what we choose. This effect of anticipated regret on decision making has also been supported empirically. Among the pioneers here are Simonson (1992) and Inman and McAlister (1994). In one study, Simonson offered participants the choice between a current, moderate sale or waiting for a later, possibly better sale. In another study, he asked participants to choose between an unknown cheap videocassette recorder (VCR) and a more expensive, well-known brand name. Half of the participants were simply asked to make a choice, and participants displayed no clear preference. The remaining participants were first asked to think about the regret they might feel after making the choice and to indicate for which of the options they would feel most regret. After this regret induction, participants predominantly chose the safer option (the current sale and the brand name VCR). Apparently, making decision makers consider future regret urges them to make decisions that shield them from those regrets. Inman and McAlister studied the fact that the usage of discount coupons shows a small but noticeable increase just before the expiration date. They modeled supermarket scanner data to describe the coupon usage by consumers and showed that a model including a regret term accounted for significantly more variance than a traditional utility-based model. In later years, these efforts have been followed up and applied in many different fields.

A THEORY OF REGRET REGULATION

Recently, we have proposed an integrative theory of regret (Pieters & Zeelenberg, 2007; Zeelenberg & Pieters, 2006b, 2007). The core idea in our approach is that people are regret averse, and that

TABLE 27.1

Propositions of Regret Regulation Theory

1. Regret is an aversive, cognitive emotion that people are motivated to regulate to maximize outcomes in the short term and learn to maximize them in the long run.

2. Regret is a comparison-based emotion of self-blame experienced when people realize or imagine that their present situation would have been better had they decided differently in the past.

3. Regret is distinct from related other specific emotions such as anger, disappointment, envy, guilt, sadness, and shame and from general negative affect on the basis of its appraisals, experiential content, and behavioral consequences.

4. Individual differences in the tendency to experience regret are reliably related to the tendency to maximize and compare one's outcomes.

5. Regret can be experienced about past (*retrospective regret*) and future (*anticipated* or *prospective regret*) decisions.

6. Anticipated regret is experienced when decisions are difficult and important and when the decision maker expects to learn the outcomes of both the chosen and the rejected options quickly.

7. Regret can stem from decisions to act and from decisions not to act: The more justifiable the decision, the less regret.

8. Regret can be experienced about decision processes (*process regret*) and decision outcomes (*outcome regret*).

9. The intensity of regret is contingent on the ease of comparing actual with counterfactual decision processes and outcomes and the importance, salience, and reversibility of the discrepancy.

10. Regret aversion is distinct from risk aversion, and they jointly and independently influence behavioral decisions.

11. Regret regulation strategies are goal, decision, alternative, or feeling focused and implemented based on their accessibility and their instrumentality to the current overarching goal.

Note: Adapted from "A Theory of Regret Regulation 1.1," by R. Pieters and M. Zeelenberg, 2007, *Journal of Consumer Psychology, 17*, 29–35.

as a consequence, they try to regulate their regrets. By this we mean that people are motivated to avoid regret, and when it happens despite these attempts, they engage in ameliorative behaviors or manage, deny, or suppress their experience of regret. Our theory is pragmatic in that it stresses how emotions exist for the sake of behavioral guidance. Put differently, the theory assumes that "feeling is for doing" (Zeelenberg & Pieters, 2006a; Zeelenberg, Nelissen, & Pieters, 2007; see also Markman, Karadogan, Lindberg, & Zell, Chapter 12, this volume). Such a pragmatic approach is needed to understand what the experience of regret entails, which behaviors it motivates, and how it can shape subsequent decision making. Our regret regulation theory thus acknowledges that regret bridges the past and the future in the present.

Our theory is consistent with other prominent theories of counterfactual thinking (e.g., Markman et al., Chapter 12, this volume; Markman & McMullen, 2003; Roese, 1997, 2005; Roese & Summerville, 2005; Zeelenberg, 1999b) that have also provided evidence indicating that retrospective regret can be "good" to the extent that it spurs further corrective action. Of course, we have benefited from these efforts and build on them. In addition, which is of particular relevance for the current chapter, we offer evidence for how decision makers cope not only with these retrospective regrets but also with the prospective form.

We do not provide a detailed description of our regret regulation theory here (but refer readers to Zeelenberg & Pieters, 2007, and Pieters & Zeelenberg, 2007). What we do, however, is illuminate that part of our theory that deals with the causes and consequences of anticipated regret. Table 27.1 shows the complete set of propositions of regret regulation theory and reflects the now-abundant knowledge of the antecedents and experience of regret and how this emotion can be differentiated from related experiences. For now, we will focus on Propositions 5, 6, 10, and 11 as these are relevant for our current discussion of anticipated regret. Along the lines of these propositions, we review research on anticipated regret, demonstrate how it enters into decision-making processes, and show how it may help and hinder decision makers in reaching their goals.

REGRET BRIDGES THE PAST AND THE FUTURE IN THE PRESENT

Our selective overview described the existence of two types of regret, both experienced in the present, but one referring to the past and the other looking toward the future. This bifurcation is captured by Proposition 5 of regret regulation theory:

> **Proposition 5:** Regret can be experienced about past (*retrospective regret*) and future (*anticipated* or *prospective regret*) decisions.

Interestingly, whether anticipated regret should be considered an emotional state has been the topic of some disagreement. Some refer to it as a rational calculation, similar to its treatment in the minimax regret tradition, and others argue that anticipated emotions are merely (cognitive) predictions about future emotions (e.g., Frijda, 2004). We, however, believe that to the extent that the anticipation of future regrets feeds into the present experience and thus acquires the experiential qualities of any other emotion, it is an emotion, albeit strongly cognitively based. In that respect, we side with Janis and Mann (1977), who, three decades ago, stated that:

> Anticipatory regret is a convenient generic term to refer to the main psychological effects of the various worries that beset a decision-maker before any losses actually materialize. ... Such worries, which include anticipatory guilt and shame, provoke hesitation and doubt, making salient the realization that even the most attractive of the available choices might turn out badly. (p. 222)

A next relevant question concerns when decision makers will engage in the anticipation of regret. The when question is relevant because only when regret is anticipated can we observe its effect on decision making. It is obvious, also from introspection, that we are not constantly anticipating regret about the choices that we make. We make so many choices on a daily basis (whether to get up in the morning, what clothes to put on, whether to have breakfast, and if so, what, etc.) that considering the potential regret for all of those would not only be a daunting task, but also would paralyze us because no time would be left for doing anything else. Fortunately, boundary conditions for anticipated regret have been suggested in the literature. For example, regret is most likely to be anticipated when decisions are difficult, such as when there is no dominant alternative, and decision makers have to trade off attributes (e.g., car A is cheaper but also less safe than car B) (Anderson, 2003; Janis & Mann, 1977). In these cases, there is ample room for self-recrimination when the chosen alternative does not result in the best outcome. Obviously, this holds most for decisions that have some relevance for decision makers or their social networks. The more important decision outcomes are, the more likely it is that decision makers simulate possible futures and their emotional reactions to them. Moreover, more important decisions will result in more intense regret when things go awry. In addition, the anticipation of regret is expected when the negative consequences that might result from the decision could start to materialize almost immediately after the decision is made. If this is not the case, however, and outcomes only become known after a considerable time, decision makers may discount the possible regret that may arise from this decision. Richard, van der Pligt, and De Vries (1996), in the context of condom use, showed that when long-term consequences are made salient before the decision, regret is anticipated and influences the decision. A final, but critical condition for the occurrence of anticipated regret is the expectation of feedback about the outcome of the rejected options (Bell, 1983). Much of our own research has dealt with that condition and is discussed later in this chapter. First, let us summarize what has just been described in the following proposition:

> **Proposition 6:** Anticipated regret is experienced when decisions are difficult and important and when the decision maker expects to learn the outcomes of both the chosen and rejected options quickly.

CONSEQUENCES OF REGRET AVERSION

Decision makers are considered to be regret averse, implying that they are motivated to avoid feeling regret (see also Proposition 1 in Table 27.1). Regret aversion has sometimes been equated to risk aversion, as illustrated by the saying that one can better be safe than sorry. Contrary to this commonly held belief, in a series of studies (Zeelenberg, Beattie, van der Pligt, & De Vries, 1996), we demonstrated that anticipated regret may promote both risk-avoiding and risk-seeking tendencies. The design of the three experiments reported in that article was as follows: Participants were given a choice between two gambles, one relatively risky and the other relatively safe. They knew that they would always learn the outcome of the gamble they chose. Importantly, feedback on the gambles was manipulated orthogonally to the riskiness of the gambles. In all experiments, there was a "safe feedback" condition, in which the outcome of the safe gamble would always become known to the participants (irrespective of whether it was chosen), and a "risky feedback" condition, in which the outcome of the risky gamble would always become known to the participants. Participants in the safe feedback condition were predicted and found to choose the safe gambles more often. The safe gamble would provide them with feedback on the chosen gamble only and thus protect them from threatening feedback on the risky gamble. Likewise, participants in the risky feedback condition, who would always learn the outcome of the risky gamble, opted more often for the risky gamble. This pattern was found in all three studies, across both high- and low-variance gambles, and with gambles involving both gains and losses. These studies thus showed that the anticipation of regret can promote risk-averse and risk-seeking tendencies.

These findings were extended to interpersonal decision making (Zeelenberg and Beattie, 1997, Experiments 2a and 2b). Here, we introduced feedback on the minimal acceptable offer in ultimatum bargaining. The ultimatum game is played by the following simple procedure: Two players are allotted a sum of money (e.g., $10). Player 1 (often called the proposer) offers some portion of the money (e.g., $4) to Player 2 (the responder). If the responder accepts, the responder gets the $4, and the proposer gets the rest ($6). If the responder rejects the offer, both players get nothing. Although economic theory prescribes and predicts that proposers should offer as little as possible, research finds that proposers are most likely to offer a 50/50 split, and responders tend to reject offers lower than 20% (for a review of ultimatum game studies, see Camerer & Thaler, 1995). How might anticipated regret influence the behavior of proposers? Proposers can regret two things: offering too little money when the offer is rejected and offering too much when the offer is accepted. If we consider the fact that the modal offer is 50%, and that offers over 20% are almost always accepted, there is a greater likelihood of regretting offers that are too high. In addition, Zeelenberg and Beattie manipulated whether proposers knew in advance that they would obtain feedback about the responder's minimal acceptable offer after they made their offer. Participants in the feedback condition were told that they would always learn the responder's minimal acceptable offer and thus that they would learn the exact amount of money that they could have or should have offered to get their offer accepted. As expected, participants in the feedback condition offered significantly less money to the responder (36% on average) than did the participants in the no feedback control condition (43%).

Larrick and Boles (1995) found similar results. In their study, participants negotiated about a signing bonus they could earn when deciding to work for a certain company. Participants either expected to learn or not to learn the offer of a competing company after they reached an agreement. Participants who expected to learn the competing offer wanted to have a higher bonus and were less likely to reach agreement than those who did not expect to learn the competing offer. In line with this, more recent work by Galinsky, Seiden, Kim, and Medvec (2002) showed that compared to those who had to negotiate multiple rounds for an agreement, negotiators whose first offer was immediately accepted were more likely to generate counterfactuals about how they could have done better and hence were less satisfied with the agreement.

Interestingly, we extended these findings concerning the role of expected feedback to real-life decision making (Zeelenberg & Pieters, 2004). We conducted four studies in which we compared people's reactions to and decisions to participate in two lotteries in the Netherlands—the Postcode Lottery and the National State Lottery. The State Lottery is a traditional lottery in which one has to buy a ticket with a number printed on it. In the Postcode Lottery, one's postcode is the ticket number, and hence even if one has chosen not to participate, one can still find out whether one would have won had one played. The results of these studies clearly show that because of the particular type of feedback that is present in the Postcode Lottery, players in that lottery not only anticipate regret over not playing, but also their decisions to continue playing are influenced by this anticipation. These participation decisions could thus be interpreted as purchasing not only a lottery ticket but at the same time an insurance against regret over not participating. Considerations of this kind were completely absent for State Lottery players, showing the moderating effect of lottery type.

It is important to note that similar findings have been obtained by several others, including Ritov (1996), Ritov and Baron (1995), Guthrie (1999), and Van Dijk and Zeelenberg (2007). Moreover, Humphrey (2004) provided a mathematical formalization of these effects in his feedback conditional regret theory. Together, these findings are summarized in the following proposition:

Proposition 10: Regret aversion is distinct from risk aversion, and they jointly and independently influence behavioral decisions.

Thus, decision makers are motivated to avoid regret, but we should also note that they are unlikely to always succeed in this. One reason is the sheer amount of decisions that we have to make. No one will make the right choice every time. The central question in our regret regulation theory is: How do we cope with these regrets? Or, phrased more appropriately for our current focus on anticipated regret: How do we prevent future regret from happening? We think that individuals make use of a number of strategies for achieving this goal, as expressed in our Proposition 11:

Proposition 11: Regret regulation strategies are goal, decision, alternative, or feeling focused and implemented based on their accessibility and their instrumentality to the current overarching goal.

The main strategic options for regret regulation are the same for anticipated and experienced regret, although the specific mechanics differ, as shown in Table 27.2. People can employ goal-focused, decision-focused, alternative-focused and feeling-focused regulation strategies. *Goal-focused strategies* of regret regulation deal with the setting of goals and the critical reference value of an outcome (below which one becomes unsatisfied). *Decision-focused strategies* are aimed at the specific decision process and outcomes at hand. *Alternative-focused strategies* deal with the non-chosen alternative. Finally, *feeling-focused strategies* address the experience of regret directly rather than indirectly as the previous two do. We proposed our classification of regret regulation strategies on the basis of previous empirical and theoretical work. An obvious and often-used classification to apply here as well would have been the distinction between problem-focused and emotion-focused coping (Folkman & Lazarus, 1980). However, we agree with Lazarus (1996): "Although it is tempting to classify any coping thought or act as either problem-focused or emotion-focused, in reality any coping thought or act can serve both or perhaps many other functions" (p. 293).

We do not expect that all regulation strategies will be equally successful, and we can even expect that some actually increase long-term regret. Before turning to the different strategies in decision makers' repertoires, it should be noted that, to date, not all possible strategies have been equally extensively researched. This makes our enterprise somewhat speculative, but at the same time it opens up many interesting avenues for future research. The different strategies are presented in Table 27.2 and described next.

TABLE 27.2

Strategies for Preventing Future Regret as Proposed by Regret Regulation Theory

1. Goal focused
   a. Decrease goal level
2. Decision focused
   a. Increase decision quality
   b. Increase decision justifiability
   c. Transfer decision responsibility
   d. Delay or avoid decision
3. Alternative focused
   a. Restrict or enlarge choice set
   b. Ensure decision reversibility
   c. Avoid feedback about forgone alternatives
4. Feeling focused
   a. Anticipate regret

Note: Adapted from "A Theory of Regret Regulation 1.1," by R. Pieters and M. Zeelenberg, 2007, *Journal of Consumer Psychology, 17*, 29–35.

ANTICIPATED REGRET REGULATION

GOAL-FOCUSED STRATEGIES

Decrease Goal Level

The simplest way of regulating negative emotions is to lower one's standards and be satisfied with what one has. In other words, better to have 1 bird in the hand than 10 in the bush. This could also be done before being confronted with bad outcomes. The pitfall might be that when we take decreasing one's goal level to the extreme, it may also take away the motivation to strive for anything better than what we currently have.

DECISION-FOCUSED STRATEGIES

Improve Decision Quality

A straightforward way to prevent future regret is to (try to) improve the quality of the decision process and resulting outcomes. There is no reason to regret a good decision. One can accomplish this, for instance, by increasing internal (i.e., in memory) or external information search (Ordóñez, Benson, & Beach, 1999). Decision makers may also attempt to do so by applying decision rules that use as much of the available information as possible, such as by using a linear-compensatory rule. Anticipated regret thereby increases decision effort, which by itself already provides insurance against regret (Van Dijk, van der Pligt, & Zeelenberg, 1999). Also, extensive information search promotes learning and should be conducive to reducing long-term regret, except when all the decision effort in hindsight turns out to have been in vain. As a recent example, it has been suggested that professional counseling about sterilization will allow both men and women to make better decisions and thereby reduce the occurrence of regret and reversal requests (Brechin & Bigrigg, 2006).

Delay or Avoid Decision

Another straightforward way to prevent future regret is by delaying decisions or avoiding them completely. Making no decision prevents regret because one simply cannot make a "wrong" decision. Thus, the anticipation of regret may result in a negative decision attitude; it can make people decision averse (Beattie, Baron, Hershey, & Spranca, 1994). However likely this is, and research shows that it is likely (Anderson, 2003), such a strategy may not be useful because many situations require a decision. In addition, there may be long-term disadvantages to decision avoidance because, as Gilovich and Medvec (1995) have convincingly shown, we may eventually regret our inactive decision attitude. Postponement or other kinds of decision delay have the same disadvantages as avoidance. In addition, to the extent that the anticipated regret of making the wrong decision enhances rumination during the period of postponement, the decision conflict may only mount, and the resulting experienced regret may be enhanced as well if indeed the decision goes awry.

Increase Decision Justifiability

The strategy to increase decision justifiability may be the best documented. A fruitful way of avoiding regrets is to opt for "normal" choices that are easily justified. This idea is central in decision justification theory (for a review, see Connolly & Zeelenberg, 2002). In this theory, it is proposed that regret consists of two components, one associated with the (comparative) evaluation of the decision outcome with outcomes forgone, the other with the feelings of responsibility and self-blame associated with having made a poor, ill-justified choice. The experience of regret is then thought to be a combination of these two components. Put differently, regret stems from bad decisions and from deciding badly. This also explains why default options generally produce less regret than switch decisions and the reversal of this effect when prior experience clearly calls for action (Inman & Zeelenberg, 2002). Moreover, it accounts for the finding that intention-behavior consistency (i.e., being a "prescriptive norm") lowers regret independent of the decision outcome (Pieters & Zeelenberg, 2005).

Transfer Decision Responsibility

As regret arises when one is personally responsible for bad decisions, one strategy for reducing future regret is the transferal of responsibility for a potentially regretful decision to others. Most frequently, this occurs when assigning responsibility to experts, such as investment advisors, doctors, marriage counselors, or partners ("I did exactly what you told me to"). There are more specific strategies for dealing with the responsibility of anticipated future regret as well. Farnsworth (1998, p. 19), in his book on regret in the context of contract law writes, "If you sometimes had 'past Regrets' because of unexpected difficulties in performing, you could allay your 'future Fears' by including in your agreement a force majeure clause, excusing you from performing should such difficulties arise." A potential drawback of this strategy, in addition to losing control over one's own decisions, is that when a suboptimal outcome arises, one can still regret transferring responsibility. This may be one of the reasons why people are reluctant to solve difficult decisions with a coin toss—it does not really take away the responsibility.

ALTERNATIVE-FOCUSED STRATEGIES

Ensure Decision Reversibility

If one cannot improve the quality of the decision (e.g., because of an inherently uncertain future), or increase decision justifiability, transfer responsibility to another agent, or postpone the decision, then decision makers may aim to increase the reversibility of a decision. That is, they may anticipate future regret that arises from being stuck with a suboptimal choice and thus aim to make reversible choices. Thus, consumers' anticipations of regret are attenuated, and their impact on choice is diminished when they receive lowest-price guarantees (McConnell et al., 2000). Plus, insurance has been shown to have similar effects (Hetts, Boninger, Armor, Gleicher, & Nathanson, 2000). Thus, when decisions or their consequences can be reversed, less regret is anticipated. Interestingly, however, it is not yet clear whether retrospective regret is influenced in a similar way. Gilbert and Ebert (2002) found that people indeed preferred reversible decisions to irreversible ones, but that irreversible decisions resulted in more satisfaction, perhaps because reversibility elicited counterfactual thinking, which then feeds regret.

Avoid Feedback About Foregone Alternatives

Because regret stems from outcome comparisons, decision makers can avoid regret by avoiding feedback about nonchosen options. This tendency was first described when we discussed our research on the consequences of regret aversion (summarized in Proposition 10).

FEELING-FOCUSED STRATEGIES

Anticipate Regret

Sometimes, the anticipation of possible regret is deemed to make the experience less aversive, as when people prepare to feel pain at the dentist. Put differently, bracing for the worst can make bad outcomes look good (see Carroll & Shepperd, Chapter 28, this volume). We must note, however, that this only works when it does not have an impact on our choices. It can in fact be counterproductive when this anticipation of regret leads people to avoid decisions or choose different options. Thus, this is typically a strategy that consumers may want to use after the decision is made but before the outcomes are known.

These regulatory aspects of anticipated regret are thus aimed at preventing regret from happening or minimizing its potential intensity. The strategies that we describe could play an important role in coping with anticipated regret and preventing future regret. We do not claim to be complete in this description and hope that future research tests our speculations and documents other ways in which decision makers cope with the threat of future regret.

CODA

Since the beginning of the 1980s, research on anticipated regret and prefactual thinking has flourished. Much has been learned, and by now it is well established that, when confronted with important and difficult choices about which outcomes and outcomes forgone will soon become known, decision makers mentally simulate what might happen and what might not. These imagination processes are not only useful in the sense that they help us to oversee the consequences of our decisions. They also facilitate the arousal of emotional reactions such as anticipated regret, which because of its motivational characteristics, may help us make better choices. We have proposed an integrative theory of regret regulation, described how the theory builds on existing knowledge about the anticipation of regret, and issued an invitation for additional research on this topic. Regret is the prototypical decision-related emotion, and anticipated regret draws heavily on our ability to mentally simulate the future. We hope that a better understanding of the psychology of regret will result in an improved understanding of the psychology of decision making and, more generally, will provide insight into the various processes that are involved in the mental simulation of alternative realities.

REFERENCES

Anderson, C. J. (2003). The psychology of doing nothing: Forms of decision avoidance result from reason and emotion. *Psychological Bulletin, 129,* 139–167.

Beattie, J., Baron, J., Hershey, J. C., & Spranca, M. D. (1994). Psychological determinants of decision attitude. *Journal of Behavioral Decision Making, 7,* 129–144.

Bell, D. E. (1982). Regret in decision making under uncertainty. *Operations Research, 30,* 961–981.

Bell, D. E. (1983). Risk premiums for decision regret. *Management Science, 29,* 1156–1166.

Brechin, S., & Bigrigg, A. (2006). Male and female sterilisation. *Current Obstetrics & Gynaecology, 16,* 39–46.

Camerer, C., & Thaler, R. H. (1995). Ultimatums, dictators and manners. *Journal of Economic Perspectives, 2,* 209–219.

Connolly, T., & Zeelenberg, M. (2002). Regret and decision making. *Current Directions in Psychological Science, 11,* 212–216.

Farnsworth, E. A. (1998). *Changing your mind: The law of regretted decisions.* New Haven, CT: Yale University Press.

Folkman, S., & Lazarus, R. S. (1980). An analysis of coping in a middle-aged community sample. *Journal of Health and Social Behavior, 21,* 219–231.

Frijda, N. H. (2004). Emotion and action. In A. S. R. Manstead, N. Frijda, & A. Fischer (Eds.), *Feelings and emotions: The Amsterdam symposium* (pp. 158–173). Cambridge, England: Cambridge University Press.

Galinsky, A. D., Seiden, V. L., Kim, P. H., & Medvec, V. H. (2002). The dissatisfaction of having your first offer accepted: The role of counterfactual thinking in negotiations. *Personality and Social Psychology Bulletin, 28,* 271–283.

Gilbert, D. T., & Ebert, J. E. J. (2002). Decisions and revisions: The affective forecasting of changeable outcomes. *Journal of Personality and Social Psychology, 82,* 503–514.

Gilovich, T., & Medvec, V. H. (1995). The experience of regret: What, when, and why. *Psychological Review, 102,* 379–395.

Gilovich, T., Medvec, V. H., & Kahneman, D. (1998). Varieties of regret: A debate and partial resolution. *Psychological Review, 105,* 602–605.

Guthrie, C. (1999). Better settle than sorry: The regret aversion theory of litigation behavior. *University of Illinois Law Review, 1999,* 43–90.

Harless, D. W. (1992). Actions versus prospects: The effect of problem presentation on regret. *American Economic Review, 82,* 634–649.

Hetts, J. J., Boninger, D. S., Armor, D. A., Gleicher, F., & Nathanson, A. (2000). The influence of anticipated counterfactual regret on behavior. *Psychology and Marketing, 17,* 345–368.

Humphrey, S. J. (2004). Feedback-conditional regret theory and testing regret-aversion in risky choice. *Journal of Economic Psychology, 25,* 839–857.

Inman, J. J., Dyer, J. S., & Jia, J. (1997). A generalized utility model of disappointment and regret effects on post-choice valuation. *Marketing Science, 16,* 97–111.

Inman, J. J., & McAlister, L. (1994). Do coupon expiration dates affect consumer behavior? *Journal of Marketing Research, 16,* 423–428.

Inman, J. J., & Zeelenberg, M. (2002). Regret repeat versus switch decisions: The attenuation role of decision justifiability. *Journal of Consumer Research, 29,* 116–128.

Janis, I. L., & Mann, L. (1977). *Decision making.* New York: Free Press.

Kahneman, D., & Tversky, A. (1982a). The psychology of preferences. *Scientific American, 246,* 160–173.

Kahneman, D., & Tversky, A. (1982b). The simulation heuristic. In D. Kahneman, P. Slovic, & A. Tversky (Eds.), *Judgment under uncertainty: Heuristics and biases* (pp. 201–208). New York: Cambridge University Press.

Landman, J. (1993). *Regret: The persistence of the possible.* New York: Oxford University Press.

Larrick, R. P., & Boles, T. L. (1995). Avoiding regret in decisions with feedback: A negotiation example. *Organizational Behavior and Human Decision Processes, 63,* 87–97.

Lazarus, R. S. (1996). The role of coping in the emotions and how coping changes over the life course. In C. Maletesta-Magni & S. H. McFadden (Eds.), *Handbook of emotion, adult development, and aging* (pp. 289–306). New York: Academic Press.

Lee, W. (1971). The effects of expected value difference and expected regret ratio on preference strength. *American Journal of Psychology, 84,* 194–204

Leland, J. W. (1998). Similarity judgments in choice under uncertainty: A reinterpretation of the predictions of regret theory. *Management Science, 44,* 659–672.

Loomes, G., & Sugden, R. (1982). Regret theory: An alternative theory of rational choice under uncertainty. *Economic Journal, 92,* 805–824.

Luce, R. D., & Raiffa, H. (1957). *Games and decisions.* New York: Wiley.

Markman, K. D., & McMullen, M. N. (2003). A reflection and evaluation model of comparative thinking. *Personality and Social Psychology Review, 7,* 244–267.

McConnell, A. R., Niedermeier, K. E., Leibold, J. M., El-Alayli, A. G., Chin, P. P., & Kuiper, N. M. (2000). What if I find it cheaper someplace else? Role of prefactual thinking and anticipated regret in consumer behavior. *Psychology and Marketing, 17,* 281–298.

Mellers, B. A., Schwartz, A., & Ritov, I. (1999). Emotion-based choice. *Journal of Experimental Psychology: General, 128,* 1–14.

Ordóñez, L. D., Benson III, L., & Beach, L. R. (1999). Testing the compatibility test: How instructions, accountability and anticipated regret affect prechoice screening of options. *Organizational Behavior and Human Decision Processes, 78,* 63–80.

Pieters, R., & Zeelenberg, M. (2005). On bad decisions and deciding badly: When intention-behavior inconsistency is regrettable. *Organizational Behavior and Human Decision Processes, 97,* 18–30.

Pieters, R., & Zeelenberg, M. (2007). A theory of regret regulation 1.1. *Journal of Consumer Psychology, 17,* 29–35.

Richard, R., van der Pligt, J., & De Vries, N. K. (1996). Anticipated regret and time perspective: Changing sexual risk-taking behavior. *Journal of Behavioral Decision Making, 9,* 185–199.

Ritov, I. (1996). Probability of regret: Anticipation of uncertainty resolution in choice. *Organizational Behavior and Human Decision Processes, 66,* 228–236.

Ritov, I., & Baron, J. (1995). Outcome knowledge, regret and omission bias. *Organizational Behavior and Human Decision Processes, 64,* 119–127.

Roese, N. J. (1997). Counterfactual thinking. *Psychological Bulletin, 121,* 133–148.

Roese, N. J. (2005). *If only.* New York: Broadway Books.

Roese, N. J., & Summerville, A. (2005). What we regret most ... and why. *Personality and Social Psychology Bulletin, 31,* 1273–1285.

Sage, A. P., & White, E. B. (1983). Decision and information structures in regret models of judgment and choice. *IEEE Transactions on Systems, Man, and Cybernetics, 13,* 136–143.

Sanna, L. J. (1996). Defensive pessimism, optimism, and simulating alternatives: Some ups and downs of prefactual and counterfactual thinking. *Journal of Personality and Social Psychology, 71,* 1020–1036.

Savage, L. J. (1951). The theory of statistical decision. *Journal of the American Statistical Association, 46,* 55–67.

Simonson, I. (1992). The influence of anticipating regret and responsibility on purchase decisions. *Journal of Consumer Research, 19,* 105–118.

Starmer, C., & Sugden, R. (1993). Testing for juxtaposition effects and event splitting. *Journal of Risk and Uncertainty, 6,* 235–54.

Taylor, K. A. (1997). A regret theory approach to assessing consumer satisfaction. *Marketing Letters, 8,* 229–238.

Van Dijk, E., & Zeelenberg, M. (2007). When curiosity killed regret: Avoiding or seeking the unknown in decision-making under uncertainty. *Journal of Experimental Social Psychology, 43,* 656–662.

Van Dijk, W. W., van der Pligt, J., & Zeelenberg, M. (1999). Effort invested in vain: The impact of effort on the intensity of disappointment and regret. *Motivation and Emotion, 23,* 203–220.

Zeelenberg, M. (1999a). Anticipated regret, expected feedback and behavioral decision-making. *Journal of Behavioral Decision Making, 12,* 93–106.

Zeelenberg, M. (1999b). The use of crying over spilled milk: A note on the rationality and functionality of regret. *Philosophical Psychology, 13,* 326–340.

Zeelenberg, M., & Beattie, J., (1997). Consequences of regret aversion: 2. Additional evidence for effects of feedback on decision making. *Organizational Behavior and Human Decision Processes, 72,* 63–78.

Zeelenberg, M., Beattie, J., van der Pligt, J., & De Vries, N. K. (1996). Consequences of regret aversion: Effects of expected feedback on risky decision making. *Organizational Behavior and Human Decision Processes, 65,* 148–158.

Zeelenberg, M., van Dijk, W. W., Manstead, A. S. R., & van der Pligt, J. (1988). The experience of regret and disappointment. *Cognition and Emotion, 12,* 221–230.

Zeelenberg, M., Inman, J. J., & Pieters, R. G. M. (2001). What we do when decisions go awry: Behavioral consequences of experienced regret. In E. U. Weber, J. Baron, & G. Loomes (Eds.), *Conflict and Tradeoffs in Decision Making* (pp. 136–155). Cambridge, England: Cambridge University Press.

Zeelenberg, M., Nelissen, R., & Pieters, R. (2007). Emotion, motivation and decision making: A feeling is for doing approach. In H. Plessner, C. Betsch, & T. Betsch (Eds.), *Intuition in judgment and decision making* (pp. 173–189). Mahwah, NJ: Erlbaum.

Zeelenberg, M., & Pieters, R. (2004). Consequences of regret aversion in real life: The case of the Dutch postcode lottery. *Organizational Behavior and Human Decision Processes, 93,* 155–168.

Zeelenberg, M., & Pieters, R. (2006a). Feeling is for doing: A pragmatic approach to the study of emotions in economic behavior. In D. De Cremer, M. Zeelenberg, & K. Murnighan (Eds.), *Social psychology and economics* (pp. 117–137). Mahwah, NJ: Erlbaum.

Zeelenberg, M., & Pieters, R. (2006b). Looking backward with an eye on the future: Propositions toward a theory of regret regulation. In L. J. Sanna & E. C. Chang (Eds.), *Judgments over time: The interplay of thoughts, feelings, and behaviors* (pp. 210–229). New York: Oxford University Press.

Zeelenberg, M., & Pieters, R. (2007). A theory of regret regulation 1.0. *Journal of Consumer Psychology, 17,* 3–18.

28 Preparedness, Mental Simulations, and Future Outlooks

Patrick Carroll and James A. Shepperd

INTRODUCTION

Among the many fables attributed to Aesop, the Greek sage from antiquity, is one about a fox encountering a boar sharpening his tusks against a tree. The fox inquires why the boar sharpens his tusk when neither hunter nor hound is nearby to pose a threat. The boar replies that it would be ill-advised for him to sharpen his weapons at the very moment that he ought to be using them (Pinkney, 2000). The fable of the boar and the fox illustrates in broad brushstrokes the guiding theme of this chapter. Successful advancement through life—even survival—demands that people not only adapt to existing demands but also anticipate and prepare for demands that may emerge in the future.

In this chapter, we discuss a fundamental need underlying much of human future-oriented behavior: the need to prepare. We begin by defining the need to prepare and the role of mental simulation in preparedness. Next, we address how future outlooks and, more importantly, changes in future outlooks reflect preparedness needs. Finally, the chapter closes by considering the conceptual and empirical implications of the claim that mental simulations provide a critical psychological mechanism that enables people to satisfy the need for preparedness via the formulation and revision of future outlooks.

PREPAREDNESS

Preparedness is an evolved need state that represents a readiness to respond to future uncertainty (Carroll, Sweeny, & Shepperd, 2006; Sweeny, Carroll, & Shepperd, 2006). Preparedness involves different things at different times (Carroll et al., 2006). Sometimes, preparedness means preparing for potential opportunities that may present themselves. At other times, preparedness means preparing for threat or potential setback. Consistent with hierarchy models of needs, preparing for threat takes priority over preparing for opportunity (Sheldon, Elliot, Kim, & Kasser, 2001). If one is unprepared for threat, being prepared for opportunity will not matter because one may not live long enough to enjoy it (Bradley, 2000; Taylor, 1991). Thus, in the face of imminent threat, motivational priority is placed on self-protection goals and pessimistic outlooks that prepare for undesired outcomes (Carroll et al., 2006). Nevertheless, being prepared extends beyond anticipatory responding to potential threat. Within novel or unstable environments, motivational priority is placed on realistic outlooks that advance accuracy goals to organize activity around preparing for potential sources of change (good, bad, or neutral) in the local environment (Carroll et al., 2006). Alternatively, being prepared can involve a readiness to respond to potential opportunity or even create new opportunity by embracing optimism. In the absence of imminent threat or environmental instability, motivational priority is placed on optimistic outlooks that advance self-enhancement goals to organize activity around preparing for goal pursuit and acquisition (Carroll et al., 2006).

Preparedness also demands distinguishing "far" from "too far" by assigning motivational priority to preparing for uncertain outcomes that are in the immediate relative to distant future (see also Amit, Algom, Trope, & Liberman, Chapter 4, this volume). A sports team needs to prepare for the game immediately ahead before it prepares for the championship game. Stated otherwise, the need to prepare for the near future is greater than the need to prepare for the distant future (Carroll et al., 2006). Preparing too far in advance may compromise preparation for more immediate states of the world. The three-shot rule of pool illustrates this rule of preparedness. Knowledgeable pool players know that successfully "running" a pool table demands that players plan three shots in advance. Any given shot is made with an eye toward setting up the second and third shot. Importantly, however, although controlling the table demands planning beyond the immediate shot, planning beyond the third short requires looking too far in the future. Such overextended outlooks tend to overextend mental resources by introducing excessive constraints that can interfere with making the first shot. Limiting planning to three shots retains the flexibility needed to run the table. In a similar vein, we propose that preparing prematurely for distant future outcomes ahead of the immediate future can compromise the ability to control important outcomes in life.

At first blush, the motivational priority against preparing too far in advance may seem at odds with self-control research, which emphasizes the value of inhibiting immediate temptations that might compromise progress toward long-term goals (Metcalfe & Mischel, 1999). However, placing priority on near goals does not mean giving in to temptation or ignoring long-term goals. Rather, it entails the implementation of self-control strategies that prioritizes the realization of short-term goals in the pursuit of long-term goals. For example, for the aspiring runner who wishes to run a marathon 3 months in the future, it entails waking early today to complete the short-term goal of a 10-mile run rather than giving in to the temptation to sleep later. In sum, the motivation to prepare for the foreseeable future first often advances rather than undermines effective self-regulation for the distant future.

Preparedness differs from other needs in important ways. For example, preparedness differs from control needs (e.g., effectance and competence) that motivate people to influence or adjust to their immediate environment so that they are better able to control important outcomes (White, 1959). Most important, unlike classic models of control needs (DeCharms, 1968; White, 1959), preparedness focuses on the sense of anticipatory readiness to respond to an uncertain future independent of the sense that the self is an effective agent of change or adjustment to one's current environmental conditions.

A study illustrated the preeminent role of preparedness among other needs. Participants were directed to recall a recent or distant past event that was either highly satisfying or highly distressing. Participants then rated the extent to which 11 needs contributed to the event feeling satisfying or distressing, and their responses were used to rank the needs from least to most important. In two separate experiments, the preparedness need was consistently ranked in the top two most important needs in determining event recollections (Carroll, Arkin, & Seidel, 2008). This ranking held regardless of whether the sample consisted of college students or survivors of a traumatic event (Hurricanes Katrina and Rita), regardless of whether participants were directed to recall a recent or distant event, and regardless of whether the event was satisfying or distressing. Indeed, preparedness was the only need that consistently emerged in the top two needs. Finally, participants' recollections of how they fulfilled their preparedness needs predicted elevations in positive affect, whereas their recollections of how they were unable to fulfill preparedness needs predicted elevations in negative affect. Most important, these effects of preparedness remained even after controlling for alternative needs such as hedonism, consistency, competence, generalized control, or even prediction and control (Carroll et al., 2008).

In sum, preparedness does not appear to represent a secondary need that derives from and thus serves some other need, such as a need for control, competence, or consistency. It also does not represent a simple attempt to reduce uncertainty (e.g., Weary & Jacobson, 1997). Rather, preparedness represents a universal and nonderivative need to ready oneself for what lies ahead and to anticipate and prepare for the cards that life may deal. As with any other need, the need for preparedness depends on specific psychological mechanisms to support its satisfaction.

MENTAL SIMULATIONS: THE ENGINE OF IMAGINATION

Preparedness cannot stand alone but depends on specific psychological mechanisms for satisfaction at the concrete level. Although while ongoing the satisfaction of preparedness may enlist a wide range of supporting processes, mental simulations may play a particularly crucial role. Mental simulations represent alternative versions of present reality (Markman & McMullen, 2003) and provide the engine of human imagination that transports people to alternate worlds past, present, and future. Mental simulations typically represent conditional propositions that specify both an antecedent (e.g., "If only I hadn't ran that red light") and a consequence (e.g., "I would not be holding this traffic ticket"). In most cases, mental simulations involve some mutation of an antecedent (e.g., stopping rather than running the red light) to arrive at some consequence (e.g., avoiding the traffic ticket) that differs from actual or expected reality.

Despite these basic shared properties, mental simulations can differ along several dimensions. For example, mental simulations may differ in terms of their tense, or temporal sign, in that one can generate *counterfactuals,* which represent alternative versions of how past outcomes could have unfolded differently, or *prefactuals,* which represent alternative versions of how actual or expected outcomes could unfold in the future (Markman & McMullen, 2003).

Beyond tense, mental simulations may also vary along the dimensions of direction and structure. Regarding direction, mental simulations can differ in their direction of deviation from actual or expected reality (Markman, Gavanski, Sherman, & McMullen, 1993, 1995; Roese, 1994). For example, mental simulations can represent *downward* simulations that change the antecedent condition to arrive at a worse outcome than the one obtained or expected. Conversely, they can represent *upward* simulations that change the antecedent condition to arrive at a better outcome than the one obtained or expected. The direction of these mental simulations has enormous impact on cognition and emotion. Downward simulations tend to evoke positive feelings when contrasted with actual or expected reality, whereas upward simulations tend to evoke negative feelings when contrasted with actual or expected reality (Markman et al., 1993; Roese, 1994; see also Markman & McMullen, 2003, for a discussion of affective assimilation effects).

Regarding structure, mental simulations differ in whether their structure involves the addition of an antecedent to reality to arrive at a different outcome (additive) or the subtraction of an antecedent from reality to arrive at a different outcome (subtractive) (Roese & Olson, 1993). Thus, for example, the student who failed his or her organic chemistry midterm may imagine how the consequence of failing the exam could have been better by mentally subtracting the antecedent of drinking several pints of beer before the exam or by adding the antecedent of attending the study session before the exam. In both cases, the obtained consequence (failing the exam) is transformed into a different imagined consequence (passing the exam). In one case, however, the transformation occurs by deleting a salient condition (e.g., drinking the pints of beer) that may have precipitated the obtained outcome (subtractive counterfactual). In the other case, the transformation occurs by inserting a salient condition (e.g., attending the study session) that may have prevented the obtained outcome (additive counterfactual).

We propose that mental simulations serve as the basis for forming expectations that enable people to prepare for the future. Expectations derived from mental simulations represent the mental translation of prior knowledge into preparedness for the future (Carroll et al., 2006; Dennett, 1991; Olson, Roese, & Zanna, 1996; Roese, 1997). This translation is possible because people have the ability to temporally sequence episodic memories within the larger structure of autobiographical narratives (e.g., knowledge of studying for a chemistry exam at the end of the fall but before Christmas) that people construct over their lifetime (Barsalou, 1988; Roberts, 2002). More important, people can mentally travel backward in time to past episodes and then project these episodes forward in time to simulate and prepare for possible future episodes (Roberts, 2002; Suddendorf & Corballis, 1997; Szpunar & McDermott, Chapter 8, this volume).

For example, students can mentally travel backward in time to consult the memory of their last exam ("When I studied for one night, I failed my exam") and project that information forward in time to guide preparations for the next exam ("If I study for one night, I will fail my next exam"). These prefactual simulations of anticipated contingencies (e.g., "If I study for 2 weeks, I will pass the next exam") provide the basis for expectations that guide plans and intentions for future action (Roberts, 2002; Roese, 1997; Suddendorf & Corballis, 1997; Tulving, 1983). In turn, commitment to specific plans and intentions ("I will study for 2 weeks rather than 1 night") derived from simulated expectations gears information processing away from extraneous cues toward goal-relevant cues that prepare people to respond effectively to the future experience (the future exam) before it actually occurs (Gollwitzer & Kinney, 1989; see also Faude, Wuerz, & Gollwitzer, Chapter 5, this volume). Ultimately, people can go beyond memories of what did and did not work in the past to simulate expectations that prepare for new, albeit similar, future experiences.

In sum, the ability to mentally simulate various future outcomes allows people to form expectations that prepare for those outcomes in advance. Of course, expectations are not static or unchanging. Rather, people sometimes revise their expectations of what the future holds. In a review, we identified two broad categories of reasons for downward shifts in expectations, both of which serve the broader need of preparedness (Carroll et al., 2006). In the following sections, we extend these arguments to consider how mental simulations provide a critical mechanism governing both sources of predictive shift that serve the need for preparedness.

DOWNWARD SHIFTS IN FUTURE OUTLOOKS

As we noted, preparedness requires a readiness to respond to what lies ahead. A growing body of research suggests, however, that people's expectations about what lies ahead can fluctuate. Often, as the moment of truth draws near, people become decidedly less optimistic in their expectations (Carroll et al., 2006; Gilovich, Kerr, & Medvec, 1993; Shepperd, Ouellette, & Fernandez, 1996; Taylor & Shepperd, 1998). For example, in one study college sophomores, juniors, and seniors estimated their starting salary in their first job after graduation. Seniors, for whom graduation was approaching rapidly, were less optimistic about their starting salary than were sophomores and juniors. Moreover, the seniors estimated a lower salary at the end of the semester, when graduation was 2 weeks away, than they did at the beginning of the semester when graduation was still several months away. In contrast, sophomores and juniors did not change their salary estimates across time (Shepperd et al., 1996).

From our perspective, the downward shift in expectations across time raises three questions. Why do people shift their expectations as the moment of truth draws near? How can preparedness account for the shift? What role do mental simulations play in the downward shift in expectations?

In a review, we identified two broad categories of reasons for the downward shifts in expectations, both of which serve the broader need of preparedness. Downward revision of expectations may reflect either a response to new information or an attempt to brace for possible undesired outcomes (Carroll et al., 2006). Mental simulations provide a critical mechanism governing both sources of predictive shift.

Response to New Information

In some instances, people shift their expectations downward in response to new information, and the shift reflects an effort to adjust expectations toward greater accuracy. The new information can reflect (a) the acquisition of new data, (b) mood as a source of information, or (c) a reexamination or greater scrutiny of existing information.

Regarding new data, as events draw near people often gain new outcome-related or control-related information, and this new information can initiate a change in expectations. For example, college students may temper their career expectations as they approach graduation in response to new information gained from their own experiences seeking employment, from career counseling, or from the experiences of their classmates. The decline in optimism often occurs in lockstep with declining perceptions of control. Initially, people may be optimistic in their predictions because expectations are intimately linked to plans and intentions via upward and additive mental simulations. Yet, plans generated from upward and additive mental simulations are more than just plans; they are plans for success. Moreover, in the absence of hard information, these plans for success are quite understandable because they are often based on intentions and clear routes for success specified in the plans.

Thus, incoming college students may be perfectly justified in their optimistic career expectations given that they only have their lofty plans to succeed in college and beyond on which to base their expectations. However, as the day of graduation approaches, the control opportunities to build a solid grade point average, to gain pregraduate experience via summer internships, and to secure a viable job following graduation evaporate. As students prepare to walk across that stage into life after graduation, they can no longer base their career expectations on what they planned to do but must focus on what they have done and what they can still do to control the outcome. Indeed, as control opportunities diminish, it may become harder to realistically imagine the successful acquisition of outcomes (Lockwood & Kunda, 1997).

Regarding mood, people may treat their current mood states as a source of information on which to base predictions (Schwarz & Clore, 1988). As outcome feedback approaches, people note their increasing anxiety and infer that if they feel this anxious it must be because things will likely turn out poorly. Mental simulations may play a critical role in the translation of the signal of negative affect into the behavioral response to potential threat (Roese, 1997; Schwarz & Bless, 1991). Specifically, prior theorists have suggested that the signal of negative affect mobilizes mental simulations to identify, evaluate, and behaviorally rectify a prospective threat (Markman, Karadogan, Lindberg, & Zell, Chapter 12, this volume; Roese, 1994; 1997; Schwarz, 1990; Schwarz & Bless, 1991). The generation of mental simulations in response to affective signals serves the adaptive function of effectively diagnosing and resolving prospective threats.

It is worth noting that this perspective treats mood as a source of information that people use to adjust predictions rather than some third variable independent of information (Schwarz & Clore, 1988). In short, people adjust their predictions because they interpret their anxiety as important information about the status of their outcome (Gilovich et al., 1993).

Finally, the downward shift in expectations may reflect a reexamination or greater use of available information, which can occur in response to increasing accountability pressures or a change in the way people construe events as they move from the distant to the near future. With regard to accountability, as events draw near, accountability pressures increase in response to the prospect that unfolding events may disconfirm personal expectations (Lerner & Tetlock, 1999). Increasing accountability pressures prompt people to process information more thoroughly and complexly, to simulate alternative outcomes to those expected, and to engage in more self-critical thinking. Even the awareness that one's predictions might be challenged can lead to a simulation of alternative outcomes and a downward shift in expectations (Armor & Taylor, 2002; McKenna & Myers, 1997; Sackett, 2002). It is even possible that people shift toward pessimistic expectations in response to increasing accountability pressures as a consequence of focusing on a negative subset of judgment-relevant cues (Lerner & Tetlock, 1999).

Regarding event construal, as events draw near, people shift from construing events at a high level to construing events at a low level (Amit et al., Chapter 4, this volume; Liberman & Trope, 1998). Changes in construal level differ from changes in accountability pressure in that the former illustrates a change in the representation (e.g., high- vs. low-construal level) of information, whereas the latter represents a change in the depth of processing (e.g., from less to more complex processing) of information. High-level construals that occur for distant events are more abstract and generalized and tend to focus on what people want to happen (desirability). Thus, when thinking about distant events (e.g., first-year students thinking about life after graduation), mental simulations tend to center on more optimistic possibilities, such as having a prestigious, high-paying job, driving a new car, and living in a beautiful, expensive home. Low-level construals that occur for near events are more concrete and specific and tend to focus more on what is likely to happen (feasibility). Thus, when thinking about near events (e.g., graduation in 1 month), mental simulations tend to center on more realistic possibilities, such as finding a job, squeezing another year out of the old jalopy, and finding roommates to share the cost of a rundown apartment. As events draw near, people shift from high-level construals to low-level construals, and their predictions for the future shift in kind. Indeed, the enhanced salience of concrete feasibility constraints as events draw near may even lead people to consider upward simulations of how the actual outcome may be harder to manage and ultimately worse than expected, prompting pessimistic predictions.

It is noteworthy that the information accounts can explain shifts in expectations for uncontrollable events such as when participants become more pessimistic over time in their predictions regarding the results of a medical test (Taylor & Shepperd, 1998). For example, as the moment of truth draws near, people may come to think more deeply and critically about their risk factors or may draw inferences that they may have neglected to draw when the medical test results were still several weeks away. In addition, rising anxiety as one awaits medical test results may be interpreted as information about what the future will reveal, perhaps suggesting that previous predictions were too optimistic.

Response to Possible Undesired Outcomes

Sometimes, downward shifts in expectations as the moment of truth draws near do not reflect a response to information but rather a response to the possibility that things may not turn out as hoped. Specifically, sometimes people alter their expectations in an attempt to influence the occurrence of an undesired outcome or to influence how they feel about an undesired outcome should one occur. In these instances, the downward shift in expectations can represent one of three proactive responses to possible bad news: (a) an attempt to brace for bad news, (b) an effort to influence or control the outcome through superstitious or magical means, and (c) the cognitive strategy of defensive pessimism.

With respect to bracing for bad news, people often must form expectations about distant events for which information pertinent to the accuracy of the expectations is nonexistent or unavailable until some distant time. The absence of information allows considerable leeway in making predictions. In addition, as noted, people's expectations are often accompanied by plans and intentions for producing desired outcomes and avoiding undesired outcomes. The result is that people may be inclined toward optimistic rather than realistic predictions (Taylor, 1991).

However, as the moment of truth draws near, people face the possibility that their optimistic outlooks might be disconfirmed. A number of studies suggest that how people feel about their outcomes is in part determined by their expectations (e.g., Medvec & Savitsky, 1997; Shepperd & McNulty, 2002). Whereas people feel elated when outcomes exceed expectations, they feel disappointed when outcomes fall short of expectations. People appear acutely sensitive to the relationship between expectations and feelings about outcomes and will lower their expectations, bracing for possible bad news, as the moment of truth draws near to avoid feelings of disappointment (Shepperd et al., 1996; Taylor & Shepperd, 1998). In a sense, people avoid feeling disappointed by making bad news seem expected rather than unexpected.

With respect to magical thinking, people sometimes believe that the mere act of making a prediction can influence the outcome that occurs. That is, they sometimes believe that meta-physical forces respond to optimistic predictions by diminishing the likelihood such predictions will come true. People thus predict the worst to avoid tempting fate (Gilovich, 2005) or "jinxing" (putting an unfavorable curse on) the outcome. This belief that the mere act of predicting an outcome can affect its occurrence illustrates a type of magical thinking. Magical thinking refers to a belief in causal forces that operate outside normal physical laws (Rozin & Nemeroff, 1990). People turn to magical thinking as a means of influencing outcomes when they can no longer influence outcomes through conventional paths. As the moment of truth draws near, opportunities to influence outcomes through conventional means decline, and people are likely to rely more and more on superstitious means. Reliance on superstitious, magical control tactics likely increases in step with declines in conventional control tactics. Indeed, people are most likely to employ magical thinking when performance or testing has ended and people merely await news of the outcome. In such instances, people may make pessimistic predictions and may even avoid mental simulations of positive outcomes because they perceive that doing otherwise increases the risk of an undesired outcome.

Although a relatively new line of inquiry, research demonstrates "jinxing" in a variety of domains, including insurance decisions, gambling, traffic violations, and sports entertainment (Gilovich, 2005; Kruger, Savitsky, & Gilovich, 1999; Risen & Gilovich, 2007a, 2007b; Risen, Gilovich, Kruger, & Savitsky, 2007). Consistent with past work on other secondary control tactics, expressions of pessimism to avoid tempting fate primarily occur when primary control opportunities have declined or completely vanished (Risen & Gilovich, 2007a, 2007b).

Finally, with respect to the cognitive strategy of defensive pessimism, research reveals that some highly capable people (i.e., defensive pessimists) mentally simulate undesirable outcomes such as failure when facing evaluation in an important performance domain (Norem & Cantor, 1986). Ironically, this pessimism serves the function of enhancing performance. Specifically, the pessimistic outlook creates anxiety, which defensive pessimists tap as energy for redoubling their efforts to avoid failure. In this sense, defensive pessimism is much like the fear of failure (Atkinson & Raynor, 1974) in that defensive pessimists use their predictions of an undesired outcome to motivate them to work harder.

Mental Simulation as the Mechanism of Change

Both categories of explanations for the changes in expectations just described (e.g., responses to new information and responses to the possibility that things may not turn out as hoped) rely on people's capacity to mentally simulate undesired outcomes. Regarding the first category, the new information promotes the mental simulation of outcomes that are alternative to the one initially expected. People shift their expectation in response to new information because the new information allows them to contemplate alternative realities. Regarding the second category, the awakening cognition that things may not turn out as hoped is in itself a mental simulation of an outcome different from the one initially expected or desired. Moreover, it is a mental simulation with motivational force in that it evokes a change in expectation and, in the case of defensive pessimism, a change in behavior.

It is noteworthy that several studies have found that the downward shift in expectations as performance draws near is often accompanied by a change in anxiety (e.g., Shepperd et al., 1996; Shepperd, Grace, Cole & Klein, 2005; Taylor & Shepperd, 1998). The change in expectations and increase in anxiety are intertwined in that both can be a cause or consequence of the other. On the one hand, as the moment of truth approaches, people mentally simulate more undesirable outcomes relative to desirable outcomes (Sanna, 1996), which can elicit heightened anxiety about the repercussions of the bad news. On the other hand, anxiety about approaching outcomes may prompt people to mentally simulate undesirable outcomes (Sanna, 1996). With this second approach, anxiety elicits mood-congruent cognitions rather than providing information (Sanna, 1996). In both cases, however, the end result is a decline in expectations. Finally, it is also possible that a downward shift in expectations can itself elicit greater anxiety and increased mental simulations of negative outcomes (Sanna & Meier, 2000).

Preparedness as the Motivation

Although mental simulations provide an important mechanism of change in future outlooks, preparedness represents the adaptive need that motivates the use of mental simulations. That is, the need for preparedness prompts people to imagine a variety of future possible outcomes, from the desired to the undesired, and to revise their outlooks in response to new information and changing circumstances. Regarding downward revisions in expectations, we have discussed how people may revise their expectations in response to new information bearing on the accuracy of their predictions (Carroll et al., 2006). The information can come from new outcome or control-relevant data that add greater precision to predictions; from current mood, which can serve as information about a forthcoming outcome (e.g., "If I feel this anxious, it must be because things will go poorly"); or from more careful consideration of existing information in response to accountability pressures or changes in event construal.

Preparedness can accommodate each of the information-based explanations for downward shifts in predictions. For example, adjusting predictions in light of new outcome or control-relevant information better prepares people to respond to what actually lies ahead. Likewise, current mood can be an important indicator for what is likely to happen in the absence of more detailed informational guideposts allowing them to formulate a response (Schwarz & Clore, 1988). Finally, preparedness can account for downward shifts in response to more careful consideration or scrutiny of existing data in response to accountability pressures or changes in event construal. Accountability pressures prompt preemptive self-criticism in which people focus on the weaknesses in their position to the relative neglect of strengths as they consider how they might defend their position relative to alternative positions (Lerner & Tetlock, 1999). The more careful and complex processing prepares people to respond to challenges even to the weakest points in their position (Lerner & Tetlock, 1999). Changes toward more concrete construals as events draw near prompt a shift in attention away from what one would like to happen toward what is likely to happen and how one should prepare and respond.

Preparedness can also accommodate each of the explanations that entail responding to the possibility that things may not turn out as hoped. With bracing for disappointment, the shift reflects an attempt to prepare for disappointment arising from outcomes that may fall short of expectations. By lowering their expectations, people minimize the impact of unexpected bad news by removing the element of surprise. With magical thinking and defensive pessimism, preparatory efforts work toward manipulating the occurrence of the undesired outcome rather than reducing its impact. In the case of magical thinking, preparatory actions are directed at avoiding thoughts or behaviors that might tempt fate and elicit an undesired outcome. In the case of defensive pessimism, people prepare by directing anxious energy arising from the prospect of an undesired outcome toward actions that ensure the undesired outcome does not occur.

UPWARD SHIFTS IN FUTURE OUTLOOKS

Thus far, we have addressed how mental simulations provide the mechanism and preparedness provides the motivation for downward shifts in future outlooks. It is important to note, however, that sometimes people exhibit upward shifts in expectations. Specifically, in the absence of imminent threat or environmental instability, the value of negative outlooks diminishes, and motivational priority shifts to positive outlooks that promote resource acquisition and personal growth. Although people may occasionally show upward shifts for reasons that have little to do with preparedness, in most instances we suspect that upward shifts are motivated by preparedness concerns.

We can think of three reasons why people might show upward shifts in future outlooks. First, the upward shift may occur as a result of new information. The new information that can prompt upward shifts parallels the kind of information that prompts downward shifts. That is, people may gain new data that suggests that their initial expectations were too conservative. Or, they may interpret a positive mood as evidence that a more positive outcome is forthcoming (see also Klein & Zajac, Chapter 21, this volume). It is also possible that changing circumstances may shift attention to successful goal attainment, which can prompt increases in positive expectations. One such change in circumstances occurs when people transition from a deliberative mindset to an implemental mind-set (Gollwitzer & Kinney, 1989). When deciding a course of action, people assume a deliberative mindset in which they hold a realistic outlook, weigh different options, and plot a path toward their goal. Once they have decided a course of action, however, people shift to an implemental mindset, and their outlook becomes more optimistic as they mentally simulate desired future prospects and put their plan of action into motion (Gollwitzer & Kinney, 1989).

Second, the upward shift may reflect a proactive coping process directed at reducing or avoiding an undesired outcome (Aspinwall & Taylor, 1997). Proactive coping bears some similarity to defensive pessimism in that it represents avoidance actions that arise in response to the looming prospect of an undesired outcome. However, proactive coping is distinct from defensive pessimism in that it entails an optimistic future outlook in which people interpret a potential stressor as a challenge that can be mastered and overcome rather than a threat that must be suffered (see Blascovich & Tomaka, 1996, for further discussion of threat/challenge distinction). The optimistic outlook gives rise to positive emotional energy that fuels efforts to overcome the stressor (Aspinwall & Taylor, 1997).

Third, the upward shift may emerge as people contemplate the future and consider possible opportunities. Preparing for an opportunity necessitates mentally simulating successful goal attainment. For instance, hopeful adolescent athletes may mentally simulate successfully making the cut on a high school sports team. To the extent that a positive mental simulation is active in working memory, it can organize, energize, and direct mental and behavioral activity around goal pursuit and enjoyment (Markus & Ruvolo, 1989). Over time, this mental simulation can become internalized as a positive possible self, which in turn leads to greater feelings of competence, mastery, and optimism as people move from the present self to the desired self (see also Oyserman & James, Chapter 25, this volume). Imagining themselves as members of the high school sports team increases adolescent athletes' belief that such a future self is possible.

The Role of Mental Simulation and Preparedness

As in the case of downward shifts in expectations, upward shifts in expectations occur in response to mental simulations (albeit of positive rather than negative outcomes). For instance, new information gives credence to alternative possible realities, and people adjust their expectations in the direction suggested by these evidence-based alternative realities. Imagining setbacks as a challenge rather than a threat can serve as a catalyst to move forward and address an impending stressor with new-found energy that can turn life's lemons into lemonade (Aspinwall & Taylor, 1997; Blascovich & Tomaka, 1996). In addition, mentally simulating positive future selves achieving goals and assuming successful roles with competence and mastery can promote a more positive outlook on the future.

Upward shifts in future outlooks serve the role of preparedness most notably via the construction of new opportunities as well as the acquisition of available opportunities. For instance, the broaden and build theory (Fredrickson, 2001) suggests that positive emotions and optimism are mutually reinforcing such that initial positive emotions engender initial optimism, which in turn cycles back to enhance positive emotions, starting the process anew. The positive emotions that flow from optimism feel good. But more important, they offer long-term benefits in that they prompt people to acquire and create new resources and opportunities (Fredrickson, 2001). Specifically, positive emotions and optimistic outlooks broaden the mental field of response possibilities to enable the creative simulation of new solutions to old problems as well as the imagination of new and larger opportunities (Fredrickson, 2001). Ultimately, the upward revision of expectations in response to new information, proactive coping, or through consideration of possible opportunities enables people to maximize their ongoing readiness to respond to changes in their local environment.

Summary

Although there are a variety of reasons why people may shift upward or downward in their future outlooks, the shifts are typically preceded by mental simulations of an alternative reality than what was initially expected. The mental simulation and revision of expectations serve the need for preparedness. Moreover, preparedness can unify the different explanations of change (upward and downward) in expectations under a single motivational system. Preparedness provides the motivational link that binds past-, present-, and future-oriented thought into adaptation over time using the engine of mental simulation.

PREPAREDNESS AS THE MOTIVATIONAL THREAD BETWEEN SIMULATIONS AND EXPECTATIONS

Thus far, we have focused on how mental simulations help people prepare for future uncertainty by allowing construction and revision of alternative future possibilities. We are not the first to suggest that mental simulations can help people prepare. The dual-function account of counterfactual thinking proposes that mental simulations can serve a preparatory as well as affective function (Markman & McMullen, 2003; Markman, McMullen, & Elizaga, 2008; Roese, 1994). Thus, for example, students can prepare themselves for the next exam by imagining how their past grade would have been better if they had reviewed the notes gradually in the weeks (rather than day) prior to the exam. People can project these counterfactuals forward in time to simulate expectations that prepare for new, albeit, similar future experiences. These prefactual simulations of anticipated contingencies (e.g., "If I study for 2 weeks, I will pass the next exam") provide the basis for expectations that guide plans and intentions to prepare for the future experience (Roberts, 2002; Roese, 1997; Suddendorf & Corballis, 1997; Tulving, 1983).

Although related, it may be apparent that our notion of the need for preparedness and the preparatory function of mental simulations differ in terms of the distinction between functions and needs. The need for preparedness, similar to other organismic needs, represents a general evolved desire common to all members of a species (Sheldon et al., 2001). Functions, by contrast, refer to the purpose for which something is designed or exists without invoking any proximal motivational drive to serve that function (Roberts, 2002).

To draw an analogue, although a crane-operated wrecking ball serves the function of destroying buildings, one would not say that the ball (or the crane that swings it) has some burning desire or need to destroy buildings. In the same way, dual-function accounts do not assume that mental simulations are, themselves, motivated by a need for preparedness (Markman & McMullen, 2003; Roese, 1994). They merely suggest that mental simulations serve the (preparatory) function of preparing people for the future. In contrast to dual-function accounts, we assume that the need for preparedness evokes a proximal goal to prepare for future uncertainty. As such, preparedness motivates not only the strategic use of mental simulations but also the use of many other cognitive mechanisms (e.g., tools of sympathetic magical thinking) that naturally serve the function of preparation for future uncertainty.[1]

The distinction between needs and functions illuminates the potential for theoretical compatibility rather than conflict between the need for preparedness and functional models of mental simulations (Oettingen & Kappes, Chapter 26, this volume; Sanna, Carter, & Burkley, 2005). In many ways, the distinction resembles that made between the roles of motivated goals and cognitive processes in biased beliefs and judgments. Specifically, the biased memory search and belief construction model (Kunda, 1990) suggested that the role of motivation was confined to the strategic generation of directional hypotheses that, ultimately, depended on cold cognitive mechanisms to garner adequate evidence to support biased conclusions. In the same way, preparedness activates the proximal goal to prepare for uncertain future outcomes within a particular situational context. However, as with goals associated with any other need (e.g., need for achievement goals), proximal goals associated with preparedness needs cannot be fulfilled in specific situational contexts without the support of cognitive mechanisms such as mental simulations.

Consistent with this point, recent work suggests that a motivation to prepare for upcoming social interactions may be fulfilled under certain conditions via the mechanism of automatic social behavior. Although this prior work is certainly noteworthy, we have proposed that the implications of preparedness extend far beyond the specific context of anticipatory responses to future social interactions to virtually all anticipatory response patterns (Carroll et al., 2006). As a pervasive motivational influence, moreover, it is naive to think that automatic social behavior represents the sole mechanism supporting the fulfillment of preparedness and its corresponding goals. In our view, mental simulations provide one of the more useful and versatile mechanisms supporting the goals that serve preparedness. As with goals associated with any other need, preparedness goals strategically enlist the support of mental simulations to shape future outlooks to satisfy the deeper need to respond to future uncertainty within that prevailing context.

In our view, this conceptual distinction between preparedness and the preparatory function of mental simulations suggests many fascinating lines of inquiry that could potentially enrich our understanding of future outlooks, preparedness, and mental simulation processes. At a basic level, the incorporation of preparedness generates several new questions about exactly when and why people use mental simulations to adjust as well as generate future outlooks. Although most investigators assume that preparation is primarily served by upward and additive counterfactuals (e.g., Roese, 1994; Sanna, 1996), we propose that downward counterfactuals can also indirectly satisfy preparedness via the positive affect derived from the favorable contrast of present reality to a worse simulated reality. This may be the case even though the comparative thought processes associated with downward simulations directly serve an affective function. Of course, these mental simulations may ultimately serve preparedness precisely because of the general value of positive affect for self-regulation. As noted, positive emotions can fuel the pursuit and acquisition of possible opportunities by broadening the mental field of response possibilities. That is, positive emotions can inspire the creative simulation of new solutions to old problems as well as the imagination of even greater opportunities.[2]

In this sense, the need to prepare for possible opportunities may trigger simulations following a setback of how life could be worse. The positive affect generated from these downward comparisons would renew motivational energy, enhance positive expectations, and reorganize attention around the acquisition of future opportunities and even extend current opportunities to bigger and better things. Thus, for example, students can feel elation by contemplating how their poor performance is still better than the simulation of how things could have been worse. The positive affect generated from the downward comparison would enhance motivation and optimism around the bright future possibilities that can still be generalized from the actual outcome obtained.

In many ways, the final suggestion for linking mental simulations to future outlooks via preparedness is the most fascinating as well as speculative. Specifically, people may prepare for possible loss via strategic bracing for undesired outcomes when they assimilate to downward simulations (Markman & McMullen, 2003). As discussed, people may forsake optimism to brace for the painful prospect of disappointment arising when their positive expectations are shattered and disconfirmed by failure. Although painful, the downward revision of expectations prepares people for disappointment by taking away the element of surprise. More important, however, the bracing model of predictive shifts suggests that forsaking optimism enhances emotional as well as cognitive preparedness. Specifically, simulating disappointment promotes emotional preparedness by allowing people to preemptively adapt to and inoculate themselves against the emotional impact of prospective disappointment before it fully emerges.

The mental simulation of an undesired outcome that characterizes bracing bears some resemblance to the intensity and durability biases. The intensity and durability biases refer to the tendency of people to overestimate the intensity and duration of their affective reactions to negative as well as positive future outcomes (Gilbert, 2006). Thus, junior faculty members are likely to overestimate the intensity and duration of their emotional reaction to being denied tenure, imagining this outcome as a crippling tragedy from which they will never fully recover.

Theorists have proposed a variety of explanations for biases in affective forecasts (Dunn, Forrin, & Ashton-James, Chapter 22, this volume; Gilbert, Pinel, Wilson, Blumberg, & Wheately, 1998). One explanation is that biases stem from focalism—people focus exclusively on specific, or focal, future outcomes to the exclusion of nonfocal outcomes when generating affective forecasts (Gilbert, 2006). The junior faculty member may focus solely on the negative event and consequences of being denied tenure and fail to consider how other future outcomes such as the birth of a first child or transition to a new and more fulfilling position will absorb attention and color general emotional states. Other theorists have argued that biases in affective forecasts stem from a peculiar tendency of people to underestimate the power of their own psychological immune system to fight off and defend against emotional setbacks (Gilbert, 2006). The integration of preparedness with the processes underlying mental simulations suggests an additional explanation for biases in affective forecasts.

Specifically, biases in affective forecasts could reflect a form of emotional inoculation. Although uncomfortable, affective assimilation to an undesirable simulation enables people to temporarily expose themselves to the emotional impact of prospective loss without incurring the actual material impact of loss. In so doing, people are able to preemptively adapt to the emotional impact of the prospective loss, making them better prepared to respond to actual loss should it occur.

Although strategically adaptive, these biases are not necessarily conscious or deliberate. As discussed, the tendency to brace represents an automatic response to anxiety associated with the prospect of disappointment. As such, emotional inoculation is primarily an automatic, adaptive consequence rather than a conscious motivational cause of bracing for the worst. Although distinct in many ways, research on affective forecasting is also consistent with the notion that preparedness concerns shape the formation and translation of past memories into future expectations. Specifically, evidence suggests that people give disproportionate weight to peak moments (marking the maximum intensity of emotional outcome) and end moments (marking the conclusion of emotional outcomes) when recalling and summarizing past emotional outcomes (Fredrickson, 2000; Fredrickson & Kahneman, 1993). Consistent with the preparedness hypothesis, peak and end moments are better remembered because they have greater implications for efforts to prepare for similar future experiences (Fredrickson, 1991, 2000).

Peak moments convey the maximum intensity of experiences and how well the person coped with that point of maximum intensity. End moments signify the absolute termination of the affective experience and allow the person to identify the peak moment as well as the duration of the affective experience with relative certainty (Fredrickson, 2000; Fredrickson, 1991). Taken together, the certain identification of a peak moment at an end moment signifies the maximum emotional intensity that the person can endure when making choices about similar future affective prospects just as past attempts to "max out" tell weight lifters how much they would be prepared to bench-press in the future. People base their choices about which emotional prospects to approach or avoid by projecting peak and end moments of past affective experiences into expectations of how prepared they would be to respond to the peak intensity of similar future experiences.

Although the mechanism of emotional inoculation is similar to the peak-end bias in the sense that it serves preparedness via affective forecasts, we are suggesting a different mechanism by which biases in affective judgments ultimately satisfy preparedness needs via emotional inoculation. Specifically, the peak-end bias serves preparedness by allowing people to quickly consult and then project the certain peak moment forward in time to guide choices about whether to embrace or eschew future emotional prospects. By contrast, the emotional inoculation mechanism serves preparedness in the sense that it maximizes emotional readiness to respond to the prospect of disappointment when people do not have the luxury of choosing to approach or avoid it in the first place. In this sense, unlike the peak-end bias, emotional inoculation is somewhat broader in that it can serve preparedness for outcomes that are not preceded by choice opportunities.

We predict that people induced to assimilate to a downward prefactual simulation (e.g., imminent performance failure) would brace more for and, in turn, be better prepared for a subsequent loss when it actually occurs. Specifically, people who temporarily experienced and strategically braced for the downward simulation of future loss would be better prepared to withstand and recover from the full emotional impact of an actual loss that subsequently occurs. In turn, the enhanced emotional resilience and recovery would minimize the drain that mood management places on mental resources, which would in turn increase cognitive preparedness for subsequent self-regulatory demands as they emerge. As such, these individuals will be better able to respond to the actual loss via effective mood regulation and ultimately better able to respond to the cognitive and behavioral demands of future self-regulatory tasks.

CONCLUDING REMARKS

Mental simulations represent the mechanism by which people generate future outlooks as well as revisions of those outlooks. Indeed, it is difficult to imagine how an expectation for a hypothetical future outcome could be generated let alone change without first assuming the role of mental simulation in generating expectations for the future as well as generating expectations for alternative possibilities. The need for preparedness, however, provides the motivational framework within which to situate the link between fluctuations in future outlooks and the mechanism of mental simulations that drive them. The value of preparedness lies in its potential to unify the various motivational and cognitive mechanisms proposed to govern the link between mental simulations and predictive shifts.

Preparedness provides a framework within which to integrate a wide and diverse array of explanations for the relation between mental simulations and predictive shifts without compromising the unique characteristics of each phenomenon. For example, the need for preparedness does not deny the preparatory or the affective functions of mental simulations. Rather, preparedness provides the proximal motivation that drives people to utilize the functions of mental simulations and expectations to prepare for possible future outcomes before they arise. In addition, preparedness provides a framework for understanding the translation of memories into mental simulations that generate the future expectations, which in turn guide plans and intentions to respond to future uncertainty. Similarly, preparedness provides a framework for understanding the various explanations for downward or upward shifts in expectations. The issue is not whether the shift represents a response to mental simulations generated from new information, accountability pressures, construal shifts, or even the possibility of undesired or desired outcomes. A shift in future outlook can occur for any or all of these reasons. However, all of these reasons converge on the common point of preparedness for future uncertainty.

In sum, framing preparedness as an adaptive need rather than a specific goal or cognitive process preserves each unique concept in its proper adaptive context relevant to anticipatory responding while at the same time unifying each concept under a single framework. Ultimately, the preparedness construct integrates mental simulations and fluctuations in future outlooks into a unified motivational psychology of anticipatory responses to future uncertainty.

ACKNOWLEDGMENTS

We thank Joann Benigno, Greg Norman, Kenneth DeMarree, Kentaro Fujita, and William Cunningham for helpful comments on portions of this chapter.

NOTES

1. Although some theorists have proposed a desire to make meaning or sense of experience as a motivational catalyst for mental simulations (Galinsky, Liljenquist, Kray, & Roese, 2005), in line with other researchers (Janoff-Bulman, 2004; Meichenbaum, 1985) we propose that the desire for meaning serves the larger goal of preparedness in social interactions and beyond. For example, the theory of stress inoculation suggests that the painful process of continually reliving a traumatic episode facilitates recovery by serving to simulate and ultimately guide the construction of more resilient worldviews and prepare for the possibility of future trauma (Meichenbaum, 1985). The revision process involves both making sense of the tragedy and mentally simulating the expectation that the previously inconceivable out-

come could recur (Janoff-Bulman, 2006; Meichenbaum, 1985). Thus, for example, recovery after 9/11 involves deleting the expectation that the United States is safe and urban attacks are inconceivable. This sense-making process would not only reconstruct but also inoculate worldviews against future trauma by simulating additional contingency plans that enhance preparedness for future trauma. Although we acknowledge the importance of the need for existential meaning and security in the reconstruction process, we believe that the purpose of the revision process is not merely to explain the previously unexpected outcome but also to incorporate the expectation for that outcome into the belief system to prepare for the possibility that it could recur.

2. Although downward mental simulations that focus on how things could be worse can generate positive affect, as suggested, so can upward simulations that focus on how things can be better. Specifically, upward simulations can inspire people to prepare for and pursue possible opportunities.

REFERENCES

Armor, D. A., & Taylor, S. E. (2002). When predictions fail: The dilemma of unrealistic optimism. In T. Gilovich, D. W. Griffin, & D. Kahneman (Eds.), *Heuristics and biases: The psychology of intuitive judgment* (pp. 334–347). New York: Cambridge University Press.

Aspinwall, L. G., & Taylor, S. E. (1997). A stitch in time: Self-regulation and proactive coping. *Psychological Bulletin, 121,* 417–436.

Atkinson, J. W., & Raynor, J. O. (1974). *Motivation and achievement.* Washington, DC: Winston.

Barsalou, L. W. (1988). The content and organization of autobiographical memories. In U. Neisser & E. Winograd (Eds.), *Remembering reconsidered: Ecological and traditional approaches to the study of memory* (pp. 193–243). New York: Cambridge University Press.

Blascovich, J., & Tomaka, J. (1996). The biopsychosocial model of arousal regulation. In M. Zanna (Ed.), *Advances in experimental social psychology* (Vol. 28, pp. 1–51). New York: Academic Press.

Bradley, M. M. (2000). Emotion and motivation. In J. T. Cacioppo, L. G. Tassinary, & G. G. Bernston (Eds.), *Handbook of psychophysiology* (2nd ed., pp. 602–635). New York: Cambridge University Press.

Carroll, P. J., Arkin, R. M., & Seidel, S. (2008). *Defining the context of needs among hurricane survivors and college students.* Unpublished manuscript.

Carroll, P. J., Sweeny, K., & Shepperd, J. A. (2006). Forsaking optimism. *The Review of General Psychology, 10,* 56–73.

DeCharms, R. (1968). *Personal causation.* New York: Academic Press.

Dennett, D. C. (1991). *Consciousness explained.* Boston: Little.

Fredrickson, B. L. (1991). Anticipated endings: An explanation for selective social interaction (Doctoral dissertation, Stanford University, 1990). *Dissertation Abstracts International, 3,* AAD91-00818.

Fredrickson, B. L. (2000). Extracting meaning from past affective experiences: The importance of peaks, ends, and specific emotions. *Cognition and Emotion, 14,* 577–606.

Fredrickson, B. L. (2001). The role of positive emotions in positive psychology: A broaden-and-build theory of positive emotions. *American Psychologist, 35,* 603–618.

Fredrickson, B. L., & Kahneman, D. (1993). Duration neglect in retrospective evaluations of affective episodes. *Journal of Personality and Social Psychology, 65,* 45–55.

Galinsky, A. D., Liljenquist, K. A., Kray, L. J., & Roese, N. R. (2005). Finding meaning from mutability: Making sense and deriving significance through counterfactual thinking. In D. R. Mandel, D. J. Hilton, & P. Catellani (Eds.), *The psychology of counterfactual thinking.* London: Routledge.

Gilbert, D. (2006). *Stumbling on happiness.* New York: Random House.

Gilbert, D. T., Pinel, E. C., Wilson, T. D., Blumberg, S. J., & Wheately, T. P. (1998). Immune neglect: A source of durability bias in affective forecasting. *Journal of Personality and Social Psychology, 75*(3), 617–638.

Gilovich, T. (2005). *The perceived likelihood of events that "tempt fate."* Paper presented at the Annual Meeting of the Society of Personality and Social Psychology, January 2005, New Orleans.

Gilovich, T., Kerr, M., & Medvec, V. H. (1993). Effect of temporal perspective on subjective confidence. *Journal of Personality and Social Psychology, 64,* 552–560.

Gollwitzer, P. M., & Kinney, R. F. (1989). Effects of deliberative and implemental mind-sets on illusions of control. *Journal of Personality and Social Psychology, 56,* 531–542.

Janoff-Bulman, R. (2004). Three exploratory models of traumatic growth. *Psychological Inquiry, 15,* 30–34.

Kruger, J., Savitsky, K., & Gilovich, T. (1999). Superstition and the regression effect. *Skeptical Inquirer, 23,* 24–29.

Kunda, Z. (1990). The case for motivated reasoning. *Psychological Bulletin, 108,* 480–498.

Lerner, J. S., & Tetlock, P. E. (1999). Accounting for the effects of accountability. *Psychological Bulletin, 125,* 255–275.

Liberman, N., & Trope, Y. (1998). The role of feasibility and desirability considerations in near and distant future decisions: A test of temporal construal theory. *Journal of Personality and Social Psychology, 75,* 5–18.

Lockwood, P., & Kunda, Z. (1997). Superstars and me: Predicting the impact of role models on the self. *Journal of Personality and Social Psychology, 73,* 91–103.

Markman, K. D., Gavanski, I., Sherman, S. J., & McMullen, M. N. (1993). The mental simulation of better and worse possible worlds. *Journal of Experimental Social Psychology, 29,* 87–109.

Markman, K. D., Gavanski, I., Sherman, S. J., & McMullen, M. N. (1995). The impact of perceived control on the imagination of better and worse possible worlds. *Personality and Social Psychology Bulletin, 21,* 588–595.

Markman, K. D., & McMullen, M. N. (2003). A reflection and evaluation model of comparative thinking. *Personality and Social Psychology Review, 7,* 244–267.

Markman, K. D., McMullen, M. N., & Elizaga, R. A. (2008). Counterfactual thinking, persistence, and performance: A test of the reflection and evaluation model. *Journal of Experimental Social Psychology, 44,* 421–428.

Markus, H., & Ruvolo, A. (1989). Possible selves: Personalized representations of goals. In L. S. Pervin (Ed.), *Goal concepts in personality and social psychology* (pp. 211–241). Hillsdale, NJ: Erlbaum.

McKenna, F. P., & Myers, L. B. (1997). Illusory self-assessments: Can they be reduced? *British Journal of Psychology, 88,* 39–51.

Medvec, V. H., & Savitsky, K. (1997). When doing better means feeling worse: The effects of categorical cutoff points on counterfactual thinking and satisfaction. *Journal of Personality and Social Psychology, 72,* 1284–1296.

Meichenbaum, D. (1985*). Stress inoculation training.* New York: Pergamon.

Metcalfe, J., & Mischel, W. (1999). A hot/cool-system analysis of delay of gratification: Dynamics of willpower. *Psychological Review, 106,* 3–19.

Norem, J. K., & Cantor, N. (1986). Defensive pessimism: Harnessing anxiety and motivation. *Journal of Personality and Social Psychology, 51,* 1208–1217.

Olson, J. M., Roese, N. J., & Zanna, M. P. (1996). Expectancies. In E. T. Higgins & A. W. Kruglanski (Eds.), *Social psychology: Handbook of basic principles* (pp. 211–238). New York: Guilford.

Pinkney, J. (2000). *Aesop's fables.* New York: SeaStar books.

Risen, J. L., & Gilovich, T. (2007a). Another look at why people are reluctant to exchange lottery tickets. *Journal of Personality and Social Psychology, 93,* 12–22.

Risen, J. L., & Gilovich, T. (2007b). *Tempting fate: The effect of negativity and accessibility on judgments of likelihood.* Manuscript in preparation.

Risen, J. L., & Gilovitch, T. (in press). Why people are reluctant to tempt fate. *Journal of Personality and Social Psychology.*

Risen, J. L., Gilovich, T., Kruger, J., & Savitsky, K. (2008). *Why calling attention to success seems to invite failure.* Manuscript submitted for publication.

Roberts, W. A. (2002). Are animals stuck in time? *Psychological Bulletin, 128,* 473–489.

Roese, N. J. (1994). The functional basis of counterfactual thinking. *Journal of Personality and Social Psychology, 66,* 805–818.

Roese, N. J. (1997). Counterfactual thinking. *Psychological Bulletin, 121,* 133–148.

Roese, N. J., & Olson, J. M. (1993). The structure of counterfactual thought. *Personality and Social Psychology Bulletin, 19,* 312–319.

Rozin, P., & Nemeroff, C. (1990). The laws of sympathetic magic: A psychological analysis of similarity and contagion. In J. W. Stigler, R. A. Shweder, & G. H. Herdt (Eds.), *Cultural psychology: Essays on comparative human development* (pp. 205–232). New York: Cambridge University Press.

Sackett, A. M. (2002). *Optimism and accuracy in performance predictions: An experimental test of the self-protection hypothesis.* Unpublished master's thesis, Yale University.

Sanna, L. J. (1996). Defensive pessimism, optimism, and simulating alternatives: Some ups and downs of prefactual and counterfactual thinking. *Journal of Personality and Social Psychology, 71,* 1020–1036.

Sanna, L. J., Carter, S. E., & Burkley, E. (2005). Yesterday, today, and tomorrow: Counterfactual thinking and beyond. In A. Strathman & J. Joiereman (Ed.), *Understanding behavior in the context of time: Theory, research, and application* (p. 165–185). Mahwah, NJ: Erlbaum.

Sanna, L. J., & Meier, S. (2000). Looking for clouds in a silver lining: Self-esteem, mental simulations, and temporal confidence changes. *Journal of Research in Personality, 34,* 236–251.

Schwarz, N. (1990). Feelings as information: Informational and motivational functions of affective states. In E. T. Higgins & R. M. Sorrentino (Eds.), *Handbook of motivation and cognition: Foundations of social behavior* (Vol. 2, pp. 527–561). New York: Guilford.

Schwarz, N., & Bless, H. (1991). Happy and mindless, but sad and smart? The impact of affective states on analytic reasoning. In J. P. Forgas (Ed.), *Emotion and social judgment* (pp. 55–72). New York: Pergamon Press.

Schwarz, N., & Clore, G. L. (1988). How do I feel about it? Informative functions of affective states. In K. Fiedler & J. Forgas (Eds.), *Affect, cognition, and social behavior* (pp. 44–62). Toronto: Hogrefe.

Sheldon, K. M., Elliot, A. J., Kim, Y., & Kasser, T. (2001). What is satisfying about satisfying events? Testing 10 candidate psychological needs. *Journal of Personality and Social Psychology, 80,* 325–339.

Shepperd, J. A., Grace, J., Cole, L., & Klein, C. T. F. (2005). Anxiety and outcome judgments. *Personality and Social Psychology Bulletin, 31,* 267–275.

Shepperd, J. A., & McNulty, J. K. (2002). The affective consequences of expected and unexpected outcomes. *Psychological Science, 13,* 85–88.

Shepperd, J. A., Ouellette, J. A., & Fernandez, J. K. (1996). Abandoning unrealistic optimism: Performance estimates and the temporal proximity of self-relevant feedback. *Journal of Personality and Social Psychology, 70,* 844–855.

Suddendorf, T., & Corballis, M. C. (1997). Mental time travel and the evolution of the human mind. *Genetic, Social, and General Psychology Monographs, 123,* 133–167.

Sweeny, K., Carroll, P. J., & Shepperd, J. A. (2006). Is optimism always the best? Future outlooks and preparedness. *Current Directions in Psychological Science, 15,* 302–306.

Taylor, K. M., & Shepperd, J. A. (1998). Bracing for the worst: Severity, testing, and feedback as moderators of the optimistic bias. *Personality and Social Psychology Bulletin, 24,* 915–926.

Taylor, S. (1991). Asymmetrical effects of positive and negative events: The mobilization-minimization hypothesis. *Psychological Bulletin, 10,* 67–85.

Tulving, E. (1983). *Elements of episodic memory.* Oxford, England: Clarendon Press.

Weary, G., & Jacobson, J. A. (1997). Causal uncertainty beliefs and diagnostic information seeking. *Journal of Personality and Social Psychology, 73,* 839–848.

White, R. (1959). Motivation reconsidered: The concept of competence. *Psychological Review, 66,* 297–333.

Author Index

Note: Reference pages are in *italic*.

Subject Index

A

Absolute *vs.* comparative judgments, 315
Abstract emotional gap, 336–338
Abstraction detail, 139
Abu Ghraib prison scandal, 183
Abu Ghraib study, 183–184
Academic motivation
    possible selves, 389
    psychological temporal distance, 353–354
ACC. *see* Anterior cingulate cortex (ACC)
Access implicit memories, 35–36
Accuracy
    memories, 105–107
    perspective taking, 296, 297, 298
Action
    correspondence to daydreams, 232
    if-then planning, 69–71
    imitation mental practice, 42
    related language comprehension, 26
    social interactions, 3–21
Activating formation, 77–78
Additive structures, 137
Adjusted empathic accuracy score, 286
Affective forecasts
    counterfactual thinking, 177
    emotions, 338, 436
    experiential system, 340
    narratives, 244
    two-systems account, 343
Affective *vs.* cognitive judgments, 314
African American students, 389
Age
    daydreaming differences, 234
    episodic future thought, 122–123
    regressed experiences, 110
AI. *see* Anterior insula (AI)
Alternatives
    counterfactual, 151, 156
    focused strategies, 418
    tense tendencies, 143
American Psychological Association (APA), 105
American Society of Clinical Hypnosis (ASCH), 105
Amnesia episodic future thought, 120–122
Analytic *vs.* holistic imagination, 332–333
Anterior cingulate cortex (ACC), 272, 273
Anterior insula (AI), 272, 273
Anticipated regret, 413–414, 416
Anticipated regret regulation, 419–421
    alternative-focused strategies, 420–421
    avoiding decisions, 420
    decision-focused strategies, 419
    decision reversibility, 420–421
    decrease goal level, 419
    delaying decisions, 420

    feeling-focused strategies, 421
    foregone alternatives, 421
    goal-focused strategies, 419
    improve decision quality, 419
    increase decision justifiability, 420
    transfer decision responsibility, 420
APA. *see* American Psychological Association (APA)
Apparent motion, 9
ASCH. *see* American Society of Clinical Hypnosis (ASCH)
Assessment method, 120
Associative creative tasks, 168
Asymmetric constraints, 131–142, 138
Asymmetric judgmental outcomes, 137–139
Asymmetric phenomenology, 136–137
Attainment
    future goals, 378
    possible selves, 374–375, 379
Attention
    bias, 198
    daydreams, 230
Auditory imagery processes, 214
Autobiographical belief, 98
    false memories, 89–99
Automatic consciousness, 120
Automaticity, 72
    daydreams, 230–231
    transportation, 245

B

Baseline accuracy, 287
Behavior
    counterfactual thinking, 178
    long-term outcomes, 356
    predictive, 321
    self-relevant impact, 378
Behavioral neuroscience approaches, 12
Bem, Daryl, 259
Bias
    applications, 201
    attenuation, 198
    case of hindsight, 198–200
    confidence changes, 201–202
    conjectures, 206–207
    emergence, 198
    familiarity, 199–200
    fluency, 199–200
    forecasting, 203
    implications, 206–207
    metacognitive model, 200–205
    planning fallacy, 202–203
    reduction, 305
    surprise, 199–200